# Lecture Notes in Computer Science 13516

More information about this series at https://link.springer.com/bookseries/558

Masaaki Kurosu · Sakae Yamamoto ·
Hirohiko Mori · Marcelo M. Soares ·
Elizabeth Rosenzweig · Aaron Marcus ·
Pei-Luen Patrick Rau · Don Harris ·
Wen-Chin Li (Eds.)

# HCI International 2022 - Late Breaking Papers

## Design, User Experience and Interaction

24th International Conference on Human-Computer Interaction
HCII 2022, Virtual Event, June 26 – July 1, 2022
Proceedings

 Springer

*Editors*
Masaaki Kurosu
The Open University of Japan
Chiba, Japan

Sakae Yamamoto
Tokyo University of Science
Tokyo, Saitama, Japan

Hirohiko Mori
Tokyo City University
Tokyo, Japan

Marcelo M. Soares
Southern University of Science
and Technology
Shenzhen, China

Elizabeth Rosenzweig
World Usability Day and Bubble Mountain
Consulting
Newton Center, MA, USA

Aaron Marcus
Aaron Marcus and Associates
Berkeley, CA, USA

Pei-Luen Patrick Rau
Tsinghua University
Beijing, China

Don Harris
Coventry University
Coventry, UK

Wen-Chin Li
Cranfield University
Cranfield, UK

ISSN 0302-9743          ISSN 1611-3349 (electronic)
Lecture Notes in Computer Science
ISBN 978-3-031-17614-2          ISBN 978-3-031-17615-9 (eBook)
https://doi.org/10.1007/978-3-031-17615-9

This Springer imprint is published by the registered company Springer Nature Switzerland AG
The registered company address is: Gewerbestrasse 11, 6330 Cham, Switzerland

# Foreword

Human-computer interaction (HCI) is acquiring an ever-increasing scientific and industrial importance, as well as having more impact on people's everyday life, as an ever-growing number of human activities are progressively moving from the physical to the digital world. This process, which has been ongoing for some time now, has been dramatically accelerated by the COVID-19 pandemic. The HCI International (HCII) conference series, held yearly, aims to respond to the compelling need to advance the exchange of knowledge and research and development efforts on the human aspects of design and use of computing systems.

The 24th International Conference on Human-Computer Interaction, HCI International 2022 (HCII 2022), was planned to be held at the Gothia Towers Hotel and Swedish Exhibition & Congress Centre, Göteborg, Sweden, during June 26 to July 1, 2022. Due to the COVID-19 pandemic and with everyone's health and safety in mind, HCII 2022 was organized and run as a virtual conference. It incorporated the 21 thematic areas and affiliated conferences listed on the following page.

A total of 5583 individuals from academia, research institutes, industry, and governmental agencies from 88 countries submitted contributions, and 1276 papers and 275 posters were included in the proceedings that were published just before the start of the conference. Additionally, 296 papers and 181 posters are included in the volumes of the proceedings published after the conference, as "Late Breaking Work". The contributions thoroughly cover the entire field of human-computer interaction, addressing major advances in knowledge and effective use of computers in a variety of application areas. These papers provide academics, researchers, engineers, scientists, practitioners, and students with state-of-the-art information on the most recent advances in HCI. The volumes constituting the full set of the HCII 2022 conference proceedings are listed in the following pages.

I would like to thank the Program Board Chairs and the members of the Program Boards of all thematic areas and affiliated conferences for their contribution and support towards the highest scientific quality and overall success of the HCI International 2022 conference; they have helped in so many ways, including session organization, paper reviewing (single-blind review process, with a minimum of two reviews per submission) and, more generally, acting as good-will ambassadors for the HCII conference.

This conference would not have been possible without the continuous and unwavering support and advice of Gavriel Salvendy, Founder, General Chair Emeritus, and Scientific Advisor. For his outstanding efforts, I would like to express my appreciation to Abbas Moallem, Communications Chair and Editor of HCI International News.

July 2022                                                    Constantine Stephanidis

# HCI International 2022 Thematic Areas and Affiliated Conferences

**Thematic Areas**

- HCI: Human-Computer Interaction
- HIMI: Human Interface and the Management of Information

**Affiliated Conferences**

- EPCE: 19th International Conference on Engineering Psychology and Cognitive Ergonomics
- AC: 16th International Conference on Augmented Cognition
- UAHCI: 16th International Conference on Universal Access in Human-Computer Interaction
- CCD: 14th International Conference on Cross-Cultural Design
- SCSM: 14th International Conference on Social Computing and Social Media
- VAMR: 14th International Conference on Virtual, Augmented and Mixed Reality
- DHM: 13th International Conference on Digital Human Modeling and Applications in Health, Safety, Ergonomics and Risk Management
- DUXU: 11th International Conference on Design, User Experience and Usability
- C&C: 10th International Conference on Culture and Computing
- DAPI: 10th International Conference on Distributed, Ambient and Pervasive Interactions
- HCIBGO: 9th International Conference on HCI in Business, Government and Organizations
- LCT: 9th International Conference on Learning and Collaboration Technologies
- ITAP: 8th International Conference on Human Aspects of IT for the Aged Population
- AIS: 4th International Conference on Adaptive Instructional Systems
- HCI-CPT: 4th International Conference on HCI for Cybersecurity, Privacy and Trust
- HCI-Games: 4th International Conference on HCI in Games
- MobiTAS: 4th International Conference on HCI in Mobility, Transport and Automotive Systems
- AI-HCI: 3rd International Conference on Artificial Intelligence in HCI
- MOBILE: 3rd International Conference on Design, Operation and Evaluation of Mobile Communications

# Conference Proceedings – Full List of Volumes

**http://2022.hci.international/proceedings**

# 24th International Conference on Human-Computer Interaction (HCII 2022)

The full list with the Program Board Chairs and the members of the Program Boards of all thematic areas and affiliated conferences is available online at:

**http://www.hci.international/board-members-2022.php**

# HCI International 2023

The 25th International Conference on Human-Computer Interaction, HCI International 2023, will be held jointly with the affiliated conferences at the AC Bella Sky Hotel and Bella Center, Copenhagen, Denmark, 23–28 July 2023. It will cover a broad spectrum of themes related to human-computer interaction, including theoretical issues, methods, tools, processes, and case studies in HCI design, as well as novel interaction techniques, interfaces, and applications. The proceedings will be published by Springer. More information will be available on the conference website: http://2023.hci.international/

General Chair
Constantine Stephanidis
University of Crete and ICS-FORTH
Heraklion, Crete, Greece
Email: general_chair@hcii2023.org

**http://2023.hci.international/**

# Contents

## User Experience Design and Evaluation Case Studies

## Cognition and Interaction

# Interaction Design Methods and Tools

# Knowledge Creation in Co-design Activities - Business-Driven Collaboration in the Development of a Digital Communication Tool

Eva Brooks$^{(\boxtimes)}$ ⓘ and Anders Kalsgaard Møller ⓘ

Aalborg University, Kroghstræde 3, 9220 Aalborg, Denmark
{eb,ankm}@ikl.aau.dk

**Abstract.** The goal of this paper was to explore the nature of university students' and company representatives' knowledge creation when they collaborated in co-design activities. Studies focusing on companies' collaboration with universities and students primarily centres around how companies contribute to students' learning of entrepreneurial skills and to the development of higher education curricula and its inclusion of entrepreneurial assets. Thus, there is a lack of understanding what kind of knowledge that students and companies jointly develop in collaborative design practices. The study applied Dewey's theory on experience highlighting matters of social conditions of experiences as well as reflective thinking. The research was generated by means of qualitative group interviews. The analytical approach was thematic and identified three themes: (1) Genuine collaborative engagement; (2) Challenges in trying new things; and (3) Knowledge creation premises. These themes revealed different kinds of knowledge creation that took place in the co-design activities. For example, how te challenges inherent in the co-design activities encouraged the students to take risks, to work in completely new ways and to try out new ways of arguing for certain choices, which helped them to actively engage in the collaboration as an equal partner. In this way, the study contributes to questions of the kinds of knowledge that students and companies collaboratively create when engaged in co-design activities. It should however be noted that this study is based on a small sample of participants and accordingly more research is needed to validate these conclusions.

**Keywords:** Knowledge creation · Co-design · Experience theory · Reflective thinking · Qualitative interviews · M.Sc. Students · Company representatives · Collaborative engagement · Challenging engagement · Knowledge creation premises

## 1 Introduction

A study by Cook-Sather et al. [1] showed that both students and faculty tend to enhance motivation and learning when they collaborate in co-design activities. Specifically, such collaboration deepens students' learning, increase their confidence, and focus on the

M. Kurosu et al. (Eds.): HCII 2022, LNCS 13516, pp. 3–17, 2022.
https://doi.org/10.1007/978-3-031-17615-9_1

process of learning rather than the outcome. For faculty, partnership-like collaboration with students develops new understanding of teaching and enhanced excitement in the classroom as well as a redefinition of teaching and learning as a collaborative process. However, while the use of co-design activities in student-teacher partnership are frequently applied, there is a lack of understanding what kind of knowledge that students develop in such collaborative design practices.

Students' participation in contributing to the design of their own learning pathways in Higher Education (HE) practices is well documented in educational and design-oriented scientific literature. These studies primarily focus on students' participation, involvement, and influence, for example in relation to design-based research, participatory design, and co-design [2–7]. Studies show that teacher-student partnership continues to increase across HE institutions encompassing a broad range of initiatives and frameworks [1, 2, 8, 9]. A study by Delpish et al. [10] showed that a co-creation framework can offer opportunities for students to take on different roles; from being involved with limited influence on decision-making to working in partnership with teachers having equal roles. Other studies focus on students' active involvement in curricula design activities, which point to positive outcomes related to how curriculum co-creation can transform students' relationships, engagement, risk taking, and academic achievement [11, 12].

HE institutions are also concerned with creating conditions for students to, within their education, collaborate and establish partnership with companies and organizations. This is particularly relevant for universities applying problem- or project-based learning models, where collaboration with companies to create academic learning opportunities outside traditional university auditorium are central [13]. Research stresses that university-business partnership has a societal value including collaboration between socio-economic stakeholders and university practices [14]. This collaboration can be in the form of exchange of knowledge, creating collaborative projects, and supporting entrepreneurship by, for example, contributing to curriculum adaptation targeting academic learning designs to be better aligned with requirements of the labour market [14]. A study by Pocol et al. [15] pointed to that companies have an interest in strengthening the relationship with universities to co-create value and develop students' entrepreneurial skills. In this regard, the authors underline that it is vital to consider both learning designs and research processes by, beside external stakeholders, such as companies, involving internal participants, such as teachers, researchers, and students. Such co-creative interactions can expand their knowledge and develop new skills. Recent years, companies have an increased focus on innovation of new products in an effort to become more market competitive [16]. In this regard, knowledge sharing is acknowledged by companies as a key issue for improving work performance and quality in new ideas and product development [16, 17]. In this sense, knowledge sharing constitutes a social, interactive, and complex process involving both tacit and explicit knowledge [18]. Nonetheless, relatively little research efforts have been paid to partnership and knowledge sharing between companies, HE institutions, and students, in particular when it comes to the consequences of such knowledge sharing. That is, what kind of knowledge is created in such knowledge sharing situations?

In the present paper, we explore processes of knowledge creation emerging from co-design activities involving four Master of Science students, two university teachers/researchers, practitioners from the elderly care domain, and three representatives from a small-sized company in northern Jutland, Denmark. The target of the co-design activities was to develop a commercial product that could support practitioners within the service sector to improve daily meeting cultures to ensure that everyone is heard and, thereby, create a sustainable team culture. The study included methods such as workshops, interviews, and prototype evaluations. In this paper, we focus on interviews carried out with the students and the company representatives. The goal of the interviews was to unfold their expectations and goals of the collaboration, and in what ways the collaboration contributed to new knowledge and development of innovative processes. The collaboration referred to both students, teachers/researchers, company representatives, and practitioners (end-users of the product).

The following section presents the background of the study followed by a section introducing related work focusing on research on collaboration and co-creation, between university teachers, students, and companies. Next, the theoretical framework based on Dewey's theory of experience [19. 20, 21] is defined as well as the co-design methodology and methods that were applied for gathering and analysing the generated interview data. Finally, the analysis is presented followed by a conclusive discussion.

## 2 Background

The background of the present paper is based on a collaboration between a university education Master of Science programme in IT, learning and organisational change, a small-sized company developing products and services targeting the healthcare sector. The master programme starts with a module where the students in collaboration with a company or organisation shall develop an IT-based learning design (10 ECTS). This module is followed by a PBL-oriented project module (15 ECTS), where the students work with a project based on a concrete problem in collaboration with an external partner. It is possible for the students to continuing to work with the design that they developed within this first module. The teachers plan for the first module by contacting companies and organisations to ask for potential problems that would include an IT-based learning design. When the students start the semester, they can choose among a range of problems to work with in collaboration with companies/organisations.

The small-sized company submitted a case proposal addressing a need for a product that could support practitioners within the service sector to improve daily meeting cultures to ensure that everyone is heard and, thereby, create a sustainable team culture. A group of four master students chose to work with this case in collaboration with the company and they continued to work with it also in the project module. The CEO of the company became the main contact and collaborator and in addition, two more employees were involved in specific co-design activities. The company had access to a user group that was involved in requirement and test activities. The teacher and researchers (authors of the paper) acted as both overall facilitators and experts in the fields of human-computer interaction, design, and learning. During the case- and project-process, the CEO and the students frequently met both physically and online. Hence, the design process included a continuity and a wide range of equal-based design-oriented interaction between the students and the different stakeholders. The case and the project were carried out during the fall semester 2021/2022 (September 2021 to January 2022).

## 3 Related Work

Co-design as a strategy intends to engage various stakeholders in collaborative design activities to foster an attitude of participation and human-centredness [22, 23]. Sanders and Stappers [24] define co-design as "the creativity of designers and people not trained in design working together in the design development process." Co-design, thus, would contribute to a design team to become better at designing as they have a better understanding of the people they are designing with and for. Co-design has been widely used in commercial as well as in public sectors to engage and involve potential users and other key stakeholders in a design process. This would enhance transparency, increase user acceptance, and reduce potential failures [25–28]. A co-design approach enables a wide range of stakeholders to contribute to developing solutions to a problem. Here, a key-component is the diversity of experts that come together to collaborate. In this sense, a co-design process has potentials to develop an equal collaboration between stakeholders while resolving a particular challenge [29]. In such a process, the designer's role shifts between being a translator of users' needs and a facilitator, which create opportunities for the people involved to engage with each other, being creative, and exchange knowledge as well as ideas [24]. In the present study, the participants had different roles. The students act as designers, the teachers/researchers as design and learning experts, the company representatives as stakeholders with a product development and business interests, and the practitioners as stakeholders with user interests.

In such co-design activities involving students collaborating with companies as part of their education, it is pivotal to expand opportunities for students' professional experience through pedagogical tools, creating and facilitate collaborative practices including external partners, and support problem-based learning structures. This would open for knowledge co-creation among students, which they can practice in other situations [30, 31], for example in collaboration with companies and business-driven collaboration. Such a knowledge co-creation teaching strategy can generate a deeper understanding, knowledge, and interest in other people and thus increase participants' motivation in collaborating [32, 33]. While these studies are related to development of curricula and collaboration between students and teachers in the HE domain, the present study relates to co-design activities, also in the HE context, but related to business-driven collaboration within a course module where students in HE should collaborate with a company to develop a service design. The collaboration was designed and co-created between students, company representatives, and end-users, and facilitated by the teacher/researcher. In general, research shows that co-design activities lead to improved learning and collaboration skills [34, 35].

The present study focuses on processes of knowledge creation in co-design activities, which can be beneficial for students, for example by opportunities to develop self-awareness, develop personal creativity, communication, skills to cope with group dynamics, and actively practice theoretical and methodical content from lectures [36–38]. Thus, as claimed by Cook-Sather et al. [1], educations offering opportunities to co-design their learning is perceived as a joint effort, where teaching and learning activities are planned with students and not for students.

Related work focusing on companies' collaboration with universities and students primarily centres around how companies contribute to students' learning of entrepreneurial skills and to the development of curricula including entrepreneurial features [14]. Hewitt-Dundas et al. [1] claim that there is evidence from international studies on the positive outcome when universities support companies to innovate. Moreover, the authors state that developing university-company collaborations, challenges a so-called 'two-worlds' paradox emerging from differences in institutional logics and priorities between businesses and universities. The outcomes from their study showed that companies' experience from collaboration can help to overcome this paradox and thus improve companies' skills to generate innovations in collaboration with universities. Considering the limited research on the knowledge creation in co-design activities between companies and universities where also students are involved, the present study contributes to identifying the kinds of knowledge that is created in such business-driven co-design activities targeting development of a service design solution to the elderly care domain.

## 4 Theoretical Framework

The theoretical framework is based on Dewey's theory on experience [21]. He highlights two aspects of the quality of experience, likes and dislike, and their significance for future experiences as well as its significance for future experiences [21]. It thus matters whether an experience produces a like or a dislike in the individual. Dewey has established two principles of experience: continuity and interaction. While continuity refers to the fact that past and present experiences influence future experiences and decisions, the interaction principle refers to the objective and internal conditions of an experience [21]. However, Dewey does not only consider experiences as individual matters. For example, he states that interaction cannot be separated from situation as an experience is grounded in the environment, including other people, in which the individual is situated. Thus, an experience is social [21], for example in the form of a conversation between the individual and the environment. In the present study, we are interested in how the continuity and interaction contributed to the experienced knowledge creation that took place during a series of joint co-design activities and conversations.

### 4.1 Reflective Thinking

Social conditions can influence what a group of people experience from a situation and hence influence the quality of the experience [19, 20] and, in the context of the present study, how this impact the complexity of knowledge creation. In relation to the concept of experience, Dewey [19] discusses the process of reflective thinking and suggests that it is an active consideration of a topic, which contribute to knowledge creation and based on this, to further actions and decisions. Reflective thinking hence constitutes a form of questioning approach to challenges opening new perspectives. Reflections can be pre-reflective where a situation creates confusion and questions that needs to be answered. Following this is a post-reflective situation which can lead to an experience when questions through a reflective process have led to ideas, solutions, or answers. Applying this understanding of reflective thinking in relation to an experience, Dewey [20] stresses that an experience as such is primarily an active-passive process; not solely cognitive. This means that our interest in the knowledge creation emerging from experiences lies in the perception of continuity or relationships to which an experience leads up. The knowledge part is thus cumulative and has a certain meaning. Within this framework, Dewey identified five phases of reflective thinking, which should be considered as a continuum rather than one phase following the other. The phases are: (1) a felt difficulty which causes a genuine interest; (2) Definition of the difficulty including analysis of the situation; (3) Proposed explanations or possible solution to the difficulty including cultivation on a variety of alternative solutions; (4) Elaboration of an idea including reasoning where implications and of any ideas are considered: (5) Corroboration of an idea and formation of a concluding belief including testing of an idea or hypothesis to see if expected outcomes indicated by the idea actually occur [19]. In the present study, this continuum of phases was used as analytical tools to explore the kinds of knowledge creation that the students and the company representatives have experienced.

## 5   Methodology

The study was carried out in March 2022 and applied a qualitative approach [39, 40] and includes interviews with the four master students and two representatives from the small-sized company. The interviews were qualitative and used a conversational mode (Yin, 2016) to create conditions for two-way interactions. An interview guide was used containing a subset of key word tailored to the topics, which were considered as relevant in relation to the aim of the study. Each key word included a set of follow-up queries and as such worked as a reminder rather than actual questions [40]. Examples of key words and topics were: (i) Expectations and goals of the collaboration; (ii) Collaboration and its contribution to new knowledge; (iii) Collaboration and its contribution to innovative processes; and (iv) Interaction with users/practitioners.

The interviews were computer-supported by means of Zoom, which is a web conferencing platform used for audio and/or video conferencing and meetings. We used the video and thus had the opportunity to meet face-to-face but however limited by not fully being able to identify bodily expressions. This was mitigated by video recording the interview sessions and thereby being able to have a closer look at for example, facial expressions. The video recording of the group interview was communicated to the participants on beforehand and all of them allowed us to record. In addition, we also started the interview session by again asking them if we still had their permission to video record the session.

The qualitative interviews were carried out as group interviews; one with the four students, and one with the two company representatives. This called for further carefulness in preparing and responding from our point of view [40]. For example, considering our attention to one of the persons and at the same time being respectful to the others so that they still felt involved. As the group interviews included a smaller size of participants, this challenge was considered but however not experienced as problematic. The interviews could be considered as summative [41] as our intention was to capture the 'big picture' and identify rather than assess the participants overall experience of the co-design collaboration. While considering the different interview topics, the participants reflections were based on the series of workshops that had taken place during the two modules, the several informal and formal meetings with the company and students respectively, as well as with the teachers/researchers and requirement- and test sessions with the end-user group.

### 5.1  Transcribing and Analysing the Generated Data

The group interviews were transcribed by highlighting incidents that were relevant in relation to the goal of the project. These incidents were transcribed verbatim. The analytical approach was hence systematic by identifying the incidents that were of concern by the participants and understanding the meaning of these concerns. This approach was inspired by Thematic Analysis and carried out in five different steps as described by Braun and Clarke [42]. The transcribed data were reviewed and coded by the authors to find patterns and initial themes in the verbal expressions. We also reviewed facial expressions that potentially could add meaning to the verbalisations. The initial themes were reviewed and defined by both authors (Table 1).

**Table 1.** Overview of the analysis process (inspired by Braun and Clarke [42].

| Phase | Description of the analysis procedure |
|---|---|
| Getting to know the data | Watching the video recordings |
| Generating initial codes | Systematically coding incidents of the data, gathering data relevant to each code |
| Searching for initial themes | Synthesising codes into initial themes, gathering data relevant to each initial theme |
| Reviewing themes | Checking if the themes make sense in relation to the coded data and the whole data set |
| Defining themes | Iteration of the analysis to refine details of each theme in relation to the research questions, generating definitions and names for each theme |

From this analysis, we identified three themes: (1) Genuine collaborative engagement; (2) Challenges in trying new things; and (3) Knowledge creation premises.

# 6  Analysis

The analysis focuses on three overall themes highlighting the outcomes that relate to the question of the kinds of knowledge that students and representatives from the small-sized company experienced while having been involved in different kinds of co-design activities. These processes included both challenges and steps towards overcoming these. Below, the identified themes are revealed.

## 6.1  Genuine Collaborative Engagement

A key factor influencing knowledge creation processes in co-design activities is the genuine collaborative engagement that both students and company representatives experienced coming from the collaborating partner. The students emphasises that the main representative from the company was very engaged and genuinely interested in the collaboration. While the students had expected a kind of sparring from the company, they experienced that it was more than that:

> They had a willingness to listen to us and our ideas and thinking, which contributed to my impression that they wanted to consider the matters that we discussed. They liked our ideas. It was a surprising experience, in a positive way, that our participation meant a lot.

The company representatives stated that it was important for them to reflect upon the project (developing a communication tool) together with the students, who were well prepared with questions, academic knowledge, and ideas:

> This collaboration opened opportunities to, together with the students, get access to new perspectives and get a deeper understanding of our product idea, in particular theories. This strengthened our goal to establish a strong foundation to realise the product as a commercial product or concept. This will confirm that the product is possible to market.

The specific challenge that the company and the students experienced as a basis for their genuine interest differed. For the company the challenge was related to developing a commercial product, which by being grounded in academic theories would strengthen aspects of what they already envisioned about the market opportunities of the product. The students experienced a challenge in balancing the companies' engagement and sometimes overwhelming optimism regarding the design and market opportunities of the product. This demonstrates how objectivity can be a challenging matter, when being emotionally engaged in a project. This adds complexity to attain an objective reflection and potentially change expectations. The students point to that this sometimes led to that the company overinterpreted outcomes from meetings with the end-users, which caused that they sometimes disagreed with the company:

> I do not know how or why this happened, what went wrong. Perhaps we had a different understanding of what the user group expressed, what the things they said meant for the product to be useful and support their work. In any case, we

*considered this challenge as the task where we really could contribute with our knowledge and more objective perspective.*

This quote from one of the students indicates that the experienced challenge resulted in a genuine interest to collaboratively work towards a useful product based on input from the end-users. On the other hand, the challenge experienced by the company was more of an academic confirmation on what they had envisioned. In conclusion, both company representatives and students experienced an increased sense of engagement and joy from collaborating in co-design activities.

## 6.2 Challenges in Trying New Things

The students described their experiences as different from what they were used to from previous bachelor studies. This resulted in that they were taking a greater responsibility for their learning and for the collaboration.

*It has really been nice that we have been 'alone' with handling the contact with the company. I mean, that you as teachers have not influenced, for example when meetings should take place and what should be on the agenda when we met. In this way, we have had the opportunity to challenge the company. We have noticed that we have done so. When we have presented a new way of understanding the use of the product, they have said that they should think about it, that what we said made sense.*

Although the students were challenged in grabbing the responsibility of the collaboration, they were at the same time inspired by the freedom that it also embraced:

*We had a lot of freedom; it was a bit difficult to see through. Did what we did make any meaning? It was challenging in a way that I was not used to being challenged. But this did not matter, the big difference was that what we were about to develop should fit into a real reality, a real practice. This was so inspiring to test. The challenge was so rewarding.*

The company representatives emphasised the importance of taking ownership and be clear about their needs. However, this required a continuity in the collaboration; it took time to reflect collectively together with the students.

*The long-term collaboration is crucial to in collaboration develop a strong and sustainable argumentation for our beliefs and for a future marketing of the product. The continuity in the collaboration with the students and the researchers have been pivotal for us to change our understanding of the product. Insights into development models and theories have forced us to clarify our visions so that the development process becomes both trustworthy and realistic. This has been a helpful journey.*

The long-termed co-design activities created a safe environment for the partners to not only collaborate, but to try out new things; it enabled them to take risks. Even though they felt uncomfortable and needed time to get used to new situations, they felt able to cross their habits and boundaries. The relation between the openness to try new things and the long-term engagement and effort spent during co-design processes was clearly addressed by both students and company representatives.

## 6.3  Knowledge Creation Premises

The before-mentioned themes, genuine collaborative engagement, and challenges in trying new things, can contribute to development of knowledge. A hight degree of engagement and sense of enjoyment was indicative for being able to elaborate, revise and consolidate existing knowledge. This guided the partners to create new kinds of understanding of and dealing with difficult situations. A student described her learning and achievement like this:

*I have learnt many things. I have gained insights into my future working life; how situations and knowledge change, nothing is constant but changes along the way. I have gained insights into practice. I have learnt the importance of being constructively critical. When someone says that 'I have a good idea', one needs to be critical by carefully reflecting on this idea. This collaboration has taught me that there is otherwise a tendency to upgrade this idea to an unrealistic level.*

Another student agrees:

*Yes, a good idea needs to be reflected upon. From many different angles. Many times. I have learnt that a long-term collaboration is beneficial as it gives me opportunity to become wiser and wiser. For example, how I shall act and what to focus on when I enter a collaboration and how to relate to the different parts included in a collaboration.*

Being critical and reflect upon ideas, solutions, and situations was a recurring theme in relation to what the students had experienced as central for knowledge creation. This was further elaborated by a student:

*I have learnt to reflect upon my own arguments; how I formulate them, what they are based on. One of the company representatives always asked very good questions, which challenged me to become clearer in my argumentations.*

The students described how co-creation activities led to extensive opportunities to practice innovation:

*We have worked innovatively. As there did not exist any similar communication tools on the market, we were forced to think freely, work iteratively and thus practice innovation. It was a competence that was growing through the iterative work.*

A powerful outcome of the co-design activities referred to the sense of being recognised as a genuine and skilled collaborator. A student expressed in this way:

*It became clear for me that the company had not only provided a case, but we were also truly recognized and respected; the work we did, the ideas we had were seriously considered. Very nice.*

The co-design environment created during collaborative sessions was described as significant for the design- as well as for the learning process. One of the company representatives spoked about this by emphasising the importance of a well well-structured process:

*For me to develop and learn, there needs to be a clear structure of the product- or concept development process. The way theory was implemented in this process was crucial for my learning.*

Both partners acknowledged the end-user group as a key to corroborating new knowledge. One of the company representatives stated:

*User involvement was central in relation to developing the product in the right direction. This has taught us about the necessity of being clear about functionalities and design features of the product/concept. The user group really pointed out the direction for the further development.*

The students pointed to the role of the user group as balancing the company's sometimes unrealistic positiveness:

*It was important to involve the user group. They were critical and mitigated the positiveness coming from the company. However, we would have needed more critical feedback from them, it tended to be more confirming than critical. It might be that we think so as we ourselves had a little doubt regarding if the product should work, and if it would make sense in the practice field.*

The analysis reveals more than genuine interest and engagement in collaborative design activities. It uncovers powerful potentials of co-design activities to influence both the students' and the company representatives' persistence with collectively develop new knowledge. For the students, this totally changed their experience of and approach to learning.

## 7   Conclusive Discussion

Returning to our original goal of this paper, to explore processes of knowledge creation emerging from co-design activities involving students, company representatives, end-users, and university teachers/researchers. We applied Dewey's theory of experience, specifically his five phases of reflection as an analytical tool to describe the kinds of knowledge creation that took place. The analysis revealed three central themes: (1) Genuine collaborative engagement; (2) Challenges in trying new things; and (3) Knowledge creation premises. In this section we conclusively discuss the implication of our findings.

The students experienced a democratic collaboration, where they had a co-ownership of the challenges they worked with together with the company. In line with the findings of Storvang et al. [29], we emphasise the engaging and democratic influence of a co-design structure when designing for collaboration that could include situations of power rather than equity. It is critical to note that even though being experienced as democratic and engaging, our findings show that the students experienced the co-design practice as challenging. However, the openness of the co-design structure generated a responsibility taking and an urge for a deeper understanding to sharpen arguments and critical considerations. In other words, the challenges could be considered as valuable and constructive when the students could see what they learned from them. This resonates with findings from Bovill et al. [32], Bovill [33], De Jans et al. [34], and Sanina et al. [35] concluding that co-design activities lead to knowledge creation and collaborative skills.

The company representatives' experience of knowledge creation differed from some of the findings in related research, which primarily focuses on how companies can contribute to students' development of entrepreneurial skills [1, 14] and become market competitive [16]. The findings from our study showed that the company acknowledged the co-design activities as they could learn from the students and from the researchers. This to improve their work processes and through a theoretical grounding deepen their knowledge as well as considering new ideas and angles. We identified examples of 'company representatives describing knowledge exchange as valuable for improving their readiness for a future marketing the product.

The students' and company representatives' reflections on their different kinds of knowledge creation are identified and can be related to Dewey's [19] reflection continuum of five phases. The finding from first theme, genuine collaborative engagement, specifically was interrelated to phases one and two. The second theme, challenges in trying new things could be connected to phase three and four and the third theme, knowledge creation premises to phase five. These interrelationships helped us to reveal the different kinds of knowledge creation that took place in the co-design activities. For example, when the students discussed how the challenges inherent in the co-design activities encouraged them to take risks, to work in completely new ways and to try out new ways of arguing for certain choices helped them to actively engage in the collaboration as an equal partner. This is aligned with findings from studies by Elsharnouby [36], Lubicz-Nawrocka [37], Brandt et al. [38], and Lubicz-Nawrocka and Bovill [11].

To conclude, in this paper we have attempted to explore the nature of students' and companies' knowledge creation when they collaborate in co-design activities. We identified students' ways of implementing new ways of acting and company representatives' new ways of adopting academic knowledge into product development processes. The participants described examples of how co-design activities created a safe and trustful framework for collaboration and knowledge creation. The study contributes to the question of the kinds of knowledge that students and companies collaboratively create when engaged in co-design activities. Furthermore, it contributes to the question of the implications of such collaboration and inherent knowledge exchange. It should however be noted that this study is based on a small sample of participants and accordingly more research is needed to validate these conclusions.

**Acknowledgements.** We thank the students and the company for their participation and sharing of experiences. We gratefully acknowledge Life Science Innovation, Aalborg, Denmark.

# References

1. Cook-Sather, A., Bovill, C., Felten, P.: Engaging Students as Partners in Learning and Teaching: A Guide for Faculty. Jossey Bass, San Francisco (2014)
2. Bovill, C.: Co-creation in learning and teaching: the case for a whole-class approach in higher education. High. Educ. **79**(6), 1023–1037 (2019). https://doi.org/10.1007/s10734-019-004 53-w
3. Bovill, C., Cook-Sather, A., Felten, P., Millard, L., Moore-Cherry, N.: Addressing potential challenges in co-creating learning and teaching: overcoming resistance, navigating institutional norms and ensuring inclusivity in student-staff partnerships. High. Educ. **71**(2), 195–208 (2016)
4. Di Salvo, B., Yip, J., Bonsignore, E., DiSalvo, C.: Participatory Design for Learning: Perspectives from Practice and Research. Routledge, Abingdon (2017)
5. Dolmans, D.H.J.M., Tigelaar, D.: Building bridges between theory and practice in medical education using a design-based research approach: AMEE Guide No. 60 **34**(1), 1–10 (2012). https://doi.org/10.3109/0142159X.2011.595437
6. Könings, K.D., Bovill, C., Woolner, P.: Towards an interdisciplinary model of practice for participatory building design in education. European Journal of Education (2017). 0.1111/ejed.12230
7. Seale, J.: Doing student voice work in higher education: an exploration of the value of participatory methods. Br. Edu. Res. J. **36**(6), 995–1015 (2010). https://doi.org/10.1080/014119 20903342038
8. Bron, J., Bovill, C., Veugelers, W.: Students experiencing and developing democratic citizenship through curriculum negotiation: the relevance of garth boomer's approach. Curriculum Perspectives **42**, 39–49. https://doi.org/10.1007/s41297-021-00155-3
9. Smith, S., Akhyani, K.: The partnership co-creation process: conditions for success? International Journal for Students as Partners **5**(2), 48-66 (2021). https://doi.org/10.15173/ijsap.v5i2.4772
10. Delpish, A., et al.: Equalizing voices: student-faculty partnerhip in course design. In: Werder, C., Otis, M. (eds.): Engaging Student Voices in the Study of Teaching and Learning, pp. 96–114. Stylus, Sterling (2010)
11. Lubicz-Nawrocka, T., Bovill, C.: Do Students experience transformation through co-creating curriculum in higher education? Teaching in Higher Education (2021). https://doi.org/10.1080/13562517.2021.1928060
12. Bergmark, U., Westman, S.: Co-creating curriculum in higher education: promoting democratic values and a multidimennsional view on learning. Int. J. Acad. Dev. **21**(1), 28–40 (2016). https://doi.org/10.1080/1360144X.2015.1120734
13. Stegeager, N., Thomassen, A.O., Laursen, E.: Problem based learning in continuous education – challenges and opportunities. J. Problem Based Learning Higher Educ. **1**(1), 151–175 (2013)
14. Pocol, C.B., Stanca, L., Dabija, D.-C., Pop, I.D., Miscoiu, S.: Knowledge Co-creation and Sustainable Education in the Labor Market-driven University-Business Environment. Frontiers in Environmental Science, 781075 (2022). https://doi.org/10.3389/fenvs.2022.781075
15. Pocol, C.B., Dumitras, D.E., Moldovan Teselios, C.: Exploring young students' attitudes towards a sustainable consumption behaviour. In: Springer, S., Grimm, H. (eds.): Professionals in Food Chains, pp. 168–173. Wageningen Academic Publishers, Wageningen (2018). https://doi.org/10.3920/978-90-8686-869-8_25
16. Gao, J., Bernard, A.: An overview of knowledge sharing in new product development. Int. J. Advanced Manufacturing Technol. **94**(5–8), 1545–1550 (2017). https://doi.org/10.1007/s00 170-017-0140-5

17. Cummings, J.N.: Work groups, structural diversity, and knowledge sharing in global organization. Manage. Sci. **50**(3), 353–364 (2004). https://doi.org/10.1287/mnsc.1030.0134
18. Polanyi, M., Sen, A.: The Tacit Dimension. University of Chicago Press, Chicago (2009)
19. Dewey, J.: How we think. Dover Publications, INC., Mineola, New York (1910/1997)
20. Dewey, J.: Democracy and Education. Simon and Brown (2011)
21. Dewey, J.: Experience and Education. Simon and Schuster (1938/2008)
22. Mattelmäki, T., Brandt, E., Vaajakallio, K.: On designing open-ended interpretations for collaborative design exploration. CoDesign. Int. J. CoCreation in Design and the Arts **7**(2), 79–93 (2011). https://doi.org/10.1080/15710882.2011.609891
23. Trischler, J., Pervan, S.J., Kelly, S.J., Scott, D.R.: The value of codesign: the effect of customer involvement in service design teams. J. Serv. Res. **21**(1), 75–100 (2018)
24. Sanders, E.B.N., Stappers, P.J.: Co-creation and the new landscapes of design. Co-Design **4**(1), 5–18 (2008). https://doi.org/10.1080/15710880701875068
25. Trischler, J., Dietrich, T., Rndle-Thiele, S.: Co-design: from expert- to user-driven ideas in public service design. Public Management Review **21**(11) (2019), 1595–1619 (2019). https://doi.org/10.1080/14719037.2019.1619810
26. Lam, B., Pitsaki, I.: Co-deign for the development of new knowledge and practices in not-for-profit organizations. Design Management J. **13**(1), 70–82 (2018). https://doi.org/10.1111/dmj.12044
27. Osborne, S.P., Radnor, Z., Strokosch, K.: Co-production and the co-creation of value in public services: a suitable case for treatment? Public Manag. Rev. **18**(5), 639–653 (2016). https://doi.org/10.1080/14719037.2015.1111927
28. Verschuere, B., Vanleene, D., Steen, T., Brandsen, T.: Democratic co-production. concepts and determinants. In: Brandsen, T., Steen, T., Verschuere, B. (eds.): Co-production and Co-creation. Engaging Citizens in Public Service, pp. 243–251 (2018). https://doi.org/10.4324/9781315204956
29. Storvang, P., Haug, A., Nguyen, B.: Stimulating consumer community creation through a co-design approach. Int. J. Market Res. **62**(2), 176 (2020). https://doi.org/10.1177/470785319858929
30. Han, S.: Reproducing the working class? incongruence between the valuation of the social-emotional skills in school and in the labor market. Sociological Perspective **64**, 467–487 (2020). https://doi.org/10.1177/07311121420956378
31. Stanca, L., Dabija, D.-C., Păcurar, E.: Community of practice: converting IT graduate students into specialists via professional knowledge sharing. Int. J. Systems & Cybernetics **51**(2), 557–581 (2021). https://doi.org/10.1108/L-10-2020-0711
32. Bovill, C., Cook-Sather, A., Felten, P.: Students as co-creators of teaching approaches, course design, and curricula: implications for academic developers. Int. J. Academic Dev. **16**(2), 133–145 (2011). https://doi.org/10.1080/1360144X.2011.568590
33. Bovill, C.: An investigation of co-created curricula within higher education in the UK, Ireland and the USA. Innov. Educ. Teach. Int. **51**(1), 15–25 (2014). https://doi.org/10.1080/14703297.2013.770264
34. De Jans, S., Van Geit, K., Cauberghe, V., Hudders, L., De Veirman, M.: Using games to raise awareness: how to co-design serious mini-games? Computers in Education **110**, 77–87 (2017). https://doi.org/10.1016/j.compedu.2017.03.009
35. Sanina, A., Kutergina, E., Balashov, A.: The co-creative approach to digital simulation games in social science education. Comput. Educ. **149**, 103813 (2020). https://doi.org/10.1016/j.compedu.2020.103813
36. Elsharnouby, T.H.: Student co-creation behavior in higher education: the role of satisfaction with the university experience. J. Mark. High. Educ. **25**(2), 238–262 (2015). https://doi.org/10.1080/08841241.2015.1059919

37. Lubicz-Nawrocka, T.M.: Students as partners in learning and teaching: the benefits of co-creation of the curriculum. Int. J. Students as Partners **2**(1), 47–63 (2018). https://doi.org/10.15173/ijsap.v2i1.3207

38. Brandt, E., Messeter, J., Binder, T.: Formatting design dialogues – games and participation. CoDesign **4**(1), 51–64 (2008). https://doi.org/10.1080/15710880809005724

39. Hewitt-Dundas, N., Gkypali, A., Roper, S.: Does learning from prior collaboration help firms to overcome the 'twoworlds' paradox in university-business collaboration? Res. Policy **48**, 1310–1322 (2019). https://doi.org/10.1016/j.respol.2019.01.016

40. Denzin, N.K., Lincoln, Y.S.: The SAGE Handbook of Qualitative Research. Sage, New York (2011)

41. Yin, R.K.: Qualitative Research from Start to Finish, 2nd edn. The Guilford Press, New York (2016)

42. Scriven, M.: The Methodology of Evaluation. Purdue University, Lafayette, Indiana, Social Science Education Consortium (1966)

43. Braun, V., Clarke, V.: Using thematic analysis in psychology. Qual. Res. Psychol. **3**(2), 77–101 (2006). https://doi.org/10.1191/1478088706qp063oa

# Holistic Multimodal Interaction and Design

Eric Chan, Gerry Chan, Assem Kroma, and Ali Arya$^{(\boxtimes)}$

School of Information Technology, Carleton University, Ottawa, Canada
{erics.chan,gerry.chan,assem.kroma,ali.arya}@carleton.ca

**Abstract.** This paper addresses the lack of an HCI framework that examines multimodal experiences in a holistic way to help design interactions where modalities are properly integrated. Such a holistic approach is important as new emerging technologies and experiences are being introduced and used frequently. The resulting multimodal experiences present new requirements and challenges which are not managed by existing HCI frameworks. Through a literature review, we propose a set of principles that define the Holistic Multimodal Interaction and Design (HMID) framework. We perform a user study as the initial evaluation of the effectiveness of this framework. The study findings showed the potential value of HMID and suggested improvements to its guiding principles.

**Keywords:** Multimodal systems · Human-computer interaction · Holism · Retail

## 1 Introduction

Human-Computer Interaction (HCI) has witnessed a trend from systems based on a single modality of interaction (i.e., method, sense, or mode of operation used to do or experience something) to multimodal ones where the user can choose which modality suits their tasks better. Emerging technologies such as the Internet of Things (IoT), wearables, and Augmented/Virtual Reality (AR/VR) have accelerated this multimodal interaction trend. Multimodal interfaces enable the user to employ different modalities such as voice, gesture, and typing for communicating with a computer [1, 2]. Various HCI frameworks such as WIMP [3], Tangible [4], Ubiquitous [5], Multimodal [1, 2], and Natural [6] have offered increasingly diverse sets of modalities and intuitive forms of interacting with computing devices. Each of these frameworks looks at the human-computer interaction from a different angle, providing its unique advantages that do not necessarily contradict other frameworks but offer complementary possibilities and increase flexibility in designing new experiences. Despite this flexibility, these frameworks and the related interfaces generally offer modalities as separate and isolated features [7–9].

Humans use their senses and modalities in a holistic way, working together to achieve goals. The notion of wholes versus parts in different domains is not a new one. It has been around since Plato discussed the relationship between parts and the whole produced by them [10]. The term "holism" was introduced by Smuts in 1926 [11]. The idea is presented based on how the world works and how it consists of many important parts that have a tendency to result in wholes that are different from those parts. The holistic notion and whole-part differences play a key role in human experiences as we work with our modalities as parts of a whole experience.

The notion of holistic user experiences is not a new one either. Some researchers argue that user experiences are holistic by nature and that demands holistic criteria for their evaluation [12]. Even in the new technologies such as driverless cars, the concept of holistic user experience is being introduced [13]. However, HCI is bigger than just user experience, and this requires an adequately defined HCI framework that outlines the principles of holistic design and interaction. While there are many design guidelines and ideas for multimodal systems [1–3, 14], there is a lack of a unifying design methodology that is based on a holistic approach to user experience and interaction design.

In this paper, we start with a thorough literature review of HCI frameworks and the notions of multimodality and holism. We argue that existing approaches, while very helpful in certain applications, suffer from one or more of the following shortcomings:

1. They do not integrate various modalities within a given experience.
2. They do not provide a seamless transition between modalities within one task.
3. They do not offer modalities in a way that is consistent (performing the same tasks and achieving the same objective) and yet complementary (offering unique advantages).
4. They do not promote a design based on personalization.

To address these shortcomings, we propose Holistic Multimodal Interaction and Design (HMID), an HCI framework for designing holistic interactions. We initially conceived of HMID based on three principles of integration, seamless transition, and consistency. To investigate the guiding principles and effectiveness of the HMID framework, we conducted a user study that resulted in a fourth principle, personalization. The study focused on an imaginary retail experience as an example. We used illustrative storyboards [15] to simulate and present three retail scenarios. These scenarios follow a character who ends up purchasing a product. Each scenario is done through a separate approach: (1) The character engages separately with just two basic modalities in the retail experience. (2) The character engages in an isolated multimodal retail experience with a variety of modalities available. (3) The character engages in a holistic, multimodal retail experience (HMID). Our study incorporated a survey to see which scenario/approach was more successful with respect to the following goals:

1. Increasing sales
2. Increasing brand awareness
3. Increasing customer engagement

The results of our study suggested that a more multimodal experience using different technologies was perceived to increase sales, brand awareness, and customer engagement. However, there was not much difference between multimodal and HMID approaches. Upon reflection, we associated this with some participants not being prepared for or interested in a full HMID experience the way we had designed. As such, HMID should be flexible and adaptive, catering to the user's needs. This resulted in our fourth guiding principle, personalization.

The following sections review the relevant literature to provide a theoretical framework for HMID, then describe and discuss our study and its findings.

## 2 Related Work

### 2.1 Holism and Whole-Part Theories

The theory of part-whole originated as a purely philosophical concept in an attempt to understand the universe and human societies. The oldest trackable mention was in Plato's work, who discussed it informally [10]. However, the first formal discussion of the idea of parts and wholes relationships was in Aristotle's work when he established metaphysics [16]. He highlighted that the whole is not the same as its parts by highlighting that it does not necessarily result in a whole which is the sum of its parts [10]. In 1901, Husserl's third Logical Investigation was one of the first to transform the part-whole theory into a formal theory [10]. This theory was loosely referred to as the Part-whole theory before becoming a whole subfield of ontology commonly known as Mereology [17].

The original formulation of mereology as a field is credited to Stanislaw Leśniewski in 1916 [17]. However, since then, there have been many extensions of mereology that are referred to by different names [17]. By definition, mereology is the field that studies parthood relationships, the logical properties of the parts, and the whole they construct. The interrelationships between these parts and the whole they form are usually called mereological relationships. The thorough study of these relationships helped researchers produce more profound interpretations of these relationships, which helped in advancing many sciences, such as set theory in math [10]. This theory is the ground on which Object-Oriented Programming and the notion of classes are formed.

In 1926, Jan Smuts [11] introduced the term "holism." The notion is based on how nature works and how it consists of many important parts that have a tendency to form wholes. He argues in his philosophical theory that nature tends to produce wholes from the ordered grouping of the parts or units and that this tendency has been seen throughout existence. The hierarchical structure of entities (wholes vs. parts, sometimes referred to as "wholism") is related but not the same as the other aspect of this notion that wholes are more than the mere sums of the existing parts.

In psychology, the Gestalt theory emerged in the early 20th century, in contrast to elementalism and atomism, which tend to see all objects and ideas as a collection of elementary building blocks [18]. It promotes the notion of "whole is more than its parts." Gestalt principles of proximity, similarity, figure-ground, continuity, closure, and connection can be used to describe how humans perceive objects and environments.

Holistic and Gestalt principles offer insights on how to design multimodal systems in a holistic way. While connection and proximity are about proper integration, similarity, figure-ground, and continuity relate to how the parts should be consistent yet complementary.

### 2.2 Main HCI Frameworks

Early computers relied on text input/output and command lines for interacting with the user. The introduction of Graphical User Interfaces (GUI) was the basis of WIMP

(Windows-Icon-Menu-Pointer), the first major HCI framework [3]. The term WIMP was coined by Merzouga Wilberts in 1980, and the framework offered a new angle to look at computing devices; it compared computers to desktops as the most common workspace, instead of the old way of comparing them to typewriters. As a result, new forms of interaction were introduced that were symbolically related to real-life experiences (e.g., folders on desktop) but still relied on visuals and hand actions and did not quite reflect real-life interactions.

WIMP was followed by a series of other frameworks (generally referred to as Post-WIMP) that tried to move away from the 2D widget-based interactions to add new modalities [19]. Tangible User Interfaces (TUI) are based on the integration of tangible modalities and the notion of embodiment [4]. TUI's special angle was that human beings need to touch and feel things to experience them. This opened the door to the utilization of haptic technologies and expanded to offer new forms of wearable technologies. However, the focus of this framework, like the rest of the frameworks, was using modalities in combinations or isolation to achieve embodiment. This is an important approach that offers significant insights but does not necessarily provide the full picture.

Augmented/Virtual Reality (AR/VR) and 3DUI looked at HCI from the angle that the world is 3D and not 2D, and therefore, the interactions should move out of the 2D widget type of interactions to an extended form of reality. Milgram et al. [20] based this framework on the reality–virtuality continuum to include both virtual and augmented realities. These realities are based on adding visual 3D modalities into the environment. As a result, this framework offered some interesting new modalities and introduced new ways of training, gaming, and so on. AR/VR/3DUI do not necessarily provide new interaction modalities but a new environment to interact. They are commonly associated with head tracking, hand controllers, head-mounted displays, and various other forms of interaction. There is very limited research on guiding principles for combining modalities in AR/VR/3DUI.

Ubiquitous Computing, and related concepts such as Ambient Computing and the Internet of Things, influenced HCI significantly [5]. This framework is based on the idea that users are surrounded by an increasing number of smart devices, each one of these devices has a function it fulfills in everyday life, and by adding interconnectivity between these devices, regardless of the type of connection, it could offer new possibilities and experiences. As the internet became the most dominant and accessible means of communication, it led to the establishment of the IoT framework by looking at it from a different angle that incorporated the internet as a means of communication. This framework showcases the importance of looking at the changing functions of parts versus the whole they constitute. However, it was applied on a very narrow application, and this highlights the importance of looking at HCI from a holistic broader angle.

Adaptive User Interfaces (AUI) are based on using intelligent adapting mechanisms to overcome usability issues [21, 22]. The angle this framework looked at was the idea that human beings adapt to each other, and the environment based on their interactions and, as a result, interactions and communications become better. While this framework is focused on the customization of interactions, it would be very interesting to look at it holistically to assess if the interrelations between its modalities would affect this customization positively or negatively in different scenarios.

Natural User Interfaces (NUI) framework [6] looked at user interactions from the angle that HCI should feel natural by incorporating the user's natural interactions. Examples of these natural interactions are gaze, speech, touch, and gesture. Similarly, the Multimodal User Interfaces (MUI) framework [1, 2] is based on the simple idea that human beings do not experience the world through one modality. Therefore, it encouraged multimodality instead of focusing on one form of modalities which was common in 2D widgets. By emphasizing this angle, most experiences turned from visual to auditory to include new unique forms of modalities. While there are many studies within the realm of NUI and MUI, there is limited research on how to design multimodal experiences in a holistic way, i.e., how to relate modalities to each other. The focus in this area has been on special applications such as AR/VR or conversational agent [23, 24], or on multimodal integration [14], i.e., when to use multiple modalities, as opposed to what design principles to follow so that the modalities can offer a holistic experience.

## 3   Research Approach

### 3.1   A Framework for Designing Holistic Multimodal Interaction

As discussed earlier, while there are many HCI frameworks, the majority are focused on the presence of modalities or the best way to utilize them in specific scenarios. Additionally, they tend to examine these modalities in isolation to solve different sets of problems. The effect of different modalities as a whole to solve a problem is different from the effect of each in isolation. Furthermore, there have been many new trends that are becoming common in new experiences. However, there is no integrated framework that systematically examines these trends and notions thoroughly as parts of a whole, rather than being optional afterthoughts.

The notion of holistic frameworks is not a new one. However, it has been mainly focused on user experience, which is only one element of HCI. These user experiences do not consider functionality or the interrelation and dynamics between modalities or mereological parts as part of the design process. For example, Pallot et al. [12] investigated different attributes of user experience design in living labs. Living labs are labs designed for studying user experiences. As a result, they produced a sample experience-illustration of a limited number of factors in a holistic user experience. They came up with a list of 10 experience types, 22 elements, and about 80 properties. They identified the following experience types: perceptual, cognitive, reciprocal, social, emotional, cultural, empathetical, technological, economical, legal, and ethical. Then each one of these experience types had elements and properties. However, this and similar studies focus only on understanding the user experience, and they do not offer guidelines on how to design multimodal experiences.

Inspired by the whole-part theories and the notions of holism and Gestalt, we propose the Holistic Multimodal Interaction and Design (HMID) framework. HMID borrows the principles of holism and holistic solutions in other fields and defines three initial principles for holistic interaction design in HCI:

1. **Integration:** This principle is the foundation of multimodal systems and states that a multimodal experience should bring together different modalities as one package.

It means that the multimodal experience is not a set of separate actions, each with one modality, but a single design that uses those modalities where and how they are more suitable.

2. **Seamless transition**: As a follow-up to integration, seamless transition means that the user should be able to switch from one modality to another at any time, even within a task, without much effort or loss of data.

3. **Consistency**: The third principle combines two seemingly opposite aspects, being compatible with being complementary. It means that while different modalities follow the same objective and communicate the same message, they complement each other by providing different advantages.

We performed an initial evaluation of HMID and its guiding principles (compared to limited modality and isolated multimodal cases) through a simulated retail experience using storyboards, as described in Sect. 4. The findings of this study (Sect. 5) suggested a fourth principle, personalization, which will be discussed in Sect. 6. Before providing the details of the study, we will briefly review the concept of storyboards and the initial validation process that prepared us for the main study.

### 3.2 Using Storyboards

To investigate the potential of a holistic approach in the context of a retail experience, we followed the approach of illustrating hypothetical scenarios by using storyboards. In the absence of actual system implementation, due to logistic restrictions and the COVID pandemic, storyboards offer a simulated experience for users to interact. We selected to use storyboards to explain what a user would experience in a common visual language so that participants can easily understand the interactions with the system. Figure 1 shows the first three panels of a simulated experience.

*User at home casually browsing the web on tablet computer*

User: My favourite brand is doing a special collaboration with an artist!

User: The new products are so cool! I can buy them online now too!

**Fig. 1.** Sample storyboard.

The design process of the storyboards followed the guidelines established by Truong et al. [15] in that we used short textual descriptions to describe the process, included people to explain the interactive experience, indicated the passage of time only when necessary, and used the minimum level of detail required to understand the scenario. All created storyboards are freely available online:

https://www.dropbox.com/sh/9rzfp4d71t2tsj0/AADdehzgIB2pzqR_xuvKoxKca.

In each of the three storyboard case scenarios (limited modality, isolated multimodal, and HMID), there is a customer engaged in a retail fashion shopping experience. The user goes through several situations that eventually lead to a product sale.

To ensure that participants understood the storyboards, we conducted a pre-study survey with five participants (3 males and 2 females) ranging in age from 30 to 39 years old. A questionnaire depicting early sketches of the three scenarios was sent asking for feedback on the clarity of the descriptions and the understanding of the scenarios. Some examples of the questions asked were: "Does the scenario make sense?", "Are the user's actions clear?", and "Do you have any suggestions for improving the pictures?". Participants were also invited to provide any general comments they had for improvement. To summarize, below were the comments we received and considered while iterating on the storyboard designs:

- Transition across the devices using voice commands is seamless and intuitive.
- The treasure hunt idea was well-liked and stimulated the most interest, yet some could not relate it to the retail experience.
- Overall, the pictures were clear. But because there is so much going on, it can be hard to keep track of. As such, in the final design, some panels were combined to shorten the story while still retaining the main idea.
- Many found that the use of QR codes was a good idea for encouraging customer engagement and interaction with the product.
- The fact that there were different payment options was not clear.

## 4 Main Study

We conducted an online survey to evaluate the preferences for scenarios. The independent variables are the three case scenarios (1) two modalities, (2) isolated multimodal, and (3) holistic multimodal. The dependent variables are increased sales, increased brand awareness, and increased customer engagement.

### 4.1 Participants

A total of 140 participants completed the survey. However, 21 of the responses were discarded as the descriptions did not properly describe the scenario, answers were too brief (e.g., one-word answers), the completion time was too short (e.g., under 3 min), or attention check questions were missed. The final data set contained 119 responses (75 men and 44 women) ranging in age from 18 to 50 years old ($M = 34.41$ years, $SD = 7.65$ years). 108 participants reported they enjoyed shopping, while 11 did not. Among the 108 respondents, 41 of them prefer to shop alone, 18 of them prefer to shop with friends and 49 prefer to shop both with friends and alone.

### 4.2 Materials and Instruments

A retail experience was the subject of our study. The goal was to design a marketing and sales campaign to increase sales, customer engagement, and brand awareness. A variety of modalities were included, such as printed material, website, mobile apps, AR advertising, a multi-platform treasure hunt to collect points, and in-store interaction.

The storyboards show a character and his interactions with technologies that were corresponded to each of the three case scenarios:

1. For the "two modalities" scenario, the user engages separately with two modalities of the retail experience.
2. For "isolated multimodal", the user engages in an isolated multimodal retail experience.
3. For "holistic multimodal", the user engages in a holistic, multimodal experience. This case is designed using the three principles of integration, seamless transition, and consistency.

The principles of HMID were implemented in the storyboard interactions by showing how the user can seamlessly switch between the different kinds of interaction modalities at hand. For HMID, we showed the same experience being available using all modalities, but each with its own conveniences. For example, a desktop browser could be simply used to collect points by answering questions. But an AR-based mobile app, while more complex, could be more convenient and allow a richer experience. We used storyboards to simulate the user experience. Figure 2 shows examples of three HMID principles at work.

To compare the performance of HMID compared to two other approaches, we considered three evaluation criteria: sales, customer engagement, and brand awareness (Table 1). Following each scenario, participants indicated their level of agreement on a 7-point (1 = strongly disagree to 7 = strongly agree) Likert scale.

### 4.3 Recruitment and Procedures

After receiving clearance from our institutional ethics review committee, the recruitment for participants commenced. Participants were recruited using Amazon Mechanical Turk (MTurk) [25]. MTurk is an online crowdsourcing platform where "workers" complete small tasks for monetary reward [26]. It is a popular method for recruiting large and diverse participants in many HCI studies [27–29]. Studies show that most workers participate out of interest or to pass the time, rather than for the sake of the reward, making these participants a good source for collecting data [30]. Participants had to be over 18 years old, must understand English, and own a computer or a mobile device with an internet connection to complete the questionnaire. A link to the questionnaire was hosted online (Qualtrics, Provo, UT) and takes approximately 30 min to complete. The questionnaire consisted of three parts. Part I collected demographic-related information (e.g., age, gender, and level of education), as well as information about shopping behaviours and preferences. Part II provided some background context to explain the scenarios, followed by the storyboards where participants were invited to look at the drawings and indicate their level of agreement or disagreement on a 7-point Likert scale to questionnaire statements that evaluated the dependent variables: increased sales, brand awareness, and customer engagement. Participants were also asked an open-ended question to share any further comments about the experience after each case scenario.

**Fig. 2.** HMID principles implemented in storyboards. Panels 7–10 and 25–28 show integration, seamless transition, and consistency.

**Table 1.** Questionnaire statements that evaluated dependent variables.

| Dependent variable | Questionnaire statements |
|---|---|
| Increase sales | I felt that the technological features were helpful in promoting increased sales |
| | I felt that the product promotion and the use of technology helped increase the sales |
| Increase customer engagement | I felt engaged with the brand campaign |
| | I felt delighted by the brand's promotional experience |
| | I felt that the technology features were easy for me to engage with the brand |
| Increase brand awareness | I felt the brand's promotional campaign and the use of technology did well in increasing brand awareness |

To ensure that respondents understood each case scenario portrayed in the story-boards, in addition to asking them to read the text provided underneath each storyboard, they were also asked to write a short description of what they thought was happening in the images before they provided a rating. At the end of each scenario, respondents were invited to provide any other thoughts they had. Attention check questions adapted from the Conscientious Responder Scale [31] were integrated into the questionnaire to verify that respondents were reading and answering the questions carefully. Participants received $2.00 USD as compensation for participating in the study.

### 4.4  Statistical Analysis

Analyses were performed using IBM SPSS for Windows Version 27.0 (SPSS, Chicago, Illinois), and prior to analyses, including the filtering process described in 4.1, the data were screened for missing values, outliers, and out-of-range values. Descriptive statistics and the Shapiro-Wilk's test of normality [32] were calculated for each of the three retail experience cases (two modalities, isolated multimodal, and holistic multimodal) with respect to the three dependent variables (increase sales, increase brand awareness, and increase engagement).

## 5   Results

### 5.1  Quantitative Results

Descriptive statistics and the Shapiro-Wilk's test were conducted to examine the normality of the sample (Table 2). Based on the shape of the distributions and the results of the Shapiro-Wilk's test, non-parametric tests were selected for analysis. An alpha level of 0.05 was set for all statistical tests.

To explore the data, 100% stacked bar charts were generated to compare each of the case scenarios with respect to the dependent measures (Fig. 3). This provided a visual representation to examine the overall distribution. Based on Fig. 3, we can see that participants preferred a more holistic experience for each of our dependent measures. It is interesting to note that for each dependent measure, the percentage between Case 2 and Case 3 showed minor differences.

A Friedman test was conducted to examine the differences between each of the three cases with respect to our dependent measures. Results showed that there were statistically significant differences between the cases for increased sales and customer engagement, but there were no statistically significant differences for brand awareness (Table 3).

Next, post-hoc tests, using the Wilcoxon signed-rank tests, were conducted between each pair of cases separately to further examine where the differences occurred.

Table 4 summarizes the results. For increased sales, case 2 is better than 1, likewise, case 3 is also better than 1, but no difference between case 2 and 3. This suggests that a holistic experience will likely increase sales. For brand awareness, case 2 is better than 1, but no differences between case 1 vs. 3 and 3 vs. 2. This suggests that a holistic experience may be similar to other cases for increasing brand awareness. For customer engagement, there were no differences between case 1 and 2, but there was a statistically significant difference between case 1 vs. 3, and 2 vs. 3. This suggests that offering a holistic experience might not necessarily increase the level of engagement.

**Table 2.** Descriptive statistics for the level of agreement for the three dependent measures: increased sales (IS), brand awareness (BA), and customer engagement (CA), with respect to each of the three cases: two modalities (TM), isolated multimodal (IM), and holistic multimodal (HM), and the Shapiro-Wilk's test of Normality.

| N = 119 | | Descriptive Statistics | | | | | Shapiro-Wilk's test | | |
|---|---|---|---|---|---|---|---|---|---|
| Case | Measure | M | SD | Mdn | Skewness | Kurtosis | W | df | p |
| TM | IS | 10.60 | 2.73 | 11.00 | − .69 | − .06 | .93 | 119 | .00 |
| | BA | 5.43 | 1.54 | 6.00 | − .96 | .29 | .86 | 119 | .00 |
| | CE | 15.00 | 3.85 | 15.00 | − .52 | .32 | .96 | 119 | .00 |
| IM | IS | 11.27 | 2.41 | 12.00 | − .80 | .16 | .91 | 119 | .00 |
| | BA | 5.79 | 1.21 | 6.00 | − .97 | .56 | .85 | 119 | .00 |
| | CE | 15.47 | 3.64 | 16.00 | − .65 | .18 | .95 | 119 | .00 |
| HM | IS | 11.41 | 1.88 | 12.00 | − .39 | − .52 | .94 | 119 | .00 |
| | BA | 5.63 | 1.34 | 6.00 | − 1.06 | .91 | .86 | 119 | .00 |
| | CE | 11.74 | 3.80 | 11.00 | .67 | − .04 | .94 | 119 | .00 |

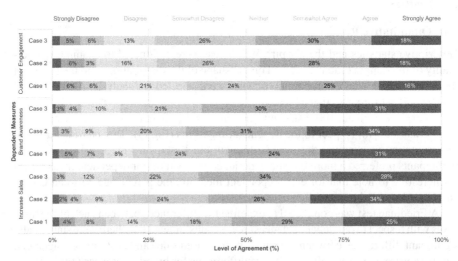

**Fig. 3.** 100% stacked bar charts for the level of agreement on dependent measures with respect to three case scenarios: (1) two modalities, (2) isolated multimodal, and (3) holistic multimodal (N = 119).

## 5.2 Qualitative Results

At the end of each case scenario, participants were given the opportunity to provide their feedback. This was helpful as it gave us insight into how the increased use of technologies, that is, from a single modality to an HMID experience, would be received from this population sample. We conducted open coding, the initial interpretive process by which

**Table 3.** Mean rank results of a Friedman test for each of the three cases with respect to the dependent measures.

| Measures | Mean Ranks | | | Friedman test statistics | | |
|---|---|---|---|---|---|---|
|  | Case 1 | Case 2 | Case 3 | $\chi^2$ | df | p |
| Increases Sales | 1.81 | 2.13 | 2.05 | 10.15 | 2 | .01 |
| Brand Awareness | 1.91 | 2.13 | 1.96 | 4.870 | 2 | .09 |
| Customer Engagement | 2.24 | 2.37 | 1.40 | 71.29 | 2 | .00 |

**Table 4.** Mean rank results of Wilcoxon's signed-rank tests for each of the three cases: (1) two modalities, (2) isolated multimodal, and (3) holistic multimodal, with respect to the dependent measures: increase sales, brand awareness, and customer engagement.

| Measures | Case comparisons | Mean Ranks | | Wilcoxon test | |
|---|---|---|---|---|---|
|  |  | Positive | Negative | $\chi^2$ | p |
| Increases sales | 1 vs 2 | 37.14 | 36.79 | − 2.61 | .01 |
|  | 1 vs 3 | 40.71 | 34.71 | − 2.56 | .01 |
|  | 2 vs 3 | 44.60 | 32.52 | − .49 | .62 |
| Brand awareness | 1 vs 2 | 34.96 | 27.19 | − 2.52 | .01 |
|  | 1 vs 3 | 37.43 | 33.20 | − 1.08 | .28 |
|  | 2 vs 3 | 36.70 | 35.55 | − 1.50 | .13 |
| Customer engagement | 1 vs 2 | 50.41 | 45.20 | − 1.09 | .28 |
|  | 1 vs 3 | 31.65 | 62.72 | − 6.92 | .00 |
|  | 2 vs 3 | 28.26 | 62.62 | − 7.92 | .00 |

raw research data are first systematically analyzed and categorized [33], followed by axial coding, a qualitative research technique that involved relating data together to uncover codes, categories, and sub-categories grounded within participants' voices within the collected data [34]. This method was appropriate not only to organize the data but was also useful for deriving potential new theories and concepts, insights that may be of value. With open coding, we deduced three categories: (1) Positives, (2) Negatives, and (3) Concerns. "Positives" relate to the positive attitudes towards the idea and user experience, while "negatives" describe the doubts and skepticisms about the idea and user experience. "Concerns" are worries that users had about the experience.

Next, we further compartmentalized participants' responses using axial coding. This was achieved by recognizing like-patterns in participants' answers, thereby collecting and categorizing them appropriately. Axial coding revealed Fun/Enjoyment, Engagement, and Immersive under Positives, Too Complex, Overwhelming, Waste of Time and Annoyed under Negatives, and Privacy and Tracking under Concerns.

In general, we found that most participants who provided feedback related to "fun and engagement" stated that they welcomed the increase in technology. For example, in Case 2, one participant (P1) wrote: "*I thought the technology made shopping a more pleasant experience in this scenario*" when comparing it with Case 1. In Case 3, another participant (P17) said: "*I thought there was a lot of technology in this scenario, and it all worked together to provide a better shopping experience*". Furthermore, participants generally thought that the experience simulated in Case 3 was engaging and exciting if the process was efficient. For example, one participant (P90) said that "*as long as steps and rewards are easy to follow and understand, then I love utilizing all the platforms to buy items*". Another participant (P33) thought that "*the brand did a great job engaging a certain segment of its customer base into buying more and being more excited by its use of technology as a marketing technique*". One more participant (P7) wrote: "*I like the idea of full use of technology like the last one and making it seamless between devices*". This suggests that the holistic experience portrayed in Case 3 was well-received.

Participants also reported negative experiences. Participants expressed that the excessiveness and the steps to use the technology to achieve the goal of purchasing products would be overwhelming. For example, in Case 2, one participant (P10) said that there are "*too many steps and too complicated*". Another participant (P38) explained that it "*seems like a lot of needless extra work to buy item*". For design, these comments suggest that it is important to make the process as simple as possible.

Interestingly, there was only one participant (P41) who raised concerns about data privacy, saying that: "*I have a concern with tracking and privacy*".

# 6   Discussion and Redesign

The result from the data supports the idea that a more multimodal experience using different technologies favour increased sales, brand awareness, and customer engagement. However, there is not much difference between multimodal Case 2 and my hypothesized HMID Case 3. There could be a variety of reasons for this. Let me explain.

It could be that the storyboards themselves needed to convey a better narrative of HMID. But a more likely explanation is that not all participants were comfortable with using various modalities/technologies in the HMID case. Reflecting on this possibility, we hypothesized that a holistic experience should be flexible and adaptive, catering the user's needs.

To informally verify this hypothesis, we ran a small mini-study with only three participants. We picked four sections of the HMID case where the user was using different modalities, and offered options such as a more convenient technology or a more familiar one. For example, Fig. 4 shows a section of the storyboard where the user received a notification on his smart watch that there is an AR-based point to collect as part of the treasure hunt. We asked if the existence of an option to save this location for the future, instead of having to use AR, adds flexibility, and so improves the HMID experience. All participants agreed with comments such as "Yes, it would improve the HMID scenario because any sort of flexibility or convenience provides a better experience for the user" (P2).

The findings of the main and follow-up studies encouraged us to add personalization as the fourth principle of holistic, multimodal interaction and design.

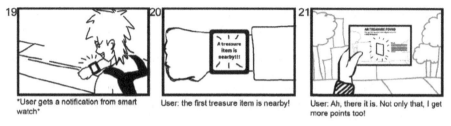

**Fig. 4.** Storyboard Sample used in follow-up mini-study.

## 7  Conclusion

Based on a review of literature on HCI frameworks and whole-part theories, we proposed a holistic, multimodal interaction and design framework based on the principles of integration, seamless transition, and consistency. Using a conceptual storyboard approach and survey research methodology, we compared the perceived effect of this framework with two other cases (limited modality and isolated multimodal) in a simulated retail scenario with the objectives of increasing sales, brand awareness, engagement, and overall satisfaction. The results from both quantitative and qualitative analyses suggested that multimodal and holistic experiences are more effective with regard to the objectives. Further reflection suggested that personalization should be added as a fourth principle to allow flexibility in holistic experiences.

As society increasingly adopts emerging technologies (such as wearables, AR/VR, amongst others), a holistic and cohesive approach for the seamless integration of data from one multimodal to another is necessary. Although this research study was specifically catered to the retail shopping scenario, we believe that HMID can potentially lay the foundation for new HCI paradigms for IoTs. Plausible future HMID research directions include education, sports, and how we engage and interact with information media platforms.

## References

1. Nigay, L., Coutaz, J.: A design space for multimodal systems. In: Proceedings of the SIGCHI conference on Human factors in computing systems - CHI '93. ACM Press, New York, New York, USA, pp 172–178 (1993)
2. Oviatt, S.: Multimodal Interfaces. human-computer Interact Handb Fundam Evol Technol Emerg Appl **14**, 405–430 (2012). https://doi.org/10.1201/b11963-22
3. Kruschitz, C., Hitz, M.: Human-computer interaction design patterns: structure, methods, and tools. Int J Adv Softw **3**, 225–237 (2010)
4. Ishii, H., Ullmer, B.: Emerging frameworks for tangible user interfaces. IBM Syst J **39**, 915–931 (2000)
5. Weiser, M.: The computer for the 21st century. Sci Am **265**, 94–104 (1991). https://doi.org/10.1038/scientificamerican0991-94
6. Jain, J., Lund, A., Wixon, D.: The future of natural user interfaces. Conf Hum Factors Comput Syst - Proc 211–214 (2011). https://doi.org/10.1145/1979742.1979527

7. Gorlewicz, J.L., Tennison, J.L., Uesbeck, P.M., et al.: Design guidelines and recommendations for multimodal, touchscreen-based graphics. ACM Trans. Access Comput. **13** (2020). https://doi.org/10.1145/3403933

8. Reeves, L.M., Martin, J.C., McTear, M., et al.: Guidelines for multimodal user interface design. Commun ACM **47**, 57–59 (2004)

9. Sarter, N.B.: Multimodal information presentation: design guidance and research challenges. Int J Ind Ergon **36**, 439–445 (2006). https://doi.org/10.1016/j.ergon.2006.01.007

10. Snyder, L.J.: Stanford Encyclopedia of Philosophy Stanford Encyclopedia of Philosophy: Implicit Bias. 1–22 (2017)

11. Smuts, J.C.: Holism and Evolution. Macmillan (1926)

12. Pallot, M., Pawar, K.: A holistic model of user experience for living lab experiential design. 2012 18th Int Conf Eng Technol Innov ICE 2012 - Conf Proc. (2012) https://doi.org/10.1109/ICE.2012.6297648

13. Luxoft Developed a Holistic Automotive User Experience Solution Based on SmartDeviceLink | Business Wire. https://www.businesswire.com/news/home/20131111006225/en/Luxoft-Developed-a-Holistic-Automotive-User-Experience-Solution-Based-on-SmartDeviceLink. Accessed 9 Jun 2022

14. Turk, M.: Multimodal interaction: a review. Pattern Recognit Lett **36**, 189–195 (2014). https://doi.org/10.1016/j.patrec.2013.07.003

15. Truong, K.N., Hayes, G.R., Abowd, G.D.: Storyboarding: an empirical determination of best practices and effective guidelines. Proc. Conf. Des. Interact Syst. Process. Pract. Methods, Tech. DIS **2006**, 12–21 (2006)

16. Mayhew, R.: Part and whole in aristotle's political philosophy. J Ethics **1**, 325–340 (1997). https://doi.org/10.1023/A:1009743012461

17. Heller, M., Simons, P.: Parts: a study in ontology. Philos. Rev. **100**, 488 (1991). https://doi.org/10.2307/2185078

18. Mather, G.: Foundations of perception. 404–427 (2006)

19. Van Dam, A.: Post-WIMP user interfaces. Commun ACM **40**, 63–67 (1997). https://doi.org/10.1145/253671.253708

20. Milgram, P., Takemura, H., Utsumi, A., Kishino, F.: Mixed Reality (MR) Reality-Virtuality (RV) Continuum. Syst Res **2351**, 282–292 (1994)

21. Raheel, S.: Improving the user experience using an intelligent Adaptive User Interface in mobile applications. 2016 IEEE Int Multidiscip Conf Eng Technol IMCET 2016 64–68 (2016). https://doi.org/10.1109/IMCET.2016.7777428

22. Hui, K.K., Liu, J., Wong, C.K.: An adaptive user interface based on personalized learning. IEEE Intell. Syst. **18**, 52–57 (2003)

23. Krishnaswamy, N., Pustejovsky, J.: An evaluation framework for multimodal interaction. Lr 2018 - 11th Int Conf Lang Resour Eval 2127–2134 (2019)

24. Rakkolainen, I., Farooq, A., Kangas, J., et al.: Technologies for multimodal interaction in extended reality—a scoping review. Multimodal Technol. Interact **5** (2021). https://doi.org/10.3390/mti5120081

25. Keith, M.G., Tay, L., Harms, P.D.: Systems perspective of amazon mechanical turk for organizational research: review and recommendations. Front Psychol **8** (2017). https://doi.org/10.3389/fpsyg.2017.01359

26. Difallah, D.E., Catasta, M., Demartini, G., et al.: The dynamics of micro-Task crowdsourcing: The case of amazon MTurk. WWW 2015 - Proc 24th Int Conf World Wide Web 238–247 (2015). https://doi.org/10.1145/2736277.2741685

27. Orji, R., Tondello, G.F., Nacke, L.E.: Personalizing persuasive strategies in gameful systems to gamification user types. Conf Hum Factors Comput Syst - Proc 2018-April (2018). https://doi.org/10.1145/3173574.3174009

28. Hirsh, J.B., Kang, S.K., Bodenhausen, G.V.: Personalized persuasion: tailoring persuasive appeals to recipients' personality traits. Psychol. Sci. **23**, 578–581 (2012). https://doi.org/10.1177/0956797611436349

29. Jia, Y., Xu, B., Karanam, Y., Voida, S.: Personality-targeted gamification: a survey study on personality traits and motivational affordances. In: Proceedings of the 2016 CHI Conference on Human Factors in Computing Systems - CHI '16. ACM Press, New York, New York, USA, pp 2001–2013 (2016)

30. Buhrmester, M., Kwang, T., Gosling, S.D.: Amazon's mechanical turk: a new source of inexpensive, yet high-quality data? Methodol issues Strateg Clin Res (4th ed) 133–139 (2015). https://doi.org/10.1037/14805-009

31. Marjanovic, Z., Struthers, C.W., Cribbie, R., Greenglass, E.R.: The conscientious responders scale: a new tool for discriminating between conscientious and random responders. SAGE Open **4** (2014). https://doi.org/10.1177/2158244014545964

32. Mohd, N., Bee, Y.: Power comparisons of Shapiro-Wilk, Kolmogorov-Smirnov, Lilliefors and Anderson-Darling tests. J. Stat. Model Anal. **2**, 13–14 (2011)

33. Mills, A., Durepos, G., Wiebe, E.: Coding: open coding. In: Encyclopedia of Case Study Research. SAGE Publications, Inc., 2455 Teller Road, Thousand Oaks California 91320 United States (2013)

34. Allen, M.: Axial coding. In: The SAGE Encyclopedia of Communication Research Methods. SAGE Publications, Inc, 2455 Teller Road, Thousand Oaks California 91320 (2017)

# Promote the Sustainable Development of Design Education Management in Private Universities by Evaluating Work

Liuying Huang and Xia Cai[✉]

Beijing Technology Institute, Zhuhai, People's Republic of China
caixia858@126.com

**Abstract.** Teaching evaluation refers to a kind of value judgment on the quality and quantity of teaching, which plays the role of guidance, control and incentive mechanism of teaching. Accurate teaching evaluation is an essential means to improve teaching quality. In view of the ineffectiveness and fuzziness of teaching evaluation caused by unknown attribution of teaching effect in the universities at present, this paper takes the sustainable development of design education management in private universities as the research object, aiming at the universities with design majors. The characteristics of design education management suggest that the improvement of teaching quality is inseparable from scientific and strict management. In order to further strengthen the management of design education in private universities, the means of "promoting construction by evaluation" should be used, and the difficulties and problems existing in the management of design education in private universities should be faced squarely, so as to actively seek countermeasures to finally realize the sustainable development of art education management in private universities.

**Keywords:** Promote construction by evaluation · Design education management · Sustainable development

## 1  Introduction

The sustainable development of China's social economy has led to the development of higher education. Private higher education is an integral part of higher education, shouldering the significant mission of training talents for the society. Private universities and their bases fully contribute to the reform of the education system. The Outline of the National Medium- and Long-Term Education Reform and Development Plan (2010–2020) clearly points out: "Private education should be robustly supported [1]. Private education is a substantial growth point in the development of education and the backbone of promoting educational reform". The growth and development of private universities has alleviated the burden of national finance, greatly met the needs of the people to receive higher education, and trained a large number of talents for the society.

The "evaluation" of this paper mainly focuses on the evaluation of the level of undergraduate teaching in the universities, which contributes to further strengthening

M. Kurosu et al. (Eds.): HCII 2022, LNCS 13516, pp. 34–42, 2022.
https://doi.org/10.1007/978-3-031-17615-9_3

the state's macro-management and guidance on the teaching work of the universities according to the level of teaching work, urging the departments in charge of education at all levels to attach importance to and support the teaching work of the universities, promoting schools to consciously implement the national educational policy, and further clarifying the guiding ideology of running a school, improving the conditions for running a school, strengthening the basic construction of teaching, strengthening teaching management, deepening teaching reform, and improving teaching quality and efficiency in an all-round way in accordance with the laws of education.

## 2  Literature Review

### 2.1  Promote Construction by Evaluation

Teaching evaluation urges private universities to establish a feasible teaching management system according to their own characteristics, optimize the educational management system, improve the informationization of teaching management, establish a routine inspection system and examination monitoring system, and establish a system of supervision, listening and evaluation. It plays an auxiliary role in improving the quality of teaching, strengthening the training and learning of teachers' scientific research, and promoting teachers to improve the level of scientific research. According to the requirements of the index system of teaching evaluation, we should earnestly take teaching work as the focus of financial input, increase the investment of teaching funds, and strengthen the construction of basic teaching conditions, and use the standard of normal evaluation to promote construction, consolidate achievements, deepen reform, improve quality, realize the coordinated development of scale, quality, structure and benefit, and cultivate high-quality talents with all-round development.

The teaching evaluation mechanism plays a critical function of guiding and standardizing in the whole teaching system. Design education falls within the scope of the art discipline. The establishment of the teaching evaluation system of design education in the universities should not replace the special standards of the art discipline with the general standards of liberal arts or science and engineering, but should completely respect and follow the law of the development of art discipline itself, grasp the characteristics of art discipline construction and construct a scientific teaching evaluation system in art universities [2]. Professor Chen Houfeng deals with the hot and difficult issues in the classification, orientation, evaluation and management of Chinese universities in his book Research on the Classification and Positioning of Chinese Higher Education Institutions, and puts forward some suggestions with policy value and reference significance around how to guide the classification and reasonable positioning of the universities [3]. In addition, a number of scholars discussed the realistic path to speed up the popularization of China's higher education and promote the leap-forward development of higher education institutions from the perspectives of practical concerns and classification and positioning of China's higher education development. In 2017, the Department and Bureau of the Ministry of Education of China organized experts to study and formulate the National Standards for Teaching Quality of Ordinary Universities Compared with Undergraduate Majors, which is the first national standard in the field of higher education in China and is of iconic significance. It defines the basic quality requirements of undergraduate specialty setting, which not only puts forward the minimum requirements for the teaching quality of all majors, but also leaves room for the specific teaching requirements of each major, because it promotes the formation of talent training characteristics of the same major in different universities, provides a reference for evaluating the quality of professional teaching, reflects the foresight of professional construction, and provides a guiding role for the sustainable development of educational construction [4]. As a fundamental link in promoting the development of education, the sustainable development of education in private universities should have the characteristics of fairness, coordination, sharing, efficiency, etc. [5].

## 2.2 Sustainable Development of Education

Sustainable development is a concept with high frequency in modern society, and contains extremely abundant connotations as a new type of social development strategy and goal. The requirement of sustainability should be added to the concept of development to produce at least four elements: sustainable use of resources, sustainable improvement of the environment, sustainable social equity and sustainable economic growth [6]. Sustainable development is the inevitable choice for human society to realize the coordinated development of economy, society, environment and population. In order to achieve this development goal, it is necessary to build the cultural basis of sustainable development as a long-term and effective cultural support for sustainable development [7]. In the past, we paid more attention to the research on education system and education policy, but in the future, we should strengthen the discussion on the micro-level issues such as curriculum, teaching and evaluation, and study the changes of talent training mode in the future, so as to serve the reform and development of education in China [8].

The formulation of sustainable development strategy in a university is inseparable from a clear development direction, which should be accurately located according to the external environment and its own characteristics, and the premise of positioning is classification. This will help form such a chain: classification-positioning-development direction-development strategy-sustainable development.

## 3 Teaching Evaluation to Promote the Construction of Design Education Management

### 3.1 Importance of Teaching Evaluation

Since it was first proposed in the Decision of the Central Committee of the Communist Party of China on the Reform of the Education System in 1985 to evaluate the school-running level of the universities, the undergraduate teaching evaluation in China has roughly gone through the stages of exploration, practice, optimization, improvement and comprehensive promotion. The State Council listed "comprehensively improving the quality of higher education" and "improving the quality of talent training" as the top priorities in the strategic development of China's higher education in the Outline of the National Medium- and Long-Term Education Reform and Development Plan (2010–2020), and has put forward a series of important measures to comprehensively implement "undergraduate teaching quality and teaching reform project in the universities", "improve teaching quality assurance system" and "improve teaching evaluation in the universities" [1].

Centering on the goal and requirements of the school's talent training program, we should follow the teaching law, establish and improve the school teaching quality monitoring and guarantee system through the formulation of rules and regulations, such as monitoring mechanism and evaluation mechanism, and constantly optimize and upgrade to ensure the sustainable development of school teaching quality.

### 3.2    Critical Role in Teaching Evaluation

In the teaching evaluation of the universities, the most closely related groups that affect the level of teaching evaluation of the universities are the evaluation organizations of teaching quality, the functional offices of the universities, teachers and students.

**Teaching Quality Evaluation Organization in the Universities.** The university teaching quality evaluation organization is responsible for further standardizing and perfecting the system construction in related fields from the aspects of the Ministry of Education and universities, effectively supporting the resource integration of evaluation data, and carrying out quantitative evaluation of all kinds of work. Accurately upload and release tasks and grasp the time node of each work. The internal teaching quality evaluation organization of the universities should be the responsibility of the commissioner, who should be familiar with the national and local teaching evaluation policies and constantly improve their own professional level. In addition to on-campus quality assessment organizations, third-party evaluation institutions outside the school should be invited. Moreover, peer evaluation is also a rare and necessary means.

**Coordination and Linkage of Various Functional Departments in the Universities.** The school evaluation office should coordinate with each functional department to formulate procedures, strengthen management, exchange information, and cooperate with the overall management of the school. Teaching management links should complement each other, so as to ensure the healthy operation of teaching management. The information-based teaching management model reduces the workload of teaching administrators. Departments should effectively coordinate and link, so that assessment data can be updated in a timely manner. Data sharing reduces duplication of work and improves accuracy.

**Group of Teachers.** Professional teachers are the core resources of professional construction and development. Teaching assessment is a means to provide teachers with the support they need to set and achieve the goals of better guiding students. The factors that affect teachers' teaching quality include teachers' objective characteristics and subjective characteristics. Teachers' objective characteristics include teachers' educational background, gender, nationality, professional title, salary, etc. [9], while teachers' subjective characteristics include teachers' professional knowledge familiarity, teachers' dedication, teachers' experience, etc. [10]. With the continuous change of education reform, the number of teachers, professional titles, awards and scientific research play a positive role in teaching evaluation. Teaching evaluation in the universities is regarded as a tool to improve classroom teaching, providing teachers with an objective direction of sustainable development, rather than eliminating weaker teachers. The evaluation of teachers' teaching quality is carried out through students' direct evaluation of teachers' efforts and abilities, but directly relying on these evaluations to reflect teachers' teaching quality will lead to incentive distortion [11].

**Student Group.** In recent years, the "student-centered" educational evaluation has attracted the attention of the domestic educational evaluation circle. From the perspective of value theory, not only students 'learning status should be regarded as the center of teaching evaluation, but also include students' demands for educational satisfaction in the content of educational evaluation. This paper takes the college students of design education as the research group, for this special group, the management work has a severe challenge. Whether they can actively cooperate with the management of schools and universities, and whether they can accept the management mode, management mode and management means of managers are also important factors that affect the sustainable development of teaching management in the universities. However, students, as the most important stakeholders, have little opportunity to participate in the evaluation. Students also play an important role in the submission of the main evidence of evaluation. Students must be the main body of teaching evaluation, and their participation runs through the whole process of teaching evaluation.

### 3.3   Optimize the Evaluation Index System

The construction of the teaching evaluation system in the universities of design education will help the competent departments of education to realize the macro-monitoring function, promote the basic construction of education, realize standardized and characteristic management, and promote the establishment of the innovation system of higher design education, so as to ensure the healthy development of higher design education. The evaluation index design of the Ministry of Education of China is mainly aimed at comprehensive schools. Without taking into account the teaching characteristics and achievement presentation of design education disciplines, classified guidance should be given to the universities with distinctive characteristics and strong personalization, such as design education universities.

The current evaluation system of the universities is relatively complete, but there are some unsuitable aspects in the index system that emphasize the award-winning and scientific research achievements of teachers and students in higher art universities, and the participation of works with strong practicality in the discipline of art and design, the holding of individual exhibitions and the success of creation have not been included in the index assessment system. In terms of teaching materials, design education can not fully use national unified teaching materials, because the consultation and updating speed of design majors is very fast, and many design works can not be seen in teaching materials.

The establishment of the teaching evaluation system of design education should fully respect and follow the law of the development of the discipline itself, grasp the characteristics of discipline construction, adhere to the principle of promoting construction by evaluation and focusing on construction, and make an in-depth discussion from the characteristics of design education and school-running characteristics. This will be more conducive to the overall promotion of the teaching evaluation system of the universities in our country.

The evaluation index system of undergraduate major evaluation index system of the universities in Guangdong Province mainly includes seven aspects: School reputation, Teaching body, Conditional resources, Cultivation process, Quality assurance and Scholastic achievement and Description of professional, as shown in Fig. 1. In the formulation of evaluation indicators and standards, the learning needs, further studies and professional needs of students in the universities should be fully taken into account. At the same time, students' real opinions and feedback on college teaching are also conducive to promoting the reform and development of higher education. How to improve the classification construction evaluation system of higher education by further deepening the reform of institutional mechanisms and comprehensively strengthening the modern governance system and governance capacity building, and comprehensively promoting and improving the systematic, systematic and comprehensive development level of China's higher education, is the deep meaning of realizing the connotative development of higher education.

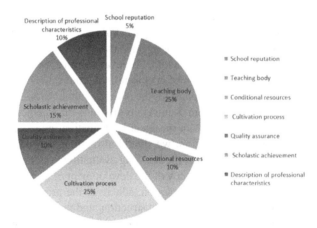

**Fig. 1.** Art Major Evaluation Index Weight

## 4 University Sustainability

With the transformation of the popularization of higher education in China from "the leap of quantity" to "the improvement of quality", private universities should strive for survival and development in the fierce competition. Due to the different educational investment system, there is a certain gap between private universities and public universities in school-running concept, talent training mode, teaching management means and the construction of teaching staff, and there are many problems in the development of private the universities, such as unstable teaching staff, lack of school-running character-istics, talent training can not meet the needs of society, etc. The sustainable development of private universities should be guided by the scientific concept of development, deeply implement the policy of "consolidation, deepening, improvement and development", and promoting the characteristics of running a school is the foundation of sustainable development. Cultural construction is the driving force of sustainable development, the construction of teachers is the foundation of sustainable development, and education and scientific research is the growing point of sustainable development.

## 4.1  Improve the Characteristics of Running a School is the Foundation of Sustainable Development

The orientation of the universities: there is an important provision in the Higher Education Law: "actively develop the cause of higher education in various forms". At present, universities pursue elite education and strive to be research universities. On the contrary, the same direction of development can not be sustainable development. The school-running characteristics of private design universities not only refer to the characteristics of the specialty itself, but also aim at the effective management methods, methods and modes established in the school-running and teaching operation of the universities. The design of the teaching evaluation system the universities should reflect the following principles: when the basic conditions of running a school are up to standard, we should focus on evaluating the innovative spirit of art universities and the teaching indicators of serving cultural and economic construction. "Innovation" and "practice" should run through the construction and evaluation of art discipline. "Innovation" emphasizes the way of thinking, while "practice" emphasizes the ability of application.

The quality of design education in a university depends on whether it has a good grasp of "innovation" and "practice". In the specific evaluation indicators, in addition to the necessary conventional indicators, we should also strengthen the evaluation of teaching practice. The establishment of the teaching evaluation system of art universi-ties should fully respect and follow the law of the development of art disciplines, grasp the characteristics of art discipline construction, adhere to the principle of promoting construction by evaluation and focusing on construction, and make an in-depth discus-sion from the characteristics of art education and the school-running characteristics of art universities, which will be more conducive to the overall promotion of the teaching evaluation system of the universities in China [2].

Taking the school-running feature of the full credit system as an example, students are enabled to freely choose courses, class hours and teachers, and arrange their own study plans. Within the flexible study period, they can apply for graduation after com-pleting the required credits according to the talent training plan. The full credit system is student-oriented, respects the individualized and differentiated development of stu-dents, and attaches great importance to quality education. The high-quality management and effectiveness of the full credit system has also become one of the characteristics of running a school today.

### 4.2 Improve the Conditions of Running Schools and Strengthen the Basic Construction of Teaching

Design education mainly involves teaching and practice, focusing on teaching infrastructure, studio construction and innovative platform construction. For example, environmental design and product design majors need model rooms, clothing sewing laboratories, digital media art majors equipped with multimedia equipment laboratories, etc., to maintain and update the equipment in a timely manner, and sign a school-enterprise cooperation platform according to the needs of different design majors to provide more internship and employment opportunities [13]. In addition, the construction of students' self-study rooms, question-and-answer platforms for teachers and students, lectures for famous teachers outside the school and sharing meetings for industry designers are also conducive to improving the learning atmosphere in the school. The tuition fees of design education majors in China are relatively high, and the financial investment of the universities should also be increased.

### 4.3 Strengthen Teaching Management and Improve Teaching Quality

Teaching management is the guarantee for the operation of various teaching activities, and occupies a core position in the management of universities. The level of teaching management directly affects the quality of teaching. The strengthening of teaching management depends on the improvement of management level and the strengthening of teaching quality monitoring. For a school to survive, it must be both effective and efficient. It is worth noting that policies must be implemented, budgets must be prepared, teachers' work must be arranged, classroom teaching must be planned and the classroom must be orderly. All of these require management to ensure the necessary tasks for the school to survive as an organization. Human, financial, material, information and other resources should be fully mobilized and utilized, so as to quickly achieve the expected educational management goals.

The professional characteristics of teaching management in the universities are obvious, with heavy responsibility and heavy load. This requires managers to have a strong dedication to work, to have a positive and correct attitude towards life, to constantly learn advanced teaching management concepts and working methods, to constantly improve the level of professional ability, to improve the incentive mechanism, and to cultivate a sense of competition. Create good conditions for development. They should actively carry out performance evaluation by continuously improving the incentive management mechanism, establish a model, play an exemplary role, form a benign competitive environment, and fully mobilize the enthusiasm and innovation of managers.

## 5  Conclusion

In order to establish the teaching evaluation system of design education, we should adhere to the principle of promoting construction by evaluation and focusing on construction, and make an in-depth discussion from the aspects of design education management. In addition, according to the requirements of the national evaluation system and the characteristics of design education, we should follow the law of discipline development to establish a teaching evaluation index system suitable for art design education. Furthermore, we should establish and improve the school teaching quality monitoring and evaluation system around the objectives and requirements of the school talent training program and follow the teaching law, and constantly optimize and upgrade to ensure the sustainable development of school teaching quality.

# References

1. The State Council: "Outline of the National Medium- and Long-Term Education and Reform and Development Plan (2010–2020)" (Articles 18 and 19) (2010)
2. Pan Lusheng, G., Qunye, D.Z., Xia, W.: Discussion on the construction of teaching evaluation system in higher art universities. Shandong Soc. Sci. **07**, 28–33 (2005)
3. Chen, H.: Research on the Classification and Positioning of Chinese Higher Education Institutions. Hunan University Press (2004)
4. "National Standards for Teaching Quality of Undergraduate Majors in Ordinary Institutions of Higher Education" Gaojiao Division No. 62 (2017)
5. Wentao, M.: An analysis of government regulation and characteristics of sustainable development of private education. Decis. Making Explor. (Middle) **08**, 67–68 (2021)
6. Wang, Z.: Sustainable development management: from indicator system to policy. Chin. Manage. Sci. **01** (1996)
7. Nanhai, Xue, Y.: Theoretical basis of sustainable development. Theor. Explor. **06**, 41–43 (2009)
8. Gu, M.: Education is a bridge for sustainable development. Educ. Sci. **05**, 1 (2021)
9. Weinberg, B.A., Hashimoto, M., Fleisher, B.M.: Evaluating teaching in higher education. J. Econ. Educ. **3** (2009)
10. Lawrence ingvarson. Recognizing accomplished teachers in Australia: Where have we been? Where are we heading? Australian J. Educ. **4** (2010)
11. White, L.J.: Efforts by departments of economics to assess teaching effectiveness: results of an informal survey. J. Econ. Educ. **1** (1995)
12. "Guangdong Provincial Universities Undergraduate Major Evaluation Index System (Trial)" Yue Jiao Gao Han No. 190 (2017)
13. Dujin, L.: Reflections on the teaching evaluation of higher art education and its index system. New Art **03**, 100–102 (2010)

# A Comparative Study of Prototyping Methods for HCI Design Using Cognitive Load-Based Measures

Naveen Kumar[1]([✉]), Jyotish Kumar[2], and Jyoti Kumar[2]

[1] School of Design, UPES Dehradun, Dehradun, India
naveenno122k@gmail.com
[2] UxLAB, Department of Design, Indian Institute of Technology Delhi,
New Delhi 110016, India

**Abstract.** Increased information complexity in HCI designs causes cognitive load on users. HCI design prototypes have been used in various stages of design process to assess the design quality and enable course correction. However, there are only a few studies reported on suitability of prototyping methods for HCI design process in testing. Also, there is a dearth of literature on cognitive load (CL) based measurement for different prototyping methods. This paper reports a comparative study of prototyping methods for HCI based control panel design from CL perspective. Comparisons of prototyping methods have been reported based on three CL measurement methods namely, subjective measure, task performance and physiological measure. Results of three CL methods were congruent and shows that, software prototype caused significantly lower CL compared to paper prototype testing. Also, it is concluded that software prototype is more suitable prototyping method in cyber physical production system scenario.

**Keywords:** Prototyping methods · Cognitive load · Physiological measurement · HCI · Industry 4.0

## 1 Introduction

Smart factory is a new concept of manufacturing in the era of Industry 4.0. The core part of smart factory is Cyber-Physical Production System (CPPS). CPPS is an intelligent production setup which is formed by connecting human and machines via cloud network [11]. CPPS deals with large amounts of smart factory data such as sensor data, managerial data, operation data, maintenance data, production planning data etc. [33]. This data can be presented on handheld, mobile human-computer interaction (HCI) based control panels [19]. Complexity of presentation of data on HCI based control panels, especially in the critical scenario of usage are cognitively challenging for CPPS operators to manage [18, 20].

Prototyping of such HCI systems is an iterative design process [21]. Different types of HCI prototyping methods are available in literature, ranging from low fidelity to high fidelity [31]. Both low and high fidelity were recommended in literature for testing of

HCI designs [34]. Design of fidelity refers to the level of detail and functionality added to the prototype. Fidelity can be varying in visuals, mode of interaction, commands, and contents [34]. High fidelity prototype is a type of prototype which uses high level of interaction, detailed computer graphics for visuals, detailed contents are presented interactively etc. whereas low fidelity prototypes are simpler, often involve manual interactions, low degree of contents and often have hand sketched visual graphics [31]. Low fidelity is often comparatively less expensive and thus is widely used for initial testing of HCI design ideas whereas high fidelity prototyping looks more realistic, often has high cost of development and thus is often used later in design process [34]. It is still not reported in literature about which prototyping methods would be useful for HCI based control panel designs. There is a need to measure the CL caused by different HCI design prototypes. The CL measurement of the designed prototypes will be required throughout the design process. However, the type of prototype itself may interfere with the CL measurement. Hence, there is a need to identify suitable prototyping methods which shows reliable CL estimation for HCI based control panel design in context of industry 4.0.

To bridge this knowledge gap, we elicit two research questions (RQs): (1) How to measure users CL to evaluate HCI prototypes? (2) Which prototyping method will have lower cognitive load and provide reliable CL estimation to access the HCI design? The aim of this paper is to highlight the need to relook at the selection of suitable prototyping method for HCI systems. Also, to propose a mix method approach to evaluate the prototyping methods from cognitive load perspective. The contributions of this paper are: (a) The method proposed for measurement of cognitive load in context of prototype evaluation (b) Identification of suitability of software prototype for HCI system in the industrial scenario of use and task execution.

## 2   Related Research

### 2.1   Prototyping Methods in Design Process

Use of prototypes for testing in early phases of design has been recommended [31] and different types of prototypes have been reported in the literature [34]. Paper prototypes are being used early in the developmental phase to get quick feedback from users and do low-cost course correction in the design process [31]. While realistic measures of actual time taken on task, response time, error rate etc. cannot be captured in the paper-based prototypes accurately. Thus, software prototypes give realistic measures of such parameters during the completion of tasks [28]. A few differences in mental complexity felt by users using paper prototype versus software prototype has been reported [3, 25]. However there is lack of studies on the measure of felt complexity of the users caused by design and complex tasks using the prototypes. Therefore, in this paper we use three cognitive load measurement methods to compare the usefulness of prototyping method in context of HCI system design.

### 2.2   Cognitive Load Types and Measuring Methods

Increase in information processing load in the working memory is known as cognitive load [22]. Three types of cognitive loads have been identified in literature, namely,

Intrinsic CL, Extraneous CL and Germane CL [22]. By definition, intrinsic CL is caused due to intrinsic nature of the information and the learning tasks. All tasks have an inherent level of difficulty [23]. The intrinsic CL is a measure of the complexity of the task. For example, adding 2-digit number causes lower intrinsic cognitive load than solving integral calculus problem. Extraneous CL has been defined as load imposed on working memory due to the way of presentation of information in the interface [23]. Complex and irrelevant information of the design needs more working memory to process information. For example, square root of a number written in alphabetical format (*SQRT*) instead of the expected symbol ($\sqrt{}$) will have different extraneous cognitive load in the user. Germane CL is defined as the load imposed due to formation of new neural schema of the learner. Learning a new way to complete a task will increase new neural schema [26]. Thus, if the tasks are new to the learner, then germane CL will increase. The three types of CL are additive in nature [22]. For example, if the task is new, task difficulty level is high, and it has added irrelevant information on interface then total CL due to the interface design will be high.

Several methods of cognitive load measurement have been reported, some of these measures are subjective while others are objective. Subjective measures often reported are NASA Task Load Index [9], Rating Scale Mental Effort (RSME) [32] and Subjective Workload Assessment Technique (SWAT) [24] etc. These subjective methods measure the 'felt' component of the task difficulty as verbally reported by the user. Some studies reported CL by assessing mental effort and task difficulty level [29]. The two CL assessing parameters (mental effort and task difficulty) were subjectively rated just after the step or task and after the completion of all the tasks [29]. Delayed ratings were found more useful and significantly higher than the average of the immediate ratings in context of cognitive load measurement [29]. Therefore, in order to validate the cognitive load differences between software and paper prototype, this paper performed subjective measurement and physiological data-based CL measurement. Correlation between them have also been done in result section.

Task performance parameters have also been reported in literature as a method of cognitive load measurement [8, 12]. Both task response time and task error have been used to understand cognitive functions [5]. Further, physiological tools such as EEG has been used for cognitive load measurement [1, 16, 17]. Electroencephalography (EEG) records microvolt fluctuations caused by neural activities of the brain. EEG signals are linear for short interval, and they are non-stationary. EEG signals are interpreted in specific bands' namely, gamma band (30–100 Hz), beta band (13–30 Hz), alpha band (8–13 Hz), theta band (4–13 Hz) and delta band (0.1–3 Hz). Frequency band power has been used in the domain of cognitive load measurement [2, 35]. It has reported that, power of alpha frequency band (8–13 Hz) remains synchronized during the resting state and become increasingly desynchronized with task difficulty [30]. Higher frequency band such as beta and gamma bands (above 13 Hz) have been reported to have higher frequency band power with increasing cognitive load [2, 16, 35]. Other researchers have proposed different feature-extraction methods for measuring cognitive load and for studying brain waves during cognitive tasks [1, 35]. As concluded from reported literature, frequency bands (especially gamma and beta band) were identified as primary features to reflect cognitive load.

Among the subjective measures of cognitive load, NASA Task Load Index (TLX) scale has often used [15]. In NASA TLX participants rate on a 10-point scale, the amount of 'felt' *'frustration'*, *'mental effort'*, *'performance'*, *'temporal demand'*, *'physical demand'* and *'mental demand'* at the end of the task [24]. Task performance (response time & error count), and physiological measures (EEG) have been used in this paper along with subjective measures.

# 3 Experiment Methodology

## 3.1 Participants

Total of 21 participants, aged between 20 to 32 years with mean age of 26.09 years and standard deviation of 3.08 years volunteered for this experiment. We showed 10 control panel elements to each participant and asked to recognize the elements. Participants who scored 7 points and above were selected for main experiment. Participants were explained about the experimental setup and a written consent was obtained before starting of the experiment.

## 3.2 Prototype Design

Two prototypes of the same control panel design were developed. Paper prototype was printed on glossy paper and the software prototype of control panel application was developed in Java and installed on an interactive touch tablet (8 in.). The *'paper prototype'* designs having a pack of 60 screens were presented manually to user and recorded their task responses manually whereas software prototype task response recorded automatically. Some of the common screens of both the prototypes are shown in Fig. 1.

The complete paper prototype set consisted of 60 screens which could be categorized in three parts based on the nature of the task and was manually operated. Whereas software prototype worked automatically on the tablet based on the coded instructions. Figure 1(a) is the starting screen for the participant and after receiving the call, machine voice explained the situation in the production process of the smart factory. With the presentation of Fig. 1(b), overall control of the production system was given to the participant and explain the critical situation of the production process with the help of an audio message.

Machine-generated auditory message was given to the test participant which made the scenario clearer, and participant felt the task more realistic. The audio message provided by the machine began when the operator received a call from the machine:

**Massage given by the machine was-**

*"Hello Sir, I am machine number #627. There is an urgent action required in plant operation.*

*In blending phase, level sensors have stopped working. System variables such as boiler temperature, pressure, motor speed and station voltage have become unstable. I have tried to set all the parameters in calculated optimum range but could not succeed. Next, I am sending you the overall machine control of the blending phase. You try to keep*

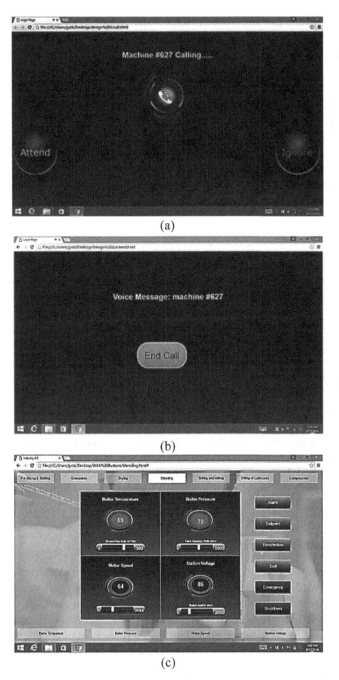

**Fig. 1.** Prototype design: (a) Starting screen (b) Intermediate screen (c) Main screen

*all the display parameters in a stable range and give your response to critical conditions only. Click END BUTTON to receive the machine control.*"

Figure 1(c) shows that two parameters of the blending phase have reached to a critical condition and the participant must control both the parameters one by one. Before that response, however, the participant must consider the machine-generated suggestions. The information provided to the participant by Fig. 1(c) established the parameters that demanded immediate controlling task from the participant.

The control panel was designed based on a hypothetical pharmaceutical manufacturing company in the context of Industry 4.0. Control panel design had four display dials namely, boiler temperature, boiler pressure, station voltage and motor speed as well as four controlling knobs namely, steam-flow rate, valve-opening width, station load, and time.

### 3.3 Task Design

Tasks namely, monitoring and controlling of the blending phase parameter, i.e., '*Temperature*', '*Pressure*', '*Motor Speed*' & '*Station Voltage*' have been given to the participants. Also, Facilitator asked participants to keep these parameters in a stable range which means, if the parameters go beyond the stable limit, then control them with suitable knobs. Stable limits were explained to the participants before the experimentation and along with scenario narration. Stable limit for the process parameters were '70 degree & below Celsius for temperature', '70 psi & below for pressure', '100 rpm & below for motor speed' and '110 V & below for station voltage'. Total task duration was 5 min (300 s) for both the prototypes and total of 16 times process parameters indicate critical limit condition within the 5 min of task. The '*response time*' and '*error counts*' were recorded manually in paper prototype by the facilitator and automatically in software prototype while controlling the critical values of the process parameters by the participants.

Two types of errors were recorded. The first type was '*wrong attempt*' when the participant touched the wrong controlling knob. The second type was '*missed chance*' when the participant did not respond within 10 s of the 'display of the critical value'. A total error was calculated by summing up both types of errors.

### 3.4 Experiment Procedure

Each prototype was tested in a 24-h gap with same participant. Physiological data using EEG were recorded during task execution and participant's task performance data was collected using response time, error counts through the application installed in the tablet and subjective self-reporting data was collected post-experiment. Experiments were conducted in an isolated room which had minimum influences of environmental noises and distractions. Experimental setup for both prototype is shown in below Fig. 2.

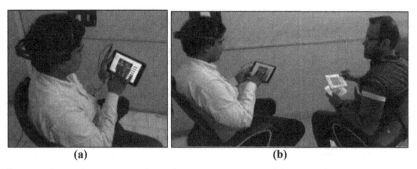

(a)                                                                      (b)

**Fig. 2.** Experimental set up (a) With software prototype, participant performing tasks alone (b) With paper prototype, screens were provided to the participant by facilitator.

Steps in the experiment for both the prototypes: Participants were explained about the EEG use in the experiment and their written consent was obtained. EEG headset was placed on the scalp of the participant according to 10–20 international system [13]. Facilitator ensured impedance of EEG sensors reached below 20 Kohm before recording of EEG signals. For software prototype, facilitator provide control panel tablet to the participant and asked them to execute the given tasks. While in paper prototype, facilitator narrate the scenario and manually provide each screen of the control panel to the participant. Assistant of the facilitator records the response time and errors of the participant during the task fulfilment. At the end of the experiment, facilitator gathered participant's feedback using NASA TLX parameters on 10-point scale. Experiment steps for both the prototype was same except the execution part (see Fig. 3).

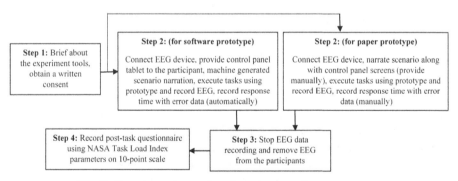

**Fig. 3.** Experimental procedure for software and paper prototype

### 3.5 EEG Data Analysis Method

Usually noise due to various electrostatic devices and muscular movements are present in raw EEG signals [27]. Standard pre-processing methods were applied to pre-process the EEG data in order to clean environmental interferences and muscle artefacts [14]. Steps followed in EEG data analysis was shown in Fig. 4.

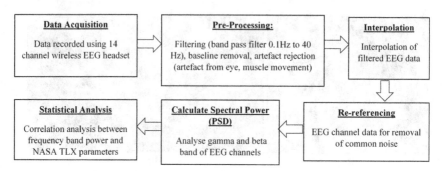

**Fig. 4.** EEG data pre-processing and analysis for CL measurement

Ten seconds of both post and prior raw EEG data was removed to get effective data set. Pre-recorded baseline was subtracted to get data related to stimuli and band pass filter (0.1 Hz to 40 Hz) was applied on the EEG channels. Interpolation of electrodes was done to bind the filtered data. Average re-referencing was performed to remove common noises from all the EEG channels with the help of EEGLAB toolbox [6]. Since EEG data contains many useful features in the frequency domain rather than time domain signals, so wavelet decomposition method was applied to transform time domain data in the frequency domain using MATLAB. For the correlation statistic, we computed the *Spearman Correlated Coefficients* between power of EEG-bands (gamma & beta) and NASA-TLX parameters. Correlation coefficient "R" and 'P' values were reported to identify the significant relationship between NASA TLX parameters with EEG band powers. Correlation between these two will be discussed in result Sect. 4.3.1.

## 4   Results and Discussion

### 4.1   Task Performance-Based CL Measurement

Total of 672 response time (2 prototypes × 21 participants x 16 controlling actions) were recorded for task performance measurement. ANOVA results shows a significant difference in mean response time ($F = 5.826$, $p < 0.05$) and error count ($F = 29.72$, $p < 0.01$) between software and paper prototypes. Figure 5 depicts that software prototype had a low mean response time which conclude that participants respond quickly in software prototype compared to paper prototype. Figure 6 shows that error count is less in software prototype compared to paper prototype which concludes that software prototype was more efficient than paper prototype.

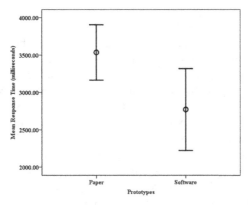

**Fig. 5.** Mean response time (millisecond) of all 21 participants for both prototypes

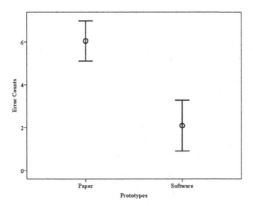

**Fig. 6.** Mean difference in error count for all 21 participants between both prototypes

Studies reported that response time and number of errors during task fulfilment reflects cognitive load of the user's [4, 5, 7]. Higher the response time and total number of errors during the task caused higher cognitive load [7]. Task performance data results showed that, participants had a smaller number of errors and less mean response time in software prototype compared to paper prototype. From subjective reporting by the participants and observation of the facilitator, it is argued here that participants had more error counts in paper prototype because of two possible reasons: (i) participants felt visually distracted due to test facilitator interacting with the functional paper prototype to replace prototype layers upon actions by users (ii) participants felt software prototype as more realistic than paper prototype and hence got optimal engaged. These results provide strong evidence that the prototype method did affect both response time and errors. Also, software prototype is more suitable for HCI system design compared to paper prototype.

## 4.2 Self-reported CL Measurement

NASA Task Load Index has been used as a self-reported method for cognitive load measurement which provide ratings on parameters such as mental demand, physical demand, temporal demand, performance, mental effort and frustration. Total of 252 NASA TLX responses (2 prototypes × 21 participants × 6 NASA TLX parameters) have been recorded for self-reported measurement of cognitive load. ANOVA between both the prototypes for six NASA TLX parameters showed that, out of six, five parameters namely, 'mental demand' (F = 15.69, $p < 0.05$), 'mental effort' (F = 18.23, $p < 0.05$), 'temporal demand' (F = 9.52, $p < 0.05$), 'performance' (F = 9.81, $p < 0.05$) and 'frustration' (F = 33.19, $p < 0.05$), were found to have significant difference between both the prototypes. Other NASA TLX parameter, 'physical demand' (F = 2.62, $p > 0.05$) did not show significant difference between the prototypes.

Several studies have reported that self-reported method alone is not a strong validation of the cognitive load caused by task complexity [8]. It has been reported that NASA TLX parameters reflects cognitive load of the user's during task fulfilment [10]. Table 1 presents the mean values and standard deviations of the NASA TLX parameters rating which indicates clear difference between the software and paper prototype.

As presented in Table 1, based on participants self-reported measures, software prototype having significantly low in 'mental demand', low in 'physical demand', low in 'temporal demand', high in 'performance', low in 'mental effort' and less in 'frustration' which is found to be more suitable for industry 4.0 scenario because of involving more reasoning and decision-making tasks. Based on the findings, it can be argued that the paper prototype does not provide a realistic environment and causes more frustration in users which congruent with task performance data. Thus, paper prototype will be helpful in the initial stage of identifying irrelevant information of the HCI but if the tasks are demanding and information is complex, like in case of Industry 4.0 HCI systems, then paper prototypes are not suitable since, it will add additional cognitive load to the users during testing.

**Table 1.** Mean and standard deviation of NASA TLX parameters ratings for both software and paper prototype

| NASA TLX parameters | Mental demand | Physical demand | Temporal demand | Performance | Mental effort | Frustration |
|---|---|---|---|---|---|---|
| *Paper* | 7.38, 1.02 | 2.47, 1.04 | 6.85, 1.27 | 5.90, 0.88 | 7.33, 0.79 | 6.95, 0.91 |
| *Software* | 3.09, 0.83 | 1.33, 0.57 | 3.19, 0.81 | 8.33, 0.96 | 2.80, 0.81 | 1.57, 0.92 |

Correlation between NASA TLX parameters for software and paper prototype for all 42 participants (21 for each prototype) have been shown in Table 2. It is evident from the correlation analysis that the 'mental demand' has a strong positive correlation with 'mental effort' and 'temporal demand'. Using Table 1, it is concluded that, mental demand of paper prototype increases with increase in time pressure and mental effort. Using paper prototype participants felt more time pressure and had high effort to attain good performance. Physical demand has a positive correlation with frustration which concludes that presenting screens by facilitator to the participant in paper prototype creates higher frustration (mean value of physical demand and frustration for paper prototype is higher than software prototype).

**Table 2.** Correlations between NASA TLX parameters for both the prototypes (*significance p > 0.05, bold style).

| NASA TLX parameters | Mental demand | Physical demand | Temporal demand | Performance | Mental effort | Frustration |
|---|---|---|---|---|---|---|
| Mental demand | 1 | −.189 .245 | **.664*** **.000** | −.020 .901 | **.473*** **.002** | −.229 .156 |
| Physical demand | | 1 | −.104 .524 | .042 .799 | .299 .061 | **.447*** **.004** |
| Temporal demand | | | 1 | .209 .195 | **.313*** **.049** | −.239 .137 |
| Performance | | | | 1 | .007 .966 | −.221 .171 |
| Mental effort | | | | | 1 | −.099 .543 |
| Frustration | | | | | | 1 |

## 4.3 Physiological CL Measurement

Total of 3.5 h (2 prototypes × 21 participants × 5-min task duration) of physiological data was recorded. Power of all the EEG channels for two frequency bands namely, beta and gamma were calculated as discussed in this section. Also, correlation analysis was performed between NASA TLX parameters and two EEG frequency band powers. Correlation coefficient 'R' and significance value 'P' of EEG band powers namely, '*gamma band*', '*beta band*' and NASA TLX parameters namely, '*mental demand*', '*temporal demand*', '*performance*', '*mental effort*', '*frustration*' have been presented in Table 3.

From Fig. 7, topography of EEG band power and NASA TLX parameters shows visual presentation of the correlation statistics (+1 represents positive correlation and −1 represents negative correlation) which indicates that EEG band power across frontal and occipital region shows a good congruence with cognitive load measure to show a significant difference between prototypes.

**Table 3.** EEG electrodes correlations (R) with spectral powers and NASA TLX parameter

| | Mental | | | Temporal | | | Performance | | | Effort | | | Frustration | | |
|---|---|---|---|---|---|---|---|---|---|---|---|---|---|---|---|
| | Elec | R value | P Value | Elec | R value | P Value | Elec | R value | P Value | Elec | R value | P Value | Elec | R value | P Value |
| **Gamma** | O1 | -0.267 | 0.105 | O1 | -0.401 | 0.013 | AF4 | 0.387 | 0.016 | FC5 | 0.394 | 0.015 | FC5 | 0.403 | 0.012 |
| | | | | | | | | | | F4 | 0.331 | 0.042 | O1 | -0.747 | 0.000 |
| **Beta** | O1 | -0.258 | 0.118 | O1 | -0.386 | 0.017 | | | | AF3 | 0.297 | 0.070 | F7 | 0.284 | 0.084 |
| | | | | | | | | | | F3 | 0.307 | 0.060 | FC5 | 0.299 | 0.068 |
| | | | | | | | | | | FC5 | 0.407 | 0.011 | O1 | -0.743 | 0.000 |
| | | | | | | | | | | T7 | 0.323 | 0.048 | | | |
| | | | | | | | | | | F4 | 0.35 | 0.031 | | | |

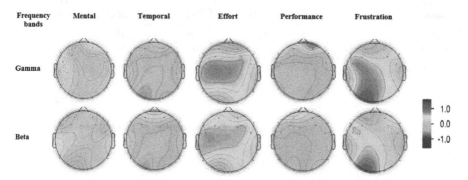

**Fig. 7.** Topography of correlation between frequency band powers with NASA TLX parameters

From Table 3, it was found that mental demand had a negative correlation with gamma (*Corr. = -0.267, P = 0.105*) and beta (*Corr. = -0.258, P = 0.118*) band power across the occipital region (O1). This showed that, frequency band power (gamma & beta) of occipital region (O1) decreases, if the '*mental demand*' of participants increases during the task fulfilment for both the prototype methods. From Table 4, it was evident that frequency band power (gamma and beta) of O1 (occipital region) is higher in software prototype compared to paper prototype. Based on the correlation analysis and ANOVA Table 4, we conclude that software prototype is less mentally demanding than paper prototype and thereby software prototype low in cognitive load.

**Table 4.** Frequency band power across EEG channels and its mean difference between software and paper prototype (ANOVA table, *significance $p > 0.05$)

| Channel/ Frequency | Software Prototype | Paper prototype | Spectral Power Difference | P-Value |
|---|---|---|---|---|
| Gamma Band Power | | | | |
| F3 | 5.1276 | 3.2011 | 1.9265 | 0.052* |
| AF4 | 12.6087 | 6.8757 | 5.7333 | 0.047* |
| FC5 | 5.3210 | 13.210 | 7.8890 | 0.031* |
| F4 | 6.2011 | 14.253 | 8.0519 | 0.025* |
| O1 | 11.337 | 2.4291 | 8.9079 | 0.010* |
| O2 | 5.5375 | 2.8667 | 2.6708 | 0.058* |
| Beta Band Power | | | | |
| AF3 | 13.5364 | 22.2137 | 8.6773 | 0.036* |
| O1 | 14.0084 | 8.0810 | 5.9274 | 0.039* |

Temporal demand (time pressure during the task) of the participants was found to have negative correlation with gamma (*Corr.* $= -0.401$, $P = 0.013$) and beta (*Corr.* $= -0.386$, $P = 0.017$) frequency bands across occipital region (O1) refer Table 3. From Table 4, it was evident that frequency band power (gamma and beta) of O1 is significantly higher in the software prototype which means software prototype had less temporal demand compared to paper prototype. In-light-of above-mentioned correlation and ANOVA results, we conclude that temporal demand was high in paper prototype because of manually presentation of the information as reported by the participants and discussed in subjective data analysis Sect. 5.2.

Performance of the participants was found to have positive correlation with gamma (*Corr.* $= 0.387$, $P = 0.016$) band power across the prefrontal region (AF4), refer Table 3. This showed that, gamma band power of prefrontal region (AF4) increases, if the '*performance*' of participants increases during the task fulfilment for both the prototype methods. As depicted from Table 4, gamma band power of AF4 was found significantly high in software prototype compared to paper prototype. In premises of these findings, authors conclude that, performance of the participants was higher in software prototype than paper prototype.

Mental effort of the participants was found to have positive correlation with gamma band power across frontal region FC5 (*Corr.* $= 0.394$, $P = 0.015$) & F4 (*Corr.* $= 0.331$, $P = 0.042$), refer Table 3. It was evident from the Table 4 that, gamma band power of frontal region is significantly higher in the paper prototype which concludes that mental effort was found higher in the paper prototype compared to software prototype. Similarly, mental effort of the participant was found to have positive correlation with beta band power across frontal region (AF3, F3, FC5, F4) AF3 (*Corr.* $= 0.297$, $P = 0.070$), F3 (*Corr.* $= 0.307$, $P = 0.060$), FC5 (*Corr.* $= 0.407$, $P = 0.011$), & F4 (*Corr.*

= *0.350, P = 0.031*). ANOVA Table 4 showed that, beta band power of frontal region (AF3) was significantly higher in paper prototype.

Frustration of the participants was found to have positive correlation with gamma band power of frontal (FC5) (*Corr. = 0.403, P = 0.012*) and negative correlation with occipital region (O1) (*Corr. = −0.747, P = 0.000*). Based on the ANOVA Table 4, gamma band power across frontal region (FC5) was observed higher for paper prototype and lower for software prototype. Gamma band power across occipital region (O1) was observed lower for paper prototype and higher for the software prototype. These results showed that frustration was higher in paper prototype compared to software prototype. As reported in literature, occipital region of the human brain is associated with visual information processing [36]. According to the post experiment self-reported data, participants reported that they had to process more irrelevant information during the task in paper prototype, which added frustration in paper prototype compared to software prototype. On the ground of these results, frustration was found higher in paper prototype, which doesn't augur well with industry 4.0 scenario for operators.

Frustration was found to have positive correlation with beta band power across frontal (F7, FC5) (*Corr. = 0.284, P = 0.084*), (*Corr. = 0.299, P = 0.068*) and negative correlation with occipital regions (O1) (*Corr. = −0.743, P = 0.000*). It was evident from Table 4 that, beta band power of O1 was significantly higher for the paper prototype, which also concludes that frustration was higher in the paper prototype.

## 5 Conclusion

In this paper, we developed two HCI design prototypes (software & Paper) considering single 'CPPS scenario of use' and 'CPPS task'. Cognitive load was measured from 21 participants during task fulfilment on the two prototypes. This paper used mix method approach to identify CL caused due to tasks in two types of prototypes.

In task performance-based CL measure, response time and error were high for paper prototype which is an indication of higher cognitive load and the reasons reported by participants were that (a) paper prototype did not give a realistic feeling due to which they responded late to the stimuli and (b) participants felt observed during task (presence of facilitator). Subjective ratings for mental demand and mental effort were high for paper prototype compared to software prototype. Physiological-based CL measurement using EEG also shows high gamma and beta band powers in paper prototype. By using mix method approach for comparing two different prototype methods gave more clarity on prototype method selection for HCI design. This comparative study between software and paper prototype is useful for industrial designers during HCI design process especially in context of Industry 4.0. Also, findings related to visual regions of the human brain (occipital region) were useful for cognitive psychologists who work on visual graphic design for HCI systems. At the end, we can conclude that software prototypes are better for designing interactive HCI based control panel than paper prototype in context of industry 4.0 as they give a more accurate estimation of the felt complexity by the users.

# References

1. Anderson, E.W., Potter, K.C., Matzen, L.E., Shepherd, J.F., Preston, G.A., Silva, C.T.: A user study of visualization effectiveness using EEG and cognitive load. Comput. Graph. Forum **30**(3), 791–800 (2011)
2. Antonenko, P., Paas, F., Grabner, R., Van Gog, T.: Using electroencephalography to measure cognitive load. Educ. Psychol. Rev. **22**(4), 425–438 (2010)
3. Archer, N.P., Yuan, Y.: Comparing telephone-computer interface designs: are software simulations as good as hardware prototypes? Int. J. Hum. Comput. Stud. **42**(2), 169–184 (1995)
4. Brünken, R., Steinbacher, S., Plass, J.L., Leutner, D.: Assessment of cognitive load in multimedia learning using dual-task methodology. Exp. Psychol. **49**(2), 109–119 (2002)
5. Cinaz, B., Arnrich, B., Tröster, G.: Monitoring of cognitive functioning by measuring reaction times with wearable devices. In: 5th International Conference on Pervasive Computing Technologies for Healthcare, pp. 514–517, Dublin, Ireland. IEEE (2011)
6. Delorme, A., Makeig, S.: EEGLAB: an open source toolbox for analysis of single-trial EEG dynamics including independent component analysis. J. Neurosci. Methods **134**(1), 9–21 (2004)
7. DeLeeuw, K.E., Mayer, R.E.: A comparison of three measures of cognitive load: evidence for separable measures of intrinsic, extraneous, and germane load. J. Educ. Psychol. **100**(1), 223–234 (2008)
8. Haapalainen, E., Kim, S., Forlizzi, J., Dey, A.: Psycho-Physiological Measures for Assessing Cognitive Load. In: 12th ACM International Conference on Ubiquitous Computing, Copenhagen, Denmark, pp. 301–310. ACM (2010)
9. Hart, S.G., Staveland, L.E.: Development of NASA-TLX (Task Load Index): results of empirical and theoretical research. Adv. Psychol. **52**, 139–183 (1988)
10. Hoonakker, P., et al.: Measuring workload of ICU nurses with a questionnaire survey: the NASA Task Load Index (TLX). IIE Trans. Healthcare Syst. Eng. **1**(2), 131–143 (2011)
11. Hozdić, E.: Smart factory for industry 4.0: a review. Int. J. Mod. Manuf. Technol. **7**(1), 28–35 (2015)
12. Hoggan, E., Brewster, S., Johnston, J.: Investigating the effectiveness of tactile feedback for mobile touchscreens. In: Proceedings of the SIGCHI Conference on Human Factors in Computing Systems, Montreal, Canada, pp. 1573–1582. ACM (2008)
13. Homan, R.W., Herman, J., Purdy, P.: Cerebral location of international 10–20 system electrode placement. Electroencephalogr. Clin. Neurophysiol. **66**(4), 376–382 (1987)
14. Klass, D.W.: The continuing challenge of artifacts in the EEG. Am. J. EEG Technol. **35**(4), 239–269 (1995)
15. Kjeldskov, J., Stage, J.: New techniques for usability evaluation of mobile systems. Int. J. Hum Comput Stud. **60**(5–6), 599–620 (2004)
16. Kumar, N., Kumar, J.: Measurement of cognitive load in HCI systems using EEG power spectrum: an experimental study. Procedia Comput. Sci. **84**, 70–78 (2016)
17. Kumar, N., Kumar, J.: Measurement of efficiency of auditory vs visual communication in HMI: a cognitive load approach. In: Proceedings of the International Conference on Advances in Human–Machine Interaction, Bangalore, India, pp. 1–8. IEEE (2016b). https://doi.org/10.1109/HMI.2016.7449168
18. Kumar, N., Kumar, J.: Efficiency 4.0 for Industry 4.0. Hum. Technol. J. **15**(1), 55–78 (2019)
19. MacDougall, W.: Industry 4.0: smart manufacturing for the future, Berlin, Germany. GTAI (2014)
20. Mittelstädt, V., Brauner, P., Blum, M., Ziefle, M.: On the visual design of ERP systems the-role of information complexity, presentation and human factors. Procedia Manuf. **3**, 448–455 (2015)

21. Norman, D.: The Design of Everyday Things. Basic Books, New York (2013)
22. Paas, F., Renkl, A., Sweller, J.: Cognitive load theory and instructional design: recent development. Educ. Psychol. **38**(1), 1–4 (2003)
23. Patricia, A.: The role of cognitive theory in human computer interface. Comput. Hum. Behav. **19**(5), 593–607 (2003)
24. Reid, G.B., Nygren, T.E.: The subjective workload assessment technique: a scaling procedure for measuring mental workload. Adv. Psychol. **52**, 185–218 (1988). https://doi.org/10.1016/S0166-4115(08)62387-0
25. Rudd, J., Stern, K., Isensee, S.: Low vs high-fidelity prototyping debate. Interactions **3**(1), 76–85 (1996)
26. Rumelhart, D.E., Norman, D.A.: Analogical processes in learning. In: Anderson, J.R. (ed.) Cognitive Skills and Their Acquisition, pp. 335–359 (1981)
27. Saeid, S., Chambers, J.A.: EEG Signal Processing. Southern Gate, Chichester, West Sussex, England: Wiley Online Library (2007)
28. Sefelin, R., Tscheligi, M., Giller, V.: Paper prototyping-what is it good for?: a comparison of paper-and computer-based low-fidelity prototyping. In: CHI 2003 Extended Abstracts on Human Factors in Computing Systems, pp. 778–779, Ft. Lauderdale, Florida, USA. ACM (2003)
29. Schmeck, A., Opfermann, M., van Gog, T., Paas, F., Leutner, D.: Measuring cognitive load with subjective rating scales during problem solving: differences between immediate and delayed ratings. Instr. Sci. **43**(1), 93–114 (2014). https://doi.org/10.1007/s11251-014-9328-3
30. Van Gog, T., Paas, F., Van Merriënboer, J.J.: Effects of process-oriented worked examples on troubleshooting transfer performance. Learn. Instr. **16**(2), 154–164 (2006)
31. Walker, M., Takayama, L., Landay, J.A.: High-fidelity or low-fidelity, paper or computer? Choosing attributes when testing web prototypes. In: 46th Annual Meeting on Human Factors and Ergonomics Society, Los Angeles, California, USA, pp. 661–665. SAGE Publications (2002)
32. Wierwille, W.W., Casali, J.G.: A validated rating scale for global mental workload measurement applications. In: Proceedings of the Human Factors Society Annual Meeting, Los Angeles, California, USA, pp. 129–133. Sage Publication (1983)
33. Wittenberg, C.: Cause the Trend Industry 4.0 in the Automated Industry to New Requirements on User Interfaces? In: Kurosu, M. (ed.) HCI 2015. LNCS, vol. 9171, pp. 238–245. Springer, Cham (2015). https://doi.org/10.1007/978-3-319-21006-3_24
34. Wong, Y.: Rough and ready prototypes: lessons from graphic design. In: SIGCHI Conference on Human Factors in Computing Systems, Monterey, CA, pp. 83–84. ACM (1992)
35. Zarjam, P., Epps, J., Chen, F.: Spectral EEG features for evaluating cognitive load. In: 2011 Annual International Conference of the IEEE Engineering in Medicine and Biology Society, Boston, USA, pp. 3841–3844 (2011)
36. Zeki, S.: A Vision of the Brain. Blackwell Scientific Publications (1993)

# Cognitive Mechanisms and Optimization Strategies in Interactive Evolutionary Design Based on Cognitive Load Theory

Chang Liu and Mao-en He$^{(\boxtimes)}$

College of Design and Innovation, Tongji University, Shanghai 200092, China
{liuc,hemaoen}@tongji.edu.cn

**Abstract.** The interactive evolutionary design (IED) approach is a human-centered design method with the design domain, which requires users to evaluate their overall satisfaction with evolutionary individuals. However, due to repeated and continuous interactions, users experience varying degrees of physical and psychological fatigue. How to alleviate user fatigue has become an important research topic. Some researchers focus on algorithm mechanisms, evaluation methods, and interface design improvements, whereas the relationship between user cognitive characteristics and interaction design has been less studied. This paper analyzed users' cognitive mechanisms and proposed optimization strategies for the IED based on cognitive load theory. First, user cognitive activities were identified during different stages, and the type of cognitive load was determined in each cognitive task. Second, combined with cognitive load effects, we proposed the optimization strategies for intrinsic, extraneous, and germane cognitive loads. Third, we adopted two existing algorithms and developed corresponding design systems to discuss the effectiveness of the proposed strategies. To achieve this, ten subjects were invited to operate systems, with experimental data recorded and cognitive load levels measured. The main findings from this paper highlighted that the proposed strategies effectively reduce the extraneous cognitive load and improve the efficiency of germane cognitive load.

**Keywords:** Cognitive load theory · Interactive evolutionary design · Human-computer interaction

## 1 Introduction

The interactive evolutionary design (IED) is an intelligent design approach based on the interactive genetic algorithm (IGA). By introducing user evaluation as individual fitness to guide population evolution, the IED has been widely utilized in various design scenarios, such as shoe and fashion design [1–3], industrial product design [4–7], pattern design [8–10], character design [11, 12], etc. Due to the limitations of human cognitive abilities, repeated interactions between users and systems lead to varying degrees of users' physical and psychological fatigue. Thus, user fatigue has become an important factor limiting the practical problem-solving ability of the IED. To alleviate this issue, many

© The Author(s), under exclusive license to Springer Nature Switzerland AG 2022
M. Kurosu et al. (Eds.): HCII 2022, LNCS 13516, pp. 59–81, 2022.
https://doi.org/10.1007/978-3-031-17615-9_5

researchers have proposed various improvement methods, such as introducing surrogate models to replace user evaluation tasks [6, 13], improving the interactive evaluation mechanism to simplify users' operations [14], adopting proper fitness representations to accurately capture user preferences [15], etc. These studies emphasized the influence of user cognitive process on algorithm performance, but few have systematically explored the user cognitive characteristics in the IED.

Based on cognitive load theory, this paper systematically analyzed the cognitive process of users in the IED. First, the information entities and specific tasks were deconstructed during the user cognition process, and the types and causes of cognitive load were clarified in different tasks. Second, corresponding improvement strategies were proposed based on cognitive load effects. Third, to verify the effectiveness of the proposed strategies, we selected the painting design for the road roller as a case. Two existing improved algorithms were selected based on the strategies, and corresponding IED systems were developed. Then, ten subjects were invited to perform design experiments, with data recorded, analyzed, and discussed.

There are three main contributions in this paper, which are: (1) A systematic study on the user cognitive process in the IED is conducted based on the cognitive load theory. This will help to explain the causes of user fatigue from the cognitive aspect; (2) the proposed corresponding improvement strategies provide new ideas for the design of specific algorithms; (3) We contribute to the development of IED system by exploring the implementation path of the proposed strategies for specific problems. It provides a reference for improving design efficiency, reducing design costs, and realizing design intelligence.

The remaining sections of this paper proceed as follows: Sect. 2 reviews the existing research on the IED and cognitive load theory, and summarizes the problems. Section 3 elaborates on the user's cognitive process, and the specific improvement strategies. Section 4 is the theoretical verification and case study. Section 5 presents the conclusions, limitations, and future research work.

## 2 Related Work

### 2.1 Interactive Evolutionary Design

The IED is a human-machine collaborative design method based on the IGA. The IGA was proposed by Dawkins [16] in 1986 and is considered to be a genetic algorithm that effectively solves the implicit objective optimization problem. In the traditional interactive genetic algorithm (TIGA), users need to evaluate the population schemes generated by the algorithm based on their preferences. Then, the algorithm utilizes the user evaluation as individual fitness to perform the selection, crossover, and mutation in sequence, and generates the next generation population.

However, the various operations increase the cognitive burden of users at different evolutionary stages in the real case, due to the limited cognitive ability of users. These stages are: (1) The early stage of evolutionary design, which is difficult for users to establish a clear relationship between design objectives and scheme characteristics. Users need to reflect and confirm the schemes repeatedly before they build a mapping relationship between the abstract objectives and the specific characteristics. This cognition ambiguity leads to evaluation noise, which interferes with the individual optimization of the IGA and reduces the algorithm efficiency. Meanwhile, repeated reflection and confirmation increase the user's cognitive load and reduces the user's cognitive efficiency. (2) The middle of evolutionary design. As the number of individuals evaluated and the duration increase, the user's cognitive load increases. Users face physical and psychological fatigue, which leads to evaluation errors. Therefore, how to reduce the cognitive load and to improve cognitive efficiency is the key to alleviating user evaluation fatigue and ensuring the feasibility of the IED in practical applications.

Aiming at the user cognitive activities in the early stage, Yang *et al.* [17] constructed a cognitive noise model to mitigate the impact of the inaccurate user evaluation. Zeng *et al.* [18] proposed a "Text-Image-Symbol" mapping strategy, which requires users to select a text description (emotional adjective) that meets the design objectives. Then, based on the selected text description the system provides stimulus pictures to help users to specify the characteristic representation of the design objective. At present, there are few studies of research on user cognition at this stage. Existing studies mainly focus on the reduction of evaluation noise caused by user cognition ambiguity, with less consideration to improving user cognitive efficiency.

For the cognitive problems in the middle stage, existing studies pay attention to improving the fitness representation, updating the evaluation mechanism, and constructing the surrogate model:

(1) Improvements for fitness representation. In the TIGA, users need to choose a number as individual fitness based on their preferences. This fitness representation method requires users to accurately distinguish the differences among population schemes, resulting in an additional psychological burden. In response to this problem, Ohsaki *et al.* [19] used discrete fitness to divide the assignment interval into fewer levels, such as the utilization of a three-points or five-points scale for individual evaluation. Besides, the relationships were also studied between the number of levels and algorithm convergence. Gong *et al.* [20] proposed a fitness representation method based on interval numbers. In this method, users need to assign two numbers as the upper and lower limits of the interval fitness. This method reduces the accuracy of user evaluation and the user's psychological burden, but complicates the evaluation operation itself. Dou *et al.* [21] improved the method of literature [20] and proposed an interval fitness based on user hesitancy. Users only assign a number as the center of the individual interval fitness. The algorithm estimates the width of the interval fitness based on the evaluation time. Gong *et al.* [22] adopted fuzzy numbers expressed by the Gaussian membership function to represent individual fitness. This method requires users to select a number as the center value of the fuzzy fitness. Then, a modal word (such as "about", "close", "very close", etc.) needs to be selected as the width of the fuzzy fitness.

(2) Improvements to the evaluation mechanism. Because user preferences are difficult to quantify, the individual evaluation that needs to assign a specific number increases the psychological burden on users. Therefore, researchers have studied non-assigned evaluation methods. Cheng *et al.* [23] calculated individual fitness by extracting user eye movement information. Takenouchi *et al.* [11] proposed an interactive genetic algorithm based on group user eye movement information. The

proposed algorithm uses the B5T007001 device to collect the eye movement information of the user group, combined with the Paired Comparison Method (PC), to infer the preferences of the user group, and output design schemes that satisfy the group.

(3) Construction of the surrogate model. These methods take individual genotypes as the input and the user evaluation results as the output to build a machine learning model to simulate user preferences and predict individual fitness. Lv *et al.* [13] presented an agent model of the user cognition based on the Back Propagation Neural Network (BPNN) to predict individual fitness and reduce user cognitive burden. [6] introduced BPNN to replace user evaluation and alleviate user fatigue.

The first category of research aims to reduce the accuracy of evaluation operations to mitigate the user's psychological load. Meanwhile, the fitness representation is designed to reflect the ambiguity and gradualness of the user's cognition. But such methods still require user assignment operations, which increases user' cognitive loads. The second category of research simplifies the evaluation operation, and users do not need to assign a specific number. The cognitive load is reduced during the evaluation. The disadvantage of these methods is that the evaluation accuracy is low, accompanied by large noise. And it is difficult to determine the general relationships between eye movement/EEG data and user preferences. The third category directly reduces the number of individuals evaluated by users. However, an accurate agent relies on a large amount of user evaluation data. The evaluation data of users are limited, and the evaluation results usually contain noise in the IGA. It is difficult for the agent to accurately fit the user preference characteristics. In short, few of the above studies can balance algorithm optimization efficiency and user cognitive load. Furthermore, the aforementioned studies seldom consider user cognitive characteristics and changes throughout the evolutionary process.

Therefore, this paper attempts to systematically study the cognitive mechanisms of users in the IED and explore optimization strategies that reduce cognitive load and improve cognitive efficiency, ensuring effectiveness in solving practical design problems.

## 2.2 Cognitive Load Theory

Cognitive load theory (CLT), was proposed by Sweller in 1988 [24]. CLT points out that the human cognitive structure consists of limited working memory and unlimited long-term memory. The human cognitive process is considered to be a process of consuming cognitive resources. Any learning and problem-solving activities are accompanied by cognitive processing behaviors. CLT aims to achieve a reasonable allocation of cognitive resources in the process of task completion. It focuses on different types of cognitive load in the instruction process, and guides the design of instructional content and material presentation. Because human cognition is closely related to many fields and applications, CLT has attracted the attention of various disciplines.

CLT divides the human cognitive load into the intrinsic cognitive load, the extraneous cognitive load, and the germane cognitive load [25]. The accumulation of three types of cognitive load equals the total cognitive load level. The intrinsic cognitive load is the cognitive load generated in the process of processing instructional materials in human working memory. It is mainly related to the complexity of the materials and tasks. Wang *et al.* [26] believed that the internal cognitive load is not easy to alleviate through external intervention. The extraneous cognitive load refers to the cognitive load caused by unreasonable instructional design or material presentation. It occupies the learner's working memory resources and leads to insufficient resources for task completion. The germane cognitive load, known as the effective cognitive load, is the cognitive load that occurs at the stage of deep processing of instructional information. It is relevant to schema construction and automation. Moderate germane cognitive load facilitates task completion and improves learning efficiency.

As mentioned in Sect. 2.1, user cognition issues reduce the effectiveness of the IED in practical applications. From the perspective of CLT, the user evaluation task in the IED is essentially a task of perceiving and identifying their preferences and characteristics of population schemes. The design of the IED systems is a design process of the instructional tasks. How to systematically inquire about the cognitive mechanisms and optimize strategies in the IED based on CLT, is worthy of further research.

# 3  Cognitive Mechanisms and Optimization Strategies

## 3.1  Information Entities and Specific Tasks in the IED

In the IED, the different cognitive processes involve different information and tasks. These include not only the presented information and the assigned tasks in the system, but also the implicit information and tasks that exist in the user's consciousness. Combined with the thinking process of designers in traditional design tasks, the information entities and specific tasks are represented in the IED, as shown in Fig. 1.

In the traditional product form design, experienced designers' thinking has typical linear characteristics [27]. Designers firstly clarify design objectives based on enterprise or user requirements (mostly expressed in descriptive text, such as adjectives, paragraphs, etc.). Then, based on personal experience and preferences, designers search for reference cases (mostly expressed in pictures or videos) that match the design objectives. Through the consideration and analysis of reference cases, the specific morphological characteristics are extracted for the expression of objective images. And the mapping relationship is constructed between abstract design objectives and tangible characteristics. Then, designers modify and integrate characteristics to sketch. Finally, it is necessary to invite design experts, enterprise representatives, and users to conduct a comprehensive evaluation of the sketch schemes. Based on the evaluation results, designers revise and iterate the sketch schemes until the design objectives are met. Therefore, in traditional design activities, the information entities that need to deal with are design objectives, reference cases, morphological characteristics, and sketch schemes. The specific tasks are respectively the search for reference cases, the extraction of characteristics, the modification and integration of characteristics, and the evaluation and iteration.

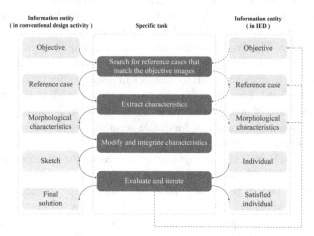

**Fig. 1.** Information entities and specific tasks in conventional design activities and that in the IED

In the IED, the explicit information entities are the population individuals (schemes) generated by the system, and the specific task is the continuous evaluation of population individuals. Given the cognitive activities in product form design, users also perform the reference search and the characteristic extraction. But these information entities and specific tasks are tacit in the user cognition, and occur in the user's working memory and long-term memory. Users need to search for references related to the design objectives from long-term memory. Based on these reference cases, morphological characteristics, which help express objective images, are refined in working memory. For inexperienced users, the number of relevant references is limited in their long-term memory. The ability to extract characteristics is also limited. It leads to low cognitive efficiency in the early stage of the IED. Users gradually clarify the mapping relationship between design objectives and individual characteristics through multiple evaluations and self-reflection. Thus, the information entities that need to be processed by users are divided into two categories: the first category is explicit and visible in the IED system, such as population individuals; the second category is implicit and invisible, which stored in the user's long-term memory, such as design objectives, reference cases, and morphological characteristics. The specific tasks also include two categories: the first category is the evaluation of population individuals; the second category is the search of reference cases, and the extraction of individual characteristics (occurring in the user's working memory).

## 3.2   Types and Causes of Cognitive Load in the IED

The relationship between the IED and the user cognition is shown in three stages, as shown in Fig. 2. Phase 1 is the association construction between design objectives and individual characteristics. Phase 2 is the user evaluation. And Phase 3 is the algorithm design. The first two phases are directly related to the user's cognitive process, and the third phase is related to the task difficulty of the IED.

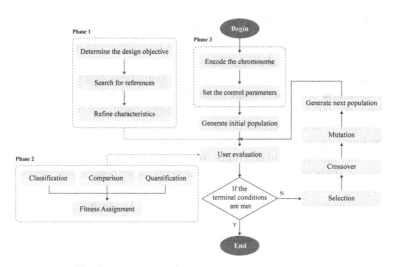

**Fig. 2.** Three phases involving cognitive load in IED

In TIED, users are not required to perform the tasks of Phase 1. However, as Sect. 3.1, associative cognitive processes are necessary for design activities. They occur spontaneously in user's working and long-term memory, and vary among users: when the design problem to be solved is in the domain familiar to the user, the user's long-term memory stores rich reference cases and clear individual characteristic extraction paths (schemas). This process occupies few cognitive resources; when the problem belongs to their unfamiliar domain, the user's long-term memory lacks relevant references. The schema for extracting individual characteristics is also insufficient. It is difficult to construct the mapping relationship between design objectives and individual characteristics in a short period. This increases the user's cognitive load, and leads to the user's cognitive fatigue for the evolutionary population, making evaluation results contain noise. According to the three types of cognitive load, the cognitive load in Phase 1 is related to the number of references and the schema of characteristic extraction in the user's long-term memory. And it is also related to the information processing ability of the working memory. As shown in Fig. 3, it is obvious that the cognitive load involved in Phase 1 belongs to the germane cognitive load.

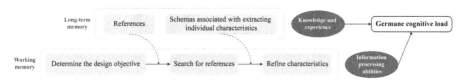

**Fig. 3.** The type of cognitive load in Phase 1

Phase 2 is the user evaluation stage. It involves the primary operation process of users in the IED. The tasks in Phase 2 require users to perform three cognitive activities in working memory, namely classification, comparison and quantification.

Classification refers to the division of individual categories based on cognitive similarity. The cognitive similarity is usually based on two dimensions: emotional and rational. The emotional dimension is derived from preference and intuition, guided by subjective factors. The rational dimension is based on objective factors such as shape, color, structure, etc. For example, products with a similar emotion (such as "modern") may have significant differences in the rational dimension (such as the product shape).

Comparison refers to the user's judgment on the pros and cons of individuals based on design objectives and preferences. Watanabe *et al.* [28] pointed out that it is difficult for users to directly assign a quantified fitness value to evaluate an individual. Users need to compare other individuals to determine their preferences for the individual. Through the comparison, users gradually understand the relationship between the individuals of the current generation, which is beneficial to the construction of the mapping relationship between design objectives and individual characteristics. Meanwhile, it also ensures the accuracy of individual evaluation.

Quantification refers to the quantification process of user preferences. Users usually first select the individuals with a deep impression, and assign an absolute number as the individual fitness based on design objectives and preferences. Through the classification and comparison, the relationship between individuals is clarified. Then, based on the fitness of the individuals evaluated, the specific fitness values of other individuals are determined.

For users who lack experience in design evaluation, the above three cognitive activities are usually incomplete and disordered. The types and causes of cognitive load involved in this stage are shown in Fig. 4. Usually, the presentation of population individuals is random in the IED. It is difficult for users to classify individuals. Users need to consume additional working memory resources to complete individual classification. Besides, in the TIED, users need to evaluate the individuals one by one, which is not conducive to comparing as a whole. The random presentation of individuals and the inappropriate evaluation mechanisms are a matter of presentation method and procedure design. On the other hand, preference quantification also involves the mapping relationship between objectives and characteristics, similar to Phase 1. Therefore, this phase involves both extraneous and germane cognitive load.

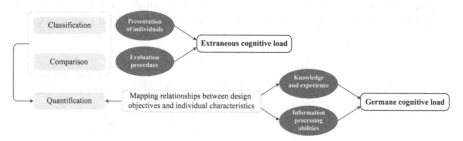

**Fig. 4.** The type of cognitive load in Phase 2

Phase 3 is the algorithm design stage. In the IED, chromosome encoding and evolution parameter settings determine the complexity of the overall evolutionary design. Generally, the number of chromosome bits is related to the objective complexity of the design task. The larger the number of chromosome bits, the more solutions the algorithm can generate, and the search process of the user's satisfactory solution set becomes more complicated. The crossover rate and mutation rate settings determine the convergence speed of the algorithm. The greater the crossover rate, the more frequent the recombination of individual alleles. The greater the mutation rate, the more frequent the change of individual alleles. The increase of both accelerates the individual change in the population. The increase of both also improves the algorithm's ability to search for unknown domains. Therefore, the crossover and mutation rate setting needs to consider a balance between convergence and unknown domain search. In short, the algorithm design in Phase 3 is directly related to the task complexity of the IED, and is usually completed by designers and developers. According to the cognitive load classification in Sect. 2.2, the cognitive load involved in this stage belongs to the intrinsic cognitive load, as shown in Fig. 5.

**Fig. 5.** The type of cognitive load in Phase 3

### 3.3 Improvement Strategies Based on Cognitive Load Effects

How to reduce the cognitive load level of taskers in the task completion process is the focus of CLT. Since the intrinsic cognitive load is related to the complexity of the task itself, it is usually not influenced by the task design. Thus, there are more studies on reducing the extraneous cognitive load and moderately increasing the germane cognitive load [29].

Researchers have concluded twelve main cognitive load effects based on theoretical research and practical experience, including the goal-free effect, the worked example effect, the completion problem effect, the split-attention effect, the modality effect, the redundancy effect, the expertise reversal effect, the guidance fading effect, the imagination effect, the element interactivity effect, the isolated interacting elements effect, and the variability effect. See [30] for a detailed description of each effect.

According to the cognitive load effects, improvement strategies are presented based on the three types of cognitive load described in Sect. 3.1 (as shown in Fig. 6).

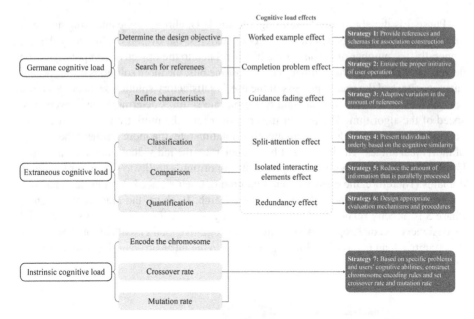

**Fig. 6.** Improvement strategies of IED based on cognitive load effects

The germane cognitive load in the IED is primarily related to the associative construction between design objectives and individual characteristics. In TIED, the processing of information entities and specific tasks completely depends on the user's working and long-term memory. Therefore, the cognitive load effects related to the example are combined to provide users with references consistent with the design objective. At the same time, the explicit schema construction also needs to be considered. Accordingly, the following strategies are proposed:

Strategy 1: Combined with the worked example effect, materialized references and step-by-step association construction schemas should be integrated into the IED system to facilitate the association between design objectives and individual characteristics in the early stage of evolutionary design.

Strategy 2: Combined with the completion problem effect, an interactive association construction procedure that promotes the user's enthusiasm and participation should be designed to mobilize the user's reflection.

Strategy 3: Combined with the guidance fading effect, the number of materialized references should be adaptively adjusted according to algorithm optimization to prevent redundant references from occupying additional cognitive resources.

For the extraneous cognitive load, it is related to user evaluation. Improvement strategies are proposed for three cognitive behaviors combined with the cognitive load effects: classification, comparison and quantification.

Strategy 4: For the classification process. Since the individual presentation is disordered in the TIED, the actual presentation of individuals with high cognitive similarity is random to the user in the system. Users spontaneously integrate and process the locations of similar individuals in working memory, which is similar to the processing of information scattered in the spatial or temporal dimension described by the split-attention effect. The classification in the user evaluation is caused by the scattered layout of similar information. Therefore, according to the user cognitive similarity, the individuals should be presented in order.

Strategy 5: For the comparison process. Since the population size is usually 6–12 in the TIED, the comparison between individuals requires users to process multiple information simultaneously in working memory, which consumes many cognitive resources. This is similar to the problem targeted by the isolated interacting elements effect. The cognitive load caused by parallel processing can be reduced through the controlled presentation of information. Accordingly, the evaluation process should be improved to reduce the number of users processing information simultaneously.

Strategy 6: For the quantification process. This process requires users to express their individual preference with an accurate number. For experienced experts, when dealing with problems closely related to rational decision-making, the assignment of a specific value helps computers obtain their precise preferences and judgments. The evolutionary efficiency is improved and the quality of the output schemes is ensured. However, the design activity itself is accompanied by emotional decision-making; the participation of human intuition and feeling is unavoidable. It is difficult to quantify them. In addition, from the perspective of the IGA, the accurate fitness value is not necessary for evolution. What is required for the algorithm evolution is the user's preference related to the individuals. The assignment of specific values is only a representation method of the preference relationship. Therefore, from the perspective of user cognition and algorithm, the assignment operation is redundant to the user evaluation process itself. Accordingly, appropriate mechanisms should be adopted to improve the individual evaluation process, such as the methods mentioned in Sect. 2.1.

The intrinsic cognitive load is related to chromosome encoding rules, crossover rate, and mutation rate settings. As mentioned in Sect. 3.2, the smaller the number of chromosomes, the smaller the search range of the solutions, which leads to a mismatch between the final output schemes and the design objectives. However, from the perspective of user cognition, the fewer the number of chromosomes, the easier the user's tasks. Therefore, the strategy 7 is proposed:

Strategy 7: The chromosome encoding rules should be formulated combined with the cognitive ability of the user group and the characteristics of the actual design problem; The crossover rate and mutation should be determined based on the comprehensive consideration of the algorithm convergence speed and searchability for the unknown domain.

## 4 Experiments and Discussions

### 4.1 Algorithm Selection

To verify the proposed strategies above, two improved IGA algorithms were chosen. These two algorithms are respectively aimed at improving the cognitive process in the early stage of evolution and the process of user evaluation.

**CA-IGA.** The CA-IGA builds on our previously proposed method [31], retaining its improved parts in the construction of association cognition. And a novel idea is added based on the proposed strategies. The algorithm flow is shown in Fig. 7, which includes three improved parts: the associative construction of "design objective-reference case", the associative construction of "reference case-individual characteristic", and the adaptive presentation of reference information.

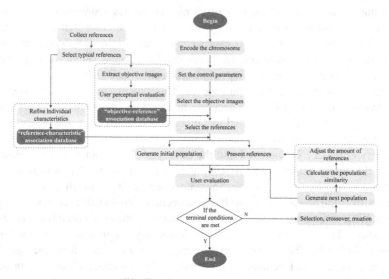

**Fig. 7.** Flow chart of CA-IGA

In the algorithm design of the CA-IGA, the associative construction of "design objective-reference case" reflects the idea of Strategy 1; the association construction of "reference case-individual characteristics" reflects the idea of Strategy 2; the adaptive number of references is presented, which embodies the idea of Strategy 3. Therefore, the CA-IGA can be used to validate the improvement strategies for the germane cognitive load in Sect. 3.3.

**AR-IGA.** The AR-IGA was the method we proposed, and its specific algorithm design is in the literature [32]. Its algorithm flow is shown in Fig. 8, including three improvements: the evaluation based on the alternation ranking method, the calculation of individual fuzzy fitness, and the comparison based on fuzzy fitness.

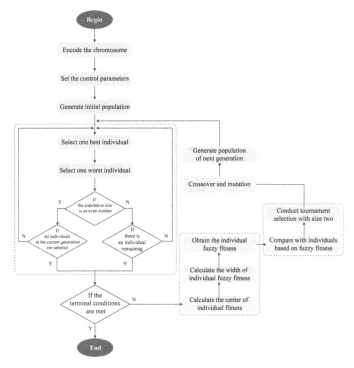

**Fig. 8.** Flow chart of AR-IGA

The algorithm design of the AR-IGA embodies the idea of strategies 5 and 6. By improving the evaluation mechanism and procedure, the AR-IGA reduces the amount of information that users need to process simultaneously and avoids the assignment and scoring operation. Thus, the AR-IGA can be used to validate the part of the improvement strategies for the extraneous cognitive load in Sect. 3.3.

### 4.2  Chromosome Encoding

The road roller painting was selected as a case study. Based on product research, the functional parts and painting area were determined. Then, the style of each painting area was summarized, and the value range of the dominant and auxiliary colors was defined. Finally, based on the proportion of phenotypes, the styles of each painting area, the values of the dominant and auxiliary colors, and the specific positions of the logo and product model were encoded, as shown in Fig. 9.

Based on the coding rules of each part, the chromosome encoding was formulated, as shown in Fig. 10. The genotype of an evolutionary individual is a binary string of 27 bits, where the first 4 bits express the dominant color, the 5th and 6th bits express the auxiliary color, the 7th, 8th, 9th, and 10th respectively express the color of the vibrating drum, the rear frame, the bumper, and the hub, the 11th to 14th bits express the painting style of the cab, the 15th to 18th bits express the painting style of the front frame, the

19th to 22nd bits express the painting style of the hood, the 23rd to 25th bits express the location of the logo, and the 26th and 27th bits express the location of the product model identification.

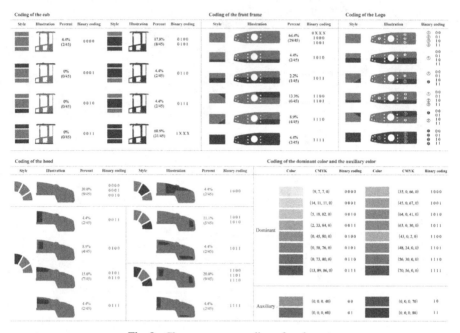

**Fig. 9.** Chromosome encoding of each part

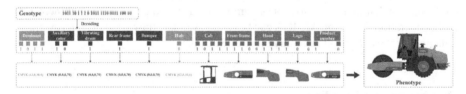

**Fig. 10.** Relationship between the genotype and phenotype of an individual

## 4.3  Parameter Setting and Terminal Condition

The population size $N$ is set to 6. The maximum number of generation T is set to 16. One-point crossover and one-point mutation mechanisms are adopted, and their rates are 0.6 and 0.03. The maximum fitness $f_{max}$ is 9, and the minimum fitness $f_{min}$ is 0. In the CA-IGA, the mid-evolution threshold $o_1$ and late-evolution threshold $o_2$ are set to $1/3$ and $2/3$. In the AR-IGA, $w_{max}$ is set to 0.288, and $\alpha_{min}$ is set to 0.5.

The terminal conditions are as follows: (1) users find four satisfactory schemes, and (2) the number of generations reaches 16. Once one of the two is met, the evolutionary process ends. If users do not find four satisfactory schemes until the generation is 16, it is believed that the algorithm cannot achieve convergence in this evolutionary iteration.

## 4.4  System Interface

Three IED systems were developed based on the TIGA, the CA-IGA, and the AR-IGA. The interfaces are shown in Fig. 11.

**Fig. 11.**  System interfaces based on three algorithms

## 4.5  Experimental Design

Ten graduate students (six males, four females, average age 24.3, standard age difference of 1.3) majoring in industrial were invited as the subjects. A color blindness test was performed to understand the color discrimination ability of the subjects. The subjects operated the IED systems for the road roller painting based on three methods (TIGA, CA-IGA, and AR-IGA). None of the subjects had engaged in work or research related to the painting design. Only one method is tested at a time. The experiments were approved by the University Ethics Committee, and all subjects received written consent before participating in the study. The two experiments are spaced three days apart to avoid the influence of the previous experiment. Before each experiment, the subjects need to learn the system operation to ensure that the subjects can operate the system proficiently.

## 4.6 Evaluation Indicator

Integrating the evaluation indicators of the IED and the cognitive load measurement, this paper proposed an evaluation method that comprehensively considers the algorithm convergence and the cognitive load measurement. The evaluation indicators are shown in Fig. 12.

In the related studies, the algorithm convergence is usually reflected in the number of generations. The smaller the number of generations when other parameters are fixed, the smaller the number of algorithm iterations, and the faster the convergence. However, too rapid convergence can make the evolution premature.

The measurement of cognitive load in the IED is a combination of the subjective and objective assessment. For the subjective evaluation of the cognitive load, Leppink *et al.* [33] pointed out that the National Aeronautics and Space Administration Task Load Index (NASA-TLX) has better applicability for cognitive load measurement in a variety of scenarios. Furthermore, the NASA-TLX scale is one of the most widely used subjective psychological stress assessment tools [34], with high user acceptance and low participant variation [35]. Therefore, the NASA-TLX was adopted to evaluate the total cognitive load level.

For the objective evaluation of cognitive load, the time for evaluating first-generation is used to reflect the germane cognitive load level, the average time for evaluating an individual is used to reflect the extraneous cognitive load level, and the total time and the number of individuals evaluated are used to reflect the total cognitive load level.

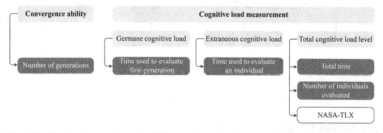

**Fig. 12.** Evaluation indices for IED combined with cognitive load measurement

## 4.7 Analysis and Discussion

The data mentioned in Sect. 4.6 were recorded. The number of generations and the number of individuals evaluated is listed in Table 1. The time used for the first generation and the total time are listed in Table 2. A paired-sample T test is suitable for studying the differences in results of the same subject under different treatments. Thus, this method is adopted to compare the effects of three different methods on the subjects' task completion.

In IBM SPSS Statistics 26, the number of generations and the number of individuals evaluated of three methods were compared by using a paired-sample T test. The results are shown in Table 3. For the number of generations, the difference between the TIGA and the CA-IGA in t is 3.50, and P = 0.007 < 0.05. It can be seen that the CA-IGA has a significant effect on the number of generations compared to the TIGA, and the average is reduced by 1.10. In the same way, AR-IGA has a significant impact on the number of generations compared to the TIGA and the CA-IGA, with 2.70 and 1.60 less. For the number of individuals evaluated, the difference between the TIGA and the CA-IGA in t is 3.19, and P = 0.011 < 0.05. It can be seen that the CA-IGA has a significant effect on the number of generations compared to the TIGA, and the average is reduced by 6.70. In the same way, AR-IGA has a significant impact on the number of individuals evaluated compared to the TIGA and the CA-IGA, with 13.70 and 7.00 less.

The time used for the first generation and the total time of the three methods were compared. The results are shown in Table 4. For the time used for the first generation, the difference between the TIGA and the CA-IGA in t is 7.31, and P = 0.000 < 0.05. It can be seen that the CA-IGA has a significant effect on the number of generations compared to the TIGA, and the average is reduced by 11.60 s. In the same way, AR-IGA has a significant impact on the number of generations compared to the TIGA with 8.80 s shorter. And the CA-IGA is 2.80 s less than the AR-IGA. For the total time, the CA-IGA is 53.60 s less than the TIGA. The AR-IGA is 133.30 s less than the TIGA and 79.70 s less than the CA-IGA.

Based on the number of individuals evaluated and the total time in Table 1 and Table 2, the average time used to evaluate an individual is calculated in Table 5. The average time of the three methods was compared, and the results are shown in Table 6. The CA-IGA is 0.41 s less than the TIGA. The AR-IGA is 1.42 s and 1.01 s less than the TIGA and the CA-IGA, respectively.

The results of the NASA-TLX scale evaluated by the subjects were averaged to reflect the total cognitive load level, as shown in Table 7. The total cognitive load level of the three methods was compared, and the results are shown in Table 8. Compared with the TIGA, CA-IGA decreases by 2.84. Similarly, the AR-IGA is 12.08 and 9.24 fewer than the TIGA and the CA-IGA.

The above results were discussed. From algorithm convergence, the CA-IGA is less than the TIGA in the number of generations. It indicates that the associative construction strategy helps users clarify the objective image, and their individual evaluation results are more consistent with the design objectives. Compared with the TIGA and the CA-IGA, the number of generations of AR-IGA decreases. It demonstrates that the alternation ranking method helps users clarify the pros and cons between individuals, which prevents deviations in the evolutionary direction.

For the germane cognitive load at the early evolution, the CA-IGA takes less time to evaluate the first generation than the TIGA and the AR-IGA. It shows that associative construction helps users build the mapping relationship between design objectives and individual characteristics, thereby alleviating the cognitive fatigue of initial evaluation. On the other hand, the references selected by users directly influence population initialization, which improves the consistency of the initial population and design objectives.

**Table 1.** Number of generations and number of individuals evaluated in the three methods

| Subject | Number of generations | | | Number of individuals evaluated | | |
|---------|------|--------|--------|------|--------|--------|
|         | TIGA | CA-IGA | AR-IGA | TIGA | CA-IGA | AR-IGA |
| 1       | 10   | 9      | 9      | 57   | 53     | 54     |
| 2       | 9    | 9      | 8      | 53   | 54     | 48     |
| 3       | 11   | 10     | 6      | 66   | 60     | 36     |
| 4       | 9    | 9      | 7      | 51   | 51     | 42     |
| 5       | 9    | 8      | 7      | 51   | 48     | 42     |
| 6       | 11   | 9      | 6      | 66   | 53     | 36     |
| 7       | 11   | 9      | 6      | 63   | 48     | 36     |
| 8       | 12   | 9      | 8      | 63   | 46     | 48     |
| 9       | 8    | 8      | 7      | 47   | 47     | 42     |
| 10      | 12   | 11     | 11     | 70   | 60     | 66     |

**Table 2.** Time used for first generation and total time by the three methods

| Subject | Time used for first generation | | | Total time | | |
|---------|------|--------|--------|------|--------|--------|
|         | TIGA | CA-IGA | AR-IGA | TIGA | CA-IGA | AR-IGA |
| 1       | 36   | 32     | 38     | 320  | 271    | 203    |
| 2       | 47   | 27     | 32     | 316  | 244    | 208    |
| 3       | 43   | 30     | 34     | 329  | 316    | 160    |
| 4       | 41   | 28     | 31     | 302  | 279    | 194    |
| 5       | 45   | 35     | 37     | 308  | 240    | 168    |
| 6       | 41   | 37     | 35     | 336  | 246    | 131    |
| 7       | 35   | 25     | 27     | 310  | 224    | 101    |
| 8       | 30   | 17     | 22     | 277  | 205    | 150    |
| 9       | 39   | 22     | 23     | 241  | 227    | 175    |
| 10      | 30   | 18     | 20     | 274  | 225    | 190    |

**Table 3.** Paired-sample T test of number of generations and number of individuals evaluated with the three methods

|  | Difference | Mean | t | Sig. (2-Tailed) |
|---|---|---|---|---|
| Number of generations | TIGA vs. CA-IGA | 1.10 | 3.50 | 0.007 |
|  | CA-IGA vs. AR-IGA | 1.60 | 3.75 | 0.005 |
|  | TIGA vs. AR-IGA | 2.70 | 4.67 | 0.001 |
| Number of individuals evaluated | TIGA vs. CA-IGA | 6.70 | 3.19 | 0.011 |
|  | CA-IGA vs. AR-IGA | 7.00 | 2.45 | 0.037 |
|  | TIGA vs. AR-IGA | 13.70 | 3.89 | 0.004 |

**Table 4.** Paired-sample T test of time used for first generation and total time with the three methods

|  | Difference | Mean | t | Sig. (2-Tailed) |
|---|---|---|---|---|
| Time used for first generation | TIGA vs. CA-IGA | 11.60 | 7.31 | 0.000 |
|  | CA-IGA vs. AR-IGA | −2.80 | −3.77 | 0.004 |
|  | TIGA vs. AR-IGA | 8.80 | 5.63 | 0.000 |
| Total time | TIGA vs. CA-IGA | 53.60 | 5.89 | 0.000 |
|  | CA-IGA vs. AR-IGA | 79.70 | 6.29 | 0.000 |
|  | TIGA vs. AR-IGA | 133.30 | 8.78 | 0.000 |

**Table 5.** Average time taken to evaluate an individual by the three methods

| Subject | TIGA | CA-IGA | AR-IGA |
|---|---|---|---|
| 1 | 5.6 | 5.1 | 3.8 |
| 2 | 6.0 | 4.5 | 4.3 |
| 3 | 5.0 | 5.3 | 4.4 |
| 4 | 5.9 | 5.5 | 4.6 |
| 5 | 6.0 | 5.0 | 4.0 |
| 6 | 5.1 | 4.6 | 3.6 |
| 7 | 4.9 | 4.7 | 2.8 |
| 8 | 4.4 | 4.5 | 3.1 |
| 9 | 5.1 | 4.8 | 4.2 |
| 10 | 3.9 | 3.8 | 2.9 |

**Table 6.** Paired-sample T test of the average time taken to evaluate an individual with the three methods

|  | Difference | Mean | t | Sig. (2-Tailed) |
|---|---|---|---|---|
| Average time taken to evaluate an individual | TIGA vs. CA-IGA | 0.41 | 2.48 | 0.035 |
|  | CA-IGA vs. AR-IGA | 1.01 | 6.97 | 0.000 |
|  | TIGA vs. AR-IGA | 1.42 | 9.13 | 0.000 |

**Table 7.** Total cognitive load level of the three methods

| Subject | TIGA | CA-IGA | AR-IGA |
|---|---|---|---|
| 1 | 42.5 | 37.5 | 26.7 |
| 2 | 40.8 | 40.0 | 31.7 |
| 3 | 39.2 | 37.5 | 33.3 |
| 4 | 41.7 | 39.2 | 28.3 |
| 5 | 45.0 | 42.5 | 31.7 |
| 6 | 42.5 | 40.8 | 31.7 |
| 7 | 39.2 | 36.7 | 30.8 |
| 8 | 40.0 | 38.3 | 29.2 |
| 9 | 45.0 | 40.8 | 29.2 |
| 10 | 43.3 | 37.5 | 25.8 |

**Table 8.** Paired-sample T test of the total cognitive load level with the three methods

|  | Difference | Mean | t | Sig. (2-Tailed) |
|---|---|---|---|---|
| Total cognitive load level | TIGA vs. CA-IGA | 2.84 | 5.54 | 0.000 |
|  | CA-IGA vs. AR-IGA | 9.24 | 11.64 | 0.000 |
|  | TIGA vs. AR-IGA | 12.08 | 10.28 | 0.000 |

For the extraneous cognitive load at the evaluation stage, the AR-IGA takes significantly less time to evaluate an individual than the TIGA and the CA-IGA. It shows that the alternation ranking method simplifies the user evaluation operation, thereby reducing the cognitive load of the evaluation process.

For the total cognitive load level, the number of individuals evaluated for the AR-IGA is significantly reduced compared with the TIGA and the CA-IGA. The total time of the AR-IGA is also reduced compared with the TIGA and the CA-IGA. This is also consistent with the results of the NASA-TLX scale.

Therefore, from the perspective of algorithm convergence and cognitive load, the AR-IGA has advantages in algorithm convergence, reducing the extraneous cognitive load and the total cognitive load level; the CA-IGA has advantages in improving the efficiency of associative cognition in the early-evolutionary period. These can prove the effectiveness of the proposed strategies to a certain extent.

# 5   Conclusions

This paper systematically analyzed the user cognitive process in the IED, and proposed the corresponding improvement strategies based on cognitive load effects. The effectiveness of the strategies was verified by system development and user experiments. However, the study in this paper has the following limitations: First, the study of cognitive processes is mainly based on theoretical research, and the physiological and psychological data related to the user cognitive activities in the IED are not studied. And the follow-up should be combined with eye movements, EEG measurements and other methods to conduct a comprehensive analysis of the user cognitive process in the IED. In addition, two algorithms were selected in this paper to verify certain proposed strategies, but not all are verified. And the actual improved algorithm research is not carried out based on the strategies in this paper. The next step should be to design the corresponding improvement algorithm to verify and correct the proposed strategies.

**Author's Contributions.** The Authors Contribute Equally. Conceptualization, CL, MH. Methodology, CL, MH. Writing of the Original Draft, CL, MH. Writing of the Editing, CL, MH.

**Funding Statement.** This Work Was Supported by China Postdoctoral Science Foundation Under Research Grant 2021M702478, and Partly Funded by Shanghai Pujiang Program (Grant Number 2020PJC110). Both Funders Had no Role in Study Design, Data Collection and Analysis, Decision to Publish, or Preparation of the Manuscript.

# References

1. Zhang, Z., Cong, H., Jiang, G., et al.: Polo shirt rapid style recommendation system based on interactive genetic algorithm. J. Text. Res. **42**(01), 138–144 (2021)
2. Mok, P., Xu, J., Wang, X., et al.: An IGA-based design support system for realistic and practical fashion designs. Comput.-Aided Des. **45**(11), 1442–1458 (2013)
3. Takenouchi, H., Tokumaru, M., Muranaka, N.: Tournament-style evaluation using kansei evaluation. Int. J. Affective Eng. **12**(3), 395–407 (2013)
4. Wang, T., Zhou, M.: A method for product form design of integrating interactive genetic algorithm with the interval hesitation time and user satisfaction. Int. J. Ind. Ergon. **76**, 102901 (2020)
5. Khan, S., Gunpinar, E., Sener, B.: GenYacht: an interactive generative design system for computer-aided yacht hull design. Ocean Eng. **191**, 106462 (2019)
6. Deng, L., Wang, G.: Application of EEG and interactive evolutionary design method in cultural and creative product design. Comput. Intell. Neurosci. **2019**, 1860921 (2019)
7. Guo, G., Chen, L., Wen, Z., et al.: Interactive genetic algorithms based on estimation of individual's fuzzy fitness. Control Decis. **33**(9), 1559–1566 (2018)
8. Cai, H.: User preference adaptive fitness of interactive genetic algorithm based ceramic disk pattern generation method. IEEE Access **8**, 95978–95986 (2020)

9. Leelathakul, N., Rimcharoen, S.: Generating Kranok patterns with an interactive evolutionary algorithm. Appl. Soft. Comput. **89**, 106121 (2020)
10. Zhang, N., Pan, R., Wang, L., et al.: Pattern design and optimization of yarn-dyed plaid fabric using modified interactive genetic algorithm. J. Text. Inst. **111**(11), 1652–1661 (2020)
11. Takenouchi, H., Tokumaru, M.: Character design generation system using multiple users' gaze information. IEICE Trans. Inf. Syst. **104**(9), 1459–1466 (2021)
12. Takenouchi, H., Tokumaru, M.: Interactive evolutionary computation system using multiple users' Gaze information considering user's partial evaluation participation. In: 2019 IEEE 10th International Conference on Awareness Science and Technology (iCAST), pp. 365–369. IEEE, New York (2019)
13. Lv, J., Zhu, M., Pan, W., et al.: Interactive genetic algorithm oriented toward the novel design of traditional patterns. Inf. **10**(2), 36 (2019)
14. Zhong, M., Li, G., Li, Y.: Spacewalker: Rapid UI design exploration using lightweight markup enhancement and crowd genetic programming. In: Kitamura, Y., Quigley, A. (eds.) 2021 CHI Conference on Human Factors in Computing Systems (CHI '21), vol. 315, pp. 1–11. ACM, New York (2021)
15. Dou, R., Guo, J., Tian, X., et al.: Interactive genetic algorithm based on customer demand. J. Manage. Sci. China **19**(01), 24–34 (2016)
16. Dawkins, R.: The Blind Watchmaker: Why the Evidence of Evolution Reveals a Universe Without Design. W. W. Notron, New York (1986)
17. Yang, Y., Tian, X.: Combining users' cognition noise with interactive genetic algorithms and trapezoidal fuzzy numbers for product color design. Comput. Intell. Neurosci. **2019**, 1019749 (2019)
18. Zeng, D., Zhou, Z., He, M., et al.: Solution to resolve cognitive ambiguity in interactive customization of product shape. Int. J. Comput. Intell. Syst. **13**(1), 565–575 (2020)
19. Ohsaki, M., Takagi, H., Ohya, K.: An input method using discrete fitness values for interactive GA. J. Intell. Fuzzy Syst. **6**(1), 131–145 (1998)
20. Gong, D., Guo, G., Lu, L., et al.: Adaptive interactive genetic algorithms with individual interval fitness. Prog. Nat. Sci. **18**(3), 359–365 (2008)
21. Dou, R., Zong, C., Li, M.: An interactive genetic algorithm with the interval arithmetic based on hesitation and its application to achieve customer collaborative product configuration design. Appl. Soft. Comput. **38**, 384–394 (2016)
22. Gong, D., Yuan, J., Sun, X.: Interactive genetic algorithms with individual's fuzzy fitness. Comput. Hum. Behav. **27**(5), 1482–1492 (2011)
23. Cheng, S., Liu, Y.: Eye-tracking based adaptive user interface: implicit human-computer interaction for preference indication. J. Multimodal User Interfaces **5**(1–2), 77–84 (2012)
24. Sweller, J.: Cognitive load during problem solving: effects on learning. Cogn. Sci. **12**(2), 257–285 (1988)
25. Sweller, J.: Element interactivity and intrinsic, extraneous, and germane cognitive load. Educ. Psychol. Rev. **22**(2), 123–138 (2010)
26. Wang, C., Cao, J., Zou, N.: The theoretical analysis of the correlationship between cognition need and cognitive load of information users. Inf. Sci. **37**(3), 141–145 (2019)
27. Zeng, D., Gong, D., Li, M., et al.: Thinking fixation strategy in product form design and its application. J. Mech. Eng. **53**(15), 58–65 (2017)
28. Watanabe, Y., Yoshikawa, T., Furuhashi, T.: A study on application of fitness inference method to PC-IGA. In: 2007 IEEE Congress on Evolutionary Computation, pp. 1450–1455. IEEE, New York (2007)
29. Pang, W.: Cognitive load theory and its teaching implications. Contemp. Educ. Sci. **12**, 23–28 (2011)
30. Sweller, J., Ayres, P., Kalyuga, S.: Cognitive Load Theory. Springer, Heidelberg (2011)

31. Zeng, D., He, M., Tang, X., et al.: Cognitive association in interactive evolutionary design process for product styling and application to SUV design. Electronics **9**(11), 1960 (2020)
32. Zeng, D., He, M., Zhou, Z., et al.: An interactive genetic algorithm with an alternation ranking method and its application to product customization. Human-Centric Comput. Inf. Sci. **11**(15), 1–24 (2021)
33. Leppink, J., Paas, F., Van der Vleuten, C.P.M., et al.: Development of an instrument for measuring different types of cognitive load. Behav. Res. Methods **45**(4), 1058–1072 (2013)
34. Yang, Y., Deng, C.: A study on the reliability and validity of NASA-TLX as a measurement of subjective fatigue after computer operation. Psychol. Res. **3**(3), 36–41 (2010)
35. Vidulich, M., Tsang, P.: Techniques of subjective workload assessment: a comparison of SWAT and the NASA-Bipolar methods. Ergonomics **29**(11), 1385–1398 (1986)

# Development History and Concept Analysis of Tangible Interaction Design

Yi Liu[1](✉) and Siyuan Xie[2](✉)

[1] Province Key Lab of Innovation and Applied Research on Industry Design,
No. 257 Changgang Road, Guangzhou, People's Republic of China
64947357@qq.com
[2] Guangzhou Academy of Fine Arts, No. 257 Changgang Road, Guangzhou,
People's Republic of China

**Abstract.** Objectives: In view of the chaotic and fuzzy phenomenon of tangible interaction design and related concepts, this study sorts out and summarizes the development history of tangible interaction design, discusses and defines the concept of tangible interaction design, and analyzes the concept development relationship of tangible interaction design. Methodology: Through literature research, this paper sorts out the development history of tangible interaction design, and defines its concept and relationship. With Hornecker's framework of tangible interaction as the prototype, this study establishes a model for interaction element analysis, and conducts a comparative analysis of the proportions of elements in the concept of tangible interaction design, thus identifying the development relationship of tangible interaction design and interaction elements. Conclusion: The development of tangible interaction design is roughly divided into three stages, namely the germination of physical input, the development of physical-digital coupling, and the transformation of experience orientation. Such concepts as Graspable Interface, Tangible Interface, and Radical Atoms all fall into the category of Tangible Interaction Design. The development of tangible interaction design and interaction elements enhance each other, from physical elements as the core to the tangible interactive interface enhancing expressiveness through technology, to the physical and expressive-based tangible interaction system with space and embodiment, reflecting the development history of experience-oriented tangible interaction design.

**Keywords:** Tangible interaction design · Interaction elements · Interactive interface

## 1 Introduction

With the rise of the "post-WIMP style" human-computer interaction paradigm, in the 1990s, the tangible interactive interface emerged as a type of post-WIMP interface interaction. In the following two decades, it attracted great attention from researchers in the field of human-computer interaction and interaction design.

M. Kurosu et al. (Eds.): HCII 2022, LNCS 13516, pp. 82–96, 2022.
https://doi.org/10.1007/978-3-031-17615-9_6

With the development of tangible interactive interface, in the early 21st century, the concept of tangible interaction design was put forward. However, the elaboration of the relationship between tangible interaction and related concepts among researchers is relatively fuzzy. Professor Hornecker summarized this situation with the "inclusive framework" [1]. Scholars not only conducted longitudinal studies on tangible interaction and tangible interaction interface from theoretical and methodological aspects, but also conducted cross-disciplinary studies from materials science, cognitive psychology, embodied interaction, intelligence technology, game design and other multidisciplinary perspectives. This study sorts out the development history of tangible interaction design, sorts out and summarizes the development history of tangible interaction design, discusses and defines the concept of tangible interaction design, analyzes the concept development relationship of tangible interaction design, hoping to gain clearer and more abstract understanding of tangible interaction design.

## 2 The Development History of Tangible Interaction Design

### 2.1 The Germination of Physical Input

In order to solve the difficulty for ordinary users to use the interface of batch processing and command line [2] in the computer, engineers have actively explored new methods of input and output. In 1970, the graphical user interface (GUI) developed by PARC (Palo Alto Research Center) in the United States was released. The WIMP paradigm based on window, icon, menu and pointer has then become the basic paradigm of human-computer interaction. The same universal input devices are basically used in any field of application, from production tools to games.

The method of WIMP interface interaction has become the mainstream, but researchers found that the WIMP interface had some shortcomings in interaction [3]. For example, it is difficult for the input devices to realize the input method participated by multiple people, and the input method basically ignores the rich actions of people in the physical space and the position of the space. In response to these problems, new input devices utilizing human's skills to interact with the real world began to emerge and solve these problems. Driven by sensing technologies, the computer's input devices broke through the input method with mouse and keyboard, and the prototype with physical input devices appeared. In 1976, Perlman [4] developed invented Slot Machine, a system representing programming with physical cards. Besides, in the early 1980s, in order to get more people participating in discussions on architectural design, Aishi et al. [5, 6] developed a 3-D modeling system using physical models as the input device. These new input devices can be classified as the first prototypes of tangible user interfaces. This new type of input method is also one of the types of post-WIMP interface interaction that emerged later.

In the late 1990s, with the miniaturization of processors and the introduction of such concepts as "ubiquitous computing", researchers of interaction design began to discuss augmented reality, and tangible interactive interfaces were formally introduced in the discussion of augmented reality. As Wellner [7] said, "We live in a complex world filled with countless objects, tools, toys, and people, and we live our lives by interacting with our environment. However, we always have to sit in front of a lighted screen connected to a mouse and keyboard for computing activities." He advocated for embedding computing into existing environments and human practices for a fluid transition between "digital" and "real", which greatly influenced the development of augmented reality and ubiquitous computing [2]. The 1970s and 1990s were the early germination stage of the tangible interface, which initially showed the basic characteristics with physical input as the core.

## 2.2  The Development Stage of Physical-Digital Coupling

From the end of the 20th century to the beginning of the 21st century, the tangible interactive interface was formally proposed, and it became a scientific research direction of interaction design alone, entering a stage of rapid development. Influenced by the concept of graspable interface put forward by Fitzmaurice et al. [8, 9] in 1995, the tangible interactive interface gradually began to develop its theoretical framework. In the same year, Professor Ishii founded the Tangible Media Group [10] in the MIT Lab, which was the first research organization on tangible interaction design. Later, in 1997, Ishii et al. [11] put forward the vision of tangible bits: bridging the gap between cyberspace and the physical environment by making digital information (bits) tangible. Based on this concept, tangible interactive interface has become a new type of interface and method of interaction.

From the perspective of technological progress, with the rapid development of software and hardware technologies such as sensors, microprocessors, virtual reality, augmented reality, artificial intelligence, and operating systems, the relatively single, fixed and precise interaction methods such as mouse and keyboard in desktop computers can no longer meet people's needs. Multi-channel, natural information acquisition and interaction methods have become the mainstream demands of users. Human-computer interaction technology has developed from the graphical user interface stage to the stage of multi channel, multimedia intelligent human-computer interaction (Mult-Modal Interaction MMI) [12]. Natural interaction based on diversified human-computer interaction technologies has become the basic direction of the current and future development of interaction design [13, 14]. The tangible interactive interface focuses on multi-channel physical input such as touch, manual, gesture, head movement, and body posture during the germination period. Later, based on technical application, the multimedia output form of coupling of tangible interface and digital information was realized as much as possible. The output form of the tangible interactive interface not only attaches importance to the physical deformation of the entity, but also combines the graphic interface, tactile sensation, sound signal, light and shadow signal and other multimedia means to carry out a unified design of physical-digital coupling.

In the early days, the research of tangible interactive interface focused on the possibility of technical application, the construction of interaction models and the description methods of systems. For example, in 2000, Ishii et al. [15] proposed the first model of tangible user interface interaction (the MCRpd model), and proposed the specific definition of tangible user interface; in 1999, Holmquist et al. [16] proposed the prototype of the "Token+constraint" system, and Ullmer et al. [17, 18] discussed it in depth and established the description method of the early tangible interactive interface. The research on tangible interactive interface is not only conducted in the field of design, but researchers in the fields of psychology, behavior, materials, space architecture and other fields have also conducted related research simultaneously. For example, in 2004, from the perspective of cognitive psychology, Fishkin [19] put forward a classification framework for tangible interactive interfaces using the scales of "metaphor" and "distance"; Sharlin et al. [20] proposed to incorporate spatiality into the design of tangible interactive interface; Djajadiningrat et al. [21] established a framework to analyze the coupling of human behavior and the functional information of tangible interface; Hoven et al. [22] focused on the influencing factors of user experience brought by the personal attributes of entities in the tangible interactive interface; in 2003, Koleva et al. [23] proposed a framework of tangible interface classification based on the degree of coupling between physical and digital objects. At this stage, "tangible interactive interface" officially became a new interaction method and a direction of interaction research. Related research mainly focused on the physical transformation of interface input and output, as well as the coupling design research of digital information and physical entities. Its core lies in how to increase the possibility of technical application to achieve better coupling with physical numbers, which is embodied in the construction of interaction models and the research on some classification frameworks.

### 2.3 The Stage of Experience-Oriented Transformation

With the development of research on tangible interactive interface in some specific application scenarios or application fields, some scholars began to pay attention to such factors as embodied effect and spatiality in tangible interactive interface. According to the prototype [24, 25] of tangible interaction interface in some group cooperation scenarios, Arias and Stanton et al. proposed the social effect in tangible interaction interface. For example, Arias [26] and Suzuki et al. [27] proposed the social affordance of tangible interactive interface; Stanton [28] believed that compared with the interaction between people and keyboards, the interaction between people and entities had a lower threshold of participation and the process of interaction was more obvious, enabling tangible interactive interface to meet the social multi-person scenarios of usage; in 2001, Dourish emphasized the social nature of the environment in Where the Action Is. The Foundations of Embodied Interaction [29]; based on the research of Dourish and the above-mentioned researchers, Hornecker et al. [1, 30] pointed out the relationship between physicality and sociality in the environment, and thus proposed the embodiment of tangible interactive interface. In addition, with the advent of some research on spatial interaction, Hornecker proposed the spatiality in tangible interactive interface [1]. For example, Bongers [31] studied the potential relationship between the concept of space and place and interactive physical space, and Ciolfi [32] studied the relationship between location and user experience in interactive space in his doctoral dissertation. These scholars focused on specific application scenarios, embodiment, and space, and turned the design of tangible interactive interface to the design of tangible interaction systems to improve user experience, thus forming a cognitive framework for tangible interaction (put forward by Hornecker et al. in 2006 [1]).

At the same time, in order to achieve better physical-digital coupling, Ishii et al. proposed the concept of Radical Atoms [33] in 2012 as a new future vision of tangible interactive interface. From the perspective of the development process of tangible interactive interaction in a broad sense, the concept of Radical Atoms is regarded as the support of digital information physical transformation technology in tangible interactive interaction, which is the ultimate form of the development of tangible interactive interface proposed so far.

Since the beginning of the 21st century, the research of tangible interaction design has begun to jump out of the research of the design of tangible interactive interface in the human-computer interaction discipline, and gradually began to discuss the design of generalized tangible interactive system under the intersection of embodied interaction, product design and interaction art, and began to focus on user experience, from the design of technology-centered tangible interactive interface to the research of tangible interaction system design aiming at user experience and social effects.

The key points and three stages of the development history of tangible interaction design are as shown in Fig. 1.

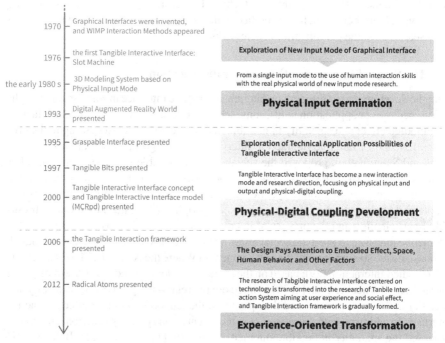

**Fig. 1.** The key points and three stages of the development history of tangible interaction design.

From the above information, the following conclusions can be drawn:

(1) From the perspective of the research content of tangible interaction design, in the early days, tangible interaction design was contained in the exploration of new methods of natural input of graphical user interfaces and multimedia output forms based on technical applicability of physical-digital coupling.

(2) From the perspective of the discipline development of tangible interaction design, tangible interaction originated from the study of human-computer interaction on interface carrier paradigm and gradually developed to the study of interaction formation factors and mechanism in interaction design. Based on the technology-centered research on tangible interactive interface, scholars put forward the concept of "tangible interaction" based on the interpretation of "tangible" from different perspectives.

(3) From the perspective of the transformation of goals in tangible interaction design, for tangible interaction, the realization of physical natural interaction is its basic goal. And with its unique "tangible" attributes, it has become its top goal to create a good social effect and a unique user experience by integrating physical and spatial elements, embodied effects and other elements.

## 3   The Concept Relationship of Tangible Interaction Design

### 3.1   The Definition and Discussion of Concepts

As mentioned above, during the emergence and development of tangible interaction from the end of the 20th century to the beginning of the 21st century, researchers from different disciplines interpreted the concept of tangible interaction from their respective research perspectives. Hornecker divided it into three perspectives, namely the perspective of digital information in computer science, the perspective of perception and action in industrial design, and the perspective of spatial interaction in architecture and art [1].

From the perspective of digital information, there are the concept of graspable interactive interface, tangible interactive interface, tangible bits, and the concept of Radical Atoms. The theory of graspable interactive interface advocates the physical representation of some virtual user interface elements that were originally in the graphical user interface. It emphasizes the "spatial reusability" of graspable input devices, the "direct grasping" of "function" in the user's mental model, as well as the spatial awareness between specific fields and situations and input devices [8, 9]. The characteristics of tangible bits basically are basically the continuation of those of the graspable interactive interface: first, the surface of the physical entity becomes an interactive interface, second, digital information and physical entity coupling, and the role of environmental media also needs to be considered: transforming physical materials in everyday architectural spaces into interactive interfaces for communication, including, for example, sound, light, flow and water movement [11]. The tangible interactive interface refers to the interactive interface generated by calculation through the coupling of digital media (such as images, audio) and physical artifacts (such as spatially operable tangible objects), using physical artifacts as the representation and control of computational media. In short, a tangible interactive interface provides the physical form for digital information [11]. Radical Atoms is the next phase of tangible interaction vision after Tangible Bits. It can also be referred to as the "Material User Interface (MUI)", emphasizing the bidirectional coupling of interface materials and underlying digital models (bits). Dynamic changes in physical form can be reflected in the digital state in real time, and vice versa [33]. The above concepts are about the theme of the physical presentation of digital information, focusing on how to use technology to break through stronger coupling. They are the basis and main line of the development of tangible interaction. Combined with the development process of tangible interaction, their basic relationship can be represented as shown in Fig. 2.

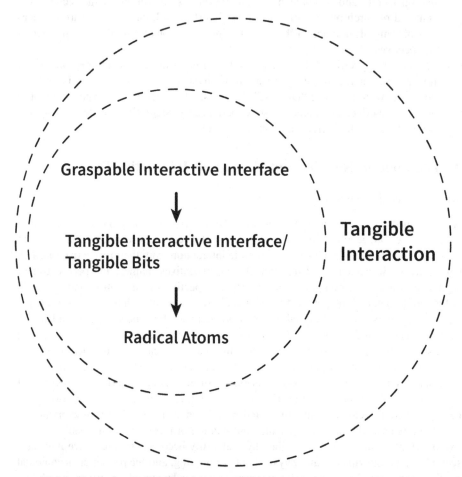

**Fig. 2.** The basic relationship between several key concepts in tangible interaction.

Djajadiningrat et al. proposed to interpret tangible interaction design from the perspective of perceived action. When discussing the "affordance" of the design of industrial product forms, they believed that designers should design the "interaction affordance" before the design of product forms, and that they could also guide some specific skills of users, so as to carry out expressive product interaction design (he used the operation actions of assembly line workers as an example), so that people could realize what actions should be taken before touching the product. To some extent, these views stem from the interaction thinking shift put forward by Dourish, that is, from the point of view of products themselves providing "affordance" to the creation of meanings in the process of product interaction [34–36].

Interpretation from the perspective of spatial interaction is mainly based on the interactive space theory of the combination of computer systems and physical spaces. The typical feature of interactive space design is to embed interactive systems into real spaces, providing opportunities for people to interact with tangible devices, triggering the display of digital content or reactive behaviors, and finally developing to full-body interaction, or using the body as an interactive device and display [31, 32, 37]. In this process, the word "tangible" is embodied in the human interaction with the entire tangible space or objects/markers in the space. At the same time, spatial interaction brings unique attributes such as "full body interaction" and "spatial location". All these can be taken into consideration in the tangible interaction system.

Although various conceptual interpretations have been put forward in the emergence of tangible interaction, we can see that none of the interpretations deny that tangible interaction is always based on the tangible properties of the physical world, and that it requires the use of physical artifacts or tangible environments coupling digital information as an interactive carrier. Depending on the possibility of technical application, the physical level of physical interaction can eventually become a natural interface similar to Radical Atoms. In addition, the physical entities themselves can bring people natural psychological feelings such as rich sensory characteristics, behavioral affordance, and spatial location, allowing tangible interactions to achieve specific user experience in specific domains or scenarios, for example, in collective collaborations, social activities and space scenarios. Therefore, it can achieve a specific user experience or interaction effect on the basis of realizing the vision of natural interactive interface. Hornecker proposed the framework of tangible interaction, but did not define the tangible interaction design in a more accurate manner [1]. Therefore, based on the description and analysis of tangible interaction in existing literature, we can define tangible interaction design in this way: tangible interaction design is the design of a tangible interaction system. The tangible interaction system takes the tangible interaction form of digital information as the carrier, uses such factors as perceived behavioral affordance, embodied effects, physical interactions, and spatial location of physical artifacts or tangible environments to endow interactions with meanings, and achieve the goal of specific interactive experiences or social effects.

### 3.2 A Comparative Analysis of Interaction Elements

An Analysis of Element Dimensions. As can be seen from the above discussion, as a research direction of interaction design, the development history of tangible interaction is very short, and some basic conceptual frameworks and classification frameworks have also been formed, but compared to MCRpd models [15, 38], "Token+constraint" system [16–18], which aim to describe and build interfaces, and classification frameworks that only consider two or more dimensions, the Tangible Interaction Framework [1] proposed by Hornecker can describe the features and interaction elements of tangible interaction design from a broad and inclusive perspective. The original framework is as shown in Fig. 3.

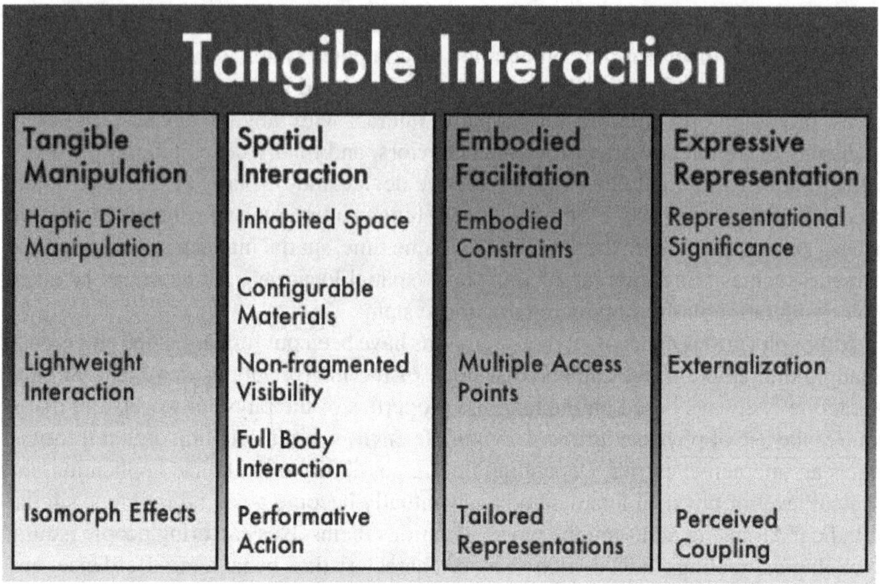

# Tangible Interaction

| Tangible Manipulation | Spatial Interaction | Embodied Facilitation | Expressive Representation |
|---|---|---|---|
| Haptic Direct Manipulation | Inhabited Space | Embodied Constraints | Representational Significance |
| | Configurable Materials | | |
| Lightweight Interaction | Non-fragmented Visibility | Multiple Access Points | Externalization |
| | Full Body Interaction | | |
| Isomorph Effects | Performative Action | Tailored Representations | Perceived Coupling |

**Fig. 3.** Hornecker's framework of tangible interaction.

In order to more comprehensively and concretely compare the differences and commonalities between related concepts of tangible interaction, according to four themes in this framework, namely tangible manipulation, spatial interaction, embodied facilitation, and expressive representation, the author has extracted four interactive elements: physicality, spatiality, embodiment, and expressiveness. Then the author established a four-dimensional analysis model based on the four interactive elements, putting each concept supplemented by typical cases under the concept in the framework, and conducts a comparative analysis of the proportion of elements according to the subdivision elements in each dimension. The subdivision elements in each dimension and dimension are described in detail in the following part.

Elements in the physical dimension: direct tactile manipulation, lightweight interaction, and isomorphic effects [1]. Physicality represents the physical interaction of a person with a physical object (device) [1]. This interaction relies on human tactile feedback (tactile manipulation) [1], which requires the interactive feedback process to be lightweight and fast, allowing people to perform multiple trial and error (lightweight interaction) [1]. The feedback and manipulation of digital information presents simultaneous, co-located, and isomorphic effects (isomorphic effects) [21].

Elements under the spatiality dimension: real space, configurable materials, non-fragmented visualization, full-body interaction, and expressive action [1]. Spatiality represents the characteristic of interactive systems embedded in real space and combining real space with virtual digital information [39]. Spatiality not only refers to the interaction system embedded in the real space, the positional relationship between the body and the space, etc. Its deeper implication is that the interaction system generates a kind of "situation space" (real space) around it during its operation [36], and it makes sense for people to move physical artifacts or their own bodies (configurable material) [1], it requires that everyone can easily observe the whole process of interaction (non-fragmented visualization) [40], and try to use the entire body of a person for action interaction (full-body interaction) [40], and interactions are expected to be expressive and convey specific meanings to the public (expressive actions) [40].

Elements in the embodied dimension: embodied constraints, multiple access points, customized representations [1]. Because people move not only in the physical space, but also metaphorically in the virtual space in the tangible interaction system. In the real space, the promoted and restricted human behaviors bring about embodied effects, which helps shape new social forms [1]. The design of the physical artifacts and physical spaces of an interactive system is intentionally done by the designer and can limit, hinder, or facilitate specific human behaviors (embodied constraints) [1, 30]. At the same time, the system should allow multiple people to participate in the interaction at the same time, preventing solo control(multiple access points) [1]. Not only does the designed system need to provide intuitive readability, but the design of the manipulable physical artifacts should also be based on the user's experience and skills (customized representation) [40].

Elements in the expressiveness dimension: representational meaning, external instrumentalization, perceptual coupling [1]. Expressiveness represents the degree of physical-digital coupling of the system and the ability to characterize physical artifacts [1]. The physical representation of the system and the underlying digital information are properly coupled and can mutually reinforce meanings (representational meanings) [40]. One can naturally use the system as an everyday tool with digital capabilities (external instrumentation) [40]. Finally, the feedback from the system is coherent and understandable with human actions. Physical artifacts are designed to fit well with the meaning of digital information they represent (perceptual coupling) [40].

In order to compare the proportion of each concept in each dimension as accurately as possible, the author gives a score of 0–3 in each dimension according to the proportion of the concept in each dimension: A score of 0 indicates that the concept does not have elements in a dimension, that is, it does not have the features; a score of 3 indicates that the concept has all the elements in a dimension and the features of the elements are obvious, that is, it fully possesses the features; a score of 1–2 indicates that the concept

| CONCEPT | CASE | INTERACTION ELEMENTS | | | | TIME |
|---|---|---|---|---|---|---|
| | | PHYSICAL | SPATIALITY | EMBODIMENT | EXPRESSIVENESS | |
| Graspable Interactive Interface | abacus | 3 | 1 | 0 | 1 | ancient |
| Graspable Interactive Interface | Bricks | 3 | 2 | 1 | 2 | 1995 |
| Graspable Interactive Interface | metadesk | 3 | 2 | 1 | 2 | 1997 |
| Graspable Interactive Interface | Marble Answering Machine | 3 | 1 | 0 | 1 | 1999 |
| Tangible Bits | transboard | 3 | 3 | 1 | 2 | 1997 |
| Tangible Bits | Ambient Room | 3 | 3 | 1 | 2 | 1997 |
| Tangible Interactive Interface | MediaBlocks | 3 | 2 | 1 | 1 | 1998 |
| Tangible Interactive Interface | Urp | 3 | 2 | 2 | 3 | 1999 |
| Tangible Interactive Interface | Sandscape | 3 | 2 | 3 | 3 | 2003 |
| Tangible Interactive Interface | PICO | 3 | 2 | 1 | 2 | 2005 |
| Tangible Interactive Interface | Relief | 3 | 2 | 1 | 2 | 2009 |
| Tangible Interactive Interface | ZreoN | 3 | 2 | 1 | 2 | 2011 |
| Radical Atoms | Perfect Red | 3 | 1 | 1 | 3 | 2012 |
| Tangible Interaction | EDC | 3 | 2 | 3 | 3 | 2002 |
| Tangible Interaction | CLAVIER | 3 | 3 | 3 | 2 | 2005 |

**Fig. 4.** Process data of the comparative analysis of element proportions.

has some elements in the dimension. The specific process data analyzed are as shown in Fig. 4. Finally, the author displays the analysis results in the form of a radar chart, as shown in Fig. 5.

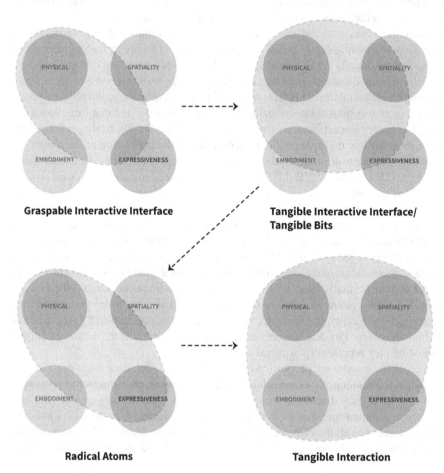

**Graspable Interactive Interface**

**Tangible Interactive Interface/ Tangible Bits**

**Radical Atoms**

**Tangible Interaction**

**Fig. 5.** Results of the comparative analysis of element proportions.

Development and Influence of Elements. As can be seen from Fig. 5, all concepts have a high proportion in the physicality dimension. Tangible bits/tangible interactive interface and tangible interaction have a high proportion in the dimension of embodiment and spatiality. Only tangible interaction and Radical Atoms have a high proportion in the dimension of expressiveness.

From the perspective of the role and development of each interaction element alone, the above results have shown that physicality is the fundamental element of the concept of tangible interaction, indicating that the development of tangible interaction is based on the tactile/bodily interaction between people and physical objects (devices). From the simple graspable interface of the desktop controlling the computer to the interactive scene of multi-person collaboration in a larger space, physicality and spatiality have become important considerations for tangible interaction. Expressiveness itself represents the degree of physical-digital coupling of the interactive system. The proportion of this element often depends on the design elements of the specific appearance of the physical artifacts. Moreover, with the progress of smart material technology (Radical Atoms) and driving technology, the expressiveness of tangible interaction systems may become stronger and stronger.

From the perspective of the overall relationship between the development of the tangible interaction concept and the interaction elements, the development of the tangible interaction design and the interaction elements promote each other: From physical elements as the core to the tangible interaction interface enhancing the performance through technology, to the tangible interaction system with space and embodiment based on physicality and performance. At the same time, the overall relationship between tangible interaction design and interaction elements also reflects the development history of tangible interaction design summarized above.

The tangible interactive interface, which has physical elements as the core and enhances the expressiveness through technology, emphasizes the exploration of how to better physically manipulate digital information. It takes technology application as the core innovation point: from passive technology, self-driving, to smart material technology [41]. These tangible interaction interfaces belong to the fundamental level of tangible interaction, and the concepts involved in this level include graspable interactive interface, tangible interactive interface (most of them), and Radical Atoms.

The physicality and expressiveness-based tangible interaction systems with spatiality and embodiment are collective systems of multi-user spatial interaction. They aim to create a spatial atmosphere of social interaction and embodied effects, and have risen from the "physical representation" of design in the physical dimension to the design of "social representation/social affordance" [1]. The concepts involved in this level are (part of) tangible interactive interface, Radical Atoms (with development potential, but no consistent design prototype has yet appeared), and tangible interaction.

## 4   Conclusion

With the rapid development of new technologies, in the future, tangible interaction design can only rely on human-computer interaction technology for more novel, diverse, convenient and efficient interaction methods, realizing a more natural interface form is the basic research direction of tangible interaction in the future, and social interaction will be an important research direction of tangible interaction design in the future. At the same time, the research of tangible interaction design has been extended from a narrow-area interaction focusing on the interaction design of computer interface to the design of a wide-area interaction that takes physical artifacts and space as the carrier to study the complex interaction between people, society and the environment. The social characteristics of tangible interaction design are becoming more and more prominent, and building a good interactive relationship between people, society and the environment will also become the focus of the research on tangible interaction design.

# References

1. Hornecker, E., Buur, J.: Getting a grip on tangible interaction: a framework on physical space and social interaction. In: Proceedings of the SIGCHI Conference on Human Factors in Computing Systems, pp. 437–446. Association for Computing Machinery, New York (2006). https://doi.org/10.1145/1124772.1124838
2. Gong, J., Wang, X.: The progress and development trend of human-computer interaction technology. J. Xidian Univ. **25**(6), 782–786 (1998). (in Chinese)
3. Shaer, O., Hornecker, E.: Tangible User Interfaces: Past, Present, and Future Directions. Now Publishers Inc., Boston (2010). https://doi.org/10.1561/1100000026
4. Perlman, R.: Using computer technology to provide a creative learning environment for preschool children. In: Artificial Intelligence Lab Publications. DSpace@MIT, Cambridge (1976)
5. Aish, R.: 3D input for CAAD systems. Comput. Aided Des. **11**(2), 66–70 (1979). https://doi.org/10.1016/0010-4485(79)90098-8
6. Aish, R., Noakes, P.: Architecture without numbers—CAAD based on a 3D modelling system. Comput. Aided Des. **16**(6), 321–328 (1984). https://doi.org/10.1016/0010-4485(84)90116-7
7. Wellner, P., Mackay, W., Gold, R.: Computer-augmented environments: back to the real world. Commun. ACM **36**(7), 24–26 (1993). https://doi.org/10.1145/159544.159555
8. Fitzmaurice, G.W., Ishii, H., Buxton, W.A.: Bricks: laying the foundations for graspable user interfaces. In: Proceedings of the SIGCHI Conference on Human Factors in Computing Systems, pp. 442–449. Association for Computing Machinery, New York (1995). https://doi.org/10.1145/223904.223964
9. Fitzmaurice, G.W.: Graspable user interfaces. University of Toronto, Toronto (1996)
10. Hiroshi Ishii Professor Homepage. https://tangible.media.mit.edu/person/hiroshi-ishii/. Accessed 11 May 2022
11. Ishii, H., Ullmer, B.: Tangible bits: toward seamless interfaces between people, bits and atoms. In: Proceedings of the ACM SIGCHI Conference on Human Factors in Computing Systems, pp. 234–241. Association for Computing Machinery, New York (1997). https://doi.org/10.1145/258549.258715
12. Dong, S.: Progress and challenge of human-computer interaction. J. Comput. Aided Des. Comput. Graph. **16**(1), 13 (2004). (in Chinese)
13. Guan, Y.: Pervasive computing and natural interface design. Zhuangshi (5), 2(2009). (in Chinese)
14. Fan, J., Tian, F., Du, Y., Liu, Z., Dai, G.: Reflections on human-computer interaction in the age of intelligence. Scientia Sinica Informationis **48**(4), 361–375 (2018). (in Chinese)
15. Ullmer, B., Ishii, H.: Emerging frameworks for tangible user interfaces. IBM Syst. J. **39**(3.4), 915–931 (2000). https://doi.org/10.1147/sj.393.0915
16. Holmquist, L.E., Redström, J., Ljungstrand, P.: Token-based access to digital information. In: Gellersen, H.-W. (ed.) HUC 1999. LNCS, vol. 1707, pp. 234–245. Springer, Heidelberg (1999). https://doi.org/10.1007/3-540-48157-5_22
17. Ullmer, B.A.: Tangible interfaces for manipulating aggregates of digital information. Doctoral dissertation, Massachusetts Institute of Technology, Cambridge (2005)
18. Ullmer, B., Ishii, H., Jacob, R.J.: Token+constraint systems for tangible interaction with digital information. In: ACM Transactions on Computer-Human Interaction, pp. 81–118. Association for Computing Machinery, New York (2005). https://doi.org/10.1145/1057237.1057242
19. Fishkin, K.P.: A taxonomy for and analysis of tangible interfaces. Pers. Ubiquit. Comput. **8**(5), 347–358 (2004). https://doi.org/10.1007/s00779-004-0297-4

20. Sharlin, E., Watson, B., Kitamura, Y., Kishino, F., Itoh, Y.: On tangible user interfaces, humans and spatiality. Pers. Ubiquit. Comput. **8**(5), 338–346 (2004). https://doi.org/10.1007/s00779-004-0296-5

21. Wensveen, S.A., Djajadiningrat, J.P., Overbeeke, C.J.: Interaction frogger: a design framework to couple action and function through feedback and feedforward. In: Designing Interactive Systems 2004, pp. 177–184. Association for Computing Machinery, New York (2004). https://doi.org/10.1145/1013115.1013140

22. van den Hoven, E., Eggen, B.: Tangible computing in everyday life: extending current frameworks for tangible user interfaces with personal objects. In: Markopoulos, P., Eggen, B., Aarts, E., Crowley, J.L. (eds.) EUSAI 2004. LNCS, vol. 3295, pp. 230–242. Springer, Heidelberg (2004). https://doi.org/10.1007/978-3-540-30473-9_22

23. Koleva, B., Benford, S., Ng, K.H., Rodden, T.: A framework for tangible user interfaces. In: Physical Interaction (PI03) Workshop on Real World User Interfaces, Udine, pp. 46–50 (2003)

24. Cohen, J., Withgott, M., Piernot, P.: Logjam: a tangible multi-person interface for video logging. In: Proceedings of the SIGCHI conference on Human Factors in Computing Systems, pp. 128–135. Association for Computing Machinery, New York (1999). https://doi.org/10.1145/302979.303013

25. Price, S., Rogers, Y.: Let's get physical: the learning benefits of interacting in digitally augmented physical spaces. Comput. Educ. **43**(1–2), 137–151 (2004). https://doi.org/10.1016/j.compedu.2003.12.009

26. Arias, E., Eden, H., Fisher, G.: Enhancing communication, facilitating shared understanding, and creating better artifacts by integrating physical and computational media for design. In: Proceedings of the 2nd Conference on Designing Interactive Systems: Processes, Practices, Methods, and Techniques, pp. 1–12. Association for Computing Machinery, New York (1997). https://doi.org/10.1145/263552.263553

27. Suzuki, H., Kata, H.: Interaction-level support for collaborative learning: AlgoBlock - an open programming language. In: The First International Conference on Computer Support for Collaborative Learning, pp. 349–355. L. Erlbaum Associates Inc., Bloomington (1997). https://doi.org/10.3115/222020.222828

28. Stanton, D., et al.: Classroom collaboration in the design of tangible interfaces for storytelling. In: Proceedings of the SIGCHI Conference on Human Factors in Computing Systems, pp. 482–489. Association for Computing Machinery, New York (2001). https://doi.org/10.1145/365024.365322

29. Dourish, P.: Where the Action Is: The Foundations of Embodied Interaction. MIT Press, Cambridge (2001)

30. Hornecker, E.: A design theme for tangible interaction: embodied facilitation. In: Gellersen, H., Schmidt, K. Beaudouin-Lafon, M., Mackay, W. (eds.) ECSCW 2005. Springer, Dordrecht (2005). https://doi.org/10.1007/1-4020-4023-7_2

31. Bongers, B.: Interactivating spaces. In: Proceedings of a Special Focus Symposium on Art and Science held as part of the 17th International Conference on Systems Research, Informatics and Cybernetics. International Institute for Advanced Studies in Systems Research and Cybernetics, Baden-Baden, Tecumseh (2005)

32. Ciolfi, L.: Situating "place" in interaction design: enhancing the user experience in interactive environments. Doctoral dissertation, University of Limerick (2004)

33. Ishii, H., Lakatos, D., Bonanni, L., Labrune, J.B.: Radical atoms: beyond tangible bits, toward transformable materials. Interactions **19**(1), 38–51 (2012). https://doi.org/10.1145/2065327.2065337

34. Jensen, M.V., Buur, J., Djajadiningrat, T.: Designing the user actions in tangible interaction. In: Proceedings of the 4th Decennial Conference on Critical Computing: Between Sense and Sensibility, pp. 9–18. Association for Computing Machinery, New York (2005). https://doi.org/10.1145/1094562.1094565

35. Djajadiningrat, T., Overbeeke, K., Wensveen, S.: But how, Donald, tell us how?: on the creation of meaning in interaction design through feedforward and inherent feedback. In: Proceedings of the 4th Conference on Designing Interactive Systems: Processes, Practices, Methods, and Techniques, pp. 285–291. Association for Computing Machinery, New York (2002). https://doi.org/10.1145/778712.778752

36. Buur, J., Jensen, M.V., Djajadiningrat, T.: Hands-only scenarios and video action walls: novel methods for tangible user interaction design. In: Proceedings of the 5th Conference on Designing Interactive Systems: Processes, Practices, Methods, and Techniques, pp. 185–192. Association for Computing Machinery, New York (2004). https://doi.org/10.1145/1013115.1013141

37. Rubidge, S., MacDonald, A.: Sensuous Geographies: a multi-user interactive/responsive installation. Digit. Creat. 15(4), 245–252 (2004). https://doi.org/10.1080/1462626048520186

38. Ishii, H.: Tangible bits: beyond pixels. In: Proceedings of the 2nd International Conference on Tangible and Embedded Interaction, pp. xv–xxv. Association for Computing Machinery, New York (2008). https://doi.org/10.1145/1347390.1347392

39. Hornecker, E.: A design framework for designing tangible interaction for collaborative use, January 2004

40. Hornecker, E.: Creative idea exploration within the structure of a guiding framework: the card brainstorming game. In: Proceedings of the Fourth International Conference on Tangible, Embedded, and Embodied Interaction, pp. 101–108. Association for Computing Machinery, New York (2010). https://doi.org/10.1145/1709886.1709905

41. Mi, H., Wang, M., Lu, Q., Xu, Y.: Tangible user interface: origins, development, and future trends. Scientia Sinica Informationis 48(4), 390–405 (2018). (in Chinese)

# A Framework for User-Requirements Analysis and Development of Creative Design Concepts

Martin Maguire[✉]

School of Design and Creative Arts, Loughborough University, Leicestershire LE11 3TU, UK
m.c.maguire@lboro.ac.uk

**Abstract.** This paper describes a framework and process for user-centred design for interactive products with an emphasis on creativity in designing solutions and the development of multiple solution concepts. The aim is to encourage more radical ideas to be put forward and for the resulting design concepts to be compared objectively using defined user requirements specification statements. The process consists of 6 stages including: identification of user problem or need, user research to generate insights and empathy, development of user requirements specification, generation of ideas synthesised into design concepts, comparison and choice of best concept, and prototyping of the concept to develop a design proposition. Classroom testing of the framework indicated that the students could use it effectively and were able to produce effective designs.

**Keywords:** User requirements · User-centred design · Design thinking · User experience design

## 1 Introduction

User requirements analysis is the process of documenting requirements or needs, described by users, for a future system or product, alongside business, administrative and technical requirements. A concept for the design may already exist, with the requirements being developed in relation to that concept. However, by starting with a single concept, this can limit creativity of the design and the potential benefit for the users.

This paper describes a process whereby having identified a problem area or user need, and explored the context of use and problem space, a process of concept creation is conducted to explore different creative ideas which can be compared so that the best concept for the users can be selected and developed. The process follows established principles of user-centred design and draws upon the Design Council's Framework for Innovation [1] and the process of Design Thinking [2]. It can be used for both the development of interactive digital or physical products to create a design that meets user needs and provides a positive user experience. The paper also refers to student work where they have developed a mobile application following a similar process.

M. Kurosu et al. (Eds.): HCII 2022, LNCS 13516, pp. 97–113, 2022.
https://doi.org/10.1007/978-3-031-17615-9_7

## 2   Overall Process

The user requirements framework is a six-stage process. Each stage is described in the following sub-sections (Fig. 1).

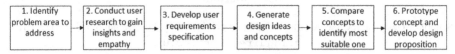

**Fig. 1.**  User requirements analysis and concept development process

### 2.1   Stage 1 – Identify a Problem Area

The starting point for the project is to identify a genuine human need or problem that, if addressed, will help improve the quality of people's lives and is both ethically and environmentally sound. It is assumed that the designer wishes to be creative and innovative, producing new and elegant ways to solve the user's problem.

In order to find a potential problem, the following strategies may be adopted:

- Look for instances of genuine human need and review available alternatives to see if new products or services could provide a better solution. Reading or watching the news can be a useful source.
- Look at everyday tasks to identify opportunities to improve the way they are done or considering how they can be carried out in different environments or by different users.
- Speak to users in an application area where there is design potential. They may own a product or be doing a job or activity that they have difficulty with, be representative of a part of society currently not well catered for or even excluded (young, old, obese, disabled, tall etc.). The goal may be to address the needs of these specific users or attempt to include their needs as part of a universal or inclusive solution.

In general, the aim is to find activities which are difficult to perform and thus have 'pain points'. It is important for the designer to be able to describe the problem clearly. One way to structure the design goal is to use a sentence template as follows, filling in the italicized sections:

This *product/application*
is to be designed for: *target users+context*
who want to: *achieve certain goals* but experiences: *pain points or constraints*

For example:

This *interactive smart app*
is to be designed for *sedentary workers*

who want to *make healthy lifestyle changes e.g. by exercising more*
but *with other commitments, lacks the time to carry out regular exercise sessions*

Note that this definition of the problem to be investigated can change as user research is conducted in the next stage of the process.

## 2.2  Stage 2 – Conduct Research to Gain Insights and Empathy

### Research Data Collection
During this stage, detailed research is conducted to gain a better understanding of the user's characteristics, environment, needs and problems in more detail. It may also identify related problems that should be considered. Ideas for solving the problem may also arise which should be recorded.

Further discussion with users will help to establish the context for the design. The answers to the following questions should help to achieve this.

*Who is the user?* – Is there more than one user (e.g., doctor and patient)? What are the essential characteristics of the user? How old are they? Where do they live and work? What special abilities or challenges do they face?

*What are the alternatives?* – How is this problem tackled currently? How do people cope now? What alternative products are already on the market? What are the drawbacks of the current solutions or products?

*What is the market?* – Where is the product to be used? Is it specific to a location, region, country or context? Does the need affect large numbers of people or very few people? What could be the impact of a clever solution?

An important part of the process is to gain empathy for the users and deeper understanding of their problems. Empathy allows the designer to set aside their own assumptions about the activity and gain insight into users and their needs. This activity involves consulting experts to find out more about the area of concern through observing, engaging and empathizing with people to understand their experiences and motivations. Being immersed in the physical environment also helps to gain a deeper understanding of the issues involved.

Commonly used methods for conducting user research include the following and are discussed in [3, 4]:

*Interviews*
This involves sitting down with someone from the target audience and ask them questions about the issues they face. What are they struggling with? What are they looking for in a product to help them? Face-to-face interviews are preferred since the interviewer can gauge the user's verbal and nonverbal reactions. However, video interviews or phone calls can also be used effectively.

*User Focus Groups*

Here a group of target users (typically 4 to 8) are brought together discuss their attitudes, emotions, and frustrations relating to an issue or product. The discussion format encourages group members to react to other opinions expressed so that it is not just a set of separate interviews. The aim is to keep the discussion flowing and encourage each person to contribute.

*Surveys*

These are questionnaires distributed to target users. They are good for finding out users' attitudes towards a specific topic with the added benefit of receiving the data as soon as the users are done with the survey. However, it is important to make sure that each question has a purpose, while care is needed not to use leading questions that could disproportionately impact the results.

*Usability Testing*

This involves asking one or more members of the target audience to test a product. For example, if the aim is to develop a new food delivery service, the researcher might ask the user to open an existing food ordering app and to order some items while observing how they act and react to using it. When completed, the researcher can then ask them questions to explore their experience and identify any problems that the new app should address. Thus, the method can help define user needs. Further details can be found in [5, 6].

Research is needed to find out what is expected from the product. This can be done by looking at existing products and reviews. Discussion can also take place with users to find out their minimum expectations of use and product functionalities. The designer should also identify any relevant standards or guidelines that the product or service should follow e.g., published by ISO (International Standards Organization), BSI (British Standards Institution), HSE (Health and Safety). Social media forums can help to learn about the audience for the product and their views about similar products and services.

**Research Data Analysis**

Several methods are available to help analyze the data collected and to draw out key themes or insights that will feed into the user requirements specification.

*Empathy Map*

An Empathy Map is a tool for plotting out knowledge and insights gained about the user in a visual form to demonstrate an understanding of the target audience [7, 8]. Empathy Maps can be shown in different formats, but generally have a common set of core elements i.e., what users are thinking, feeling, doing and saying, based on the data collected. The technique has the following advantages:

• The most important insights about the user are presented
• Helps communicate a better understanding of the end user
• Quick and cheap to use; easy to adapt (Fig. 2)

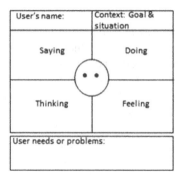

**Fig. 2.** Example template for user empathy map

*Persona*

A persona is a description of a fictional character, based upon the research, to represent the different user types for the product. The process of creating personas helps to understand users' needs, experiences, behaviors and goals better [7, 8]. A persona layout will present the users name, a tagline about them and a profile picture. It will normally contain sections such as background information, pain points, task goals and experience goals.

Personas helps the design team identify with the target users and to keep their characteristics and needs in mind during the design process. They also help ensure a consistent perspective on the user (Table 1).

**Table 1.** Example persona for health and activity application

| William – aiming to exercise more and be healthier | Overview | Interests |
|---|---|---|
|  | A software developer who lives with partner and two children, (boys: age 7 and 9 years). Recent health check recommends weight loss. William is popular, has good sense of humor, is sociable, kind and caring. | Sports fan, particularly football and has the full sports package on TV. An adventurous cook, he also enjoys wine with food but beer with sports. Spends several hours per week on computer gaming. |
| **Pain points** | **Task goals** | **Experience goals** |
| Has a sedentary job, working from home. Very busy with lots of MS Teams meetings each day. Misses the social aspect of meeting colleagues at work. Time/access to exercise is limited by wife's shifts and transporting children to attend lots of clubs. | To lose one stone in weight and be fit enough to easily manage to play football with the children for 30 minutes. Go on holiday to a beach resort with the family and take part in beach games and water sports. | Increased confidence and self-esteem and to feel healthier. To enjoy a family holiday and make some good memories. |

*User Journey Map*
A User Journey Map (also known as a Customer Journey Map) is a diagram that visually illustrates the user flow through an activity including interaction systems and software, starting with initial contact or discovery, and continuing through the process of engagement into long-term loyalty and advocacy. It identifies key interactions and touchpoints with the system or mobile app and describes in detail the user's or customer's goals, motivations, and feelings at each stage [9, 10] (Fig. 3).

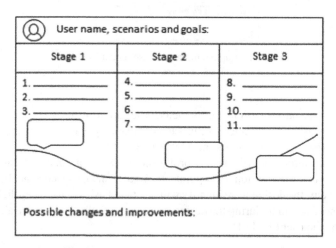

**Fig. 3.** Typical structure of user journey map

*Affinity Map or Sticky Note Analysis*
These are methods can be used to analyze research data by recording individual data items onto post-its and placing them to identify groups and themes. The method may be used to analyze by activity, events, relationships, or perspectives (Fig. 4).

*Task Analysis and Activity Analysis*
Task analysis is the process of learning about ordinary users by observing them in action to understand in detail how they perform their tasks and achieve their intended goals. The output is a flow chart showing the order and hierarchical structure of the individual actions [11].

A similar method is Activity Analysis which is the process of breaking down an activity into steps and detailed subparts and examining these components. Within an organization, it includes identification and description of activities that the organization carries out. For each activity data collected includes: details of the activity executed, time required to execute it, the number of people involved and their roles, the resources consumed and value to the organization of the activity.

The data required to carry out Task and Activity analyses can come from direct observation, interviews, questionnaires, and reviews of work records [3].

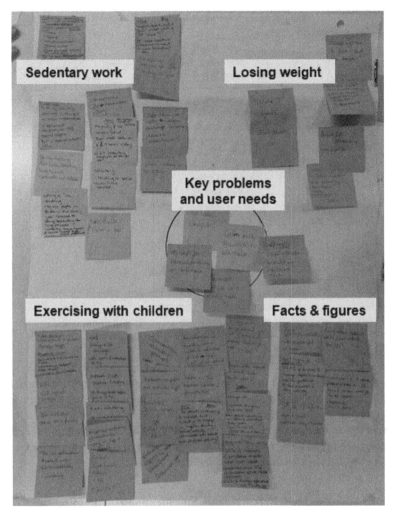

**Fig. 4.** Affinity map relating to exercise and health app

*Use Cases*

A use case is a written description of how users will perform a task to achieve a goal with the system and can be used to show the relationship between multiple user roles to specify their general needs [12]. Each use case is represented (often in graphical form) as a sequence of simple steps, beginning with the user's goal and ending when that goal is fulfilled. It is thus useful in the user-centered design process, to be able to identify which are the key use cases to concentrate upon for user requirements specification (Fig. 5).

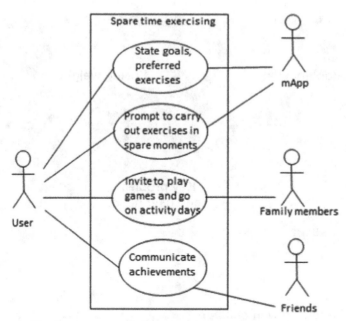

**Fig. 5.** Use case diagram example for exercise and health app

The technique of *user stories* can help to identify use cases and possible system functions that may be required to support them. A user story is a short, informal, plain language description of what a user might want to do with the system or app, to gain something they find valuable Each story may be documented in the form "As a [type of user], I want [an action], so that I can [a benefit/value]" [13]. For example: *"If I become a long-term user of the app, I will want to be able to adjust my weight loss goal to maintain my motivation to continue using it."*

### 2.3 Stage 3 – Create User Requirements Specification Highlighting the Key Needs and Constraints

The user research and analysis tools provide the resources for specifying the user requirements for the product or application. The requirements are a set of statements or human-centered criteria that the design should meet before creating a design solution and sums up the desirable outcomes of the design. There may also be a general design specification document, containing all the requirements collected (business, administration, technical) including user requirements. General guidance on the content of a design specification is provided in [14].

*Example user requirements criteria include:*

- Physical dimensions e.g., what percentile of the population should the product fit?
- Features e.g., presentation of certain data for the user to guide them.
- Experience needs e.g., being fun to use, aesthetics, sense of achievement.

- Usability needs e.g., learning time, avoiding errors, maximum steps to reach goal, security, follows platform user interface guidelines.
- Accessibility needs e.g., minimum screen contrast or size of lettering.
- Environmental needs e.g., ability to work in unfavorable weather conditions.
- Health and safety e.g., needing to meet health and safety requirements or relevant laws.

The example below shows the user requirements specification (feature and constraints) for the exercise and health app. It is good practice to include an indication or measure to show whether each requirement has been achieved, or to what extent. This can assist in the concept generation and comparison stages 4 and 5, or during testing of early prototypes of the concept in stage 6 (Table 2).

**Table 2.** User requirements specification for health and activity app

| Criteria category | Criteria |
| --- | --- |
| Usability | Must be easy to use. Basic functions must be learnable within 5 min |
| | Should be able to personalize to own lifestyle needs |
| Accessibility | Must use default font size of no less than 10 point and good contrast ratio |
| Features | Must provide feedback on activity over time<br>Should provide feedback on weight and trend over time |
| Experience | Must be visually appealing (achieving an average score on a 5-point scale of 3.5+ from an appropriate questionnaire) |
| | Must be fun to use (achieving an average score on a 5-point scale of 3.5+ from an appropriate questionnaire) |
| | Should encourage social interaction with others i.e., friends and family |
| Environmental needs | Must be suitable to use outside in different weather conditions |
| Health and safety | Must avoid requiring completion of exercise that is too strenuous for user's current state of health and current fitness level |

Within some development environments, there will be a distinction between functional and non-functional requirements [15]. The former is concerned with what the system should do e.g., "Send an email when a new customer signs up" or "The product must allow up to 8 cups of coffee to be carried". The latter describes how the system performs a certain function and what limits there are on its functionality e.g., "The email must be sent within 10 min of the user signing up", or "The design must allow the person transporting the coffee sufficient vision ahead to reduce hazards". Non-functional requirements are often referred to as system qualities.

It may be necessary therefore to make this distinction when specifying user requirements.

## 2.4   Stage 4 – Generate Several Concepts that Meet the PDS and Address the Goal

The next stage is to start generating ideas for the app which can be quite specific or general. These can then be reviewed and formed into concepts that can be regarded as alternative solutions to the design problem.

The benefits of generating multiple concepts are:

- initial or most obvious idea may not be the best solution.
- stepping beyond initial ideas helps increase the innovation potential of the solution.
- can give a broader perspective on the problem itself.

Generating the different concepts, requires the designer or design team to think creatively to identify new solutions to the problem statement and bear in mind the user requirements specification. The tendency may be to consider concepts based on digital user interfaces, but benefit can be obtained by thinking about tangible user interfaces where the user interacts with physical controls which can perform a small number of specific functions that simplifies the user interface and may provide a more enjoyable experience [16].

There are many ideation techniques such as: brainstorming, 'how-might-we' statements, worst possible idea, metaphorical thinking and reversal [17]. Another technique called brainwriting is a variation on brainstorming where participants write down their ideas about a particular question for a few minutes without talking. Then, each person passes his or her ideas to the next person who may add to them or use them as a trigger for refining their own ideas. This technique is a good way to ensure that everyone contributes, not just those who are the most confident in the group setting.

Typically, these creativity methods are used to stimulate free thinking and to expand the problem space. Team members build on each other's responses and ideas with the aim of generating as many potential solutions as possible as a basis for concept generation. The ideas can then be categorized, combined and narrowed down to form a series of interesting design concepts.

Crazy 8's, is another method often used to stimulate creativity [18, 19]. It is a fast-sketching exercise that challenges people to sketch eight distinct ideas in eight minutes. The goal is to push beyond the first most obvious idea, frequently the least innovative, and to generate a variety of solutions. It may happen that these weird and seemingly impractical ideas give way to inspired and useful ones.

The example below shows a Crazy 8's layout for the health and exercise application, to encourage more physical exercise among busy people with limited time (Fig. 6):

**Fig. 6.** Example Crazy 8 sketches

After all the ideas have been generated and collected together, they are used as a basis for concept generation as solutions to the design problem. Typically, between three and five concepts should be generated with each one containing one or more of the ideas generated. Each concept should be accompanied with a short explanation and a simple visual representation (e.g., a sketch) to distinguish them and enable easy comparison. Based on the previous Crazy 8 sketches, three different concepts were produced (Table 3).

**Table 3.** Design concepts developed for health and activity app

| | |
|---|---|
| 1. Inactivity identification with option to include family and friends on a dashboard | |
| 2. Smart schedule for calendars at work and home to identify potential activity gaps | |
| 3. Invitation for local friends to join activity e.g., football, cricket, yoga, at short notice | |

While the generation of creative solutions is important, the designer will need to apply their business knowledge, analytical thinking, and empathy to really understand a problem set and how potential design solutions would work within that context.

### 2.5 Stage 5 – Compare Concepts to Identify the Most Suitable One

When concept forming is completed, participants must then select the best solution to take forward and develop.

A scoring system can be used to rate each concept against each of the user requirements criteria. The total score of each concept can then be calculated to help determine which one is the most suitable to develop further. The three concepts for the health and exercise activity are compared below (Table 4):

**Table 4.** Comparison of concepts against user requirements specification

| Criteria scored on a scale of **1 to 5**. | Inactivity identification | Smart Schedule to identify activity gaps | Short notice activity invitation. |
|---|---|---|---|
| 1. Easy to use | 4 | 3 | 5 |
| 2. Visually appealing | 4 | 3 | 3 |
| 3. Able to personalize to own lifestyle needs | 4 | 5 | 2 |
| 4. Minimal costs | 5 | 5 | 4 |
| 5. Provide feedback on weight | 4 | 0 | 0 |
| 6. Provide feedback on activity | 4 | 2 | 2 |
| 7. Be fun to use | 3 | 2 | 5 |
| 8. Encourage social interaction | 2 | 2 | 5 |
| Total Score | **30** | 22 | 26 |

The concept with the highest score would generally be the chosen concept to develop. However other considerations may come in to play related to business requirements or technical requirements so the concept may also need to be adapted to meet these other requirements e.g., practicality, cost, fitting company's business model. Also, some concepts may not relate to all the criteria so putting a 0 into the table for some criteria may produce an artificially low score. One way to cater for this would be to adjust the table scores, taking account of non-applicable criteria.

It is helpful to develop a storyboard of the chosen product concept to help communicate it to the rest of the design team [20]. The storyboard consists of a series of sketched pictures of the application in use but focusing on the broader experience e.g., emotions and actions, rather than functions (close ups of screen interaction). A comic strip style is suitable for this activity (Fig. 7).

**Fig. 7.** Storyboard of design concept for exercise and health app

## 2.6  Stage 6 – Prototype Design Concept and Develop Design Proposition

Development of the chosen design concept now proceeds through prototyping starting with low-fidelity sketches or wireframes working up to higher fidelity versions. The aim is to see how well the design concept addresses the design problem. Prototyping allows the design concept to be envisioned and tested quickly to see what improvements need to be made [21].

Each prototype does not need to be a simulation of the whole concept. Prototypes can be scaled down versions showing specific features found within the product concept. Each one is then either accepted, improved and re-examined, or rejected on the basis of the users' experience and feedback. Prototypes may be shared and tested within an organization, or with people from outside who can be considered user representatives.

By the end of this stage, the design team will have a better idea of how real users would behave, think, and feel when interacting with the end-product and how well their problems and needs have been addressed (Fig. 8 and Table 5).

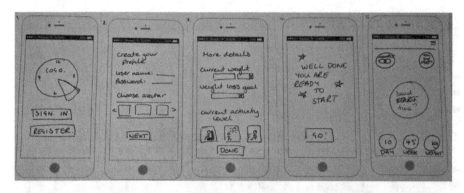

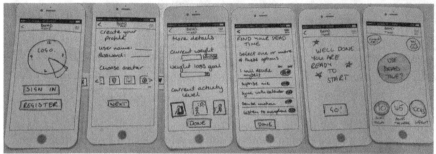

**Fig. 8.** Original and updated version of paper prototype

**Table 5.** User comments on original prototype and changes made in response to them

| Test | User comment | Outcome |
|------|-------------|---------|
| 1 | a) Use color and clearer picture for selecting activity level on screen 3 | a) Clearer activity selection (screen 3) using color |
|   | b) Unclear how "dead-time" will be identified | b) Extra screen would be good to help identify permissions for dead time identification |
| 2 | a) There is unclear wording in the big button on screen 5 | a) Words on button updated to be clearer |

The outcome of this stage is a design proposition that solves the problems that have been identified and that has been reached using critical thinking and evidence-based design.

It is important to communicate the design proposition in an effective way. The designer may produce a short report that describes the process that took place based on the above stages. An important part of this document is to justify the design decisions made and to show that they were based on user-centered or ergonomics criteria rather than assumptions or personal designer preference.

The report should be supported by design boards that show certain elements in a visual form. They may in include:

- a storyboard showing how the product user meets their needs in context
- a user interface board showing sequences of screens, or other interactive components, that the user will interact with
- a development board showing the physical product labelled with annotations about how it is constructed, its measurements and materials, etc.

## 3   Use of Framework Within Student Work

The framework for user-requirements analysis and early design has been used on a Master's degree course where students were required to design an application concept within 3 days. The chart below shows the average ratings for the received by 5 groups of students for their reporting of each stage of the framework (Fig. 9).

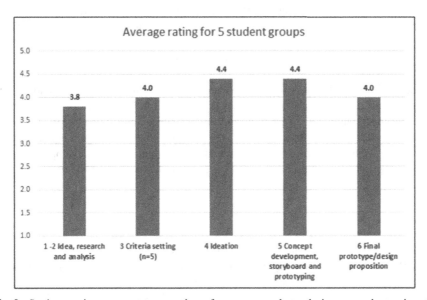

**Fig. 9.** Student assignment category ratings for group work to design a product using the framework

Each rating along the x-axis corresponds to the stages defined in the framework. The rating scale indicators were 5 = excellent, 4 = very good, 3 = good, 2 = satisfactory, 1 = poor. Thus, the average ratings for 'idea identification and user research' was 3.8 out of 5, i.e. between good and very good.

The chart shows that the work carried out was of a high standard across all the design stages. The user research stage was mainly based on secondary research and the student's own experiences as within the short period of the project and during the pandemic, the students were limited in their ability to locate and interview or survey users.

The criteria setting stage was carried out well with a good mixture of task related items and general qualities. Further improvement could be achieved by making the criteria more explicit in places. The ideation stage that was carried out as a basis for concept generation was effective and good use was made of the Crazy 8 method. It was seen that the different concepts were sometimes addressing different aspects of the problem although this enabled the chosen concept to include elements of the other concepts. The students showed enthusiasm to generate paper prototypes and to test them with others in the classroom. The final designs and proposition for a future project were convincing. In general, the students enjoyed follow the framework method and were pleased with the outcome of their work.

## 4  Conclusion

This paper describes a method to create future design proposition to address a user problem or need that is based upon having a clear understanding of that problem or need, specification of the related user requirements, generation of contrasting potential design concepts, and development of the best concept as a basis of an interactive product.

The aim is not to reach a complete design resolution, but to show how user requirements can be used to progress a design concept that has been prototyped to some degree and taken forward for development with a degree of confidence that it will meet user needs.

One of the main features of the six-stage process is that knowledge acquired at the later stages can feedback to earlier stages. Information is continually used both to inform the understanding of the problem and solution spaces, and to redefine the problem if necessary. Within this iteration process, the designer continues to gain new insights, develop new ways of viewing the product and its possible uses and develop, not only the product proposition, but also acquires a deeper understanding of the users and the problems they face.

## References

1. Design Council: What is the framework for innovation? Design Council's evolved Double Diamond. https://www.designcouncil.org.uk/news-opinion/what-framework-innovation-design-councils-evolved-double-diamond. Accessed 11 May 2022
2. Damm, R. F.: 5 stages in the design thinking process. Interaction Design Foundation. https://www.interaction-design.org/literature/article/5-stages-in-the-design-thinking-process. Accessed 11 May 2022
3. Robson, C., McCartan, K.: Real World Research: A Resource for Users of Social Research Methods in Applied Settings, 4th edn. Wiley, Chichester (2015)
4. Maguire, M.: Methods to support human-centred design. Int. J. Hum. Comput. Stud. 55(4), 587–634 (2001)
5. Nielsen, J.: Usability Engineering. Academic Press, New York (1993)
6. Rubin, J., Chisnell, D.: Handbook of Usability Testing: How to Plan, Design, and Conduct Effective Tests, 2nd edn. Wiley, New York (2008)
7. Ferreira, B., Conte, T., Barbosa, S.D.J.: Eliciting requirements using personas and empathy map to enhance the user experience. In: 2015 29th Brazilian Symposium on Software Engineering, pp. 80–89. IEEE (2015)

8. Ferreira, B., Silva, W., Oliveira, E., Conte, T.: Designing personas with empathy map. In: SEKE (Semantic Scholar), vol. 152, July 2015. https://doi.org/10.18293/SEKE2015-152

9. Rosenbaum, M.S., Otalora, M.L., Ramírez, G.C.: How to create a realistic customer journey map. Bus. Horiz. **60**(1), 143–150 (2017)

10. Gibbons, S.: Journey mapping 101, Nielsen Norman Group, December 2018. https://www.nngroup.com/articles/journey-mapping-101/. Accessed 11 May 2022

11. Usability.gov: Task analysis. https://www.usability.gov/how-to-and-tools/methods/task-analysis.html. Accessed 11 May 2022

12. Brush, K.: Use case (2020). https://www.techtarget.com/searchsoftwarequality/definition/use-case. Accessed 11 May 2022

13. Cohn, M.: User Stories Applied: For Agile Software Development. Addison-Wesley, Reading (2009)

14. Holishevska, A.: How to write the design specification? [quick guide], Northell (2021). https://northell.design/blog/how-to-write-the-design-specifications-quick-guide/. Accessed 6 May 2022

15. ReQtest: Why is the difference between functional and non-functional requirements important? April 2012 (2012). https://reqtest.com/requirements-blog/functional-vs-non-functional-requirements/. Accessed 11 May 2022

16. Holmquist, E.H.: The future of tangible user interfaces. Forum – interaction technologies. Interactions **26**, 82–85 (2019)

17. MindTools: Creativity Tools. https://www.mindtools.com/pages/main/newMN_CT.htm. Accessed 6 May 2022

18. Stevenson, H.: How to run a crazy eights workshop (2019). https://blog.prototypr.io/how-to-run-a-crazy-eights-workshop-60d0a67b29a. Accessed 11 May 2022

19. McNeish, D., Maguire, M.: A participatory approach to helicopter user interface design. In: Ergonomics & Human Factors (EHF 2019); Contemporary Ergonomics & Human Factors 2019, Stratford on Avon. Chartered Institute of Ergonomics & Human Factors (CIEHF), 29 April–01 May 2019

20. Krause, R.: Storyboards help visualize UX ideas, July 2018. https://www.nngroup.com/articles/storyboards-visualize-ideas/. Accessed 11 May 2022

21. Dam, R.F., Siang, T.Y.: Design thinking: get started with prototyping. https://www.interaction-design.org/literature/article/design-thinking-get-started-with-prototyping. Accessed 11 May 2022

# Design for Meaningful Work Experiences: A Holistic Approach to Human-Work Interaction Design

Maylis Saigot[(⊠)]

Copenhagen Business School, Copenhagen, Denmark
msa.digi@cbs.dk

**Abstract.** Promoting meaningful experiences at work is essential to employees' wellness and constitutes a strategic investment toward sustainable growth. Interactive work tools appear to have been excluded from most academic efforts to determine meaningful work. Yet, user experience for work tools can optimize interaction with technology, improve employee well-being, and give a more exciting, satisfying, and meaningful perception of the activity for workers. We conduct a two-stage qualitative study to develop a model of Design for Meaningful Work Experiences, aiming to answer the following question: how can researchers and designers approach work tool design to stimulate human flourishing through more meaningful work experiences? Based on a preliminary case study and a follow-up study consisting of 9 qualitative interviews, we develop a model that describes a new methodology to integrate Positive Design into the relationship between Human Work and Interaction Design. Creative inversion is introduced as an emergent design technique that can help foster creativity by facilitating communication between researchers, designers, and users.

**Keywords:** Human work · Interaction design · Positive design

## 1 Introduction

Employee well-being has received increasing attention in the past few years and became especially preponderant in the context of the COVID-19 pandemic, which has redefined people's relationship with work in many ways. Promoting meaningful experiences at work is essential to employees' wellness and constitutes a strategic organizational investment toward sustainable growth [1–3]. In a world increasingly demanding evidence and research-based products and services [4], the research agenda needs to adapt to the globally increasing interest in employee well-being and expand academic knowledge across fields. Although job characteristics and individual attributes have been well explored as determinants of meaningful work [2], interactive work tools[1] appear to have been excluded from most academic efforts [5]. Yet, user experience for work tools can

---

[1] Interactive work tools refer to any information system that an employee needs to interact with to complete some or all of their work-related tasks.

M. Kurosu et al. (Eds.): HCII 2022, LNCS 13516, pp. 114–135, 2022.
https://doi.org/10.1007/978-3-031-17615-9_8

optimize interaction with technology, improve employee well-being, and give a more exciting, satisfying, and meaningful perception of worker activities [6, 7]. This paper reports the results of a two-fold study asking: *how can researchers and designers approach work tool design to stimulate human flourishing through more meaningful work experiences?* Based on a preliminary case study, we developed a sensitizing model of Design for Meaningful Work Experiences (DMWE). We then performed an empirical test of our model by conducting additional qualitative interviews outside the scope of the case study. The purpose of this article is thus to demonstrate how the DMWE can inform the design of features that not only help improve work efficiency but also create work experiences that enhance human flourishing[2].

## 2   Theoretical Framework

### 2.1   Problem-Driven Work Tool Design

**Human Work Interaction Design.** Because employee well-being is a complex construct, designing for it calls for HCI research that can account for several social levels while still focusing on interaction design. Moreover, it is important that HCI research can contribute to practice by (i) being able to make design recommendations and (ii) acknowledging the environmental context as an integral part of the analysis [9]. *Human work interaction design (HWID)* adopts both technical and social perspectives as it considers the three areas of *human work, interaction design,* and *environmental context* as integral parts of its analytical potential [9]. This approach is particularly useful to study the connection between human work and interaction design in concrete cases through artifact design [10]. Consistent with HWID, most of the existing research on enhancing employee experience through tool design mostly focuses on pragmatic design [5].

**Paradigmatic Innovation for Design Practice.** While designers have historically been encouraged to pursue problem-solving (as per the *industrial paradigm*), there is now a call for adopting a possibility-seeking approach that better suits newer paradigms of innovation [5, 11]. Consistent with arguments of the Paradigmatic Innovation for Design Practice framework [11], workplace practices have arguably been characterized by a paradigmatic shift that emphasizes systems approaches to organizational development. This means that thriving organizations are now those capable of offering value to their customers, employees, and stakeholders in a dynamic fashion while considering factors such as experience, knowledge, and sustainability [11–13]. The same applies to design, with the emerging preponderance of human-centered approaches [11, 14, 15]. The main difference thus lies in the emerging importance of a cohesive flow between all the elements related to an object of study rather than them standing as silos. As this trend emerges, we see an increased focus on organizations or artifact design as a system, making it important that researchers and practitioners take into account factors that used to be considered beyond the scope of an organization or artifact (e.g., sustainability used to be considered separately from an organization's overall strategy, employee well-being used to be considered separately from work tool design, etc.).

---

[2] Human flourishing focuses on "meaning and self-realization and defines well-being in terms of the degree to which a person is fully functioning" [8].

## 2.2 Possibility-Driven Work Tool Design

**Experience Design.** The distinction between *welfare* and *well-being* is gaining more relevance as economies drift away from the industrial paradigm. While welfare is often focused on economic utility [16], well-being is less measurable and includes non-rational variables that contribute to human flourishing – closer to the eudaimonic tradition [17, 18]. Experience Design is a practice that prioritizes experience over usability and aesthetics [5]. Traditional approaches to the design of work tools have focused on providing features that are useful to human work while conveniently improving the interface aesthetics and usability of the interface. Instead, designers should place experience and human needs first and design experience-driven core functionality that directly addresses these goals [7, 19]. In line with the goal of Experience Design, Positive or Happiness Design has emerged as a practice with a specific focus on contributing to experiences of positive affect – such as happiness and pleasure [20–22]. However, practical applications of such practices can be challenging at two main levels: (i) defining the experience goals and (ii) designing features that fulfill these goals [5].

**Positive Design.** The Positive Design Framework is a helpful tool to navigate these challenges. It proposes three main components for design artifacts that enable or stimulate human flourishing: virtue (i.e., "being a morally good person"), personal significance (i.e., "pursuing personal goals"), and pleasure (i.e., "experiencing positive affect") [23]. Much of the value of this framework comes from its general applicability to a broad range of contexts and cultures. The framework does not prescribe specific elements or instantiations of virtue, pleasure, and personal significance, but instead focuses on universal factors of subjective well-being [5, 23].

**Work Experience.** The increased focus on experience and subjective well-being naturally questions the nature and the meaning of work. While work primarily fulfills welfare-based needs, a rich stream of literature shows that meaningful experiences are also embedded into our work lives, suggesting that work can contribute to positive affect and human flourishing [1, 3, 5, 24]. In a theoretical integration and review of the literature about the meaning of work, Rosso et al. [24] develop a framework that describes the Mechanisms of Meaningful Work (MMW). These 13 mechanisms are either self-oriented or other-oriented. They include self-concordance, identity affirmation, personal engagement, control or autonomy, competence, perceived impact, self-esteem, significance of work, value systems, social identification, interpersonal connectedness, interconnection, and self-abnegation [24].

**Positive Design Framework for Work.** Experience design [19, 22, 25, 26], positive design [23], and happiness design [27, 28] have become well-known approaches for consumer products, but have been under-represented in the design of work tools – despite the growing interest in work-related happiness. The PDFWork is one of the few instances of academic attempts to improve employee well-being through work tool design. It was developed to help designers embody "meaningful experiences at work and a future of flourishing, motivated employees" [5] by leveraging experience and positive design principles. The PDFWork contributes to discussions about employee experience, experience design, and interaction design by proposing a model that integrates important elements of work-related happiness and experience design into a streamlined design methodology. The authors argue that the first step to designing work tools that contribute to employee happiness is to define experience goals. A suggested approach to defining meaningful experience goals is to use basic human needs as a starting point.

*Psychological Needs.* Based on 10 original human needs [29] and models of user experience, Hassenzahl et al. [21] suggest that 6 needs are fundamentally relevant in the context of Interaction Design: autonomy, competence, relatedness, popularity, stimulation, and security. However, these are considered potential sources of positive affect, meaning that they do not constitute a fixed set of rigid categories – researchers and practitioners should feel free to add and remove needs from the list as they see fit. In the context of this study, we choose to use the toolbox of 8 psychological needs proposed by the Experience and Interaction Design working group as sources of positive experiences [30] (based on [21, 29, 31, 32]), which adds physicalness and meaning to the original 6 needs.

# 3   Method

This study unfolds through a two-step methodology using an abductive approach. We first conduct a case study and then build upon our findings to conduct a second qualitative study and develop a design model.

## 3.1   Case Description

We investigate the case of a customer relationship management system used in the MBA admission office of a Danish university. MBAs are a strategic area of the university's educational offering, as they are the most financially retributive. As a highly strategic department, the MBA admissions Office's functioning is closer to that of a corporate organization than the rest of the programs it offers. To support its recruitment activities, the MBA Office implemented a Customer Relationship Management system specialized in the student life cycle. This case study will focus on two specific MBA programs as they both use the same CRM system – as opposed to their neighboring offices. While the two programs have their respective admission teams, they share supporting functions, such as the Marketing team. The team consists of one admissions manager and two student assistants (one for each program).

The CRM system is used for a wide range of admissions-related tasks, including collecting and organizing potential candidate data, conducting email campaigns, creating event sign-ups, and processing applications. The scope of this investigation is narrowed down to focusing on the email campaign function of the system.

Because the admission team delegates the task of formulating and sending email campaigns to the student assistants in the marketing team, the primary users in this study are the student assistants of the two programs.

## 3.2 Methodology

The case was selected because it is a critical example of a work tool primarily designed to fulfill functional needs while providing usability. We conducted semi-structured qualitative interviews with two student workers who are the main users of the CRM system – two 24-year-old female employees with respectively 1.5 years and 4 months of employment at the MBA admission office.

In the first round of interviews, we used the HWID approach to discover the main pain points of our users and use this insight as a basis for proposing a prototype. With the first worker, we used contextual inquiry to unveil her role, goals, tasks, and pains while understanding how she interacted with the CRM system. Based on this, we developed the first iteration of a prototype using Adobe XD. In the interview with the second participant, we conducted a usability test based on a think-aloud protocol to maximize the rigor and replicability of the test. After the test, the prototype, as well as the CRM system, served as probes to understand the participant's role, goals, tasks, and pains during our interview.

During our interview with the second participant, we were surprised to learn that after only a few months of employment, she had just handed in her resignation from the position. As this insight stood out during our analysis of the data, we decided to search the literature to make sense of this new information and explore opportunities for improving the experience of future employees. We used select elements of the Positive Practice Canvas (PPC) [33] to guide follow-up interviews with both participants and collect data that ultimately informed a sensitizing theoretical extension of HWID – the Design for Meaningful Work Experiences model. The PPC is a tool developed to "support designers with identifying concrete opportunities to improve wellbeing through design" [33]. It is a visual interview guide made of different sections: profile, practice, meaning, needs, skills, and material. The sections help identify a positive practice, understand what needs it fulfills, and the required materials (or interfaces) and skills used during the practice. The canvas was created to support "anecdotal design", where specific and sometimes individual practices are used as starting points for design ideation. Using the anecdotal practices as inspirations, designers can come up with creative ideas for new features or functionality that can be useful to other people as well as other contexts [33].

For this case study, the PPC served as inspiration in structuring user interviews. Specifically, "practice", "meaning", "needs" and "skills" were used to build an interview guide that was adapted to an online format and mindful of the fact that this interview was a follow-up. The remaining sections ("profile" and "material") were irrelevant in this case, as these details were already provided in the first interviews. We analyzed this data using the PDFWork and developed a user task flow based on the experience goals we defined from the data. We also developed the second iteration of our prototype to integrate the newly suggested features and functionality.

In the second stage of our research, we set out to refine and validate our proposed model. We, therefore, recruited nine participants working in the fields of sales, marketing, and management whose tasks involved the extensive use of an ERP, CRM, or collaborative file-sharing system. Our goal was to expand the context of our model while remaining within the scope of digital services. The participants were aged 22 to 35 and were located in Denmark (1), the United Kingdom (1), and the United States (7). A gift card of a value of approximately 10 USD was offered as compensation for the participants' time. The interviews took place on Zoom, lasted between 32 and 46 min, and were recorded and transcribed using Konch.ai (all resulting transcripts were processed manually to ensure correctness). We used the same interview technique as during the second round of our first-stage interviews: the Positive Practice Canvas. We analyzed the data using the PDFWork and defined experience goals along with feature suggestions.

# 4 Findings

## 4.1 Findings from the Human Work Interaction Design Analysis

**Users' Tasks and Characteristics.** The student assistants are in charge of sending out campaigns and their tasks are similar. Tasks, characteristics, needs, and pain points of the users were the main comparison elements in the study. Both users are 24-year-old females, with no prior experience working with CRM systems. The first participant has worked for the MBA office for 1.5 years, while the second participant had less experience – 4 months. According to Participant 1, her and Participant 2's tasks are similar, with differences in how they execute them. Participant 2's tasks focus on an MBA program that receives fewer applicants, so she is more personally engaged in contacting the applicants (i.e., phone calls, also resulting in a different way of selecting email recipients). Participant 1 uses the email campaign function more often and is engaged in more marketing tasks since she assists the marketing department, while Participant 2's job is more administrative and HR-related. For this paper, only tasks related to the marketing campaign function of the CRM system were analyzed.

**Users' Problems and Needs.** Both participants emphasized that the system is easy to learn and use. Additionally, Participant 2 mentioned that the CRM system's customer support is fast and helpful. Participant 1 specified that the process of sending out campaigns is intuitive. However, we found that Participant 2's work is very manual and that she sees certain functionalities as inconvenient or useless. Similarly, Participant 1 found some functions inconvenient or lacking customization. The main user pain points during the campaign setup process include messaging, audience sorting, and sending out test emails. A sample of supporting quotes is presented in Table 1.

*Messaging.* This refers to the part of the campaign setup where email templates, visuals, and copy are done. Besides limited editing possibilities, email templates can be accessed in two places, which confuses the users. The main problems with the messaging functions could be summarized as lacking customization, unintuitive, and leaving little room for creativity.

*Audience Sorting.* Within an email campaign, users can select relevant recipients using filters and tags. As it seems, users are involved in large amounts of manual tasks – Participant 2 searches each recipient manually on a separate page because she cannot find the relevant filters on the campaign level, while Participant 1 spends a lot of time navigating filters and selecting each of them. Both users may therefore benefit from improved audience sorting, especially in terms of geographical sorting.

*Sending Out Test Emails.* Lastly, both users recognized that it is only possible to send out test emails to their own email addresses. Since both users have to confirm campaigns with their manager, improving this functionality could be beneficial.

**Table 1.** Sample of supporting quotes for the human work analysis

|  | Messaging | Audience sorting | Test emails |
|---|---|---|---|
| Problem | Limited customization; hard to express one's creativity; non-intuitive work-flow since templates can be accessed on two separate pages | A lot of manual work to find relevant recipients; the system lacks relevant filtering options that would help narrow down the audience; many useless functions; the overwhelming amount of filters | Only possible to send test emails to oneself |
| User quotes | "Formatting is very limited, lacks visual elements such as content boxes, video formats"; "Lack of functionality limits creativity and that's why I only copy campaigns"; "Campaign functions are not put together nicely" | "It takes too long to create rules so I just search for people manually"; "I don't think it would be possible to make useful filters, I don't see how, because there are so many different people"; "There are many useless illogical functions when filtering audiences on the campaign"; "It's almost like there's too much customization, too many possibilities"; "I just stick to what I know" | "I have to confirm everything with my manager before sending out the campaign"; "I can't send test emails to anyone else" |

The HWID analysis unveiled that users are engaged in a variety of manual tasks and they need improved efficiency. The main pain points were identified as messaging, audience sorting, and sending out test emails. Based on the insights and discussion's themes (functionality, user critically reflecting on how the system works), it appeared that both shared a need for improved usability so they can become more competent. When asked about specific usability elements that could be improved, both participants indicated that the performance and stability of the system were satisfactory, whereas task efficiency had room for improvement.

This stage of the research aims to propose a prototype based on the pain points identified in the above analysis, consequently creating value within the Industrial Paradigm through faster production of email campaigns and less manual labor required to execute them [11]. Consequently, a prototype was constructed to address these issues and served as a connection between HW and ID (see Appendix I).

## 4.2   Findings from the Positive Design Analysis

The Positive Practice Canvas helped identify tasks and activities that constitute positive experiences for the users. Specifically, both interviewees mentioned design and copywriting activities as great sources of positive affect. Therefore, this is the positive practice that we chose to analyze. Through discussing the participants' creative practices (email design and copywriting), we were able to understand what were some of their important psychological needs, and specifically how the creative activities help fulfill them. Table 2 present a sample of quotes that helped us discover each psychological need.

**Table 2.** Psychological needs and sample of supporting quotes (case study)

| Psychological need | Sample of quotes |
|---|---|
| Meaning | "I want to learn more practical things that are relevant to my studies"; "I want to get experience with things that would help in my career"; "Creativity is important because then the work would be more meaningful"; "I feel I'm doing more valuable work for myself and the company when I'm creating like I'm spending my time more usefully" |
| Stimulation | "When I'm designing, I don't even feel like I'm working"; "Marketing-related tasks are the most exciting"; "You enjoy work more if you can do your own ideas"; "I like creative things like design, it doesn't really feel like work" |
| Autonomy | "I appreciate that my colleagues trust my copywriting skills enough that they don't feel they have to supervise me"; "I like to have brief guidelines and then create"; "Boundaries like feedback, timelines are important for me but it's also important that they would let me do my own thing"; "Flexibility and independence reflect my lifestyle" |

Gaining a deeper understanding of the basic needs of our participants helped us identify the mechanisms that made their work meaningful to them. This further helped us define experience goals for redesigning the email campaign functionality of their CRM system in a way that would address these needs and directly contribute to the identified mechanisms.

Specifically, we found that creative tasks were a common and redundant theme among our participants because they triggered feelings of *self-concordance*, *personal engagement*, and *independence*. These mechanisms of meaningful work could be mapped into the Positive Design Framework for Work components, leading to the adoption of experience goals based on the following three psychological needs: meaning, stimulation, and autonomy. This analysis helped design a proposal for a digital experience that would let users complete their work tasks in a more meaningful way, thereby improving their job satisfaction and subjective well-being. A summary of our analysis can be found in Table 3.

Based on our analysis, several features were considered as suggestions for improving the user's experience using the CRM's email campaign function. Based on these features, we developed user stories as a roadmap for our improved prototype.

**Table 3.** Defining experience goals

| Experience goals | Explanation | PDF component | Mechanism of meaningful work |
| --- | --- | --- | --- |
| Meaning | Realizing the user's own goals and objectives through accomplishing work tasks | Virtue | Self-concordance |
| Stimulation | Getting enjoyment from work tasks by embedding personal hobbies into practices | Pleasure | Personal engagement |
| Autonomy | Feeling that one is the cause of their own actions, rather than being directed into specific tasks | Personal significance | Independence |

The user stories induced from the HW analysis are: (i) users should be able to schedule campaigns, (ii) users should be able to sort campaigns based on the recipient's geo-localization and/or citizenship, and (iii) users should be able to send test emails to other employees.

With regards to the Positive Design analysis and newly defined experience goals, we opted to combine all three into an element-based design section within the CRM system – in the current version of the system, the design tab is hard to access and inflexible, leading to the assistants sticking to the same templates. The user stories for creating a positive experience that fulfills the needs for "meaning", "stimulation" and "autonomy" are: (iv) users should be able to add and edit text, (v) users should be able to change existing colors and add custom colors, (vi) users should be able to add and edit elements and (vii) multimedia files. The resulting user flow is visualized in Fig. 1 (the dotted lines represent tasks that were visually included in our prototype but not functional).

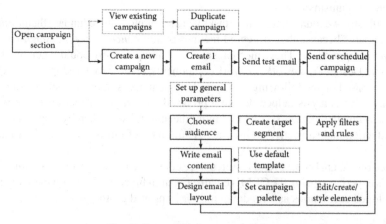

**Fig. 1.** Suggested new user task flow

### 4.3   A Sensitizing Model of Design for Meaningful Work Experiences

Because our data revealed new insight, we chose to trust the research process and embrace the pivot. As a result, the afore data collection and analysis constitutes a combination of Human Work (HW), Interaction Design (ID), and Positive Design (PD). Given the power of this combined approach, we propose to conceptualize it into a sensitizing Design for Meaningful Work Experiences model (see Fig. 2).

We argue that Human Work and Interaction Design provide the groundwork for solving functional issues, including informing about users' characteristics, problems, and needs, the technology they work with, and how they interact with it. Positive Design builds upon this practical understanding of a given case to help create an experience that addresses pain points but also has the potential to improve employee experience and job satisfaction. Importantly, Positive Design contributes to human flourishing by helping design features that increase feelings of pleasure, virtue, and/or personal significance.

While it is common to only address one of the three areas in one design, such a proposal should "avoid imparting any negative effects on the other two" [23]. In our case, we learned from the interview that several features of the existing artifact were pain points for the users – which means that other aspects of the design could negatively impact the positive experience we were designing. Therefore, we deemed it necessary to also address functional pain points that did not directly result in meaningful experiences, because we believed that the negative emotions they could generate would likely undermine the positive effects of our proposed design. We thus want to emphasize that all three approaches have much to learn from one another and benefit from being combined. While human work alone lacks the human-centered elements that unlock meaningful experiences at work, positive design may lack the functional and contextual understanding of a work environment. Finally, interaction design must learn from both HW and PD so it can support functional and meaningful user experiences – but interaction design also has great potential to contribute to HW and PD by acting as a probe and supporting effective communication between users, designers, and researchers.

The environment wherein an organization is embedded inevitably impacts all aspects of the design and is reciprocally impacted by the users' experiences – as such, it permeates the whole structure. Our case revealed several instances of interaction between work, the artifact, the workers, and the environment. One of the most telling examples was that at the time of the data collection in April 2020, most of the Danish workforce had been sent home to work remotely due to the COVID-19 pandemic. At the time, the CRM system was desktop-based, and as a result, the student workers could not access it remotely – therefore Participant 1 emphasized that an area for potential improvement would be to make the software available on the browser and via a mobile application. Both participants also acknowledged the customer support team of their CRM provider who regularly makes adjustments to the system based on their feedback. This is not only an example of the role of external stakeholders in the work experiences, but it also shows that workers can influence their environment.

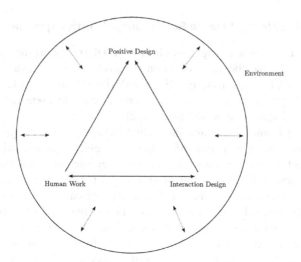

**Fig. 2.** Design for Meaningful Work Experiences (DMWE) sensitizing model

### 4.4   A Validation of the DMWE Model

To test our sensitizing model, we conducted a new round of 9 semi-structured interviews in May 2022. We summarize our findings hereafter.

**Human Work.** We started the interviews by asking users to describe their roles, goals, and some challenges they encounter at work and when interacting with their work tools. This provided a context for the discussion that followed – about their positive practices and psychological needs. The participants' goals varied from supervision duties (P4) to marketing activities (P5, P6, P9), including data analysis (P3), customer satisfaction (P2), project management (P7), etc. Many participants encountered relatively minor technical challenges and software limitations, including lagging performance (P1, P9), system complexity (P3, P6, P7), and a lack of integration of other business processes in the main system (P4, P5, P6, P7). The bulk of their occupational challenges however is entangled in their work environment. For example, P5 explains that a lag in customer responses to feedback surveys slows her down and impedes her progress ("Delay in receiving a response from satisfaction surveys. It discourages me because I need feedback from customers so I can improve. When I don't get it leaves me with no idea what to do"). P4 recounts how a lack of direct interaction with customers led the company to set up a physical suggestion book directly in the store. Every Friday, the sales team picks up the book and uploads the suggestions to the CRM system where managers can access it and further act on it. However, sales associates often linger in reporting the suggestions which causes the managerial team to be stuck in their work and have to put in extra work to go retrieve the suggestions. Workers develop interesting practices to overcome some of these challenges, thereby being actors in their work environment. For instance, P5 reports using WhatsApp conversations to overcome the inequalities in access to her company CRM system's internal communication channels. P6 explains how his team adapted to a lack of integration by using two different laptops when performing data analysis on SPSS and going through qualitative customer feedback on Microsoft tools or dividing all projects into different parts so that different employees take care of different parts of the analysis ("Right now you have to use two laptops, which makes work more tedious. We're used to it"; "Most times it doesn't make me feel comfortable because what I do so I don't have so much stress, I assign most of the work to my colleague"; "I would be happier, I would be grateful because it would [...] make our work, our duty run very smoothly. Because we would be able to scale our target").

**Positive Design.** During the second part of the interviews, we employed the Positive Practice Canvas to steer the conversation away from problem-solving and towards possibility-seeking instead.

Table 4 provides an overview of the positive practices identified and discussed during the interviews. Some of them who were redundant across several participants were clustered to simplify the analysis and demonstrate the transferability of anecdotal insight. The analysis of positive practices helped identify and illustrate the different psychological needs that workers evoked (see Table 5 for a sample of supporting quotes for each of the eight needs).

To clarify the process, we can consider the specific instance of "learning". P1, P2, and P3 all reported experiencing positive affect when engaging in activities such as reading, studying, or doing research. These activities created feelings of discovery, richness, and excitement which are indicative of a psychological need for *stimulation*. They were also sources of feelings of liberty, independence, and self-reliance – fulfilling the participants' need for *autonomy*. Finally, participants shared described feelings of self-realization, meaningfulness, and fulfillment through these activities, which we argue contribute to their need for *meaning*. We further identified that these learning activities require time-management skills (e.g., setting time apart to dedicate to learning, or making sure that learning practices do not overflow on work tasks of higher priority) and the ability to focus. Moreover, participants reported using a range of materials when they engage in learning practices, including sources of content such as digital and physical documents, note-taking tools (e.g., Microsoft Word), and ways to bridge this practice to other areas of their work environment (e.g., shared documents to engage in collaborative learning, calendar applications to define boundaries between learning activities and immediate duties).

**Table 4.** Identifying positive practices

| Positive practice | Participants | Social practice |
|---|---|---|
| Learning (reading, studying, researching) | P1, P2, P3 | **Psychological needs:** stimulation, autonomy, meaning<br>**Skills:** time-management, focus<br>**Materials:** YouTube, web browser, books, white papers, calendar app, Microsoft Word |

(*continued*)

**Table 4.** (*continued*)

| Positive practice | Participants | Social practice |
|---|---|---|
| Having conversations with co-workers | P4, P5, P8 | **Psychological needs:** relatedness, meaning, stimulation<br>**Skills:** communication, availability<br>**Materials:** lunch break, office |
| Energizing snack | P2 | **Psychological needs:** physicalness<br>**Skills:** know what to choose<br>**Materials:** coffee, juice, meal |
| Writing content | P3, P9 | **Psychological needs:** meaning, stimulation<br>**Skills:** proficiency, vocabulary, competence<br>**Materials:** pen and paper, Microsoft Word, digital notepad |
| Organize company trips | P4 | **Psychological needs:** stimulation, relatedness<br>**Skills:** relationship management<br>**Materials:** trophies, budget, employees |
| Listen to music | P6 | **Psychological needs:** stimulation, meaning<br>**Skills:** focus, music selection<br>**Materials:** iTunes, playlists, AirPods |
| Stretching | P6 | **Psychological needs:** physicalness<br>**Skills:** be quick and effective<br>**Materials:** none |
| Time-pressured tasks | P7 | **Psychological needs:** competence, stimulation, popularity<br>**Skills:** efficiency, organization, Excel skills, focus, prioritization, time flexibility<br>**Materials:** Evernote, Excel, iMessage/WhatsApp, |
| Helping co-workers | P1, P3, P5, P7 | **Psychological needs:** popularity, competence, meaning, stimulation, relatedness<br>**Skills:** leadership, social, communication, counseling, charity, care, accountability, professionalism<br>**Materials:** coffee, lunch, online resources about mental health |
| Keeping paper records | P1 | **Psychological needs:** security, competence<br>**Skills:** professionalism, accountability<br>**Materials:** printer, digital and physical diaries, sheets of paper, digital and physical records |

**Table 5.** Psychological needs and sample of supporting quotes (validating study)

| Psychological need | Interview quotes |
| --- | --- |
| Stimulation | "I like to work on pressure"; "Sometimes, even if it's a boring task – but something different than what I usually do on my day-to-day basis, I like to change a little bit"; "It's fun for me on a daily basis because I learn each and every day"; "Often, I go for lunch with colleagues, making fun, having chats of different software, how the future is going to look like in the software market. It's often very fun and interesting"; "I love researching more, reading more about a particular product that might be new"; "What I love about writing is that you know, you get to come across new words and this helps increase your vocabulary"; "Music gives me more energy, it serves as a renewal, it gives me more motivation" |
| Competence | "The whole process wasn't something I'd done before. And I was happy, I was able to do it right the first time"; "Wow, well my day is always hectic but at the same time, I love my day because I always accomplish whatever I have to do for the day"; "What really interests me is see how the content gets to generate more sales. I love it when I see those contents attract people, it makes me feel good about myself, it shows the work I'm doing is productive" |
| Popularity | "They trust me to do it. I like it. […] So I feel really happy if I know that they chose me to do something"; "When someone acknowledges you, saying 'thank you', when the person sees your worth, you feel valued. And you feel happy"; |
| Autonomy | "And I also really appreciate how he gives me like freedom and flexibility to do things my own way"; "As you're working, you don't need to wait for your boss to come out and tell you everything"; |
| Meaning | "I choose to be professional because I want to be professional, because I want to do a good job, because I want my company to actually stand strong, I want customers to always give us a 5-star feedback"; "[Learning] is important to me because I'm doing it for the better mental, and to broaden my knowledge"; "When I'm writing I really get inspired, you know? I love writing. It's part of me. I think it's one of my favorite activities, I love it"; "[Knowing how my colleagues feel] is very important to me because I believe in teamwork"; "If we should have music in the software it would actually change the orientation because I would feel like I'm working for myself, I'm working in my home – this is my project and I'm not working for the business. If I feel like I'm working for someone, then I can't really concentrate" |

(*continued*)

**Table 5.** (*continued*)

| Psychological need | Interview quotes |
| --- | --- |
| Physicalness | "[Drinking coffee] makes my brain to be calm, my nerves to be calm, and I feel relaxed while using the computer"; "I stretch, it's some exercise – if someone can sit for 6 h, man! You start to feel the pain. You need to stand up, stretch, sit down and continue working"; "[Taking care of your physical health even when you're at work] is the major priority, because if you're not physically fit, you can't work for long, then you can't meet your goals" |
| Relatedness | "I have the love for everyone around me, and I love my social network, the community"; "Sometimes if I'm lost or if I need their help on something I go and ask and they will be willing to help me and they will not ask for anything in return. And they will do this thing to just help me with what I just showed them – and I'll feel happy"; "My happiness is when my employees are happy"; "[When my colleagues are struggling] it gives me the urge to encourage the person"; |
| Security | "I have a diary, I keep physical records. It's compulsory [...], to do a good job, you also need to have backup plans"; "Prompt responses to duties by my co-workers – that makes me so happy my co-workers responding to their duties" |

**Experience Goals.** Based on our Human Work analysis and Positive Design insights, we were able to use the psychological needs to develop experience goals. These experience goals served as guidelines to develop creative ideas for features that enable or stimulate human flourishing. They do so by fostering positive affective experiences, but also by alleviating pain points through functional or "palliative" design. Table 6 provides a sample of selected experience goals. To define a new experience that bridges positive design and meaningful work, we collected interview quotes supporting each psychological need and sought to understand how they relate to elements of the Positive Design Framework and the Mechanisms of Meaningful Work, following the methodology of the PDFWork.

**Table 6.** A sample of experience goals

| Psychological need | Definition of experience goal | PDF components | Mechanism of meaningful work |
| --- | --- | --- | --- |
| Stimulation | Giving the user opportunities for self-fulfillment through autonomous discovery and exploration while doing their job | Pleasure, virtue, personal significance | Personal engagement, autonomy |

(*continued*)

**Table 6.**  (*continued*)

| Psychological need | Definition of experience goal | PDF components | Mechanism of meaningful work |
|---|---|---|---|
| Relatedness | Help users develop and nurture healthy relationships with co-workers | Virtue, personal significance | Interpersonal connectedness, interpersonal sensemaking |
| Meaning | Make it possible for workers to embed their personal passions and values into some of their work tasks | Pleasure, virtue, personal significance | Self-concordance, identity affirmation, personal engagement |
| Competence | Automate the instantiation of workers' ability to achieve their goals | Virtue, personal significance | Personal control, self-efficacy |

The newly defined experience goals then served as probes for us to ideate new features or functionality to be implemented into the work tools discussed with the interviewees. Table 7 provides a brief sample of the output of the ideation process. These proposed features are not meant as unique or ideal solutions but serve as evidence that combining human work analysis with the sharing of positive anecdotes can generate potentially valuable creative output.

**Table 7.**  Examples of new features based on experience goals

| Experience goals | Example 1 | Example 2 | Example 3 |
|---|---|---|---|
| Stimulation | AI-powered chatbot that recommends online resources for self-paced learning based on worker's repeated tasks | Development of e-learning modules in partnerships with universities and MOOC platforms | Designated notebook available within the main work system to facilitate and centralize learning |
| Relatedness | Develop a communication system based on topical channels using conversation prompts with different levels of privacy based on role and hierarchy | AI-powered calendar feature to find free times and probe workers to use them for social activities | Create a function within a collaborative system to send digital/physical gifts to co-workers when they complete a task or assignment |

(*continued*)

Table 7. (*continued*)

| Experience goals | Example 1 | Example 2 | Example 3 |
|---|---|---|---|
| Meaning | Create a personal dashboard where workers can curate content that helps them feel better (e.g., music playlists, mindfulness exercises, stretches) | Scatter artwork, pop-up inspirational quotes, and well-being tips throughout the interface | Generate a cyclic survey that asks workers about the alignment between their personal preferences and work tasks |
| Competence | Track worker's completed tasks (e.g., sent email, launched campaign, reconciled transaction) and show a list of completed tasks when the worker logs off | Create a space where co-workers can keep track of their achievements (i.e., journal or diary) | Automatically prompt the worker to create a printed record of newly created digital transactions |

## 5   A Refined Model of Design for Meaningful Work Experiences (DMWE)

The first stage of this study was a stepping stone to understanding the complexity of improving work experiences through work tool design – and discovering the relationships between Human Work, Interaction Design, and Positive Design. It enabled the creation of a sensitizing model that stimulated the second stage of our study and encouraged us to further explore the potential of our research opportunity. The second round of interviews provided a variety of experiences and contexts that were lacking in the initial study. This richness helped better capture coherent patterns and relationships that were only emergent in our sensitizing model.

In our refined model of Design for Meaningful Work Experiences (see Fig. 3), we first clarify the relationships between Human Work, Interaction Design, and Positive Design. We argue that Human Work has a revelatory role in Positive Design. Because it emphasizes employees' roles, goals, and challenges, it facilitates the discussion between researcher/designer and worker in a way that reveals positive practices at work. In many cases, positive practices emerge where workers experience challenges or achievements concerning their roles and goals. For example, P6 evokes challenges in the configuration of some of his tasks, which generate stress and make his work tedious. Soon after, when we probed him to think about positive practices, he immediately thought of listening to music – which he does when he feels stressed ("I play my music to ease the stress, so I get to worry less"). This naturally led him to come up with the idea of embedding a music player within the CRM system he uses for work. We argue that moving from functional design/problem resolution toward positive design results in a "creative inversion" where we turn negative practices or experiences into opportunities for positive experiences. This creative inversion results in concrete artifacts (design guidelines, prototypes, features) that contribute to human flourishing. In other words, we suggest that Positive Design is a mediator between Human Work and Interaction Design in that it prevents researchers, designers, and users to get stalled and instead fosters open conversations conducive to creative ideas.

Second, we refine the role of the environment. Our data showed that the role of the environment is complex, plural, and multidirectional. It primarily acts as an enabler or as an inhibitor. In the relationship between Human Work and Positive Design, the environment can be an inhibitor to how people exteriorize or even experience negative experiences, challenging the process of creative inversion. On the other hand, it may in some instances serve as an enabler of Positive Design. Returning to the example of P6's music – he can use AirPods at work, which enables him to turn stressful triggers into an experience that he describes as meaningful and significant. If his work environment made it impossible to use earbuds in the office (organizational culture, corporate policy, large amount of phone calls or meetings, etc.), it would act as an inhibitor instead. The environment similarly impacts the development of Interaction Design through Positive Design. In our case study, the CRM system used at the Danish university has a customer support team who is willing and able to make quick customizations to the software based on direct conversations with the student workers. In this case, the environment acts as an enabler. Less accessible vendors would instead inhibit the development of Interaction Design through Positive Design. Finally, we emphasize that users, artifacts, and practices reciprocally influence the environment, by enabling or inhibiting environmental change – either in the way they relate their work experiences to positive experiences (Human Work to Positive Design) or in the way that they interact with positive artifacts (Positive Design to Interaction Design).

We would like to note that the relationship between Human Work and Interaction Design in our model of Design for Meaningful Work is faithful to what is described in the Human Work Interaction Design framework [9, 10].

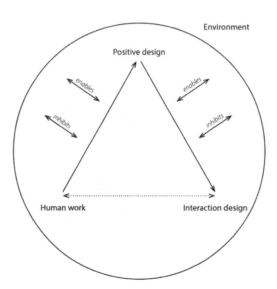

**Fig. 3.** Design for Meaningful Work Experiences (DMWE)

# 6    Conclusion

Our model describes a new methodology that emerges through the implementation of Positive Design into the relationship between Human Work and Interaction. Creative inversion is an emergent design technique that can help foster creativity by facilitating communication between researchers, designers, and users. User experience research has developed several studies and frameworks using Positive Design. However, less research was conducted in the workplace, and most was focused on pragmatic design [5].

First, we successfully applied the Positive Practice Canvas to a workplace context, suggesting that the guide is also relevant for fostering communication around interaction with work products and not only consumer products.

Second, we expand the empirical field of work tool design and contribute to research on positive/experience design and work experience by using the PDFWork and developing a new model of Design for Meaningful Work Experiences. The first iteration of our model had already received attention from Human-Computer Interaction scholars, suggesting that there is a need for continuing academic research that can build bridges between Human Work, Interaction Design, and Positive Design [34]. We, therefore, encourage other researchers and practitioners to use our model to inform their work and stimulate fruitful conversation with users – for example, an action design study could help validate the model through a real-life intervention that would make it possible to measure the concrete outcomes of the model.

**Acknowledgments.** I would like to express my gratitude to Torkil Clemmensen for his thoughtful feedback and continued encouragement to pursue this study, as well as to Gabija Bogdzeviciute and Yeeun Kim for their contributions to the data collection and analysis of the preliminary case study.

# Appendices

### Appendix I

See Figs. 4, 5, 6 and 7.

**Fig. 4.** From left to right, original FF and prototype.

**Fig. 5.** From left to right, entering the campaign area and audience rules settings.

**Fig. 6.** "Email content" area on the prototype.

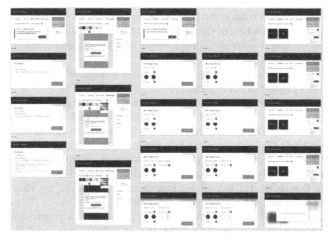

**Fig. 7.** Full overview of the prototype (A recorded demo of the prototype can be viewed here (https://youtu.be/7baPqqMsNYM)).

## References

1. Bergs, J.: Effect of healthy workplaces on well-being and productivity of office workers. In: Proceedings of International Plants for People Symposium (2002)
2. Wright, T.A., Walton, A.P.: Affect, psychological well-being and creativity: results of a field study. J. Bus. Manag. **9**, 21–32 (2003)

3. Lips-Wiersma, M., Morris, L.: The Map of Meaning: A Guide to Sustaining Our Humanity in the World of Work, 1st edn. Routledge, Abingdon (2017)
4. Sein, M.K., Henfridsson, O., Purao, S., Rossi, M., Lindgren, R.: Action design research. MIS Q. **35**, 37–56 (2011). https://doi.org/10.2307/23043488
5. Lu, Y., Roto, V.: Evoking meaningful experiences at work – a positive design framework for work tools. J. Eng. Des. **26**, 99–120 (2015). https://doi.org/10.1080/09544828.2015.1041461
6. Grundgeiger, T., Hurtienne, J., Happel, O.: Why and how to approach user experience in safety-critical domains: the example of health care. Hum. Factors **63**, 821–832 (2021). https://doi.org/10.1177/0018720819887575
7. Savioja, P., Liinasuo, M., Koskinen, H.: User experience: does it matter in complex systems? Cogn. Technol. Work **16**(4), 429–449 (2013). https://doi.org/10.1007/s10111-013-0271-x
8. Ryan, R.M., Deci, E.L.: On happiness and human potentials: a review of research on hedonic and eudaimonic well-being. Annu. Rev. Psychol. **52**, 141–166 (2001). https://doi.org/10.1146/annurev.psych.52.1.141
9. Abdelnour-Nocera, J., Clemmensen, T.: Theorizing about socio-technical approaches to HCI. In: Barricelli, B.R., et al. (eds.) HWID 2018. IFIP AICT, vol. 544, pp. 242–262. Springer, Cham (2019). https://doi.org/10.1007/978-3-030-05297-3_17
10. Clemmensen, T.: A Human Work Interaction Design (HWID) case study in e-government and public information systems. Int. J. Public Inf. Syst. **7**, 105–113 (2011)
11. Gardien, P., Djajadiningrat, T., Hummels, C., Brombacher, A.: Changing your hammer: the implications of paradigmatic innovation for design practice. Int. J. Des. **8**, 119–139 (2014)
12. Schwaninger, M.: Managing complexity—the path toward intelligent organizations. Syst. Pract. Action Res. **13**, 207–241 (2000). https://doi.org/10.1023/A:1009546721353
13. Schwaninger, M.: Intelligent organizations: an integrative framework. Syst. Res. Behav. Sci. **18**, 137–158 (2001). https://doi.org/10.1002/sres.408
14. British Design Council: What is the framework for innovation? Design Council's evolved Double Diamond. British Design Council (2015). https://www.designcouncil.org.uk/news-opinion/what-framework-innovation-design-councils-evolved-double-diamond. Accessed 17 Mar 2022
15. Brown, T., Katz, B.: Change by design. J. Prod. Innov. Manag. **28**, 381–383 (2011). https://doi.org/10.1111/j.1540 5885.2011.00806.x
16. Maximo, M.: The difference between welfare and wellbeing and how objective the concept of a good life can be. In: International Conference Economic Philosophy (1987)
17. Deci, E.L., Ryan, R.M.: Hedonia, eudaimonia, and well-being: an introduction. J Happiness Stud **9**, 1–11 (2008). https://doi.org/10.1007/s10902-006-9018-1
18. Ryff, C.D.: Psychological well-being revisited: advances in the science and practice of eudaimonia. PPS **83**, 10–28 (2014). https://doi.org/10.1159/000353263
19. Sanders, E., Dandavate, U.: Design for experiencing: new tools. In: First International Conference on Design and Emotion, TU Delft (1999)
20. Yoon, J., Pohlmeyer, A.E., Desmet, P.M.A., Kim, C.: Designing for positive emotions: issues and emerging research directions. Des. J. **24**, 167–187 (2021). https://doi.org/10.1080/14606925.2020.1845434
21. Hassenzahl, M., Eckoldt, K., Diefenbach, S.: Designing moments of meaning and pleasure. Experience design and happiness. Int. J. Des. **7**, 12 (2013)
22. Jordan, P.W.: Human factors for pleasure in product use. Appl. Ergon. **29**, 25–33 (1998). https://doi.org/10.1016/S0003-6870(97)00022-7
23. Desmet, P., Pohlmeyer, A.: Positive design: an introduction to design for subjective well-being. Int. J. Des. **7**, 5–19 (2013)
24. Rosso, B.D., Dekas, K.H., Wrzesniewski, A.: On the meaning of work: a theoretical integration and review. Res. Organ. Behav. **30**, 91–127 (2010). https://doi.org/10.1016/j.riob.2010.09.001

25. Hassenzahl, M.: Experience design: technology for all the right reasons. Synth. Lect. Hum. Cent. Informa. **3**, 1–95 (2010). https://doi.org/10.2200/S00261ED1V01Y201003HCI008

26. Hekkert, P., Mostert, M., Stompff, G.; Dancing with a machine: a case of experience-driven design. In: Proceedings of the 2003 International Conference on Designing Pleasurable Products and Interfaces, pp 114–119. Association for Computing Machinery, New York (2003)

27. Desmet, P., Hassenzahl, M.: Towards happiness: possibility-driven design. In: Zacarias, M., de Oliveira, J.V. (eds.) Human-Computer Interaction: The Agency Perspective. SCI, vol. 396, pp. 3–27. Springer, Heidelberg (2012). https://doi.org/10.1007/978-3-642-25691-2_1

28. Desmet, P.M., Pohlmeyer, A.E., Forlizzi, J.: Special issue editorial: design for subjective well-being. Int. J. Des. **7**, 1–3 (2013)

29. Sheldon, K.M., Elliot, A.J., Kim, Y., Kasser, T.: What is satisfying about satisfying events? Testing 10 candidate psychological needs. J. Pers. Soc. Psychol. **80**, 325–339 (2001). https://doi.org/10.1037/0022-3514.80.2.325

30. Hassenzahl, M., et al.: 8 needs as a starting point for designing interactive technology (2022)

31. Hassenzahl, M., Diefenbach, S.: Well-being, need fulfillment, and experience design. In: Designing Well-being Workshop (2012). Accessed Aug 2013

32. Hassenzahl, M., Diefenbach, S., Göritz, A.: Needs, affect, and interactive products – facets of user experience. Interact. Comput. **22**, 353–362 (2010). https://doi.org/10.1016/j.intcom.2010.04.002

33. Klapperich, H., Laschke, M., Hassenzahl, M.: The positive practice canvas: gathering inspiration for wellbeing-driven design. In: Proceedings of the 10th Nordic Conference on Human-Computer Interaction, Oslo, Norway, pp 74–81. Association for Computing Machinery (2018)

34. Clemmensen, T.: Human Work Interaction Design: A Platform for Theory and Action. Springer, Cham (2021). https://doi.org/10.1007/978-3-030-71796-4

# Triple Diamond Design Process

## Human-centered Design for Data-Driven Innovation

Johannes Schleith$^{(\boxtimes)}$ and Daniella Tsar

Thomson Reuters Labs, London, UK
johannes@schleith.org

**Abstract.** Innovation is a team sport that requires interdisciplinary collaboration. This study discusses how design thinking methods can be adapted to support such collaborative AI innovation and Human centred AI (HCAI). We propose an enhancement to the traditional double diamond framework, by adding a notion of "data discovery" alongside problem discovery. Further we propose the use of "data user stories" to not only communicate user tasks and user goals, but also document input and output data of a given process.

**Keywords:** Design thinking · Artificial intelligence · Machine learning · Requirements engineering · Design process

## 1 Introduction

Problem-solving with AI should involve multiple interdisciplinary perspectives with contributions from domain experts, designers, end users and other stake holders, who might not have a scientific or technical background - in addition to scientists and engineers who represent the AI/ML expertise.

In this short paper, we make a case for enhancements to the design process and design thinking methodology in order to provide a framework for a more inclusive and participatory AI innovation process. We discuss the need for a data discovery, alongside a focus on information handling and cognitive tasks for the discovery and definition of the problem space, as well as the need for semi-functional prototyping and experimental evaluation of user centered metrics for content that is dynamically created in early AI experimentation.

## 2 Background

Design Thinking describes a human-centered approach to requirements engineering and the design of products and services [1]. Such approach commonly considers "end-users" (i.e. people that are going to use the system or service), "domain experts" (i.e. people that have knowledge about the domain, systems, processes or data in the scenario under investigation) or other "stakeholders"

M. Kurosu et al. (Eds.): HCII 2022, LNCS 13516, pp. 136–146, 2022.
https://doi.org/10.1007/978-3-031-17615-9_9

(i.e. individuals or groups that are impacted by the system) [2]. Design thinking methods can also be applied to AI innovation [3].

Human Centered AI has been adopted as an umbrella term to describe methods for the design of AI systems [4], and related challenges for human involvement in the creation of Machine Learning (ML) systems [5], human computer interaction (HCI) with AI systems [6], AI explainability [7], interactive Machine Learning (ML) [8] and human in the loop systems [9].

Frameworks for data science exploration, such as Knowledge Discovery in Databases (KDD) [10] or CRISP-DM [11], tend to focus more strongly on data processing and data-driven solution exploration. The gap of frameworks for problem discovery, problem definition, problem-led requirements engineering and creative problem solving for AI innovation motivated this paper.

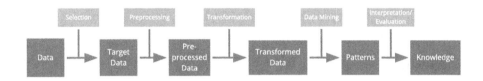

**Fig. 1.** Illustration, Knowledge Discovery in Databases (KDD) [10]

Knowledge Discovery in Databases (KDD) [10] provides a framework for data pre-processing, transformation and data mining, see Fig. 1. CRISP-DM [11] describes phases to understand the business need, gather and clean data, model and evaluate the results, see Fig. 2. Both frameworks informed the definition of the data discovery phase (Sect. 4.2). Steps described in CRISP-DM for initial requirements gathering and interaction with business stakeholders further informed the problem discovery phase (Sect. 4.1).

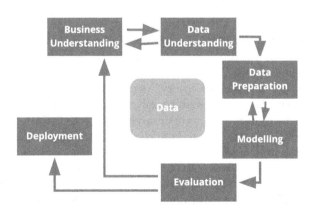

**Fig. 2.** Illustration, CRISP-DM [11]

Standards and frameworks for user-centered design [2,12], and design thinking [13] present phases for requirements gathering, design and user-centered evaluation, which informed the description of problem discovery (Sect. 4.1), solution exploration and prototyping (Sect. 4.4), see Fig. 3.

**Fig. 3.** Illustration double diamond design process [13]

## 3    Method

The exploratory approach presented in this paper (Sect. 4) has been developed based on a review and combination of existing frameworks for data science experimentation and design thinking (Sect. 2). The framework has been validated and refined through review with internal subject matter experts. It further has been applied to structure phases for discovery and experimentation in internal innovation projects with interdisciplinary teams of data scientists, designers and developers. While this study does not present a formal evaluation of the framework, we could observe how a shared terminology helps project teams and project stakeholders to articulate and align on project phases, manage expectations and project resources.

## 4    Triple Diamond

A double diamond framework [13] has commonly been used to describe a design process that focuses on "problem discovery" first, and problem led "solution exploration" second, see Fig. 3.

Activities during "problem discovery" (e.g. semi-structured interviews, qualitative and quantitative user research and problem definition) aim to understand "what" is the right problem worth solving, whereas "solution exploration" (e.g. design sprints, conceptual and detailed design, and user testing) focuses on "how" to solve the problem right. Design thinking, with its focus on the investigation of the problem space and collaborative creative problem solving can infuse AI innovation with a richer and more appropriate problem definition, empathy with end users and co-design with domain experts. While frameworks for data science exploration focus on investigation of data constraints and opportunities for data analysis, they might lack such a human-centered perspective.

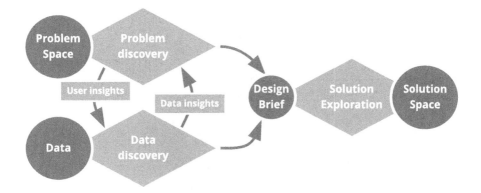

**Fig. 4.** Illustration, triple diamond design process

The balance between "user need" and "data constraints" might seem like a "chicken and egg" problem. However we argue that strong opportunities for AI innovation need to stem from both, a detailed understanding of the problem space, end-user pain points and current processes, as well as constraints and opportunities based on data, its availability and accessibility. We therefore propose a framework that adds a third "diamond" for "data discovery" to the design process, see Fig. 4.

On the one hand, both discovery streams *"filter"* the set of relevant problems, from a perspective of problems that are relevant to the user, as well as problems that can be related to data. On the other hand, both activities also *"update"* the understanding of the problem space. Learnings from user research might offer a more systematic view beyond individual silos. Insight from the data discovery might flow back and update the understanding about the business problem.

### 4.1   Problem Discovery

When it comes to problem discovery, user research helps prioritize and "filter" problems that are relevant to end users.

On the one hand, limited knowledge about customer workflows and pain points has been shown to pose the highest difficulty for the design of Machine Learning (ML) based systems [14]. Frameworks for requirement engineering describe elicitation and analysis of requirements [15], but often lack phases for user research and requirements elicitation with end users or stakeholders and hence lack contextual understanding to inform requirements. On the other hand, existing user research methods, such as task analysis or "Jobs To Be Done" (JTBD) [16], provide great tools to investigate and analyse end user tasks and desired outcomes but lack precision for the identification of problems worth solving with AI systems.

We therefore argue that problem discovery for AI innovation ideally combines established user research methods with methods that further focus in on the

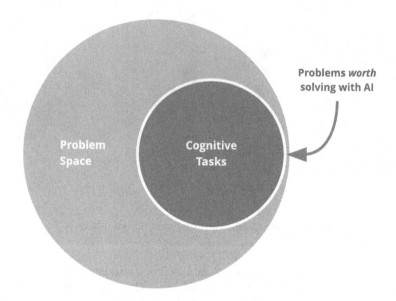

**Fig. 5.** Subset of problems worth solving with AI

investigation of "information handling" and "cognitive tasks", see Fig. 5. Such tasks might involve handling and manipulation of information and data. Cognitive tasks might for example involve *learning* about new unknown information, *searching* for specific, known, information, *relating* information and data points, or *creating* new information. In previous research, we show that refining user stories with a focus on such "cognitive tasks" can enable workshop participants to come up with ideas that are more relevant for AI innovation [17].

## 4.2  Data Discovery

Problems worth solving with AI, are problems that represent a real pain point for end users or other stakeholders, as well as problems that are related to data, see Fig. 6. AI driven solutions require information that is available and accessible as digital data. Data structure, formats and access inform and limit the choice of AI methods during solution exploration.

Data can be defined as facts or information used usually to calculate, analyze, or plan something, or any information that is produced or stored by a computer [18]. In the context of the proposed methodology, we consider it as information that is accessible to the AI/ML system. Exploratory data analysis constrains the problem space to problems that are related to accessible and available data. Drawing parallels from research in creative problem solving and the "double diamond" framework [13], we propose to add yet another "diamond" for "data discovery", see Fig. 4. Divergent parts of such data discovery involves all steps necessary to source and explore data sets. Convergent parts of this phase

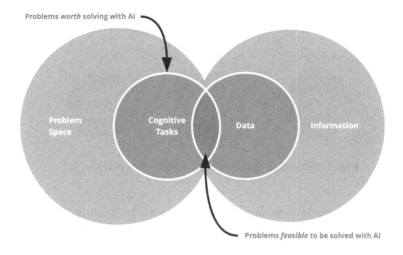

**Fig. 6.** Subset of problems feasible *and* worth solving with AI

include initial analysis of the data, creation of a "data inventory" with descriptive statistics and example data points, as well as transformation of the data, and preliminary testing.

A data inventory phase might help represent and quantify the problem area more holistically. Descriptive statistics help understand the current state. Inferential statistics enable us to abstract assumptions beyond the available data to the entire problem area often in a form of various hypotheses. In the past few years the use of AI and ML technologies grew exponentially, however, the widespread sophistication of matching problem statements and use cases did not. Research in this area aligns to the perceived need for a more robust and human centered requirements engineering process for AI/ML systems [19]. While often being seen as a technical and quantitative process, requirements engineering has qualitative aspects [20] and can be seen as a creative problem solving process [21]. These qualitative aspects are'uniquely human' and'of intuitive nature' and are the basis of human-in-the-loop requirements engineering [20].

Without initial problem discovery and problem definition, technical professionals with limited or no understanding of the subject matter, struggle with designing the right AI/ML systems [14]. Typically, the technical focus shifts to the search for further data sources, analysis of the data, defining technical specifications (e.g.: explanaibility), as well as agreeing verification and validation [15], rather than challenging or delving deeper into the initial problem definition.

### 4.3  Data User Stories

Requirements are commonly captured in "user stories" [22], that describe *user persona*, *task* and *user goal*, see Fig. 8. In such a form they might be used throughout a design sprint, or agile software development. However, such requirements might lack details about the data lifecycle that are required by data scientists to choose relevant AI methods and approaches (Fig. 7).

**Fig. 7.** Simplified illustration of a user story, see also [22]

General business process management frameworks, such as "SIPOC" (Six Sigma [23]), require not only the description of the *supplier* and *customer*, but also description of the specific *input* and *output* of a business process. Data scientists' creative problem solving require more specific detail on "input data" and "output data" [17], in order to come up with suitable approaches.

**Fig. 8.** Illustration of a data user story

We therefore propose the notion of "data user stories" that encapsulate both, the end users' goals as well as the data that is involved in the process. We propose to enhance "user stories" as defined by Patton and Economy [22], with detail on the "data" that is used in a task or process [17], see Fig. 8. This would allow to enrich requirements definition with a notion of "expected input data" as well as "desired output data". "Expected input data" incorporates any information or requirements around the data sets, features, or human readable information that is required for a task, prior to any further data manipulation. While "desired output data" outlines the expected output, formats of output, ranges of data after the manipulation in the main task that is described in the user story.

### 4.4   Prototyping and User Centered AI Metrics

Finally, the creation of prototypes during solution exploration has been presented as a major challenge for AI Innovation [24]. On the one hand, user experience (UX) methods support prototyping and testing of conceptual designs, interaction design and end user experience - such as *Wizard of Oz* [25] experiments or interactive prototyping (e.g. Axure[1], Figma[2]). However most tools only support testing with *static* content, i.e. content or interaction that has been defined by a designer prior to the experiment. On the other hand, data science tools, such as programming environments (e.g. juypter notebooks[3] [26]), semi-functional prototyping (e.g. Streamlit[4], Shiny[5]) and web app development (e.g. Flask[6]) enable a scientist or developer to experiment with *dynamically generated content* and code, but only support design and testing with end users in a limited way. There seems to be a gap for rapid prototyping with *dynamically generated content* [27] and experimentation with end users and other stakeholders. Prototyping and testing AI/ML systems poses challenges:

- For dynamically generated content, the system would need to show pretrained results. Retraining models during testing would likely introduce unacceptable latency.
- Testing the performance of the modelling requires the model to have been trained on a broad range of the data. Certain subsets of the data could give misleading results.
- Model Ops - the architecture layer to dynamically generated content is difficult to create as a low-fidelity option.

While there is a wealth of statistical and mathematical methods to assess AI and ML systems on data centric methods (e.g. f1/precision/recall [28], loss functions [25]), we argue that HCAI lacks a framework and metrics for the early evaluation of end users' experience with *"dynamic content"* [27], i.e. content, hierarchies, classification or navigation that are generated at runtime. Previous research [29] explored the interaction of "precision" and "recall" [28] and a notion of "task support" in an experimental setup. A dimension to this consideration is that non-technical domain experts evaluating the dynamic content often lack understanding of technical performance measures [15].

Similar to the development of tools for the evaluation of information architecture (e.g. OptimalWorkshop[7], UserZoom[8]), further work should expand on a framework of experimental methods and metrics. Such guidance could facilitate collaboration between User Experience (UX) and Data Science professionals, in order to allow for evaluation and testing of *dynamic content* in throwaway prototypes or surveys with end users as early as possible with the least amount of effort.

---

[1] Axure RP, http://axure.com.
[2] Figma, http://figma.com.
[3] Jupyter, http://jupyter.org.
[4] Streamlit, http://streamlit.io.
[5] Shiny, http://shiny.rstudio.com.
[6] Flask, https://palletsprojects.com/p/flask/.
[7] OptimalWorkshop, https://www.optimalworkshop.com.
[8] UserZoom, https://www.userzoom.com.

# 5    Discussion

In this short paper we presented a number of different ideas how existing design thinking practice and process could be adapted to support AI innovation. We presented the analogy of a *triple diamond*, that integrates a data discovery step, the notion of a *data user story* to capture requirements relevant to data science and finally the need for experimentation with *dynamic content* and user centered AI metrics. We hope that these ideas might assist interdisciplinary teams to coordinate the discovery of user needs and problem space alongside the study of constraints and opportunities based on available and accessible data.

We argue for the need to bridge the gap and facilitate collaboration between scientists and domain experts, in order to not only explore the art of the possible in terms of technology and science, but also solutions to relevant problems in terms of domain and context. We provide a framework with some terminology to support various levels of discovery and prototyping.

Further research and a more in-depth look at the cadence and sequence of interaction of different stakeholders during discovery is needed, in order to better understand how problem discovery and data discovery can "update" problem definition as well as "filter" the problem area to problems that are both relevant to end users and domain experts and feasible for AI driven solutions. We hope that the ideas presented in this paper can build upon and link together references in design thinking and data science experimentation.

# References

1. Tschimmel, K.: Design thinking as an effective toolkit for innovation. In: ISPIM Conference Proceedings, page 1. The International Society for Professional Innovation Management (ISPIM) (2012)
2. Ergonomics of human-system interaction - Part 110. Standard, International Organization for Standardization, Geneva, CH, March 2020
3. Stackowiak, K.: Design thinking in software and AI projects: proving ideas through rapid prototyping. In: Design Thinking in Software and AI Projects: Proving Ideas Through Rapid Prototyping (2020)
4. Shneiderman, B.: Human-Centered AI. Oxford University Press, Oxford (2022)
5. Gillies, M., et al.: Human-centred machine learning. In: Proceedings of the 2016 CHI Conference Extended Abstracts on Human Factors in Computing Systems, CHI EA 2016, pp. 3558–3565. Association for Computing Machinery, New York, NY, USA (2016)
6. Amershi, S., et al.: Guidelines for human-AI interaction. In: Proceedings of the 2019 CHI Conference on Human Factors in Computing Systems, CHI 2019, pp.. 1–13. Association for Computing Machinery, New York, NY, USA (2019)
7. Vera Liao, Q., Gruen, D., Miller, S.: Questioning the AI: informing design practices for explainable AI user experiences. In: Proceedings of the 2020 CHI Conference on Human Factors in Computing Systems, pp. 1–15. ACM, Honolulu HI USA, April 2020

8. Sanchez, T., Caramiaux, B., Françoise, J., Bevilacqua, F., Mackay, W.: How do people train a machine? Strategies and (Mis)understandings. In: CSCW 2021 - The 24th ACM Conference on Computer-Supported Cooperative Work and Social Computing, Virtual, United States, October 2021
9. Shneiderman, B.: Human-centered artificial intelligence: three fresh ideas. AIS Trans. Human Comput. Interact. **12**, 109–124 (2020)
10. Maimon, O., Rokach, L.: Data Mining and Knowledge Discovery Handbook, 2nd edn. Springer, New York (2010). https://doi.org/10.1007/b107408
11. Shearer, C.: The CRISP-DM model: the new blueprint for data mining. J. Data Warehous. **5**(4), 13–22 (2000)
12. Norman, D.A.: User Centered System Design: New Perspectives on Human-computer Interaction. CRC Press, Cambridge (1986)
13. British Design Council: What is the framework for innovation? Design council's evolved double diamond. (2004). Accessed 30 May 2022
14. Ishikawa, F., Yoshioka, N.: How do engineers perceive difficulties in engineering of machine-learning systems? - questionnaire survey. In: 2019 IEEE/ACM Joint 7th International Workshop on Conducting Empirical Studies in Industry (CESI) and 6th International Workshop on Software Engineering Research and Industrial Practice (SER IP), pp. 2–9 (2019)
15. Vogelsang, A., Borg, M.: Requirements engineering for machine learning: perspectives from data scientists. CoRR, abs/1908.04674 (2019)
16. Lucassen, G., Keuken, M., Dalpiaz, F., Brinkkemper, S., Sloof, G., Schlingmann, J.: Jobs-to-be-Done Oriented Requirements Engineering: A Method for Defining Job Stories, pp. 227–243, March 2018
17. Schleith, J., Norkute, M., Mikhail, M., Tsar, D.: Cognitive strategies prompts: creativity triggers for human centered AI opportunity detection. In: Creativity and Cognition (C&C 2022), Venice, Italy (2022)
18. The Britannica Dictionary. Data
19. Villamizar, H., Escovedo, T., Kalinowski, M.: Requirements engineering for machine learning: a systematic mapping study. In: 2021 47th Euromicro Conference on Software Engineering and Advanced Applications (SEAA), pp. 29–36 (2021)
20. Kostova, B., Gurses, S., Wegmann, A.: On the interplay between requirements, engineering, and artificial intelligence. In: Sabetzadeh, M., (eds.) et al. Joint Proceedings of REFSQ-2020 Workshops, Doctoral Symposium, Live Studies Track, and Poster Track co-located with the 26th International Conference on Requirements Engineering: Foundation for Software Quality (REFSQ 2020), Pisa, Italy, March 24, 2020, vol. 2584, CEUR Workshop Proceedings. CEUR-WS.org (2020)
21. Maiden, N., Jones, S., Karlsen, I.K., Neill, .R, Zachos, K., Milne, A.: Requirements engineering as creative problem solving: a research agenda for idea finding. In: 2010 18th IEEE International on Requirements Engineering Conference (RE), pp. 57–66. IEEE Computer Society (2010)
22. Patton, J., Economy, P.: User Story Mapping: Discover the Whole Story, Build the Right Product. O'Reilly Media, Sebastopol (2014)
23. Vivekananthamoorthy, N., Sankar, S.: Lean six sigma. In: Coskun, A. (ed.) Six Sigma. IntechOpen, Rijeka (2011)
24. The Prototypers Dilemma [EUROIA 2018]. https://www.slideshare.net/jbaeck/the-prototypers-dilemma-euroia-2018-117320114. Accessed 30 May 2022
25. Hanington, B., Martin, B.: Universal Methods of Design Expanded and Revised. Rockport Publishers, Beverly (2019)
26. Jupyter. http://jupyter.org. Accessed 30 May 2022

27. Schleith, J.: Human-centered evaluation of dynamic content (2021)
28. Arora, M., Kanjilal, U., Varshney, D.: Evaluation of information retrieval: precision and recall. Int. J. Indian Cult. Bus. Manage. **12**(2), 224–236 (2016)
29. Johannes Schleith, Nina Hristozova, Brian Chechmanek, Carolyn Bussey, and Leszek Michalak. Noise over fear of missing out. In Carolin Wienrich, Philipp Wintersberger, and Benjamin Weyers, editors, Mensch und Computer 2021 - Workshopband, Bonn, 2021. Gesellschaft für Informatik e.V

# Leveraging Design Thinking Towards the Convergence of AI, IoT and Blockchain: Strategic Drivers and Human-Centered Use Cases

Maximilian Tigges<sup>(✉)</sup>, Chloé Ipert, and René Mauer

Jean Baptiste Say Institute for Entrepreneurship, ESCP Wirtschaftshochschule,
Heubnerweg 8-10, Berlin, Germany
{mtigges,cipert,rmauer}@escp.eu

**Abstract.** Artificial Intelligence (AI) is increasingly transforming and reshaping human interactions, severely impacting organizational processes and operations. However, it faces substantial challenges, such as collecting, evaluating, and anonymizing data, which brings along privacy risks for sensitive user data and tends to diminish the human perspective as the principal focus of many activities in our world. The relationship between Design Thinking (DT) and AI is meaningful on two interrelated and reciprocal levels: (1) The impact and perceived benefits of AI on the DT process; (2) DT as an important concept to understand the opportunities offered by the combination of AI with Blockchain and the Internet of Things. Hence, we investigate human-centered use-cases building on AI, Blockchain, and IoT by interviewing experts such as entrepreneurs, technology researchers, investors, and academics. We find that AI significantly affects streamlining and enhancing the DT process while the DT process offers great potential to create human-centered use cases leveraging AI, Blockchain, and IoT. Notably, we suggest that the DT process should pay particular attention to industrial and organizational capabilities during the empathize and define stages, the process performance requirements throughout the ideation and prototyping stages, and the output at the testing stage.

**Keywords:** Design thinking · Artificial intelligence · Convergence · Blockchain · Internet of Things · Autonomous systems

## 1 Introduction

Artificial Intelligence (AI) is playing an increasingly important role in our world today, impacting individuals, societies, organizations, and ecosystems [1–3]. While few AI-driven technologies already exist in the form of self-driving vehicles and self-learning algorithms, credible and scientifically grounded short to mid-term future scenarios predict an outlook where AI will play a significantly more substantial role than it already does today [4, 5]. Governments, states, cities, and organizations will all be linked to and impacted by AI-driven networks that help such entities make sense of the ever-increasing

M. Kurosu et al. (Eds.): HCII 2022, LNCS 13516, pp. 147–162, 2022.
https://doi.org/10.1007/978-3-031-17615-9_10

amount of data generated by human and non-human actors worldwide [6]. However, individuals will also be progressively affected by AI, as it will help humans organize their lives, careers, hobbies, and personal networks and eventually might even help them find the best-suited relatives[7]. With the concept of Design Thinking (DT) having proven to be one of the most used organizational innovation practices in recent years [8], we rely on its foundational principles to discover the key drivers of human-centered use cases based on AI, Blockchain, and IoT.

Vitalik Buterin introduced Decentralized Autonomous Organizations (DAO) as autonomous organizations living upon the Blockchain and fostering "automation at the center and humans at the edge" [9]. In that case, we inquire about a framework for "autonomously run systems" based on AI, IoT, and Blockchain, featuring humans at the center and automation at the edge. By extending the scope of the need for further DT and AI research to AI, Blockchain, and the IoT, we attempt to provide a canvas for resolving the structural complexity of potential AI, Blockchain, and IoT-based solutions to real-world problems. Our research follows the principles of design as aggregated by Lietdka et al. [10] and augmented by Verganti et al. [11]: people-centric, abductive, and iterative.

Our findings contribute to the industry-specific literature [12] and the technological convergence discussion [13] while adding to the understanding of AI in the DT process. From an industry perspective, Sodhi's [12] survey on supply chain managers' user experience with emerging technologies outlines the lack of user-centricity as one of the constraints to broader adoption. The article further encourages research on failure, success factors, and conceptual models with affordances, constraints, and goals. From a technological convergence perspective, Sick et al. [13] call for models highlighting convergence patterns and drivers and exploring the political, societal, and environmental drivers of convergence. Our results add elements to the conversations mentioned above as we offer a design framework for human-centered autonomous systems based on AI, IoT, and Blockchain, and secondly, display the drivers of the technological convergence of Blockchain, AI, and IoT.

## 2   Design Thinking and Technology

### 2.1   Extant Knowledge About Design Thinking and AI

While AI plays a significant and growing role in our societies, our human behavior trains AI and therefore lays the foundations for smart artificial systems to learn from. AI, however, is not only limited in its role to increase levels of efficiency and effectiveness throughout organizations but is also as a key driver of sustainability - by reducing human activities' energy intensity [14]. Ultimately, AI will not only undermine the basic principles of design but also impact design practices by creating instantaneous feedback loops beyond traditional quantity and speed limits [11]. Design Thinking (DT) plays a crucial role in embedding intelligent algorithms into our lives, organizations, and workflow patterns [15]. The DT concept "helps us take a step back and remain open-minded, consider alternative points of view, watch for bias, recognize adjacent possibilities, and innovate" [16]. The Design Thinking method consists of five well-defined key steps, which we will carefully investigate for their suitability with artificial intelligence. The five steps are: Empathize, Define, Ideate, Prototype, and Test [17–20]. In the following section, we will investigate each stage of the DT process and its interplays with AI.

**Empathize.** The initial stage of DT aims at empathizing with a situation by gathering the relevant pieces of information needed afterwards. Empathize stage's activities often involve interviews, surveys, literature research, and open conversations [21]. AI is particularly suited to aggregate, process, categorize and analyze vast amounts of data that can directly or indirectly influence the decision-making processes [22]. Thus, by expanding the set of the Empathize stage using Alternative Data, data richness reach a threshold previously impossible [23]. While AI enables to tap into Alternative Data funnels, such as social media platforms, it can also be used to mine more traditional sites such as blogs, websites, newspapers, and archives [24]. These steadily increasing data pools either require the availability of tremendous human resources or AI-enhanced processing capabilities to streamline and "make sense" of the data [25]. AI can therefore substitute not only the described data gathering and extraction processes but also the storing, classification, codification, and preliminary analysis of the information, saving humans significant time and creative potential, which can be redirected at more promising stages of the DT process [15].

**Define.** While the gathering and collecting of extensive feedback data build the critical foundation for the following stages of the DT process, the resulting organization and categorization of information around the situational needs, problems and expectations is a structurally complex and challenging task [26]. If it is essential during the Empathize stage to gather neutral and non-judgmental feedback to better understand the situation at hand [19], the Define-stage narrows feedback down and classifies feedback segments into appropriate clusters. In that regard, AI is particularly suited to perform tasks such as categorizing and labeling large amounts of data, either by applying inductive or deductive technologies such as neural networks, group method of data handling (GMDH), statistics, inductive production rule generation, genetic algorithms, or case-based reasoning [27]. AI supports humans in distilling the most relevant information from the data pool, defining the problems, and funneling the information into distinguishable, relevant, and concrete artifacts featuring a respective function, behavior, and structure [28]. Once the artifacts have been elaborated, AI can further assist with organizing group encounters, storing the findings safely in cloud architectures. It also has the ability to improve the challenging traditional archival processes, prone to document loss and theft, and preventing the possibility of reassessing and reevaluating years after, meaning that many of the then undiscovered learnings were lost forever [29].

**Ideate.** As the number of ideas gathered plays a major role in the Ideation stage and at least temporarily trumps quality [26], AI is an important toolkit to enhance this step. It is imperative to withhold instant feedback and judgmental comments concerning the quality of ideas and artifacts obtained during the Define stage. Therefore, potential shortcomings of AI-based reasoning and decision-making algorithms [30] play a lesser role than during other stages of the DT process, while human reasoning and abstraction have a greater stake. With a particular emphasis being placed on the novelty aspect of the ideas being generated during this stage [19], AI can further assist by applying specific filters such as date, time, range, region, and topic in addition to real-time statistical analysis on parameters such as keyword/public interest over time or keyword/availability/price of resource over time [31]. However,, AI's most significant potential during the Ideate stage may lay within the controlled use of alternative data. While the information gathered during the Empathize stage and the artifacts established during the Define stage provide excellent training data for AI systems, the algorithm's consistency and reach can significantly contribute to the quantity and diversity of ideas gathered. If, in the traditional process, the quantity and diversity of ideas gathered are bound to the number and background of people involved, AI has the potential to enlarge that pool and bring ideas to the participants that otherwise neither could have been considered nor discussed or evaluated [15]. By supporting an organization to overcome many hurdles within the DT process, such as scalability, and increasing its learning and adaptation capacities in instant feedback loops, AI directly impacts and at least partially solves some of the problems encountered during the Ideation stage of a human-centered DT process [11].

**Prototype.** AI plays a critical role during the final stages of the DT process [15]. The creative processes are streamlined during this stage into actionable prototypes, and ideas become a reality [20]. While the previous ideation phase focuses on the unrestricted generation of a diverse and broad range of ideas and visions, the final stages involve selecting the 'best' or most 'fit' or 'promising' ideas from the ideas pool gathered during the previous stages [21]. This selection is crucial since it might not be possible to build a unique prototype for each idea, hence the human, financial and technological resources will necessarily influence decision-making processes. However, it is essential during this stage to distinguish between digital and virtual prototypes on the one side and physical prototypes on the other [32]. Creating digital and virtual prototypes such as online platforms, can be assisted by AI, which can extract data from massive established databases and interconnect distinct data silos [33]. Therefore, its ability to assist in constructing physical, 'real-world' prototypes is less significant than digital and virtual prototypes. AI can still support the construction of physical prototypes by relying on knowledge-based systems, fuzzy logic, inductive learning, neural networks, and genetic algorithms [34]. Practically, it can support process automation, enhance the functionality, productivity, and consistency of the tools and materials used during the construction phase, help with the decision-making process, and offer 'unbiased' criticism through an iterative feedback loop which can be further augmented by interconnecting smart devices through the Internet of Things [35].

**Test.** The final step of the DT process is directly linked to the previously established artifacts and prototypes [21]. After applying qualitative judgment to define the limiting parameters of the ideas and prototypes,, it is crucial to gather and evaluate critical feedback data as early as possible [20]. Since AI is particularly well suited to gather, organize, categorize, synthesize, and evaluate large amounts of data by user needs and preferences [25], it can notably suport the gathering, accumulation, and evaluation of feedback from the user-tested prototypes [15]. This is particularly pertinent to test virtual and digital prototypes, as AI can assess large pools of users data in real-time and increase the test stage's speed and accuracy. It can be done through statistical methods and by expanding the sample size beyond the limits of a human DT team [31]. With the amount of testing and the quality of the following evaluation methods being crucial to the success of the test stage [36], AI also enables faster feedback loops and (re-)iterations of prototypes established during the previous stage, which contributes to a competitive advantage in the medium to long run [37].

## 2.2   Challenges Deriving from the Technological Convergence Between AI, IoT and Blockchain

The first definition of technological convergence was given by Rosenberg in 1963 [38]. Rosenberg noticed that in preindustrial economies, "skills and techniques tend to be specific and tied down to individual vertical sequence whereas, in industrial economies, similar skills, techniques, and facilities are involved in the production of a wide range of products". Rosenberg refers to this phenomenon of converging techniques within distinct industries as "technological convergence". Later, Adner and Levinthal [39] pictured technological convergence through the example of the CAT scanner, which results from the combination of two disparate technologies: x-ray and computer technology. While these two technologies used to have two different domains of application: x-ray being dedicated to medical imaging and computer technology for data processing, their technological convergence thereby led to the advent of the scanner.

In 2010, Hackin et al. [40] elaborated a model representing the different stages of convergence to uncover the process of inter-industry innovation. The first step, labeled knowledge convergence, leads to associating several technological components, also referred to as technological convergence. Technological convergence then leads to applicational convergence: the integration of previously intersected technologies uniformizing novel applications across industries. The last step of the process is industrial convergence, where disparates industries use a substituent technology base [40]. According to Hacklin et al., the phenomenon of convergence can be seen as the technological change process, which starts with the impetus of knowledge spillovers and results in applied levels of convergence, sometimes even in the merging of several industries.

In the same vein, Schuelke-Leech established a model to understand the magnitude of disruptive technologies [41]. She distinguishes between first-order disruption, which has a localized impact, and second-order disruption, which ripples through society. She also suggests that combining several first-order disruption technologies can lead to second-order disruptions and outlines that AI, Blockchain, and IoT are already first-order disruptions. If Blockchain, IoT, and AI are already mentioned altogether - keyword network analysis [42], literature review [43, 44], industrial perspectives [45] - due to their potential synergies, their integration faced some challenges which eventually led to disappointment [12]. Thus, Sodhi et al. titled "Why emerging supply chain technologies initially disappoint: Blockchain, IoT, and AI?". Building on Gartner's hype cycle [46] and affordance theory [47], they deduct out a quantitative study of the supply chain operations management that expectations were higher than the resulting experience, leading to disillusionment [12]. This might be partly related to the fact that Blockchain technology is an institutional innovation [48], enabling new ways of coordinating economic activities [49] precisely due to its decentralized architecture. As an illustration, the startup LO3 Energy diffuses a unique model of microgrid connecting electricity consumers and producers to trade energy in a decentralized manner and independently from the utility network [50], involving the use of AI, IoT et Blockchain. The prototype led to further replicating such systems in different regions (US, Europe, Asia) and enabled autonomous communities of electricity prosumers and consumers to exchange electricity daily. As reasoning through the lens of decentralization is undoubtedly one of the most significant adoption challenges, appropriate frameworks could support this shift.

In 2014, Vitalik Buterin, the visionary brain behind the Ethereum Blockchain, introduced the concept of Decentralized Autonomous Organization (DAO) [9]. Buterin pictured a DAO as an organization in which humans are at the edge and technologies at the center, as opposed to traditional organizations which feature technologies at the edge and humans at the center [9]. As inspired by the case of LO3 [50], we suggest that there could exist a concept of autonomously run systems based on AI, Blockchain, and IoT, featuring humans at the center and automation at the edge. The disillusions at the operational management level [12], compared with the hype's phase over-expectations [42], emphasize the need to research this phenomenon further. That is why our study aims at uncovering the intertwined effects of AI, BL, and IoT on each other; the strategic drivers of such technological integration, and providing framework to support the ideation of human-centered autonomous systems based on AI, IoT, and Blockchain.

## 3   Methodology

To enhance our understanding beyond our rigorous literature review and given the newness of our topic and its relative complexity, we employed an exploratory perspective, aimed at outilining preliminary hypotheses and new ideas [51]. We conducted forty expert interviews within two different yet related industries: the automotive and the supply chain. The interviews aimed at uncovering the usage, challenges, pain points, and success drivers of using AI, Blockchain, and IoT altogether. Our interview guidelines followed design thinking principles in that they are people-centric, abductive, and iterative [10, 11].

Hence, we exchanged with users directly involved with one of these three technologies from various perspectives, such as entrepreneurs, consultants, institutional, engineers, and investors. Additionally, we did not present them with a set of pre-established perspectives but instead favored open discussions on their pain points and challenges when it comes to using these technologies. Lastly, we adopted an iterative process in the sense that we were first suggesting an independent usage of these three technologies and, in a second step, ignited reflection upon the three technologies altogether, which often provoked iterations of the previously mentioned use cases with the technological add-on. Also, since we used the Gioia methodology [52] for our data analysis, we paid particular attention to giving voice to the interviewees and adjusting our interview protocol based on their answers. For example, we interviewed an entrepreneur who used to work on a project involving IoT, AI, and Blockchain, which failed. We encouraged him to explain the story of his entrepreneurial venture and the reasons for its failure.

Regarding data collection, potential participants of the interviews were contacted according to their expertise in one of the three technologies and one of the industries concerned. The data was collected with the interviewees' consent. The audio recordings were anonymously transcribed, and some transcripts were submitted to the interviewees for final checking. The interviews were conducted both in German and English. The German interviews were subsequently transcribed into English to allow for a unified and cohesive coding system. The audio recordings were then deleted. For data analysis, we used the Gioia methodology, which is an inductive qualitative approach. As an example, for the framework displaying the drivers of AI with Blockchain, and IoT, we coded 314 first-order themes centered on the interviewees, which we then transformed into over 60 s-order theory-centric themes that were afterward aggregated into 30 dimensions and clustered into four axes. Concerning software, we used Trint to facilitate the transcription process and coded the interviews with MaxQDA.

## 4   Results

We will first display the positive and negative influences of AI, Blockchain, and IoT, we will then provide a design framework for the ideation of autonomous systems, and lastly, we will highlight the drivers of the design thinking process when it comes to design AI, IoT, and Blockchain-based autonomous systems.

### 4.1   Positive and Negative Influences of AI, Blockchain, and IoT

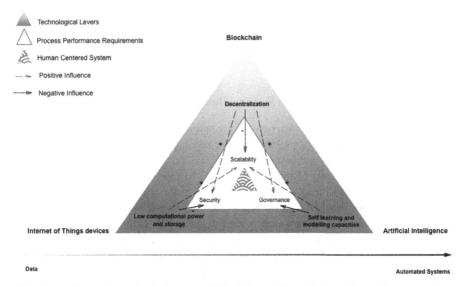

**Fig. 1.** Positive and negative influences of Blockchain, AI, and IoT, Authors' own conception

If scalability is usually blamed as one of the biggest hurdles to Blockchain adoption [53], concrete solutions such as Lighting networks, second layer applications, and tailor-made Blockchain solutions such as the IOTA ecosystems were mentioned as tentatively resolving this issue. One interviewee even qualified scalability as a "growth factor" in a sense that it spurs technological advancement. As Fig. 1 displays, several interviewees noted that IoT devices' low computational power and storage capacity would compensate for the need for scalability and positively influence the system's efficiency, making IoT devices particularly suitable for Blockchain architectures. To a lesser extent, the self-learning et modeling capabilities of AI agents would enable the optimization of the autonomous system to decrease its scalability needs. On the other hand, networks of IoT devices are often under the scrutiny of cyber hackers since their core characteristics, low computational power and storage capacity, make them vulnerable to attacks. Also, a data breach within a single device can lead to a generalized network attack. Conversely, Bitcoin, the first occurrence of Blockchain technology, due to its decentralized architecture and consensus mechanism, would require a coordinated attack of 51% of the network to be hacked [54]. Solutions such as Fog computing enable the distribution of computational power and the storage of "the data not in a centralized silo which might be prone to hacking attacks". Hence, several interviewees mentioned that the decentralized architecture of Blockchain technology could provide a "secure identity management for the IoT devices so they can be somewhat autonomous". Lastly, Blockchain's characteristics engender several specificities: it is by nature transparent and immutable. While AI experiences governance-related issues, such as opacity and arbitrary decision-making, Blockchain can be leveraged as a governance mechanism. Thus, Blockchain integration prevents data manipulation and "informs data integrity to some extent, which is also vital for AI". Another participant stated that IoT devices and AI agents need "a way of being governed". Conversely, if transparency is a significant driver of Blockchain technology's usage, it might become a problem regarding data privacy. Participants mentioned several solutions, such as the mix of off-chain and on-chain storage, hence "storing the data centrally and encrypting it with ashes on the Blockchain", or employing AI, offering "solutions to privacy via federated machine learning".

## 4.2  Frameword for Autonomous Systems Based on AI, Blockchain, and IoT

We derived from Fig. 1 a design framework for autonomous systems featuring humans at the center and technologies at the edge while enabling advanced value gained through automation. The labeling "autonomous system" is consistent with the results of our interviews. As stated by one of the interviewees: "to run an autonomous system or a remote system, we need the combination of those technologies coming together". If we keep separate, for now, "the world of humans and the world of automated things", the disintermediation of these two worlds would lead to "a Cambrian explosion of new business models, new revenue structures, and new ways of humans working alongside robots in society". However, nailing down a business model for such an automated system is not a trivial task. That is likely why "if the company is seeking to use technology to address a problem framed within the current business model [...] the project will fail". Therefore, the system's technological components are influencing the model and the business model to be explored "requires a more decentralized approach to things" as specified by another participant.

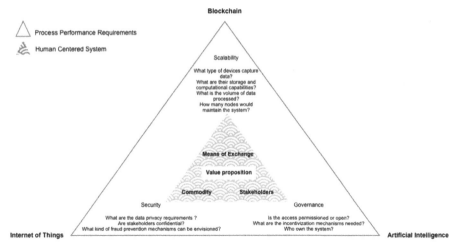

**Fig. 2.** Framework for autonomous systems based on AI, IoT, and Blockchain, Authors' own conception

We highlighted in Fig. 2 the main characteristics to consider when ideating an autonomous system based on AI, Blockchain, and IoT. As displayed on the framework, governance and scalability were the key design features tackled by the participants. On the governance dimension, one participant pinpointed the most important questions to study: "What are the rules for incumbents to exit if they want? And what are the rules relating to data permissions and data governance?". In contrast, another participant emphasized the importance of distinguishing between different data types to make the data available only to "authorized, relevant recipients". Regarding scalability features, one of the participants mentioned that it depends upon the "number of participants or performance or volumes of data or throughput". He then added that the careful selection of the technological architecture or technology enables to bypass scalability issues. Also, as specified by one of the participants, when using Blockchain, "there is a certain trade-off between capacity, electricity costs and security". The more decentralized the architecture is, the more secure the network is, but this comes along with lower scalability. This exhorts the necessity to pre-define the minimal requirements in terms of security to adjust the overall system design.

### 4.3 Drivers of the Design Thinking Process for AI, IoT, and Blockchain Based Autonomous Systems

Lastly, based on our interviewees, we built a model displaying the drivers of the DT process when it comes to designing autonomous systems based on AI, Blockchain, and IoT. Thus, as displayed in the figure below, particular attention must be given to the industrial and organizational requirements in the Empathize and define stages. Then, the ideation and prototyping steps must ensure that the drivers' performance requirements are met. Finally, much caution should be given to the output drivers during the testing phase.

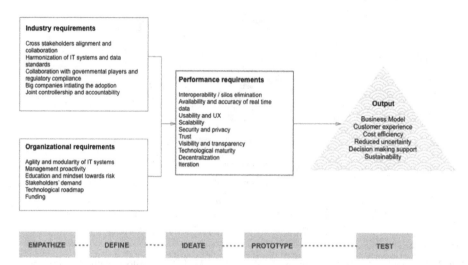

**Fig. 3.** Drivers of the design thinking process for AI, IoT, and Blockchain-based autonomous systems, Authors' own conception.

For the empathize and define stages, the industrial and organizational clusters need to be considered. From an industry perspective, the most emphasized driver across interviews is the necessity for stakeholders to collaborate "to build consensus amongst a varied group of individuals and cultures and companies with their own goals and missions". The "stakeholders' alignment" process requires agreement on data sharing and technical standards. This cooperation might be facilitated with the standardization of data formats and IT. Thirdly, the industry's big players are generally seen as powerful innovation drivers since they have the capabilities, are embedded in a continuous innovation process, and are thus quite often at the forefront of emerging technologies. A few participants mentioned the concept of joint controllership, "a Blockchain that is not operated publicly, like Bitcoin, but in a consortium where companies each operate a node". Such Joint controllership, in which stakeholders take joint responsibility for the database, might comply with GDPR. Concerning regulation, it is seen as an enabler when it imposes constraints on companies that must be met with digitization or pull out regulatory incentivization and limitations regarding compliance. Lastly, some interviewees emphasized the pioneering roles of institutions due to the inherent characteristics of autonomous systems and advocated for the need for "neutral parties to bring these people together". From an organizational perspective, the interviewees emphasized the need for an "IT environment that is agile" and "modular", which eventually needs to be built from scratch according to the features of the autonomous system. In terms of management, there needs to be a genuine willingness to integrate these technologies and involve, educate, and train the employees. This goes hand in hand with a "cooperative IT department supporting" the project and the organization's stakeholders and a "technological roadmap". Also, among the mentioned drivers, customers' and contractors' demands were considered to have immense potential. Lastly, the funding capacity of the organization is an important factor since the creation of the IT environment might be from a greenfield.

During the ideation and prototyping stage, the focus should be on the performance requirements to ensure that potential prototypes are appropriate. In terms of performance requirements, interviewees outlined the need to "eliminate data silos" and favor interoperability amid various IT systems, as well as the availability of real-time data. Since usability is the biggest blame addressed to the three technologies, particularly Blockchain, it is of utmost importance to create user-friendly autonomous systems. Security, privacy, and trust were also mentioned as drivers of the implementation of AI, Blockchain, and IoT. Visibility and transparency are also considered drivers, particularly since most of the use cases discussed during the interviews were traceability driven. In the same vein, decentralization is considered a driving factor, enabling the emergence of autonomous systems. Lastly, several interviewees emphasized the need for iteration and agility within the process. As one of them spelled out, "you need to be able to adapt quickly and to listen fast". Particularly given the fast technological evolution pace.

Lastly, during the DT testing stage, attention shall be driven toward the output drivers. It does not mean that the final autonomous system must include all these drivers but making sure that at least one of them is significant. Participants enforced that having a sustainable business model is an absolute must. They also underlined the need for an outstanding customer experience to spur adoption. Also, if the autonomous system is aimed at enforcing collaboration among stakeholders, expected output could be cost efficiency, and reduced uncertainty (time and error reduction, prediction, fraud detection). Autonomous systems might also be used to provide "state-of-the-art decision support tools for operators, enabling them to maximize their operational efficiency while at the same time having an effective continuous improvement process". Finally, sustainability has also been mentioned as a potential driver for the implementation of Blockchain, AI, and IoT, which is consistent with our introductory example: the case of LO3 energy. Indeed "the new climate emergency" situation requires extremely efficient systems which could be fostered by AI, Blockchain, and IoT.

## 5   Discussion

We will, in the first step, discuss the impact of Blockchain, ai and IoT, and DT, then display our study's limitations and potential avenues for further exploration. Lastly, we'll address the practical implications, both from a regulatory and an entrepreneurial perspective.

If we acknowledge that AI particularly influences the DT process and that there are various success drivers to take into account during the DT stages when it comes to Blockchain, AI, and IoT, there seems to be also room for AI, Blockchain, and IoT as strong supporters for DT. Security is a critical aspect of various stages of the DT process. While during the early stages of DT (Empathize, Ideate), it is particularly important to gather and evaluate information in an anonymized way to protect the privacy of the interviewees, it is equally important to store the information in a secure manner so that not only the privacy of individuals but also the data itself is protected from competitors and data leakage [55]. As the implementation of AI, IoT, and Blockchain systems within a pre-existing organizational IT infrastructure often comes with security and privacy challenges [56], trust becomes a critical concern for all stakeholders involved in the process. In the case of the DT process, this means that due to its decentralized architecture, the convergence of AI, Blockchain, and IoT can play a significant role in mitigating trust-related concerns that might arise not only among DT team members during the entire process but also between interviewers and interviewees, especially during the Empathize and Test stages [57]. Lastly, while most organizations and particularly start-ups that employ DT to enhance their innovation processes, strive for scalability, it remains a difficult hurdle to overcome [58]. The critical phase between the final stages of the DT process (Ideate, Prototype, Test) and wider success in national and international markets cannot only be enhanced by successful employment of the DT concept but also by exploiting the efficiencies created by the convergence.

## 5.1 Limitations

Even though we carefully applied the principles of design thinking, as outlined by Liedtka [10] and Vergantini [11], we do think that there is a lot of potential in experimenting with the whole DT process to create an AI, Blockchain, and IoT based autonomous system. Also, we do think that interactions among our interviewees and greater collaboration would have fostered participants' creativity and magnified our findings. Despite our effort to have a diverse sample of participants, most of the interviewees were men. Therefore, we advocate reducing gender bias for further research. Finally, as pointed out by one of the interviewees, having an in-depth knowledge of one of these three technologies is admirable, but having expertise in the three technologies seems barely doable. Thus, we sometimes faced interviewees' incertitude and limited ability to answer when it comes to the combination of the technologies. At the convergence level, this article draws insights into the DT process' drivers fostering the successful implementation of Blockchain, AI, and IoT, but these findings can't be extended to alternative emerging technologies. Further research could attempt to explore a different subset of technologies to compare our findings. Lastly, our findings resonate with the supply chain and automotive industries. Additional research could explore the drivers within different industries, especially the ones that are at the forefront of innovation, such as the financial sector.

## 5.2 Avenues for Further Research

Direct follow-up research would be to confirm or infirm the influences between the three technologies highlighted in Fig. 1 with larger sample size and eventually a different research design. Thus, the influences tentatively highlighted in the first figure can be used as initial hypotheses for quantitative research. Also, based on Fig. 2 and Fig. 3, further research could employ Design Science Research Methods to create a real-world solution [59, 60]. The same logic can be undertaken with an Action Research perspective [61], as an example, by taking part in an organization's innovation process to leverage these technologies. Finally, further research could employ Delphi methods, which are often used for forecasting purposes. Delphi enables "the identification and prioritization of issues for managerial decision-making" [62] out of a several-round expert surveying process. Besides that, since the existence of business cases was a central concern of our experts, it might be worth inquiring about the potential cost-efficient business models for autonomously run systems. Indeed, open-source economic models [63] and circular business models [64]. On another dimension, one of the participants explained an entrepreneurial attempt that occurred to fail. As already voiced out by Sodhi et al. [12], further research could gain insights on already existing failing cases, eventually through a multiple case study research design.

### 5.3  Implications

From a regulatory perspective, first and foremost, regulators need to have a good understanding of emerging technologies. On the other hand, organizations willing to employ and design such frameworks need to build them in an adequation with regulations. As an example, the European GDPR features the right to be forgotten for personal data. This might imply that at the customer's request, personal data stored shall be erased. If this is not possible to erase a data entry from the Blockchain, it is possible to adapt the technological design. Hence, one of the interviewees suggested storing data in different ways, referencing the Blockchain while storing sensitive information locally. Hence, through the transaction reference, the identity of the query can be verified, and if the access is authorized, redirect to the personal data stored on a local server. As one of the interviewees further points out: "this is not a question of technology, but a question of technology design". While entrepreneurs entering that space could face potential hurdles due to the technological complexity, regulatory voids, and lack of resources, following a lean process would be particularly beneficial. Hence, agility is a necessity since "the technology's progressing at a certain rate, and if you're not able to adopt that change very quickly and iterate with the customers or end-stakeholders, you will not be able to do anything". The one entrepreneur who initiated a venture within that field and which failed afterward confessed that they were sustainable, making revenues selling "Proof-of-Concept" to companies but did not manage to convince them to use their product. As they could not find any "sustainability" in their business model, they decided to wind down. Reasons invoked for that failure were wrong timing, "too early", and not enough funding, as well as "not doing the convergence in the first place", since they integrated AI to their product only in a second step.

## 6  Conclusion

As our study has shown, due to the interwoven specificities of AI, Blockchain, and IoT, autonomous systems based on these technologies must be designed thoughtfully, especially for the governance, scalability, and security aspects. We also noticed that specific drivers need to be considered along the design thinking process. Thus, Empathize and define steps should rely on organizational and industrial drivers, while the ideation-prototyping phases should pay attention to the Performance requirements drivers. Lastly, the testing stage should pay particular attention to output drivers. Also, there is a reciprocity between technology and DT; on the one hand, technology such as AI heavily impacts and enhances the DT process, while we also relied on DT principles to investigate the undergoing convergence of AI, IoT, and Blockchain. Each of the five DT stages bears the different potential to be impacted by AI: data collection for empathizing stage, data analysis for the define stage, artifacts building in the ideation stage, assisting the prototyping in the prototyping phase, and classifying, and evaluating feedback with real-time data during the last step. If AI, therefore, has the potential to expand DT far beyond human limitations, the addition of Blockchain and IoT would have a greater impact on DT since it would reinforce the security and the trust of the DT process.

# References

1. Braganza, A., et al.: Productive employment and decent work: the impact of AI adoption on psychological contracts, job engagement and employee trust. J. Bus. Res. **131**, 485–494 (2021)
2. Csaszar, F., Steinberger, T.: Organizations as artificial intelligences: the use of artificial intelligence analogies in organization theory. Acad. Manag. Ann. **16**, 1–37 (2021)
3. George, G., Merrill, R.K., Schillebeeckx, S.J.D.: Digital sustainability and entrepreneurship: how digital innovations are helping tackle climate change and sustainable development. Entrep. Theory Pract. **45**(5), 999–1027 (2021)
4. Alvarez, S.A., et al.: Developing a theory of the firm for the 21st century. Acad. Manag. Rev. **45**(4), 711–716 (2020)
5. Nambisan, S., Wright, M., Feldman, M.: The digital transformation of innovation and entrepreneurship: Progress, challenges and key themes. Res. Policy **48**(8), 103773 (2019)
6. Hilb, M.: Toward artificial governance? The role of artificial intelligence in shaping the future of corporate governance. J. Manag. Gov. **24**(4), 851–870 (2020). https://doi.org/10.1007/s10 997-020-09519-9
7. Misselhorn, C.: Artificial systems with moral capacities? A research design and its implementation in a geriatric care system. Artif. Intell. **278**, 103179 (2020)
8. Dell'Era, C., et al.: Four kinds of design thinking: from ideating to making, engaging, and criticizing. Creat. Innov. Manag. **29**(2), 324–344 (2020)
9. Buterin, V.. A next-generation smart contract and decentralized application platform. White Paper 3.37, p. 2-1 (2014)
10. Liedtka, J.: Perspective: Linking design thinking with innovation outcomes through cognitive bias reduction. J. Prod. Innov. Manag. **32**(6), 925–938 (2015)
11. Verganti, R., Vendraminelli, L., Iansiti, M.: Innovation and design in the age of artificial intelligence. J. Prod. Innov. Manag. **37**(3), 212–227 (2020)
12. Sodhi, M.M.S., et al.: Why emerging supply chain technologies initially disappoint: Blockchain, IoT, and AI. Prod. Oper. Manag. (2022)
13. Sick, N., Bröring, S.: Exploring the research landscape of convergence from a TIM perspective: a review and research agenda. Technol. Forecast. Soc. Chang. **175**, 121321 (2021)
14. Nishant, R., Kennedy, M., Corbett, J.: Artificial intelligence for sustainability: challenges, opportunities, and a research agenda. Int. J. Inf. Manag. **53**, 102104 (2020)
15. Cautela, C., et al.: The impact of artificial intelligence on design thinking practice: insights from the ecosystem of startups. Strat. Des. Res. J. **12**(1), 114–134 (2019)
16. Weller, A.J.: Design Thinking for a user-centered approach to artificial intelligence. She Ji J. Des. Econ. Innov. **5**(4), 394–396 (2019)
17. Buchanan, R.: Wicked problems in design thinking. Des. Issues **8**(2), 5–21 (1992)
18. Dorst, K.: The core of 'design thinking' and its application. Des. Stud. **32**(6), 521–532 (2011)
19. Kimbell, L.: Rethinking design thinking: Part I. Des. Cult. **3**(3), 285–306 (2011)

20. Razzouk, R., Shute, V.: What is design thinking and why is it important? Rev. Educ. Res. **82**(3), 330–348 (2012)
21. Brown, T.: Design thinking. Harv. Bus. Rev. **86**(6), 84 (2008)
22. Novak, A., Bennett, D., Kliestik, T.: Product decision-making information systems, real-time sensor networks, and artificial intelligence-driven big data analytics in sustainable Industry 4.0. Econ. Manag. Financ. Mark. **16**(2), 62–72 (2021)
23. Erhard, L., McBride, B., Safir, A.: A framework for the evaluation and use of alternative data in the consumer expenditure surveys. Mon. Lab. Rev. **144**, 1 (2021)
24. Hansen, K.B., Borch, C.: Alternative data and sentiment analysis: prospecting non-standard data in machine learning-driven finance. Big Data Soc. **9**(1), 20539517211070700 (2022)
25. Duan, Y., Edwards, J.S., Dwivedi, Y.K.: Artificial intelligence for decision making in the era of Big Data–evolution, challenges and research agenda. Int. J. Inf. Manag. **48**, 63–71 (2019)
26. Brenner, W., Uebernickel, F., Abrell, T.: Design thinking as mindset, process, and toolbox. In: Brenner, W., Uebernickel, F. (eds.) Design Thinking for Innovation, pp. 3–21. Springer, Cham (2016). https://doi.org/10.1007/978-3-319-26100-3_1
27. Nemati, H.R., et al.: Knowledge warehouse: an architectural integration of knowledge management, decision support, artificial intelligence and data warehousing. Decis. Support Syst. **33**(2), 143–161 (2002)
28. Kannengiesser, U., Gero, J.S.: Design thinking, fast and slow: a framework for Kahneman's dual-system theory in design. Des. Sci. **5** (2019)
29. Rolan, G., et al.: More human than human? Artificial intelligence in the archive. Arch. Manuscr. **47**(2), 179–203 (2019)
30. Trunk, A., Birkel, H., Hartmann, E.: On the current state of combining human and artificial intelligence for strategic organizational decision making. Bus. Res. **13**(3), 875–919 (2020). https://doi.org/10.1007/s40685-020-00133-x
31. Nagorny, K., et al.: Big data analysis in smart manufacturing: a review. Int. J. Commun. Netw. Syst. Sci. **10**(3), 31–58 (2017)
32. Ahmed, B., Dannhauser, T., Philip, N.; A lean design thinking methodology (LDTM) for machine learning and modern data projects. In: 2018 10th Computer Science and Electronic Engineering (CEEC). IEEE (2018)
33. Garrido, A.L., Sangiao, S., Cardiel, O.: Improving the generation of infoboxes from data silos through machine learning and the use of semantic repositories. Int. J. Artif. Intell. Tools **26**(05), 1760022 (2017)
34. Pham, D.T., Pham, P.T.N.: Artificial intelligence in engineering. Int. J. Mach. Tools Manuf **39**(6), 937–949 (1999)
35. Javaid, M., et al.: Artificial intelligence applications for Industry 4.0: a literature-based study. J. Ind. Integr. Manag. **7**(01), 83–111 (2022)
36. Micheli, P., et al.: Doing design thinking: conceptual review, synthesis, and research agenda. J. Prod. Innov. Manag. **36**(2), 124–148 (2019)
37. Cousins, B.: Design thinking: organizational learning in VUCA environments. Acad. Strateg. Manag. J. **17**(2), 1–18 (2018)
38. Rosenberg, N.: Technological change in the machine tool industry, 1840–1910. J. Econ. Hist. **23**(4), 414–443 (1963)
39. Adner, R., Levinthal, D.A.: The emergence of emerging technologies. Calif. Mana. Rev. **45**(1), 50–66 (2002)
40. Hacklin, F., Marxt, C., Fahrni, F.: An evolutionary perspective on convergence: inducing a stage model of inter-industry innovation. Int. J. Technol. Manag. **49**(1–3), 220–249 (2010)
41. Schuelke-Leech, B.-A.: A model for understanding the orders of magnitude of disruptive technologies. Technol. Forecast. Soc. Chang. **129**, 261–274 (2018)
42. Centobelli, P., et al.: Surfing Blockchain wave, or drowning? Shaping the future of distributed ledgers and decentralized technologies. Technol. Forecast. Soc. Chang. **165**, 120463 (2021)

43. Parker, B., Bach, C.: The synthesis of Blockchain, artificial intelligence and internet of things. Eur. J. Eng. Technol. Res. **5**(5), 588–593 (2020)
44. Montes, G.A., Goertzel, B.: Distributed, decentralized, and democratized artificial intelligence. Technol. Forecast. Soc. Chang. **141**, 354–358 (2019)
45. Singh, S.K., Rathore, S., Park, J.H.: Blockiotintelligence: a Blockchain-enabled intelligent IoT architecture with artificial intelligence. Future Gener. Comput. Syst. **110**, 721–743 (2020)
46. Dedehayir, O., Steinert, M.: The hype cycle model: a review and future directions. Technol. Forecast. Soc. Chang. **108**, 28–41 (2016)
47. Leonardi, P.M.: When flexible routines meet flexible technologies: affordance, constraint, and the imbrication of human and material agencies. MIS Q. **35**, 147–167 (2011)
48. Davidson, S., De Filippi, P., Potts, J.: Blockchains and the economic institutions of capitalism. J. Inst. Econ. **14**(4), 639–658 (2018)
49. Lumineau, F., Wang, W., Schilke, O.: Blockchain governance—a new way of organizing collaborations? Organ. Sci. **32**(2), 500–521 (2021)
50. Lacity, M.C.: Addressing key challenges to making enterprise Blockchain applications a reality. MIS Q. Exec. **17**(3), 201–222 (2018)
51. Swedberg, R.: Exploratory research. In: The Production of Knowledge: Enhancing Progress in Social Science, pp. 17–41 (2020)
52. Gioia, D.A., Corley, K.G., Hamilton, A.L.: Seeking qualitative rigor in inductive research: notes on the Gioia methodology. Organ. Res. Methods **16**(1), 15–31 (2013)
53. Sanka, A.I., Cheung, R.C.C.: A systematic review of Blockchain scalability: issues, solutions, analysis and future research. J. Netw. Comput. Appl. **195**, 103232 (2021)
54. Nakamoto, S.: Bitcoin: a peer-to-peer electronic cash system. Decent. Bus. Rev., 21260 (2008)
55. Hajli, N., et al.: Towards an understanding of privacy management architecture in big data: an experimental research. Br. J. Manag. **32**(2), 548–565 (2021)
56. Mohanta, B.K., et al.: Survey on IoT security: challenges and solution using machine learning, artificial intelligence and Blockchain technology. Internet Things **11**, 100227 (2020)
57. Hussain, A.A., Al-Turjman, F.: Artificial intelligence and Blockchain: a review. Trans. Emerg. Telecommun. Technol. **32**(9), e4268 (2021)
58. Sanz, J.L.C., Zhu, Y.: Toward scalable artificial intelligence in finance. In: 2021 IEEE International Conference on Services Computing (SCC). IEEE (2021)
59. Pfeffers, K., et al.: The design science research process: a model for producing and presenting information systems research. In: Proceedings of the First International Conference on Design Science Research in Information Systems and Technology (DESRIST 2006), Claremont, CA, USA (2006)
60. Dresch, A., Lacerda, D.P., Antunes, J.A.V.: Design science research. In: Dresch, A., Lacerda, D.P., Antunes, J.A.V. (eds.) Design science research, pp. 67–102. Springer, Cham (2015). https://doi.org/10.1007/978-3-319-07374-3_4
61. Avison, D.E., et al.: Action research. Commun. ACM **42**(1), 94–97 (1999)
62. Okoli, C., Pawlowski, S.D.: The Delphi method as a research tool: an example, design considerations and applications. Inf. Manag. **42**(1), 15–29 (2004)
63. Lerner, J., Tirole, J.: Some simple economics of open source. J. Ind. Econ. **50**(2), 197–234 (2002)
64. Lüdeke-Freund, F., Gold, S., Bocken, N.M.P.: A review and typology of circular economy business model patterns. J. Ind. Ecol. **23**(1), 36–61 (2019)

# Rethinking Mobile Interaction Design Within Service

Zhen Xiao[1] and Baisong Liu[2(✉)]

[1] Zhejiang Normal University, Zhejiang, China
[2] Eindhoven University of Technology, Eindhoven, The Netherlands
b.liu2@tue.nl

**Abstract.** Along with the explosion of mobile access across the globe, service experience has evolved. Now there is a myriad of service settings in which mobile interactive artifacts are used in providing service, ranging from express, shopping to healthcare, and more. Those interactive products in service consequently not only enable to interact with users but also aim to offer high-quality service. In this paper, we find mobile interaction design evolved by taking advantage of service design. To better understand the difference and competence of mobile applications within service, we compare the independence tool mobile applications and the service embedded mobile applications in four paradigms: communication actors, design objective, value, process. There is an obvious feature that from "linear analysis" to "open system analysis". Then summarizing the benefits of rethinking from a service perspective: sequence thinking of content rhythm; a holistic lens in solving the problem; multi-role stakeholders' co-creation. Based on service measuring methods, we deduce the evaluation dimensions content of service embedded mobile applications. Finally, To validate the evaluation scheme, we conducted a pilot study in mobile courier applications by collecting and classifying service functions to propose mobile courier applications design constraints from service dimension view. In this way, we try to give a contribution to the development of service-embedded mobile interaction design.

**Keywords:** Interaction design · Mobile application · Service-embedded application

## 1 Introduction

With the advent of the mobile Internet, mobile applications are increasingly affecting the lives of people. Users can access the Internet via mobile devices anytime, anywhere to enjoy a variety of products and services. Because of the applications of mobile devices, a lot of traditional services have enabled consumers to enjoy split-new service experiences, which refers to unlimited infinite channels of information exchanging flow, more efficient dissemination of information as well as reconstruction of the way of disseminating service information. So the widespread use of mobile devices - particularly smartphones - accelerates the transformation of the traditional service to a new model - "software integrate hardware plus APP" [1].

© The Author(s), under exclusive license to Springer Nature Switzerland AG 2022
M. Kurosu et al. (Eds.): HCII 2022, LNCS 13516, pp. 163–174, 2022.
https://doi.org/10.1007/978-3-031-17615-9_11

In this particular situation, mobile internet acts as both an interactive platform and a service-enabling infrastructure, whilst the mobile platform is raised be an important medium constructing the whole service system. Owing to it is mobile features, it plays an indispensable role in information flow and financial flow and connecting users (service receivers), managers (service providers), and other products no matter when and where among this new model service system to deliver a higher quality service. Under such a background, the mobile application has been embodied both interaction and service characters.

Yet the service features of mobile applications have not been given enough attention and the adoption of service design concepts and methods in HCI has been sporadic over the past decade [2]. When it comes to mobile interaction, it is generally designed from the interface details or human-machine interactions perspective, therefore lacking comprehensive concern about following the overall service objectives and values, making the mobile application aligned and assimilated into the service system.

This paper has focused on the interaction design of mobile applications in a service system that may include physical hardware and digital software services, as a subject for which the implementation and outcome would depend significantly on what kind of quality of service the managers and users desire. This article starts from the evolution of mobile interaction design, following the comparison between an independent tool and a service embedded mobile application, with paradigmatic concerns on the subjects such as communicating actors, design objective, value and process are brought into the system. Then choosing the mobile courier applications as a pilot to explore the mobile interaction design constraints from a service evaluation perspective, which considering the mobile application as one of the touchpoints in the express service system, shedding the light on the detailed interaction design suggestions from the holistic service quality requirements in the system.

## 2 Mobile Interaction Design Within Service

### 2.1 Mobile Interaction Design

In recent years mobiles became an integrated part of life for billions of users. It is vastly believed that wireless devices will help us to communicate and relate in better ways, be more creative, more informed, and more efficient and effective in our working lives. Under this circumstance, we have to cater to the everyday needs people have, shifting the design perspective away from technology and concentrating on usability; in other words, developing interfaces and devices with a great deal of sensitivity to human needs, desires, and capabilities [3]. Designers attach more importance to user aspects.

Most modern, mobile devices employ touch screens, which provide their own set of opportunities and constraints. We use them not only to view content but also to interact with that content. These forces designers to consider ergonomics, gestures, transitions, and finally, mobile-specific interaction patterns (Main navigation, Selecting content, Signing in, Using forms) [4]. When it comes to the concrete mobile interaction design, those implementation points are generally oriented by some specific interface features.

## 2.2 Mobile Interaction Design Within Service

Interactive artifacts are being introduced into service settings to a larger degree than before. We tend to rely on these artifacts as one, or sometimes the sole, possibility to do banking, to declare our taxes, etc. [5]. This interaction paradigm uses a mobile device to extract information and use it to more intuitively and easily invoke the associated service. A common approach to mobile and service interaction is primarily through smartphones, where applications act as intermediaries between interactive agents and different physical objects [6]. Not only can we treat the application as an interactive product, but also consider it as a digital touchpoint among the service system. UX work is changing, and understanding this change is important to maintain the relevance of UX research [7].

Jodi Forlizzi and John Zimmerman, two professors from Carnegie Mellon's HCI Institute and School of Design, state a pioneer exploration to promote service design as a core practice in interaction design. They point out that interaction designers who employ user experience and user-centered design practices most often work to specify the behavior of a single computer system, whereas service designers work to envision a multi-stakeholders service system, starting with an explorative phase that includes fieldwork, competitive analysis, log analysis, etc. They give examples of interaction design that benefit from a service perspective. One mobile application, called Flip-board, creating a magazine-like reading experience was instanced. With Flipboard, end-users co-produce value with the social networks, and service design thinking helps interaction designers to understand the exchanged role and value amongst the stakeholders (content providers, advertisers) to drive co-production [8]. Daisy et al. [9] address that in a shift to the service-centric design paradigm, it is important to recognize design researchers as distinct stakeholders, who actively interact with systems and services intending to fulfill their values and achieve desired outcomes. By a case study of new digital services for public libraries, they provide an extended value co-creation model that clarifies the position of design researchers within the sociocultural context in which they practice design and visualize how their positions impact the value co-creation, and in turn, the design outcome.

## 3 Comparison Between an Independent Tool and a Service Embedded Mobile Application

To differentiate and understand the characters and competence of service-embedded mobile applications from the independent tool type, we compared the two kinds of mobile applications in four paradigms: communication actors, design objective, design value as well as design process (Table 1).

**Table 1.** Four subjects as compared

| Subjects | The independent tool app | The service embedded app |
| --- | --- | --- |
| Communication actors | Target users | Target users (service receivers), managers, staff (service providers), hardware products, software platforms |
| Design objective | To achieve specific functions for meeting target needs | To provide quality services for collaborative services with other touchpoints in a system) |
| Design value | User-centered | User-centered, social value |
| Design process | Linear | Multi-factors |

- Communication Actors

When designing the app as a mini tool in our smartphone, we tend to concentrate or immerse in our target users. Because the app mainly communicates with the target users who have the dominant access and right to experience and evaluate.

While considering the app in a service system, this app is in touch with multi-stakeholder, which relate to target users (service receivers), managers (back-stage), staff (service providers) as well as other service modes which contain physical hardware products and digital software platforms.

- Design Objective

In terms to design an independent tool type application, designers are prone to implement specific functions by acquiring and researching the needs of target users. For example, the weather application is for offering information on the weather forecast during the day or the week.

On the other hand, the service embedded application is for providing quality services - collaborative services - that design specialists for helping develop and deliver great services, regarding coordinate with another physical or digital touchpoint in a system, which forms a harmonious convergence of services. The courier application is a typical example to provide an express service. In the whole express service, the courier application plays a continuous role in supporting express service with the self-service terminal machine in front-stage and the express management system back-stage.. It is not only used by consumers but rather acting as an information posting platform serving for couriers and managers. It is also an interactive platform between the consumers and couriers, and communicating with other terminal machines by information timely sharing.

- Design value

In designing an independent tool type application, user-centered design thinking leads the design orientation and value-creating by observing, interviewing, and responding to the users in their subtle using behaviors and desires. Like using the calendar applications, the user habits - when most users use it? What do users want and do when using it? Why do they use it? etc. - all oriented by target users.

Nevertheless, the service-embedded application design needs to take consideration of use, satisfaction, loyalty about users and sustainability, transformation, profit about a society that is a perspective from service design [10]. For instance, the banking services applications, a time-saving way to transfer, check or record for users with transparent and timely information service, at the same time, also an effective approach to improving capital circulation, labor savings, or cutting costs for society and companies. It helps promote the upgrade of the traditional banking service model.

- Design process

The design process of independent tool mobile applications is linear, starting from finding users' needs then defining mobile application functions, after that setting the application architecture, and finally drawing the interface. It is quite a tool target-oriented with focusing on the target users.

For example, mobile dictionary applications are focusing on those who want to know, learn or use foreign languages. Designers have to know the various subtle needs when users consult the mobile dictionary application, such as looking for words, phrases, or sentences. Moving to the defining functions section and keeping going to set the architectures until the final drawing of the hi-fi interfaces, there is an obvious logical deducing process. The next step development mainly depends on the step before, and the first stage, finding users' needs, is the significant ground of the whole design line.

On the contrary, service embedded mobile applications' design process does not rigidly follow an order. The ubiquitous it is formed by multiple factors simultaneously, mainly from the environment, information, relationship, and products aspects. The four factors are not fixed and separate alone, rather they affect and penetrate each other, which leads to some more complex factors existing - those involve or combine two or more elements. In the meantime, the factors have a flexible effect on design, which means sometimes not every factor contributes to it, and not every factor has the same amount of impact.

The environment is an extrinsic element. It refers to the potential scenarios where we might use the mobile application for any service. For instance, healthcare applications can be used in a hospital, a home, a pharmacy, and so on. In those different circumstances, different demands may be stimulated. The relationship factor is about the connection amongst almost all stakeholders. It is a critical role, not simply unidirectional relation from users to managers. Like the nurses as service providers role to patients, whereas facing the doctors they act as information service receivers. The information is an internal factor, that about it is self-ability scope - what source, information, service that can afford, like providing online hospital registration channels, expertise information of various sections, etc. The products as peer parts in the system, which means the corporation

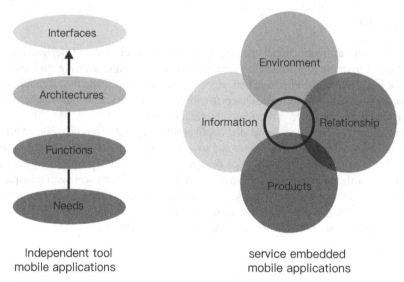

**Fig. 1.** A design process comparison between independent tool APP and service-embedded APP

between the other products and the mobile application. Like the self-service ticket terminal and display of calling all coordinate with a mobile application to provide service in a hospital (Fig. 1).

## 4   The Benefits of Rethinking from Service Perspective

Service design is an emerging field that focuses on creating good ideas by using a combination of intangible and tangible mediums. While applied to industries such as retail, banking, transportation, and healthcare, it offers many benefits for the end-user experience [10], and the holistic approach of setting other design disciplines into a wider social and active context. An integrated aspect is IxD's focus on the design of interactive artifacts, while service design focuses on the design of services, and interactive artifacts are part of it [8]. In this way, designing service-embedded mobile applications can take advantage of service perspective in sequence thinking of content rhythm.

### 4.1   Sequence Thinking of Content Rhythm

The service needs to be displayed in a logical, rhythmic manner, which is the same in a mobile application that the service is a dynamic process over some time, with consecutive leveraging or chiming in with other service instruments and interacting with service receivers or providers. Therefore timeline is very important to the users, which means service rhythm is also pretty significant that will affect the user's emotions.

No longer just considering a few physical contacts between mobile applications and users, even more, take consideration into the whole service process that includes tangible and intangible service to explore the participation possibilities of mobile applications. From interaction to trajectories for designing coherent journeys through user experiences [11]. For instance, when using a courier application to send express, users have the chance to access the application during the three service processes: before sending, sending, after sending. Designers ought to think from the integral three service process, regardless of whether interact with the app or not. Then choreographing the process in a brand new and desiring way, such as outputting the electronic order at mobile application, a convenient and time-saving mode to prevent anxiety and time consumption from a brick and mortar express shop. So design ought to link users and services with sequence rhythm in every interaction content to express a nice story together.

## 4.2  Holistic Lens in Solving Problem

Service provides a holistic, systemic, or integrated lens that lets designers envision problems solving solutions that are larger than a single computer part, that means satisfying the needs of a great number of stakeholders linked together in complex relationships for better adapting to the challenges of social computing and innovation [8, 10]. For service designers, the service design is not user research plus service blueprint, more importantly, from the perspective of holistic thinking, attempting to guide rather than follow, to create a more integral and valuable experience, reflecting through the service process in a variety of touchpoints.

This view helps designers design every touchpoint problem-solving solution under a holistic lens of the whole system pursuit. For example, the alphabetical arrangement of the typing keyboard in the bank app is disordered. Compared to the ordinary keyboard, the input experience is not friendly, because the user needs to spend the time to determine the location of each letter, but the security is higher than the general keyboard. When the user was accidentally seen by a stranger typing the password, the stranger can not know the user's password number only judging by is the place user's finger clicked. This is a design from the holistic, systematic lens, in financial applications, the importance of security is far higher than ease of use.

## 4.3  Multi-role Stakeholders' Co-creation

Service connotation and environment have endowed mobile application touching numerous stakeholders in different roles and identities. In the meanwhile, the ubiquitous mobile network enables stakeholders to co-create anytime and anywhere, it also provides a new creation mode because people are involved in activities with strong motivations to change the process and experience of interaction in collaborative services [12]. One stakeholder's character differs on facing or interacting with different participants due to the mazy mobile platform. The diversified role of stakeholders means a stakeholder can be both a service provider and a service receiver. In other words, the user's role has evolved from consumers to prosumers. And the completion of service is the result of multiple stakeholders involved.

## 5 The Evaluation of Mobile Applications Within Service

The evaluation of research artifacts is an important step to validate research contributions [13]. Service evaluation as a measuring standard of service, starting from the desired design results, which can improve service quality with clear directions. Design evaluation guide to design. As service-embedded mobile applications possess obvious service characters and competence, we can see them as an interactive product or a service touchpoint. When we consider it as a service, how can we assess it and what is the norm?

Cross-fertilization between marketing/management-centric and design-centric service designs is mutually beneficial [14]. In 1988 A. Parasurman, Valarie Zeithaml, and Leonard L. Berry represented a breakthrough in the measurement methods used for service quality research by capturing respondents' expectations and perceptions along the five dimensions. Reliability: the ability to perform the promised service dependably and accurately. Assurance: the ability to perform the promised service dependably and accurately. Tangibles: the appearance of physical facilities, equipment, personnel, and communication materials. Empathy: the provision of caring, individualized attention to customers. Responsiveness: the willingness to help customers and to provide prompt service [15]. Their measurement tools have been used by many researchers in a wide range of service industries and environments such as healthcare, banking, financial services, and education.

Given the widespread use of mobile internet and e-service, we sought to explore the measure dimensions of service embedded mobile applications' quality based on PZB research.

- Reliability is the ability of the service provider to fulfill the service commitment accurately and reliably. Reliable mobile applications are in line with user needs and expectations and mean that the service is in the same way with the promise to complete on time.
- Assurance namely the customer's trust in the brand, the application, and the service. The service-embedded mobile applications convey a high-quality brand image to stimulate user reliance. Brand image consistency promotes the formation and accumulation of consumer brand experience and eventually has become the primary factor in developing user loyalty.
- Tangibles in mobile applications reflect on information communication. In the knowledge paradigm, users are never lacking information, instead of how to get valuable information more conveniently. Mobile application tangibles focus on how to accurately and quickly transform the information into "visual".
- Empathy emphasizes inspiring and activating from the experience of others by observing people's real reactions, seeking user participation. Investigating the needs under specific different scenarios combined with digging potential emotional demands.
- Responsiveness in the service embedded mobile application reflects in quickly responding to user actions and feedback to problems, while in invisible service refers to the desire to help customers and provide services quickly.

## 6 Pilot Study in Mobile Courier Applications

With the rising of online shopping in the mobile internet environment, an express service model combined with mobile applications has become one of the most popular, labor-saving, and cost-cutting service models. Mobile platform plays an important intermediary role in the whole express service system in information service and logistics flow, which means the mobile platform is a key online service touchpoint. Chinese express companies have launched mobile applications, scrambling to seize the online market. First, collecting service function points of 6 popular domestic mobile courier applications in China (Table 2). Considering that PZB divides the evaluation dimension according to the characteristics of intangible services, we project this thinking into tangible mobile applications. The service feature of mobile applications mainly performs in the service function points. Second, analyze the relationship between the service dimensions and the mobile application service functions, and find the corresponding link (Fig. 2). Third, proposing interaction design constraints of mobile courier applications from service dimensions.

**Table 2.** Service functions collection of mobile courier applications

| Service functions points | Shunfeng | Shengtong | Yuantong | Zhongtong | Yunda | Cainiao Guoguo |
|---|---|---|---|---|---|---|
| searching history | √ | √ | √ | √ | √ | √ |
| package searching: input tracking | √ | √ | √ | √ | √ | √ |
| package searching: scan QD code | √ | √ | √ | √ | √ | √ |
| logistical detail | √ | √ | √ | √ | √ | √ |
| branch nearby | √ | √ | | √ | √ | |
| fill sending form online | √ | √ | √ | √ | √ | √ |
| collect restriction | √ | √ | | | √ | |
| sending history | √ | √ | √ | √ | √ | |
| remark | √ | | | √ | | |
| complaints and suggestions | √ | √ | √ | | √ | √ |
| custom service online | √ | √ | √ | √ | √ | |
| timeline inquiry | √ | √ | √ | √ | | √ |
| transportation expenses inquiry | √ | √ | √ | | √ | √ |
| delivery range | √ | | √ | | | |
| address administration | √ | √ | √ | √ | √ | √ |
| delivery standard | √ | | | √ | | |
| sending procedure | | | | | | |
| clearance service | √ | | | | | |
| member points | √ | | | | √ | √ |
| membership card | √ | | | √ | √ | |
| message center | √ | √ | | √ | √ | √ |
| address book | | | | | √ | |
| security service | √ | | | √ | √ | |

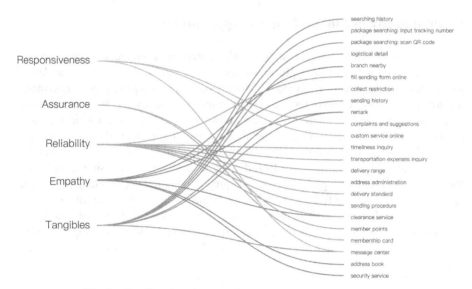

**Fig. 2.** Classification of service functions points into dimensions

- Delivering accurate and timely information is particularly valuable when using mobile devices.

  Transparent express tracking and visual package delivery path can give users a sense of security and help users access the distribution process and result more straightforward.

  First, the logical classification makes the target information easier to be positioned and understood. Second, various information display forms such as graphical forms improve the efficiency of communication and reduce the user's cognitive burden.
- Fit currently users' behavioral needs; dig potential emotional value of products.

  In the context of the experience economy, using scenario and emotional design methods become key factors in enhancing the user experience. First, analyze the operation scenario of users so that the service steps of an application can be closer to the current user behavior. Second, based on the current need, giving users an emotional experience that is beyond expectation can make the service impressive.
- Predictable results of the service and implementing functions effectively.

  The more clear blueprint the users have for the upcoming service, the faster speed the decisions been made, and also users will more confide to the service providers. For example, calculating the aging freight before making the order and providing the information of the courier in detail, etc., all these things can help users make better decisions through constructing psychological expectations.
- Unify interactive actions logic and visual perception feelings.

  In the process of establishing the brand image of mobile application services, the unity of interactive logic and visual experience plays an important role. Maintain the navigation between pages, icon features, and interactive efficiency of the same, so that user's operation phases can be similar when using different pages of the application.

The visual effect is reflected in the unity of interface form (font size, element size), color (hue, purity, brightness), and texture (muscle, shadow thickness).

- Response to users' actions quickly

   The response to users' behavior can help succeed sending promptly, which results in the positive effect of service. In the process of filling the cumbersome sending information tablets, the rational use of the response function can reduce the text inputting burden.

## 7  Conclusion

Mobile interaction design within service is something holistically more than mobile digital interface design, encompassing human interaction with objects, people, environments, and systems. It is a more holistic, multi-dimension, integrative field in mobile interaction design by embedding service as a critical new lens, that is essential in a knowledge-driven economy.

By analyzing the difference and competence of service embedded mobile applications from independent tool mobile applications. We found that this service-embedded mobile application has the advantages and characteristics of the service paradigm in the aspect of communication actors, design objective, design value as well as the design process. There is an obvious feature that from "linear analysis" to "open system analysis".

When we rethink mobile interaction design, we can gain benefits from the three aspects: sequence thinking of content rhythm; a holistic lens in solving the problem; multi-role stakeholders' co-creation. And while we describe the evaluation content from service quality dimensions, the thinking clue, and attention points are obtained in a different but integrated way.

Finally, we attempt to do a pilot study in mobile courier applications, a kind of typical service-embedded mobile application. Through collecting and classifying their service functions points into service dimensions, we put forward design constraints from the evaluation paradigm.

## References

1. Luo, S.-J., Hu, Y.: Model innovation driven by service design. Pack. Eng. **36**(12), 1–4 (2015)
2. Yap, C.E.L., Lee, J.-J., Roto, V.: How HCI interprets service design: a systematic literature review. In: Ardito, C., et al. (eds.) INTERACT 2021. LNCS, vol. 12933, pp. 259–280. Springer, Cham (2021). https://doi.org/10.1007/978-3-030-85616-8_16
3. Matt, J., Gary, M.: Mobile Interaction Design, 1st edn. Wiley, New York (2006)
4. Elaine, M.: Designing for Mobile, Part 2: Interaction Design. http://www.uxbooth.com/articles/designing-for-mobile-part-2-interaction-design/. Accessed 20 Jan 2022
5. Stefan, H.: Interaction design and service design: expanding a comparison of design disciplines. Des. Inq. **2**, 1–8 (2007)
6. Gregor, B., et al.: Supporting mobile service usage through physical mobile interaction. In: Fifth Annual IEEE International Conference on Pervasive Computing and Communications. IEEE Press (2007)

7. Virpi, R., Jung, J.-L., Lai, C., John, Z.: The overlaps and boundaries between service design and user experience design. In: Proceeding of DIS 2021, pp. 1915–1926. ACM, New York (2021)

8. Jodi, F., John, Z.: Promoting service design as a core practice in interaction design. In: The 5th IASDR World Conference on Design Research, pp. 1–13. Springer (2013)

9. Daisy, Y., Anya, E., Sofia, S., Eva, E., Peter, D.: Service design in HCI research: the extended value co-creation model. In: Proceeding of the Halfway to the Future Symposium 2019, pp. 1–8. ACM, New York (2019)

10. Marc, S., Jakob, S.: This is Service Design Thinking: Basics, Tools, Cases, 1st edn. BIS Publishers, Amsterdam (2012)

11. Steve, B., Gabriella, G., Boriana, K., Tom, R.: From interaction to trajectories: designing coherent journeys through user experiences. In: Proceedings of the SIGCHI Conference on Human Factors in Computing Systems, pp. 709–718. ACM, New York (2009)

12. Gong, M., Manzini, E., Casalegno, F.: Mobilized collaborative services in ubiquitous network. In: Rau, P.L.P. (ed.) IDGD 2011. LNCS, vol. 6775, pp. 504–513. Springer, Heidelberg (2011). https://doi.org/10.1007/978-3-642-21660-2_57

13. Remy, C., et al: Evaluation beyond usability: validating sustainable HCI research. In: Proceedings of CHI 2018, p. 216. ACM, New York (2018)

14. Yu, E.: Toward an integrative service design framework and future agendas. Des. Issues **36**(2), 41–57 (2020)

15. Parasuraman, A., Ziethaml, V., Berry, L.L.: SERVQUAL: a multiple- item scale for measuring consumer perceptions of service quality. J. Retail. **62**(1), 12–40 (1988)

# On the Transformation of Audience-Designer Relationship from the Perspective of Speculative Design

Jindou Yao[✉]

China Academy of Art, Hangzhou 311115, Zhejiang, People's Republic of China
20202483@caa.edu.cn

**Abstract.** Art, which is a short process of "happen here", has the function of social communication. Works of art have changed from a simple mirror image of the social background to a platform for public discussion, and have changed from didactic critical design to speculative design that stimulate discussion of various possibilities. As a social medium, art invites the public to participate in discussions and picture the future. From then on, the identity of the audience and the designer have changed and have transformed to a new audience-designer relationship. Among them, the opening authority, single acceptance and selection of audience, that achieved by the performance of props and technical means in speculative design, become the invitation from the designer to explore the audience's participation and possibility. In addition, through the blank space of the construction from artifacts, which is the props, designer and audience explore and change the reality together from the fictional archaeology. The process of thinking and understanding from designer and the participants together is the very first step to change the direction of reality.

**Keywords:** Speculative design · Form of participation · Audience-designer relationship · Props

## 1 Art as a Social Medium

### 1.1 Penetration and Implanted Intention

Art, which is a short process of "happen here", has the function of social communication [1]. However, art, as one of the appearance of the designer, its internal expression was often ignored by the public. People usually define "form" only as the appearance corresponding to the "content" and judge the work by it's shape of the appearance, denying that the form has also contained the extended expression of the work. While there is no form, that contain the extended expression, in nature. It is only by seeing that we have this idea. In the same way, the work of art turns into a real object only when people communicate and interact with it.

Art has penetrated the appearance of "being" and establishes a profound and intimate relationship with the audience. The work of art is also a kind of the extended expression of the designer. As a one-way viewer, audience will not give a deep understanding for the core of the art work, the reason of its appearance that has been made. The art work should be negotiated and completed in the process of sharing and understanding. Artist shows the work through its form, and invites the audience to join in the dialogue by his art. How to connect the designer and audience through the work, and how to let both get spiritual satisfaction and get more enlightening discussion became the theme of thinking and the direction to pursue that relate to stimulate the form creating in 1990s and after. The work has what the designer intended to implant, and it is also the product of the age for what Nicolas Bourriaud refers to "penetration" that comes with the production of human work [1]. This "penetration" connects the space-time with the designer. However, when presenting and communicating, the art work is the product of the time first, and then is the manifestation of the designer's intention. This concept originates from the de-formalization of artistic expression, that is, a free selection or creation of the external shape of the work and the expression of the idea. The famous work "Marilyn Monroe" by Andy Warhol is a depiction of the mechanical indifference by the dominance of industry. Because of the "infinite drive", the freedom and changeability of art enable it to exploration and exchange with the world, commerce and even philosophy. Through aesthetic practice, artists endow works with "activity" and explore the connection between the public and the reality to stimulate more imagination, fiction and thinking.

## 1.2   Participation and Transmission of the Art from 90s

Nicolas Bourriaud said that the art activity is like a game. According to the evolution of the time and society, the form, modality, function and even the nature of the art activity will change as well [1]. Political modernity emerged together with the philosophy of enlightenment emphasized the ideological emancipation of the individual. However, due to the existence of multiple versions of modernism, the 20th century was dominated by the competition between rationalism, irrationalism and utilitarianism; the rational conception developed from 18th century modernism and the irrationalist philosophy of liberation represented by Dadda, surrealism and situationism, were both antagonistic to authoritarian forces that seek to dictate human relations and enslave individuals or utilitarianism. The progressive and "rational" industrial technology, which should lead and create a better society, did not bring the liberation to the public as anticipation. However, people blindly devoted themselves to the worship of machines. As a result, the modern plan for liberation suffered a failure [6].

From a blind optimism of technology and enlightening other possibilities for design, Antony Dunne and Fiona first introduced the concept of critical design in the 1990s, in order to arouse the attention of the public to the reconciliation of technology and humanities [1]. What used to be called progressive grew out of modern rationalism, where design was more often a product of the industry. Thoughtless assembly line, a capital orientation, was deliberately undermined by its negative effects. From a global perspective since the 1990s, art has begun to intervene the community for the purpose of contemporary art practice. Art and design are reborn through different philosophies, cultures, and the society assumptions. The concept of critical design overlaps with the new needs of artists in the context of the times. Art works are constantly being tried and updated through experimental, critical and participatory models. And they tried to get close to the Enlightenment philosophers continuing struggling against with the direction suggested by Dadda or Piet Mondrian that depreciated the improving of living and working conditions. Art is no longer a cautious stay in the world, but a declaration and whoop for the possibility of shaping the future. For example, the functional product that used to be all over the world is no longer universally accepted by the public [6]. "Problem-solving" is no longer the end-point of the design, as artists construct the existing lifestyles and behavior patterns in arbitrary patterns and invite audiences to participate in them. The process of discovery and experience has become a new way for artists or designers to give feedback for the society through works and design archetypes.

Participation, as an ideology of contemporary art, focuses on social intervention and participation subject. The relationship between people and art works is inter-subjectivity when the art works are regarded as the stand-in of "human" and concept. As a concept which is close to formal dialogue, transmission, which constitutes the specific content of the work, negates the specific "art space" and it becomes the important nature of the work. In another words, a art work without "transmission" becomes a "dead thing" that loses its vitality. The Eugène Delacroix argues that a good oil painting condenses the viewer's vision, which mean, it briefly solidifies the viewer's vision and the emotions and gives the viewer and the work a silent, interactive space, and gives emotional feedback to the painting as a new "life" of activity [1]. Artist is no longer the producer of the work, but the architect of the scene, is the guide who embeds an idea into the work and faces the audience. For example, ethnic Thai artist Rikrit Tiravanijia has moved daily activities into the exhibition space several times since 1990s. He uses himself as a catalyst in his work, inviting others to step in and share their experiences, and it gives the work a deeper meaning and a range of possibilities [7].

In 1990s, as the relationship between arts and the audience were getting closer, art was presented in a variety of forms: sculpture, installation, even performance and social action. At the same time, audiences also have a sense of participation through the public opinion and this operate mode began to become a norm. Art has the characteristic of social communication. And the relational art puts the human interaction and the "world" formed by social context on the same theoretical level. From then on, the art work is no longer a breathing space under some kind of centralization, and no longer confined to the symbolic space that proclaims autonomy and privacy. In stead it serves as a starting point for open-ended discussion and an experiential process. Works of art take transitivity as a part of expression, and design the negotiation state and the interactivity of the audience while interacting with the work. At this point, audience and artists, as different subjects, were interweaving and "deducing" the works together.

### 1.3 The Cooperation of "SPeculative" and "Technology" After 90s

The word "speculative" has been mentioned since the very past. Its critical design, though taking criticism as the external appearance, also includes the internal logic of speculative, and is opposite from the "definite design", which emphasizes solving and strengthening the present situation [2]. The core of critical design is to "question everything", to challenge preconceived narrow assumptions, and to reject the only certainty by using non-verbal objects concretely and visually. It also points out that it is more important to identify the problem than to solve it in some specific situations. The transformation from critical design to speculative design is similar to the transformation from radical design to critical design and from modernism to internationalism. When critical design is fixed as the "trend" of the times by the public, its critical thinking and pioneering ideology are gradually ignored and forgotten [1].

At this time, the concept of speculative design is put forward, which calls back people's attention to the activity of design as a research and as a critical medium. Speculative design is a new concept proposed by Antony Dunne and Fiona after critical design with the book《Speculative Everything: Design, Fiction and Social Dreams》. It is a new plan for the artistic creation to face the post-industrial age. "Speculative" in the Oxford dictionary means to infer and speculate. Zhang Li, as a translator, refers it to the word "speculate" in the Oxford dictionary as: a theory or conjecture formed by thinking without sufficient knowledge, and at the same time, it also has the meaning of "conjecture", which is, subjective speculation and imagination. In the field of philosophy and psychology, the concept and extension of "speculation" have already been stable. In the field of psychology, speculation emphasizes the psychological instinct and instability. In philosophy, however, speculation is based on pure thinking without emotional prejudice, and makes a bold analysis of the irrationality of the real world through the deduction of things and concepts. As Immanuel Kant mentioned, it is a purely rational philosophical inference based on the absence of the experienced object, and it is a corollary to the purely conceptual dialectical object, as Hegel put it [2].

"Speculation" is the central focus, while "design" is the medium and means,.. Dunne put forward that the practical significance of speculative design is to guide people to act together to catalyze the realization of social dreams [2]. Compared with the single discourse of critical design, speculative design is more inclusive and can guide the audience's active thinking and imagination. Speculative design puts the object of speculative philosophy on the object of "technology", and it advocates the discussion of many future possibilities based on the real technology as a mode of thinking, And it also invites the public to participate in the discussion and learn more about the present. The "speculative" part of speculative design is focused on the level of thinking towards the abstract concept, and the "design" part is implemented in the specific practical links. Speculative design encourages bold ideas of different forms and content, similar to design a fiction, but more based on real technologies that can extrapolate other possibilities of the future. Rather than celebrating technological progress, subversion of reality is the ultimate goal of speculative design [2]. Criticism is also one of the angles to observe the practical technology in speculative design. In the speculative design, "design" as a mean of communication and performance connects participants and designer, guiding their active thinking, trying to build the field of communication between the work, audience and designers.

## 2 "View-Acting" and "Authority"

### 2.1 "Props" and "Connections" in Speculative Design

Through the way of making up the future, speculative design pushes the functionality and aesthetics of technology to the extreme. It subvert people's single understanding of reality and activate people's active participation in the discussion and action of "the future of technology". Speculative design defines "props" as the characters, that complete narration and deliberate roles, to make up for the lack of details, and it regards "props" as an important expression and essential element during speculative design. In the connection of imagination and technology, props and their given fictional context constitute a local manifestation of a parallel space-time intercepted by the creators. And their ability of fiction is also a necessary attribute to distinguish reality. Like the famous work "Architecture of the Imagination" by EL Ultimo Grito, its design is based on a exterior vitrification as an imaginary urban building. The use of props as both the reality and the audience's imagination of the non-reality of aesthetics, giving the urban architecture vague and poetic expression [1]. Since props is used to celebrate the non-reality, speculative design would love to design objects as props and models.

Physical props are the only element of non-realistic aesthetics and the most important characteristic of speculative design [2]. When the creator attempts to construct a new, blank reality without the basic appearance of the real world, it will lead to the occurrence and discussion of various possibilities. In addition, how to allow the audiences to participate more quickly and bring themselves into different scenarios is also a critical design consideration. Its field, atmosphere and identity structure are also the effective mediums to convey ideas and values. For example, the identity structure of a character can also explain and promote the values and social system of the world itself. From the fictional time-and-space background, the character's occupation and his personality traits, any superposition of the three attributes can create a more complete non-reality role of the "activity", and can feedback the work through the role of emotion and behavior. The mapping of place and atmosphere, the distortion of daily life, reflecting the phenomena of extended work (even the new problems of audience communication that the creator ignores), through the occurrence of imaginary props, characters or specific events, and non-places. The problems it produces are bound to coincide with real life. The combination of setting and atmosphere brings the audience into the work better. These expressions are the embodiment of "props" in the speculative design, which is an important channel for the work to connect reality and imagination.

Based on the above conditions, when a work is given a special definition or assumption, it will form an independent "world" or a local projection in the field of the work. Artist becomes closer to the identity of the receiver, connecting the audience with the work, and construct the communication symbols that linking the two "worlds". Instead of a single passing of ideas or a brief reference to a painting, as Eugène Delacroix mentioned, the communication formally invites the audience to participate and discuss, and use props to stimulate thinking and imagination of more possibilities.

## 2.2 The Relationship Between Audience and Designer in Creating

From the relationship between audience and performance of drama and the definition of Jerzy Grotowski, the relationship between audience and designer or performance is not only the sum of the two factors, but also the "field" of interaction and exchange that forms the core of the whole work. The relationship between audience and performance comes from the division of stage and audience by drama [2]. Drama, as the carrier of ideology, has always played an important role in influencing and guiding the existence of society. The medium of theatrical expression is to establish communication with the audience through the effective performance of the actors. In the process of design and creation, based on the creative diversity brought about by speculative design, works become a media for designers to convey their ideas and invite the public to participate in the common fiction of the future and activate more possibilities. The creative design prototype is also separated from the pure performance under the industrial technology and the time centralization. It is based on the physical props because of the creator changing the present situation and the imaginary future reflection and the strong intention. Accepting change and thinking how to change is something that designers should consider again. Based on the two types of viewing space in drama, the single-latitude viewing space and the multi-dimensional compound space, there are three types of participation art.

One is a kind of "report" like the one-way output of drama text and actors to the audience [4]. The audience in this mode will accept the idea of centralization in the social background and other ideas reflected by the works, or simply tour and browse. At the same time, painting can focus the audience's attention and the field around the work for a short stay. In this mode, there is no real audience involvement and participation, only the audience in the imaginary space of the work of sporadic interpretation and a single response. From the perspective of speculative design, there is also only one-sided, sporadic dialectical thinking or critical discourse of the audience.

The second is "theatrical", with a "two-way output" model in which actors interact and explore with the audience. Such as the polemical drama of Antonin Artaud and the immersive drama influenced by it. It is quite different from the first type mentioned above, that the boundary between the audience and the actors is blurred and the estrangement disappears. Based on this, the artistic creation began to invite the audience, the work is no longer a certain doctrine or concept of oppression, but with the participation of the creator and the audience to re-endow the "vitality". For example, in 1990s, the public opinion about radical happenstance art was involved in the stimulation of many possibilities under the mode of participatory art and speculative design with formal audience intervention. Works of art have become a platform for making declarations and communicating in the times. The designers and the participants, used to be spectators, constitute the purpose of daydreaming, thinking about the future world and trying to change the present situation.

The third type is to break the traditional single theater space. By using multi-dimension or multi-space performances, performers and audience exist in the exchange of identity under the work [4]. Audience and the plot are also under the interaction of mutual influence. It is called a compound, multi-channel input-output model of the audience. With the cross-disciplinary creation of art, art works form from the screen, physical props move onto the use of virtual technology. When art creation has a sense of participation and identity change, there is also a closer connection and a more accurate discussion of society and the world.

### 2.3 "Speculative Design" and the "Authority" of Participants

Based on the discussion and exploration of the boundary between technology and non-reality aesthetics, the purpose of the open authority is to allow participants to visualize the real outcome of their work, to explore the possibilities and transformations of reality, and to redefine the relationship between human beings and technology. Based on the combination of drama and performance and the exploration of the possibility from the perspective of speculative design, the creator has established a closer relationship with the audience through his works. In fact, audiences do not have a full authority freedom in the drama, actually they are more driven by the script. Most scholars believe that the immersion drama subverts the traditional power relationship between performers and audiences so that the audiences can control the performance. Rather than control, audience is the participant who has the right to choose, the authority is still in the hands of the produce team and the audience is only the decision maker of the independent aesthetic trend. The issue of the exposition of props and the opening authority of the work expression in speculative design is discussed privately. From the refraction of the imaginary world and reality in terms of props, the work that stays in this state has the permission to open up the audience's imagination mentally. While the combination of participatory art is an invitation to the audience. From single indoctrination to speculation, one-way acceptance to participation, the two-way output of the performance relationship is an open test of the audience's authority. Audience, from spectator to participant in the thorough transformation, plays an essential role in the work. In this mode, there are two levels of the authority trial. Participation (authority of selection) and change node, that means without far from the only direction of the work's concept and give multiple choices by stacking out multiple plot structures. However, the third kind of authority that completely submit to audience will lead to a totally different ending and even out of control. For example, Marina Abramovic's most influential film, rhythm 0, is an example and discussion of open authority. Marina signed a waiver contract to assure the audience that she would participate. Under a six hour physiological anaesthetic, she hands over her body, her props and her performance to the audience. From flowers to guns, from touching to hurts, the performance pushes the boundaries of human morality to the limit. Even the artist's own life was almost taken by the gun which audience took from the prop. And the work became a moral test of reality.

## 3    "Blank" Artifacts

The text that presents the direction of the work and constructed by the worldview of the designer is a certainty of the sage-like speech guide. When it leaves more space for audience to have more opportunities of imagination and intervention, the blank space in the text is particularly important, since it weakens the redundant descriptions while retaining the core worldview; by breaking the certainty of the text, it achieves the creative goal of leaving the blank space in order to stimulate the audience to think, and the goal of replenishing the work with the actions and emotions of the audience. In this kind of audience-designer relationship, as a receiver and participant, the audience's initiative creation has also been reflected.

Props, as a very important element, connects reality and non-reality in speculative design. And it is a medium of "permission" that opens the public imagination space. The various external manifestations of the props, including the role, the field, and the certain object, give the "active" opportunity to creation. At this point, the activation of thinking and the opening of authority of the speculative design do not emphasis on whether the problem is solved after the work is finished. What they care most is how the atmosphere under the collision of thinking becomes call of the world. Most of the works today are constructed by the existing civilizations or societies or the facts. So whether or not we can deduce from the opposite direction by giving a hint to the audience with constructing artificial artifacts and creating a fictional civilization, to allows the viewer to think and imagine in a different direction through the work. This is also a way of thinking through design, even though the end point is all about reality and the present. But different directions of deduction can also provide new stimulation for thoughts. When we construct props that can span the space-time, it will no longer be the mirror condensates of a particular space-time. It will rather be the complaints of multiple social problems, or the "canvas" of another direction in a parallel time and space. The transformation from the viewer to a participant becomes both the leader of the canvas and the writer of the ending of a text.

When we go through the elements from space and time to create an alternative and fictional artifacts called "props", the blank and imagined space it left provides the opportunity for personal interpretation of the audience. Through the cooperation of various audience-designer relations and props, people can understand and interpret reality from many angles or avoid the possibility, going beyond the concrete practice of using design as a medium. The public can also link props with self-imagination in speculative design, and even as a speculative material culture, deducing fictional archaeology and imaginary anthropology. What we can decide is to give the participants "authority" and guidance to let participants really become the main part of the deduction and begin dialogue with the world. The designer, on the other hand, guides the behavior and emotion of the participants and control the works through the setting of "Props". The artistic creation forms based on the speculative design, in addition to the direct verbal communication with the audience, in the process of feeling the work, the thought and the feeling is the communication with the creator's soul and the mutual acceptance with the work, which has become a kind of very romantic art form that needs ponder.

Based on the reality of a variety of possible future imagination and structure of the parallel world, physical props as an important representation of speculative design, will lead to some problems and their reflections. How to guide the audience to think and react, the open authority and the participants, whether they can lead the exploration of more possibilities? These issues will continue to revolve around the designer's overall planning of creative ideas and continuous practice for the works.

## References

1. Bourriaud, N.: Translated by Huang Jianhong. Relationship Aesthetics. Jincheng Press, Beijing (2013)
2. Dunne, A., Fiona: Everything: Design, Fiction, and Social Dreams. Jiangsu Phoenix Fine Arts Publishing House (2017)
3. Yan, Y.: Using science and technology as media – research on speculative design creation. Art Watch **2021**(10), 154–155 (2021)
4. Pubo. On the Three Forms of Dramatic Space. Shanghai Theatre Academy (2011)
5. Kimberly, J., Yu, K.: Use and abuse of Antonin Artaud. Theatre Arts **2011**(05), 5–12 (2011). 10.13737
6. Intellectual restlessness, interview with Claire Bishop and Julia Bryan Wilson. Mousse magazine (2012). http://www.artda.cn/view.php?tid=7526&cid=39
7. Claire. Antagonism and relational aesthetics, October 2010. http://www.artda.cn/yishuzhexue

# User Experience Evaluation Methods and Tools

# AI-Based Emotion Recognition to Study Users' Perception of Dark Patterns

Simone Avolicino[✉] [iD], Marianna Di Gregorio[iD], Fabio Palomba[iD],
Marco Romano[iD], Monica Sebillo[iD], and Giuliana Vitiello[iD]

University of Salerno, 08544 Fisciano, SA, Italy
{savolicino,madigregorio,fpalomba,marromano,msebillo,
gvitiello}@unisa.it

**Abstract.** Dark Patterns are design patterns used to trick users into acting against their real interest. The web provides an infinite number of services accessible to anyone, which do not always promote a good user experience and are often structured with the aim of leading the user to perform unwanted actions or discourage him from making decisions that could damage the company. This is a very common practice, especially in neuromarketing. Human behavioral and perceptual patterns are cleverly exploited to achieve a specific goal. For this reason, dark pattern developers try to create an environment that invites as much purchase as possible by stimulating the customer's unconscious. Among the areas in which these strategies are adopted is tourism: online travel agency websites promote "fake discounts" for the products/services they are selling, display inaccurate pricing information leading to incorrect pricing assumptions, thus misleading consumers. One of the goals of this work is to identify which dark patterns are most used in online travel agencies and once identified, they will be used to run scenarios that will simulate booking a vacation online. During the execution of the tests, users will be filmed via webcam tracking their expressions and emotions through AI-based facial recognition. Finally, the data obtained from the tests will be analyzed to study the emotions and feelings that a user feels when he/she is confronted with dark patterns, to understand which users are more at risk and which are the types of dark patterns to which they are more vulnerable.

**Keywords:** Dark patterns · Emotion recognition · User experience

## 1 Introduction

User Experience (UX) Design is focused on the creation of pleasant and satisfying user experiences. It is achieved by putting the user at the center of the design process. It is a crucial component in business activities, indeed, a good UX supports growing credibility associated with the brand [24], and, consequently, the potential growth of customer loyalty during the time. Often, however, this proportional relationship is underestimated by companies, looking for short-term benefits. For example, some online companies hide from their customers some of the costs of their services until the moment of payment.

M. Kurosu et al. (Eds.): HCII 2022, LNCS 13516, pp. 185–203, 2022.
https://doi.org/10.1007/978-3-031-17615-9_13

Such a strategy is commonly called "dark pattern": tricks used in websites and apps that make you do things that you didn't mean to, like buying or signing up for something [5]. However, UX is affected during all the steps of the consumer's interaction with the brand, starting from the first contact until the purchase of the product. For this reason, the main objective of UX design is not the enhancement of the product, brand, or service but the construction of a relationship as satisfying as possible for the consumer from an emotional and functional point of view.

In this work, we investigated the effects on the customer experience of the most common dark patterns. To do so, we exploited the potentiality of the AI and neural networks to monitor and extract users' emotions while interacting with an online travel agency in a controlled experiment.

## 2 Related Works

The interface design is one of the disciplines that for several years now contributes deeply to our daily life, making fundamental digital services and products more intuitive and usable [20, 24, 25, 7]. However, there is a mischievous current of thought of who voluntarily decides to design an interface to force the user to make some actions, that most of the time benefit just the service provider. Dark patterns, so-called for the first time by UX Researcher Harry Brignull in 2010 [5], are interface elements carefully designed and combined to confuse the users, lead them to perform unwanted actions, or discourage them to make decisions that could damage the company. In addition, dark patterns may put users with disabilities at greater risk [6]. The website platform darkpatterns.org [5] presents a collection of categorized common dark patterns used in the web. It allows users to add new undiscovered dark patterns. It has a twofold function: on one hand it represents a guide for users and aims to be a tool to help them protect themselves in the "dark world" of the web; on the other hand, given the scarcity of tools for the identification of dark patterns, the public defamation of these sites could lead the owners of such applications to take steps to correct the website in order to improve the overall experience of their users.

### 2.1 Dark Patterns Taxonomy

The phenomenon of dark patterns was brought to light by Harry Brignull, who also provided a first and fundamental classification on the website darkpattern.org [5].

Numerous researchers, over the years, have also shown other examples of classification in articles, on personal websites, and through other media [8, 9, 10]. This has therefore led to an expansion of the different types of present. A further classification was presented by Gray et al. [1], who following analysis and comparisons on the various typologies found, provided a proposal in which the patterns identified were classified within 5 macro-categories, represented in Fig. 1. These considerations arose as a result of the fact that many of the typologies concerned specific types of content (advertising, e-commerce), while others indicated more general strategies (e.g., operations to divert the user, bait and switch). These show that dark patterns are evolving as the web evolves.

| | Nagging | Obstruction | Sneaking | Interface interference | Forced action |
|---|---|---|---|---|---|
| Description | Redirection of expected functionality that persists beyond one or more interactions. | Making a process more difficult than it needs to be, with the intent of dissuading certain action(s). | Attempting to hide, disguise, or delay the divulging of information that is relevant to the user. | Manipulation of the use interface that privileges certain actions over others. | Requiring the user to perform a certain action to access (or continue to access certain functionality |
| Dark Patterns included | | Price Comparison Prevention, Intermediate Currency | Forced Continuity, Hidden costs, Sneak into basket, Bait and switch. | Hidden information, Preselection, Aesthetic manipulation, Toying with emotion, False Hierarchy, Disguised Ad, Trick questions. | Social Pyramid, Privacy suckering, Gamification. |

**Fig. 1.** Classification of dark patterns by Gray et al.

## 2.2 Dark Patterns in Online Travel Agency

Online travel agencies are becoming increasingly popular in today's world. People come across one of these websites taken by the desire to travel, and they, probably, do not pay attention to the many tricks that companies use to get them where they want. Such dark patterns, which, being a little-known phenomenon, succeed to deceive the users using apparently convenient prices and availability.

The establishment of laws to counteract them led dark pattern creators to define new approaches and strategies that could circumvent them [5]. Also, the purchase and sale of products online, have significantly intensified in many fields, leading to define new patterns that could be used during any purchasing process, such as fake time offers, fake reviews to promote a product or, in general, techniques to generate in the user feelings of urgency and scarcity. Because of the scale and sophistication with which digital marketplaces and online stores may target people, market manipulation becomes even more successful [11]. Another factor to consider is that economic markets can manipulate both sellers (hosts) and buyers (travelers) [12].

In [2], the authors inspected various public domain lawsuits on online travel agencies from 2016 to 2020 to identify dark patterns in online travel agency websites. The main categories of these documents include civil lawsuits and final judgments. The dark patterns identified are "Low Stock Message", "Activity Notification", "High Demand Message", "Limit Time Message", "Hidden Cost". In further, we explored other online travel agency websites encountering the following dark patterns in addition to the above: "Pre-selection" and "Aesthetic Manipulation".

Each of these Dark Pattern's tactics affects cognitive biases that can influence consumer decision making. The goal of each is to rush the user into taking a certain action, which in this case is buying a ticket.

### Hidden Cost
Brignull's "Hidden Costs" pattern provides users with a late disclosure of certain costs. In this pattern, a certain price is advertised for a good or service, only to later be changed

due to the addition of taxes and fees, limited time conditions, or unusually high shipping costs [1].

**Activity Notification**
In the "activity notification" pattern, online travel agencies' websites drag users' attention to particular product pages by indicating the online activities of other users. When online travel agencies' websites display the activities of other users, consumers are more motivated to buy the product/service [2].

**High Demand Message, Limit Time Message, and Low Stock Message**
To create a sense of competition among consumers, online travel agencies use the scarcity effect as a pressure strategy to encourage purchasing. The websites of online travel agencies can use several types of dark pattern tactics to create scarcity bias. By emphasizing that the deal/sale will close soon without specifying a deadline, the limited-time message tactic creates urgency and uncertainty. The "low-stock message" indicates that the product is out of stock. Finally, the "high-demand message" tactic aims to remind users that the products/services are in high demand and will sell out quickly [2].

**Pre-selection**
Any situation in which an option is selected by default prior to user interaction is referred to as a "pre-selection" pattern. "Pre-selection" is typically represented as a default choice that the product's shareholder wishes the user to make; however, this choice is frequently in the user's best interests or may have unintended consequences [1].

**Aesthetic Manipulation**
"Aesthetic Manipulation" is any user interface manipulation that is more concerned with form than function. This includes design choices that draw the user's attention to one thing to redirect their attention from or persuade them to believe in something else [1].

### 2.3 Classification and Recognition Techniques of Emotions

Measuring emotions has been a subject of research for many scientists, to be able to classify them and demonstrate their universality. According to the International Organization for Standardization (ISO) the user experience concept includes "Users' perceptions and responses include the users' emotions, beliefs, preferences, perceptions, comfort, behaviours, and accomplishments that occur before, during and after use" [4]. Paul Ekman [3] showed, through experimenting with people from different places, the possibility to classify emotions and demonstrated their universality. He also engaged in cataloguing human expressions, creating a coding system of facial actions (FACS). To do so, he took thousands of photos of facial expressions and associated each one with a value based on the facial muscles involved. The researcher argued that there are universal emotions that is common emotions that are the same for everyone in all cultures and can be defined as primary, such as anger, fear, sadness, happiness, surprise, and disgust, and secondary, such as amusement, contempt, contentment, embarrassment, excitement, guilt, pride, relief, pleasure, shame. For a long time, facial expression recognition and analysis, particularly FACS detection [13] and discrete emotion detection, has been a hot area in computer science, with numerous promising algorithms [14, 15, 16]. Nowadays several methods and technologies allow the recognition of human emotions, which differ in the level of intrusiveness. The use of invasive tools (e.g. ECG or EEG, biometric sensors) [17, 18] can influence the behavior of subjects and in particular can adulterate their spontaneity and, consequently, the emotions experienced by them, introducing biases that inevitably end up compromising the expected results. Most of these techniques, methods and tools refer to three areas of research: facial emotion analysis, speech recognition analysis and biofeedback emotion analysis. Facial emotion analysis aims to recognize patterns from facial expressions facial expressions and linking them to emotions. For this analysis, AI comes into play with algorithms of Deep Learning, particularly based on Convolutional Neural Networks (CNN). It is a mathematical model of Deep Learning that takes in input different types of images and makes predictions based on the trained model. CNN is not only used for emotion recognition [19, 21], but also for gestures [22, 23].

## 3   Study on Emotion Recognition in Relation to Dark Patterns

To identify the user's emotions when dealing with different types of dark models, 3 tests were conducted. The first one is to understand the technological skills and knowledge that the participants possess. The second, which is the main point of this work is divided into several tasks, one for each dark model. These tasks are about booking a ticket online, be it an airline ticket or a hotel reservation. Through this test, it will be possible to know the emotions of the users while viewing the dark patterns. The last test is used to understand the influence that these dark patterns have on purchases on websites. Moreover, it is useful to validate the data obtained from emotion recognition from test 2. The tests are conducted individually and in a specific environment.

### 3.1   Participants

To analyze users' emotions while viewing the dark models, users of different ages and with different technological backgrounds were chosen. Participants' age ranged from 19 to 66 (M = 35.5, SD = 14,7). Users are equally divided between participants under 35 years of age and those over 35. For this reason, in the study and analysis participants were divided into 2 categories: under 35 and over 35.

### 3.2   Choice of Tasks

The types of dark patterns are countless, so in this work we considered all those dark patterns that can be encountered in online travel agencies ("Low Stock Message", "Activity Notification", "High Demand Message", "Pre-selection", "Limit Time Message", "Aesthetic Manipulation", "Hidden Cost"). We have selected some of the most famous sites that contain the presence of dark patterns, and they are listed in the Fig. 2. We asked the participants to carried out come tasks on them to verify their efficiency during the booking of a travel online and to understand if they provoked particular emotions on them. The table in Fig. 2 shows the websites selected for testing and their corresponding dark patterns.

| | Low Stock Message | High Demand Message | Limit Time Message | Activity Notification | Hidden Cost | Pre-Selection | Aesthetic Manipulation |
|---|---|---|---|---|---|---|---|
| Booking | | | X | | | | |
| Ryanair | X | | | | | | |
| E-Dreams | X | | X | | | | |
| Expedia | | | | | | X | |
| Volagratis | | | | | | | X |
| Mytrip | | | | | | | X |
| B-Rent | | | | | X | | |
| Rentalcars | | X | | X | | | |
| Nautal | | X | | X | | | |

**Fig. 2.** Dark patterns contained in the websites tested in this work.

### 3.3 Test Preparation and Tool Used

The test was conducted in a controlled environment and video/audio recording tools, a data collection system, etc. were set up. The study execution was conducted in person, for it we used the following tools: - DeskShare: Screen Recorder Pro[1] for recording two screens simultaneously; - Google Forms[2] for surveys; - Excel to track results; - MorphCast Emotional AI[3] for emotion recognition. MorphCast Emotional AI is a software application that uses machine learning and face recognition, as well as gender, age, and the six primary FACS emotions, to determine a user's level of attention without asking for personal information. The software is client-side (JavaScript), allowing it to avoid sending biometric data to the server. In addition, the software is browser-based, allowing it to be used simultaneously with other applications. This is an important characteristic allowing us to watch the evolution of emotions on a screen, while users working on a task using a second screen.

### 3.4 Background Survey

The background survey was used to learn about users' technological experiences and skills. The questions in this survey were: How frequently do you use smartphones, computers, tablets, etc.? How frequently do you browse the web during the day? Do you prefer to book your vacations using online services or in traditional physical agencies?

### 3.5 Tasks Presentation and Execution

Two test scenarios were identified, both of which contained websites with the same number and type of dark patterns. The first scenario includes the following tasks: - Flight booking on E-Dreams[4]; - Hotel room booking on E-Dreams; - Car rental on B-Rent[5]; - Boat rental on Nautal[6]; - Hotel room booking on Expedia[7]; - Flight booking

---

[1] https://www.deskshare.com.

[2] https://docs.google.com/forms/.

[3] https://www.morphcast.com/sdk/.

[4] https://www.edreams.it.

[5] https://www.b-rent.com.

[6] https://www.nautal.it.

[7] https://www.expedia.it.

on Volagratis[8]. The second instead: - Booking a flight on Ryanair[9]; - Booking a hotel room on Booking[10]; - Booking a car on B-Rent; - Booking a hotel room on Expedia; - Booking a car on Rentalcars[11]; - Booking a flight on MyTrip[12]. Once the instructions for conducting the test were explained, the user could choose which scenario to complete. The instructions provided indicated how to explore the websites to visualize the dark patterns and how to position oneself in front of the camera so that the recognition of the expressions would be as reliable as possible. During the execution of the various tasks, the users' emotions were analyzed by webcam through AI-based emotion recognition, as shown in Fig. 3. When a dark pattern is executed, the system captures the user's expression, and the conductor records it in an excel sheet. In addition, the researchers wrote down all the comments of the participants regarding the dark patterns they met.

**Fig. 3.** A test case that shows the participant during the experiment.

### 3.6  User Experience Questionnaire

The UX questionnaire was used to learn more about the tasks performed and was divided into 7 sections. Each section referred to a website and the dark patterns encountered. The questions for each section were 4 and were addressed to the experience had with the dark pattern displayed. The proposed questions were used to understand the influence of each dark pattern on each of the users. The questions of the survey have been: (1) Did you notice the presence of the dark pattern x? (2) Did the presence of the dark pattern influence the decision to complete the purchase? (3) Do you think that without the presence of the dark pattern you would not have completed the purchase? (4) How did you feel about the presence of the dark pattern?

Although the emotions have been analyzed by a specific software, it was useful to know the feelings that the users themselves declared to compare them with the results obtained by the software and understand whether they were related or not.

---

[8] https://www.volagratis.com.

[9] https://www.ryanair.com.

[10] https://www.booking.com.

[11] https://www.rentalcars.com.

[12] https://www.it.mytrip.com.

# 4   Analysis of Results

In this section we show the results obtained through the previously mentioned surveys and those obtained through facial emotion recognition. Finally, the data obtained were compared to see their reliability.

## 4.1   Background Survey Results

From the data regarding the background survey, we found that users over the age of 35 were the participants with the poorest backgrounds. For this reason, it was chosen to divide the users in the following way: users under 35 years of age and users with an age greater than or equal to 35 years of age. This classification is useful for analyzing the data for the upcoming tests.

## 4.2   Emotion Recognition Results

This section discusses the data obtained from facial emotions recognition through MorphCast Emotional AI. Just as with the background survey, there were 50 test participants. The emotions analyzed are the primary ones cited in the above paragraph.

So, anger, fear, sadness, happiness, surprise, and disgust were measured. In addition, another emotion was added: indifference, which indicates a neutral expression that can be found when the participant does not reproduce any expression.

The graph in Fig. 4 shows the emotions of all users for each dark pattern found. The Fig. 5 shows the graph of emotions of all users under 35 years old for each dark pattern found. The Fig. 6 instead, represents the emotions of all the users with age superior or equal to 35 years for every dark pattern found.

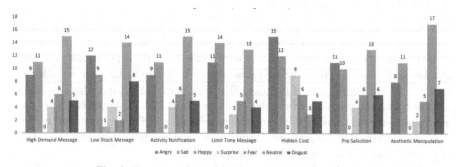

**Fig. 4.** Emotions of all users for each dark pattern found.

Table 1 reports for each dark pattern the predominant emotion resulting from the study.

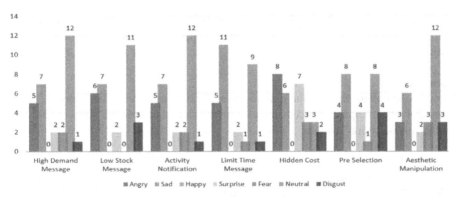

**Fig. 5.** Emotions of all users under 35 years old for each dark pattern found.

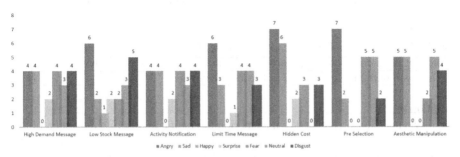

**Fig. 6.** Emotions of all users over 35 years old for each dark pattern found.

**Table 1.** Predominant emotions for each dark pattern.

| Dark pattern | Under 35 | Over 35 | Totality |
|---|---|---|---|
| Low stock message | Indifference | Angry | Indifference |
| High demand message | Indifference | Indifference, Sadness, Angry, Disgust | Indifference |
| Activity notification | Indifference | Indifference, Sadness, Angry, Disgust | Indifference |
| Limit time message | Sadness | Angry | Sadness |
| pre-selection | Sadness/Indifference | Angry | Indifference |
| Aesthetic manipulation | Sadness | Indifference, Sadness, Angry | Indifference |
| Hidden cost | Angry | Angry | Angry |

### 4.3 User Experience Questionnaire Results

The goals of the UX questionnaire are many: - To understand how many people notice the presence of dark patterns; - To understand how much the presence of dark patterns effects the choice of purchase; - To compare the data obtained from emotion recognition with the emotions obtained from the UX questionnaire to verify the reliability of the results.

**Question 1**
From the data obtained from the first question ("Did you notice the dark model?") we found that all participants noticed all dark patterns, only those over 35 years old did not see the "pre-selection" pattern.

**Question 2**
From the data obtained by the second question ("Did the presence of the dark pattern influence the choice to complete the purchase?") we have discovered that only the following four dark patterns have influenced the choice to complete the purchase: "low stock message", "hidden cost", "limit time message" and "aesthetic manipulation".

**Question 3**
The third question ("Do you think that without the presence of the dark pattern you would not have completed the purchase?") shows that users would have bought the product even without the presence of the dark patterns.

**Question 4**
The fourth question was related to the emotion felt by the user during the vision of the dark pattern. Specifically, it was asked: "How did you feel in the presence of the dark pattern?" for each of the patterns analyzed. Table 2 shows the predominant emotion (highest percentage) regarding this question.

**Table 2.** Predominant emotion regarding the fourth question.

| Dark pattern | Under 35 | Over 35 | Totality |
| --- | --- | --- | --- |
| Low stock message | Indifference | Angry | Indifference |
| High demand message | Indifference | Indifference | Indifference |
| Activity notification | Indifference | Indifference | Indifference |
| Limit time message | Sadness | Indifference | Sadness |
| Pre-selection | Sadness | Indifference | Sadness |
| Aesthetic manipulation | Sadness | Sadness | Sadness |
| Hidden cost | Angry | Angry | Angry |

## 4.4 Comparison Between Data Obtained Through Emotion Recognition and Data Collected from the UX Questionnaire

In this section we will compare the data obtained through the recognition of emotions and the data received from the UX questionnaire. In the previous sections are the results for each dark pattern, however it is necessary to validate these data, to understand or not if the outcomes of the different tests are correlated with each other. Also in this analysis, as in the previous ones, the users will be divided by age. The dark patterns "high demand message" and "activity notification" are shown in the same web site, therefore graphs of the dark pattern "high demand message", that they will follow, are equal to the dark pattern "activity notification", that will not be shown because they have given the same results. The comparison of data will follow in the following order: (1) Comparison of emotions considering the totality of users; (2) Comparison of emotions examining users under 35 years old; (3) Comparison of emotions examining users over 35 years old.

### 4.5  Comparison of Emotions Considering the Totality of Users

In this paragraph, the colors of the graphs indicate: - Yellow: results obtained from the UX questionnaire; - Blue: results obtained by emotion recognition.

**High Demand Message and Activity Notification**
The graph in Fig. 7 shows a close correlation between almost all the emotions. The expression anger did not assume the same value for both the tests, but the predominant emotions predominant for both are sadness and indifference, thus confirming the reliability of this result.

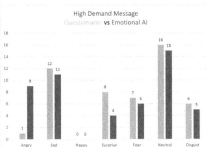 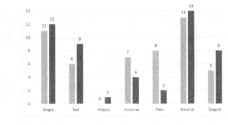

**Fig. 7.** Comparison of questionnaire and emotion recognition of total users' high-demand message and task notification patterns.

**Fig. 8.** Comparison of questionnaire and emotion recognition of total users' low stock message pattern.

**Low Stock Message**
The comparison of the emotions coming from the dark pattern "low stock message" results coherent. In fact, the graph in Fig. 8 shows an almost equal relationship in the greater part of the emotions, except for fear, that assumes different values.

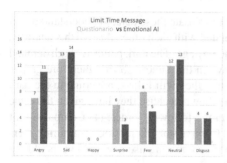

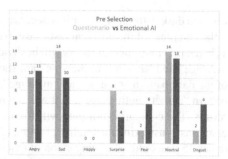

**Fig. 9.** Comparison of questionnaire and emotion recognition of total users' limit time message pattern.

**Fig. 10.** Comparison of questionnaire and emotion recognition of total users' pre-selection pattern.

### Limit Time Message

The relationship of the predominant values of the dark pattern "limit time message" is nearly equal, as we can see in the graph in Fig. 9.

### Pre-selection

For the dark pattern "Pre-selection", the predominant emotions remain Sadness, Anger, and Indifference, even if, as we can notice from the graph in Fig. 10, Sadness took on a slightly different value, although it remained among the top three.

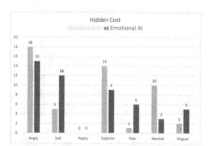

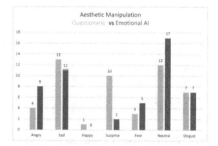

**Fig. 11.** Comparison of questionnaire and emotion recognition of total users' hidden cost pattern.

**Fig. 12.** Comparison of questionnaire and emotion recognition of total users' aesthetic manipulation pattern.

### Hidden Cost

From the graph illustrated in Fig. 11, anger can be confirmed as the predominant emotion, however, an alteration can be seen in the emotion's sadness and surprise. They would lead to confirm surprise as the second highest value and sadness as third.

### Aesthetic Manipulation

The graph in Fig. 12 shows two primary emotions: indifference and sadness. Although the two tests provided two dominant emotions different, the values for each of them are close. We can therefore validate the results obtained.

### 4.6  Comparison of Emotions Examining Users Under 35 Years Old

In this paragraph the colors of the graphs indicate: - Blue: results obtained from the UX questionnaire; - Orange: results obtained through the recognition of emotions.

**High Demand Message and Activity Notification**
What can be observed from the graph in Fig. 13 is a close correlation between almost all the emotions, in particular sadness and indifference. The expression anger did not assume the same value for both tests, but the predominant emotions however, for both result to be similar, confirming therefore the reliability of such result.

**Low Stock Message**
The comparison of the emotions coming from the dark pattern "low stock message" results coherent. In fact, the graph in Fig. 14 shows an almost equal comparison for anger and sadness. The indifference, indicated from the voice "neutral", remains the dominant expression, despite the values of the various tests are not close between them.

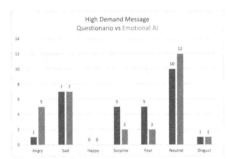

**Fig. 13.** Comparison of questionnaire and emotion recognition of under 35 years old users' high demand message and activity notification patterns.

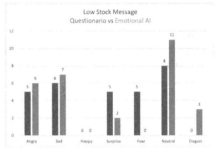

**Fig. 14.** Comparison of questionnaire and emotion recognition of under 35 years old users' low stock message pattern.

**Limit Time Message**
The ratio of the predominant values of the dark pattern "limit time message" is fair for sadness and indifference, which are confirmed as the main emotions for this dark pattern, as we can see in the graph in Fig. 15.

**Pre-selection**
For the dark pattern "Pre-selection", the predominant emotions are sadness, anger, and indifference. Even surprise, however, as we can see from the graph in Fig. 16, has reached a value like anger.

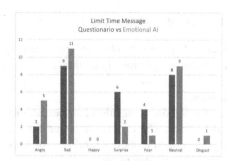

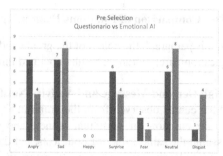

**Fig. 15.** Comparison of questionnaire and emotion recognition of under 35 years old users' limit time message pattern.

**Fig. 16.** Comparison of questionnaire and emotion recognition of under 35 years old users' pre-selection pattern.

**Hidden Cost**

From the graph illustrated in Fig. 17 we can confirm anger as the predominant emotion, followed by surprise. However, it is possible to notice an alteration of the emotions: sadness and indifference.

**Aesthetic Manipulation**

The highest values concern anger and indifference, as shown in the graph in Fig. 18. It can be seen that the questionnaire reported higher values for surprise.

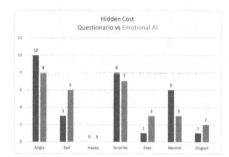

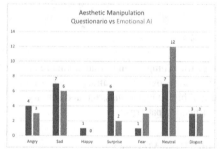

**Fig. 17.** Comparison of questionnaire and emotion recognition of under 35 years old users' hidden cost pattern.

**Fig. 18.** Comparison of questionnaire and emotion recognition of under 35 years old users' aesthetic manipulation pattern.

## 4.7  Comparison of Emotions by Examining Users Aged 35 Years and Older

In this paragraph, the colors of the graphs indicate: - Blue: results obtained from the UX questionnaire; - Green: results obtained by emotion recognition.

**High Demand Message and Activity Notification**
The values of almost all the emotions are similar, as can be seen from the graph represented in Fig. 19. Disgust and sadness remain the highest values, fear instead has decreased from the results of the UX questionnaire. Same for anger, which was zero in the UX questionnaire. Indifference is also confirmed as one of the highest values.

**Low Stock Message**
From the diagram in Fig. 20 the same values of anger and disgust can be noticed, that represent the highest. The indifference has reached a higher value from the data of the questionnaire, but it remains however in third higher, confirming the results obtained from the test.

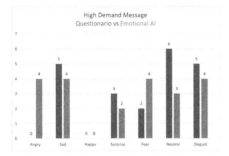 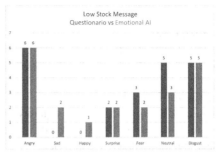

**Fig. 19.** Comparison of questionnaire and emotion recognition of over 35 years old users' high demand message and activity notification patterns.

**Fig. 20.** Comparison of questionnaire and emotion recognition of over 35 years old users' low stock message pattern.

**Limit Time Message**
The emotions detected for the dark pattern "limit time message" were the most truthful, from the graph in Fig. 21 it can be observed how the values of all the emotions are tightly close.

**Pre-selection**
From the relationship illustrated by the graph in Fig. 22, only two emotions can be confirmed: "indifference" and "anger". The fear and sadness found by the software for the detection of emotions was not validated by the questionnaire.

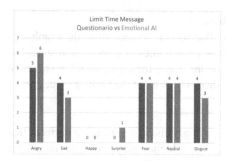

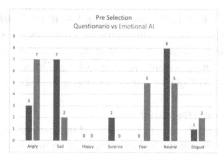

**Fig. 21.** Comparison of questionnaire and emotion recognition of over 35 years old users' limit time message pattern.

**Fig. 22.** Comparison of questionnaire and emotion recognition of over 35 years old users' pre-selection pattern.

**Hidden Cost**

From the graph illustrated in Fig. 23 we can confirm "anger" as the predominant emotion. However, the remaining values are discordant.

**Aesthetic Manipulation**

The graph in Fig. 24 shows the equality of the values inherent to disgust, indifference, and fear; sadness is also confirmed as the highest value. It is different instead for two other emotions, anger, and surprise.

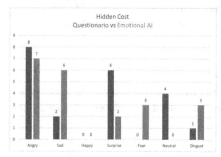

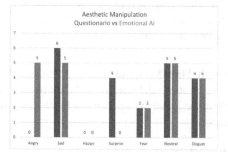

**Fig. 23.** Comparison of questionnaire and emotion recognition of over 35 years old users' hidden cost pattern.

**Fig. 24.** Comparison of questionnaire and emotion recognition of over 35 years old users' aesthetic manipulation pattern.

## 4.8 Analysis

After analyzing the results, shown in the previous section, several considerations emerged.

- The under 35 represent the users with a more advanced technological background and are accustomed to such strategies and tricks, this explains the indifference for most of the dark patterns. For the patterns "limit time message" and "pre-selection" instead the perceived emotion is sadness. While anger for the dark pattern "hidden cost".

- The over 35 are more vulnerable users because they use less frequently online travel agencies to book their vacations. The emotions detected are in fact different for each dark pattern.

  - Aesthetic manipulation: sadness
  - Low stock message: anger and disgust
  - Limit time message: anger
  - Hidden cost: anger
  - Activity notification and high demand message: sadness and disgust
  - Pre-selection: indifference

- The "pre-selection" pattern has not been noticed by most users.
- The dark patterns that influence most the customer during the purchase of a product/service online are: (1) "Low stock message", (2) "Hidden cost", (3) "Aesthetic manipulation".
- The users would buy the products if they were really interested, but the dark patterns incentivize them to complete the purchases in the shortest possible time.
- The dark pattern "Hidden cost" is the one perceived with the highest values of anger probably because it is the most tangible form of deception among all the dark patterns.
- The anger, especially on users over 35, detected by facial recognition can be linked to a visual effort of the users, assuming a deep look and contracted eyebrows.

## 5   Conclusion and Future Research

In this paper, we dealt with dark patterns and the effects they cause on users. We identified the most commonly used dark patterns in online travel agencies and we investigated their effects on the customer experience by carrying out a study involving 50 participants and 9 websites. During the test, the users have been filmed via webcam in order to track their expressions and emotions through AI-based facial recognition. At the end of the task, to validate the results, we conducted a final questionnaire where all users indicated the emotion they felt during the test. The results were compared with the AI-based emotion recognition results, and we found that the over 35 are more vulnerable to dark patterns than those under 35. We realized that technological background greatly affects the emotions users may feel when interfacing with dark patterns. Not being familiar with the web makes inexperienced users easily fooled by strategies and tricks, such as dark patterns. The under 35 s are more experienced users with online travel agencies and are accustomed to such dark patterns, as opposed to the over 35 s, who less frequently use websites to book their vacations. Indeed, for those under 35 we have found the indifference for most of the dark patterns. For the "limit time message" and "pre-selection" patterns the manifested emotion was sadness. While anger for the "hidden cost" dark pattern. For the over 35, instead, we found different emotions for each pattern: sadness and disgust for "activity notification" and "high demand message" patterns, anger for "limit time message" and "hidden cost" patterns, for the "aesthetic manipulation" pattern the emotion was sadness and finally indifference for "pre-selection" pattern.

In the future considering that the over 35 were the ones who manifested emotions other than indifference in all dark patterns, except for "pre-selection" pattern, we plan to extend the test to other over 35 users, in order to learn more about the effects of dark patterns.

In the next future, on the basis of the study results, we are going to formalize a set of design guidelines to support practitioners during the development of web interfaces for online travel agencies, in a way to design effective interfaces while avoiding dark patterns that would negatively affect the user experience.

# References

1. Gray, C., Kou, Y., Battles, B., Hoggatt, J., Toombs, A.: The dark (patterns) side of UX design (2018). https://doi.org/10.1145/3173574.3174108
2. Kim, W.G., Pillai, S.G., Haldorai, K., Ahmad, W.: Dark patterns used by online travel agency websites. Ann. Tour. Res. **88**(C) (2021). https://doi.org/10.1016/j.annals.2020.103055
3. Matsumoto, D.: Paul Ekman and the legacy of universals. J. Res. Pers. **38**, 45–51 (2004). https://doi.org/10.1016/j.jrp.2003.09.005
4. International Organization for Standardization. ISO 9241-11 (2018)
5. Brignull, H.: Dark patterns. Technical report. Harry Brignull dark patterns website, deceptive design (2019). www.darkpatterns.org
6. Battistoni, P., Sebillo, M., Di Gregorio, M., Vitiello, G., Romano, M.: ProSign+ a cloud-based platform supporting inclusiveness in public communication. In: 2020 IEEE 17th Annual Consumer Communications & Networking Conference (CCNC), pp. 1–5. IEEE, January 2020
7. Di Chiara, G., et al.: The framy user interface for visually-impaired users. In: 2011 Sixth International Conference on Digital Information Management, pp. 36–41. IEEE, September 2011
8. Conti, G., Sobiesk, E.: Malicious interface design: exploiting the user. In: Proceedings of the International Conference on World Wide Web, pp. 271–280 (2010)
9. Mathur, A., et al.: Dark patterns at scale: findings from a crawl of 11k shopping websites. In: Proceedings of the ACM on Human-Computer Interaction 3, CSCW, Article 81, 32 pages, November 2019. https://doi.org/10.1145/3359183
10. Di Geronimo, L., Braz, L., Fregnan, E., Palomba, F., Bacchelli, A.: UI dark patterns and where to find them: a study on mobile applications and user perception. In: Proceedings of the 2020 CHI Conference on Human Factors in Computing Systems, pp. 1–14. Association for Computing Machinery, New York (2020). https://doi.org/10.1145/3313831.3376600
11. Calo, R.: Digital market manipulation. Geo. Wash. L. Rev. **82**, 995 (2014). https://digitalcommons.law.uw.edu/faculty-articles/25
12. Calo, R., Rosenblat, A.: The taking economy: uber, information, and power. Colum. L. Rev. **117**, 1623 (2017). https://digitalcommons.law.uw.edu/faculty-articles/47
13. Ekman, P., Friesen, W.V., Hager, J.C.: A human Face (Firm). Facial Action Coding System. A Human Face, Salt Lake City, UT (2002)
14. Pantic, M., Rothkrantz, L.: Automatic analysis of facial expressions: the state of the art. IEEE Trans. Pattern Anal. Mach. Intell. **22**, 1424–1445 (2001). https://doi.org/10.1109/34.895976
15. Zeng, Z., Pantic, M., Reisman, G.I., Huang, T.S.: A survey of affect recognition methods: audio, visual, and spontaneous expressions. IEEE Trans. Pattern Anal. Mach. Intell. **31**(1), 39–58 (2009). https://doi.org/10.1109/TPAMI.2008.52

16. Valstar, M.F., Jiang, B., Mehu, M., Pantic, M., Scherer, K.:The first facial expression recognition and analysis challenge. In: 2011 IEEE International Conference on Automatic Face & Gesture Recognition (FG), pp. 921–926 (2011). https://doi.org/10.1109/FG.2011.5771374
17. Bos, D.O.: EEG-based emotion recognition. Influ. Vis. Audit. Stimuli **56**(3), 1–17 (2006)
18. Torres, E.P., Torres, E.A., Hernández-Álvarez, M., Yoo, S.G.: EEG-based BCI emotion recognition: a survey. Sensors **20**, 5083 (2020). https://doi.org/10.3390/s20185083
19. Deng, L., Dong, Y.: deep learning: methods and applications. Found. Trends Signal Process. **7**, 197–387 (2014)
20. Di Gregorio, M., Nota, G., Romano, M., Sebillo, M., Vitiello, G.: Designing usable interfaces for the industry 4.0. In: Proceedings of the International Conference on Advanced Visual Interfaces, pp. 1–9, September 2020
21. Battistoni, P., Di Gregorio, M. Romano, M., Sebillo, M., Vitiello, G.: AI at the edge for sign language learning support. Int. J. Humaniz. Comput. Commun. (IJHCC) **1**(1), 23–42 (2020)
22. Battistoni, P., Di Gregorio, M., Romano, M., Sebillo, M., Vitiello, G., Solimando, G.: Sign language interactive learning - measuring the user engagement. In: Zaphiris, P., Ioannou, A. (eds.) HCII 2020. LNCS, vol. 12206, pp. 3–12. Springer, Cham (2020). https://doi.org/10.1007/978-3-030-50506-6_1
23. Battistoni, P., Di Gregorio, M., Sebillo, M., Vitiello, G.: AI at the edge for sign language learning support. In: 2019 IEEE International Conference on Humanized Computing and Communication (HCC), pp. 16–23. IEEE, September 2019
24. Battistoni, P., Di Gregorio, M., Romano, M., Sebillo, M., Vitiello, G., Brancaccio, A.: Interaction design patterns for augmented reality fitting rooms. Sensors **22**(3), 982 (2022)
25. Ginige, A., Romano, M., Sebillo, M., Vitiello, G., Di Giovanni, P.: Spatial data and mobile applications: general solutions for interface design. In: Proceedings of the International Working Conference on Advanced Visual Interfaces, pp. 189–196, May 2012

# Defining an A/B Testing Process for Usability and User Experience Evaluation Through the Analysis of the Results of a Literature Review

Ítalo Fernandes[1], Simara Rocha[1], Carlos Portela[1],
Geraldo Braz Junior[1], João Almeida[1], Aristofanes Silva[1], Davi Viana[1],
Jacilane Rabelo[2], Anselmo Paiva[1], and Luis Rivero[1][✉]

[1] PPGCC, Universidade Federal do Maranhão, São Luis, Brazil
`italo.fernandes@discente.ufma.br,`
`{simara.rocha,carlos.castro,geraldo.braz,joao.dallyson,ac.silva,`
`davi.viana,anselmo.paiva,luis.rivero}@ufma.br`
[2] Universidade Federal do Ceará, Russas, Brazil
`jacilane.rabelo@ufc.br`

**Abstract.** Usability and User Experience are high-impact quality factors for the design of interactive systems, since they impact how we use them in daily life activities. Despite the importance of these quality attributes, several users report problems when interacting with information systems. Considering the need to meet different quality standards, software testing is an important area for identifying software defects. Despite the proposal of different approaches for A/B testing in the context of Usability and UX evaluation, there are still some improvement opportunities. For instance, after carrying out a literature review, we did not identify an A/B testing process that could be applied for identifying both usability and user experience problems. Furthermore, most of the A/B testing processes in the context of human computer interaction do not gather qualitative data, which makes it difficult to identify what to improve in the selected version of a software to meet the users' needs. Considering the above, this paper proposes a new A/B testing process that allows the evaluation of both usability and user experience attributes. For each of the A/B testing processes found in our literature review, we gathered data on the categorization of the process, its activities, the roles within the process, and the artifacts that were employed during the planning, conducting and reporting of the test. We then organized our results creating a new process that would consider all relevant activities and artifacts from previous work.

**Keywords:** A/B Testing · Usability · User experience · Evaluation methods · Comparative testing · Evaluation process

M. Kurosu et al. (Eds.): HCII 2022, LNCS 13516, pp. 204–213, 2022.
https://doi.org/10.1007/978-3-031-17615-9_14

# 1  Introduction

Usability is one of the most important quality factors for the design of interactive systems, since it impacts how we use them in daily life activities [4]. An interactive system with a low degree of usability may become difficult to use and turn the user less productive when carrying out tasks [3]. Additionally, User Experience (UX) is a concept for understanding and studying the quality in use of interactive products. According to AllAboutUX.org[1], there are at least 27 definitions on UX. For instance, UX is defined by the International Organization for Standardization [9] as a person's perceptions and responses that result from the use or anticipated use of a product, system or service.

According to Borsci et al. [2] the relation-ship between user experience and usability is still under discussion; and some UX researchers [7,13,20] state that UX goes beyond the task-oriented approach of traditional usability by bringing out aspects such as beauty, fun, pleasure, and personal growth that satisfy general human needs but have little instrumental value. Consequently, traditional usability measures related to the ease of use and usefulness of an application can be employed to assess its user experience. However, evaluating traditional usability attributes may not be sufficient as UX considers attributes beyond the instrumental such as users' emotions before, during and after their interaction with a software application [20]. Therefore, to transmit a positive experience, it is necessary that applications provide functionality and easy means to access it [8]. Hence, usability principals must be respected when developing the user interface of a mobile application, while also considering users' emotions and reactions towards the application.

Considering the need to meet different quality standards, software testing is an important area for identifying software defects [6]. Several evaluation methods have been proposed to capture users' thoughts, expectations and emotions towards software applications [1]. Among the different software testing approaches, A/B testing has emerged as an alternative for comparing different types of software in a given context [12]. A/B testing proposes to split the universe of users in two or more groups with the purpose of testing different versions of an idea with each group and comparing the effect of each version [12]. The obtained information within these tests can be used for defining the impact of changes in different versions of a software, or evaluating the impact of choosing between two or more concurrent information systems. Traditionally, A/B testing allows comparing functional requirements of an information system. However, new approaches were developed to allow evaluating usability and user experience when comparing two or more information systems [18].

Despite the proposal of different approaches for A/B testing in the context of Usability and UX evaluation, there are still some improvement opportunities. For instance, we did not identify an A/B testing process that could be applied for identifying both usability and user experience problems. Considering the above, this paper proposes a new A/B testing process that allows the evaluation of both usability and user experience attributes. To do so, for each of the A/B testing

---

[1] All about UX Website: http://www.allaboutux.org/ux-definitions.

processes found in a literature review, we gathered data on the categorization of the process, its activities, the roles within the process, and the artifacts that were employed during the planning, conducting and reporting of the test.

The remainder of this paper is organized as follows. In Sect. 2, we discuss work related with this research. In Sect. 3, we present our research methodology, which allowed us to identify the activities for A/B Usability and UX evaluation. Section 4 presents our results with the proposal of a nee process Usability and UX A/B Testing. Finally, our conclusions and future work are described in Sect. 5.

## 2   Related Work

According to Kujala et al. (2014), evaluating the UX and usability features of a system is a challenging task, as users may find it difficult to express their experiences if directly asked to. Hence, besides objective usability measures such as task execution time or the number of errors, it is necessary to develop evaluation approaches that determine what is relevant from the user point of view [20].

To investigate the different available evaluation approaches, a number of reviews has been performed [17]. Based on these reviews, several types of evaluation methods can be listed. For instance, forms have become essential as they have been developed considering usability and new evaluated UX factors [14]. Other questionnaires focus on extracting users' motivations and attitudes by providing open questions or means for the users to describe their emotions themselves [13].

In the experience sampling category, users report their experience at specific moments of their day. While a device periodically senses their physiological responses to stimulus or tracks the context of their day, users are asked how they are feeling [15]. The main advantage of employing experience sampling methods is having users experience the applications in real usage scenarios, gathering valuable information to understand the context of use. Nevertheless, to gather complete data, these methods may take long to be applied, may disrupt the interaction with the evaluated application and may make users feel tired [11].

We can also gather usage data from the direct observation of users or by monitoring their physiological responses towards the evaluated application. For instance, Marco et al. (2013) employed video recording to analyze the degree of fun and children's engagement. The video stream allowed the children's gestures and verbal expressions while interacting with each other to be transcribed, as well as their engagement by means of observing the focus of the children's attention. During the analysis, it is also possible to include stamps to indicate interaction problems.

When using the above mentioned methods, we can also compare different types of software aimed at achieving similar goals. In that context, A/B testing proposes to split the universe of visitors in two or more groups with the purpose of testing different versions of an idea with each group and comparing the effect of each version [4]. Traditionally, A/B testing allows comparing functional requirements of an information system. However, a similar approach may be used to improve usability. Hence, new approaches were developed to allow evaluating usability and user experience when comparing two or more information systems [18].

Among these approaches, Firmenich et al. (2019) proposes an iterative method supported by a toolkit that allows usability experts to design user tests, run them remotely, analyze results, and assess alternative solutions to usability problems similarly to A/B testing. According to the authors, each solution is created by applying client-side web refactorings, i.e., changes to the web pages in the client which are meant to improve usability. The main benefit of their approach is that it reduces the overall cost of user testing and particularly, A/B testing, by applying refactorings to create alternative solutions without modifying the application's server code.

In another paper, Speicher et al. (2014) developed the Usability-based Split Testing which is an A/B testing approach with leverage considering user interactions for deriving quantitative metrics of usability. The authors developed WaPPU, which is a tool realized as a service with a central repository, which enables developers to create and monitor A/B testing projects. In the tool, it is possible to choose from a range of 27 predefined interaction features including clicks, length of the cursor trail and amount of scrolling. The tool was able to detect the predicted difference in usability with statistical significance for the largest and most representative user group.

Finally, some papers describe usability A/B testing approaches using traditional A/B testing considering traditional usability instruments (e.g. System Usability Scale) [10] or attributes (ease of operation, number of steps, ergonomics, visual preference, others) [16,19], or specific UX features in embedded automated machine learning models [5]. For instance, Jabbar et al. (2021) carried out an A/B testing to improve a website's interactivity. In their research, design trends were applied on the Website of Quaid-e-Awam University of Engineering, Science and Technology (QUEST) to make it more interactive for students. The usability of the old version and new version was measured in order to recommend better design trends. The study was designed with pre-test and post-test questionnaire designed using system usability scale (SUS) measuring three attributes of usability that are effectiveness, efficiency and satisfaction.

Despite the proposal or application of different approaches for A/B testing in the context of Usability and UX evaluation, there are still some improvement opportunities. For instance, after carrying out a literature review combining the terms "A/B testing", "Split testing", "Multivalued Testing", "Comparative Testing", "Usability" and "User experience", we did not identify an A/B testing process that could be applied for identifying both usability and user experience problems. Furthermore, most of the A/B testing processes in the context of human computer interaction do not gather qualitative data, which makes it difficult to identify what to improve in the selected version of a software to meet the users' needs. Finally, although remote testing is important for gathering real usage data, most of the identified A/B testing processes were performed this way instead of laboratory setting or in the field, which, in turn, can be useful to gather further information from the point of view of users, such as user feedback and emotional responses.

Considering the above, there is a need to develop specific Usability/UX A/B testing evaluation approaches that can be useful in the evaluation of different versions of a software idea or concurrent software. Also, these approaches could be useful for defining the set of steps necessary for carrying out an A/B testing. In the following section, we present the steps for identifying the activities within A/B testing for usability and/or UX evaluation, while also proposing an evaluation process that considers these activities and describes what is necessary to perform them.

## 3   Research Methodology

For each of the A/B testing processes found in our forementioned literature review, we gathered data on the categorization of the process, its activities, the roles within the process, and the artifacts that were employed during the planning, conducting and reporting of the test. In all, six publications [4,5,10, 16,18,19] were considered during our literature review.

**Table 1.** Identified activities within the A/B testing process for usability evaluation by Firmenich et al. (2019)

| Code | Optional | Activity Description | Role | Resources |
|---|---|---|---|---|
| ACTV01 | | Select a specific use case to be tested in this interaction, defining it as "Usability Testing" | Expert Designer | Scenario Recorder |
| ACTV02 | Yes | Decompose the functionality of the selected Usability test at the level of tasks to be performed (For example: "Create a new user account", "Login"), etc. | Expert Designer | Scenario Recorder |
| ACTV03 | Yes | Assemble tasks into groups to create a Usability Test Scenario Template | Expert Designer | Scenario Editor |
| ACTV04 | | Define the metrics and which tools will be used in the test scenario, when it is executed | Expert Designer | Scenario Editor |
| ACTV05 | | Recruit participants to run test scenarios | Expert Designer | Not Defined |
| ACTV06 | | Answer the demographic questionnaire with the participants | Participants | Scenario Player |
| ACTV07 | | Carry out the tests of the test scenarios following the guided steps (For example: Create a new user account", "Login", "Search for products", "Add products to cart" and "Check-out") | Participants | Scenario Player |
| ACTV08 | | At the end of the test, answer a usability questionnaire for the participants | Participants | Scenario Player—SUS Questionnaire |
| ACTV09 | | Analyze results to discover usability issues (For example: "Abandoned form", "Undescriptive element", and "Misleading link") | Expert Designer | Test Analysis Tool (VisualA) |
| ACTV10 | Yes | Create different versions of the application as solutions to try to solve usability issues (For example: "Abandoned form", "Undescriptive element", and "Misleading link") | Expert Designer | CSWR Framework—Vi tool |
| ACTV11 | Yes | Reapply usability test | Expert Designer | Not Defined |
| ACTV12 | | Analyze test execution results | Expert Designer | Test Analysis Tool |
| ACTV13 | | Decide on the best evaluated solution (A/B/n) | Expert Designer | Not Defined |
| ACTV14 | Yes | Produce the specification and implementation project of the best identified solution | Developers | CSWR Framework—Vi tool |
| ACTV15 | Yes | Develop the solution | Developers | Not Defined |
| ACTV16 | Yes | Make the interface available in the production environment | Developers | Not Defined |
| ACTV17 | Yes | Retest for usability (cycle restart) | Developers | Not Defined |

Table 1 shows an example of such extraction from the research by Firmenich et al. (2019). In this example, we defined the code for each of the activities of the process described by the authors for carrying out a usability A/B testing. Note that some activities have been marked as optional. This happened due to the fact that, in some cases, the authors carried out specific activities that were not generic, or that would require specific tools to be carried out. When this happened, we marked these activities as optional, in order to indicate whenever specific requirements or actions could be required. Note that this example also indicates who carried out the activity or is the main actor for its execution, while also indicating the resources that were necessary for their execution. In case the authors of an analyzed paper did not provide this information, we inferred this information. When there was no way of inferring the information, we indicated "Not defined". At the end of the analysis process all mandatory and optional activities were registered in sex tables, each for analyzed paper within our literature review.

After identifying the set of activities for each of the identified usability/UX A/B testing processes, we carried out an analysis in order to merge the mandatory and optional activities. The analysis was performed as follows. We listed the identified activities within each A/B testing process and ordered according to the order indicated in the papers describing them. Then, we grouped activities if two or more processes referred to the same activity. After that, the best (i.e. the most clear and detailed) description for each activity was selected as prime description for the an activity within our process, yielding a list of single descriptions. For example, two processes referred to the same activity: (1) Define the metrics and which tools will be used in the test scenario, when it is executed [4]; and (2) Define quantitative metrics as dependent variables, or user responses [19]. These activities were considered a group and the first description by Firmenich et al. (2019) used as main description of the activity as it was more clear and understandable from the point of view of the researchers. In the following section, we present the final version of our process considering usability and UX A/B testing processes found in the literature.

## 4 Result

We created a new process that would consider all relevant activities and artifacts from previous work. As mentioned before, if an activity was cited more than one time among the considered processes, we combined its description with the other activities' descriptions to make a single activity that would be more understandable and thoroughly described.

Tables 2, 3 and 4 show the proposed process, which differentiates from others by combining the basic processes' activities, artifacts and evaluation criteria, suggesting metrics for evaluating both usability and user experience. When considering all activities within the process, Table 2 shows all activities that must be performed in order to carry out the A/B testing usability or UX evaluation. Nevertheless, some activities may be substituted, such as ACTV20, in which an

**Table 2.** Proposed A/B testing process for Usability and UX evaluation - Mandatory Activities

| Code | Substitute | Activity description | [4] | [18] | [10] | [19] | [16] | [5] |
|---|---|---|---|---|---|---|---|---|
| ACTV01 | | Select a specific use case to be tested in this interaction, defining it as "Usability Testing" | X | | | | | |
| ACTV02 | | Determine user intent | | X | | | | |
| ACTV03 | Can be substituted by OP-ACTV-01 | Make the current version of the system available for testing | | | X | | | |
| ACTV04 | | Define the metrics and which tools will be used in the test scenario, when it is executed | X | | | X | | |
| ACTV05 | | Set scores for the variants and metrics and interface being evaluated | | | | | | X |
| ACTV06 | | Define semi-structured tasks for executing the tasks on the site | | X | | | | |
| ACTV07 | | Prepare the experiment with design variants and objects | | | | X | | |
| ACTV08 | | Define the start and end dates of the test, textual and graphical instructions, consent form, number of comparisons and the demographic data to be captured | | | | X | | |
| ACTV09 | | Define criteria for inclusion and exclusion of participants | | | | | X | |
| ACTV10 | | Recruit participants for the application of test scenarios | X | X | X | | X | |
| ACTV11 | | Collect demographic data by interview or questionnaire | X | X | X | | | |
| ACTV12 | | Present to the participant the guidelines for performing the test | | | | X | | |
| ACTV13 | | Split participants between the two available test interfaces | | X | X | X | | |
| ACTV14 | | Monitor the balance of participants by application version | | | | X | | |
| ACTV15 | Can be substituted by OP-ACTV-02 | Carry out the tests of the test scenarios following the guided steps | X | X | X | X | | X |
| ACTV16 | | Track user behavior in a test's interfaces during execution | | X | | | | |
| ACTV17 | | Evaluate user interaction effort in different interfaces | | | | | | X |
| ACTV18 | | Report test completion | | X | | | | |
| ACTV19 | | Answer a usability questionnaire at the end of the test (for participants) | X | X | X | | X | |
| ACTV20 | Can be substituted by OP-ACTV-03 | Analyze results to discover usability issues | X | X | X | X | X | X |
| ACTV21 | | Decide on the best evaluated solution (A/B/n) | X | | | X | X | |
| | | Total Number of Contributions per Paper | 8 | 10 | 7 | 9 | 5 | 4 |

analysis could be performed through machine learning algorithms. If that is the case, the development team could check reference [5] for information on how to perform this activity. This information is provided in both Tables 2 and 3, by checking the code of possible substitute activities. Finally, extra activities that are not mandatory nor substitutes for mandatory activities can be found in Table 4. These activities have not been ordered as they may appear according to the specific needs of the development team.

**Table 3.** Proposed A/B testing process for Usability and UX evaluation - Optional activities that could be performed to substitute mandatory activities

| Code | Activity description | [4] | [18] | [10] | [19] | [16] | [5] |
|------|----------------------|-----|------|------|------|------|-----|
| OP-ACTV-01 | Create web application versions with usability problem assessment techniques | | | X | | | X |
| OP-ACTV-02 | Create versions of web applications with semi-automatic evaluation techniques for usability problems to be found through interaction analysis | | | | | | X |
| OP-ACTV-03 | Use Machine Learning techniques for interaction analysis | | | | | | X |
| | Total Number of Contributions per Paper | 0 | 0 | 1 | 0 | 0 | 3 |

**Table 4.** Proposed A/B testing process for Usability and UX evaluation - Optional Extra Activities that could be performed if needed by the development team

| Code | Activity description | [4] | [18] | [10] | [19] | [16] | [5] |
|------|----------------------|-----|------|------|------|------|-----|
| OP-ACTV-04 | Break down test functionality into tasks to be selected Usability | X | | | | | |
| OP-ACTV-05 | Assemble tasks into groups to create a Usability Test Scenario Template | X | | | | | |
| OP-ACTV-06 | Create app versions as solutions to usability issues | X | | | | | |
| OP-ACTV-07 | Reapply usability testing | X | | | | | |
| OP-ACTV-08 | Produce implementation specification of the best identified solution and project design | X | | | | | |
| OP-ACTV-09 | Produce implementation specification of the best identified solution and project design | X | | | | | |
| OP-ACTV-10 | Implement as improvements of the best results | X | | X | | | |
| OP-ACTV-11 | Make the interface available in the production environment | X | | | | | |
| OP-ACTV-12 | Guide participants to unlock AD Blocks from their web browsers (browsers) | | X | | | | |
| OP-ACTV-13 | Redesign the application with support from UX professionals | | X | | | | |
| OP-ACTV-14 | Load the used pool of properties performed in the experiment as variants in a package | | | | X | | |
| OP-ACTV-15 | Carry out the test in the tool (for example: clicks on a variant or on "It's a draw") | | | | X | | |
| OP-ACTV-16 | Perform statistical tests to validate research data | | | | | X | |
| OP-ACTV-17 | Explore positive (solutions) and negative (solutions) behavior through the usability tool | | | | | | X |
| OP-ACTV-18 | Select the element with usability problem | | | | | | X |
| OP-ACTV-19 | Investigate method to do as web tool | | | | | | X |
| OP-ACTV-20 | Discover micro measures so that each element can be averaged and evaluated for a semi-automatic UX assessment | | | | | | X |
| OP-ACTV-21 | Definition of the decision tree through micro-measures | | | | | | X |
| OP-ACTV-22 | Feedback or Machine Learning algorithm to improve a semi-automatic analysis | | | | | | X |
| | Total Number of Contributions per Paper | 8 | 2 | 1 | 2 | 1 | 6 |

## 5   Conclusions and Future Work

Based on the analysis of 6 papers describing processes for A/B testing for evaluating usability and UX in different types of systems, we managed to develop a new and more complete process containing 21 mandatory activities and 22 optional activities, from which 3 can substitute mandatory activities and 19 can be added to a traditional usability and UX A/B testing. Through the process, we also identified who carries out the tasks during the evaluation and what tools/artifacts may be necessary for the execution of the A/B testing.

We are currently applying the new process in a power multinational company to test two concurrent software, to make decisions into which software best meets users' needs and expectations. As future work, we intend to gather data during these evaluations in real contexts to verify to what extent the new process allows collecting relevant usability and UX data from the point of view of users. Furthermore, we intend to evaluate the artifacts we are developing for the execution of the mandatory activities within our process. By providing a process and a set of artifacts for evaluating both usability and UX, we intend to support the software development industry in identifying usability and UX problems, as well as supporting the correction of those problems, improving the quality of future software and the experience of users' while carrying out tasks and achieving goals in information systems and applications.

## References

1. Bargas-Avila, J.A., Hornbæk, K.: Old wine in new bottles or novel challenges: a critical analysis of empirical studies of user experience. In: Proceedings of the SIGCHI Conference on Human Factors in Computing Systems, pp. 2689–2698 (2011)
2. Borsci, S., Kurosu, M., Federici, S., Mele, M.L.: Computer systems experiences of users with and without disabilities (2014)
3. Fernandez, A., Insfran, E., Abrahão, S.: Usability evaluation methods for the web: a systematic mapping study. Inf. Softw. Technol. 53(8), 789–817 (2011)
4. Firmenich, S., Garrido, A., Grigera, J., Rivero, J.M., Rossi, G.: Usability improvement through a/b testing and refactoring. Software Qual. J. 27(1), 203–240 (2019)
5. Gardey, J.C., Garrido, A.: User experience evaluation through automatic a/b testing. In: Proceedings of the 25th International Conference on Intelligent User Interfaces Companion, pp. 25–26 (2020)
6. Garousi, V., Rainer, A., Lauvås, P., Jr., Arcuri, A.: Software-testing education: a systematic literature mapping. J. Syst. Softw. 165, 110570 (2020)
7. Gegner, L., Runonen, M.: For what it is worth: Anticipated experience evaluation. In: Proceedings of the 8th International Conference on Design and Emotions. Central Saint Martins University of the Arts London and the Design and . . . (2012)
8. Hassenzahl, M., Tractinsky, N.: User experience-a research agenda. Beha. Inform. Technol. 25(2), 91–97 (2006)
9. ISO, B., STANDARD, B.: Ergonomics of human-system interaction (2010)
10. Jabbar, A., Memon, R.N., Memon, I., Arain, A.A., Sodhar, I.N.: Web design trends and their usability by a— b testing method. Int. J. Sci. Technol. Res. 10(05), 25–30 (2021)

11. Kahneman, D., Krueger, A.B., Schkade, D.A., Schwarz, N., Stone, A.A.: A survey method for characterizing daily life experience: the day reconstruction method. Science **306**(5702), 1776–1780 (2004)
12. Kohavi, R., Longbotham, R.: Online controlled experiments and a/b testing. Encyclopedia Mach. Learn. Data Mining **7**(8), 922–929 (2017)
13. Kujala, S., Roto, V., Väänänen-Vainio-Mattila, K., Karapanos, E., Sinnelä, A.: Ux curve: a method for evaluating long-term user experience. Interact. Comput. **23**(5), 473–483 (2011)
14. Law, E.L.C.: The measurability and predictability of user experience. In: Proceedings of the 3rd ACM SIGCHI Symposium on Engineering interactive Computing Systems, pp. 1–10 (2011)
15. Niforatos, E., Karapanos, E.: Emosnaps: a mobile application for emotion recall from facial expressions. Pers. Ubiquit. Comput. **19**(2), 425–444 (2015)
16. Prasetyo, Y.T., Soliman, K.O.S.: Usability evaluation of erp systems: a comparison between sap s/4 hana & oracle cloud. In: 2021 IEEE 8th International Conference on Industrial Engineering and Applications (ICIEA), pp. 120–125. IEEE (2021)
17. Rivero, L., Conte, T.: A systematic mapping study on research contributions on ux evaluation technologies. In: Proceedings of the XVI Brazilian Symposium on Human Factors in Computing Systems, pp. 1–10 (2017)
18. Speicher, M., Both, A., Gaedke, M.: WaPPU: usability-based A/B testing. In: Casteleyn, S., Rossi, G., Winckler, M. (eds.) ICWE 2014. LNCS, vol. 8541, pp. 545–549. Springer, Cham (2014). https://doi.org/10.1007/978-3-319-08245-5_47
19. Vanderdonckt, J., Zen, M., Vatavu, R.D.: Ab4web: an on-line a/b tester for comparing user interface design alternatives. In: Proceedings of the ACM on Human-Computer Interaction 3(EICS), pp. 1–28 (2019)
20. Vermeeren, A.P., Law, E.L.C., Roto, V., Obrist, M., Hoonhout, J., Väänänen-Vainio-Mattila, K.: User experience evaluation methods: current state and development needs. In: Proceedings of the 6th Nordic Conference on Human-Computer Interaction: Extending Boundaries, pp. 521–530 (2010)

# AnyMApp Framework: Anonymous Digital Twin Human-App Interactions

Ana Ferreira[1]([⊠]) [iD], Rui Chilro[2], and Ricardo Cruz-Correia[1] [iD]

[1] CINTESIS@RISE, MEDCIDS, Faculty of Medicine, University of Porto, Rua Plácido Costa, 4200-450 Porto, Portugal
{amlaf,rcorreia}@med.up.pt
[2] Porto, Portugal
rchilro@gmail.com

**Abstract.** As technology is more than ever part of everyday life and activities, their benefits and potential have to be optimized. Currently, this is not happening and technology adherence and continued use is very low. We need to have simple but clear means to understand why that is so and what needs to be done to improve it close to the technology itself and its users. This work introduces AnyMApp, an anonymous digital twin human-app interactions framework to provide online anonymous testing of mock-up applications. These applications may or may not exist and even be in different stages of their deployment. The main goal of AnyMApp is to provide an easy, online way to collect data from users' interactions with the application and complement these with questions to the user regarding contextual, demographic and domain specific. Collected data will be used to quickly detect usability and interactional problems but can also be used to explore relations between humans and technology, and identify experiences and behavioural patterns of the target population.

**Keywords:** Anonymous usability testing · Digital twin · Mobile application interactions · Usage data analysis

## 1 Introduction

There is an increased and generalized use of mobile applications (mApps) to perform the most diverse activities however, human-technology symbiosis, human-environment interactions, as well as privacy and security are still great challenges to be attained [1]. Clearly, existing advances have not been enough to promote the potential that technology has in extending and improving human capabilities [2]; or technology has evolved faster than the human could adapt to them [3].

On average, mApps lose 65% of their users in the first week, while very popular ones lose 35% [4]. The success of mApps highly depends on their acceptance by the users [5, 6], so usage behaviour information can help developing better mApps as well as optimizing their uptake and continued use [4, 6, 7]. The study of usage logs in mApps

---

R. Chilro—Independent Researcher.

can provide identification of typical usability problems [8] as well as determine the extent to which the system resonates with the user or what features are most persuasive [9]. Further, users' engagement can be determined by other factors, for instance, users' characteristics or contextual variables, indicating that particular groups or goals should be targeted differently [10].

Testing is ideal but testing user acceptance in a lab is usually costly as well as time and resource-consuming, and with physical constraints [5], moreover with the current pandemic. Other commonly used techniques, such as user surveys with statistical analysis, could also draw biased conclusions [11] because frequently, the correlation between mApps self-reports and log data, is not high. "What you say you do, is not really what you do" [12]. New evaluation methods are required, and these must include log and usage data analytics and/or implementing new frameworks for usability [13].

With all these requirements in mind, the aim of this work is to present AnyMApp framework, a digital twin framework aiming to anonymously simulate and analyse interactions and usability online between humans and mobile applications (fictitious or existing). The AnyMApp framework provides easy means, with mock-up made interfaces (low or high fidelity) allied to anonymous survey data, to integrate useful data regarding what the user really does in specific contexts, with specific goals, and how they think/feel about it.

Next section presents the state of the art while Sect. 3 describes the proposed framework with its detailed architecture. Section 4 details privacy and security issues regarding the framework development and use and Sect. 5 discusses expected outcomes and impacts from the framework implementation and use by the research community. Section 6 concludes the paper.

## 2 Background

Research shows that there is a correlation between mobile applications (mApps) usage and the multitude of factors (e.g., gender, age, previous experience, health status, etc.) that intervene in the interactions between humans and mApps [14–18]. Those factors can also comprise security and privacy perception [14–16], but because we are not the same from one moment to the other, each interaction is unique [15]. This adds to the complexity of predicting and supporting a stable and continued use of technology [1, 10].

Frequently, studying and testing each specific interaction as well as sets of interactions in mApps, together with influencing factors, and with real users, can provide a wealth of opportunities to tailor particular mApps features, to a particular individual's needs [15,16, 18].

However, usability studies can have limitations, even more with the current pandemic, where setting lab experiments or even face-to-face dialogs is not advisable. Lab studies can be useful for pretesting ideas [19] but they can take a long time to: organizing, recruiting participants, monitoring them, gathering all data (frequently in manual form), transferring data to more automated means of analysis and then extracting some meaning.

Usability lab tests are also limited in terms of physical space and sample size and they fail to capture users' interactions in-situ. Other methods such as self-reporting and diary studies highly depend on participants' willingness to describe their context and details of their searches, and on their ability to accurately recall their interactions and behaviours [20]. These methods mostly rely on users' perception [21].

When performing studies with human users, ethical, privacy and legal issues are also a concern, as these are required to avoid privacy breaches or harm to the participants.

Usability experiments are usually not anonymous (although analysis can be performed on pseudonymized data) and need to comply with legal requirements (e.g., GDRP [22] in Europe). Ethics requirements include a study approval from an Ethics Commission, confirming the study has low or no associated risks, but may have a positive impact on the participants or society in general. These procedures are also time and resource consuming thus ideally, usability or interactional experiments should be done anonymously. Although this can limit the collection of some relevant data, it is still possible to recruit more people and collect more data in shorter periods of time, while still being able to predict personal demographics, as well as correlate main mApps' functionalities to their usage patterns [23].

As more aspects of human life get mediated by mobile phone applications (mApps), new directions are essential to overcome the aforementioned limitations. These include user log data and usage data analytics and/or implementing new frameworks for usability, to automatically infer users' privacy attitudes, or other factors, that influence interactions with mApps [13, 21]. User log data can be considered more reliable than traditional data collection methods such as questionnaires, diaries and interviews as they can capture natural observations and interactions of the user in their own environment [24]. Moreover, event logs can be statistically exchangeable and comparable to more traditional methods, opening promising new ways to perform usability testing cost-effectively and at greater scale [8].

However, there is also a limit to what can be learned through automated analyses, so the additional use of traditional quantitative and qualitative techniques such as surveys and interviews will yield a more complete picture of how the user interacts and evaluates mApps [9]. In this case, developing visualization and simulation tools that make data mining methods and results more accessible to researchers and developers, with limited data mining skills, is highly encouraged [25].

Yet, within the current research literature, most existing tools to explore mApps usage data focus in finding particular faults in their functionality [2] or providing usage analytics for marketing and profiling purposes, many times to be shared with third-party companies. This tool (AppTrace) automatically collects Android Apps logs and provides visualization of those logs as graphs, in a temporal ordering of collection [26].

Unfortunately, there is not much information available about its features but the tool outcomes include essentially telemetry data such as: usage statistics, overall and on a daily basis, per country, the app rating and ranking comparison with other mApps. It also refers the inclusion of sentiment analysis but this must refer to the star rating scale from the users or is not an available feature for public perusal. Many works also focus on studying the way users interact with different apps simultaneously and how they multitask among them [27].

In summary, there is a lack of research and advancement in providing easy, fast means to perform usability studies online, anonymously, to test customized and interactive mockup mApps interfaces (before, during or after their development) and their interactions and behaviors with real users [6].

AnyMApp proposes to build just that, while also complementing usage log analytics with mixed studies from data gathered directly from the users, e.g., online survey questions integrated within the tool features, specific to each use-case.

## 3  AnyMApp Framework

The aim of this work is not to reinvent the wheel but re-using working techniques and technologies for user's research and usability, which are made available in a simple to use infrastructure.

### 3.1  Front-End Architecture

This section describes the AnyMApp framework from the users' perspective as well as regarding the processing of collected data.

Figure 1 presents the AnyMApp Framework general architecture.

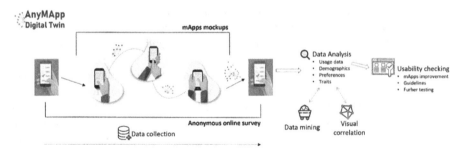

**Fig. 1.** AnyMApp framework front-end architecture proposed in this work.

AnyMApp framework is divided in two parts. Part 1 (Fig. 1, on the left), comprises the integration of the following:

a)  *mApps mock-ups*: the interfaces of the mobile application that we want to test. This may include the full application screenshots or just specific use case scenarios. The idea is to present the user with a prototype of the scenario that the tester wants to evaluate. While the tester may only want to test a specific functionality, it may also validate an idea of what a specific interactional flow could be of an mApp, already existing or not. This would obviously save time as it would quickly give the tester feedback to their ideas and possibly follow the direction dictated by the framework feedback. Moreover, data may also indicate that more tests are required or that exploring a specific case or flow is necessary. In this case, adapting the mock-ups to those needs would not imply many changes but to add/alter screens, their flow or simply, their action buttons;

b)  *Anonymous online survey questions*: to complement the previous point (e.g., the mock-ups) anonymous questions can be setup before and/or after the interaction with the mock-ups, or even during, if necessary. These questions could be closely linked with the main goal of the tester. For instance, understanding if the look and feel of the mApp is well accepted; if the interactions and flow are easy to follow and learn/understand; if there are any main difficulties associated with a specific target population (e.g., accessibility of patients, elderly); or if any ambiguities, errors or even privacy issues have been missed in the mApp's conception. Various types of data, from users' demographics, experiences, opinions, to perceptions, satisfaction and clarity of language, can be gathered. And all this needs to be done without mentioning or integrating identifiable data for that user, even for aggregated data. For more details on these aspects please see Sect. 4.

Part 2 (Fig. 1, on the right), subsequent analysis of the data collected in Part 1, hidden from the user. This analysis needs to integrate data from a), the interactional data gathered from the use of the mockups by the users, as well as data from b), the questionnaires or the various questions that were setup for that specific test. The tools used for this analysis will depend on the content and type of collected data as well as the objectives for the test. Type a) data will not vary much as it will include log, objective data from what buttons or links were clicked, at what time, which pages were visited, for how long, etc. While type b) data may include both quantitative and qualitative data from the user side. Identifying patterns of use, experiences, influencing factors and perceptions can be drawn so that we better understand if that application will have a good usability and adherence.

There is a range of technologies that can be used here which range from Machine learning techniques to find patterns of use as well as visualization techniques, from network science indicators, used to group and correlate actions and behaviours for a more complete and integrated view of those found patterns. More common qualitative analysis relating to the assessment of usability heuristics such as users' satisfaction, language understanding, quality of visual assets or easiness/quickness of use, can also be attained. All these data choices will depend on the primary objective of the testing and the maturity of the idea/application to be tested.

## 3.2   Assessment Report

In the end, the framework needs to provide an assessment report of the analysis that was performed, giving possibly more detail to specific issues regarding unique characteristics (e.g., context of use, more technical content, specific target population or accessibility features, and so on) of the tested mApp. To clarify, participants in the testing will not have feedback regarding the testing itself. They will be guided into the process and be warned and thanked once they reach the end of its execution. On the other hand, the team, researcher or responsible parties who are testing the mApp, will be able to access an assessment report regarding the testing. Contents of this report may vary but they can range from descriptive statistics to more interactional details on the success of tasks completion or the pleasantness of experience with that specific mApp.

Example of an extract of a simulated assessment report is shown in Fig. 2.

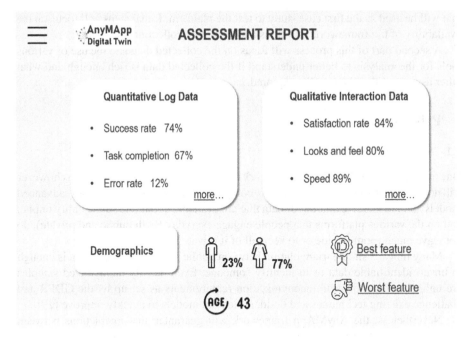

**Fig. 2.** Example of an extract of an assessment report.

### 3.3 Back-End Architecture

This section gives just an overview of the required technologies and associated architecture to deploy the AnyMApp Framework.

Being part of a short exploratory project, AnyMApp framework needs to be proto-typed and tested in practice quickly. The aim is not to develop or test new technologies but, instead, re-use existing ones that are free/open source to use, but at the same time, robust and which can give high-performance.

We will have a webserver (Apache with PHP) with the required front-end webpages (both with questions and mock-ups) available for the testers. Besides common access and action logs and answers to simple questions, not much data or high requirements and structure for data will be needed. We will have a relational database to store collected data (e.g., MySQL) but this may also depend on the type of data to be collected. NoSQL or simply text based data such as from open questions etc., could also be one option.

A separate analysis tool will be deployed to mine and analyse collected data from the database storage (and other sources). The technologies for analysis still need to be defined as they will depend on the usability as well as exploration requirements of each application to be tested.

### 3.4 Current Stage

Currently, the requirements of AnyMApp framework are being defined and there is already a choice of one mobile application for patient's monitoring of high blood pressure that will be used as the first case study to test the platform. Initial steps will focus on the availability of the framework as well as adequate data collection and storage.

A second part of this process will focus on the collected data and the use of various tools for the analysis to better understand if the collected data is rich enough and what other aspects of that data can be explored.

## 4  Privacy

### 4.1  Anonynimisation

One main goal of the AnyMApp framework is to be completely anonymous. It is however still not possible to guarantee that data are completely anonymous. Technology, advanced models and the massive amount of data that are available about one single entity online, and on the various platforms that people engage everyday (both public and private), do not leave much room to hide or to keep all of it private [28].

Many times, a simple triangulation between public data and social media is enough to unveil identifiable data or to identify someone. Even heavily anonymized samples are unlikely to comply with anonymization requirements as set up by the GDPR and challenge existing techniques and de-identification models to quickly improve [29].

Nevertheless, the AnyMApp framework will guarantee that interactions between participants and the platform should be similar to those of anonymous online surveys where questions about a specific theme are asked and only basic demographic, non-personal and non-identifiable data, are requested from the participants. Although not required by GDPR (as there is no identifiable data around), informed consent will always be asked of participants prior to participate in the study and use the AnyMApp framework. An initial page will be provided with information regarding the purpose of the study, type of data collected, how processing will be performed and contact details in case of any doubts. Only after this prior information confirmation will the participants be allowed to interact with the platform and proceed with the testing.

On a more technical level, anonymisation verification and privacy preservation techniques will also be used to identify possible aggregation issues before questions and interactions are available to be tested by the public and data are collected [30, 31]. The most widely used solution is called *de-identification* (or *anonymization*), which removes identifying information from the dataset. Another option is to allow only aggregate queries, such as an average over the data. Unfortunately, neither approach provides strong privacy protection. De-identified datasets are subject to database-linkage attacks. Aggregation only protects privacy if the groups being aggregated are sufficiently large, and even then, privacy attacks are still possible.

One novel privacy preserving technique is Differential Privacy [30] where data can be aggregated and shared without giving information regarding identifiers in the group. This is the case even if the group has identifiable information which, according to the AnyMApp framework, it normally will not.

Other techniques use anonymity algorithms such as k-anonymity or l-diversity [31], which by combining sets of data with similar attributes, identifying information about any one of the individuals contributing to that data, can be obscured. k-Anonymization is often referred to as the power of 'hiding in the crowd.'

All these techniques will be assessed and contribute to the anonymization of the AnyMApp framework.

**Advantages of Anonymized Interactions and Data Collection**

- Collect data from a bigger sample, as online we can reach wider populations;
- Collect more data in shorter periods of time, relevant for smaller iteration projects or MVPs (Minimum Viable Products), saving this way more time and resources;
- Anonymized data are not obliged to be processed in accordance with GDPR;
- Although data are anonymized, it is still possible to gather rich information, such as predicting personal demographics, as well as correlating main mApps' functionalities to their usage patterns [23].

**Disadvantages of Anonymized Interactions and Data Collection**

- With anonymized data is harder to guarantee data quality and verifiability of inserted data; however, even in identifiable questionnaires or interviews people can make up identities and provide fake data in order to hide themselves online;
- Due to the previous lack of guaranties, there is the need to be more careful in assessing collected data validity as well as verify errors and inconsistencies;
- It is also harder to collect richer qualitative data, however the project aims to overcome this by including more questions directed to users, which can complement this issue. Non-identifiable data can bring also much richness and most of it actually relies on asking the right complementary questions to the context, domain, and technologies and situations that are being tested.

### 4.2  Not Anonymous

It may be the case where some studies may have the need to be performed without being anonymous. The case of integrated usability studies with other projects that are performing studies such as using technology to monitor chronic patients' indicators. These may, for instance, require the processing of pseudonimized data or even original data. However, these specific cases can be delimited both in time as well as technologically and both ethics and GDPR compliance will be guaranteed from the beginning.

These type of studies have requirements that need to be set up upfront, before they even start. With all considerations taken care of, AnyMApp framework will be prepared to handle these securely with the inclusion of a Digital Informed Consent to be signed online by every participant before they start interacting with the framework. Also, these data will be separated from any other collected data and their processing will not be integrated within major groups of processing, unless data are anonymised first, and obviously following the procedures defined in the study protocol.

# 5 Expected Outcomes and Impact

## 5.1 It is Very Difficult to Test

Even without pandemic issues around, organizing, recruiting participants and performing usability tests in person is very difficult. We need to setup a physical, dedicated and quite space, and still people may not feel at ease to share their real experiences, feelings and behaviours. There is only the need to please and the fear that they themselves are being tested. But this is when they come to perform the test. In the end, people may give up or find unanticipated situations and not be able to participate at all.

To overcome some of these issues, and during pandemic times, usability tests were performed online, or not at all. However, with the need to share the screen, relying on the participants technical abilities and available materials together with the privacy issues involved in audio or video recording of the sessions, still many obstacles were complex and many times hard to control. When mediated by the technology there is still a communication gap that can be difficult to overcome in order to try to explaining and solving issues and helping people from a distance. This is certainly not ideal and can lead to skewed and/or incomplete results.

In previous situations the required sample is not high, but still, the richness of data collected would not be ideal and no detailed data regarding usage logs, execution times and accurate interactions would be so easily provided.

The AnyMapp framework aims to overcome most of these issues with automated online testing, anonymously, and reaching a wider range of people for the creation of rich clusters of users, interactions and behaviours. It can also, this way, overcome physical barriers as any person in the world can be a tester and identifiable information is not essential to provide sets of rich data which are useful to evaluate an mApp.

Research communities aiming to develop and introduce new technology to specific audiences will much benefit from such framework to easily provide a testbed for their prototype, MVP or full product.

## 5.2 Every User, Every Application and Every Interaction is Unique

For common usability tests the required sample size is usually very low compared with the one required from, for instance, online questionnaires. This is so because the main goal of usability tests is to explore specific features of a specific product quickly, to find the most obvious problems in terms of interaction, information content and structure as well as understanding the learning curve, memory issues, and satisfaction of visualization and layout aspects.

However, normally it is not possible to repeat those tests and explore other users' characteristics with more users. To explore more about the relations that can be created between human users and their mApps we need certainly more data and ideally more time. Nevertheless, the more and richer data we can gather quickly the more it can make up for the time variable as we can learn more and try to understand also more.

# 6 Conclusions

The main barriers to technology adherence and continued use are still privacy and usability issues together with the lack of motivation and engagement of users with their applications. AnyMAp framework can certainly tackle all these issues at once and help understand and create more personalized technology, adapted to the needs and wishes of specific types of users. AnyMApp can help fulfill mApps full potential of extending human capabilities and supporting their needs by optimizing their daily activities.

Beyond usability related aspects, AnyMApp will open the possibility to easily and anonymously study other behavioural and interactional variables, still difficult to study with current solutions. These can comprise a better understanding of: behaviour interaction with mApps as well as detecting personality and victimization traits or even mental, cognitive and even ageing related issues [6, 32].

Next steps include the development of the AnyMApp framework prototype and its testing with live users for a pre-defined case study.

**Acknowledgements.** This work is financed by project AnyMApp - Anonymous Digital Twin for Human-App Interactions (EXPL/CCI-COM/0052/2021) (FCT – Fundação para a Ciência e Tecnologia).

# References

1. Stephanidis, C., et al.: Seven HCI grand challenges. Int. J. Hum. Comput. Interact. **35**(14), 1229–1269 (2019). https://doi.org/10.1080/10447318.2019.1619259
2. Chiaramida, V., Pinci, F., Buy, U., Gjomemo, R.: AppSeer: discovering flawed interactions among Android components. In: Proceedings of the 1st International Workshop on Advances in Mobile App Analysis (A-Mobile 2018), pp. 29–34. Association for Computing Machinery, New York (2018). https://doi.org/10.1145/3243218.3243225
3. The Human Factor: Technology Changes Faster Than Humans. The State of Security. Tripwire Guest Authors. https://www.tripwire.com/state-of-security/off-topic/human-factor-tec hnology-changes-faster-humans/. Accessed 16 Feb 2021
4. Sigg, S., Lagerspetz, E., Peltonen, E., Nurmi, P., Tarkoma, S.: Exploiting usage to predict instantaneous app popularity: trend filters and retention rates. ACM Trans. Web **13**(2), Article no. 13, 25 p., April 2019. https://doi.org/10.1145/3199677
5. Mennig, P., Scherr, S.A., Elberzhager, F.: Supporting rapid product changes through emotional tracking. In: 2019 IEEE/ACM 4th International Workshop on Emotion Awareness in Software Engineering (SEmotion), Montreal, QC, Canada, pp. 8–12 (2019). https://doi.org/10.1109/SEmotion.2019.00009
6. Donker, T., Petrie, K., Proudfoot, J., Clarke, J., Birch, M.R., Christensen, H.: Smartphones forsmarter delivery of mental health programs: a systematic review. J. Med. Internet Res. **15**(11), e247 (2013 15). https://doi.org/10.2196/jmir.2791. PMID: 24240579; PMCID: PMC3841358
7. Boateng, G., Batsis, J.A., Halter, R., Kotz, D.: ActivityAware: an app for real-time daily activity level monitoring on the Amulet wrist-worn device. In: 2017 IEEE International Conference on Pervasive Computing and Communications Workshops (PerComWorkshops), Kona, HI, pp. 431–435 (2017). https://doi.org/10.1109/PERCOMW.2017.7917601

8. Ferre, X., Villalba, E., Julio, H., Zhu, H.: Extending mobile app analytics for usability test logging. In: Bernhaupt, R., Dalvi, G., Joshi, A., K. Balkrishan, D., O'Neill, J., Winckler, M. (eds.) INTERACT 2017. LNCS, vol. 10515, pp. 114–131. Springer, Cham (2017). https://doi.org/10.1007/978-3-319-67687-6_9

9. Turkington, R., Mulvenna, M., Bond, R., O'Neill, S., Armour, C.: The application of user event log data for mental health and wellbeing analysis. In: Proceedings of the 32nd International BCS Human Computer Interaction Conference (HCI 2018), Swindon, GBR, Article no. 4, pp. 1–14. BCS Learning & Development Ltd. (2018). https://doi.org/10.14236/ewic/HCI2018.4

10. Böhm, A.K., Jensen, M.L., Sørensen, M.R., Stargardt, T.: Real-world evidence of user engagement with mobile health for diabetes management: longitudinal observational study. JMIR Mhealth Uhealth. 8(11), e22212 (2020). https://doi.org/10.2196/22212. PMID:32975198; PMCID: PMC7679206

11. Deng, T., et al.: Measuring smartphone usage and task switching with log tracking and self-reports. Mobile Media Commun. 7, 23–33 (2019)

12. Boase, J., Ling, R.: Measuring mobile phone use: self-report versus log data. J. Comput. Med. Commun. 18(4), 508–519 (2013). https://doi.org/10.1111/jcc4.12021

13. Herselman, M.: A scoping review of the use of data analytics for the evaluation of mhealth applications (2020). sun.ac.za

14. Ferreira, A., Muchagata, J., Vieira-Marques, P., Abrantes, D., Teles, S.: Perceptions of security and privacy in mHealth. In: Moallem, A. (eds.) HCII 2021. LNCS, vol. 12788, pp. 297–309. Springer, Cham (2021). https://doi.org/10.1007/978-3-030-77392-2_19

15. Moura, P., Fazendeiro, P., Inácio, P.R.M., Vieira-Marques, P., Ferreira, A.: Assessing access control risk for mHealth: a Delphi study to categorize security of health data and provide risk assessment for mobile apps. J. Healthc. Eng., Article no. 5601068, 14 p. (2020). https://doi.org/10.1155/2020/5601068

16. Ferreira, A., Muchagata, J.: TagUBig - taming your big data. In: 2018 International Carnahan Conference on Security Technology (ICCST), Montreal, QC, Canada, pp. 1–5 (2018). https://doi.org/10.1109/CCST.2018.8585539

17. Billmann, M., Böhm, M., Krcmar, H.: Use of workplace health promotion apps: analysis of employee log data. Health Policy Technol. 9(3), 285–293 (2020). ISSN 2211-8837. https://doi.org/10.1016/j.hlpt.2020.06.003

18. Tian, Y., Zhou, K., Lalmas, M., Liu, Y., Pelleg, D.: Cohort modeling based app category usage prediction. In: Proceedings of the 28th ACM Conference on User Modeling, Adaptation and Personalization (UMAP 2020), pp. 248–256. Association for Computing Machinery, New York (2020). https://doi.org/10.1145/3340631.3394849

19. Ferreira, A., Vieira-Marques, P., Almeida, R., Fernandes, J., Fonseca, J.: How inspiring is your app: a usability take on an app for asthma medication adherence. In: 11th International Conference on e-Health, pp. 225–229 (2019)

20. Aliannejadi, M., Harvey, M., Costa, L., Pointon, M., Crestani, F.: Understanding mobile search task relevance and user behaviour in context. In: Proceedings of the 2019 Conference on Human Information Interaction and Retrieval (CHIIR 2019), pp. 143–151. Association for Computing Machinery, New York (2019). https://doi.org/10.1145/3295750.3298923

21. McCallum, C., Rooksby, J., Gray, C.M.: Evaluating the impact of physical activity apps and wearables: interdisciplinary review. JMIR Mhealth Uhealth 6(3), e58 (2018). https://doi.org/10.2196/mhealth.9054. PMID: 29572200; PMCID: PMC5889496

22. General Data Protection Regulation (EU) 2016/679 of the European Parliament and of the Council L 119. Official Journal of the European Union

23. Qin, Z., et al.: Demographic information prediction based on smartphone application usage. In: 2014 International Conference on Smart Computing, Hong Kong, China, pp. 183–190 (2014). https://doi.org/10.1109/SMARTCOMP.2014.7043857

24. Olson, J.S., Kellogg, W.A.: Ways of Knowing in HCI, Springer, New York (2014). https://doi.org/10.1007/978-1-4939-0378-8
25. Stragier, J., et al.: Data mining in the development of mobile health apps: assessing in-app navigation through Markov chain analysis. J. Med. Internet Res. **21**(6), e11934 (2019)
26. Qiu, L., Zhang, Z., Shen, Z., Sun, G.: AppTrace: dynamic trace on android devices. In: 2015 IEEE International Conference on Communications (ICC), London, UK, pp. 7145–7150 (2015). https://doi.org/10.1109/ICC.2015.7249466
27. De Nadai, M., Cardoso, A., Lima, A., et al.: Strategies and limitations in app usage and human mobility. Sci. Rep. **9**, 10935 (2019). https://doi.org/10.1038/s41598-019-47493-x
28. Gruschka, N., Mavroeidis, V., Vishi, K., Jensen, M.: Privacy issues and data protection in big data: a case study analysis under GDPR. In: 2018 IEEE International Conference on Big Data (Big Data), pp. 5027–5033 (2018). https://doi.org/10.1109/BigData.2018.8622621
29. Rocher, L., Hendrickx, J.M., de Montjoye, Y.A.: Estimating the success of re-identifications in incomplete datasets using generative models. Nat. Commun. **10**, 3069 (2019). https://doi.org/10.1038/s41467-019-10933-3
30. De-Identification tools. Privacy Engineering Program. NIST – Information Technology Laboratory/Applied Sybersecurity Division. https://www.nist.gov/itl/applied-cybersecurity/privacy-engineering/collaboration-space/focus-areas/de-id/tools. Accessed 25 May 2022
31. Valli Kumari, V., Varma, N.S., Sri Krishna, A., Ramana, K.V., Raju, K.V.S.V.N.: Checking anonymity levels for anonymized data. In: Natarajan, R., Ojo, A. (eds.) ICDCIT 2011. LNCS, vol. 6536, pp. 278–289. Springer, Heidelberg (2011). https://doi.org/10.1007/978-3-642-19056-8_21
32. Gordon, M.L., Gatys, L., Guestrin, C., Bigham, J.P., Trister, A., Patel, K.: App usage predicts cognitive ability in older adults. In: Proceedings of the 2019 CHI Conference on Human Factors in Computing Systems (CHI 2019), paper 168, pp. 1–12. Association for Computing Machinery, New York (2019). https://doi.org/10.1145/3290605.3300398

# Construction of an Instrument for the Quantitative Assessment of Experience in the Use of Conversational Agents

Andressa Ferreira[✉], Thiago Gama, and Francisco Oliveira

Ceará State University, Fortaleza, CE, Brazil
magdandressa@gmail.com, thiago.dias@aluno.uece.br,
fran.oliveira@uece.br

**Abstract.** Relational conversational agents represent a new frontier in human-computer interaction. They can be handy, for example, in interacting with the elderly public. Considering the increase in life expectancy, longevity came to be seen as a gain and a concern for society. The number of older people grows at a more significant proportion than the number of professionals specialized in their care, often causing an overload in the work of these professionals. In this context, we argue that the technology of voice assistants has the potential to become a promising solution to alleviate problems such as the greater demand for care services for the elderly, contributing not only to assisting caregiver's activities as well as for the recovery of the independence of the elderly. However, the lack of tools for evaluating users' experiences with these voice interfaces is remarkable, mainly when used by the elderly. Thus, this work contributes to filling this gap, providing as its main contribution an instrument that quantitatively measures the experience obtained by an older user when using a conversational agent. The application of a tool like this can decisively help design and evolve a voice interface. Applying a tool like this can decisively help plan and grow a voice interface. Furthermore, our instrument can help from observing points of improvement in the system to the degree of suitability of the product to the user, being helpful to get validation with the user from the beginning of the development cycle.

**Keywords:** Older adults · Voice interaction · Conversational agents · User experience · Engagement · Cronbach's alpha · Wizard of Oz

## 1 Introduction

Worldwide, the number of people aged 60 and over is growing at a much higher percentage than any other age group. The elderly community, people aged 60 and over, increased by about 7.3 million between 1980 and 2000, totaling more than 14.5 million in 2000. It is estimated that Brazil, by 2025, will be the sixth-largest country in the world in terms of the number of older people [43]. This visible accelerated growth of

M. Kurosu et al. (Eds.): HCII 2022, LNCS 13516, pp. 226–243, 2022.
https://doi.org/10.1007/978-3-031-17615-9_16

the elderly population represents significant challenges for families and society, mainly due to the decrease in health professionals to the number of older people.

Thus, to alleviate this problem of a constant greater demand for care services for the elderly, the use of intelligent voice assistants appears to be a promising solution, contributing not only to assisting in the activities of caregivers and family members as well as for the recovery of the independence of the elderly. These assistants can also bring the elderly community closer to new technologies, as many show a particular technological aversion. Despite its potential impact, several factors contribute to the low adherence to mobile solutions among the elderly, such as low visual acuity, memory loss, and decreased manual dexterity [26]. These factors we were able to help with the use of voice interfaces. Several scholars argue that speaking is the most natural form of communication and that audio interfaces are, therefore, a priori, highly usable by many types of people in many situations [37]. Initial studies pointed to a higher quality of user experience during the interaction between voice agents and older users [10]. However, how to effectively evaluate this experience of using voice agents used by seniors?

With this question in mind, we performed several searches in academic libraries, such as the IEEE Xplore and ACM Digital Library, and we noticed a lack in this area. Thus, our main contribution lies in constructing and refining an instrument that quantitatively measures the experience between conversational agents and older users. In collaboration with the planning, execution, and data collection in the experimental procedure described in Gama and Oliveira [13], we built this instrument and evaluated it quantitatively and qualitatively.

## 2   Related Works

### 2.1   Evaluation of a Chatbot in the Educational Context: An Experience with Metis

In this study, the Metis chatbot is evaluated as a support tool in distance education activities. We emphasize that this agent does not communicate with the user by voice. This evaluation was based on data collected through a questionnaire developed by the authors, conversation logs with two groups of students provided by the chatbot, and analysis of access to support materials of a discipline. The questionnaire developed in this study consisted of twenty-six objective questions divided into five categories: learning, reliability, relationships, engagement, and overview. All questions had a five-point Likert scale response option, ranging from "strongly disagree" to "strongly agree".

The purpose of creating this instrument was to complement the data collected in the logs and access to support materials. The study had a more qualitative focus to assess the usability and engagement of the system with students. To verify the reliability of the questionnaire, the authors used Cronbach's Alpha coefficient to measure the correlation between the answers given by the participants. Their result was an alpha of 0.9524, considered a high reliability. It was reported that, according to the results of the analysis of the data collected, there was an increase in the general average of the grades obtained by the two groups of analyzed students. This proves that the technology achieved satisfactory results in terms of dialogue efficiency, influence on student engagement in the classroom, and even that intelligent agent technology has proved to be quite efficient in helping students perform various activities.

However, in this work, we point out that its alpha was so high. The reliability of Cronbach's alpha varies between 0 and 1, and the minimum acceptable value for alpha is 0.70. The internal consistency of the scale items is considered low for values below this limit. In contrast, the maximum target value for alpha is 0.90, as larger values may represent the presence of redundancy or duplication, which may suggest that multiple items are measuring precisely the same element of a construct. In this case, it is indicated that the redundant or duplicated elements are eliminated [38]. This was not done in this study. We also miss more details of the study, such as how the choice of factors addressed in the categories of questions of the instrument was made and how this experiment was organized and carried out, which had two groups of students, one with eleven and the other with twelve participants. It would also be essential to inform the age group of the participants. User groups at different stages of life tend to behave differently with specific technologies. Several authors report, for example, in their studies that the elderly tend to personify agent technologies more than younger people and tend to perceive such technology more as a life companion than a simple tool [4]. However, despite these criticisms, this work helped us a lot in our methodological procedure.

## 2.2 Older Users Interaction with Conversational Agent

The authors explore how users behave when interacting with a conversational agent in this work. The study included 19 people aged between 30 and 70 years, 12 older adults, and seven younger adults. Here, participants over 50 were classified as older adults. Initially, the Clova agent was introduced and explained before the start of the experiment. Then, with the introduction completed, the Clova, a voice-controlled conversational agent like Amazon's Alexa, was made available for use.

The interviews were conducted after the participants had interacted with the agent for two weeks. During the interviews, the subjects were asked about the frequently used functions and the satisfactory and unsatisfactory aspects of the agent. The interview scripts were analyzed with NLP techniques using Python. For a comparison between the two groups of users, the interview scripts were separated between older and younger adults; for each group, a keyword and sentiment analysis were conducted using the "KoNLPy" library. The conventional analysis method by interview was also used to understand the context of the use of each word.

The study indicated that participants over 50 years of age mentioned musical functions at a much higher rate than other functions, suggesting that it is of great importance to them. In contrast, respondents under 50 said the various functionalities of the agent more equally, meaning that convenience is the most critical factor for them. In addition, older adults were reported to personify the agent more than younger adults and tend to perceive the agent more as a life partner than a simple tool.

Although this study did not provide more detailed data on participants' reports with the agent or analyze the user-agent interaction experience, it did provide us with a lot of insights from its findings. This trend towards the humanization of agents by users, especially the older ones, was seen in other works collected in our searches. Such authors reported, for example, that older users expected that such computational entities could become good conversation partners [41]. This humanization factor has been shown to positively affect the experience of the elderly with the agents in both works cited. This fact led us to incorporate the humanization in our Instrument for Quantitative Assessment of Experience among Seniors and Conversational Agents.

### 2.3   Design and Evaluation of a Smart Home Voice Interface for the Elderly: Acceptability and Objection Aspects

In this study, the authors describe the development of a new intelligent home system, designed to be used by elderly users in their homes, called Sweet-Home, whose primary interaction mode is based on voice command technology. The system is designed to control objects such as blinds, lights, and kitchen utensils. The project intends to enable the growing number of older people to continue living in their own homes for as long as possible and in a more autonomous way.

However, before developing the SWEET-HOME system, the authors raised some questions: would an independent elderly and his family be interested in this technology? What would make it acceptable to this audience? Thus, the objective of this study was to answer these questions, carrying out an evaluation with the user. In addition, the experiment consisted in asking the elderly to perform realistic tasks in a smart home environment.

The authors used an experimental platform called DOMUS that was designed and implemented by the MULTICOM team at the Grenoble Computer Laboratory to validate their approach. The assessment involved 18 participants, eight healthy older people aged between 71 and 88, seven family members (informal caregivers), and three professional caregivers. For about 45 min, participants were questioned about their discoveries of commands on the DOMUS platform, alternating between interview periods and periods interacting with the Wizard of Oz (WOz).

Each test was composed of an interviewer, an assistant (researcher hidden in the DOMUS technical room operating the system remotely), and a pair composed of an older adult with a family member (except an older adult who was alone). Participants and the interviewer were inside the smart home throughout the test, except for some parts of the scenarios where the family member moved to another room (by videoconference). This study aimed to evaluate the acceptability of the SWEET-HOME system. However, there is no standard definition of user acceptability in this domain. Thus, most of the experiment was conducted to determine if potential users would appreciate the new features provided by the system. Furthermore, to guide the development of SWEET-HOME, aspects of utility, usability, personalization, interactivity, proactivity, intrusiveness, social interaction, and security were investigated.

Thus, the planned experiment was divided into four scenarios: voice control, communication with the outside world, interruption of the human activity system, and electronic agenda. In each of these scenarios, the elderlies were asked to interact with the environment and answer questions related to this interaction. The results revealed that the elderly prefer to use voice interfaces over other interaction methods, such as typing or touch interfaces. In addition, these interfaces have shown great potential to facilitate the daily lives of these users. And when considering the elderly still healthy and independent in the user's evaluation, an exciting finding that emerged was their general acceptance, as long as the system does not induce them to a lazy lifestyle, taking control of everything.

This work was our primary reference for planning our experiment. In addition, this work provided us with exciting reports, such as the preference of elderly users for using applications by voice commands, the fact that we also encountered in our initial study [10]. In addition, the aspects investigated in the experiment to assess appreciation with the SWEET-HOME system served as a reference for us in search of the factors to build our evaluative instrument.

## 3  Background

### 3.1  Usability and User Experience (UX)

The UX has become one of the main characteristics of the evaluations of an interactive system. Nielsen [30] states that the first requirement to obtain a UX model is to meet the user's needs without complications. Furthermore, the author points out that actual UX goes far beyond just giving users what they say they want. Unfortunately, many people get pretty confused about differentiating what is UX and what is usability. So, in this section, we seek to characterize and distinguish them.

Nielsen [28] argues that usability measures the quality of a user's experience when interacting with a system. The term usability began to be used in the early 1980s and has its origins in cognitive science, psychology, and ergonomics [6]. Usability analyzes interaction via the interface, that is, the way a user performs their tasks and interacts with a given product, considering different needs and types of users. On the other hand, the User Experience is a set of disciplines that comprise usability and many other areas, such as information architecture, interaction design, interface design, and even metrics and factors. So, usability is a part of the user experience, but it's not everything.

We can yet distinguish the UX from the usability according to the search for continuous engagement. Usability focuses primarily on the task, aiming for efficiency and learnability as a matter of performance. Traditional usability concepts include effectiveness, efficiency, and satisfaction [27]. While effectiveness and efficiency are related to the user's ability to perform a task through the product, satisfaction presents a different perspective. User satisfaction encompasses many aspects that focus on whether the system provided them with a good experience and met their specific needs. This also has a direct relationship with user engagement.

### 3.2  User Experience (UX) with Voice Interfaces

The UX evaluation is essential for developing any conversational assistant, as it provides a greater understanding of the direction to be taken to improve the system [20]. Over the years, there has been a greater emphasis on UX analysis focused on voice interfaces. However, as it is a different form of interaction from conventional ones, it is essential to consider these differences when evaluating these systems. Unlike graphical interfaces that can visually display hidden functionality and information, conversational interfaces are more complex to perform, as they have little or no visual content. As they do not have a way to visually present functionalities such as menus and options, they must resort to other techniques to obtain a better interaction [40].

Some authors point out that the biggest obstacle for designers and developers in thinking about usability and UX is precisely in the reorganization of the process of interaction flows [39]. This scenario tends to be even more problematic when dealing with voice interfaces, as the interaction model undergoes even more significant changes. Navigation needs to be fluid and more natural. The steps of this navigation and the user's actions tend to be much more unpredictable than interacting with a text field or visual interface.

The use of methods to monitor the use of a system by actual users, the observation, and the definition of factors for quantitative and qualitative assessment are necessary to evaluate an interface. Knowing which paradigms, techniques, and assessment factors are most appropriate for voice interfaces is essential. However, despite advances in conversational systems, UX aspects are still an area to be explored.

### 3.3  Wizard of Oz Technique

The term Wizard of Oz (WOz) was created by Jeff Kelley around the 1980s to describe the experimental method he created in his work. This technique allows a user to interact with an interface, not knowing that the responses are being generated by a hidden human and not a machine, having someone behind the scenes who is pushing buttons and switches. This technique allows researchers to test a concept by having one person acting as Moderator leading the face-to-face session with each user. In contrast, another person works as an Assistant controlling the responses sent to the user via the chosen method. This technique can be beneficial for testing interfaces of systems that rely on artificial intelligence technologies and voice recognition systems.

The technique's name refers to the 1939 Wizard of Oz movie. In the film, a character presents himself to the story's protagonists as a giant flaming head until this head is unmasked and exposed as a persona of a human being controlled through various mechanisms behind a curtain. He did this to deceive everyone who wanted to talk to him. Similarly, the Wizard of Oz method consists of a person hiding somewhere, generating responses to the user's inputs who is testing a prototype and who is unaware of the existence of the "Wizard". This is an essential point for this method's successful execution. Test participants can never suspect that the entity they are talking to is not a machine but a human being pretending to be one.

### 3.4  Reliability Analysis Through Cronbach's Alpha Coefficient

According to the objectives of this study, design, and validation of an Instrument for Quantitative Assessment of Experience among Seniors and Conversational Agents, it is necessary to proceed with an analysis of the instrument's metric qualities. In this way, we will study its reliability. For this, we used the reliability calculation through Cronbach's alpha coefficient. The coefficient is one of the most relevant statistical tools used in research involving making tests and their application. The alpha measures the correlation between responses to a questionnaire by studying the profile of answers given by respondents. This is an average correlation between the questions.

The reliability of Cronbach's alpha coefficient varies typically between 0 and 1. The minimum acceptable value for alpha is 0.70. The internal consistency of the scale items is considered low for values below this limit. In contrast, the maximum target value for alpha is 0.90, as larger values may represent the presence of redundancy or duplication, which may suggest that multiple items are measuring the same element of a construct. Redundant or duplicated elements must be eliminated [38]. Finally, we present the reliability classification of Cronbach's Alpha Coefficient [12]:

1. $\alpha \leq 0.30$ – Very low;
2. $0.30 < \alpha \leq 0.60$ - Low;
3. $0.60 < \alpha \leq 0.75$ - Moderate;
4. $0.75 < \alpha \leq 0.90$ - High;
5. $\alpha > 0.90$ – Very high.

## 4    Engagement, Factors and User Experience (UX)

Although several areas have sought and studied its essence, the engagement remains a complex concept with several definitions [14]. Engagement can be defined as the state in which people are so involved in an activity that nothing else seems to matter [42]. This concept leads us to two factors with which we can observe and analyze a user's engagement and experience with a system: **immersion** and **satisfaction**. Satisfaction is also directly related to the **pleasure** factor.

Lalmas [21] also addresses these factors in his definition of engagement. She argues that engagement connects three facets: emotional (user feelings such as happiness and sadness), cognitive (user mental states such as immersed and dispersed), and behavioral (user actions such as comments and shares). It refers to the connection that exists at a specific time and for some time between a user and a technological resource. For Akgün [1], engagement is about the way we nurture and build the community. It is the emotional, cognitive, and/or behavioral connection that exists, at any moment and for any period of time, between a user and a technological resource.

When a product manages to get the user to build this connection, we can observe the degree of involvement and the user experience. This link can be constructed and metrified in several ways. We can mention, for example, the personification/humanization factor of these agents. In several studies, we find reports of the tendency of older adults to see a system of agents as something more than a mere tool [4, 41]. Studies also indicate that humanized resources such as the voice, the demonstration of emotions, and empathy help people have more confidence, pleasure, and companionship when interacting with a system [9].

Some interactive systems have incorporated adaptation to individuals, generally receiving greater involvement than the same systems without adaptation [7, 18, 31]. The change in the agent's speech and behavior over time can be crucial in maintaining engagement across multiple encounters and in building a long-term relationship [3, 19, 23]. The importance of the adaptability factor of systems to their users is evident, especially users who suffer from some type of limitation. This factor is also directly related to the accessibility of the system. Another critical factor is retention. This factor is related to the number of users returning to the system and is one of the most used metrics [36]. We can also consider this factor as evidence of engagement and UX. A user would not continue to use something that did not involve them or did not provide them with a good experience.

We can also mention the novelty factor as an indication when measuring engagement. An individual experience that is entirely new to a user can profoundly affect initial satisfaction. So much so that users often overlook usability issues or ignore the content of the experience, they show a greater tolerance [35]. Users experiencing voice-controlled intelligent agent technologies for the first time may experience an overwhelming sense of curiosity and wonder, an emotion that can have various positive and/or adverse effects.

From these definitions, we observe the link between engagement and UX. Both shares, among other points, the interest in resorting to the user's emotions and feelings when using a system. Authors further report that user experience has been at the forefront of the HCI to determine the overall value of ideas such as aesthetics, affection, and fun [16]. Thus, we can consider engagement as a UX quality that emphasizes the positive aspects of interaction. In this sense, he deepens and focuses on the UX characteristic that relates to the positive or negative perception of a given service and how the user commits to it.

## 5 Metholodogy

To substantiate our study, we planned and executed an experiment, carried out in collaboration with Gama and Oliveira [13], with a group of participants with seven older people aged between 61 and 81 years old. Regarding the type of approach to the problem, our research can be defined as mixed, quantitative, and qualitative. Part of our analysis was based on data and numbers, using statistical techniques such as reliability analysis using Cronbach's alpha. As for the qualitative side of the study, we detailed and analyzed in detail all the interactions between the elderly and the conversational agents.

Regarding the objectives, we can classify this study, in general, as exploratory. This area of study of intelligent agents used by older users is plenty new, which still does not have many contributions. Thus, after a systematic mapping in academic libraries and the analysis of what was being written about it, we realized that it would be an exciting area to venture into and that this line of research would potentially generate numerous ramifications for future studies. This interest motivated us to develop an instrument that could measure quantitatively the degree of experience in the elderly-agent interaction focused mainly on engagement with the system. In the following subsection, we detail the experimental protocol adopted and some details of its execution.

### 5.1 Experimental Design

Gama and Oliveira [13] directed their efforts to study the common ground, while here, we focus on the study of UX and engagement between agents and the elderly. Initially, was developed and refined a tool to collect information from family members about the elderly participants in the study, without the elderly being aware of it, in a previous way, that is, before the elderly came into contact with the prototyped agent using the WOz technique.

Firstly, we explained the entire process to the family members to help us complete the Common Ground questionnaire [13] and convince the elderly to participate in the study. We also asked family members not to leak to the elderly about the existence of this questionnaire. At no time did we inform any of the participants, whether they were family members, caregivers, or the elderly, that the elderly would not be talking to a computational entity, but rather with a human being impersonating this entity using a tool to make his voice sound robotic. These details and the hiding of specific information are essential requirements for using the WOz technique.

With the common ground questionnaires answered, specific conversational scenarios were created for each of the seven older people based on the responses collected [13]. The scenarios created were elaborate and sufficient to guide the interaction throughout the experimental period of four days per participant. After making the scenarios, a member of the research team went to the residence of each older adult to install an Echo Dot. The wizard never had contact with the elderly. The only information he had about the elderly was the data collected through the answers to the common ground questionnaire, with which he elaborated his scenarios.

When the researcher arrived at the elderly's home to configure the Echo, which consisted of plugging it into an energy source and connecting it to the home's Wi-Fi network, he also used the opportunity to deliver and read the Free and Informed Consent Form and collect the participant's signature. We highlight that the Echo installed in the older person's house was already previously paired with the wizard's Echo, so the older person's device always automatically answered all the calls that the wizard made using the device's Drop In function. In this way, we were able to simulate the functioning of a more active intelligent voice assistant with the functionality of spontaneous speech [41]. After this step, we started the execution of the experiment.

Upon completing the four-day trial period per participant, we immediately started phase three of the trial period, applying the Instrument for Quantitative Assessment of Experience among Seniors and Conversational Agents. To avoid unnecessary contact and take care of the participants' health and the team of researchers, data collection was done through telephone interviews. Remembering that we were already in a period of Covid-19. Thus, a researcher called to each one of the elderlies requested permission to record the call to review details by listening to the audios later, and finally was read the questions in the instrument, available in Ferreira [11], and collected the answers that, in addition, to provide by the elderly, were always justified or had some comment from the respondent. These comments are exposed in Sect. 7.2.

After collecting the responses, we used the IBM SPSS Statistics tool to analyze reliability using Cronbach's Alpha and incrementally refined it to obtain the highest alpha possible. Finally, we arrived at a final version of ten items for our instrument, available in Ferreira [11]. We used the SUS calculation rules to obtain a quantitative value for the experience between the elderly and the agent. This refinement and calculation are explained in detail in Sect. 7.1. Briefly, our experiment took place in three phases: application of the common ground questionnaire to family members, usability test using the WOz technique, and application of the Instrument for Quantitative Assessment of Experience.

## 6  Construction and Refinement of the Evaluative Instrument of the Experience

Based on the factors raised and explained in Sect. 4 and others discussed below, we developed a tool with a central focus on analyzing the experience among the elderly and intelligent conversational agents. The factors used were Immersion, Adaptability, Satisfaction, Minimization of Errors, Recommendation, Safety, Humanization, Efficiency, Naturalness of Dialogue, Retention, Reliability, and Common Ground. We detail them below.

1.  **Immersion**: translates into the system's ability to involve the user, disconnecting him from his natural environment, sinking his senses into actions and interactions. According to Laurel [22], the key to immersion lies in achieving user engagement.
2.  **Adaptability**: we can define this factor as the system's ability to adapt to different environments without intervention [17]. In this work, we focus on adapting the product to the user.
3.  **Satisfaction**: evaluates the user's level of satisfaction with a system and its experience. Nielsen [29] argues that the system should be used pleasantly to satisfy users with its use.
4.  **Error minimization**: the interface should prevent possible errors by users [8].
5.  **Recommendation**: this factor is related to the act of the user of a given product to recommend it to other users, who report to other people their personal experience with it. The recommendation is directly related to user experience, reliability, and satisfaction. This factor is also addressed in the Net Promoter Score (NPS) [34].
6.  **Security**: can be described as the ability to predict and recover from errors by the system and keep users away from failures [29]. Here we give a new meaning to this factor. For us, it has to do with the system's ability to protect its user's data and maintain their privacy.
7.  **Humanization**: this characteristic involves both the way of speaking and the way of visualizing the figure that represents the conversational entity. Among several features, we can mention its ability to provide fluid conversations, easy to understand, suitable for each language, with a lot of naturalness and personality, in front of its users. As a result, users tend to see such an agent more as a life companion than a simple tool [4].
8.  **Efficiency**: the system must be efficient so that the user, after knowing how to use it, can achieve good productivity [29].
9.  **Naturalness of the Dialogue**: the dialogue must be natural and capable of not disappointing the user's expectations. An unnatural dialogue leads users to give up using the system and think it is not prepared to meet their needs [8].
10.  **Retention**: Measures the percentage of users who return to the product [35]. This factor also seeks to demonstrate how your users behave in the face of changes (or lack thereof) in your system over time.

11. **Reliability**: for ISO/IEC 9126-1 [17], software reliability is the ability of the software product to maintain a specified level of performance when used under specified conditions. In our context, we give a new meaning to this factor. For us, it has to do with the belief in the integrity of the information provided by the system, such as the suggestions provided by agents to their users.

12. **Common Ground**: we can describe it, in a simplified way, as a theory of HCI related to the previous knowledge that a subject has of another with which he will interact. This prior knowledge is one of the keys to getting engagement. Given that with this knowledge base on issues such as tastes, habits, and preferences of a subject, an individual can develop a conversational flow in a more engaging way for another.

Based on these factors associated with usability, engagement, and user experience, we wrote a questionnaire with a total of 22 items [11]. The questions had answer alternatives arranged on a 5-point Likert scale ranging from 1 ("Strongly Disagree") to 5 ("Strongly Agree"). As can be seen, each item of the questionnaire focuses on one of these factors raised, which are indicated question by question. After completing the user test performed with seven older people, aged between 61 and 81 years, and a simulated agent using the WOz technique [13], we applied our Instrument through telephone interviews. As discussed earlier, we found ourselves in a period of a pandemic in which very few people had already had access to the vaccine, access that our research group had not yet obtained. Thus, to preserve the health of our research participants, this distance protocol was agreed upon.

We called the elderly, read the questions, and collected their answers. Interestingly, the elderlies were not limited to merely answering the questions. They always provided us with justifications, making the experience and data collection even more prosperous. To avoid losing any information, we recorded the audio of the entire data collection with the agreement and permission of the research participant. After applying and collecting the responses of the seven participants, we decided to analyze their reliability using Cronbach's Alpha Coefficient. For this, we use the IBM SPSS Statistics tool as an aid, which is very useful to perform statistical tests, such as correlation, multicollinearity, and hypothesis tests.

Before any refinement with IBM SPSS Statistics, we already had an alpha of 0.702, indicating moderate reliability [12]. The IBM tool not only provides the general measure of all questionnaire items, but it also provides the final alpha value if a given item is excluded. As a result, we could incrementally refine our Experience Assessment Tool until it reached a maximum alpha. By analyzing the item-total statistics table generated by SPSS Statistics, we decided which items to eliminate in the first refinement. They were seven: 2, 3, 5, 9, 11, 14, 15. After that, we repeat the steps for the third refinement. Item-total analysis. Choice of items, in this case, we eliminated two more: 4 and 21. Reliability analysis, which changed to 0.851. In the third refinement, we eliminated items 8 and 18, obtaining a tool with 11 items and a reliability of 0.853, which is considered high reliability. We noticed that this was our maximum alpha and that eliminating any item would decrease it from that point on.

However, we had eleven items at that moment, a number very close to the number of items in the SUS, which is a quantitative questionnaire with a specific calculation to infer a value at the end. Furthermore, the SUS questions are also based on UX-related metrics, factors, and heuristics. Thus, our idea of carrying out one more refinement emerged so that our instrument would fit into the logic of the SUS calculation, and we could obtain good reliability and a quantitative value at the end. So, we looked at the item-total statistics table in SPSS and observed that we could eliminate both items 6 or 7, and we would get a tool with a final alpha of 0.851, also considered high. So, we opted for a random elimination and had item 6 chosen for the final removal in the fourth refinement section. The refinement step by step, the final version of the instrument, and the factors associated with each item of the tool can be seen in Ferreira [11].

# 7 Assessing Our Proposed Instrument

In Sect. 6, we detail the steps of building and refining our instrument. Here we aim to document the application of the tool to the elderly participants, describe a little about the reports of their experience, and expose the final result obtained by each participant according to the calculation of the instrument in its final version, after the four refinement sessions. We have divided this section into the two subsections below to organize better and discuss findings.

## 7.1 Quantitative Validation

The quantitative analysis of the results took place after the four refinement sections of the instrument, explained in Sect. 6, with which we limited the number of items to ten and ordered them to conform to the standard of the SUS questionnaire. Table 1 displays the user's responses to each of the questions that remained after the four refinement sections of the instrument. Note that in the final version of our tool and the SUS, odd questions positively affect UX at its maximum value on the Likert scale, while even questions negatively impact the experience with the system [11]. We exemplify this below with the questions copied from the final instrument.

1. I liked talking to Lady Laura so much that sometimes I even lost track of time (positive impact on the experience).
2. I kept hearing noises while Lady Laura spoke (negative impact on experience).

The SUS calculation is straightforward, to reach the final result, we must follow the following three steps:

1. For odd questions (1, 3, 5, 7, 9), subtract one from the score the user answered.
2. For even questions (2, 4, 6, 8, 10), subtract 5 (5-X) from the score the user answered.
3. Add the values of the ten questions and multiply by 2.5.

**Table 1.** Participants' answers by instrument item in its final version.

| Identifier | Q01 | Q12 | Q10 | Q13 | Q06 | Q16 | Q19 | Q17 | Q20 | Q22 |
|------------|-----|-----|-----|-----|-----|-----|-----|-----|-----|-----|
| P1 | 5 | 1 | 5 | 4 | 5 | 2 | 5 | 2 | 5 | 5 |
| P2 | 4 | 2 | 4 | 1 | 1 | 1 | 4 | 2 | 4 | 3 |
| P3 | 5 | 2 | 3 | 1 | 4 | 2 | 4 | 1 | 3 | 4 |
| P4 | 5 | 5 | 5 | 5 | 5 | 5 | 5 | 4 | 5 | 5 |
| P5 | 4 | 1 | 4 | 5 | 5 | 1 | 4 | 1 | 4 | 5 |
| P6 | 5 | 1 | 5 | 4 | 5 | 1 | 5 | 1 | 5 | 3 |
| P7 | 5 | 4 | 5 | 5 | 3 | 5 | 5 | 5 | 4 | 5 |

The SUS scores range from 0 to 100 and have 68 points. Systems with at least 90 points have the best possible usability. Those who get between 80 and 90 points have excellent usability. Systems that score between 70 and 80 points have good usability but have points to improve. Those that reach between 60 and 70 points are considered "OK" and have significant improvements to be made. Finally, all those below 60 points are those whose usability degree is deemed to be unacceptable [2]. Bringing this definition to our context, we used this scale to measure the participants' experience with the voice assistant prototyped with the WOz technique. This was possible due to the number of items in our instrument, our ordering, and the types of factors used to prepare the questions. The results of each participant are shown below in Table 2.

**Table 2.** Results of the quantitative analysis by participant.

| Identifier | Score | Experience |
|------------|-------|------------|
| P1 | 87.5 | Excellent |
| P2 | 70 | Good |
| P3 | 77.5 | Good |
| P4 | 62.5 | Ok |
| P5 | 80 | Good |
| P6 | 87.5 | Excellent |
| P7 | 55 | Unacceptable |

The results proved to be plenty consistent with the users' reports. Those who were more interested in the technology, who expressed their desire to continue talking to the agent and even personified him, ended up having a higher score than those who were more insecure with the use, for reasons such as security and inexperience with technologies in general. However, as we can see from the data analysis, in general, we had an excellent result not only with the acceptance of the technology but with the validation of the questionnaire, which proved to be very consistent with the reports provided by the older participants and their families, messages that were presented in the Subsect. 7.2 below.

## 7.2 Qualitative Validation

Firstly, we highlight the positive points of the distance protocol adopted due to the Covid-19. Due to the application of the instrument in the format of interviews by telephone calls, we were able to obtain the audio recording of the conversations to review details, clarify possible doubts of the interviewees about some items, and still have the guarantee that the respondent was only the elderly participant, without the influence of third parties, such as their family members. With this collection method, we could still obtain general reflections about the system. The elderly always made a point of commenting on each of their answers and also exposing their feelings with the system. The application of the instrument and data collection took place immediately after the conclusion of the four days in which the older user was in contact with the technology at his home so that your memories with the system were still plenty recent. Among the most exciting feedback, we had from the participants were those related to the personification of the agent.

One of the participants, who we call P1, mentioned that the agent's way of speaking, the method of expressing himself, and the words used by the agent sent her memories of an old friend with whom P1 had not talked in a while. This led her to have a strong nostalgic feeling and the desire to extend the stay of technology in her home. Another report in this context occurred with participant P6. She was pretty satisfied with the topics addressed by the conversation agent because, according to P6, it seemed that both had a lot of tastes in common, with that the agent became a person with whom P6 felt great pleasure when talking. P6 also reported his desire to speak to the agent again in the future. We highlighted to this participant is the question she asked the researcher when the instrument's items were already answered. She wanted to know if we would bring the technology into her home again or if she could still buy the technology for personal use because she felt very lonely at home and would love the opportunity to have someone to talk to daily. Both these reports demonstrate that the humanization factor of agents is directly related to engagement, retention, and user experience with the system.

Participant P2 also presented us with exciting reports. He was our most learned participant, both educationally and technologically. He told us that he was very suspicious about the application's security. The same was afraid that the agent would somehow leak their conversation. One of the topics he liked to talk about was politics, a topic that he thought was quite controversial, and he didn't want his opinion to be shared with anyone else. The same reported that due to this, he even limited certain information in the conversations he had with the agent due to fear of information leakage. Another report by P2 was related to the agent's intelligence level. P2 did not have as much confidence in the accuracy of the information provided on specific subjects or even in the agent's ability to delve deeper into particular topics. He informed that he regretted not having tested the agent's intelligence more, analyzing how far he could deepen his conversations in a debate. In this report, we note the dominance of reliability and safety factors.

Participant P3 also surprised us, mainly due to his behavior with the agent. He was the only one who provided untrue information during conversations with the agent. We validated the integrity of this information passed by P3 to the agent through the Common

Ground questionnaire [13], applied before the test period with users. The family members in residence with this older person reported this point to our research team, finding this behavior funny, as the older person somehow felt the need to please the agent, leading to its humanization.

We highlight that P3 was 81 years old at the time, is a retired, illiterate farmer, and lives in the countryside of a small town in Ceará with his daughter and a granddaughter. He did not report any problems using the Echo Dot during the experiment, even without having ever seen this type of technology. As we left the device at the older person's residence previously paired with the other Echo of the researcher playing the wizard's role, the older person did not need to act when the wizard called. His Echo automatically answered the call. In P3's reports, the presence of humanization and novelty factors is clear. He was so fascinated with the technology that he ended up humanizing the agent and still feeling the need to please him as if he had just been introduced to a person that he had a great appreciation for.

P5 reported that he found the technology exciting and that it was the first time he used this type of system, which made him more curious. He also noted that he had, at times, asked the agent to repeat what it had said. However, the participant added that he lives on a bustling street and that sound cars often pass in front of his residence. Continuing the report, he mentioned that when he could not hear what the agent was saying well, it was due to some external noise. This report mainly demonstrates the presence of the error minimization factor, given that the tool was prepared for communication repairs. Some of the participants also reported having requested the repetition of some information due to some external noise or even an instability with the internet connection.

Participants P4 and P7 were the most opposed to their participation in the experiment. Recruiting both of them was challenging for our research team, and we relied heavily on their family members' help to help us convince them. Among the main reasons they did not want to participate in our study, that the older women confessed to their relatives who passed on this information to us, were reasons related to insecurity with the use of this type of technology and lack of time. These two participants were the last to participate in the experiment. Participant P4 was one of the most difficult to schedule the technology installation in her home by one of our researchers, who cleaned the Echo with alcohol, used masks, and maintained an appropriate distance from all participants. We schedule several times until we get availability from the participant. She did not provide further insights into the experiment other than noticing noises on the call. She pondered that some instability in the internet connection caused them.

Participant P7 was quite hesitant. She didn't consider herself able to help in this kind of experiment, as she didn't even have a cell phone. She had no experience with any more modern technology, in addition to having a particular aversion to them. Her daughter and our recruiter talked a lot with the participant before convincing her to participate. P7 commented that she found the technology exciting and had no problem using it. It is worth mentioning that this participant was also illiterate, but still managed to use the technology without any issues. However, she reported that she would not be interested in using this type of technology and does not have the time to do so, as she is a housewife and takes care of several family members who live with her or close to her home. She also made comments about noises on the call and the fact of asking the agent to repeat some information, both for the sake of understanding certain words and for noises in the environment she was in. In the reports of P4 and P7, we see factors like error minimization, reliability, adaptation, and user satisfaction. Below in Table 3, we summarize the main characteristics of our study participants, aspects raised through the Common Ground questionnaire prepared by Gama and Oliveira [13].

**Table 3.** Main characteristics of participants.

| Identifier | Gender | Age | Profession | Education level |
|---|---|---|---|---|
| P1 | Female | 71 | Housewife | Complete high school |
| P2 | Male | 67 | Retired | Complete higher education |
| P3 | Male | 81 | Retired farmer | No schooling |
| P4 | Female | 79 | Retired | Complete high school |
| P5 | Male | 61 | Retired | Incomplete elementary school |
| P6 | Female | 66 | Retired | Complete high school |
| P7 | Female | 75 | Housewife | No schooling |

# 8 Conclusion

This section exposes the conclusions of this study, summarizing its contributions and future perspectives, which point out some directions for continuing research in the area of voice-controlled intelligent agents.

## 8.1 Main Contributions

As one of the main contributions, we can mention our survey of the UX, Engagement, and Usability factors, applicable in the context of voice interfaces. Other researchers can use them to build their assessment instruments in their specific contexts. The significant additional contribution of this study is the Instrument for Quantitative Assessment of Experience among Seniors and Conversational Agents. Our questionnaire can be reused by others interested in this technology to determine the degree of experience between user and agent.

## 8.2 Future Works

As future works, we intend to focus on strategies for repairing disengagement in the context of voice agents and also on sustaining engagement over long periods. We initially have to review the literature on the prevalence, antecedents, and consequences of boredom in the user experience with this type of technology. A key to maintaining engagement with a given system is the distance from boredom, which can be done, for example, by including new features in the system.

# References

1. Akgün, A., Keskin, H., Byrne, J.: Organizational emotional capability, product and process innovation, and firm performance: an empirical analysis. J. Eng. Tech. Manag. **26**, 103–130 (2009)
2. Bangor, A., Kortum, P., Miller, J.: Determining what individual SUS scores mean: adding an adjective rating scale. J. Usability Stud. **4**, 114–123 (2009)
3. Bickmore, T., Schulman, D., Yin, L.: Maintaining engagement in long-term interventions with relational agents. Appl. Artif. Intell. **24**, 648–666 (2010)
4. Chung, K., Oh, Y., Ju, D.: Elderly users' interaction with conversational agent. In: Proceedings of the 7th International Conference on Human-Agent Interaction (2019)
5. Cronbach, L., Shavelson, R.: My current thoughts on coefficient alpha and successor procedures. Educ. Psychol. Measur. **64**, 391–418 (2004)
6. Dias, C.: Usabilidade Na Web: Criando Portais Mais Acessíveis. Alta Books, Rio de Janeiro (2007)
7. D'mello, S., Graesser, A.: AutoTutor and affective autotutor: learning by talking with cognitively and emotionally intelligent computers that talk back. ACM Trans. Interact. Intell. Syst. **2**, 1–39 (2012)
8. Dybkjær, L., Bernsen, N., Dybkjær, H.: A methodology for diagnostic evaluation of spoken human—machine dialogue. Int. J. Hum Comput Stud. **48**, 605–625 (1998)
9. Fank, J., Diermeyer, F.: "Look me in the eyes!" Analyzing the effects of embodiment in humanized human-machine interaction in heavy trucks. In: 2021 IEEE Intelligent Vehicles Symposium (IV) (2021)
10. Ferreira, A., Oliveira, F., Damasceno, A., Cortés, M.: Conversational agents for the elderly, the guardian platform. In: Anais do XI Computer on the Beach - COTB 2020 (2020)
11. Ferreira, A.: Instrument for Quantitative Assessment of Experience among Seniors and Conversational Agents (2022). https://drive.google.com/file/d/1yXztMXOX_6TedubLOasZA OxlF7aQ4FXO/view?usp=sharing
12. Freitas, A., Rodrigues, S.: A avaliação da confiabilidade de questionário: uma análise utilizando o coeficiente alfa de Cronbach. In: Simpósio de Engenharia de Produção. Anais... Bauru-SP: UNESP (2005)
13. Gama, T., Oliveira, F.: Diretrizes para o Desenvolvimento de Agentes Relacionais Baseados em Common Ground para Idosos Brasileiros. Ceará State University (2022)
14. Glas, N., Pelachaud, C.: Definitions of engagement in human-agent interaction. In: 2015 International Conference on Affective Computing and Intelligent Interaction (ACII), pp. 944–949 (2015)
15. Gould, J., Conti, J., Hovanyecz, T.: Composing letters with a simulated listening typewriter. Commun. ACM **26**, 295–308 (1983)
16. Hassenzahl, M., Tractinsky, N.: User experience - a research agenda. Behav. Inf. Technol. **25**, 91–97 (2006)
17. ISO/IEC 9126-1: Software Engineering-Product Quality-Part 1: Quality model. International Organization for Standardization, Geneva, Switzerland (2001)
18. Kasap, Z., Magnenat-Thalmann, N.: Building long-term relationships with virtual and robotic characters: the role of remembering. Vis. Comput. **28**, 87–97 (2011)
19. Kidd, C., Breazeal, C.: Robots at home: understanding long-term human-robot interaction. In: 2008 IEEE/RSJ International Conference on Intelligent Robots and Systems (2008)
20. Kiseleva, J., Williams, K., Hassan Awadallah, A., Crook, A., Zitouni, I., Anastasakos, T.: Predicting user satisfaction with intelligent assistants. In: Proceedings of the 39th International ACM SIGIR Conference on Research and Development in Information Retrieval (2016)
21. Lalmas, M.: Measuring web user engagement: a cauldron of many things (2013)

22. Laurel, B.: Computers as Theatre. Addison-Wesley, Upper Saddle River (2014)
23. Lee, M., Forlizzi, J., Kiesler, S., Rybski, P., Antanitis, J., Savetsila, S.: Personalization in HRI: a longitudinal field experiment. In: 2012 7th ACM/IEEE International Conference on Human-Robot Interaction (HRI), pp. 319–326 (2012)
24. Leontitsis, A., Pagge, J.: A simulation approach on Cronbach's alpha statistical significance. Math. Comput. Simul. **73**, 336–340 (2007)
25. Lucchesi, I., Silva, A., Abreu, C., Tarouco, L.: Evaluation of a chatbot in the educational context: an experience with Metis. RENOTE 16 (2018)
26. Milošević, M., Shrove, M., Jovanov, E.: Applications of smartphones for ubiquitous health monitoring and wellbeing management. JITA J. Inf. Technol. Appl. (Banja Luka) - APEIRON **1** (2011)
27. Monk, A.: Common ground in electronically mediated communication: clark's theory of language use. In: HCI Models, Theories, and Frameworks: Toward a Multidisciplinary Science, pp. 265–289 (2003)
28. Nielsen, J.: Iterative user-interface design. Computer **26**, 32–41 (1993)
29. Nielsen, J.: Usability inspection methods. In: Conference Companion on Human Factors in Computing Systems - CHI 1994 (1994)
30. Nielsen, J.: The Definition of User Experience (UX). https://www.nngroup.com/articles/definition-user-experience/. Accessed 07 Jan 2022
31. Peters, C., Castellano, G., de Freitas, S.: An exploration of user engagement in HCI. In: Proceedings of the International Workshop on Affective-Aware Virtual Agents and Social Robots - AFFINE 2009 (2009)
32. Rogers, Y., Sharp, H., Preece, J.: Design de interação. Bookman, Porto Alegre (2013)
33. Portet, F., Vacher, M., Golanski, C., Roux, C., Meillon, B.: Design and evaluation of a smart home voice interface for the elderly: acceptability and objection aspects. Pers. Ubiquit. Comput. **17**, 127–144 (2011)
34. Reichheld, F.: The one number you need to grow. Harv. Bus. Rev. **81**, 46–55 (2003)
35. Roussou, M.: Immersive interactive virtual reality and informal education. In: Proceedings of User Interfaces for All: Interactive Learning Environments for Children, pp. 1–9 (2000)
36. Seufert, E.: Freemium Economics: Leveraging Analytics and User Segmentation to Drive Revenue. Morgan Kaufmann Publishers (2014)
37. Slavík, P., Němec, V., Sporka, A.J.: Speech based user interface for users with special needs. In: Matoušek, V., Mautner, P., Pavelka, T. (eds.) TSD 2005. LNCS (LNAI), vol. 3658, pp. 45–55. Springer, Heidelberg (2005). https://doi.org/10.1007/11551874_6
38. Streiner, D.: Being inconsistent about consistency: when coefficient alpha does and doesn't matter. J. Pers. Assess. **80**, 217–222 (2003)
39. Teixeira, F.: Desenhando interfaces conversacionais: o desafio de UX. https://brasil.uxdesign.cc/desenhando-interfaces-conversacionais-o-desafio-de-ux-5d94cce7e82. Accessed 07 Jan 2022
40. Yankelovich, N.: How do users know what to say? Interactions **3**, 32–43 (1996)
41. Yamada, S., Kitakoshi, D., Yamashita, A., Suzuki, K., Suzuki, M.: Development of an intelligent dialogue agent with smart devices for older adults: a preliminary study. In: 2018 Conference on Technologies and Applications of Artificial Intelligence (TAAI) (2018)
42. Webster, J., Ahuja, J.: Enhancing the design of web navigation systems: the influence of user disorientation on engagement and performance. MIS Q. **30**, 661 (2006)
43. World Health Organization (WHO): Envelhecimento ativo: uma política de saúde, p. 60 (2005)

# To Discover Novice Expert Paradigm: Sequence-Based Time-Domain and Graph-Based Frequency-Domain Analysis Method of Eye Movement

Dian Jin[1], Weiwei Yu[1]([✉]), Xinliang Yang[2], Haiyang Wang[2], and Ran Peng[2]

[1] School of Mechanical Engineering, Northwestern Polytechnical University,
Xi'an 710072, China
yuweiwei@nwpu.edu.cn
[2] Avionics Research Institute, Chinese Flight Test Establishment,
Xi'an 710089, China

**Abstract.** Eye movement data can show the cognitive process in performing tasks to a certain extent. The existing researches on eye movement analysis are usually based on statistics, and it is difficult to show the correlation between the information associated with the scene. Other probabilistic algorithms usually focus on user feature recognition based on eye movement representation. In this paper, the concept of time-domain and frequency-domain analysis of eye movement area of interest is proposed, within which, the frequent pattern mining method and visual cognitive graph model are constructed to mine the relationship between the areas of interest. Finally, some application examples of this model in the novice expert paradigm are presented.

**Keywords:** Area of interest · Novice expert paradigm ·
Human-computer interaction · Domain analysis of AOI · Graph model

## 1 Introduction

The research of eye movement is the most effective means of visual information processing [19]. Research [15] reveals that eye-movement data provide an excellent online indication of the cognitive processes underlying visual search and reading.

HCI (Human-Computer interface) refers to the interfaces between computer technology and people as users [12]. Some studies focus on the presentation of individual information or interactive element aiming to provide a new HCI design: In [21], eye movement physiological experiments are conducted to evaluate the size, shape, and spacing of the card in the interface. [17] analyzed the

Supported by the Key Research and Development Program of Shaanxi 2020SF-152, and Educational reform research project 2022JGY10.

technique of reading a colorful early map by examining eye movement parameters, where it was observed that test subjects spend more time studying the cluttered area, but this effect can be related to eccentricity. The experiences and the obtained results can contribute to the design and development of modern user interfaces.

In addition to guiding interface design, the study of eye movement can also be used to analyze expert paradigms for novice training. [18] examined eye movement parameters in the context of the acquisition of IT skills. The results show that differences in gaze movement can be detected in students with different levels of knowledge, from which conclusions can be stated and related to the effectiveness, success, or failure of learning. Focusing on the map-reading skills, [10] provides a new approach to facilitate the quantitative assessment of map-reading skills based on eye-tracking. The results indicated that map-reading skills could be reflected in metrics like the measure of the first fixation, the measure of processing, and the measure of search. [13] proposed that the evaluation of the eye movement parameters could serve as a support for measuring different abilities. It examined the forms and effectiveness of the debugging phase of software development through eye movement tracking with the involvement of test subjects. After examining the results, it can be seen that test subjects who made many minor modifications as well as more frequent compilations and runs with less efficiency and more time required, discovered and corrected more hidden errors in the source code than those who placed more emphasis on interpretation, and they used the ability to compile and run the application less often.

For the analysis of eye movement data, many methods have been proposed. Heat map, also called visual attention map, is one of the simplest and most used eye-tracking visualization techniques [1]. A method that makes use of heat maps and gaze stripes, as well as attention clouds is presented in [6]. The results are aiming to help public transport map designers and producers gain feedback and insights on how the current design of the map can be further improved, by leveraging the visualization tool. In order to find eye movement patterns and similar strategies between participants, [3] presented a graph comparison method using radial graphs that show AOIs and their transitions. Those graphs can be analyzed based on dwell times, directed transitions, and temporal AOI sequences. Two graphs can be compared directly and temporal changes may be analyzed. In [5], an interactive and web-based visual analytics tool combining linked visualization techniques and algorithmic approaches for exploring the hierarchical visual scanning behavior of a group of people when solving tasks in a static stimulus is proposed. The methods included visual attention map, hierarchical flow, and interactive Sankey diagram. This has the benefit that the recorded eye movement data can be observed in a more structured way to find patterns in the common scanning behavior of a group of eye-tracked people. Scarf plot is an excellent AOI visualization method [14]. Nevertheless, scarf plots are ineffective when there are many AOIs. To help analysts explore long temporal patterns, [20] presented Alpscarf, an extension of scarf plots with mountains and valleys to visualize order-conformity and revisits. Gaze Entropy [7] defined the degree

of disorder and distribution of gaze fixations to evaluate mobile crane operator's gaze pattern to discriminate the effects of skills and performance. This can
be used as development of work support or guidance system to facilitate crane
operation.

These methods reflect part of the association between AOIs, but the deep
relationship between AOIs can hardly be explored. For example, these studies
did not consider the role of each AOI in the process of AOI transfer, while not
considering the context information.

There exist eye movement analysis based on the Probability model: In [9],
hidden Markov models (HMM) were used to model eye searching patterns of
people with different cultures in face recognition. Results suggest that active
retrieval of facial feature information through an analytic eye movement pattern
may be optimal for face recognition regardless of culture. Another research [8]
also constructed an HMM model to analyze eye movement data in cognitive
tasks involving cognitive state changes. In research [16], a cognitive model of
individual reading was constructed based on eye movement data and Bayesian
estimation. Besides these methods, Deep Neural Network is also used in eye
movement analysis [11], aiming to achieve emotion recognition via eye movement
data, eye image, and EEG data.

These methods are also more or less based on traditional eye movement
indicators. Besides, they mainly focus on user traits, such as user state or user
feature recognition.

This paper focuses on the relationship between the information of the AOI
under different scenes and constructed two models. These two models facilitate
mathematical analysis, and not only can be used to guide the interface design
and analyze the novice expert paradigm but can be used to reveal the underlying
knowledge of decision making.

## 2  Methods

### 2.1  Time and Frequency-Domain Analysis of AOIs

This paper proposed the concept of time and frequency-domain analysis of AOIs.
Generally speaking, time-domain and frequency-domain analysis are used to
analyze waveform signals: A sine wave signal is a sinusoidal signal in one direction
(time-domain) and a straight line in the other direction (frequency-domain).
Based on this idea, this paper constructed time-domain and frequency-domain
models for AOI analysis, as shown in Fig. 1. It is a sequence of events from one
direction (time-domain) and a graph model from the other direction (frequency-
domain).

### 2.2  Frequent Pattern

As a sequence, the AOI can be mined by using many sequence data mining
methods, for example, frequent pattern mining. When a Remotely Piloted Aircraft (RPA) pilot is performing an operation, his/her AOI subsequences tend to

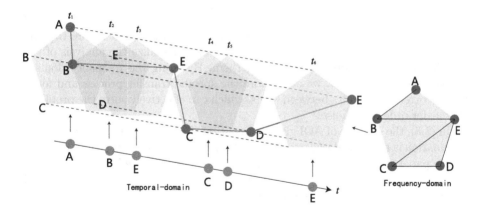

**Fig. 1.** Time and frequency-domain analysis of AOI.

show patterns, for example, during the climb, there are frequent AOI transitions between the front view and flight altitude information. We attribute this type of analysis to time-domain analysis.

**Sequence Matching.** A simple idea to mine frequent patterns is Sequence matching: Set the pattern length $k$ and then iterate through the original AOI sequence, recording the number of occurrences of each sequence:

$$N_s = \sum_{i=1}^{n-k+1} \mathbb{1}(s, S_{(i,i+k-1)}) \tag{1}$$

where $s$ is the frequent pattern candidate with length $k$, $N_s$ denotes the count. $S_{(i,i+k-1)}$ denotes the subsequence from item $i$ to item $i+k-1$, and $\mathbb{1}$ denotes:

$$\mathbb{1}(s_1, s_2) = \begin{cases} 1 & s_1 = s_2 \\ 0 & s_1 \neq s_2 \end{cases} \tag{2}$$

Frequent patterns for each experiment $\hat{S} = \{\hat{s}_1, \cdots, \hat{s}_m\}$ can be chosen via setting threshold or using topk method. For multiple experiments, the frequent patterns that appear in multiple experiments were selected, and the number of occurrences is called the support.

### 2.3   Visual Cognitive Graph

The time-domain analysis method can only see the pattern information of eye movement and the correlation between the AOIs on the temporal sequence. However, for a task, different people may acquire information in a different order, and there may be a lot of noise in the process of acquiring information. For analysis methods in the frequency domain, traditional eye movement analysis methods like Gaze plot and heat map usually consider the statistical characteristics of AOIs, such as fixation times (e.g. eye movement heat map), but ignore the correlation between AOIs. This kind of method can not realize the analysis of the AOI itself and the correlation between them. By using the frequency-domain analysis method of AOIs, we can ignore the specific transfer process and focus on the correlation results between AOIs, which can effectively solve the problems of transfer order and noise.

In [2,5], the concept of AOI graph is mentioned. However, the context (scene) information is not considered, and the relationship between AOIs is not analyzed. In this paper, the flight scene is divided and AOIs are analyzed under tasks. For each stage, the graph theory related indicators and analysis methods are used to mine the information association between AOIs.

**Graph Construction.** The frequency-domain analysis of AOI is based on graph model. Each node of the graph represents the AOI, and the edges between nodes represent the association relations, such as the number of transitions, etc., which can also be measured by various graph theory related indicators such as random walk. Node size represents an attribute of the AOI, such as the frequency of occurrence, and can also be measured by graph theory indicators such as betweenness centrality.

*Task Division.* For the flight scene, the eye movement pattern is very different in different flight tasks. Therefore, we need to link the analysis content with the flight tasks. Therefore, before the construction of the graph, a task division is indispensable.

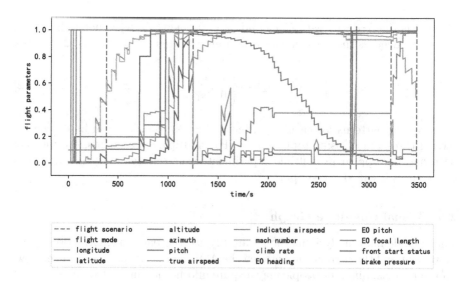

**Fig. 2.** Task division result

After the task division, we can start building graphs.

*Graph Building and Merging.* Take mission $p$, task $q$ as an example:
Construct an $N \times N$ zero matrix $\mathbf{T}_{p,q}$, where $N$ represents the number of AOIs. For AOI $i$ and subsequent AOI $j$ in AOI sequence $S$, add $\mathbf{T}_{p,q}(i,j)$ with 1. Then, an adjacent matrix $\mathbf{T}_{p,q}$ of the transition graph is built, whose row $i$, column $j$ represents that eye movement shifts from AOI $i$ to AOI $j$ for $\mathbf{T}_{p,q}(i,j)$ times.

However, this is only the transition graph of task $q$ under mission $p$, which may have a lot of randomness and noise. Therefore, we considered merging the eye tracker of the same task under multiple missions.

Considering task $q$ in multiple missions, the merged adjacent matrix is:

$$\mathbf{T}_q = \sum_{p=0}^{n} \mathbf{T}_{p,q} \tag{3}$$

**Graph Analysis**
*Random Walk.* The random walk algorithm measures the probability of one node moving directly or indirectly to another node (Fig. 2).

Let $\boldsymbol{P}_A$ as the transition probability matrix of attribute augmented graph $G_a$. Considering $c \in (0,1)$ as restart probability, the original random walk distance $\boldsymbol{R}$ of $G_a$ is determined as:

$$\boldsymbol{R} = c\left[\boldsymbol{E} - (1-c)\boldsymbol{P}_A\right]^{-1} \tag{4}$$

Since $G$ is a directed graph, we defined the random walk distance as the average of the original random walk distance from node to node. Thus the random walk distance is:

$$\boldsymbol{R}_A = \frac{\left(\boldsymbol{R} + \boldsymbol{R}^T\right)}{2} \tag{5}$$

We use random walk algorithm to measure the importance of nodes and to measure the direct and indirect relationships between nodes.

*Betweenness Centrality.* Betweenness centrality [4] of a node $v$ is the sum of the fraction of all-pairs shortest paths that pass through $v$.

$$c_B(v) = \sum_{s,t \in V} \frac{\sigma(s,t \mid v)}{\sigma(s,t)} \tag{6}$$

where $V$ represents the set of nodes, $\sigma(s,t)$ shows the number of shortest $(s,t)$-paths, and $\sigma(s,t \mid v)$ is the number of paths passing through some node $v$ other than $s,t$. If $s = t, \sigma(s,t) = 1$, and if $v \in s,t, \sigma(s,t \mid v) = 0$.

We used betweenness centrality to evaluate the importance of an AOI as a bridge connecting other AOIs.

*Distance Closeness.* Theoretically, we measure the distance closeness by:

$$\mathbf{W_c} = \mathbf{D} \cdot \mathbf{T} \tag{7}$$

where $\mathbf{W_c}$ represents the distance closeness matrix which measures the total distance between AOIs. $\mathbf{D}$ is the distance matrix, e.g. $\mathbf{D}(i, j)$ measures the distance between AOI $i$ and $j$. Due to the accuracy of eye tracker, our AOIs are big. To improve accuracy, we sum up each path length:

$$\mathbf{W_c}'(i, j) = \sum_{k=1}^{n-1} \mathbb{1}_{k,(i,j)} \cdot d_k \tag{8}$$

where $\mathbf{W_c}'$ represents the closeness matrix which measures the total distance between AOIs accurately. $\mathbb{1}_{k,(i,j)}$ equals to 1 if $s_k$ represents the transition from AOI $i$ to $j$:

$$\mathbb{1}_{k,(i,j)} = \begin{cases} 1 & s_k : i \to j \\ 0 & \text{else} \end{cases} \tag{9}$$

The distance closeness reveals the transition distance between AOIs. Thus can be used to guide the design of interface layout.

## 3    Experiments

The experiments are based on a search-and-rescue mission of RPA. All the experiments were done on the simulator of the RPA operation platform (as shown in Fig. 3). The platform can record the eye movement data of the operator, the operation data of the operator, and the flight parameters of the simulator simultaneously.

Table 1. Abbreviations of AOIs

| AOI | Abbreviation |
|---|---|
| Operation interface | OP |
| State interface | ST |
| CCD view | CCD |
| Front view | FR |
| Throttle speed | TH |
| Roll angle | RO |
| Flight speed | SP |
| Flight altitude | AL |
| Flight path | PA |

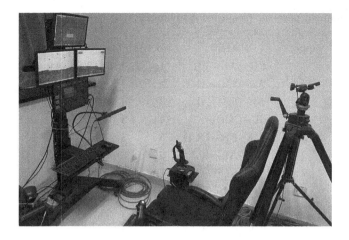

**Fig. 3.** Flight simulator platform

The display of this platform includes 9 functional areas, which are called AOIs: Operation interface, State interface, CCD view, Front view, Throttle speed, Roll angle, Flight speed, Flight altitude, and Flight path (Abbreviations are shown in Table 1). Different flight tasks can be simulated on the platform, such as "take-off", "climb", "cruise", "search target", and "flight return".

Each experiment included one flight mission. Each mission is made up of the above six flight tasks. The subjects were an expert pilot and a novice pilot. The expert pilot has three years of experience in RPA operation, the novice pilot only has basic training. For each subject, four experiments were conducted.

## 4    Results and Analysis

### 4.1    Results Based on Time-Domain Analysis

The data of "climb" stage is analyzed with the Sequence matching method to demonstrate the time-domain analysis.

The result of the Sequence matching is shown in Table 2. We can discover that the novice pilot and expert pilot have many similar patterns (highlighted in different colors). However, it can also be found that the eye movement sequences of the expert pilot are more structured and own higher support. Besides, "AL" often appears in the patterns of an expert pilot, which means that the expert paid more attention to altitude information than the novice.

### 4.2    Results Based on Frequency-Domain Analysis

The constructed graph of "climb" stage is shown in Fig. 4. In Fig. 4(a) Graph based on traditional statistical indicators: The size of the node represents the fixation count. The width of the line represents the transition count; In Fig. 4(b)

**Table 2.** Frequent patterns (sequence matching, $k = 3$): novice (left), expert (right)

| No. | Support | Pattern | No. | Support | Pattern |
|-----|---------|---------|-----|---------|---------|
| 1 | 4 | FR→AL→FR | 1 | 4 | FR→AL→FR |
| 2 | 4 | AL→FR→AL | 2 | 4 | AL→FR→AL |
| 3 | 3 | AL→PA→AL | 3 | 4 | AL→PA→AL |
| 4 | 2 | FR→CCD→FR | 4 | 3 | FR→AL→PA |
| 5 | 2 | CCD→FR→CCD | 5 | 3 | PA→AL→PA |
| 6 | 2 | RO→AL→RO | 6 | 3 | AL→RO→AL |
| 7 | 2 | AL→RO→AL | 7 | 2 | AL→PA→FR |
| 8 | 2 | RO→AL→PA | 8 | 2 | AL→CCD→FR |
| 9 | 2 | PA→FR→AL | 9 | 2 | PA→FR→AL |
| 10 | 2 | FR→AL→RO | 10 | 2 | FR→AL→CCD |

Graph based on betweenness centrality and distance closeness: The size of the node represents their betweenness centrality, which indicates the importance of the AOI as a bridge connecting other information. Such information is used as a reference in the pilot's decision-making process. The width of the line represents the transition distance, and shows the total saccade distance between AOIs; In Fig. 4(c) Graph based on random walk distance: The size of the node represents the sum of random walk distance between itself and other nodes, which indicates their importance. The width of the line represents the random walk distance, which indicates the direct and indirect relationships between AOIs.

Observe Fig. 4, the graph structure of experts and novice are similar, while some differences exist:

Comparing Fig. 4(a) and (b), although the novice pilot did not pay much attention to "OP", he did use "OP" as reference information, as he's looking past it in the process. However, the "OP" is not an important operation during the "climb" stage, the expert pilot use "AL" as reference information significantly better than the novice pilot. In Fig. 4(a), the line between "AL" and "FR" is wide, which indicates the transition is frequent. Judging by this alone, designers are likely to see this as an optimization direction. However, in Fig. 4(b), the width is thin, which means the total saccade distance is small. This is because the "AL" and "FR" are relatively close to each other. In Fig. 4(b)expert, the width between "AL" and "PA" is wide, which means the expert pilot costs a long saccade distance between these two AOIs. This might be optimized by reducing the distance between interfaces, or summarizing complex information with a brief message on the main interface.

Focusing on Fig. 4(c), node "AL" of expert converges more information as it has a strong connection with multiple nodes. This means that while the pilot pays attention to altitude, he is also very good at obtaining other information to make overall decisions. Novice pilots, by contrast, have a more chaotic structure.

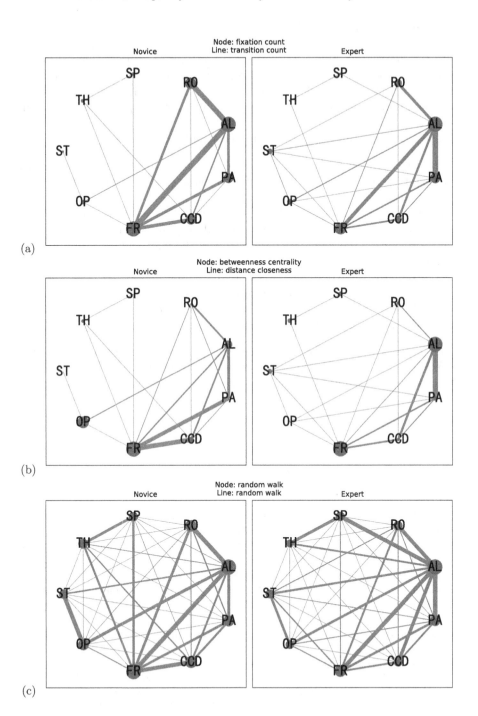

**Fig. 4.** Novice expert comparison: novice (left), expert (right).

## 5   Conclusion

With the application of eye tracker, more and more researches related to eye movement appear. This paper proposed the concept of time and frequency-domain analysis of AOI, which takes sequence model and graph model to eye movement data analysis, and discovered the novice expert paradigm via a comparative experiment.

The contribution of this paper can be concluded as follows:

1. The time-domain analysis of eye movement based on the sequence mining method is proposed, from which information acquisition rules and cognitive patterns can be mined;
2. The frequency-domain analysis of eye movement based on the graph model is proposed, within which, several indicators derived from graph theory are proposed to reveal the underlying knowledge of the pilot while decision making in a simulated flight task.
3. In a comparative experiment between novice pilot and expert pilot, the proposed method is used to realize the discovery of the novice expert paradigm and the analysis of the expert decision-making process. The results can be directly used to guide novice pilots and guide interactive system design.

In future work, more sequence mining methods can be used, such as the PrefixSpan algorithm. But the result of the algorithm must be well explainable. Besides, this research can be used to implement an adaptive interaction system in the future.

## References

1. Blascheck, T., Kurzhals, K., Raschke, M., Burch, M., Weiskopf, D., Ertl, T.: Visualization of eye tracking data: a taxonomy and survey. In: Computer Graphics Forum, vol. 36, pp. 260–284. Wiley Online Library (2017)
2. Blascheck, T., Kurzhals, K., Raschke, M., Strohmaier, S., Weiskopf, D., Ertl, T.: Aoi hierarchies for visual exploration of fixation sequences. In: Proceedings of the Ninth Biennial ACM Symposium on Eye Tracking Research and Applications. ETRA 2016, pp. 111–118. Association for Computing Machinery, New York (2016). https://doi.org/10.1145/2857491.2857524
3. Blascheck, T., Schweizer, M., Beck, F., Ertl, T.: Visual comparison of eye movement patterns. In: Computer Graphics Forum, vol. 36, pp. 87–97. Wiley Online Library (2017)
4. Brandes, U.: A faster algorithm for betweenness centrality. J. Math. Sociol. **25**(2), 163–177 (2001)
5. Burch, M., Kumar, A., Timmermans, N.: An interactive web-based visual analytics tool for detecting strategic eye movement patterns. In: Proceedings of the 11th ACM Symposium on Eye Tracking Research and Applications. ETRA 2019. Association for Computing Machinery, New York (2019). https://doi.org/10.1145/3317960.3321615

6. Burch, M., Veneri, A., Sun, B.: Eyeclouds: a visualization and analysis tool for exploring eye movement data. In: Proceedings of the 12th International Symposium on Visual Information Communication and Interaction. VINCI'2019. Association for Computing Machinery, New York (2019). https://doi.org/10.1145/3356422. 3356423
7. Chew, J.Y., Ohtomi, K., Suzuki, H.: Monitoring attention of crane operators during load oscillations using gaze entropy measures. In: Stephanidis, C., et al. (eds.) HCII 2021. LNCS, vol. 13096, pp. 44–61. Springer, Cham (2021). https://doi.org/10. 1007/978-3-030-90328-2_3
8. Chuk, T., Chan, A.B., Shimojo, S., Hsiao, J.H.: Eye movement analysis with switching hidden Markov models. Behav. Res. Methods **52**(3), 1026–1043 (2020)
9. Chuk, T., Crookes, K., Hayward, W.G., Chan, A.B., Hsiao, J.H.: Hidden Markov model analysis reveals the advantage of analytic eye movement patterns in face recognition across cultures. Cognition **169**, 102–117 (2017)
10. Dong, W., Jiang, Y., Zheng, L., Liu, B., Meng, L.: Assessing map-reading skills using eye tracking and Bayesian structural equation modelling. Sustainability **10**(9) (2018). https://doi.org/10.3390/su10093050
11. Guo, J.J., Zhou, R., Zhao, L.M., Lu, B.L.: Multimodal emotion recognition from eye image, eye movement and EEG using deep neural networks. In: 2019 41st Annual International Conference of the IEEE Engineering in Medicine and Biology Society (EMBC), pp. 3071–3074. IEEE (2019)
12. Katona, J.: A review of human-computer interaction and virtual reality research fields in cognitive infocommunications. Appl. Sci. **11**(6) (2021). https://doi.org/ 10.3390/app11062646
13. Kovari, A., Katona, J., Costescu, C.: Evaluation of eye-movement metrics in a software debbuging task using gp3 eye tracker. Acta Polytechnica Hungarica **17**(2), 57–76 (2020)
14. Kurzhals, K., Hlawatsch, M., Seeger, C., Weiskopf, D.: Visual analytics for mobile eye tracking. IEEE Trans. Visual Comput. Graphics **23**(1), 301–310 (2017). https://doi.org/10.1109/TVCG.2016.2598695
15. Liversedge, S.P., Findlay, J.M.: Saccadic eye movements and cognition. Trends Cogn. Sci. **4**(1), 6–14 (2000)
16. Seelig, S.A., Rabe, M.M., Malem-Shinitski, N., Risse, S., Reich, S., Engbert, R.: Bayesian parameter estimation for the swift model of eye-movement control during reading. J. Math. Psychol. **95**, 102313 (2020)
17. Török, Á., Török, Z.G., Tölgyesi, B.: Cluttered centres: interaction between eccentricity and clutter in attracting visual attention of readers of a 16th century map. In: 2017 8th IEEE International Conference on Cognitive Infocommunications (CogInfoCom), pp. 000433–000438. IEEE (2017)
18. Ujbanyi, T., Katona, J., Sziladi, G., Kovari, A.: Eye-tracking analysis of computer networks exam question besides different skilled groups. In: 2016 7th IEEE International Conference on Cognitive Infocommunications (CogInfoCom), pp. 000277– 000282. IEEE (2016)
19. Xiong, W., Wang, Yu., Zhou, Q., Liu, Z., Zhang, X.: The research of eye movement behavior of expert and novice in flight simulation of landing. In: Harris, D. (ed.) EPCE 2016. LNCS (LNAI), vol. 9736, pp. 485–493. Springer, Cham (2016). https://doi.org/10.1007/978-3-319-40030-3_47

20. Yang, C.K., Wacharamanotham, C.: AlpScarf: augmenting scarf plots for exploring temporal gaze patterns. In: Extended Abstracts of the 2018 CHI Conference on Human Factors in Computing Systems, pp. 1–6 (2018)
21. Zhang, L., Ma, G., Zhou, J., Jia, F.: Human-computer interface design of intelligent spinning factory monitoring system based on eye tracking technology. In: Ahram, T.Z., Falcão, C.S. (eds.) AHFE 2021. LNNS, vol. 275, pp. 579–586. Springer, Cham (2021). https://doi.org/10.1007/978-3-030-80091-8_69

# Evaluation of a Virtual Working Environment via Psychophysiological Indices

Seiji Kikuchi, Ryosuke Konishi, Reiji Goda, Yusuke Kan'no, Shinji Miyake, and Daiji Kobayashi[(✉)] [iD]

Chitose Institute of Science and Technology, Chitose, Hokkaido, Japan
{m2210080,d-kobaya}@photon.chitose.ac.jp

**Abstract.** Many studies have suggested that natural landscapes could relieve stressful sentiments regardless of how the virtual nature is presented. Thus, we investigated the effect of a virtual working environment on workers' mental and physiological states using psychophysiological measures and subjective assessments. Twenty-two healthy male students ($22.0 \pm 0.9$ yrs.) voluntary participated in the study. The results indicated that the finger plethysmogram (PTG) amplitude measured in a forest environment was significantly lower than that measured in an office environment. However, the differences in subjective fatigue and stress between the two environments were negligible. Therefore, we assumed that the forest environment could enhance sympathetic activity owing to an excited-pleasurable working experience. However, other more sophisticated measures should be introduced. Furthermore, it is necessary to investigate the subtle effects of nature using more sensitive methods.

**Keywords:** Virtual environment · Working environment · Psychophysiological indices

## 1 Introduction

The evaluation of psychological and physiological stress caused by office work has been a crucial issue addressed by both ergonomic practitioners and researchers [1]. Modern office working environments using human-computer interfaces can be further stressors for workers [2]; therefore, new work styles based on information communication technologies, including computer network infrastructure, have been discussed by Japanese ergonomists. On the other hand, the Japanese government has recommended that office workers in business districts should work in leafy suburbs to not only control COVID-19 transmission rates but also reform the contemporary work style. Hence, many companies and organisations expect a natural environment to have certain positive effects on their workers, enabling them to focus more on their work while relaxing in a natural scenery. Subsequently, such new work styles in leafy scenic areas have been introduced, although the effect of the working environment surrounded by nature on the worker's performance is not extensively studied. Thus, this study aims to investigate the effect of being exposed to natural environments on workers' psychological and physiological

M. Kurosu et al. (Eds.): HCII 2022, LNCS 13516, pp. 257–266, 2022.
https://doi.org/10.1007/978-3-031-17615-9_18

states for proposing novel work style guidelines, despite the existing knowledge about the experimental design procedures being limited.

A study in which a natural scenery was presented using videotapes of six different natural and urban settings for evaluating the stress relief levels of people in different situations reported that the natural landscape can effectively relieve stress [3]. Furthermore, the method of presenting natural landscapes based on psychophysiological indices has been evaluated in the literature [4, 5]. More recently, it was reported that a virtual natural scenery projected on a head-mounted display (HMD) provided a greater relief compared with that observed using a desktop display using psychophysiological measures [6]. Furthermore, presenting high-resolution digital images of a natural environment using an HMD affected the restoration rate from a stressful situation which was constructed using the Stroop colour task based on an electroencephalogram [7]. Previous studies have reported the effectiveness of natural environments in relieving stressful sentiments based on psychophysiological viewpoints, regardless of whether it is presented via videotapes, photographs on a wall, or an HMD.

Regarding the effectiveness of stress relief provided by leafy and other urban environments, it was reported that a virtual forest environment could have a positive impact on psychological health, while a virtual urban environment could have a negative impact. Contrarily, Chia-pin et al. reported that forest environments and urban environments did not have significant differences in influencing participants' physiological states, although they indicated that the reason may be insufficient visual and auditory stimuli [8]. Accordingly, the effectiveness of natural sounds integrated with virtual environments has been pointed out [9]; however, it is not always possible for office workers in leafy areas to work outdoors. More commonly they can enjoy nature scenery while they work inside without the sound of nature. Therefore, it is appropriate to investigate how workers' psychophysiological states affect task performance when they work in a leafy environment without natural sounds.

From another perspective, a biophilic design approach which promotes the integration of natural elements into building environment has been studied to determine the restorative effects of experiencing the natural environment in person. In this discipline, virtual environments (VEs) are applied as research tools for investigating different types of stimuli. Generally, it is assumed that exposure to simulated or mediated nature can be an alternative to actual nature and result in similar restorative effects [10]. For example, several types of virtual biophilic designs have been evaluated based on their restorative effect after a stress-inducing task based on psychophysiological measures [11].

Considering the abovementioned studies, VE can be applied to evaluate the effect of work environments, such as an office and leafy scenic area, on workers' psychophysiological states and observing how the psychophysiological state is affected by stress-induction tasks. Thus, we investigated the effect of natural VE and an office on workers' psychological and physiological states using psychophysiological measures and subjective assessments.

# 2   Method

## 2.1   Design and Participants

The participants executed a mental arithmetic (MA) task in two different VEs in a sequential manner so that we can observe their psychophysiological states while working and resting.

Twenty-two healthy male students participated voluntarily in the study who were divided into two groups, with 11 males in each group, for counterbalancing. The participants' average age was $22.0 \pm 0.9$ years.

This study was conducted respecting the guidelines provided by the ethical review board of Chitose Institute of Science and Technology. Informed consent was obtained from all participants in advance.

## 2.2   Virtual Work Environment

Two VEs without environmental sounds were created to provide the visual stimuli in this study, shown in Fig. 1. The virtual computer monitor was placed in the virtual working space. In the forest condition, the natural landscape can be observed through the window. An urban office building is outside the window in the office condition. Many digits (39 $\times$ 21) were displayed on the PC screen. The participants were instructed to add adjacent figures horizontally and answer one digit by pressing a ten-key keypad on an actual desk. The participant could not look at the ten-key keypad which was connected to a note PC while wearing the HMD (HTC VIVE Pro Eye). However, the actual screen feed from the note PC was captured and displayed on the PC screen in VEs using our virtual reality system consisting of a desktop PC and software developed using Microsoft Visual Studio 2019 running on Microsoft Windows 11 Pro (Fig. 2).

**Fig. 1.** Two VEs displayed in HMD for the office (left panel) and forest conditions (right panel).

**Fig. 2.** Participants execute mental arithmetic tasks wearing the HMD and using a ten-key keypad.

## 2.3 Procedure and Psychophysiological Measures

Upon arrival to the laboratory, participants studied the mental arithmetic task for seven minutes. Then, they sat quietly for five minutes, the resting period (Rest 1), followed by a ten-minute adaptation period with HMD, in which a bright room surrounded by grey walls is displayed. Participants were asked to perform the MA at their own pace for five minutes (Task). They sat quietly for five minutes again after the task (Rest 2). They repeated this session twice under different VEs successively with 10-min intervals between sessions (Fig. 3). The order of these conditions was counterbalanced among participants.

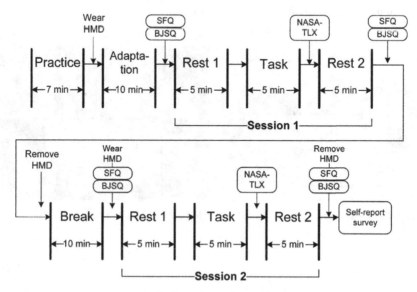

**Fig. 3.** Experimental procedure.

Subjective fatigue was assessed using the subjective fatigue questionnaire (SFQ) before and after attempting the tasks. Psychological stress reactions were also assessed using 18 questionnaire items taken from the brief job stress questionnaire (BJSQ) [12, 13]. The subjective mental workload was evaluated using the National Aeronautics Space Administration Task Load Index (NASA-TLX). All questionnaires were presented on a virtual PC screen in each VEs. Participants responded using a ten-key keypad installed on the desk in an actual environment, shown in Fig. 2.

### 2.4  Physiological Measures

A fingertip photoelectric plethysmogram (PTG) and skin conductance level (SCL) were measured (BIOPAC Systems. PPG100C, EDA100C) to evaluate stress and emotional strain due to the MA task in both VEs. Low PTG amplitude was associated with stress and emotional strain. Moreover, high SCL is another indicator of physiological stress and emotional strain. Both are mediated by the sympathetic nervous system. Electrocardiograms (ECG) were also recorded using a multi-telemeter (Nihonkoden WEB-9500), using which the basic heart rate and high-frequency (HF) and low-frequency (LF) components of the heart rate variability power spectrum were obtained. The abovementioned physiological indices were measured during all experimental blocks, including before and after the resting periods.

### 2.5  Statistical Analysis

All physiological indices were standardised across all blocks for each participant. Repeated two-way (2 conditions × 3 blocks) analysis of variance with Greenhouse and Geisser correction of degree of freedom ($\varepsilon$) was applied to physiological indices. When the main effect of the block was significant, post-hoc analysis (Ryan-Einot-Gabriel-Welsch) was used. Subjective fatigue and stress scores were tested before and after the tasks using a paired t-test. NASA-TLX scores were compared between the conditions using a paired t-test. For all analyses, the significance level was set to $p < 0.05$, while marginally significant level was $p < 0.10$. All statistical tests were performed using SPSS ver. 27.

## 3  Results and Discussions

### 3.1  Physiological Measures

Table 1 displays repeated analysis of variance (ANOVA) results.

**Table 1.** ANOVA results.

|   |   | df | F | ε | 1 − β | η² | p |
|---|---|---|---|---|---|---|---|
| HR | Condition | 1 | 0.045 | 1 | 0.055 | 0.002 | 0.834 |
|  | Block | 1.584 | 14.806 | 0.846 | 0.993 | 0.414 | 0.000*** |
|  | Condition × Block | 1.696 | 1.945 | 0.914 | 0.347 | 0.085 | 0.163 |
| LF | Condition | 1 | 0.106 | 1 | 0.061 | 0.005 | 0.748 |
|  | Block | 1.951 | 18.124 | 1 | 1 | 0.463 | 0.000*** |
|  | Condition × Block | 1.621 | 1.495 | 0.869 | 0.27 | 0.066 | 0.238 |
| HF | Condition | 1 | 0.136 | 1 | 0.064 | 0.006 | 0.716 |
|  | Block | 1.814 | 6.421 | 0.998 | 0.856 | 0.234 | 0.005*** |
|  | Condition × Block | 1.985 | 0.008 | 1 | 0.051 | 0 | 0.992 |
| PTG | Condition | 1 | 8.723 | 1 | 0.804 | 0.293 | 0.008*** |
|  | Block | 1.923 | 17.173 | 1 | 0.999 | 0.45 | 0.000*** |
|  | Condition × Block | 1.988 | 0.123 | 1 | 0.068 | 0.006 | 0.885 |
| SCL | Condition | 1 | 0.24 | 1 | 0.075 | 0.011 | 0.629 |
|  | Block | 1.716 | 18.151 | 0.927 | 0.999 | 0.464 | 0.000*** |
|  | Condition × Block | 1.625 | 0.212 | 0.871 | 0.078 | 0.01 | 0.764 |

## 3.2 Heart Rate

Repeated ANOVA measures revealed a significant main effect of the block ($F = 14.08$, $\eta^2 = 0.414$, $p < .001$). The heart rate was significantly higher during the task than before the task and after the resting period. However, no significant effect of condition was observed (Fig. 4).

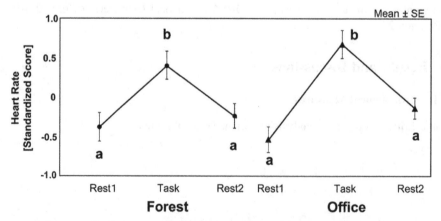

**Fig. 4.** Changes in heart rate. Small letters indicate homogeneous subsets. If small letters are different for two averages, they are significantly different.

### 3.3 Heart Rate Variability

The block main effect was significant in both the LF ($F = 18.124$, $\eta^2 = 0.463$, $p <$ .001) and HF ($F = 6.421$, $\eta^2 = 0.234$, $p < .01$) components. The LF component was significantly smaller during the task than both before the task and after the resting period, shown in Fig. 5. However, the HF component was significantly smaller than that after the resting period (Fig. 6). No significant main effect of condition was found on the LF and HF components. These results and the heart rate increase indicated that the task induced parasympathetic inhibition of the heart.

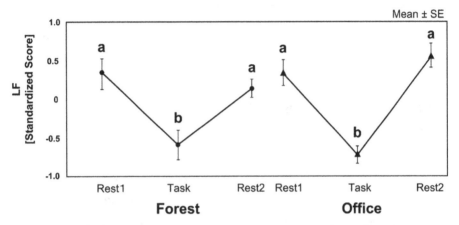

**Fig. 5.** Changes in the LF component. See Fig. 4 caption for small letters.

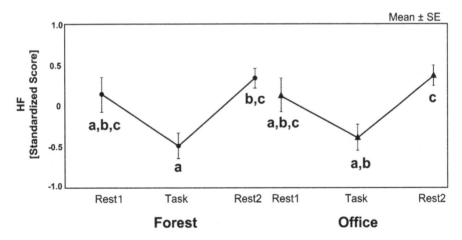

**Fig. 6.** Changes in the HF component. See Fig. 4 caption for small letters.

### 3.4 Fingertip Photoelectric Plethysmogram

A significant main effect of condition ($F = 8.723$, $\eta^2 = 0.293$, $p < .01$) and block ($F = 17.173$, $\eta^2 = 0.45$, $p < .001$) were detected. A smaller amplitude during the task block indicates that the MA task activated the α-adrenal sympathetic response that evokes vasoconstriction, resulting in a decrease in PTG amplitude. A lower PTG amplitude in the forest condition may suggest that participants felt a pleasant feeling in the natural setting (Fig. 7).

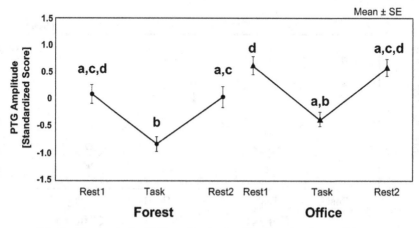

**Fig. 7.** Changes in the PTG amplitude. See Fig. 4 caption for small letters.

### 3.5 Skin Conductance Level

The block main effect ($F = 18.151$, $\eta^2 = 0.464$, $p < .001$) indicated sympathetic activation by MA. This result was comparable to that of the PTG amplitude change. No significant main effect of condition was detected (Fig. 8).

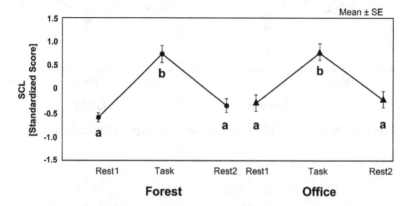

**Fig. 8.** Changes in the SCL. See Fig. 4 caption for small letters.

## 3.6   Subjective Assessment

See Figs. 9, 10 and 11.

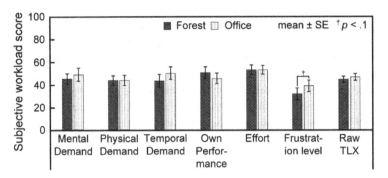

**Fig. 9.**  NASA-TLX

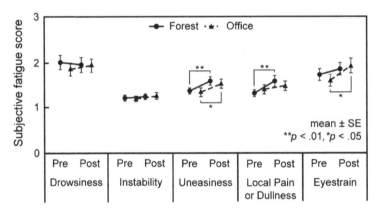

**Fig. 10.**  SFQ

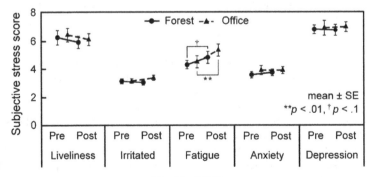

**Fig. 11.**  BJSQ

# 4   Conclusion

The results indicated that the finger plethysmogram (PTG) amplitude measured under the forest condition was significantly lower than that measured under the office condition. However, the differences in subjective fatigue and stress between the conditions were small. In other words, the working condition with the natural scene tested experimentally in this study could not sufficiently evoke a significant difference from the office condition. Therefore, a wider field of view may be necessary to evaluate the effect of the work environment integrated with a natural scene on worker stress levels.

In this study, we used "minimum" physiological signals and indices. Therefore, more sophisticated and varied measures should be introduced. It is necessary to investigate the subtle effects of nature using more sensitive methods.

# References

1. Monika, F., Pawel, W.: Literature survey on how different factors influence human comfort in indoor environments. Build. Environ. **46**(4), 922–937 (2011)
2. Nis, H., Dag, R., Anne, K.B., Nils, F., Ulf, L., Karen, S.: The effect of mental stress on heart rate variability and blood pressure during computer work. Eur. J. Appl. Physiol. **92**, 84–89 (2004)
3. Roger, S.U., Robert, F.S., Barbara, D.L., Evelyn, F., Mark, A.M., Michael, Z.: Stress recovery during exposure to natural and urban environments. J. Environ. Psychol. **11**, 201–230 (1991)
4. Yeo, N.L., et al.: What is the best way of delivering virtual nature for improving mood? An experimental comparison of high-definition TV, 360∘ video, and computer generated virtual reality. J. Environ. **72**, 101500 (2020)
5. https://files.eric.ed.gov/fulltext/EJ1131318.pdf. Accessed 23 May 2022
6. Stefan, L., Linda, G., Maic, M.: The relaxing effect of virtual nature - immersive technology provides relief in acute stress situations. Ann. Rev. Cyber Ther. Telemed. **16**, 87–93 (2018)
7. Gao, T., Zhang, T., Zhu, L., Gao, Y., Qiu, L.: Exploring psychophysiological restoration and individual preference in the different environments based on virtual reality. Int. J. Environ. Res. Public Health **16**, 3102 (2019)
8. Chia-Pin, Y., Hsiao-Yun, L., Xiang-Yi, L.: The effect of virtual reality forest and urban environments on physiological and psychological responses. Urban For. Urban Green. **35**, 106–114 (2018)
9. Matilda, A., et al.: Inducing physiological stress recovery with sounds of nature in a virtual reality forest—results from a pilot study. Physiol. Behav. **118**, 240–250 (2013)
10. Maryam, M., Yimin, Z.: Application of virtual environments for biophilic design: a critical review. Building **11**(4), 148 (2021)
11. Jie, Y., Jing, Y., Nastaran, A., Paul, J.C., Joseph, G.A., John, D.S.: Effects of biophilic in-door environment on stress and anxiety recovery: a between-subjects experiment in virtual reality. Environ. Int. **136**, 105427 (2020)
12. Inoue, A., Kawakami, N., Shimomitsu, T., Tsutsumi, A., Haratani, T., Yoshikawa, T., et al.: Development of a short version of the new brief job stress questionnaire. Ind. Health **2014**(52), 535–540 (2014)
13. Tsutsumi, A., Inoue, A., Eguchi, H.: How accurately does the Brief Job Stress Questionnaire identify workers with or without potential psychological distress? J. Occup. Health **2017**(59), 356–360 (2017)

# Towards a Methodology to Evaluate User Experience with Personalized Questionnaires for the Developments of Custom Systems

Jenny Morales[1]([⊠]) [iD], Germán Rojas[2] [iD], and Gamadiel Cerda[3] [iD]

[1] Facultad de Ciencias Sociales y Económicas, Departamento de Economía y Administración, Universidad Católica del Maule, Av. San Miguel 3605, Talca, Chile
jmoralesb@ucm.cl
[2] Facultad de Ingeniería, Universidad Autónoma de Chile, Av. 5 Poniente 1670, Talca, Chile
german.rojas@cloud.uautonoma.cl
[3] Quimval SpA, 30 Oriente 1420, Oficina 402, Talca, Chile
gcerda@quimvalspa.cl

**Abstract.** Systems are considered essential in organizations. These systems can be standard implementations, such as Enterprise Resource Planning (ERP) or custom developments to address specific problems. Considering custom developments, how do we evaluate usability and User eXperience (UX) to obtain indicators of improvements related to one domine? One methodology widely used is the user test, which is accomplished through surveys to collect information. Several questionnaires collect general information about usability and UX. Although, the information provided is broad and partially covers the feedback needed to improve specific areas of the systems. What hinders the decision-making process for improving the system in particular aspects of usability and UX. For this reason, it is necessary to adapt the general questionnaires to the needs of the system developed. In this work, we present a preliminary methodology that allows considering different available questionnaires to evaluate the usability and/or UX and relate them to a specific context, emphasizing the particularities of custom development. The proposed methodology considers eight stages, and this methodology was used in a practical case to evaluate a custom system developed for a company that produces and markets products. The results showed specific information that supported decision-making for improving usability and user experience about navigation, search, and visualization of the information displayed in the interface. Improve the minimalist design associated with the portable system version, improving efficiency to achieve specific activities, among other things. Future work intends to use the methodology in different case studies, refine it and establish an implementation guide.

**Keywords:** User eXperience · Usability · Personalized questionnaires methodology · Evaluation custom development

© The Author(s), under exclusive license to Springer Nature Switzerland AG 2022
M. Kurosu et al. (Eds.): HCII 2022, LNCS 13516, pp. 267–281, 2022.
https://doi.org/10.1007/978-3-031-17615-9_19

# 1   Introduction

Today there is a growing concern for the user experience, usability, and in its broadest concept, the consumer experience. The systems that support various processes in companies or organizations are crucial to achieving competitive advantages [1] and are considered essential. Considering the uniqueness of organizations and processes, custom developments are produced to solve specific problems. Considering these developments, how do we evaluate usability and User eXperience (UX) to obtain particular indicators of improvement? Although there are several methods to evaluate usability and user experience, there exists difficulty in establishing the essential aspects of UX to be evaluated in software [2].

Generally, in usability and UX evaluation, a user test is followed by standardized questionnaires, for example, System Usability Scale (SUS) [3], Software Usability Measurement Inventory SUMI [4], among others. The information collected is extensive and partially covers the need for feedback to improve specific areas of the systems. This hinders the decision-making process from improving the system in particular aspects of usability and UX. Therefore, the need arises to adapt the questionnaires.

In this work, we present a preliminary methodology that allows considering different general questionnaires to evaluate usability and/or UX and relate them to a specific context considering users and clients, emphasizing the particularities of custom development. The proposed methodology considers eight stages that are: stage 1, understand the systems and evaluation needs; stage 2, literature review; stage 3, adjustment of the questionnaire; stage 4 initial validation; stage 5, specification of the questionnaire ad-hoc; stage 6, application of the questionnaire; stage 7, documentation of results; and finally, stage 8, verify the relevance of the results obtained. The methodology proposal was used in a practical case to evaluate a custom system developed for a Chilean organization. The system manages equipment maintenance information. The methodology was applied in each of its stages and allowed making decisions to improve the system under development in various aspects of usability and UX, which were well-valued by customers and users.

The paper is organized as follows: Sect. 2 introduces the theoretical background; Sect. 3, presents questionnaires used to evaluate usability and UX; Sect. 4, presents the proposed methodology and the case of study; finally, in Sect. 5 we present conclusions and future work.

# 2   Theoretical Background

## 2.1   User eXperience

User experience is defined as follows: "user's perceptions and responses that result from the use and/or anticipated use of a system, product, or service" [5]. To explain the elements in the user experience, there are several models. The honeycomb is a UX model that consider the following aspects: (i) useful, to satisfy some needs; (ii) usable, related to ease to use; (iii) desirable, associated to aesthetical aspect; (iv) findable, related to the ease to navigate or finding information; (v) accessible, considering different users with their capabilities or disabilities; (vi) credible, give user confidence; and (vii) valuable, to deliver value to whoever uses it [6]. The elements of user experience model proposed by Garret consist of several overlapping planes from the most abstract at the bottom to the most concrete at the top. This model considers functional and informative aspects of what is being developed. The functional aspects consider those that allow the user to perform a task, and the informative ones, which aim to communicate with the user [7]. The Wheel is a model that contains the value in the center, considering that it adds value for both customers and suppliers. This model has different phases: useful, findable, accessible, desirable, usable, and credible. Each of these phases has factors that constitute it. The model should start with the search engine factor and then go through all the remaining elements [8]. Both Honeycomb and The Wheel expose the same seven aspects, both focused on the goal of generating value. In The Wheel model makes explicit the value for both customers and providers. The difference is that The Wheel model is more structured and procedural, recommended to start with the search engine strategy and go through the thirty factors exposed. The Honeycomb model covers the same aspects of the user experience. It is more general and is open to new connections and dimensions.

## 2.2  Usability

Usability is an important UX factor. However, it is not the only within UX models reviewed in 2.1. The usability is defined as follows: "the extent to which a system, product or service can be used by specified users to achieve specified goals with effectiveness, efficiency and satisfaction in a specified context of use" [9]. Effectiveness, related to users and the correct performance of specific tasks. Efficiency, referring to the resources used by users to achieve the performance of specific tasks. Satisfaction, it is one of the most subjective terms since it depends on personal factors (emotional, physical, among others). It is related to the satisfaction of the needs and expectations of the user [9].

## 2.3  Custom Developments

Systems are essential for organizations as they allow them to manage and administer various processes. Enterprise resource planning (ERP) systems integrate and support the functional operations of a business [1]. However, on many occasions, companies or organizations decide and need custom systems development and manage specific problems of its operation and management. For decades the elements concerning custom system developments have been studied. In [10] authors established that these developments are built to satisfy specific user needs. It is crucial to establish forms of development that actively incorporate the users involved.

On another note, with the increase in the use of smartphones, the development of mobile applications for different fields and domains has also increased. It is important then that the models for the development of the applications are adequate. In mobile, some models were identified that specifically contemplate aspects, such as user experience, security, among others [11].

# 3  Questionnaires Used to Evaluate User eXperience and Usability

We could evaluate usability through user testing and/or inspection methods. In previous works related to the programmer experience, we found that user tests were widely used, and the collection of information was mostly done with questionnaires and interviews. In the case of inspections, they were used to a much lesser extent than tests with users. The inspection method that presented the most repeated use was heuristic evaluation [12]. In turn, studies related to UX evaluation techniques match with the wide use of self-prepared questionnaires and standardized questionnaires, in addition to the use of interviews [13]. Next, we present a brief review of some widely used questionnaires.

### 3.1 System Usability Scale

In 1986 Brooke created the System Usability Scale (SUS), which allows evaluating practically any type of system. SUS has ten items in total, with responses on a Likert scale ranging from 1 to 5. 5 that means strongly agree, and 1 means strongly disagree. Calculating the results is carried out for the odd questions, the score obtained minus 1, and even questions 5 minus the score obtained. Then the sum of the scores of the 10 items is multiplied by 2.5. The total score in SUS is 100 and the minimum score to be considered usable is 68 [3]. The items of SUS are shown in Table 1.

**Table 1.** Items system usability scale [3].

| N° | Item | | | | |
|----|------|---|---|---|---|
| 1 | I think that I would like to use this system frequently | | | | |
| | (1)<br>Strongly disagree | (2) | (3) | (4) | (5)<br>Strongly agree |
| 2 | I found the system unnecessarily complex | | | | |
| | (1)<br>Strongly disagree | (2) | (3) | (4) | (5)<br>Strongly agree |
| 3 | I thought the system was easy to use | | | | |
| | (1)<br>Strongly disagree | (2) | (3) | (4) | (5)<br>Strongly agree |
| 4 | I think that I would need the support of a technical person to be able to use this system | | | | |
| | (1)<br>Strongly disagree | (2) | (3) | (4) | (5)<br>Strongly agree |
| 5 | I found the various functions in this system were well integrated | | | | |
| | (1)<br>Strongly disagree | (2) | (3) | (4) | (5)<br>Strongly agree |
| 6 | I thought there was too much inconsistency in this system | | | | |

(*continued*)

**Table 1.** (*continued*)

| N° | Item | | | | |
|----|------|---|---|---|---|
| | (1)<br>Strongly disagree | (2) | (3) | (4) | (5)<br>Strongly agree |
| 7 | I would imagine that most people would learn to use this system very quickly | | | | |
| | (1)<br>Strongly disagree | (2) | (3) | (4) | (5)<br>Strongly agree |
| 8 | I found the system very cumbersome to use | | | | |
| | (1)<br>Strongly disagree | (2) | (3) | (4) | (5)<br>Strongly agree |
| 9 | I felt very confident using the system | | | | |
| | (1)<br>Strongly disagree | (2) | (3) | (4) | (5)<br>Strongly agree |
| 10 | I needed to learn a lot of things before I could get going with this system | | | | |
| | (1)<br>Strongly disagree | (2) | (3) | (4) | (5)<br>Strongly agree |

### 3.2 Questionnaire for User Interface Satisfaction

Questionnaire for User Interface Satisfaction (QUIS) was developed by researchers at the University of Maryland in 1988 to evaluate user satisfaction. QUIS 5.0 had parts containing 4 to 6 items each. The scale associated with each item was 0 to 9, considering 0 the lowest compliance and 9 the highest compliance of item [14]. Table 2 shows QUIS 5.0. Currently, the questionnaire exists in version 7.0.

**Table 2.** Items questionnaire for user interface satisfaction [14].

| OVERALL REACTIONS TO THE SOFTWARE | | |
|---|---|---|
| Terrible | 0 1 2 3 4 5 6 7 8 9 | Wonderful |
| Difficult | 0 1 2 3 4 5 6 7 8 9 | Easy |
| Frustrating | 0 1 2 3 4 5 6 7 8 9 | Satisfying |
| Inadequate power | 0 1 2 3 4 5 6 7 8 9 | Adequate power |
| Dull | 0 1 2 3 4 5 6 7 8 9 | Stimulating |
| Rigid | 0 1 2 3 4 5 6 7 8 9 | Flexible |
| SCREEN | | |
| Characters on the computer screen | | |
| Hard to read | 0 1 2 3 4 5 6 7 8 9 | Easy to read |
| Highlighting on the screen simplifies task | | |

(continued)

**Table 2.** (*continued*)

| SCREEN | | |
|---|---|---|
| Not at all | 0 1 2 3 4 5 6 7 8 9 | Very much |
| Organization of information on screen | | |
| Confusing | 0 1 2 3 4 5 6 7 8 9 | Very clear |
| Sequence of screens | | |
| Confusing | 0 1 2 3 4 5 6 7 8 9 | Very clear |
| TERMINOLOGY AND SYSTEM INFORMATION | | |
| Use of terms throughout system | | |
| Inconsistent | 0 1 2 3 4 5 6 7 8 9 | Consistent |
| Computer terminology is related to the task you are doing | | |
| Never | 0 1 2 3 4 5 6 7 8 9 | Always |
| Position of messages on screen | | |
| Inconsistent | 0 1 2 3 4 5 6 7 8 9 | Consistent |
| Messages on screen which prompt user for input | | |
| Confusing | 0 1 2 3 4 5 6 7 8 9 | Clear |
| Computer keeps you informed about what it is doing | | |
| Never | 0 1 2 3 4 5 6 7 8 9 | Always |
| Error messages | | |
| Unhelpful | 0 1 2 3 4 5 6 7 8 9 | Helpful |
| LEARNING | | |
| Learning to operate the system | | |
| Difficult | 0 1 2 3 4 5 6 7 8 9 | Easy |
| Exploring new features by trial and error | | |
| Difficult | 0 1 2 3 4 5 6 7 8 9 | Easy |
| Remembering names and use of commands | | |
| Difficult | 0 1 2 3 4 5 6 7 8 9 | Easy |
| Tasks can be performed in a straight-forward manner | | |
| Never | 0 1 2 3 4 5 6 7 8 9 | Always |
| Help messages on the screen | | |
| Unhelpful | 0 1 2 3 4 5 6 7 8 9 | Helpful |
| Supplemental reference materials | | |
| Confusing | 0 1 2 3 4 5 6 7 8 9 | Clear |

(*continued*)

**Table 2.** (*continued*)

| SYSTEM CAPABILITIES | | |
|---|---|---|
| System speed | | |
| Too slow | 0 1 2 3 4 5 6 7 8 9 | Fast enough |
| System reliability | | |
| Unreliable | 0 1 2 3 4 5 6 7 8 9 | Reliable |
| System tends to be | | |
| Noisy | 0 1 2 3 4 5 6 7 8 9 | Quiet |
| Correcting your mistakes | | |
| Difficult | 0 1 2 3 4 5 6 7 8 9 | Easy |
| Experienced and inexperienced users' needs are taken into consideration | | |
| Never | 0 1 2 3 4 5 6 7 8 9 | Always |

## 3.3 User Experience Questionnaire

User Experience Questionnaire (UEQ) is a questionnaire that contains 26 items divided into six scales: attractiveness, perspicuity, efficiency, dependability, stimulation, and novelty. The items follow a certain order, and their responses have complementary polarities. The response scale ranges from 1 to 7 [15]. In order to facilitate its application, the questionnaire is available in more than 30 languages. It also has a spreadsheet to facilitate its application [16]. Table 3 shows the items of UEQ in English version.

**Table 3.** Items user experience questionnaire [15].

| | 1 | 2 | 3 | 4 | 5 | 6 | 7 | | |
|---|---|---|---|---|---|---|---|---|---|
| Annoying | O | O | O | O | O | O | O | Enjoyable | 1 |
| Not understandable | O | O | O | O | O | O | O | Understandable | 2 |
| Creative | O | O | O | O | O | O | O | Dull | 3 |
| Easy to learn | O | O | O | O | O | O | O | Difficult to learn | 4 |
| Valuable | O | O | O | O | O | O | O | Inferior | 5 |
| Boring | O | O | O | O | O | O | O | Exciting | 6 |
| Not interesting | O | O | O | O | O | O | O | Interesting | 7 |
| Unpredictable | O | O | O | O | O | O | O | Predictable | 8 |
| Fast | O | O | O | O | O | O | O | Slow | 9 |
| Inventive | O | O | O | O | O | O | O | Conventional | 10 |

(*continued*)

**Table 3.** (*continued*)

| | 1 | 2 | 3 | 4 | 5 | 6 | 7 | | |
|---|---|---|---|---|---|---|---|---|---|
| Obstructive | O | O | O | O | O | O | O | Supportive | 11 |
| Good | O | O | O | O | O | O | O | Bad | 12 |
| Complicated | O | O | O | O | O | O | O | Easy | 13 |
| Unlikable | O | O | O | O | O | O | O | Pleasing | 14 |
| Usual | O | O | O | O | O | O | O | Leading edge | 15 |
| Unpleasant | O | O | O | O | O | O | O | Pleasant | 16 |
| Secure | O | O | O | O | O | O | O | Not secure | 17 |
| Motivating | O | O | O | O | O | O | O | Demotivating | 18 |
| Meets expectations | O | O | O | O | O | O | O | Does not meet expectations | 19 |
| Inefficient | O | O | O | O | O | O | O | Efficient | 20 |
| Clear | O | O | O | O | O | O | O | Confusing | 21 |
| Impractical | O | O | O | O | O | O | O | Practical | 22 |
| Organized | O | O | O | O | O | O | O | Cluttered | 23 |
| Attractive | O | O | O | O | O | O | O | Unattractive | 24 |
| Friendly | O | O | O | O | O | O | O | Unfriendly | 25 |
| Conservative | O | O | O | O | O | O | O | Innovative | 26 |

### 3.4 Usefulness, Satisfaction, and Ease of Use Questionnaire

The usefulness, satisfaction, and ease of use (USE) questionnaire contains three factors that, according to the authors, emerged with greater force during the development of the questionnaire. The authors suggest that usefulness and ease of use are correlated, contributing to improve satisfaction. The questionnaire has a 7-point Likert scale, ranging from strongly disagree to strongly agree. Table 4 shows the questionnaire with the three dimensions and the ease of learning, which is closely related to ease of use. The items written in italics represent elements with less weight in the factors [17].

Different systems are evaluated with these questionnaires and commonly accompanied by another method. SUS for instance can be used for a wide variety of systems, we have found articles that use it in various domains, such as evaluating usability in visual programming languages [18], education technology systems [19], among others. Also, we found studies that use SUS and QUIS to evaluate virtual training systems [20].

On the other hand, we also found valuations of user experience through UEQ in education to evaluate an information system that supports thesis management. In that work, the authors found excellent results of the system evaluated in the six aspects of the questionnaire and complemented this questionnaire with a heuristic evaluation [21].

Other questionnaires are used, but are more extensive. The SUMI is one of them, it contains 50 items to evaluate the perception of usability of the software, which provides usability problems in detail. It was developed considering the definition of ISO 9241

**Table 4.** Items usefulness, satisfaction, and ease of use [17].

| Items |
| --- |
| USEFULNESS |
| It helps me be more effective |
| It helps me be more productive |
| It is useful |
| It gives me more control over the activities in my life |
| It makes the things I want to accomplish easier to get done |
| *It saves me time when I use it* |
| *It meets my needs* |
| *It does everything I would expect it to do* |
| EASE OF USE |
| It is easy to use |
| It is simple to use |
| It is user friendly |
| It requires the fewest steps possible to accomplish what I want to do with it |
| *It is flexible* |
| *Using it is effortless* |
| *I can use it without written instructions* |
| *I don't notice any inconsistencies as I use it* |
| *Both occasional and regular users would like it* |
| *I can recover from mistakes quickly and easily* |
| *I can use it successfully every time* |
| EASE OF LEARNING |
| I learned to use it quickly |
| I easily remember how to use it |
| It is easy to learn to use it |
| *I quickly became skillful with it* |
| SATISFACTION |
| I am satisfied with it |
| I would recommend it to a friend |
| It is fun to use |
| It works the way I want it to work |
| It is wonderful |
| *I feel I need to have it* |

(*continued*)

**Table 4.** (*continued*)

| Items |
| --- |
| *It is pleasant to use* |

and the European Directive on Health and Safety Standards for Workers with Data Visualization Equipment [4].

In [22] the authors applied SUMI and other methods to evaluate an Integrated Development Environment (IDE). The authors successfully found several usability problems using the questionnaire and complemented it with the other methods.

## 4 Proposed Methodology

Standard questionnaires do not provide enough usability and UX information required for business decision making. For this reason, we consider necessary to incorporate elements of the system domain to discover significant usability and UX aspects for the system context. To discover specific aspects to improve, we started to develop a proposal methodology, which contains eight stages.

Stages 1. Understand the systems and evaluation needs. At this stage, it is necessary to establish the information requirements related to the user test to be carried out. Include understanding the system domain, its functionalities, purpose, and the information needs for decision making of the key actors in custom development.

- Input: list system requirements documents, description of the problem that the system solves, system implementation environment, and other documents that describe the context of the system. The information of the key actors of the software development system and client (who needs the system and pays for it). To obtain this information, we suggest interviews, meetings, or other ways that allow us to know the key actors.
- Output: list relevant aspects of usability and UX to consider in the questionnaire.

Stage 2. Literature review. Consideration of the literature review and state of the art on different instruments available to evaluate usability and/or UX.

- Input: scientific articles of questionnaires to evaluate usability and UX in systems.
- Output: list of questionnaires that can be useful in the usability and UX evaluation of the software. The selection focuses on the factors previously established in stage 1.

Stage 3. Adjustment of the questionnaire. Analysis gaps, it is necessary to review each questionnaire selected and determine if there are missing elements to incorporate them, modify some questionnaires, and/or partially select items. Also, choose the response scale to use and the length of the questionnaire.

- Input: questionnaires selected and specific usability and UX factors.
- Output: first version of the questionnaire ad-hoc to apply.

Stage 4. Initial validation. The questionnaire is sent to experts and key development actors for validation at this stage. The perception of validity is carried out through questionnaires with satisfaction scales and interviews.

- Input: questionnaire ad-hoc to apply.
- Output: responses from experts and key development actors.

Stage 5. Specification of the questionnaire ad-hoc. The questionnaire to be applied is defined in its adjusted and validated version. The application protocol must be defined considering the time, ways, and environment, among others.

- Input: results of the initial validation.
- Output: questionnaire to apply and the application protocol.

Stage 6. Application of the questionnaire. The questionnaire is ready. Users have already tested the system and worked with it, so they are prepared to answer the questionnaire. The application protocol defined gives the guidelines for the effective use of the questionnaire.

- Input: the questionnaire and the protocol to apply the questionnaire.
- Output: user responses.

Step 7. Documentation of results. The results of the questionnaires are analyzed, and the usability and UX problems are identified. Each issue is related to the particular elements of the system to be improved.

- Input: questionnaire user responses.
- Output: results report with critical indicators and list of improvement opportunities related to usability and user experience problems detected. List the set of feasible decisions regarding the improvement of the system.

Stage 8. Verify the relevance of the results obtained. We verify the usefulness of the results in relation to making feasible decisions. We collect the feedback with focus groups, interviews, and a survey for key actors, including the clients. This stage includes determining the proposals associated with the information provided by the questionnaire and optionally economically valuing the suggestions.

- Input: results report.
- Output: impact of the results in the system development process. Build an analysis matrix relating the decisions to improve the system and the dimensions of usability and UX in systems.

### 4.1  Initial Case of Study

The methodology was applied in one custom system developed for a company that produces and markets products. This company is Chilean and has a presence in several

Latin American countries. Contextualizing, the system addresses the maintenance of the factory's production equipment. The correct planning of maintenance tasks and a timely record of the progress of each of the tasks allow decisions to be made in real-time. In this way, the decisions of reassignment, prioritization, cancellation, etc., of each task are based on the information provided by the system implemented, with the "S" curve being one of the primary information artifacts consulted. Subsequently, the system delivers detailed reports of each of the equipment with feedback from the maintenance manager, for which the following planning will consider the data obtained from the system. The intention is to carry out planning that adjusts to the productive reality of the external companies that carry out the maintenance of the equipment. The system consists of two parts, the web system for internal users of the company and the mobile application (app) for external users who perform maintenance.

In summary, Table 5 shows the inputs and outputs of each stage.

In the stage 1, the specification documents were requested, which allowed us to understand the problem that the system solves, the scope, and the context of use. In addition, an unstructured interview was developed with the client and one key user to determine which aspects of usability and UX seemed relevant to evaluate (see Table 5).

In stage 2, we searched scientific articles in different databases, including Scopus, IEEE Xplore, and Google Scholar. The selection of the questionnaire was based on the usability and UX factors they evaluated and the number of citations after the article. An exciting aspect to check was also if it had a reliability index.

In stage 3, we considered using the questionnaires SUS for usability and some items of usefulness and satisfaction of USE.

In stage 4, the first questionnaire was sent to key users and clients. Subsequently, we interviewed to collect doubts and adjust the questionnaire. In this interview, concerns arose about the generality of some items associated with the system's usefulness. The length of the survey was also an element of the discussion.

In stage 5, it was determined to use SUS as a global measure of usability and use the first two satisfaction items of USE. In the case of usefulness, given the generality of the USE items and the need identified with customers and key users for specific usefulness aspects to be evaluated related to system functionalities, four items were added for app users and five items for users of the web system. We specified a questionnaire application protocol, which consisted of using the system by the users at different times and according to real test cases. Then, we defined a time of 1 day to answer the questionnaire. We sent it by email.

Stage 6, the questionnaire was applied according to the protocol, and the resulting information was collected.

Stage 7, in this stage, the information obtained from the questionnaire is analyzed, and a set of usability, usefulness, and satisfaction result indicators are expressed. 25 app users and 13 web users responded to the survey. The results were good for the case of the perception of usability evaluated with SUS obtaining both web and app 66 points. The ease of being learned stands out within the usability in both cases. In the case of usefulness, the scores in both cases are between neutral and in agree, so it is evident that there are usefulness elements to improve. For example, we detected difficulties in timely communication between both types of users. This communication goes both ways, and users of the web and app indicated the same lack of usefulness due to visibility problems and relevant information shown to the user. In the case of satisfaction, the results were lower and closer to neutral in web and app cases. In the analysis of the information derived from the open question, we detected two factors: one external, which is the lack of connectivity, the flexibility of use related to search filters, and the minimalist design associated with displaying the relevant information of the interface. In Fig. 1 we can see the usefulness and satisfaction score.

Stage 8, when presenting the analysis of the results, we requested an unstructured interview with the client and a key user that would allow knowing if these aspects detected in the surveys were relevant. In the case of chat, it is critical that the system aims to have updated information for timely decision-making, that results translate into a more extended machine downtime in maintenance. Therefore, an economic loss for the company. In the case of the flexibility of use of the filters, it also turned out to be an essential element to correct to make the selection of information faster, shortening

**Table 5.** Inputs and outputs of each stage.

| Stage | Input | Output |
|---|---|---|
| Stage1 | • System requirements specification<br>• Usability and UX factor need to be evaluated | • Aspects to evaluate usability, usefulness, and satisfaction |
| Stage 2 | • Analysis of several questionnaires in scientific articles and their application | • SUS<br>• USE |
| Stage 3 | • Aspects to evaluate usability, usefulness, and satisfaction<br>• SUS and USE | • SUS in all items<br>• USE on some factors (satisfaction and usefulness) |
| Stage 4 | • First version of questionnaire includes SUS and USE selected factors | • Results of key actors' interview |
| Stage 5 | • Results of key actors' interview | • SUS in all items<br>• USE the first two items of satisfaction<br>• Including the characterization items<br>• Including four items to evaluate the app usefulness<br>• Including five items to evaluate the web usefulness<br>• Including one open question<br>• Likert scale of 5 points<br>• Application protocol |
| Stage 6 | • Questionnaire<br>• Application protocol | • Results of evaluation |
| Stage 7 | • Results of evaluation | • Indicators of usability, usefulness, and satisfaction |
| Stage 8 | • Indicators of usability, usefulness, and satisfaction | • Validation through interview |

the time for the user. Finally, the display of relevant information for the user is more valuable in the app case because it is a device with smaller screen size.

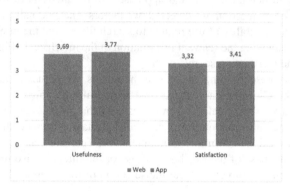

**Fig. 1.** Results of usefulness and satisfaction.

## 5    Conclusion and Future Work

Considering the context of custom-developed systems and the need to evaluate the user experience in them, we presented an initial methodology that allows evaluating UX with personalized questionnaires, considering the context of custom-developed systems, including users and clients, in such a way as to promote decision-making and improvements associated with the results obtained. The methodology was used in a case study to evaluate a custom system developed for a Chilean company that produces and markets products in several Latin American countries. Specifically, the case study was a system developed to manage information about the maintenance of company equipment. The methodology was applied in each of its stages, obtaining specific information from the evaluated system that supported decision-making to improve usability and user experience, improving navigation, search, and visualization of the information displayed on the interface. Improve the minimalist design associated with the version of the portable system, allowing elements to be better distributed in the interface improving efficiency to achieve specific activities, among other things. Future work aims to specify the methodology in detail, considering statistical indicators of reliability of the questionnaires, process diagram, and incorporation of key indicators of the user experience. In addition, the methodology should be used in new case studies to refine it. Finally, we hope to implement the guide to facilitate its application.

**Acknowledgment.** We thank Quimval SpA, which allowed us to apply the methodology in the company's actual project.

## References

1. Cohen, D., Lares, E.: Tecnologías de la Información en los Negocios. Quinta Edición. McGrawHill (2009)

2. Meiners, A.L., Kollmorgen, J., Schrepp, M., Thomaschewski, J.: Which UX aspects are important for a software product? Importance ratings of UX aspects for software products for measurement with the UEQ+. In: Mensch und Computer 2021, pp. 136–139 (2021)
3. Brooke, J.: SUS-a quick and dirty usability scale. Usability Eval. Ind. **189**(194), 4–7 (1996)
4. Kirakowski, J., Corbett, M.: SUMI: the software usability measurement inventory. Br. J. Edu. Technol. **24**(3), 210–212 (1993)
5. ISO 9241–210: Ergonomics of human-system interaction- Part 11: Usability: Definitions and concepts, International Organization for Standardization, Geneva (2018)
6. Morville, P.: User experience honeycomb. http://semanticstudios.com/user_experience_des ign/. Accessed 7 Jan 2022
7. Garrett, J.J.: Customer loyalty and the elements of user experience. Des. Manag. Rev. **17**(1), 35–39 (2006)
8. Revang, M.: The User Experience Wheel. http://userexperienceproject.blogspot.cl/. Accessed 2 Jan 2022
9. ISO 9241–11: Ergonomics of human-system interaction- Part 11: Usability: Definitions and concepts, International Organization for Standardization, Geneva (2018)
10. Ovaska, P.: A case study of systems development in custom IS organizational culture. In: Proceedings of the Information Systems Development, pp. 405–416. Springer, Boston, MA (2009). https://doi.org/10.1007/978-0-387-68772-8_31
11. Jabangwe, R., Edison, H., Duc, A.N.: Software engineering process models for mobile app development: a systematic literature review. J. Syst. Softw. **145**, 98–111 (2018)
12. Morales, J., Rusu, C., Botella, F., Quiñones, D.: Programmer eXperience: a systematic literature review. IEEE Access **7**, 71079–71094 (2019)
13. Pettersson, I., Lachner, F., Frison, A.K., Riener, A., Butz, A.: A bermuda triangle? A review of method application and triangulation in user experience evaluation. In: Proceedings of the 2018 CHI Conference on Human Factors in Computing Systems, pp. 1–16 (2018)
14. Chin, J.P., Diehl, V.A., Norman, K.L.: Development of an instrument measuring user satisfaction of the human-computer interface. In: Proceedings of the SIGCHI Conference on Human Factors in Computing System, pp. 213–218 (1988)
15. Laugwitz, B., Held, T., Schrepp, M.: Construction and evaluation of a user experience questionnaire. In: Holzinger, A. (ed.) USAB 2008. LNCS, vol. 5298, pp. 63–76. Springer, Heidelberg (2008). https://doi.org/10.1007/978-3-540-89350-9_6
16. Schrepp, M.: UEQ User Experience Questionnaire. https://www.ueq-online.org/. Accessed 5 Jan 2022
17. Lund, A.M.: Measuring usability with the use questionnaire. Usability Interface **8**(2), 3–6 (2001)
18. Morales, J., Rusu, C.: Usability perception of visual programming language: A case study. In: Proceedings of the CEUR Workshop, vol. 2747, pp. 83–88 (2020)
19. Vlachogianni, P., Tselios, N.: Perceived usability evaluation of educational technology using the system usability scale (SUS): a systematic review. J. Res. Technol. Educ., 1–18 (2021)
20. Delamarre, A., Shernoff, E., Buche, C., Frazier, S., Gabbard, J., Lisetti, C.: The interactive virtual training for teachers (IVT-T) to practice classroom behavior management. Int. J. Hum. Comput. Stud. **152**, 102646 (2021)
21. Paramitha, A.I.I., Dantes, G.R., Indrawan, G.: The evaluation of web based academic progress information system using heuristic evaluation and user experience questionnaire (UEQ). In: Proceedings of the 2018 Third International Conference on Informatics and Computing (ICIC), pp. 1–6. IEEE (2018)
22. Kline, R.B., Seffah, A.: Evaluation of integrated software development environments: challenges and results from three empirical studies. Int. J. Hum. Comput. Stud. **63**(6), 607–627 (2005)

# EmoFrame: Prototype of a Framework to Assess Users' Emotional Responses

Suzane Santos dos Santos[✉], Erick Modesto Campos,
and Kamila Rios da Hora Rodrigues[iD]

University of São Paulo, São Carlos, São Paulo, Brazil
suzanesantos@usp.br, erick.c.modesto@gmail.com, kamila.rios@icmc.usp.br

**Abstract.** Analyzing users' emotional aspects when interacting with computational solutions is a challenge for Computing professionals. In several situations, this kind of evaluation is the responsibility of the domain specialist. This study seeks to bring together different instruments for evaluating emotional responses in a framework named EmoFrame. It is possible to guide computer professionals in choosing the appropriate artifacts for their evaluations, depending on the solution developed and their use context. We developed a medium-fidelity prototype of the framework, and a first validation was carried out by Health and Computer specialists. It is also in the interest of this research to identify possible assessment protocols or instruments from other domains, which can be computerized with the support of these domain professionals and, later, become part of the EmoFrame.

**Keywords:** Computational systems evaluation · Emotional aspects · Emotional response · Framework · EmoFrame

## 1 Introduction

Human-Computer Interaction (HCI) is an area of research in Computer Science in which the evaluation stage is very relevant. During the evaluation, the user interface and interaction problems, not noticed in the design and development stages, are identified and corrected. This way, after a rigorous evaluation, the user has the chance to receive a safer, more effective product that does not harm they experience during the use of the product. Discussing evaluation in the context of the HCI generally leads to the concept of usability. For example, Nilsen [19] defines usability as an attribute of software quality that assesses the ease of use of user interfaces [3].

Still, in the context of evaluation and HCI, another concept intrinsically associated with usability is the concept of User Experience (UX). According to Nielsen [20], the UX covers all aspects of the end user's interaction with its services and products. More specifically, UX is about how people feel about a product and what their pleasure and satisfaction are with using it [24]. The user's emotion, in turn, is no longer just related to the system's unexpected

© The Author(s), under exclusive license to Springer Nature Switzerland AG 2022
M. Kurosu et al. (Eds.): HCII 2022, LNCS 13516, pp. 282–301, 2022.
https://doi.org/10.1007/978-3-031-17615-9_20

response or frustration with an incomprehensible error message. The researchers now understand that a wide range of emotions plays a vital role in all tasks performed on the Computer. When interacting with computer systems, users' emotions are a fundamental aspect to help understand the user experience [29].

The recent change in the user's emotion concerning interactive systems has raised the need to understand better what emotion is and how it influences the user during the interaction. However, even though the term "emotion" is often used, there is no consensus on the concept [27]. The definition of Scherer [26] states that: "Emotion is defined as an episode of synchronized and interrelated changes in the states of all or most of the five subsystems of the organism in response to the evaluation of a stimulus event external or internal as relevant to the main concerns of the organism". Therefore, we adopted this definition in this study. The rationale behind this choice lies in the fact that this definition is one of the most comprehensive.

The project presented in this paper seeks to bring together different assessment tools, especially for assessing emotional responses, in a framework named EmoFrame. The framework has the function of: a) helping the Computer professional to find suitable tools for the target audience of the application—taking into account the particularities of the users, as well as the context of use and the requirement to be evaluated (ex.: usability, accessibility, emotional response); b) assist professionals, especially in the Health area, to apply their instruments in a computerized way and with a quick view of the results; and c) enable Computer professionals, with the support of the domain specialist, to also be able to use instruments and protocols from other areas (those possible), in order to obtain results on the effectiveness in the use of its computational solution.

In this paper, Computing instruments that can be computerized will be presented, which can facilitate their application remotely, a strategy that is especially welcome at times like the current—of social detachment due to the pandemic of COVID-19. We organized this paper into nine sections. In Related Works (Sect. 2), we discuss previous works about emotion evaluation. In the Method section (Sect. 3), we make a brief description of the techniques applied during the prototype conception. In the Selected Instruments section (Sect. 4), we detail the protocols and instruments chosen to be prototyped. In the section entitled EmoFrame Prototype (Sect. 5), we describe the screens and features of the prototyped framework. In the Evaluations and Discussion section (Sect. 6), we deal with the formal evaluation of the prototype with the project's partner specialists. Finally, we present the final considerations in the section (Sect. 7).

## 2    Related Works

In this section, we present some works related to the topic of interest of this research.

The study proposed by Silva et al. [32] investigates with four instruments – a set of emojis, the Self-Assessment Manikin, scroll sliders, and Semantic Emotional Space - to discover which provides information about a subjective feeling closer to an existing emotion. The experiments conducted by the authors involved 29 volunteers taking part in four experimental rounds. A volunteer watched a movie or part of a video clip in each round and later randomly interacted with one of the instruments in a user interface. The results suggested that the scroll slider leads to more excellent proximity to the pre-classified emotions.

The work done by Xavier, Garcia and Neris [34] presents a study on the impact that elements of interfaces in computer systems have on the human emotional response. The idea was to verify how the interaction in systems with "bad" interfaces affects negative emotional responses to help build interface design. The authors chose the Ten Heuristics method [6] to evaluate users' emotions, and the target audience was older adults. The experiment consisted of carrying out a usability test of a particular system with users. Every step of user interaction with the system was filmed. The results showed that the study of emotional responses is an excellent analysis to be considered in the interface design process. This work shows the importance of evaluating users' emotional responses and how they can positively affect the quality of computational solutions.

In the study proposed by Moreira, dos Reis and Baranauskas [17], the authors developed and evaluated the TangiSAM environment, which consists of tangible artifacts designed and built to carry out assessments of affective states from the SAM, an instrument for assessing emotion often used in the area of Computing. TangiSAM includes sets of three-dimensional concrete dolls that use tangible technologies to assess affective states playfully. In this study, conducting a study in a real educational space with children and teachers is detailed to understand if TangiSAM's tangible artifacts favor a better self-assessment experience. The authors found that participants preferred TangiSAM when compared to other proposals for the representation of affective states. This study influenced our choice of an alternative form of the SAM instrument to compose the EmoFrame.

The use of emojis to assess emotional aspects occurs in the study presented by Hall, Hume and Tazzyman, [10]. The authors focus on achieving optimal responses through supporting children's judgments, using Smiley Face Likert scales as a rating scale for quantitative questions in evaluations. The paper outlines a range of studies, identifying that to achieve differentiated data and full use of rating scales by children that face positive emotions should be used within Smiley Face Likert scales. The authors used the proposed rating method (the Five Degrees of Happiness Smiley Face Likert scale) in a large-scale summative evaluation of a Serious Game. Their results highlight that the traditional Smiley Face Likert, with emotions from very happy to very unhappy, has doubtful utility as an effective method for communicating with this age group.

Our initial idea was to try to bring other works or tools that group evaluation instruments and provide a way to apply them and present results. Unfortunately, even in our best attempts, within the consulted literature, we did not find studies with this scope, so the theoretical framework is in reporting instruments for assessing emotional responses.

# 3   Methods

For the construction of the framework, we adopted the Participatory Design [28] methodology added to the Evolutionary Prototyping from Software Engineering [22]. In evaluating computational solutions, it is crucial to have access to the people who use the system. Participatory Design works with users to analyze claims for their current practices and then generate design ideas that address the issues raised by shared analysis. Although users generally do not have practical knowledge about the development of the application, they are very good at reacting to concrete projects that they do not like or that will not work in practice [25].

In the evolutionary prototyping technique, the developer or the development team first builds a prototype. After receiving initial customer feedback, subsequent prototypes are produced by the team, each with additional features or improvements, until the final product appears [31]. We want to emphasize that during the design/conception stage of Emoframe, we had the support of a specialist in gerontology and a specialist in psychology. They participated in workshops to support the framework's design and evaluation steps.

Initially, we conducted a study of the literature on emotional response evaluation instruments. After the study collection, there were brainstorming sessions with partner professionals; in these sessions, we discussed which instruments amongst those found in the literature (considering the case studies) we could choose. Therefore, the construction process took place through a first round in which we collected ideas and discussed the literature. Later, in a second round, we presented the prototype. Specialists validated the prototype and suggested adjustments. The next section describes the instruments chosen to compose the EmoFrame.

# 4   Selected Instruments

This section details the protocols and instruments that we prototyped as proof of concept for constructing the framework. The instruments selected to compose the preliminary prototype version of EmoFrame evaluate the usability of computational solutions or users' emotional responses to interactive systems. The following subsections describe such instruments. We include SUS (System Usability Scale) and SD (Semantic Differential) instruments that assess usability and UX (User eXperience) issues because we understand these issues as a requirement that leads to user satisfaction and therefore affects emotional issues.

The instruments that are part of the prototype can be applied by people other than specialists, such as psychologists or occupational therapists, which are freely distributed and have a validated translation into Brazilian Portuguese. In addition, the instruments fit the needs of the research group of the authors of this study. These needs relate mainly to two case studies, which involve both children and the elderly. The specialist also suggested an instrument that did not appear in the literature research: the WHOQOL (World Health Organization Instrument to Evaluate Quality of Life).

## 4.1    Geriatric Depression Scale (GDS—15)

The first instrument added to EmoFrame was the Geriatric Depression Scale (GDS) is a screening test developed, initially, by Yesavage et al. [35] and used to identify symptoms of depression in elderly. The original scale is a 30-item self-report instrument that uses a "Yes/No" response. Professionals can administer the scale with healthy adults, clinically ill adults, and those with mild to moderate cognitive impairments. The GDS scale was tested and used extensively with the elderly population. In evaluating depression in old age, the GDS scale is currently one of the most used self-reports of depression. Although specialists cannot diagnose depression exclusively based on the GDS result, they usually include its result as a part of the diagnostic evaluation due to the scale's established reliability and validity [13].

Taking into account that the GDS-30 is relatively time-consuming, an abbreviated version consisting of 15 questions (GDS-15) was developed in 1986 by Sheikh e Yesavage [30]. Among the 15 items, 10 usually indicate depression when answered positively, while the others usually indicate depression when answered negatively [9]. The scale was translated and validated for the elderly Brazilian population [1]. As mentioned above, one of the studies developed by the authors' research group is conducted with elderly people. Such studies make use of gerontology instruments to collect information about the quality of life and feelings of this population. Given this context, the GDS was incorporated into EmoFrame by: a) evaluating emotional aspects; b) attending the context of study with the elderly, being particularly important for the research group.

## 4.2    Profile of Mood States (POMS)

The Profile of the States of Mood is a 65-item psychological self-report instrument intended for adults aged 18 and over. POMS assesses short-term moods that are considered transient and often fluctuating [12,16]. POMS is a multidimensional Likert self-report scale, originally developed to assess the response of psychiatric patients to pharmacological and psychotherapeutic treatment. This instrument, however, quickly became applied to sport and exercise psychology, as well as to assess coping among people with chronic diseases.

The 65 items of the POMS represent six subscales that assess: tension (T), depression (D), hostility (H), fatigue (F), confusion (C), and vigor (V). A composite score—Total Mood Disturbance (TMD)—is obtained by adding five negative affect subscales and subtracting the vigor score, reflecting the total mood disturbance. POMS quickly became a trendy instrument, with adaptations for other languages. The version used in this work is the Portuguese version of the reduced version, adapted by Viana, Almeida and Santos [33]. This adapted version consists of 36 items, each of the six scales having six items. In addition, the Portuguese version (from Portugal) also features six additional items that make up the Training Misfit Scale, a complementary instrument developed by Raglin and Morgan [23], which allows assisting in the diagnosis of overtraining syndrome alerts.

Each POMS adjective is rated on a 5-point scale (0 = Never; 1 = A little; 2 = Moderately; 3 = Very; 4 = Very much). All items are quoted in the same direction, except for one item on the Tension scale and two items on the Confusion scale. In these cases, the specialist must reverse the response to the item before adding to the others. In the response instructions, we ask the users to say how they felt over a certain period. That period usually corresponds to a day or a week. In this study, we adopted the period that comprises the mood swings of the user over the last week. We obtain the POMS result in two steps: add the result of each dimension and apply the values in the TMD formula, as shown below.

$$PTH = [(T + D + H + F + C) - V] + 100 \qquad (1)$$

The POMS was chosen for this work because it is a tool that assesses emotional response and can be applied to both case study audiences; we especially favored POMS because it includes a scale geared towards athletes, an area that is also our psychology collaborator's specialty.

### 4.3 Self-Assessment Manikin (SAM)

The Self-Assessment Manikin is an image-based questionnaire developed by Bradley and Lang [4] to measure emotional response. The questionnaire, widely used in evaluations by Computing professionals, was designed to measure three characteristics of an emotional response (pleasure, arousal and dominance), identified as central to emotion in research conducted by Lang et al. [14]. SAM can be considered free of language; that is, any individual, of any schooling, can answer it. SAM is also not limited to any culture and can be easily understood and suitable for different countries. Hayashi et al. [11] proposed an alternative form of SAM, emoti-SAM, in which they adopted different representations of the original figures. The authors created emoti-SAM due to the feedback that children gave spontaneously about the original assessment tool. According to them, most children did not like the look and colors of the original SAM. The children thought the original scale was "ugly" and did not make much sense. In response to their feedback, Hayashi et al. [11] replaced each figure in the original SAM with a corresponding emoji or emoticon—similar to those commonly used in social media and instant messaging apps. We used an adaptation of emoti-SAM in the EmoFrame.

The SAM questionnaire was chosen for this work because the version included in the framework is an adaptation aimed at children, one of the audiences that are part of the case study of interest to the research. In addition, the SAM is an instrument that is already well established in the field of Computing.

### 4.4 Semantic Differential (SD)

Developed by Osgood, Suci, and Tannenbaum [21], the Semantic Differential (SD) generally takes the form of a 5 or 7 point bipolar adjective scale. The authors created this method when they realized the need to assess the affectivity and qualities of a concept and quantify the affective meaning of attitudes, opinions, perceptions, social image, personality, preferences, and interests of people [15]. Semantic scales tend to have poles and, in each pole, opposite adjectives, through which the subjects evaluate the concept, verifying the one that most expresses their feelings. One end is considered "positive" and the other end "negative", for example, stimulating and discouraging. There is a possibility of adding some questions on special interest issues, but it is usually customary to keep the questionnaire short to maximize the response rate.

SD is one instrument often used to assess people's affective perception of the objective and subjective situations faced in their daily lives. It is possible to express the concept by a word, phrase, or figure and has a psychological meaning that varies according to the group that evaluates it.

## 4.5  System Usability Scale (SUS)

The System Usability Scale (SUS) is a commonly used questionnaire, distributed free and reliable. The original SUS instrument was proposed by Brooke [5] and is composed of 10 statements that are scored on a 5-point agreement strength scale. The questionnaire score results in a usability score in the range 0–100. A positive feature of SUS is that it provides an exclusive reference score for participants' opinions on the usability of a product. The ease of administration and scoring of SUS makes it a popular choice among usability professionals. In addition to being a popular choice for online usability research, SUS can be used as a subjective follow-up measure after testing the usability of functional systems as a pre-and post-test component [2, 7].

We choose an adaptation of the original SUS to compose the prototype of the EmoFrame. The adapted version is composed of 28 items that comprise the ten original items.

## 4.6  The World Health Organization Instrument to Evaluate Quality of Life (WHOQOL-BREF)

The WHOQOL Group developed the WHOQOL-100 quality of life assessment with fifteen international field centers simultaneously to develop a quality of life assessment cross-culturally applicable.

The WHOQOL-100 allows a detailed assessment of each facet related to the quality of life. In some instances, however, the WHOQOL-100 may be too long for practical use. Therefore, the WHOQOL-BREF was developed to provide a summary assessment of the quality of life that analyzes domain level profiles, using data from the WHOQOL-100 pilot assessment. An item from each of the 24 facets of the WHOQOL-100 was included to provide a broad and comprehensive assessment. In addition, two items from the General quality of life and General health facet were included (questions 1 and 2) [8].

We choose the WHOQOL for this work at the suggestion of a specialist in gerontology. WHOQOL is an instrument validated by the WHO and evaluates very relevant aspects for the population in general. Our interest is to know how the elderly population perceives their quality of life and health.

The next section describes how the framework containing the aforementioned instruments was developed.

# 5 EmoFrame Prototype

After analyzing and choosing the instruments to be adopted in the EmoFrame, which we will use in two case studies, we implemented an interactive prototype (medium-high fidelity) from EmoFrame. We emphasize that the term framework is used in the context of this work in the broadest sense as a structure composed of mechanisms, artifacts, and systems used in planning and decision-making regarding software evaluation. The prototyped interface of EmoFrame, available in the images below, represents the evaluated version to specialists to assess with their populations of interest. The specialists, in general, will have access to the instruments and be able to register users and could consult the results of the evaluations conducted by them. The user will access the system when registered by a specialist and have access only to the tools and not to the results.

The EmoFrame provides accessibility features, such as: increase the font, decrease the font, and contrast. To register, the specialist must provide the following information: Name; Social Name; Specialty; Phone Number; Gender; Date of birth; E-mail; and Password. After completing the registration, the specialist can enter the system by providing an e-mail and password.

## 5.1 Used Instruments and Instructions

Upon entering the system, the specialist has access to three main pages: tools, registering users, and results. The Fig. 1 illustrates the tool screen.

This tab contains the six instruments selected to compose the framework, until now. All instruments have an initial sentence, a kind of instruction to answer the test. In addition, they also have a button called "instructions" that contains examples of how to answer the scales.

## 5.2 User Registration on EmoFrame

In the second tab, the specialist can register new users to have access to the tools. The register is essential so that the different data are collected so that possible correlations between the data obtained through the questionnaires and socio-demographic data, for example, can be traced. In addition, with the user registered on the system, it is possible to store, in a safe and adequately anonymized manner—if necessary, the results of the instruments and specialists will be able to access this data whenever necessary. The requested data are as follows: Name; Social Name; Nationality; Naturalness; Address; Telephone; Gender; Marital Status; Education; Individual Monthly Income; Monthly Family Income; Date of birth; and Email.

**Fig. 1.** Instruments—EmoFrame.

## 5.3 EmoFrame Results

The results are available to the specialists who applied the instruments. A specialist who applied SAM, for example, to 100 users, will only have access to the data of those users. Access control is a crucial part of protecting this sensitive data. The results can be filtered by the user's name or by the six available instruments. The following subsections describe how the results are made available for each instrument.

**SUS Results.** We divided the SUS result into three types of visualizations. The first is a score combined with a reference table, described in Table 1. The second view is a horizontal bar chart that illustrates all the questions and answers given by the user. The last response visualization is a "curve" that illustrates the response variation. In addition, at the bottom of the screen, there is a button that, when clicked, illustrates how we calculate the SUS score.

**GDS Results.** The GDS result has a score and a reference table, in addition to the button on how to calculate. The reference we adopted is shown in Table 2.

**Table 1.** SUS score reference table.

| Score | Usability Status |
|---|---|
| Less than 60 | Unacceptable |
| 60–70 | Ok. |
| 70–80 | Good. |
| 80–90 | Excellent. |
| Greater than 90 | Best possible usability |

**Table 2.** GDS reference table.

| Score | Result |
|---|---|
| 1–5 | Low risk for depression indication |
| 6–10 | Moderate risk for depression indication |
| 11–15 | Severe risk for depression indication |

**POMS Results.** The result consists of two different scores, a TMD result and a result referring to the training misfit scale. We show the results references of Total Mood Disturbance (TMD) in Table 3.

**Table 3.** POMS reference table.

| Score | Result |
|---|---|
| High TMD score | Indicate worsening of mood |
| Low TMD score | Indicate improvement of mood |

To know the result of the training misfit scale, add the results of the questions related to this domain to the PTH. A high value indicates overtraining, and a low value implies that the exercise practitioner is healthy.

**SD Results.** We illustrate the SD result using a chart with two axes representing opposite poles. We plot the user responses in the form of a line that demonstrates the user's trend. In addition, the SD results page also contains a table with responses, which range from -3 to 3.

**WHOQOL Results.** The WHOQOL result is divided between the scores for four domains and the answers for two general questions. Each domain has an individual score, and the domain scores are scaled positively. That is, higher scores indicate higher quality of life. The results page contains a table showing each score for each domain, a vertical bar chart, and a table showing the score for the two general questions.

**SAM Results.** SAM evaluates three domains, and its result is given in the form of a table, where each row represents one of the domains. The table is graded by colors and each color indicates the tendencies of the responses: red—negative; yellow—neutral; and green—positive. Examples of results from each of the aforementioned instruments can be viewed in the project's repository[1].

### 5.4   Final Considerations About the Prototype

The Computing area is broad and plural; that is, it covers many areas and, consequently, the most diverse users. Therefore, the motivation to build EmoFrame arose from finding appropriate instruments to evaluate specific solutions that meet the most diverse needs scenarios. Furthermore, because we believe that evaluating the quality/efficiency of solutions is a difficulty faced by other areas, we seek to make EmoFrame a valuable tool for many professionals. Hence, we intend that specialists access the framework and filter an instrument that suits their solution and meets the target audience's demands. In addition, we expect that, even if these specialists have never seen the instrument, they will use it correctly, following the instructions and guidelines that EmoFrame may offer.

The results pages are essential so that specialists from other research areas can understand users' opinions and feelings when interacting with solutions or interventions proposed by them. The results of SUS and SD show an overview of the usability and quality of solutions. From the users' answers, the tester can know the strengths and weaknesses of the evaluated solution. With the GDS result it is possible to refer the user to a more rigorous and detailed assessment if the user presents a high indication of depression, so the instrument can be considered a powerful way of screening for some disorders. The WHOQOL result is an essential piece of data to understand the users' perception of quality of life and health. It is an instrument that assesses, above all, the user's understanding of situations such as housing and support systems. Although simple, the SAM result tells us if a user felt good when using a particular solution, if users feel in control (safe, for example) and if what was proposed by the developers can motivate them.

## 6   Evaluation and Discussion

In the first evaluation of the framework, the specialists (psychologist, gerontologist, and HCI specialists) freely evaluated all EmoFrame screens. We did not pre-set any script or scenario. During the interaction with the prototype, they asked several questions and suggestions, such as increasing the font size, changing the initial sentences of some instruments, adding or removing buttons, for example. All EmoFrame screens have changed after this first assessment, but in general, the specialists approved most of the features of EmoFrame, considered an interface "clean" and very similar to the instruments applied on paper.

---

[1] https://drive.google.com/file/d/1wGMyyJlItWHtI2ThUReVwibRwdQ4Xozn/view?usp=sharing.

After the first evaluation, we conduct a second evaluation (user test) with the specialists who participated in the previous evaluation (gerontologist and psychologist). We also invited three other specialists in HCI, who are also part of the research group. To conduct the validation, we set up three different fictional scenarios: A, B, and C. For the three scenarios, we ask specialists to carried out a series of tasks, namely: (1) To access the EmoFrame; (2) To carry out the registration as a specialist; (3) To register a user; (4) To evaluate the tools of the scenario to which they were assigned; (5) To open the results page of the instruments evaluated by them; (6) To answer the SUS questionnaire, evaluating the EmoFrame and (7) Log out.

In scenario A, the personas are elderly people who participate in a digital literacy course. In this context, users learned to use various applications for smartphones and tablets, such as Instagram® and YouTube®. At the end of the course, it is interesting for the researchers responsible for students' course feedback on their experience. In this scenario, the focus is on evaluating the students' experience during the course, for which we used two instruments. The first is the GDS, and the second is WHOQOL. As the public in this scenario are elderly people, the gerontologist evaluated the instruments of this scenario.

In scenario B, the personas are high school students practicing sports and sedentary students. In the suggested context, the school board asked the institution's psychologist to investigate the students' emotional state and compare the results of active students of some sport (who were part of a team) with students who do not practice any sport actively. The instruments used were POMS and SD. The POMS is a scale for assessing mood states and also includes the Training Misfit Scale (TMS). To report how they felt when answering POMS, the students answered the SD. The specialist responsible for evaluating this scenario was the psychologist.

In scenario C, the specialists used EmoFrame to evaluate an educational game. The game has three phases. At each stage played, the specialists responded to the SAM to say how they felt when interacting with the computational solution. When completing this step, the specialists should carry out the tasks listed above, evaluating the SAM and SUS instruments. We have assigned the three HCI specialists to this scenario.

### 6.1 Scenario Discussions

When starting the evaluation of Scenario A, the specialist noticed that when she entered the system after registering, her username did not appear anywhere on the screen, leaving her confused and uncertain about completing the registration. Another observation made by the gerontologist concerns the initial WHOQOL sentence. The specialist stressed the importance of informing the user that the World Health Organization validates the instrument. One of the main contributions made in this scenario involves the date of the test. The specialist said this topic: *"It is important that I have the results, the name, the age and the date of application of the test. With the date of application, you can follow the evolution of the users if they are under treatment."*.

Regarding scenario B, the psychologist made several suggestions. One of them was to include an option in all questionnaires that says: "I do not know/I do not want to answer" according to the specialist, users do not have to answer what they do not want. Regarding POMS, the psychologist believes that it is better to remove the numbers from the POMS questions and change the order of the items if the intention is to do a "pre and post test". In addition to these specific suggestions, the specialist stated that it would be positive to add a field to insert comments on the questionnaires in the form of text, video, or audio. Regarding the user registration, the suggestions were to add a field to inform who is responding to the user registration (responsible or the individual himself), add the field "race" to the questionnaire, and put the options in alphabetical order. He also suggests dividing the fields "The first name" and "The last name", adding an option "I do not know/I prefer not to say" in the gender question. Regarding the SD instruction, the psychologist said: *"The instructions are perfect, it is important to define what is between the extremes. The example with the 3 points is the recommended one"*.

In scenario C, HCI specialists suggested adding feedback whenever the user sends a response or fills out a form. In addition, they stressed the need to include a field for reporting errors. One of the specialists made the following comment: *"I really liked it. I found the interface very well done. The emojis used, [...] were very well chosen. As much as the person doesn't read the description, you can understand what each one represents. The texts are clear and objective."*

## 6.2   SUS Evaluation

After carrying out the requested tasks, the specialists answered the SUS instrument about the EmoFrame interface. We categorize SUS questions according to Nilsen's usability heuristics [18].

**Match Between System and the Real World.** According to the definition of this heuristic, the design must follow real world conventions, making the information appear in a natural and logical order. The SUS questions that we consider to fall into this category are listed below:

- Question 8: *"Navigating the application's menus and screens was easy."*;
- Question 12: *"It is easy to remember how to do things in this application."*;
- Question 23: *"The terminology used in the button texts was easy to understand. "*.

Figure 2 illustrates the responses of the 5 specialists who evaluate the framework. The positive responses regarding this heuristic infer that terms, concepts, icons and images seem perfectly clear to users.

**User Control and Freedom.** We consider that the questions below are related to this heuristic:

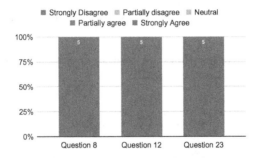

**Fig. 2.** Match between system and the real world.

- Question 4: *"I felt in charge using this app."*;
- Question 7: *"It is easy to do what I want using this application."*;
- Question 25: *"I felt comfortable using this app."*.

Based on the users' responses, shown in Fig. 3, we can consider that the framework promotes a sense of freedom and confidence to the specialists. Only one specialist was neutral in this category when it came to one of the questions. The specialist would like more tools available in the framework.

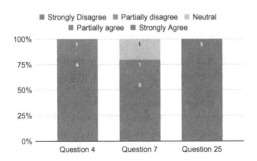

**Fig. 3.** User control and freedom.

**Consistency and Standards.** Conceptually, according to this heuristic, users should not ask themselves if different words, situations, or actions mean the same thing. That is, the system follows a pattern. The questions regarding this concept are listed below:

- Question 11: *"I found the app consistent. For example, all functions can be performed similarly."*;
- Question 20: *"The symbols and icons are clear and intuitive."*;
- Question 26: *"The application behaved as I expected."*;

– Question 28: *"I found that the various functions of the application are well integrated."*.

The 5 specialists agree that the tool is consistent and follows a well-established pattern, as shown in Fig. 4.

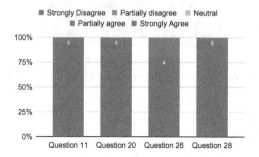

**Fig. 4.** Consistency and standards.

**Help Users Recognize, Diagnose, and Recover from Errors.** Two questions present in the SUS related to this heuristic are listed below. According to Nilsen, the error messages must be expressed in simple language, accurately indicate the problem, and suggest a solution constructively.

– Question 2: *"When I make a mistake, it is easy to correct it."*;
– Question 3: *"Error messages help to correct problems."*.

The users' responses show a flaw in the framework. According to the specialists, they are not faced with any error message and no field to report these errors. We consider this as a usability problem. The responses of the 5 specialists can be seen in Fig. 5.

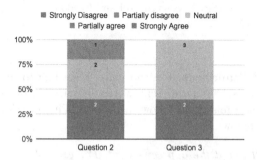

**Fig. 5.** Help users recognize, diagnose, and recover from errors.

**Recognition Rather Than Recall.** This heuristic says that the user should not remember information from one part of the interface to another. That is, the information needed to use the design must be visible or easily retrievable when necessary. The questions listed below refer to this Nielsen's heuristic:

– Question 6: *"It was easy to learn how to use this app."*;
– Question 14: *"The organization of menus and action commands (such as buttons and links) is logical, allowing you to find them easily on the screen."*;
– Question 17: *"The application provides all the information necessary to complete the tasks clearly and understandably."*.

The specialists' positive responses, shown in Fig. 6, to the EmoFrame interface suggest that it promotes recognizing actions and reduces the amount of cognitive effort required from users to carry out tasks within the framework.

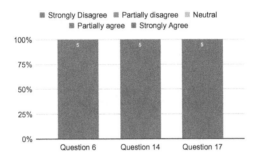

**Fig. 6.** Recognition rather than recall.

The questions below are also related to this heuristic. However, they make negative statements about the framework. Therefore, the adverse responses are positive about EmoFrame, as we show in Fig. 7.

– Question 18: *"I found the app very complicated to use."*;
– Question 19: *"I needed to learn many things to use this application."*;
– Question 22: *"I found the application unnecessarily complex. I had to remember, research or think hard to complete the tasks."*;
– Question 24: *"I would need support from a person to use this app."*.

**Flexibility and Efficiency of Use.** This heuristic concerns efficiency when executing actions within the system; flexibility implies that the different users can execute the many processes in different ways to choose the method that works for them. The related questions are:

– Question 1: *"I found it easy to enter data into this application."*;
– Question 5: *"I thought the time it took to complete the tasks was adequate."*;

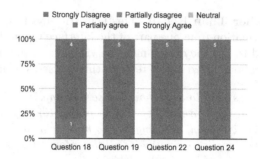

**Fig. 7.** Recognition rather than recall (reverse scale).

- Question 9: *"The application meets my needs."*;
- Question 10: *"I would recommend this app to others."*;
- Question 13: *"I would use this app frequently."*;
- Question 16: *"I enjoyed using this app."*.

We show the specialists' responses in Fig. 8.

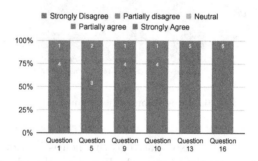

**Fig. 8.** Flexibility and efficiency of use.

**Aesthetic and Minimalist Design.** Nielsen says that the interfaces should not contain irrelevant or rarely needed information. Each extra unit of information in an interface competes with the relevant information units and decreases their relative visibility. The two SUS questions that we consider related to these aspects are:

- Question 15: *"The app's interface design is attractive."*;
- Question 21: *"I found the texts easy to read."*.

We show the specialists' responses in Fig. 9. According to the answers, we can infer that the design pleased the users or that at least it did not bother them to the point of impairing the interaction.

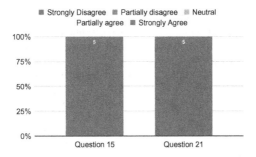

**Fig. 9.** Aesthetic and minimalist design.

# 7 Final Remarks

We presented a medium-high fidelity prototype of the EmoFrame. The technologies we used to develop the prototype were HTML, CSS, and JavaScript. We concluded during this study that it is also necessary to include guidelines to compose the framework and a set of instruments. As a contribution, we hope to offer the EmoFrame as an artifact, together with the synthesized instruments.

A work in progress is the development of the EmoFrame in high fidelity. It is in the interest of the research group to carry out new studies also in the tool's interface, as well as to use it in the context of research with the populations of interest of the group's specialists. In the future, it is expected that the specialist can receive recommendations for instruments to be used in their studies, based on input data offered by these specialists, such as the desire to assess emotional responses with children, the elderly, carriers disability, among other audiences, for example, and also for different types of emotional responses.

**Acknowledgments.** The authors would like to thank the financial support from Brazilian agency: CAPES and also to thank the participants in the evaluation.

# References

1. Almeida, O.P., Almeida, S.A.: Confiabilidade da versão brasileira da Escala de Depressão em Geriatria (GDS) versão reduzida. Arquivos de Neuro-Psiquiatria. **57**, 421–426 (1999). http://www.scielo.br/scielo.php?script=sci_arttext&pid=S0004-282X1999000300013&nrm=iso
2. Bangor, A., Kortum, P.T., Miller, J.T.: An empirical evaluation of the system usability scale. Int. J. Human Comput. Interact. **24**(6), 574–594 (2008). https://doi.org/10.1080/10447310802205776
3. Barbosa, S., Silva, B.: Interação Humano-Computador. Elsevier Brasil (2010). https://books.google.com.br/books?id=qk0skwr_cewC
4. Bradley, M.M., Lang, P.J.: Measuring emotion: the self-assessment manikin and the semantic differential. J. Behav. Ther. Exp. Psych. **25**(1), 49–59 (1994)
5. Brooke, J.: SUS: a quick and dirty usability scale. Usabil. Eval. Ind. **189**, 4–7 (1995)

6. De Lera, E., Garreta-Domingo, M.: Ten emotion heuristics: guidelines for assessing the user's affective dimension easily and cost-effectively. In: Proceedings of HCI 2007 The 21st British HCI Group Annual Conference University of Lancaster, UK, vol. 21, pp. 1–4 (2007)

7. Finstad, K.: The system usability scale and non-native English speakers. J. Usabil. Stud. 1(4), 185–188 (2006)

8. Fleck, M.P., et al.: Aplicação da versão em português do instrumento abreviado de avaliação da qualidade de vida "WHOQOL-bref". Revista de Saúde Pública 34, 178–183 (2000). http://www.scielo.br/scielo.php?script=sci_arttext&pid=S0034-89102000000200012&nrm=iso

9. Greenberg, S.A.: The geriatric depression scale (GDS). Best Pract. Nurs. Care Older Adults 4(1), 1–2 (2012)

10. Hall, L., Hume, C., Tazzyman, S.: Five degrees of happiness: Effective smiley face Likert scales for evaluating with children, pp. 311–321, June 2016. https://doi.org/10.1145/2930674.2930719

11. Hayashi, E.C.S., Posada, J.E.G., Maike, V.R.M.L., Baranauskas, M.C.C.: Exploring new formats of the self-assessment manikin in the design with children. In: IHC 2016, Association for Computing Machinery, New York, NY, USA (2016). https://doi.org/10.1145/3033701.3033728

12. Heuchert, J.P., McNair, D.M.: Profile of mood states 2nd edition™ (2012)

13. Lach, H., Chang, Y.P., Edwards, D.: Can older adults with dementia accurately report depression using brief forms? J. Gerontol. Nurs. 36, 30–37 (2010). https://doi.org/10.3928/00989134-20100303-01

14. Lang, P.J., Greenwald, M.K., Bradley, M.M., Hamm, A.O.: Looking at pictures: affective, facial, visceral, and behavioral reactions. Psychophysiology 30(3), 261–273 (1993)

15. Lopes, J.L., Nogueira-Martins, L.A., Andrade, A.L., Barros, A.L.B.L.: Escala de diferencial semmântico para avaliação da percepção de pacientes hospitalizados frente ao banho. Acta Paulista de Enfermagem. 24, 815–820 (2011). http://www.scielo.br/scielo.php?script=sci_arttext&pid=S0103-21002011000600015&nrm=iso

16. McNair, D.M., et al.: Manual profile of mood states (1971)

17. Moreira, E., dos Reis, J., Baranauskas, M.C.: Artefatos tangíveis e a avaliação de estados afetivos por crianças. Revista Brasileira de Informática na Educação. 27, 58 (2019). https://doi.org/10.5753/rbie.2019.27.01.58

18. Nielsen, J.: 10 usability heuristics for user interface design. https://www.nngroup.com/articles/ten-usability-heuristics/ (1994). acesso em 02 Fev 2021

19. Nielsen, J.: Usability 101: Introduction to usability. https://www.nngroup.com/articles/usability-101-introduction-to-usability/ (2012). acesso em 02 Fev. 2021

20. Norman, D., Nielsen, J.: The definition of user experience (UX). https://www.nngroup.com/articles/definition-user-experience/ (2006). acesso em 02 Fev. 2021

21. Osgood, C.E., Suci, G.J., Tannenbaum, P.H.: The Measurement of Meaning. No. 47, University of Illinois press (1957)

22. Pressman, R., Maxim, B.: Engenharia de Software-8ª Edição. McGraw Hill, Brazil (2016)

23. Raglin, J., Morgan, W.: Development of a scale to measure training-induced distress. Med. Sci. Sports Exer. 21, S50 (1980). https://doi.org/10.1249/00005768-198004001-00299

24. Rogers, Y., Sharp, H., Preece, J.: Interaction Design: Beyond Human-computer Interaction. John Wiley & Sons, Hoboken (2011)

25. Rosson, M.B., Carroll, J.M.: Usability Engineering: Scenario-Based Development of Human-computer Interaction. Morgan Kaufmann, Burlington (2002)

26. Scherer, K.R.: Appraisal considered as a process of multilevel sequential checking. Apprais. Process. Emot. Theory Methods Res. **92**(120), 57 (2001)
27. Scherer, K.R.: What are emotions? and how can they be measured? Soc. Sci. Inf. **44**(4), 695–729 (2005). https://doi.org/10.1177/0539018405058216
28. Schuler, D., Namioka, A.: Participatory Design: Principles and Practices. CRC Press, Boca Raton (1993)
29. Sears, A., Jacko, J.A.: Human-computer Interaction Fundamentals. CRC Press, Boca Raton (2009)
30. Sheikh, J.I., Yesavage, J.A.: Geriatric depression scale (GDS): recent evidence and development of a shorter version. Clin. Gerontol. J. Aging Mental Health. (1986)
31. Sherrell, L.: Evolutionary Prototyping. In: Runehov, A.L.C., Oviedo, L. (eds.) Encyclopedia of Sciences and Religions, pp. 803–803. Springer, Netherlands, Dordrecht (2013). https://doi.org/10.1007/978-1-4020-8265-8_201039
32. Silva, L.G.Z., Guimarães, P.D., de Souza Gomes, L.O., de Almeida Neris, V.P.: A comparative study of users' subjective feeling collection instruments. In: Proceedings of the 19th Brazilian Symposium on Human Factors in Computing Systems, pp. 1–10 (2020)
33. Viana, M.F., Almeida, P.L.d., Santos, R.C.: Adaptação portuguesa da versão reduzida do Perfil de Estados de Humor: POMS. Análise Psicológica. **19**, 77–92 (2001). http://www.scielo.mec.pt/scielo.php?script=sci_arttext&pid=S0870-82312001000100008&nrm=iso
34. Xavier, R., Garcia, F., Neris, V.: Decisões de design de interfaces ruins e o impacto delas na interação: um estudo preliminar considerando o estado emocional de idosos, pp. 127–136 (2012)
35. Yesavage, J.A., et al.: Development and validation of a geriatric depression screening scale: a preliminary report. J. Psych. Res. **17**(1), 37–49 (1982)

# A Systematic Mapping Study of Emotional Response Evaluation Instruments

Suzane Santos dos Santos[✉] and Kamila Rios da Hora Rodrigues[ID]

University of São Paulo, São Carlos, São Paulo, Brazil
suzanesantos@usp.br, kamila.rios@icmc.usp.br

**Abstract.** In the context of the study of emotions, the limits that define it can be so confusing that everything can be easily characterized as an emotion. Experts are not unanimous about what is an emotion and what is not, and if this is a challenge for experts, for other professionals it is an even bigger barrier. For example, analyzing users' emotional aspects when interacting with interactive computational solutions is very difficult for Computer professionals, in several situations, this evaluation is the responsibility of the specialist professionals in the studied domain. In an attempt to alleviate this problem, this systematic mapping study seeks to identify different instruments for evaluating emotional responses from different contexts to help professionals of many domains choose suitable artifacts for their evaluations. We identified 32 studies that describe 18 different instruments, these instruments are mainly from the field of Psychology and aimed at adults.

**Keywords:** Computational systems evaluation · Emotional aspects · Emotional response · Systematic mapping

## 1 Introduction

There are different ways to evaluate a product, whether it is a physical good, a service provided, or a computational solution. In order to conduct a practical assessment, it is crucial to know how and when to use the different types of assessment available in the literature. Human-Computer Interaction (HCI) is a research area of Computer Science in which evaluation has high relevance. During the evaluation stage, problems in the interface and user interaction, not noticed in the design and development stages, are identified and corrected. Thus, after a systematic and careful evaluation, the user has the chance to receive a safer, more effective product that, above all, does not harm their experience while using the product.

In the context of evaluation and HCI, another concept intrinsically associated with usability is the concept of User eXperience (UX). According to Nilsen [36], the user experience encompasses all aspects of the end user's interaction with its

© The Author(s), under exclusive license to Springer Nature Switzerland AG 2022
M. Kurosu et al. (Eds.): HCII 2022, LNCS 13516, pp. 302–317, 2022.
https://doi.org/10.1007/978-3-031-17615-9_21

services and products. More specifically, UX is related to how people feel about a product and their pleasure and satisfaction when using it.

User emotion, in turn, is no longer just related to unexpected system response or frustration with an incomprehensible error message. It is now understood that a wide range of emotions plays an essential role in all tasks performed on the computer. When interacting with computer systems, users' emotions are a fundamental aspect to help understand the user experience [4,47].

This recent change in user emotion concerning interactive systems has raised the need to understand better what emotion is and how it influences the user during interaction. However, even though the term emotion is used very often, and several studies in the literature address this issue, there is no consensus on the concept, which is controversial even for specialists in the field [46].

Given that HCI is the intersection between Psychology and Social Sciences on the one hand and the combination of Computer Science and technology on the other, it is crucial to understand how different areas of knowledge understand and assess individuals' emotional responses. Hence, we conducted a Systematic Mapping (SM) study whose objective is to identify instruments for evaluating emotional responses and find instruments from other fields that can be systematized and incorporated into the area of Computing or other areas.

This paper is divided as follows: Sect. 2 describes the theoretical foundation, Sect. 3 describes the protocol for planning, conducting and reporting the systematic mapping. Section 4 contains the synthesis of the results obtained through the mapping. In Sect. 5 we make the final considerations and our conclusions on the subject.

## 2    Theoretical Foundation

In this section, we present a summary of the study of emotions. In the literature, there are several definitions of emotion. According to Young [60], emotion is an acute disorder of the individual, of psychological origin, involving behavior, conscious experience, and visceral functioning. For Ekman [12], emotion refers to the process by which an elicitor is assessed automatically or in an extended way. An affect program may or may not be triggered, organized responses may occur, although more or less managed by attempts to control emotional behavior.

According to Izard [21], emotion is a complex concept with neurophysiological, neuromuscular, and phenomenological aspects. At the neurophysiological level, emotion is defined primarily in terms of patterns of electrochemical activity in the nervous system. At the neuromuscular level, emotion is primarily a facial activity, and facial patterns and secondary is a bodily response. At the phenomenological level, emotion is essentially a motivating experience or experience that has immediate meaning and importance. These definitions were found in the work proposed by Kleinginna and Kleinginna [25], in which the authors compiled a compilation of 92 definitions and nine skeptical statements from a variety of sources in the emotion literature.

For Coan and Allen [9], emotion is too broad a class of events to be a single scientific category. As psychologists use the term, it includes the euphoria of winning an Olympic gold medal, a brief startle with an unexpected noise, a deep, unrelenting pain, the fleeting pleasant sensations of a warm breeze. While it can also mean cardiovascular changes in response to the display of a movie, stalking and murder of an innocent victim, lifelong love for a child, feeling excited about no known reason, and interest in a newsletter.

The boundaries of emotion can be so confusing that everything can easily be characterized as emotion. Experts are not unanimous about what is an emotion and what is not. All the different types of events included in this term are essential, some of the vital importance. Nevertheless, it is increasingly evident that not all events can be explained in the same way. No description and evaluation framework can do justice to this heterogeneous class of events without differentiating one type of event from another [9].

## 2.1  Emotion Evaluation

The definition of Scherer [45] states that: "Emotion is defined as an episode of synchronized and interrelated changes in the states of all or most of the five subsystems of the organism in response to the evaluation of a stimulus event external or internal as relevant to the main concerns of the organism". Therefore, we adopted this definition in this study. The rationale behind this choice lies in the fact that this definition is one of the most comprehensive. The five components are:

1. Cognitive evaluations, which have the function of evaluating objects and events;
2. Behavioral trends (action trends), responsible for preparing and directing activities;
3. Motor expressions (facial and vocal expressions), which communicate reactions and behavioral intentions;
4. Physiological reactions (physical symptoms), responsible for regulating the body;
5. Subjective feelings (conscious experience), which monitors the organism's internal state and interaction with the environment.

This study focuses on the subjective feelings component. This means that we only considered self-report instruments for the systematic mapping study. In the field of Psychology, a self-report is any test, measure, or survey that is based on an individual's own account of their symptoms, behaviors, beliefs, or feelings. Examples that are widely used are interviews (structured or not) and questionnaires, which are usually applied using paper and pencil, or online.

## 3  Methodology

This section outlines the protocol used to carry out this study. The protocol consists of five activities: defining the research questions, the search process, research strategy (inclusion/exclusion criteria), data extraction strategy, and synthesis of the extracted data.

### 3.1    Research Question

The present systematic mapping study addresses one leading research question, which we named RQ: "What self-report instruments are used to evaluate individuals' emotional responses?".

By answering this research question, we can discover which self-report instruments are used to assess individuals' emotional responses. Since this is a broad question and is not limited to a specific area, the results may include well-known and widely used instruments, as well as innovative instruments that may be discovered and disseminated.

### 3.2    Search Process

The search process aimed at identifying studies that will answer our research question. In order to achieve this goal, we create a search string for the search process, gathering the most relevant terms related to the search question and combining them by logical operators. To obtain relevant and valuable results for this study, some iterations were carried out until reaching the terms that composed the following string used: (**"emotion evaluation" OR "emotional evaluation" OR "emotional response evaluation" OR "evaluation of emotion"**).

The procedure consisted of an automated search into well-known digital libraries in both Computing and Health areas. The electronic search was performed on:

- ACM Digital Library[1];
- IEEE Xplore[2];
- PubMed digital libraries[3];
- Scielo[4];
- Scopus[5];
- Virtual Health Library[6];
- Web of Science[7].

### 3.3    Search Strategy

Inclusion (IC) and exclusion (EC) criteria were defined for the studies returned by the search string, as shown in Table 1.

---

[1] https://dl.acm.org/.
[2] https://ieeexplore.ieee.org.
[3] https://pubmed.ncbi.nlm.nih.gov/.
[4] https://www.scielo.br/.
[5] https://www.scopus.com/.
[6] https://bvsalud.org/en/.
[7] https://www.webofscience.com/.

**Table 1.** Selection Criteria.

| Criteria | Code | Description |
|---|---|---|
| Inclusion | IC.1 | Study that explicitly addresses the evaluation of users' emotional responses. |
| Exclusion | EC.1 | Study that does not address the evaluation of users' emotional response |
| | EC.2 | Study that presents instruments that are not self-report |
| | EC.3 | Study written in languages other than English |

The selection process followed six steps:

1. Execution of the search on the bases previously chosen;
2. Removal of duplicates studies;
3. Selection through title and abstract;
4. Application of selection criteria in the studies selected in step 3, in the full text;
5. Application of quality criteria in the final set of selected studies;
6. And finally, data extraction.

Quality criteria (see Table 2) were adopted to ensure that the selected studies were relevant to answering the research question raised. The possible answers to the questions were "yes", "partially", or "no", quantified with the values "1", "0.5", and "0", respectively. For the paper to be considered sufficient quality to have its data extracted for the research, it was necessary to reach a minimum score of 3.5 points. The studies that did not reach the minimum score were eliminated. The quality criteria applied to the studies are described in Table 2.

**Table 2.** Quality Criteria

| Quality Criteria | Question |
|---|---|
| QC.1 | Does the study define who the target audience is? |
| QC.2 | Does the study describe which emotions it assesses? |
| QC.3 | Is the assessment procedure replicable? |
| QC.4 | Can the instrument be digitized? |

The database search returned a total of 1410 studies, of which 736 were duplicates. Thus, only 674 went through the first iteration of the inclusion and exclusion criteria. At this stage, based on reading the title and abstract, we selected 70 studies. In the second iteration of the selection criteria, we read the full text of the remaining studies and applied the quality criteria, the final set of studies consisted of 52 studies. The identified works are described in Table 3.

**Table 3.** Set of studies identified.

| Id | Authors and Year | Source | Instrument |
|---|---|---|---|
| 1 | Müller et al. (2021) [34] | Scopus | University of California, Los Angeles Loneliness Scale (UCLA-3) |
| 2 | Bojan et al. (2021) [6] | Scopus | Positive and Negative Affect Schedule (PANAS) |
| 3 | Önder (2020) [35] | Scopus | The Oxford Happiness Questionnaire (OHP) |
| 4 | Oh et al. (2019) [37] | Scopus | The Profile of Mood States (POMS) and Semantic Differential (SD) |
| 6 | Racine (2017) [42] | Scopus | Self-Assessment Manikin (SAM) |
| 7 | Park et al. (2017) [40] | Scopus | A modified semantic differential (SD) and Profile of Mood States (POMS) |
| 8 | Carmel et al. (2017) [8] | Scopus | State Trait Anxiety Inventor (STAI) |
| 9 | Miśkiewicz et al. (2016) [33] | Scopus | Positive and Negative Affect Schedule (PANAS) |
| 10 | Balconi et al. (2016) [3] | Scopus | Self-Assessment Manikin (SAM) |
| 11 | Maffei et al. (2015) [30] | Web of Science | Self-Assessment Manikin (SAM) |
| 12 | Balconi et al. (2015) [2] | Scopus | An adapted version of SAM |
| 13 | Ermes et al. (2014) [14] | Scopus | PAD Semantic Scale and EmoCards |
| 14 | Melnyk et al. (2013) [32] | Scopus | Beck Youth Inventory (2nd Edition: BYI II) |
| 15 | Xavier and Neris (2012) [58] | Scopus | Self-Assessment Manikin (SAM) |
| 16 | Somaini et al.(2011) [49] | Scopus | State-Trait Anxiety Inventory Y-1 (STAI) Self-Assessment Manikin (SAM) |
| 17 | Vuoskoski and Eerola (2011) [56] | Scopus | POMS-A |
| 18 | Emery and Hess (2008) [13] | Scopus | Positive and Negative Affect Schedule (PANAS) |
| 19 | Gaina et al. (2004) [16] | Scopus | Profile of Mood States (POMS) |
| 20 | Shibata et al. (1993) [48] | Scopus | Semantic Differential (SD) |
| 21 | Park and Chong (2019) [39] | Web of Science | Music emotion assessment tool (MEAT) |
| 22 | Aguilar et al. (2008) [1] | Web Of Science | Self-Assessment Manikin (SAM) |
| 23 | Wood and Moreau (2006) [57] | Web Of Science | Modification of Differential Emotions Scale (DES-II) |
| 24 | Jayanthi et al. (2018) [23] | Web Of Science | Rosenberg Self-esteem Scale (RSE) |
| 25 | Gozansky et al. (2021) [18] | PubMed | The Revised University of California, Los Angeles (R-UCLA) Loneliness Scale and The Short Depression, Anxiety and Stress Scale (DASS-21) |

(*continued*)

**Table 3.** (*continued*)

| Id | Authors and Year | Source | Instrument |
|----|------------------|--------|------------|
| 26 | Igasaki *et al.* (2020) [20] | PubMed | Profile of Mood States 2nd Edition (POMS 2) |
| 27 | Philpott *et al.* (2016) [41] | PubMed | Hospital Anxiety and Depression Scale (HADS) |
| 28 | St. Jacques *et al.* (2015) [51] | PubMed | Self-Assessment Manikin (SAM) and Positive and Negative Affect Schedule (PANAS) |
| 29 | Tempesta *et al.* (2010) [54] | PubMed | Self-Assessment Manikin (SAM) |
| 30 | Gil *et al.* (2011) [17] | PubMed | State Trait Anxiety Inventor (STAI) and Edinburgh Postnatal Depression Scale (EPDS) |
| 31 | Martinez *et al.* (2018) [31] | Virtual Health Library | Geriatric Depression Scale (GDS) |
| 32 | Firoozi *et al.* (2013) [15] | Virtual Health Library | Beck Depression Inventory (BDI) |

### 3.4 Data Analysis

The data extraction process was carried out systematically, throughout a form for recording the information necessary for answer the research question, containing the following fields:

1. Study identifier (ID);
2. Title;
3. Authors;
4. Year;
5. Search base;
6. Evaluation instrument;
7. Instrument origin field;
8. Emotions evaluated by the instrument;
9. Target audience;
10. and Evaluation procedure.

In Table 3 we show the ID, authors, year, source and the evaluation instrument, and Table 4, in turn, shows the instruments used in the studies described in Table 3. In total, we identified 19 assessment instruments, some instruments, such as the POMS, have variations and only one version appears in the table.

## 4   Results

The instruments described in the tables were divided into four categories: screening instruments, non-verbal instruments, instruments based on rating scales, and instruments based on the semantic differential.

**Table 4.** Instruments identified.

| Instrument | Origin field | Target audience | Emotional Aspects involved |
|---|---|---|---|
| UCLA-3 | Psychology | Teens and adults | Subjective feelings of loneliness |
| PANAS | Psychology | Adults | Positive and negative affect |
| OHQ | Psychology | No restrictions described | Happiness |
| POMS | Psychology | Adults | Tension-anxiety, depression-dejection, anger-hostility, fatigue, confusion and vigor |
| SD | Psychology | No restrictions described | Connotative meaning of objects, events, and concepts |
| SAM | Psychology | No restrictions described | Valence/Pleasure, arousal and dominance/control |
| STAI | Psychology | Adults | State anxiety and trait anxiety |
| PAD Semantic Scale | Psychology | No restrictions described | Pleasure, arousal and dominance |
| EmoCards | Psychology | No restrictions described | Excited (neutral or pleasant), average pleasant, calm (pleasant, neutral or unpleasant), average unpleasant and excited unpleasant |
| BYI | Psychology | Children and adolescents | Depression, anxiety, anger, disruptive behavior, and self-concept |
| MEAT | Psychology of Music | Adults | Happiness, sadness, anger, and fear |
| DES-II | Psychology | No restrictions described | Seven positives and seven negatives emotions variables |
| RES | Psychology | Teens | Both positive and negative feelings about the self |
| DASS-II | Psychology | Adults | The negative emotional states of depression, anxiety, and Stress/tension |
| HADS | Psychology | No restrictions described | States of depression and anxiety in the setting of an hospital medical outpatient clinic |
| EPDS | Psychology | Cisgender women | Postpartum depression symptoms on the third day after childbirth |
| GDS | GeriatricPsychiatry | Older adults | Symptoms of depression |
| BDI | Psychology | 13 years old and above | Key symptoms of depression including mood, pessimism, sense of failure, etc. |

## 4.1   Screening Instruments

A screening test is done to detect potential health disorders or diseases in people who do not have any disease symptoms. The goal is early detection and lifestyle changes or surveillance to reduce the risk of disease or detect it early enough to treat it most effectively. Brief psychological measures can be used to screen individuals for a range of mental health conditions. Screening measures are often questionnaires completed by clients. Screening tends to be quick to administer, but results are only indicative: if a positive result is found on a screening test, then the screening test can be followed up by a more definitive test [55]. The ID's of instruments that fall into this category are: 14, 23, 25, 27, 30, 31 ans 32.

The following is a brief description of the instruments in this category:

- Beck Youth Inventory (BYI II): this instrument uses five self-report inventories to assess symptoms of depression, anxiety, anger, disruptive behavior, and self-concept in children and adolescents [52];
- Differential Emotion Sacale (DES-II): the DES is a standardized instrument that reliably divides the individual's description of emotion experience into validated, discrete categories of emotion [22];
- The Short Depression, Anxiety and Stress Scale (DASS-21): The Depression, Anxiety and Stress Scale - 21 Items (DASS-21) is a set of three self-report scales designed to measure the emotional states of depression, anxiety and stress. Each of the three DASS-21 scales contains 7 items, divided into subscales with similar content [29];
- Hospital Anxiety and Depression Scale (HADS): This instrument measure anxiety and depression in a general medical population of patients. HADS focuses on non-physical symptoms so that it can be used to diagnose depression in people with significant physical ill-health [53];
- Edinburgh Postnatal Depression Scale (EPDS): The 10-question Edinburgh Postnatal Depression Scale (EPDS) is a valuable and efficient way of identifying patients at risk for "perinatal" depression. The EPDS is easy to administer and has proven to be an effective screening tool. This instrument can only be applied by a specialist [10];
- Geriatric Depression Scale (GDS): GDS is a self-report measure of depression in older adults. Users respond in a "Yes/No" format. This form can be completed in approximately 5 to 7 min, making it ideal for people who are easily fatigued or are limited in their ability to concentrate for longer periods of time. GDS is a scale widely used and it is an instrument that non-specialists can administer [59];
- Beck Depression Inventory (BDI): The Beck Depression Inventory (BDI) is a 21-item, self-report rating inventory that measures characteristic attitudes and symptoms of depression. The BDI has been developed in different forms, including several computerized forms [5].

Screening tests for emotional disorders are usually administered by trained professionals. Systematizing them would be possible with the help of domain experts.

## 4.2   Non-verbal Instruments

Non-verbal instruments have no age restriction. They can be applied to children, the elderly, people with communication difficulties, and low education. The Self-Assessment Manikin (SAM)(ID's: 6,10, 11, 12, 15, 16, 22 and 28) is a non-verbal instrument that is also based on a 9-point Likert Scale.

The Self-Assessment Manikin (see Fig. 1) is an image-based questionnaire developed by Bradley and Lang [7] to measure emotional response. The questionnaire, widely used in evaluations by Computing professionals, was designed to measure three characteristics of an emotional response (pleasure, arousal and dominance), identified as central to emotion in research conducted by Lang et al. [27]. SAM can be considered free of language; that is, any individual, of any schooling, can answer it.

EmoCards (2) is an instrument made up of eight cards and is manually administered. The Emocard was inspired by the model of [44] and has eight emotions, each of these emotions is represented by a male and female face, totaling 16 cards, as shown in Fig. 2.

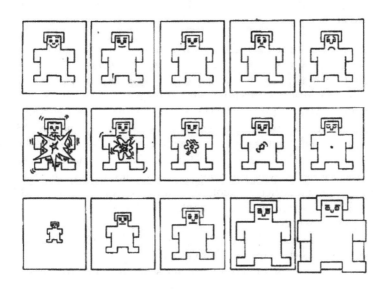

Fig. 1. SAM (Extracted from Bradley and Lang [7]).

Fig. 2. EmoCards (Extracted from Russell [44]).

## 4.3    Instruments Based on Rating Scales

One of the most common rating scales is the Likert scale. The original Likert scale is a set of statements offered for a real or hypothetical situation under study. Participants are asked to show their level of agreement (from strongly disagree to agree strongly) with the given statement (items) on a metric scale. Here all the statements in combination reveal the specific dimension of the attitude towards the issue, hence, necessarily inter-linked with each other [24].

UCLA (1, 25) POMS (4, 7, 17, 19, 26), PANAS (2, 9, 18, 28), STAI (8, 16, 30), and OHQ (3), are instruments based on a Likert scale, as follows they will be briefly described.

- University of California, Los Angeles Loneliness Scale (UCLA): The UCLA Loneliness Scale is a commonly used measure of loneliness. It was originally released in 1978 as a 20-item scale. It has since been revised several times and shorter versions have been introduced [43];
- The Profile of Mood States (POMS): POMS questionnaires contain a series of descriptive words/statements that describe feelings people have. Subjects self report on each of these areas using a 5-point Likert scale. There are several versions of the POMS questionnaire. Currently, the most commonly used is the POMS 2, which is available for adults aged 18 years and older (POMS 2-A) and another for adolescents 13 to 17 years of age (POMS 2-Y). Both POMS 2 instruments are available as full-length (65 items) and short versions (35 items) [26];
- : Positive and Negative Affect Schedule (PANAS): PANAS is a self-report questionnaire consisting of two 10-item scales to measure positive and negative affect. Each item is rated on a 5-point scale from 1 to 5 [11];
- State-Trait Anxiety Inventory (STAI): The State-Trait Anxiety Inventory (STAI) is a commonly used measure of trait and state anxiety. It can be used in clinical settings to diagnose anxiety and to distinguish it from depressive syndromes. Form Y, its most popular version, has 20 items for assessing trait anxiety and 20 for state anxiety. All items are rated on a 4-point scale [50];
- The Oxford Happiness Questionnaire (OHP): The Oxford Happiness Questionnaire (OHQ) is a widely-used scale for assessment of personal happiness. Each item of questionnaire each presented as a single statement can be endorsed on a uniform six-point Likert scale [19].

## 4.4    Instruments Based on the Semantic Differential

Developed by Osgood, Suci and Tannenbaum [38], the Semantic Differential usually takes a bipolar adjective scale of 5 or 7 points. This form usually differs according to the number of points on the scale, the degree, and marking of these points. The authors created this method when they realized the need to assess the affectivity and qualities of a concept, as well as ways to quantify the effective meaning of attitudes, opinions, perceptions, social image, personality, preferences, and interests of people or patients with content related to their health, treatment, and illness, which are not directly measurable. The works whose ID's are 4, 7 and 20 use instruments based on the semantic differential [28].

The next section describes the potential threats related to the systematic mapping conducted

### 4.5 Threats to Validity

This subsection aims at presenting the most common threats to validity of this research. Such threats are described as follows:

- Study inclusion/exclusion bias: If inclusion/exclusion criteria are conflicting, or very generic ones;
- Construction of the search string: Problems with string construction can result in the search returning a large number of studies (including many irrelevant ones) or missing some relevant studies;
- Data extraction bias: The data extraction phase can be hampered by the use of "open questions" on the variables collected, whose treatment is not explicitly discussed in the protocol;
- Researcher bias: Finally, this threat refers to potential bias the authors of studies may have, while interpreting or synthesizing the extracted results.

## 5    Final Remarks

This study describes a systematic mapping of emotion evaluation instruments. Its contributions are the protocol planning and the mapping results. For each study selected, we extracted and summarized their information. The self-report instruments found in this study are mainly from the Psychology field and are aimed at adults. Most instruments are administered manually. Some instruments are already used in the Computing area.

The mapping also answered our research question and brought us several self-report instruments used in different domains to assess different emotions. Our objective is to offer a framework composed of a system with several of these systematized instruments (with the support of domain professionals), so that professionals can carry out their assessments and obtain data and results in real time.

We identified 32 papers that describe 18 different instruments. For each of these techniques we extracted and summarized their information. The self-report instruments that are used to assess the emotional responses of users listed in this study are mainly from the field of Psychology and aimed at adults. Most instruments are administered manually. Some instruments are already used in the Computing area, such as the SAM, the Semantic Differential and EmoCards.

We believe that this study is relevant for our field because computer professionals develop applications for several other areas, a frequent example of the tools focused on the Health area. In many cases, the application developer does not have feedback from the end-user or the specialist, and this occurs because, in most situations, the evaluation is in charge of the domain specialists themselves. Therefore, it is of utmost importance that the professionals who work to create them have the necessary tools to evaluate them. One way to achieve this goal is to analyze users' emotional responses to these interactive systems. The identification of instruments that assess users' emotional responses in different areas is, therefore, essential so that new instruments can be disseminated.

**Acknowledgments.** The authors would like to thank the CAPES, Brazilian agency, for their financial support.

# References

1. Aguilar de Arcos, F., et al.: Dysregulation of emotional response in current and abstinent heroin users: negative heightening and positive blunting. Psychopharmacology **198**(2), 159–166 (2008)
2. Balconi, M., et al.: Understanding emotions in frontotemporal dementia: the explicit and implicit emotional cue mismatch. J. Alzheimer's Disease **46**(1), 211–225 (2015)
3. Balconi, M., et al.: Facial feedback and autonomic responsiveness reflect impaired emotional processing in Parkinson's disease. Sci. Rep. **6**, 31453 (2016). https://doi.org/10.1038/srep31453
4. Barbosa, S., Silva, B.: Interação Humano-Computador. Elsevier, Brasil (2010). https://books.google.com.br/books?id=qk0skwr_cewC
5. Beck, A.T., Ward, C.H., Mendelson, M., Mock, J., Erbaugh, J.: An inventory for measuring depression. Archiv. Gen. Psychiatry **4**(6), 561–571 (1961)
6. Bojan, K., et al.: The effects of playing the Cosma cognitive games in dementia. Int. J. Ser. Games **8** (2021). https://doi.org/10.17083/ijsg.v8i1.412
7. Bradley, M.M., Lang, P.J.: Measuring emotion: the self-assessment manikin and the semantic differential. J. Behav. Therapy Exper. Psychiat. **25**(1), 49–59 (1994)
8. Carmel, S., King, D., O'Rourke, N., Bachner, Y.: Subjective well-being: gender differences in holocaust survivors-specific and cross-national effects. Aging Mental Health **21**, 668–675 (2017). https://doi.org/10.1080/13607863.2016.1148660
9. Coan, J.A., Allen, J.J.: Handbook of Emotion Elicitation and Assessment. Oxford University Press, Oxford (2007)
10. Cox, J.L., Holden, J.M., Sagovsky, R.: Detection of postnatal depression: development of the 10-item Edinburgh postnatal depression scale. Br. J. Psychiat. **150**(6), 782–786 (1987)
11. Crawford, J.R., Henry, J.D.: The positive and negative affect schedule (PANAS): construct validity, measurement properties and normative data in a large nonclinical sample. Br. J. Clin. Psychol. **43**(3), 245–265 (2004). https://doi.org/10.1348/0144665031752934
12. Ekman, P.: Biological and cultural contributions to body and facial movement. The anthropology of the body (1977)
13. Emery, L., Hess, T.M.: Viewing instructions impact emotional memory differently in older and young adults. Psychol. Aging **23**(1), 2 (2008)
14. Ermes, V., Janß, A., Radermacher, K., Röcker, C.: Analyzing the benefits of integrative multi-dimensional assessments of usability features in interaction-centered

user studies. In: Proceedings of the 8th International Conference on Pervasive Computing Technologies for Healthcare, p. 227–230. PervasiveHealth '14, ICST (Institute for Computer Sciences, Social-Informatics and Telecommunications Engineering), Brussels, BEL (2014). https://doi.org/10.4108/icst.pervasivehealth.2014. 255142

15. Firoozi, M., Besharat, M.A., Boogar, E.: Emotional regulation and adjustment to childhood cancer: role of the biological, psychological and social regulators on pediatric oncology adjustment. Iran. J. Cancer Prevent. **6**, 65–72 (2013)

16. Gaina, A., et al.: Improvement of daytime rapid eye movement parameters following a hot bath in night-shift workers. Sleep Biol. Rhythm. **2**(2), 144–149 (2004). https://doi.org/10.1111/j.1479-8425.2004.00137.x

17. Gil, S., Teissèdre, F., Chambres, P.: The evaluation of emotional facial expressions in early postpartum depression mood: a difference between adult and baby faces? Psychiat. Res. **186**, 281–286 (2011). https://doi.org/10.1016/j.psychres.2010.06. 015

18. Gozansky, E., Moscona, G., Okon-Singer, H.: Identifying variables that predict depression following the general lockdown during the covid-19 pandemic. Front. Psychol. **12** (2021). https://doi.org/10.3389/fpsyg.2021.680768

19. Hills, P., Argyle, M.: The oxford happiness questionnaire: a compact scale for the measurement of psychological well-being. Personal. Individ. Diff. **33**(7), 1073–1082 (2002). https://doi.org/10.1016/S0191-8869(01)00213-6

20. Igasaki, T., Hiramatsu, S., Yanagihara, D., Baba, Y.: Emotion evaluation during working on a puzzle by spatiotemporal pattern of band power of electroencephalogram, vol. 2020, pp. 1043–1046 (2020). https://doi.org/10.1109/EMBC44109.2020. 9176312

21. Izard, C.E.: The Face of Emotion (1971)

22. Izard, C.E.: Patterns of Emotions: A New Analysis of Anxiety and Depression. Academic Press, New York (2013)

23. Jayanthi, M., Kumar, R., Swathi, S.: Investigation on association of self-esteem and students' performance in academics. Int. J. Grid Utility Comput. **9**, 211 (2018). https://doi.org/10.1504/IJGUC.2018.093976

24. Joshi, A., Kale, S., Chandel, S., Pal, D.K.: Likert scale: explored and explained. Br. J. Appl. Sci. Technol. **7**(4), 396 (2015)

25. Kleinginna, P.R., Kleinginna, A.M.: A categorized list of emotion definitions, with suggestions for a consensual definition. Motivat. Emotion **5**(4), 345–379 (1981)

26. Lane, A., Terry, P., Fogarty, G.: Construct Validity of the Profile of Mood States (2007)

27. Lang, P.J., Greenwald, M.K., Bradley, M.M., Hamm, A.O.: Looking at pictures: affective, facial, visceral, and behavioral reactions. Psychophysiology **30**(3), 261–273 (1993)

28. Lopes, J.D.L., Nogueira-Martins, L.A., Andrade, A.L.D., Barros, A.L.B.L.D.: Escala de diferencial semmântico para avaliação da percepção de pacientes hospitalizados frente ao banho. Acta Paul. Enfermag. **24**, 815–820 (2011). http://www. scielo.br/scielo.php?script=sci_arttext&pid=S0103-21002011000600015&nrm=iso

29. Lovibond, P.F., Lovibond, S.H.: The structure of negative emotional states: comparison of the depression anxiety stress scales (DASS) with the beck depression and anxiety inventories. Behav. Res. Therapy **33**(3), 335–343 (1995)

30. Maffei, A., Vencato, V., Angrilli, A.: Sex differences in emotional evaluation of film clips: interaction with five high arousal emotional categories. PLOS ONE 10(12), 1–13 (2016). https://doi.org/10.1371/journal.pone.0145562

31. Martinez, M., et al.: Emotion detection deficits and decreased empathy in patients with Alzheimer's disease and Parkinson's disease affect caregiver mood and burden. Front. Aging Neurosci. **10** (2018). https://doi.org/10.3389/fnagi.2018.00120

32. Melnyk, B., Kelly, S., Lusk, P.: Outcomes and feasibility of a manualized cognitive-behavioral skills building intervention: group cope for depressed and anxious adolescents in school settings. J. Child Adolesc. Psychiat. Nurs. Assoc. Child Adolesc. Psychiatr. Nurses, Inc. **27** (2013). https://doi.org/10.1111/jcap.12058

33. Miśkiewicz, H., Antoszewski, B., Iljin, A.: Personality traits and decision on breast reconstruction in women after mastectomy. Polish J. Surg. **88**, 209–214 (2016)

34. Müller, F., Röhr, S., Reininghaus, U., Riedel-Heller, S.G.: Social isolation and loneliness during covid-19 lockdown: associations with depressive symptoms in the German old-age population. Int. J. Environ. Res. Publ. Health **18**(7) (2021). https://doi.org/10.3390/ijerph18073615

35. Önder, I.: Association of happiness with morningness - eveningness preference, sleep-related variables and academic performance in university students. Biol. Rhythm Res. (2020). https://doi.org/10.1080/09291016.2020.1848266

36. Norman, D., Nielsen, J.: The Definition of User Experience (UX) (2006). https://www.nngroup.com/articles/definition-user-experience/. Accessed 2 Feb 2021

37. Oh, Y.A., Kim, S.O., Park, S.A.: Real foliage plants as visual stimuli to improve concentration and attention in elementary students. Int. J. Environ. Res. Publ. Health **16**, 796 (2019). https://doi.org/10.3390/ijerph16050796

38. Osgood, C.E., Suci, G.J., Tannenbaum, P.H.: The Measurement of Meaning, No. 47. University of Illinois Press (1957)

39. Park, H.Y., Chong, H.J.: A comparative study of the perception of music emotion between adults with and without visual impairment. Psychol. Music **47**(2), 225–240 (2019). https://doi.org/10.1177/0305735617745148

40. Park, S.A., Song, C., Oh, Y.A., Miyazaki, Y., Son, K.C.: Comparison of physiological and psychological relaxation using measurements of heart rate variability, prefrontal cortex activity, and subjective indexes after completing tasks with and without foliage plants. Int. J. Environ. Res. Publ. Health **14**, 1087 (2017). https://doi.org/10.3390/ijerph14091087

41. Philpott, A.L., Andrews, S.C., Staios, M., Churchyard, A., Fisher, F.: Emotion evaluation and social inference impairments in Huntington's disease. J. Huntington's Dis. **5**(2), 175–183 (2016)

42. Racine, S.: Emotional ratings of high- and low-calorie food are differentially associated with cognitive restraint and dietary restriction. Appetite **121** (2017). https://doi.org/10.1016/j.appet.2017.11.104

43. Russell, D., Peplau, L., Cutrona, C.: The revised UCLA loneliness scale: concurrent and discriminate validity evidence. J. Personal. Soc. Psychol. **39**, 472–480 (1980). https://doi.org/10.1037/0022-3514.39.3.472

44. Russell, J.: A circumplex model of affect. J. Personal. Soc. Psychol. **39**, 1161–1178 (1980). https://doi.org/10.1037/h0077714

45. Scherer, K.R.: Appraisal considered as a process of multilevel sequential checking. Apprais. Process. Emot. Theory Methods Res. **92**(120), 57 (2001)

46. Scherer, K.R.: What are emotions? and how can they be measured? Soc. Sci. Inf. **44**(4), 695–729 (2005). https://doi.org/10.1177/0539018405058216

47. Sears, A., Jacko, J.A.: Human-Computer Interaction Fundamentals. CRC Press (2009)

48. Shibata, S., Ohba, K., Inooka, N.: Emotional evaluation of human arm motion models. In: Proceedings of 1993 2nd IEEE International Workshop on Robot and Human Communication, pp. 346–351 (1993)

49. Somaini, L., et al.: Psychobiological responses to unpleasant emotions in cannabis users. Eur. Archiv. Psychiat. Clin. Neurosci. **262**, 47–57 (2011). https://doi.org/10.1007/s00406-011-0223-5

50. Spielberger, C.D., Gonzalez-Reigosa, F., Martinez-Urrutia, A., Natalicio, L.F., Natalicio, D.S.: The state-trait anxiety inventory. Rev. Interamer. Psicolog./Interamer. J. Psychol. **5**(3 & 4) (1971)

51. St. Jacques, P.L., Grady, C., Davidson, P.S., Chow, T.W.: Emotional evaluation and memory in behavioral variant frontotemporal dementia. Neurocase **21**(4), 429–437 (2015)

52. Steer, R.A., Kumar, G., Beck, J.S., Beck, A.T.: Evidence for the construct validities of the beck youth inventories with child psychiatric outpatients. Psychol. Rep. **89**(3), 559–565 (2001)

53. Stern, A.F.: The hospital anxiety and depression scale. Occup. Med. **64**(5), 393–394 (2014). https://doi.org/10.1093/occmed/kqu024

54. Tempesta, D., et al.: Lack of sleep affects the evaluation of emotional stimuli. Brain Res. Bullet. **82**, 104–108 (2010). https://doi.org/10.1016/j.brainresbull.2010.01.014

55. Tools, P.: Psychological assessment tools for mental health (2021). https://www.psychologytools.com/download-scales-and-measures/. Accessed 2 Feb 2021

56. Vuoskoski, J.K., Eerola, T.: The role of mood and personality in the perception of emotions represented by music. Cortex **47**(9), 1099–1106 (2011). https://doi.org/10.1016/j.cortex.2011.04.011

57. Wood, S., Moreau, C.: From fear to loathing? how emotion influence the evaluation and early use of innovations. J. Market. **70**, 44–57 (2006). https://doi.org/10.1509/jmkg.70.3.44

58. Xavier, R., Neris, V.: A hybrid evaluation approach for the emotional state of information systems users. In: Proceedings of the 14th International Conference on Enterprise Information Systems (ICEIS 2012), vol. 3, pp. 45–53 (2012)

59. Yesavage, J.A., et al.: Development and validation of a geriatric depression screening scale: a preliminary report. J. Psychiat. Res. **17**(1), 37–49 (1982)

60. Young, P.T.: Emotion in man and animal; its nature and relation to attitude and motive (1943)

# Developing a Framework for Trustworthy AI-Supported Knowledge Management in the Governance of Risk and Change

Rebecca Vining[1]([✉]) [iD], Nick McDonald[1], Lucy McKenna[2] [iD], Marie E. Ward[1,3] [iD], Brian Doyle[1,4] [iD], Junli Liang[2], Julio Hernandez[2] [iD], John Guilfoyle[4], Arwa Shuhaiber[5], Una Geary[3], Mary Fogarty[3], and Rob Brennan[2] [iD]

[1] Centre for Innovative Human Systems, School of Psychology, Trinity College, The University of Dublin, Dublin 02 PN40, Ireland
rvining@tcd.ie
[2] ADAPT Centre, School of Computing, Dublin City University, Dublin 09 PX21, Ireland
[3] Quality and Safety Improvement Directorate, St James's Hospital Dublin, Dublin 08 NHY1, Ireland
[4] Health and Safety Unit, Dublin Fire Brigade, Dublin 02 RY99, Ireland
[5] Beacon Renal, Sandyford Business Park, Dublin 18 TH56, Ireland

**Abstract.** This paper proposes a framework for developing a trustworthy artificial intelligence (AI) supported knowledge management system (KMS) by integrating existing approaches to trustworthy AI, trust in data, and trust in organisations. We argue that improvement in three core dimensions (data governance, validation of evidence, and reciprocal obligation to act) will lead to the development of trust in the three domains of the data, the AI technology, and the organisation. The framework was informed by a case study implementing the Access-Risk-Knowledge (ARK) platform for mindful risk governance across three collaborating healthcare organisations. Subsequently, the framework was applied within each organisation with the aim of measuring trust to this point and generating objectives for future ARK platform development. The resulting discussion of ARK and the framework has implications for the development of KMSs, the development of trustworthy AI, and the management of risk and change in complex socio-technical systems.

**Keywords:** Access-Risk-Knowledge (ARK) · Socio-technical systems analysis · Risk governance · Artificial intelligence · Trust

## 1 Introduction

Safety regulation increasingly calls for a strategy that goes beyond compliance to being proactive, predictive, and preventive [1]. Under such a strategy, effective organisational risk governance relies on evidence-based knowledge, which can be leveraged in support of actions to mitigate risk. A sophisticated knowledge management system (KMS) is needed to oversee this mechanism. While many organisations, particularly in high-risk domains, are generating large amounts of data from diverse sources, the challenge for

M. Kurosu et al. (Eds.): HCII 2022, LNCS 13516, pp. 318–333, 2022.
https://doi.org/10.1007/978-3-031-17615-9_22

risk and safety management is to base operational and strategic decision-making on a coherent, integrated body of data and evidence (knowledge). Our work develops such a system through the case study of deploying an artificial-intelligence (AI)-based software platform that manages risk among three healthcare organisations. There is an ethical obligation to build trustworthiness into AI technology [2], but this obligation must be extended to incorporate issues of trustworthiness in complex socio-technical systems (STS). This paper explores how this extension can be achieved, integrating strategies for building trust in AI and in organisations in order to develop a framework for trustworthy AI-supported knowledge management. This suggests two research questions:

1. What are the components of a trustworthy AI-supported KMS?
2. How can these components be achieved in the development and deployment of a software platform for mindful risk governance?

The Access-Risk-Knowledge (ARK) Platform [3] is a software platform that supports the management of risk and change in complex operational systems. The platform deploys the Cube framework for socio-technical systems analysis (STSA) [4–8] along with a risk register, an evidence service, risk mitigation project management tools, analytics, and reports. Risk assessments can be imported from an existing risk register or completed within the platform and are then linked to safety projects. These features enable what we define as mindful governance of risk by leveraging human- and machine-based knowledge to analyse causal relationships. The result of a completed ARK project is an evidence-based analysis of a risk mitigation project throughout the full project management cycle. Projects can also be interlinked in order to synthesise results or to compare results, evidence, or domains. Results can be disseminated to the organisation using the customisable report generation feature.

ARK-Virus is a collaborative project between an academic research team from both the computer science and organisational psychology disciplines, as well as a Community of Practice (CoP) involving quality and safety staff from a 1000-bed urban academic teaching hospital, medical staff from a private renal dialysis service, and management staff from a large urban fire and emergency medical services (EMS) provider. The aim of the project is to develop the ARK platform via a use case relating to infection prevention and control (IPC) in each of the three participating organisations. There are four ARK platform development trials planned; at the time of writing, the project is between the third and fourth of these. A fuller description of each trial and the research activities involved is outlined in a previous paper [7]; the focus of this paper is to develop a framework for trustworthy AI-supported knowledge management, which spans all four of the trials.

In earlier stages of ARK-Virus, our research focused on issues relating to usability, but trust has become increasingly important. Discussions with users centred around a key set of issues: how to make sense of the data, how to do something useful with it, and how to generate a sound basis for engaging others within the organisation. Trust in the platform's ability to deliver this may be a key mechanism for understanding the relationships between the ARK platform, knowledge, users, and the organisation. In this paper, we draw upon the literature on trust in organisations, AI technology, and data, and upon several decades of research on risk in aviation and healthcare, to outline a framework for the development of a trustworthy KMS that is supported by AI technologies. As the ARK-virus project continues, we aim to apply this framework so that trust can be built into future platform development stages.

Our work is situated at the intersection of technology and people, and there is a clear link between trust in these two domains. Building trustworthy AI involves the full organisational context of implementation, while building trust in the organisation similarly requires taking into account the role of technology supported knowledge as evidence as a rational basis for action. The convergence of knowledge between technology and people inevitably means that technology-based knowledge is a critical resource for human decision-making, as it can generate leverage to address complex problems. Risk and safety management must be based on data and evidence that is integrated into operational decision making. As trust is core to the management of safety and the implementation of change, a unified view of trust that bridges risk management and trust in AI is needed.

Our model of trust incorporates existing theories of organisational trust [9, 10], governance of risk [11], and data governance [12]. Drawing upon several decades of research, dialogue with collaborators, and the literature, three core dimensions of trust were identified: data governance, validation of evidence, and reciprocal obligation to act. By supporting improvements in these three dimensions, trust is improved at the level of trust in the organisation [10, 13], trust in the AI technology [2], and trust in the data [14]. The framework is outlined in Fig. 1.

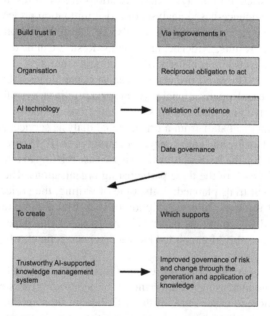

**Fig. 1.** Framework for developing a trustworthy AI-supported KMS for risk governance.

The ARK platform instantiates this model to support human-directed decision-making and implementation as part of an accountable governance framework. **Data governance** is at the core of ARK's services. **Validation of evidence** is the core activity of STSA Cube analysis, deploying the flexible schemata of Knowledge Graphs to bring together diverse data sources to support analysis, decision-making and project management by quality and safety experts. **The reciprocal obligation to act** is engendered by the mindful governance of a risk project from problem state to verified outcome.

In this paper, five stages are outlined in the development of trust in such a system. The trust model is used to analyse and assess the ARK platform's deployment within each collaborating organisation. Over the course of the previous ARK-Virus trials, trust has been developed through a variety of strategies in each organisation. Using the model of trust as an explanatory concept in this way provides a set of objectives for future development of the project. This suggests the possibility of a capability maturity model (CMM) to provide guidance in development of trustworthy governance of system risk based on verifiable outcomes to demonstrate the effective mitigation of system risk.

## 2   A Framework for Trustworthy AI-Supported Knowledge Management

Trust has been defined in the literature on trustworthy AI as "(1) a set of specific beliefs dealing with benevolence, competence, integrity, and predictability (trusting beliefs); (2) the willingness of one party to depend on another in a risky situation (trusting intention); or (3) the combination of these elements" [15]. The European Union Ethical Principles for Trustworthy AI [2] outline a set of seven requirements for trustworthiness; our work supports and extends these principles by integrating trustworthy AI, trust in data, and trust in organisations.

Mollering offers a model that helps us build an understanding of the problems with trust relating to our work [9]. Trust is defined as a strategy to cope with the complexity, uncertainty, and risk in the world at large; the necessity to assume a level of certainty projected to the future is based on a combination of reason, routine, and reflexivity. Keymolen applies this model to analyse the relation between trust in other individuals, trust in an organisation and trust in technology [16]. Ward, through a series of case studies in an aviation organisation, illustrates the dynamic nature of the factors that combine to develop trust in an organisational context: understanding and sharing common goals; open communication of information and knowledge; building relationships in resolving conflicts in the process of work; together reviewing and adjusting work-as-imagined based on how work actually happens; it also implies a belief in the future and establishes the basis for future action [10].

The three components of Mollering's model provide a powerful framework to analyse the nature of trust in a data-rich organisational system that is dedicated to managing risk (achieving certain outcomes) through the deployment of diverse dedicated roles and relationships. Figure 2 illustrates the connections between that model and the trust dimensions identified in our work.

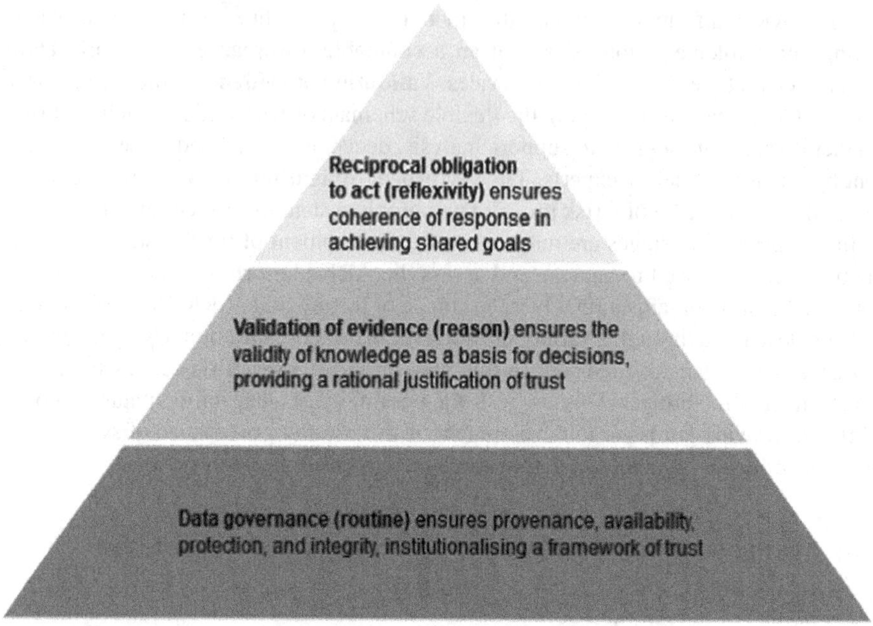

**Fig. 2.**  Mollering's triad and the core trust dimensions.

At a basic level there are three objects of a trusting relationship (trust domains):

- Trust in the data itself.
- Trust in the processing or transformation of data into usable information and knowledge (Trustworthy AI).
- Trust in the sharing of knowledge with colleagues and building trusting relationships, leading in turn to trust in the organisational processes that deploy and use that information and knowledge.

Trustworthy data governance ensures high-quality data and efficient, effective use of the data, thus leading to more meaningful and trustworthy evidence. Validation of that evidence in turn links data governance to reciprocal obligation to act by linking cause to effect. In turn, the obligation to act drives a need for continued collection of high-quality, trustworthy data. What results is a cyclical pathway driving continuous improvement of trust in the KMS.

Table 1 illustrates from a theoretical perspective how each dimension (data governance, validation of evidence and obligation to act) builds trust in each domain (data, AI technology, organisation), explaining the key mechanism by which improvements in the core dimensions will result in the development of trust in each domain. Each column in Table 1 represents the impacts of improvements in that dimension on each of the three trust domains (i.e., the column labelled 'Data Governance' describes how good data governance improves trust in data, trust in AI technology, and trust in the organisation).

The row labelled 'AI Technology' draws directly on the requirements set forward in the European Union Ethical Principles [2].

**Table 1.** Impacts of core dimensions on trust domains

| Domain | Data governance | Validation of evidence | Reciprocal obligation |
|---|---|---|---|
| Data | Ensures data quality and efficient/effective use | Generates trust-related metadata and trustworthy data as an outcome of cause and effect | Action based on data validates the data based on action outcomes - if the outcome works, it increases the confidence in the data |
| AI Tech | Supports human agency and oversight, privacy and data governance, transparency, accountability, diversity and fairness, and technical robustness and safety | Ensures human agency and oversight, transparency, diversity and fairness, societal and environmental wellbeing, and technical robustness and safety | Sustains human agency and oversight, accountability |
| Organisation | Leads organisational decisions to be data-driven and ensures data decisions are aligned with organisational goals | Ensures that data-driven decisions are grounded in causal relations | Sustains coherent response throughout the project cycle, including stakeholder feedback |

# 3 The ARK (Access-Risk-Knowledge) Platform and Trust

ARK (Fig. 3) is a software platform that builds and maintains a Resource Description Framework (RDF)-based unified knowledge graph [17] of risks and projects to link available datasets on practices, risks, and evidence. This bridges traditional qualitative risk evidence and quantitative operational or analytics data, which in turn makes large-scale evidence collection and risk analysis more tractable. Through ARK, human-oriented quantitative risk information is transformed into structured, machine-readable data suitable for automated analysis, querying, and reasoning. A privacy by design approach is taken and data governance principles are followed to ensure support for evidence linkage, classification, and search. The ARK platform is designed to support human-directed decision-making and implementation as part of an accountable governance framework. Data governance, data protection and confidentiality are key features of the design. Knowledge graphs are a natural way to bring together such diverse data sources due to their flexible schemata and through use of uplift to common ontologies, ontology alignment techniques, Natural Language Processing (NLP)-based knowledge extraction and metadata-based integration, e.g., data catalogues.

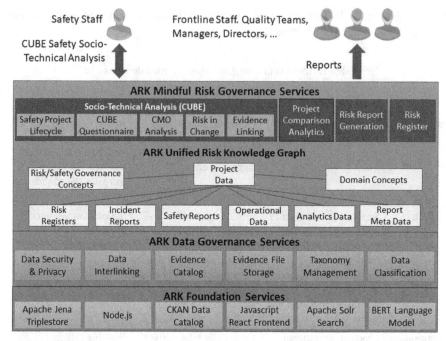

**Fig. 3.** The ARK platform risk governance services, risk knowledge graph, data governance services, and foundation services.

ARK supports the development of trust via the key pathway of leveraging data to create knowledge in support of action by embedding the trust dimensions as described below.

**Data governance** is at the core of ARK's services since it supports Khatri and Brown's data governance decision domains of data principles, data quality, lifecycle, metadata, and access [18] to manage projects, evidence, and risk. The Comprehensive Knowledge Archive Network (CKAN) data catalogue is used to build the ARK Evidence Service. This enables collecting and tracking of extensive metadata on all evidence, relating to provenance, verifiability, reputation, and licensing. Within the Cube knowledge graph, World Wide Web Consortium (W3C) standards for provenance, classification, identity and access control [19] have been used to capture this metadata on all data entities within the graph and a flexible policy-driven, General Data Protection Regulation (GDPR) enabled, context-aware access control system has been implemented to enable federated data sharing within and between organisations [20].

**Validation of evidence** is the core activity of STSA, where quality and safety experts use ARK to perform a structured analysis of risks and safety projects linking them to a wider range of data sources to support synthesis (with operational data) to give evidence-based assessment of risk and create new knowledge via that synthesis. The structured user interface of ARK exposes multiple views of an underlying ontology that unifies the analysis and enables the combination of traditional qualitative textual analysis fields with structured data in the form of evidence datasets, risk, and domain classification taxonomies. A natural language processing component based on the BERT language model [21] suggests appropriate taxonomy terms and these are approved by the human expert. Uploading of new evidence (as opposed to evidence linking) is an access-controlled activity and only users with sufficient permissions can do this, to facilitate manual validation of evidence prior to upload.

**The reciprocal obligation to act** is made explicit in numerous parts of the ARK platform. Firstly, the platform is arranged around the sequence of project stages through verification of the outcome, which gives information about the outcome as well as how the entire sequence works. The Cube summary, project analysis, reporting and synthesis interfaces all contribute to exposing the importance of the problem, the effectiveness of the solution and the viability of the pathway that underlie the obligation to act. Finally, the use of knowledge graphs and feature for linking multiple projects in hierarchies or more general graphs enable a development of a new level of organisational knowledge, facilitating innovative meta-projects rather than reinforcing what's already known. This understanding is leveraged for effective action, responsibility for which can be distributed explicitly to individuals within the organisation.

## 4   Stages in the Acquisition of Trust

Analysing progress in the three core dimensions provides an enriched understanding of the evolution of trust in ARK-Virus. Understanding the dimensions and the interactions between them develops trust into an explanatory concept, which can be used to inform a set of development objectives. In Table 2 we have outlined five stages in the acquisition of trust, from neophyte to multiple organisations. In the upcoming phase of the ARK-Virus project, the goal is for each organisation to progress up a stage: Organisation 1 from single projects to multiple; Organisation 2 from neophyte to intermediate; and Organisation 3 from intermediate to single projects. This table offers a way of measuring where each organisation is in the trust development process, which will be useful as a point of comparison in the future and support us in determining the key issues to be addressed at that point in time.

**Table 2.** Stages in the acquisition of trust

| Stage | Data governance | Evidence validation | Reciprocal obligation |
| --- | --- | --- | --- |
| 1. Neophyte | Resolve issues of access and privacy | Plausible interpretation and evidence gathering | Initial individual use. Potential for collaboration |
| 2. Intermediate | Assemble and begin integrating relevant data sources | Gathers evidence and performs effective analysis | Engages people in real projects that require collaboration |

*(continued)*

**Table 2.** (*continued*)

| Stage | Data governance | Evidence validation | Reciprocal obligation |
|---|---|---|---|
| 3. Single projects | Develop knowledge graphs to generate project-level knowledge. Catalogue data source provenance | Diverse evidence synthesised & validated as representing process & outcome | Embedded in tactical organisational processes that provide accountable action and outcome |
| 4. Multiple projects, organisational level | Link data at the level of multiple projects to further develop knowledge graphs and generate organisation-level knowledge. Assure data quality | Synthesis of evidence provides a basis for policy | Engage strategic & operational loops of knowledge lifecycle across & beyond organisation |
| 5. Multiple organisations, sector level | Fully developed private & public knowledge space, routine transformation of private into public | Evidence provides a basis for guidance, regulation or publication | Guidance feeds back into the evidence base |

# 5   Application of the Trust Model to a Community of Practice

In this exercise, we applied our model of trust to the ARK-Virus project within each of the three participating organisations, asking users to reflect on the ways in which trust had been developed to this point and the next steps for further development. The results of this exercise in each organisation are outlined in the subsections below.

Several commonalities emerged in terms of needs moving forward. Firstly, it was noted that many of the more salient issues for the CoP were related to data governance. For Organisation 1, this was the acquisition of data from different stakeholders within the organisation; for Organisation 2, data privacy and obtaining formal permissions to enter information into the platform; for Organisation 3, the resolution of data complexity and organising data from a large number of different sources. Secondly, there is a clear need across all three organisations to extend the user base to encompass the full range of relevant decision-makers. This expansion improves capacity in all three dimensions, but in particular the reciprocal obligation to act. Thirdly, there is a pragmatic need to gather and disseminate evidence showing that actions from ARK projects lead to good outcomes at the organisational level, thus increasing trust in all three dimensions.

## 5.1   Organisation 1

Organisation 1 developed a project examining personnel compliance with COVID-19 IPC risk management and control measures. At the onset, the organisational representatives hoped to collect data measuring personnel compliance in rest areas, as these were suspected to be a key source of staff-to-staff COVID-19 transmission. However, this was deemed unfeasible as there was a need to develop trust in the project among personnel before such data could be collected. Instead, data was drawn from what was available in terms of occupational health data, guidelines and control measures over time, impact of limited personnel availability on service provision, and implicit/explicit knowledge about the linkages between the evidence sources from the organisation's ARK-Virus project team. The ARK platform then enabled the project team to analyse a complex and intractable problem for a full project cycle (from problem to embedment). The structured approach to STSA helped frame the problem and identify possible solutions, which were transposed into an implementable operational solution. The platform was also utilised to effectively communicate and implement the solution and verify the efficacy of the solution. Further projects utilising the ARK platform within the organisation have been initiated, indicating the organisation's trust in the platform.

**Data Governance:** Data Protection (DPA) and Non-Disclosure (NDA) Agreements guaranteed a level of data protection that was acceptable to the organisation. However, access to more granular data remained restricted due to concerns about anonymity of personnel. While there were difficulties in acquiring granular data and evidence, the process of seeking this evidence for use on the platform resulted in the acquisition of knowledge from within the organisation which verified the efficacy of the implemented solution.

**Validation of Evidence:** Gathering of evidence was somewhat restricted due to privacy issues, the organisation's work practises, and the organisation's clinical environment. The evidence gathered was done so utilising a top-down/bottom-up approach, with stakeholders from various departments, including operations, health and safety, and logistics, gathering, interpreting, and validating the uploaded evidence.

**Reciprocal Obligation to Act:** Organisation 1 has a fairly strict hierarchical rank structure, with a promotional process that means senior managers have fulfilled operational roles, sometimes alongside personnel they now manage. This structure was felt to enhance the level of social trust across ranks in the organisation, contributing to a peer-driven environment where personnel are amenable to the idea of change based on that trust. Initially, there were three personnel from the organisation who engaged directly with the platform, from middle and senior management and health and safety. However, input was also sought from other areas of the organisation, including operations, resources allocation, health and safety, and senior management. To strengthen reciprocal obligation to act, there is a need to involve these stakeholders more formally, in particular by training more personnel as ARK users.

## 5.2  Organisation 2

Organisation 2 aimed to assess patient compliance with PPE measures upon arrival. Six months of data on patient compliance were collected by front desk staff, a timeframe which covered two different sets of PPE requirements. There were, however, significant issues with obtaining access to the data, with the DPA and NPA taking nearly a full year to complete. In the meantime, users from the organisation were able to fill out sample projects on the platform and participate fully in the other aspects of the project such as the CoP meetings and workshops. In Trial 3, the goal for Organisation 2 is to move from the first stage of trust to the second. The risk is currently being actively managed at the local level (clinical frontline), but having overcome data governance barriers, a thorough analysis of evidence will enable the organisation to strengthen its management of that risk.

**Data Governance:** Access to data was granted just one week prior to writing of this paper (the datasets remain within the organisation only, while analysis of the data is accessible to others within the ARK-Virus project). Trust in data governance as it relates purely to data has been heightened through the formalisation of data governance procedures via the DPA and NPA, but there is still much progress to be made in terms of data governance and trust in the AI technology and the organisation.

**Validation of Evidence:** The organisation is at the stage of moving from data collection to analysis and use of the data. Moving forward, the organisation is working to identify variables in the data and complete the STSA component of an ARK project, which will allow for further exploration and validation of the predictors and/or outcomes of PPE compliance.

**Reciprocal Obligation to Act:** At this stage, operational staff are the primary user group; an important development will be the engagement of a wider variety of users, particularly in more strategic or risk management roles.

### 5.3   Organisation 3

Early on in the project, it became apparent that a key issue for Organisation 3 was the vast amount of data being produced and reviewed, with no unified structure for tracking all of the data. Over 100 discrete performance indicators are currently monitored in relation to the actions taken for the prevention and control of healthcare-associated infections (PCHCAI), and the processes for capturing, reporting on, collating, and presenting the data can be fragmented and time consuming. As a result of the organisation's experiences completing an ARK project related to environment hygiene and the wider PCHCAI programme, the organisation conducted a data governance mapping exercise. PCHCAI metrics were mapped along dimensions of data governance including the purpose of the metric; type of metric; basis of metric (numerator and denominator); owner; reporting; tools or platforms used for gathering, analysing and reporting the data; whether it could be considered an outcome, process, structure or balancing measure; and the national and international benchmarks and regulatory basis of the data.

**Data Governance:** Progress was made in terms of data governance processes, addressing the issue of the large amount of data and how to turn it into a more manageable data catalogue that provides a clear rationale for management and use. What remains to be done is to expand and embed the data governance processes so that subsequent actions and outcomes can be obtained and measured. The fact that the platform created a strong rationale for compiling and auditing data is an argument in favour of understanding the entire data system prior to initiating a real-world project; in other words, to avoid prematurely structuring an evidence trail without first having agreement on the purpose of each of the metrics.

**Validation of Evidence:** The organisation is moving from the validation and use of individual data sets to the validation and use of knowledge, which will be undertaken by quality and safety improvement staff and PCHCAI programme contributors using the STSA components of the ARK platform.

**Reciprocal Obligation to Act:** To this point, work on this ARK trial has been situated in the core quality and safety improvement team, with some level of engagement via production of the stakeholder report in the previous trial. The results of this trial will strengthen this engagement, forming the basis for drawing additional stakeholders into a collaborative programme and widening the ARK platform user base. Building interpersonal trust within the local team is the first step to engaging a wider stakeholder group and building an organisational basis for trust (and subsequently organisational obligation to act).

### 5.4    Capability Maturity in Trust in AI and the Organisation

The idea that there are phases in the development of a trustworthy AI-supported KMS suggests the possibility of a CMM that would provide a framework for verifying progress through these phases and provide guidance in development and application. De Bruin, et al. discuss the development of CMMs and provide a relevant example of a Knowledge Management Capability Assessment metric with progressive stages in the sharing, managing, and improving of knowledge assets [22]. An example from safety management in aviation is the Civil Air Navigation Services Organisation (CANSO) model of excellence in safety management for Air Traffic Control Organisations [23]. For the development of the ARK platform, we need a hybrid combination that spans between the technology, the AI, and the organisation.

Table 3 outlines two phases in the development of the platform: Trials 1 and 2, and Trial 3. Trial 1 and 2 measurements were collected in the earlier phase of the project. Trial 3 trust measurements will be collected in the upcoming phase of the project, as will measurements on platform usability and effectiveness. The strategic requirements for achieving advancements in trust are outlined in the middle column, Trial 3 Strategy. Table 3 represents a synthesis of the first two tables and an initial attempt to define and measure progress at this point in ARK-Virus towards the development of a trustworthy AI-supported KMS.

**Table 3.** Trust-related measurements and development strategy

| Dimension | Trial 1 and 2 measurements | Trial 3 strategy | Trial 3 measurements |
|---|---|---|---|
| Data governance | ISO27001 Security Assessment | Security (advanced access control policies to enable federated sharing) GDPR compliance (privacy by design, compliance reporting, etc.) Privacy-aware data interlinking mechanisms | Trustworthy data metrics to measure provenance, verifiability, reputation, and licensing [14] |
| Validation of evidence | Develop and distribute stakeholder report on findings | Analyse and better illustrate quality of causal relations Validate sequence of activity and outcome Meta-analysis of multiple projects to support proposal of new guidance | Develop guidance material based on evidence Initiate new projects based on expectation of outcomes of value |
| Reciprocal obligation to act | Build internal user groups Propose credible solutions to the identified problem | Represent different user roles in platform Represent relationships between reports and their owners in platform Engage stakeholders within and outside of CoP organisations | Build set of expert users and widen user base Engagement with implementation of guidance material |

## 6   Discussion

In order to move the ARK platform along the pathway from development to implementation to embedment, it is crucial that the technology and the system it engenders are trusted by the participating user organisations. Operationally, the ARK platform is for management of risk and change, which involves analysing the issues to do with causal relationships, outcomes, and changing the outcomes. The key mechanism for changing outcomes is the leveraging of knowledge as evidence. A better understanding of this process can help explain the differential success of change projects, impacting at the level of the organisation, sector, and society.

The ARK-Virus project has been a strong stimulus to organise evidence in the participating organisations. Although so far that collection has not been highly sophisticated in terms of AI, and while there has not been the opportunity for in-depth AI supported analysis, there is confidence that the platform will deliver this in the future. The organisation of evidence is a necessary first step. In addition, this exercise showed that the first step is to build trust at the local level; trust is developed in stages, and overestimating the level of trust already achieved within an organisation should be avoided. Trust was built locally by enhancing relationships with working colleagues at the level of the research team, the CoP, and the user groups from each organisation.

Access to data presented key challenges in terms of project progress across the participating organisations. This highlights a need for updated data governance models that enable effective action, rather than solely protecting privacy, aligning with the work of Janssen, et al. [24]. Inter-organisational trust in data governance practices, in particular with regards to protecting anonymity of personnel, appears to play a role in securing access to data, though legal agreements are also necessary.

The ARK-Virus project is a work in progress. This exercise enabled us to develop a structured framework for examining the stages in development of the project and the ARK platform. Analysing trust has helped us to outline a plan for moving forward in the project in a way that supports the embedment of the platform in existing risk management processes within the participating organisations and led to the selection of key outcome measures relating to the development of trust, constituting the first step in developing a CMM.

## 7 Conclusions

In this exercise, we outlined a framework for developing a trustworthy AI-supported KMS. In the proposed model, three key dimensions (data governance, validation of evidence, and reciprocal obligation to act) contribute to improved trust in three domains (organisation, AI technology, and data). There are five stages in the development of trust, against which organisations can measure their progress. We then applied the framework to the ARK-Virus project, which deploys a risk management platform in three participating healthcare organisations. This application resulted in a set of objectives that, when achieved, will improve trust in each organisation, as well as a measurement strategy that can be used to track the development of trust. This suggests the possibility of a CMM to provide guidance in development of trustworthy governance of system risk based on verifiable outcomes to demonstrate the effective mitigation of system risk.

Over the course of the previous ARK-Virus trials, trust has been developed through a variety of strategies in each organisation, including participation in the CoP, active feedback loops, engagement of key stakeholders, comprehensive data protection agreements, and building a better understanding of the data. We aim to continue focusing on trust moving forward by measuring the level of trust and developing trial objectives that specifically support its development. There is currently a high level of trust in the platform and its future deployment, particularly in Organisation 1 as evidenced by their selection of the ARK to support additional projects in the coming months. However, there is room for improvement as well. The most salient issues identified were related to data governance, meaning a focus on this area in the coming months will be key. Core needs also included the expansion of the ARK platform user base and the production of a follow-up stakeholder report which consolidates the evidence for beneficial organisational outcomes as a result of ARK projects. These needs will be addressed in subsequent development trials.

Integration of a technology-based knowledge system has social implications, meaning that beyond trust in data or technology, the organisational dimensions of trust must be considered. At the same time, the role of knowledge and evidence is critical for developing trust in the organisation; it is not merely a question of social relationships or expectations. There is a need for frameworks guiding the development of trust in this holistic way. There is also a need to develop guiding principles for AI implementation that support and extend the European Union principles for ethical AI, in particular focusing on the organisational dimension having to do with implementation, action, and outcome. In this exercise, we have contributed to the resolution of this gap by operationalising Mollering's triad [9] to outline a framework for the development of trust in an AI-supported KMS. While our focus has been on a system that has formal structures for looking at risk and change, any complex STS would benefit from practical examination of a technology-based KMS in terms of trust.

**Acknowledgments.** This research was conducted with the financial support of Science Foundation Ireland under Grant Agreement No. 20/COV/8463 at the ADAPT SFI Research Centre at Dublin City University and Trinity College Dublin. This research was conducted with the financial support of Science Foundation Ireland at ADAPT, the SFI Research Centre for AI-Driven Digital Content Technology at DCU [13/RC/2106_P2]. For the purpose of Open Access, the author has applied CC BY public copyright licence to any Author Accepted Manuscript version arising from this submission.

# References

1. Hollnagel, E., Wears, R.L., Braithwaite, J.: From Safety-I to Safety-II: A White Paper. The Resilient Health Care Net. University of Southern Denmark, University of Florida, USA, and Macquarie University, Australia (2015)
2. European Commission High-Level Expert Group on Artificial Intelligence: Ethics Guidelines for Trustworthy Artificial Intelligence. Brussels, Belgium (2019)
3. Crotti Junior, A., Basereh, M., Abgaz, Y., Liang, J., Duda, N., McDonald, N., Brennan, R.: The ARK platform: enabling risk management through semantic web technologies. In: Proceedings of the 11th International Conference on Biomedical Ontologies, Bolzano, Italy (2020)
4. Ward, M., McDonald, N., Morrison, R., Gaynor, D., Nugent, T.: A performance improvement case study in aircraft maintenance and its implications for hazard identification. Ergonomics **53**(2), 247–267 (2010)
5. Ulfvengren, P., Corrigan, S.: Development and implementation of a safety management system in a lean airline. Cogn. Technol. Work **17**(2), 219–236 (2014). https://doi.org/10.1007/s10111-014-0297-8
6. Corrigan, S., et al.: Socio-technical exploration for reducing & mitigating the risk of retained foreign objects. Int. J. Environ. Res. Public Health **15**(4), 714 (2018)
7. McDonald, N., et al.: Evaluation of an access-risk-knowledge (ARK) platform for governance of risk and change in complex socio-technical systems. Int. J. Environ. Res. Public Health **18**(23), 12572 (2021)

8. Geary, U., Ward, M.E., Callan, V., McDonald, N., Corrigan, S.: A socio-technical systems analysis of the application of RFID-enabled technology to the transport of precious laboratory samples in a large acute teaching hospital. Appl. Ergon. **102**, 103759 (2022)

9. Möllering, G.: Trust: Reason, Routine Reflexivity. Elsevier, Amsterdam, Netherlands (2006)

10. Ward, M.: Contributions to human factors from three case studies in aircraft maintenance [Doctoral thesis]. Trinity College Dublin (2006)

11. McDonald, N., Callari, T.C., Baranzini, D., Mattei, F.: A mindful governance model for ultra-safe organisations. Saf. Sci. **120**, 753–763 (2019)

12. Brous, P., Janssen, M.: Trusted decision-making: data governance for creating trust in data science decision outcomes. Adm. Sci. **10**(4), 81 (2020)

13. Blomqvist, K., Stahle, P.: Building organizational trust. In: 16th Annual IMP Conference, Bath, U.K (2000)

14. Zaveri, A., Rula, A., Maurino, A., Pietrobon, R., Lehman, J., Auer, S.: Quality assessment for linked data: a survey. Semantic Web **7**(1), 63–93 (2016)

15. Siau, K., Wang, W.: Building trust in artificial intelligence, machine learning, and robotics. Cutter Bus. Technol. J. **31**, 47–53 (2018)

16. Keymolen, E.: Trust on the line: a philosophical exploration of trust in the networked era [Doctoral thesis]. Erasmus University Rotterdam (2016)

17. World Wide Web Consortium. RDF 1.1 Concepts and Abstract Syntax. In: Cyganiak, R., Woods, D., Lanthaler, M. (eds.) W3C Recommendation. https://www.w3.org/TR/rdf11-con cepts/. Accessed 3 Apr 2022

18. Khatri, V., Brown, C.V.: Designing data governance. Commun. ACM **53**(1), 148–152 (2010)

19. World Wide Web Consortium (W3C) Standards. https://www.w3.org/standards/. Accessed 27 Apr 2022

20. Hernandez, J., McKenna, L., Brennan, R.: TKID: A trusted integrated knowledge datas-pace for sensitive healthcare data sharing. In: IEEE 45th Annual Computers, Software, and Applications Conference, pp. 1855–1860 (2021)

21. Devlin, J., Chang, M.W., Lee, K., Toutanova, K.: Bert: Pretraining of deep bidirectional transformers for language understanding. https://arxiv.org/abs/1810.04805. Accessed 27 Apr 2022

22. de Bruin, T., Rosemann, M., Freeze, R., Kulkarni, U., Carey, W.: Understanding the main phases of developing a maturity assessment model. In: 16th Australasian Conference on Information Systems, Sydney, Australia (2005)

23. Civil Air Navigation Services Organisation: CANSO Standard of Excellence in Safety Management Systems. https://canso.org/publication/canso-standard-of-excellence-in-safety-man agement-systems/. Accessed 3 Apr 2022

24. Janssen, M., Brous, P., Estevez, E., Barbosa, L.D., Janowski, T.: Data governance: organizing data for trustworthy artificial intelligence. Gov. Inf. Q. **37**(3), 101493 (2020)

# User Experience Design and Evaluation Case Studies

# End-User Adoption of Cryptocurrency: A Literature Review

Saeed Abooleet[✉] and Xiaowen Fang

School of Computing, College of CDM, DePaul University, 243 S. Wabash Avenue, Chicago, IL 60604, USA
saboolee@depaul.edu, Xfang@cdm.depaul.edu

**Abstract.** The increasing presence of cryptocurrency has disrupted various areas such as financial, e-commerce, etc. This has attracted many scholars to investigate this technology, including its adoption. Yet, end-users adoption remains low despite numerous attempts to study the adoption. This paper conducts a systematic literature review of empirical studies on cryptocurrency adoption from individuals' perspectives, aiming to identify research gaps that need to be addressed. A total of 50 articles were collected and reviewed. We illustrate that the majority of papers are quantitative, and the most widely utilized theories are TAM and UTAUT. Most of the reviewed studies investigate the adoption without context. Trust is the most critical factor impacting cryptocurrency adoption. Several gaps in the current literature have been identified and discussed. Consequently, future research agendas are suggested.

**Keywords:** Cryptocurrency · Adoption · Bitcoin · Trust

## 1 Introduction

As of January 2022, the cryptocurrency market cap hit $1.52 trillion, where Bitcoin (BTC) leads, representing 40% of all cryptocurrencies, followed by Ether (ETH), 19% (Coinmarketcap[1]). The number of cryptocurrencies has grown exponentially to reach 6,000 cryptocurrencies in 2022. Cryptocurrency is a digital currency that relies on sophisticated encryption techniques that enable financial transactions [1]. It is estimated that there are 101 million unique cryptocurrency users worldwide in 2020 [2]. Glaser et al. [3] argue that the uses of cryptocurrencies take two forms: a speculative digital asset and a currency. Hileman and Rauchs [4] introduce four categories for cryptocurrency uses: investment, medium of exchange, payment rail, and non-monetary use cases (e.g., Ethereum smart contracts).

Only 7.6% of the world's population uses cryptocurrencies [5]. Only 1.4% of Americans own at least one cryptocurrency [6]. Compared to the volume of transactions and the number of cryptocurrencies, and despite numerous adoption studies, it is evident that the adoption rate is still low. Indeed, cryptocurrency's long survival is dependent on the

---

[1] https://coinmarketcap.com/.

M. Kurosu et al. (Eds.): HCII 2022, LNCS 13516, pp. 337–349, 2022.
https://doi.org/10.1007/978-3-031-17615-9_23

mass adoption that leads to leveraging its full potential. To encourage more adoption, it is necessary to examine previous adoption research to identify possible research gaps.

Al-Amri et al. [7] have conducted a systematic literature review reviewing 25 cryptocurrency adoption papers, attempting to address the gaps in the field. They emphasize several ones, including the lack of studies that use adoption theories and models, the small sample size, the rarity of end-user adoption research and the shortage of mixed-method papers. Nevertheless, the number of empirical studies has more than doubled since then, emphasizing the need for further review. Also, their work lacks empirical focus in general and on end-user specifically, whereas this research addresses both. Besides, this paper aims to determine the most potent factors influencing end-user adoption decisions of cryptocurrency. Finally, this review seeks to address the gaps in the current literature and suggest research agenda for future work on cryptocurrency adoption.

Therefore, this paper conducts a systematic literature review of studies investigating cryptocurrency adoption from individuals' perspectives. We attempt to answer three research questions.

- R1: What models and theories are utilized in previous cryptocurrency adoption studies, and what factors are referenced the most?;
- R2: What are the contexts of these studies?;
- R3: What are the current research gaps, and how can future research address them?

The rest of the paper is structured as follows: Cryptocurrency Background is presented next, followed by the research Methodology section. Thirdly, the Result section is introduced, where we categorize the reviewed papers and highlight the most vital factor of cryptocurrency adoption, Trust. Next, the Discussion section evaluates the findings. Finally, we end with the Conclusion and Future Research Agenda.

## 2   Cryptocurrency Background

Cryptocurrencies are defined as "digital assets designed to work as media of exchange using cryptography to secure the transactions and control the creation of additional units of the currency" [8]. Nakamoto [9], the creator of the first cryptocurrency (Bitcoin), asserts that there should be an electronic system that relies on cryptographic proof rather than trust. Individuals can transfer money directly without the need for a central authority. The underlying technology of cryptocurrency is blockchain. Blockchain is a tamper-evident and tamper-resistant distributed ledger that is usually decentralized [10]. Blockchain is defined as a digital, distributed transaction ledger, with identical copies maintained on multiple computer systems controlled by different entities" [11]. Each block has a block header containing metadata and block data comprising a set of transactions. The header of each block, except for the very first one (i.e., the genesis block), contains a hash that links it to the previous block [10]. Cryptographic techniques enforce the rules of the network that prevent tampering and equivocation of data [12]. As new blocks are added, the previous blocks become near impossible to alter. New blocks are replicated across copies of the ledger within the network, and any conflicts are resolved automatically using established rules (i.e., consensus mechanism). Nodes in the network aim to reach a consensus regarding the following block to append utilizing a consensus protocol. Such a protocol is the core of the blockchain, as it ultimately ensures decentralized governance, quorum, performance, authentication, integrity, nonrepudiation, and byzantine fault tolerance [13].

## 3  Methodology

We followed Webster and Watson's [14] recommendations. First, we defined the scope, which is to include articles that empirically investigated the factors influencing end-user adoption of cryptocurrency. Following this scope, we identified the search keywords: Cryptocurrency OR Bitcoin AND Adoption OR Acceptance OR Use. Any combination of these keywords should be in at least one of these places: the paper's title, abstract, or keywords. Had we set no such boundaries, the first round of collected studies would have consisted of unmanageable returns (e.g., searching for "bitcoin" and "adoption" in ABI Inform = 1,290 results, excluding non-scholarly returns). Next, we searched ACM, IEEE Xplore, ABI Inform, AIS library, and Science Direct databases. We utilized Google Scholar as a complementary source to lookup papers referenced in any article from the aforementioned databases. By reading the title and abstract of the returned results, we ended up with a total of 80 papers. The inclusion criteria that these 80 papers should meet to be reviewed include: they should be written in English, have empirical results, and investigate cryptocurrency from individuals' perspectives. The final round of inspection resulted in excluding four papers that did not collect data, one non-English paper, and 25 papers that were not empirical nor from the end-user perspective. Searching was concluded on Oct 26, 2021.

## 4  Results

A total of 50 papers have investigated the factors impacting end-users adoption of cryptocurrency. Table 1 shows an overview of these studies based on their types (qualitative, quantitative, and mixed-method), the theory utilized, and finally, their contexts. It is illustrated that most papers are quantitative, 40 papers, whereas the most widely utilized theory is the technology acceptance model (TAM), followed by the unified theory of acceptance and use of technology (UTAUT). Most of these papers explore the adoption without context, where participants are inquired about the general use of cryptocurrency. However, cryptocurrency as a form of money or payment system (9 papers), as an investment tool (3 papers), and finally for gaming purposes (1 paper) represent the contexts that some of the reviewed papers utilized. Across all articles, trust is the most referenced factor affecting cryptocurrency adoption across all articles, followed by perceived usefulness, facilitating conditions, ease of use, and performance expectancy. Trust has been identified in 17 papers where it has been operationalized differently, unidimensional or multidimensional. The Trust as Main Contributor subsection below elaborates more.

Review papers should be concept-centric [14]; thus, we classify the studies collected based on their research methodology, qualitative, quantitative, and mixed-method. Then, we further elaborate on these classifications by focusing on the adoption theory or model used. These classifications are further discussed next.

**Table 1.** Overview of the reviewed papers

| Type | Qualitative | | Quantitative | | | | Mixed studies |
|---|---|---|---|---|---|---|---|
| #studies | 6 | | 40 | | | | 4 |
| Theory | TAM | UTAUT | TPB | DOI | No Theory used | TRA | TCE; SST; ECT; SNSP; TRI; Utility Theory; Hofstede's[a] |
| #studies[b] | 20 | 13 | 9 | 7 | 5 | 2 | 1 |
| Context | No context (i.e., general use) | | As a form of money or payment system | | As an investment tool | | For gaming purposes |
| # studies | 37 | | 9 | | 3 | | 1 |

[a]Each of these theories once.

[b]Some papers used more than one theory, so the total of papers exceeds 50.

TPB = Theory of planned behavior; DOI = Diffusion of innovation theory; TRA = Theory of reasoned actions; TCE = Transaction cost economics; SST = Social support theory; ECT = Expectation confirmation theory; SNSP = Social network self-protection model; TRI = Technology readiness index.

## 4.1 Qualitative Studies

Although research is scarce in qualitative studies (i.e., six papers), researchers vary in employing adoption and acceptance theories. The DOI [15] is the most referred to theory [16–18], where Spenkelink [18] is among the first studies that look at Bitcoin adoption using DOI through the lens of technical aspects. She identifies three main pillars for future mass adoption; ease of use, price stability, and improved governance. The TAM [19] is also adopted in this research venue. Perceived ease of use and usefulness have been identified as the main drivers for using cryptocurrency [20]. Other researchers highlight ideological motivations such as engaging in a monetary revolution and financial inclusion in addition to pure financial gains, while others emphasize users' technological curiosity [17, 21, 22].

## 4.2 Quantitative Studies

The majority of research is quantitative; 40 studies. Unsurprisingly, the TAM model is utilized the most, followed by UTAUT. Hence, perceived ease of use, perceived usefulness, facilitating conditions, effort expectancy, and performance expectancy are among the factors explaining the adoption [23–26]. Yet, the most dominant factor is trust, which affects the adoption decision in ten studies within different contexts. For instance, Mendoza-Tello et al. [27] explore the role of social media in increasing trust and intention to adopt cryptocurrency while making electronic payments. They conclude that trust is the second direct impacting adoption intention. Also, Abbasi et al. [23] add trust to the UTAUT factors to predict cryptocurrency adoption and conclude that it has a significant direct effect. Other researchers suggest that regulatory support and experience increase users' trust in cryptocurrency, positively impacting their attitude to use it [28].

Moreover, Gagarina et al. [29] argue that distrust of social institutions is directly linked to young people's intentions to use cryptocurrency. Quantitative studies reviewed reveal many other attributes linked to cryptocurrency adoption, including compatibility, awareness, perceived enjoyment, subjective norms, etc. The wide range of factors is mainly attributed to the different adoption theories. Table 2 shows the complete list of papers and their main findings.

**Table 2.** Summary of quantitative research[a]

| Paper | Theory | Main findings |
|---|---|---|
| [24, 27, 30–43] | TAM | Perceived benefits; perceived usefulness; trust; perceived ease of use; social influence; security; social commerce; awareness |
| [23, 25, 26, 28, 34, 44–50] | UTAUT | Trust; price value; effort expectancy; performance expectancy; facilitating conditions; social influence; behavioral intention; hedonic motivations; security; regulations |
| [1, 28, 33, 37, 42, 51–53] | TPB | Trust; regulations; social media; attitude; perceived behavioral control; social norms |
| [33, 53–55] | DOI | Relative advantage; compatibility; anxiety; trialability |
| [29, 56–58] | NA (No theory used) | Distrust in social institutions; perceived value; perceived self-efficacy |
| [43, 59] | TRI | Optimism; innovativeness |
| [24, 27, 37, 53, 60, 61] | TCE; SST; ECT; SNSP; TRA; Hofstede's Model | Perceived benefits; social commerce; trust; enjoyment; satisfaction; social norms; spatial distance; social distance; hypothetical distance |

[a]Same citations in different rows means papers utilize multiple theories at once.

### 4.3 Mixed Method Studies

The final classification is the mixed-method studies—four papers incorporated both qualitative and quantitative methods while exploring cryptocurrency adoption [62–65].

These studies incorporate the TAM and UTAUT models either in whole or in combination with other models emphasizing factors such as perceived usefulness, perceived ease of use, facilitating conditions, and performance expectancy. For instance, Walton and Johnston [62] conclude that perceived benefit, attitude, and behavioral control are the strongest direct predictors of adoption, while perceived usefulness and trust risk have the highest indirect impact. One research employs utility theory in conjunction with UTAUT [65], where researchers interview cryptocurrency users and non-users to identify a set of positive utilities (i.e., benefits) such as perceived anonymity and negative utilities (i.e., risks) such as lack of regulations that are associated with using Bitcoin. Participants also are asked to identify the social factors affecting bitcoin adoption. Then, they use the information from these interviews to conduct their quantitative study. They conclude that network effect, regulation, attitude, self-efficacy, and innovativeness are the strongest predictors of adoption.

### 4.4 Trust as Main Contributor

Our review concludes that trust is the most potent factor that impacts cryptocurrency adoption. Out of all papers, 17 studies have proved trust significance. Scholars differ in their conceptualizations of trust. Most studies treat it as a unidimensional construct (e.g., [54, 62, 64]) while others present it as multidimensional. For instance, Voskobojnikov et al. [66] follow Gefen et al. [67] conceptualization of institutional trust consisting of situational normality and structural assurances. The former means the perception that a situation or a transaction is normal, while the latter asserts the existence of safety nets that involve guarantees and regulations. They conclude that trust has the most substantial impact on non-user intentions to adopt cryptocurrency while their self-efficacy increases this trust. Similarly, Shahzad et al. [41] argue that trust in monetary systems has two aspects; trust in money and purchasing power and system functionality. Their results determine that Chinese users' trust in Bitcoin has the potent effect on their intention to use it.

Trust antecedents vary widely among researchers. Mendoza-Tello et al. [36] argue that trust impacts perceived usefulness since trust absence cannot guarantee that customers execute financial transactions even if they are useful. On the contrary, Paschalie et al. [39] claim the opposite because users' belief of the usefulness of cryptocurrency enhances their trust in it and, eventually, their adoption intentions. The latter also adds social commerce as a second antecedent of trust. This conclusion aligns with Mendoza-Tello et al.'s [27] findings where they debate that the support generated in social communities improves confidence and commitment to using a cryptocurrency, proving social support as an antecedent to trust. Other researchers argue that web quality, e-word-of-mouth, and perceived risk are significant antecedents of trust, with e-word-of-mouth providing the greatest weight [34].

Novendra et al. [47] argue that Indonesians' trust in Bitcoin is represented through their expectations of cryptocurrency performance (i.e., Performance expectancy), as well as their trust in the facility and infrastructure that support it (i.e., Facilitating conditions). Gagarina et al. [29] emphasize the role of social aspects. They conclude that Russian youths' connection of distrust of both cryptocurrencies and people behind them (e.g., developers) accompanied by their confidence in the government regulation of new technologies suggests that emotional distress is primarily experienced by those who fear reducing control over the financial sphere. Kimmerl [16] conducts an interviews-based study to develop a framework for cryptocurrency adoption. Some participants criticize cryptocurrency issuers, while others question the underlying technology (i.e., distributed ledgers). She concludes that perceived trust constitutes trust in the technology and the people behind it.

## 5 Discussion

This paper conducts a systematic literature review on cryptocurrency adoption. The goal is to explore: 1) what theories researchers have employed and what factors matter the most; 2) what context they conducted their studies in, and 3) what gaps need to be addressed by future research. We have reviewed 50 papers with empirical evidence on the issue, classifying them into qualitative, quantitative, and mixed-method studies. Trust significantly affects users' cryptocurrency adoption, while TAM and UTAUT are utilized the most.

Researchers rely heavily on adoption theories that provide high statistical power, such as the UTAUT and TAM. Table 1 answers our R1, where we conclude that few studies have attempted to approach the issue utilizing unpopular theories in IS, such as SST and SNSP. We believe that prevalent adoption theories (e.g., TAM and UTAUT) are efficient in explaining technology adoption in an organizational context since they shed light on the role of task and productivity. However, they might not be the most applicable theories to explain cryptocurrency usage. Although mixed-method studies are essential since they enhance the validity of the research through triangulation and convergence of various sources [68], they are scarce, representing only 25% of the reviewed studies. Not only are they rare, but they also follow the same trend in quantitative, where TAM and UTAUT models are dominating.

Some researchers attempt to complement these widespread theories by incorporating them with other ones (e.g., [27, 53]), while others focus on being creative in the analysis methodology, such as the use of Artificial Neural Networks (ANN) analysis [23, 43, 59]. Yet, the complexity of this technology calls for different treatment due to the various adoption facets (e.g., phycological, environmental, technical, cultural). Indeed, the reviewed studies appear to oversight the economic side of the technology, which obscures our vision of the issue. For instance, cryptocurrency virtuality resembles virtual items/goods in games. Researchers have concluded that economic rationality is rated as the most important reason behind gamers' purchase of in-game content (e.g., [69]). However, such lenses have not been employed yet when studying cryptocurrency adoption.

From a context standpoint (R2), most research provides no context for cryptocurrency use (Table 1). This should not prevent us from getting well-established feedback, yet neglecting the context results in an incomplete examination. Different usages of cryptocurrency can result in different adoption intentions. Nadim [25] includes a question about the usages of cryptocurrency, concluding that 74% of the participants' primary goal is investing; however, the conclusion does not provide insights on whether different uses impact the way users perceive cryptocurrency. Likewise, Shahzad et al. [41] investigate gamers' perceptions of using Bitcoin for game purposes only and conclude that players' trust in Bitcoin has the highest positive impact on their adoption decisions. Yet, this does not necessarily mean that they trust other cryptocurrencies the same way. This is yet to be discovered due to the lack of focus on different types of cryptocurrencies (e.g., bitcoin, ether, shiba inu, etc.). Indeed, scholars investigating Bitcoin, for instance, might present some biases to the participants since it is the most popular cryptocurrency. Only two of the reviewed studies explore different forms of cryptocurrency, stable coins (e.g., Libra) [16, 54], whereas the rest of the studies either investigate bitcoin or "cryptocurrency" in general.

The gaps in the current research (R3) can be summarized into five themes. 1) there is still a lack of empirical studies. Fifty research initiatives are insufficient if we consider the vast spectrum of the technology (e.g., 6,000 cryptocurrencies). This has also been highlighted by Al-Amri et al. [7], even though the number of studies has doubled since their review. Not only the lack of studies but also the variety of the research is limited. The majority of studies are quantitative that employ famous adoption models with high statistical powers. 2) it is evident that the non-adoption of cryptocurrency has not been the focus of researchers except for Voskobojnikov et al. [66], who investigate users' and non-users adoption of cryptocurrency. But, their conclusion does not provide how they differ. 3) convenience sampling appears to be dominant, which might prevent the extraction of new knowledge. For example, many cryptocurrency communities are overlooked by the current research. This asserts our second argument that different populations are not represented enough; hence, flawed inferences might be made. 4) none of the reviewed papers explore cryptocurrency through the lens of game literature, especially when they share the same virtuality. For instance, in VWs and online games, currencies and items are sold and bought in marketplaces in closed communities. These transactions could also occur outside these marketplaces (e.g., eBay). These platforms are regulated by governments which helps in establishing trust in them. Yet, the decentralized nature of cryptocurrencies' projects complicates this process due to the nonexistence of regulations. Reviewed studies lack such focus. 5) There is no clear justification of the antecedents of trust where researchers' findings show some contradictions. For example, some claim that perceived usefulness is an antecedent of trust, while others believe the opposite. Similarly, the same result is noticed in the ease of use and trust constructs. We believe this is due to the lack of understanding of the "trust" factor. Indeed, while this construct is heavily used in the IS field, researchers seem to overlook its complexity, especially in decentralized systems [70].

## 6    Conclusion and Research Agenda

The purpose of this paper is to conduct a systematic literature review of cryptocurrency adoption research. A total of 50 empirically validated studies are collected and reviewed. We argue that although the number of papers seems sufficient, well-designed cryptocurrency adoption studies are needed. The complexity of the technology and its applications, in addition to the variety of stakeholders involved, call for more attention.

We argue that a digital innovation can have different dimensions: 1) Use (personal vs. task-related); 2) Value (utilitarian vs. hedonic); 3) Materiality (virtual vs. non-virtual); 4)

Governance (centralized vs. decentralized); 5) Purpose (economic vs. non-economic). Cryptocurrency technology is unique since it involves multiple dimensions, emphasizing the adoption complexity. For example, adopting cryptocurrency can be because of its hedonic value to users (e.g., thrill), its utility (e.g., quick cross-border transactions), or both. Also, although cryptocurrency is developed as a decentralized technology, many cryptocurrencies are not fully decentralized, where the teams behind the advances of these currencies are centralized in nature. Also, scholars argue that the role of intermediaries is essential to making cryptocurrencies (e.g., Bitcoin) global currencies despite their decentralized nature [71]. For example, the absence of exchange companies makes it harder for a potential user to acquire a cryptocurrency since mining is a complicated task to comprehend for the average user [30].

Therefore, these dimensions can be an initial guide for future research evaluating cryptocurrency adoption. Previous studies ignore some major facets of these dimensions. For instance, the economic aspect of cryptocurrency has not been the focus of prior studies, although cryptocurrency has emerged as a replacement for fiat money. Also, cryptocurrency's decentralized nature helps users conduct trust-less transactions more efficiently and securely. However, establishing trust in a decentralized technology is distinct, calling for a closer look at this construct in the context of cryptocurrency. Based on this review results and the dimensions above, future research agendas are suggested.

First, future research should address the difference in users' and non-users' motivations behind their adoption of cryptocurrency. Second, scholars are urged to explore the role of cryptocurrency types (i.e., bitcoin vs. ether) in the adoption. For instance, how users perceived different cryptocurrency projects considering their popularity, the team behind them, public figures who support them, etc. Indeed, according to Sas and Khairuddin [70], the current utilizations of trust models and principles fail to address trust in decentralization systems. They argue that Bitcoin is a unique system that involves many stakeholders where the trust needs to be addressed across all of them (Government, users, miners, exchanges, and merchants). In addition, the level of trust in bitcoin includes (institutional trust, social trust, and technological trust). Finally, the virtual economic side of cryptocurrency ought to be examined, such as users' valuation process of cryptocurrency, considering its virtuality. Indeed, we can be inspired by the research on games' virtual items. In fact, cryptocurrencies have been compared to virtual objects in MMORPG [72, 73]. Bitcoin, for instance, has been interpreted as a game where computer nodes (i.e., miners) are rewarded with incentives to keep the network safe [74, 75]. Although the products are virtual, the economic systems are not, which asserts the role of economic factors and virtuality in cryptocurrency adoption studies.

# References

1. Mazambani, L., Mutambara, E.: Predicting fintech innovation adoption in South Africa: the case of cryptocurrency. African J. Econ. Manag. Stud. (2019). https://doi.org/10.1108/AJEMS-04-2019-0152
2. Blandin, A., et al.: 3rd global cryptoasset benchmarking study. SSRN Electron. J. (2020). https://doi.org/10.2139/ssrn.3700822
3. Glaser, F., Zimmermann, K., Christian Weber, M.: Bitcoin-Asset or currency? Revealing users' hidden intentions Management of Market Price Risks: Regulation and Coordination

of Volatility Interruptions in Europe View project Social Media Management View project BITCOIN-ASSET OR CURRENCY? REVEALING USERS' HIDDEN INTENTIONS (2014)

4. Hileman, G., Rauchs, M.: Global cryptocurrency benchmarking study. Cambridge Cent. Altern. Financ. (2017)
5. Wang, K.: Measuring Global Crypto Users A Study to Measure Market Size Using On-Chain Metrics (2021)
6. Auer, R., Tercero-Lucas, D.: Distrust or Speculation? The Socioeconomic Drivers of U.S. Cryptocurrency Investments (2021)
7. Al-Amri, R., Zakaria, N.H., Habbal, A., Hassan, S.: Cryptocurrency adoption: current stage, opportunities, and open challenges. Int. J. Adv. Comput. Res. 9, 293–307 (2019). https://doi.org/10.19101/ijacr.pid43
8. Chu, J., Chan, S., Nadarajah, S., Osterrieder, J.: GARCH modelling of cryptocurrencies. J. Risk Financ. Manag. 10, 17 (2017). https://doi.org/10.3390/jrfm10040017
9. Nakamoto, S.: Bitcoin: A Peer-to-Peer Electronic Cash System. (2008)
10. Yaga, D., Mell, P., Roby, N., Scarfone, K.: Blockchain technology overview. Natl. Inst. Stand. Technol., 1–68 (2018)
11. Schatsky, D., Muraskin, C.: Beyond bitcoin : blockchain is coming to disrupt your industry. Deloitte Univ. Press., 1–27 (2015)
12. Narayanan, A., Bonneau, J., Felten, E., Miller, A., Goldfeder, S., Clark, J.: Bitcoin and cryptocurrency technologies introduction to the book (2016)
13. Garriga, M., Dalla Palma, S., Arias, M., De Renzis, A., Pareschi, R., Andrew Tamburri, D.: Blockchain and cryptocurrencies: a classification and comparison of architecture drivers. Concurrency and Comput. Pract. Exp. 33, e5992 (2021). John Wiley and Sons Ltd
14. Webster, J., Watson, R.T.: Analyzing the Past to Prepare for the Future: Writing a Literature Review (2002)
15. Rogers, E.M.: Diffusion of Innovation. Free Press, New York (2003)
16. Kimmerl, J.: Understanding Users' Perception on the Adoption of Stablecoins-Understanding Users' Perception on the Adoption of Stablecoins - The Libra Case, 6–22 (2020)
17. Presthus, W., O'Malley, N.O.: Motivations and barriers for end-user adoption of bitcoin as digital currency. Procedia Comput. Sci. 121, 89–97 (2017). Elsevier B.V.
18. Spenkelink, H.: The adoption process of cryptocurrencies (2014). https://www.taylorfrancis.com/books/9781317766162/chapters/https://doi.org/10.4324/9781315801643-12
19. Davis, F.D.: Perceived usefulness, perceived ease of use, and user acceptance of information technology. MIS Q. Manag. Inf. Syst. 13, 319–339 (1989). https://doi.org/10.2307/249008
20. Baur, A.W., Bühler, J., Bick, M., Bonorden, C.S.: Cryptocurrencies as a disruption? empirical findings on user adoption and future potential of bitcoin and co. In: Janssen, M., Mäntymäki, M., Hidders, J., Klievink, B., Lamersdorf, W., van Loenen, B., Zuiderwijk, A. (eds.) I3E 2015. LNCS, vol. 9373, pp. 63–80. Springer, Cham (2015). https://doi.org/10.1007/978-3-319-250 13-7_6
21. Cousins, K., Subramanian, H., Esmaeilzadeh, P.: A value-sensitive design perspective of cryptocurrencies: a research agenda. Commun. Assoc. Inf. Syst. 45, 27 (2019). https://doi.org/10.17705/1CAIS.04527
22. Khairuddin, I.E., Sas, C., Clinch, S., Davies, N.: Exploring motivations among bitcoin users. In: Proceedings of the Conference on Human Factors in Computing Systems, pp. 2872–2878. Association for Computing Machinery (2016)
23. Abbasi, G.A., Tiew, L.Y., Tang, J., Goh, Y.N., Thurasamy, R.: The adoption of cryptocurrency as a disruptive force: deep learning-based dual stage structural equation modelling and artificial neural network analysis. PLoS ONE 16, e0247582 (2021). https://doi.org/10.1371/journal.pone.0247582

24. Nadeem, M.A., Liu, Z., Pitafi, A.H., Younis, A., Xu, Y.: Investigating the repurchase intention of bitcoin: empirical evidence from China. Data Technol. Appl. **54**, 625–642 (2020). https://doi.org/10.1108/DTA-10-2019-0182
25. Nadim, M.: Understanding consumer adoption of cryptocurrencies (2017)
26. Tamphakdiphanit, J., Laokulrach, M.: Regulations and behavioral intention for use cryptocurrency in Thailand. J. Appl. Econ. Sci. **3**, 523–531 (2020). https://doi.org/10.14505/jaes.v15.3(69).01
27. Mendoza-Tello, J.C., Mora, H., Pujol-López, F.A., Lytras, M.D.: Social commerce as a driver to enhance trust and intention to use cryptocurrencies for electronic payments. IEEE Access **6**, 50737–50751 (2018). https://doi.org/10.1109/ACCESS.2018.2869359
28. Albayati, H., Kim, S.K., Rho, J.J.: Accepting financial transactions using blockchain technology and cryptocurrency: a customer perspective approach. Technol. Soc. **62**, 101320 (2020). https://doi.org/10.1016/j.techsoc.2020.101320
29. Gagarina, M., Nestik, T., Drobysheva, T.: Social and psychological predictors of youths' attitudes to cryptocurrency. Behav. Sci. (Basel) **9**, 118 (2019). https://doi.org/10.3390/bs9120118
30. Abramova, S., Böhme, R.: Perceived Benefit and Risk as Multidimensional Determinants of Bitcoin Use: A Quantitative Exploratory Study (2016)
31. Almuraqab, N.A.: Predicting determinants of the intention to use digital currency in the UAE: an empirical study. Electron. J. Inf. Syst. Dev. Ctries. **86**, e12125 (2020). https://doi.org/10.1002/isd2.12125
32. Alqaryouti, O., Siyam, N., Alkashri, Z., Shaalan, K.: Cryptocurrency usage impact on perceived benefits and users' behaviour. In: Themistocleous, M., Papadaki, M. (eds.) EMCIS 2019. LNBIP, vol. 381, pp. 123–136. Springer, Cham (2020). https://doi.org/10.1007/978-3-030-44322-1_10
33. Ayedh, A., Echchabi, A., Battour, M., Omar, M.: Malaysian Muslim investors' behaviour towards the blockchain-based bitcoin cryptocurrency market. J. Islam. Mark. **12**, 690–704 (2020). https://doi.org/10.1108/JIMA-04-2019-0081
34. Gil-Cordero, E., Cabrera-Sánchez, J.P., Arrás-Cortés, M.J.: Cryptocurrencies as a financial tool: acceptance factors. Mathematics **8**, 1–16 (2020). https://doi.org/10.3390/math8111974
35. Lee, W.-J.: Understanding consumer acceptance of fintech service : an extension of the TAM model to understand bitcoin. **20**, 34–37 (2018). https://doi.org/10.9790/487X-2007023437
36. Mendoza-Tello, J.C., Mora, H., Pujol-López, F.A., Lytras, M.D.: Disruptive innovation of cryptocurrencies in consumer acceptance and trust. IseB **17**(2–4), 195–222 (2019). https://doi.org/10.1007/s10257-019-00415-w
37. Murko, A., Vrhovec, S.L.R.: Bitcoin adoption: scams and anonymity may not matter but trust into bitcoin security does. In: ACM International Conference Proceeding Series. Association for Computing Machinery (2019)
38. Nadeem, M.A., Liu, Z., Pitafi, A.H., Younis, A., Xu, Y.: Investigating the adoption factors of cryptocurrencies—a case of bitcoin: empirical evidence from China. SAGE Open **11**, 2158244021998704 (2021). https://doi.org/10.1177/2158244021998704
39. Paschalie, L.E., Santoso, A.S.: Cryptocurrencies as investment instrument: a social commerce and subscription-based service perspective. J. Bus. Econ. Anal. **3**, 106–132 (2020). https://doi.org/10.36924/sbe.2020.3202
40. Rodenrijs, N., Wokke, J.: Will social media make or break the acceptance in new technology ? (2018). https://api.semanticscholar.org/CorpusID:49471950
41. Shahzad, F., Xiu, G.Y., Wang, J., Shahbaz, M.: An empirical investigation on the adoption of cryptocurrencies among the people of mainland China. Technol. Soc. **55**, 33–40 (2018). https://doi.org/10.1016/j.techsoc.2018.05.006
42. Siquian, J.V.: Examining the Influence of Gender and Age on Acceptance Rates of Bitcoin (2020)

43. Sohaib, O., Hussain, W., Asif, M., Ahmad, M., Mazzara, M.: A PLS-SEM neural network approach for understanding cryptocurrency adoption. IEEE Access **8**, 13138–13150 (2020). https://doi.org/10.1109/ACCESS.2019.2960083

44. Arias-Oliva, M., Pelegrín-Borondo, J., Matías-Clavero, G.: Variables influencing cryptocurrency use: a technology acceptance model in Spain. Front. Psychol. **10**, 1–13 (2019). https://doi.org/10.3389/fpsyg.2019.00475

45. Gunawan, F.E., Novendra, R.: An analysis of bitcoin acceptance in Indonesia. ComTech Comput. Math. Eng. Appl. **8**, 241–247 (2017). https://doi.org/10.21512/comtech.v8i4.3885

46. Hutchison, M.: Acceptance of Electronic Monetary Exchanges, Specifically Bitcoin, by Information Security Professionals: A Quantitative Study Using the Unified Theory of Acceptance and Use of Technology (UTAUT) Model (2017)

47. Novendra, R., Gunawan, F.E.: Analysis of technology acceptance and customer trust in bitcoin in Indonesia using UTAUT framework. KSII Trans. Internet Inf. Syst., 1–18 (2017)

48. Putra, I.G.N.A.P., Darma, G.S.: Is bitcoin accepted in Indonesia? Int. J. Innov. Sci. Res. Technol. **4**, 424–430 (2019)

49. Silinskyte, J.: Understanding Bitcoin adoption: Unified Theory of Acceptance and Use of Technology (UTAUT) application (2014)

50. Ter Ji-Xi, J., Salamzadeh, Y., Teoh, A.P.: Behavioral intention to use cryptocurrency in Malaysia: an empirical study. Bottom Line **34**, 170–197 (2021). https://doi.org/10.1108/BL-08-2020-0053

51. Anser, M.K., Zaigham, G.H.K., Imran Rasheed, M., Pitafi, A.H., Iqbal, J., Luqman, A.: Social media usage and individuals' intentions toward adopting Bitcoin: The role of the theory of planned behavior and perceived risk. Int. J. Commun. Syst. **33**, e4590 (2020). https://doi.org/10.1002/dac.4590

52. Schaupp, L.C., Festa, M.: Cryptocurrency adoption and the road to regulation. In: ACM International Conference Proceeding Series. Association for Computing Machinery (2018)

53. Yoo, K., Bae, K., Park, E., Yang, T.: Understanding the diffusion and adoption of bitcoin transaction services: the integrated approach. Telemat. Inf. **53**, 101302 (2020). https://doi.org/10.1016/j.tele.2019.101302

54. Ajouz, M., Abdullah, A., Kassim, S.: Acceptance of Sharīʿah-compliant precious metal-backed cryptocurrency as an alternative currency: an empirical validation of adoption of innovation theory. Thunderbird Int. Bus. Rev. **62**, 171–181 (2020). https://doi.org/10.1002/tie.22106

55. Hoens, T.: The Adoption of Cryptocurrencies as Speculative Investment by Users from Netherlands (2019)

56. Huang, W.: The impact on people's holding intention of bitcoin by their perceived risk and value. Econ. Res. Istraz. **32**, 3570–3585 (2019). https://doi.org/10.1080/1331677X.2019.1667257

57. Pakrou, M., Amir, K.: The Relationship between Perceived Value and the Intention of Using Bitcoin (2016)

58. Voskobojnikov, A., Wiese, O., Koushki, M.M.: The u in crypto stands for usable: an empirical study of user experience with mobile cryptocurrency wallets. In: Proceedings of the Conference on Human Factors Computing Systems (2021). https://doi.org/10.1145/3411764.3445407

59. Alharbi, A., Sohaib, O.: Technology readiness and cryptocurrency adoption: PLS-SEM and deep learning neural network analysis. IEEE Access **9**, 21388–21394 (2021). https://doi.org/10.1109/ACCESS.2021.3055785

60. Alaklabi, S., Kang, K.: Perceptions towards cryptocurrency adoption: a case of Saudi Arabian citizens. IBIMA Bus. Rev. **2021**, 1–17 (2021). https://doi.org/10.5171/2021.110411

61. Abraham, J., Sutiksno, D.U., Kurniasih, N., Warokka, A.: Acceptance and penetration of bitcoin: the role of psychological distance and national culture. SAGE Open **9**, 1–14 (2019). https://doi.org/10.1177/2158244019865813
62. Walton, A., Johnston, K.: Exploring perceptions of bitcoin adoption: the south african virtual community perspective. Interdiscip. J. Inf. Knowl. Manag. **13**, 165–182 (2018). https://doi.org/10.28945/4080
63. Arias-Oliva, M., de Andrés-Sánchez, J., Pelegrín-Borondo, J.: Fuzzy set qualitative comparative analysis of factors influencing the use of cryptocurrencies in spanish households. Mathematics **9**, 1–19 (2021). https://doi.org/10.3390/math9040324
64. Göbert, M.: End-user Adaptation of Cryptocurrencies (2018)
65. Esmaeilzadeh, P., Cousins, K., Subramanian, H.: A utility theory model for individual adoption of bitcoin. In: Proceedings of the International Conference on Information Resources Management (CONF-IRM) (2020)
66. Voskobojnikov, A., Abramova, S., Beznosov, K., Böhme, R.: Non-Adoption of Crypto-Assets: Exploring the Role of Trust, Self-Efficacy, and Risk (2021)
67. Gefen, K.: Straub: trust and TAM in online shopping: an integrated model. MIS Q. **27**, 51 (2003). https://doi.org/10.2307/30036519
68. Venkatesh, V., Brown, S.A., Bala, H.: Bridging the Qualitative-Quantitative Divide: Guidelines for Conducting Mixed Methods Research in Information Systems Quarterly Bridging the Qualitative-Quantitative Divide: Guidelines for Conducting Mixed Methods Research in Information Systems1 (2013)
69. Hamari, J., Keronen, L.: Why do people buy virtual goods: a meta-analysis. Comput. Human Behav. **71**, 59–69 (2017). https://doi.org/10.1016/j.chb.2017.01.042
70. Sas, C., Khairuddin, I.E.: Exploring trust in bitcoin technology: a framework for HCI research. In: Proceedings of the OzCHI 2015 Conference on Being Human, pp. 338–342 (2015). https://doi.org/10.1145/2838739.2838821
71. Möser, M., Böhme, R.: Trends, Tips, Tolls: A Longitudinal Study of Bitcoin Transaction Fees. Presented at the (2015)
72. Spiegelman, A., Keidat, I., Tennenholtz, M.: Game of coins. In: Proceedings of the International Conference on Distributed Computing Systems, 2021-July, pp. 954–964 (2021). https://doi.org/10.1109/ICDCS51616.2021.00095
73. Tsabary, I., Eyal, I.: The Gap Game, 132–132 (2018). https://doi.org/10.1145/3211890.321 1905
74. Kavanagh, D., Miscione, G., Dylan-Ennis, P.: The bitcoin game: ethno-resonance as method. Organization **26**, 517–536 (2019). https://doi.org/10.1177/1350508419828567
75. Verduyn, M.C.-: Bitcoin and Beyond Cryptocurrencies, Blockchains, and Global Governance. Routledge (2018)

# A Study on User Experience of Non-linguistic Communication: Focusing on the Interactive Emojis in On-line Meeting Platforms

Sunghee Ahn[✉]

School of Design Convergence, Hongik University, Seoul, South Korea
sahn2002@hongik.ac.kr

**Abstract.** The pandemic period spanning over two years has shifted most offline meetings and working processes online. People still say that online communication is less accurate in terms of satisfaction with communication as much as face-to-face communication because many parts of human communication can be clearly communicated through verbal expressions, as well as facial expressions, hand gestures, and gestures.

The hypothesis of this research is to increase the satisfaction and accuracy of communication in non-face-to-face communication, it is necessary to study user experience on non-face-to-face communication methods.

The aim of this research is to analyze the non- linguistic communication tools in meeting platform, especially on emojis that can be added in real time during the on-line meeting. For this, among the recently used online meeting platforms, four were selected and the user experience of using emoji to help non-verbal communication between participants was analyzed. The participants of user test are mainly 20 s and 30 s who have online education experience or work experience as well as personal on -line real time face-to face chatting in daily lives. This paper carried out FGI user test with closed format of 5 different key stages in every platform.

As a result, this paper finds out your hidden needs in non-linguistic communication in on-line meetings. It also followed by comprehensive evaluation of user's satisfaction analysis. Since these platforms are in rapid upgrading and changes, Platforms are upgrading and evolving too quickly now, but people's complex and convergence methods for communication are elements that have been together in people's society for a long time, so 'cultural human factors' have common characteristics and needs. Therefore, the results of this study are expected to contribute as basic research to the design and technology development from the user's point of view better in the future in non-face-to-face communication. Also, from the future perspectives of development of HCI technology, this paper shows further close location of cultural and humane needs.

**Keywords:** On-line meeting platform UT · Non-linguistic communication · Interactive emoji · UXR

# 1   Research Background

Traditionally, media-mediated communication has been centered on letters, which are symbols, but since such text-centered communication involves an abstraction process, there are limitations in the expression of information to be conveyed. It is because cultural and social influence factors were overlooked when creating emoticons. The use of emoticons reflects the cultural sentiment agreed by the social group, and it can be said that this culture is transmitted while using it. In addition to the technical aspect, cultural influence is also the most decisive factor in human behavior [1] Through the process of learning the spoken language, various non-verbal movement languages that are culturally hardened in the society are also learned.

In this context, non-verbal communication can be said to be a very important part of communication that exists along with verbal communication. People speak with their mouths and hear them with their ears, and when they speak with their hearts, they hear them with their hearts. People are more sympathetic to sadness when a single tear drops from their eyes than a hundred sentence of sadness.

# 2   Literature Reviews

## 2.1   MERIvion's Law and the Ratio of Human Nonverbal Communication

People rely largely on verbal and non-verbal means to communicate. However, it is not an exaggeration to say that people have only been interested in communication by verbal means, and most of them are not adopted as public evidence for communication made by non-verbal means and have been almost ignored especially in online communication. In addition, several studies have already demonstrated that people tend to trust non-verbal messages more when verbal and non-verbal messages conflict.According to sociologist Albert Mehrabian, in the communicating process, the verbal component (the content of speech) accounts for 7%, and the non-verbal component accounts for the remaining 93%. Visual information (attitude/gesture/hand gestures) 55% and sound information (speech, intonation, tone, tone, etc.) 38% are the parts that feel the language contradiction in the expressions of others, and the actual verbal content is only 7% [2] Although there is a difference in degree, if these arguments are accepted, the proportion of non-verbal communication in actual communication is much larger than that of verbal communication.

## 2.2   On-line Meeting Platform

On-line meeting makes the people join from every different location and in a pre-agreed time using on line platforms [3]. Due to pandemic, this kind of on-line, virtual meeting become usual. Zoom, for instance, had 10 million daily meeting participants in December 2019, but by April 2020, that number had risen to over 300 million [4]. Other video conferencing platforms, such as Google Meet™ and Microsoft Teams, have also experienced significant increases in daily participants [5, 6]. Furthermore, it is likely that the use of videoconferencing will continue long after the pandemic ends, as Gartner predicts that only 25% of business meetings will take place in-person by 2024 [7].

### 2.3 Interactive Emojis

An emoticon is a compound word of emotion and icon. It is a visual sign that can express emotions in the form of pictures, and is also called emoji. In 1997, as graphic emoticons in Gif file format were published online by Nicholas Lufrani, graphic emojis began to be used [8], and the use of graphic emojis became popular in the 21st century especially among young generations. Alshenqeeti (2016) sees the emojis are creating new language for the new generation [9, 10]. An emoticon is a symbolic image that symbolizes a specific meaning. These symbolic images are socially learned, reinterpreted and reproduced. Because of this influence, Apple in 2016 responded to public criticism, such as that realistic gun-shaped emojis could make children familiar with guns or that white male-centered emojis could instill discriminatory views about gender and race. In this context, Google also replaced some emoticons in 2018. This is because cultural and social influence factors were overlooked when creating emojis. The use of emoticons reflects the cultural sentiment agreed by the social group, and it can be said that this culture is transmitted through use.

In today's multimedia-based SNS communication, emoticons are complementary to texts and enable rich emotions to be delivered. The biggest characteristic of emoticons is to enrich the expression of emotions between users in media-mediated communication and to diversify the symbols and methods of communication. This activation of the use of emoticons also influenced the formation of a new cultural content industry, such as the 'Kakao Friends' character industry.

## 3   Analysis on Interactive Emojis in On-line Meeting Platforms

### 3.1   User Test Platform 01_Zoom

- The 'reaction' icon is located as the default icon on the screen, so it is convenient to communicate opinions in the middle of the meeting.
- In the case of a button to replace the video filter, it is not easily visible, and it is not easy to replace it during a video conference because it has to go through several steps.
- Face recognition is natural, and the video filters are varied and interesting.
- Basic 5 types of virtual backgrounds and 59 types of video filters are provided.
- Filters with small shapes are not visible on the screen (Fig. 1).

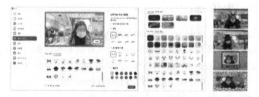

**Fig. 1.**  Zoom user test screen

## 3.2   Test Platform 02_Webex

– The face icon button is located on the menu bar below the video conference screen for quick access.
– When you press the face icon button, a total of 8 icons (Like, Clap, Congratulation, Smile, Haha, Wow, Sad Tears, Dislike) appear and disappear for about 5 s saying 'Send response'.
– If you recognize a total of three hand gestures (like, clap, and dislike) and recognize the hand gesture on the screen, the 'Like' icon will appear on the screen during the meeting without pressing the button (Fig. 2).

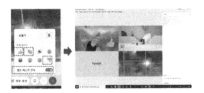

**Fig. 2.**   Webex user test screen

## 3.3   Test Platform 03_Justalk

The icon has a motion effect, and the user can change the size and position of the icon at will (Fig. 3).

**Fig. 3.**   Justtalk user test screen

## 3.4   Test Platform 04_Facebook-Messenger

– Click the effect icon on the screen during video call.
– There are emoticon stickers and text stickers, so you can attach stickers to any screen location you want.
– For animated characters and special effects, the effect is automatically applied by recognizing a face (Fig. 4).

**Fig. 4.** Facebook-Messenger user test screen

### 3.5  Test Platform 05_Kakaotalk

– Click the face icon on the video call screen > Emoji filter can be selected.
– It is arranged with slightly exaggerated facial expressions and text to increase the understanding of expressions.
– When the black border line of the picture is composited into the background, it has a noticeable effect (Fig. 5).

**Fig. 5.** Kakaotalk user test screen

### 3.6  Test Platform 06_Facetime

– If you click the face icon on the camera screen > select the effect button, the face is recognized and the filter is applied.
– Animation effects and filters focusing on character faces are applied (Fig. 6 and 7).

**Fig. 6.** Facetime filter application process

**Fig. 7.** Facetime user test screen_Types of filters

# 4 Comprehensive Analysis

## 4.1 Analysis of User Experience on Interaction

(Table 1 and 2).

**Table 1.** Evaluation 1_User Interaction

| Platform | Advantages | Disadvantage |
|---|---|---|
| Zoom | + Two screen layout configurations selectable<br>+ User and participant screen order can be changed in gallery view mode<br>+ The Raise Hand emoticon keeps raising your hand until the user clicks the button again, which is convenient when requesting a speech during a meeting | - There are many steps to apply the face sticker effect and it is cumbersome. (You need to go to the video settings window and apply it) |
| Webex | + Two screen layout configurations selectable<br>+ 'Responsive' menu tab is intuitive and convenient with fewer steps to select right on the screen<br>+ The 'reaction' effect automatically disappears after a certain period (about 5 s), which is convenient because the user don't need to cancel the setting | - Unable to move user's screen position. (if the screen is fixed in the down position, the camera's position will not match, and the gaze will be downwards when looking at your own screen) |
| Justalk | + There are 3 types of screen composition layouts for users to select<br>+ You can freely adjust the rotation and size of the sticker effect using gestures | - Layout can be changed during a two-person video call, but the position and size of the screen cannot be adjusted<br>- You cannot change the screen layout in a group meeting of 3 or more people |

*(continued)*

**Table 1.** (*continued*)

| Platform | Advantages | Disadvantage |
|----------|-----------|--------------|
| Facebook-Messenger | + User screen position can be moved. (limited to borders) | - Unable to resize user screen<br>- Unable to change screen layout |
| Kakaotalk | + User screen position can be moved. (limited to borders) | - Unable to resize user screen<br>- Unable to change screen layout |
| Apple-Facetime | + User screen position can be moved. (limited to borders)<br>+ You can freely adjust the rotation and size of the sticker effect using gestures | - Unable to adjust user screen size<br>- The screen layout continuously fluctuates during group meetings to disperse concentration<br>- You cannot see the other users while emoji is being applied<br>- The sticker delete button on the screen is small and difficult to operate, and it is difficult to edit when stickers are overlapped |

**Table 2.** Evaluation 2_Function & technology

| Platform | Advantages | Disadvantage |
|----------|-----------|--------------|
| Zoom | + Face recognition is good even when wearing a mask, so there is no difference in using stickers and makeup effects<br>+ You can set the background concept as a wallpaper with the picture you want | - If you change a filter during a meeting, the filter you selected is continuously applied not only on the preview screen of the filter but also on the meeting progress screen, making it inconvenient to change the filter during a meeting |
| Webex | + By recognizing the gesture of raising the thumb and the clapping gesture, the good and clap icons appear as animation effects in a large size, so you can send emoticons without pressing a button<br>+ There is a survey and function, so it can be used to ask the opinions of those in attendance<br>+ You can set the background concept as a wallpaper with the picture you want | - Inconvenient to use due to poor gesture recognition<br>- There is no filter or decoration function, so it is suitable for a formal meeting, but it is static for use in a casual environment |
| Justalk | + There is a drawing tool, so it is useful to draw and communicate when you can't hear the other person's voice, and can be used as a fun element such as graffiti on the face | - Interaction effect is not supported for group video calls of 3 or more people |

(*continued*)

**Table 2.** (*continued*)

| Platform | Advantages | Disadvantage |
|---|---|---|
| Facebook-Messenger | + Ability to take pictures during video calls<br>+ Creates a natural background synthesizing effect depending on the camera position<br>+ Can be used as a fun factor with voice modulation function | - No preview function before applying the sticker |
| Kakaotalk | + Face recognition works well even when wearing a mask | - Stickers only available on mobile<br>- No preview function before applying the sticker |
| Apple-Facetime | + Ability to take pictures during video calls<br>+ If you move the sticker close to the face, the sticker will follow the face | - Face recognition does not work well when using a mask |

## 4.2 Analysis of User Experience on Functional Factor and Technology

## 4.3 Analysis of User Experience on Visual Factors

The table below summarizes the 'visual factors' among the three analysis frame groups conducted in this study (Table 3).

**Table 3.** Evaluation 3_Visual design

| Platform | Advantages | Disadvantage |
|---|---|---|
| Zoom | + Various fun face recognition filters allow you to decorate your own face, so it can be used in a casual environment<br>+ User background setting is possible, which can be used professionally in a conference environment, such as setting a background with a meeting topic in the background | - Except for the background effect, the face recognition sticker effect is inconspicuous on a small screen<br>- There are many filters (59), but the main function of the filter is a decoration function, so it is not suitable for a meeting or office environment except for 7 emoticons including raising a hand on the main screen |

(*continued*)

**Table 3.** (*continued*)

| Platform | Advantages | Disadvantage |
|---|---|---|
| Webex | + Emoji size is large and animated, so it's easy to spot on a small screen<br>+ New emoticons are added every season (Christmas, winter, etc.) to give users freshness<br>+ User background setting is possible, which can be used professionally in a conference environment, such as setting a background with a meeting topic in the background | - The 'Raise Hand' effect is inconspicuous with a gray background and a white icon<br>- Graphics are not differentiated from commonly used icons |
| Justalk | + The icon graphic is cute and the emoticons have various and intuitive expressions | - Focus on images that can be used in a casual atmosphere rather than an official meeting |
| Facebook-Messenger | + There are various types such as funny facial recognition animation stickers that can be used casually | - Feeling of heterogeneity in facial recognition graphics or makeup effects. (facial distortion effects that do not match Korean emotions, etc.)<br>- Not suitable for formal meetings |
| Kakaotalk | + Provides a sticker that combines text and graphics to express emotions such as resolute and great<br>+ The color of the border of the graphic is dark and clear, so the expression effect is noticeable even on a small screen | - There are not many types of developed stickers<br>- Focus on images that can be used in a casual atmosphere rather than an official meeting |
| Apple-Facetime | + Various effects. (AR emoji, text, animated emoticons, etc.)<br>+ You can communicate by typing text directly into a sticker | - Focus on images that can be used in a casual atmosphere rather than an official meeting |

### 4.4 Comprehensive Analysis

Below image is the visualization of comprehensive user experience on emojis of on-line meting platform. Altogether 18 elements of user experience have been evaluated by 4 levels (Fig. 8).

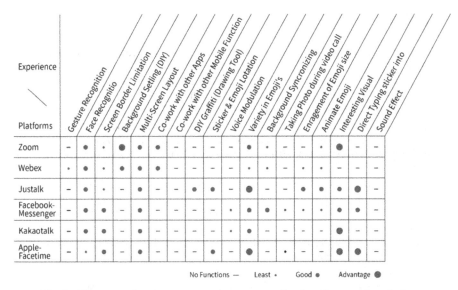

**Fig. 8.** The comprehensive user experience on emojis of on-line meeting platforms

## 5  Conclusion

Human relationships are formed through various types of communication. The problem is that non-verbal communication skills are becoming an important medium in life relationships day by day. Now, in setting the direction of new HCI technologies such as deep learning, the importance of non-verbal communication, which accounts for most of human communication, should be recognized again, and this part should not be overlooked in establishing the direction of technology development. The development and application of HCI technology from a human-centered point of view is very necessary from this point of view. In online communication using computers or mobile phones, it is necessary to ensure that sufficient understanding can accompany each other by considering individual needs and emotions centered on people rather than aligning people with a uniform systemic method. The value accumulated by habits and cultural characteristics based on the experiences people have lived for a long time is a factor that must be considered in terms of technology as well.

The limitation of this study is that there may be some differences from 2020, when this study was conducted, as online platforms are being upgraded at a very fast rate recently.

Nevertheless, the expression technique of 'emoji' based on mutual communication is a major communication method that can increase the satisfaction of communication in meetings for various purposes, such as meetings or education, using real-time based online meeting platforms. It is meaningful in that it was assure that it was a channel.

# References

1. Kotler, N., Kotler, P.: Estrategias y Marketing de los Museos, Ariel (eds.). Patrimonio Histórico (2001)
2. Mehrabian, A.: Some referents and measures of nonverbal behavior. Behav. Res. Meth. Instru. **1**, 203–207 (1968). https://doi.org/10.3758/BF03208096
3. Dermawan, D.A., Wibawa, R.P., Susanti, M.D.: Analysis of the use of virtual meeting in the implementation of proposal/thesis examination during Covid-19 pandemic. In: International Joint Conference on Science and Engineering (IJCSE 2020), pp. 65–69. Atlantis Press (2020)
4. Evans, B.: The Zoom revolution: 10 eye-popping stats from tech's new superstar. Cloud Wars (2020)
5. Peters, P.: Google's Meet teleconferencing service now adding about 3 million users per day. The Verge (2020)
6. Thorp-Lancaster, D.: Microsoft Teams hits 75 million daily active users, up from 44 million in March. Windows Central (2020)
7. Standaert, W., Muylle, S., Basu, A.: How shall we meet? Understanding the importance of meeting mode capabilities for different meeting objectives. Information & Management **58**(1), 103393 (2021)
8. Quann, J.: A picture paints a thousand words: Today is World Emoji Day. News Talk (2015)
9. Alshenqeeti, H.: Are emojis creating a new or old visual language for new generations? A socio-semiotic study. Adv. Lang. Literacy Stud. **7**(6), 56–60 (2016)
10. Hu, T., et al.: Spice up your chat: The intentions and sentiment effect of using emojis. In: The proceedings of the 11th International AAAI Conference on Social Media, pp. 102–112 (2017)

# Remote Workers' Perceptions on Employee Monitoring

Yusuf Albayram$^{(\boxtimes)}$, Richard DeWald, and John Althen

Department of Computer Science, Central Connecticut State University,
New Britain, CT, USA
yusuf.albayram@ccsu.edu, {dewaldr,althenj}@my.ccsu.edu

**Abstract.** With the prevalence of working from home, more and more
organizations are adopting monitoring methods to keep track of their
employees' work activities electronically. Understanding how employees
respond to various monitoring methods and what factors affect their attitudes and perceptions towards monitoring is important to maintain a
healthy employee-employer relationship and productivity in workplaces.
To explore employees' perceptions, concerns, attitudes and knowledge of
commonly used monitoring methods, we conducted an online survey with
197 remote workers. We found that the use of cameras, microphones and
screen recorders were among the most disapproved monitoring methods
that would cause participants to refuse a job offer, promotion or even quit
their current job. Our qualitative findings indicated that the most commonly cited reasons behind their disapproval were concerns about invasion of privacy and safety. Participants were found to be more opposed
to remote monitoring than monitoring at office/location. We also identified factors influencing employee satisfaction, employee loyalty, faith in
intentions of management, intention to disclose, trust in employers, and
openness to employer monitoring. Implications of our findings towards
better monitoring practices are also discussed in the paper.

**Keywords:** Monitoring · Remote work · Privacy · Trust in employers

## 1 Introduction

The number of employees working from home (i.e., remotely) has vastly increased
across the globe after COVID-19 related measures took effect [22]. Many companies have reported plans to continue working remotely even after the pandemic is
over, as both employees and organizations are seeing benefits in terms of cost savings, reduced commute costs, savings in time and organizational resources, and
higher employee satisfaction [4,33]. The rise of remote work has likewise intensified the level of monitoring employers use to track employees' activities while
working remotely. There are a variety of monitoring tools used by organizations
today, which can range from recording via a camera or microphone, keyboard
recorders (e.g., keyboard strokes), screen recorder (can be used to take screenshots at regular intervals), monitoring email usage and content, websites visited

© The Author(s), under exclusive license to Springer Nature Switzerland AG 2022
M. Kurosu et al. (Eds.): HCII 2022, LNCS 13516, pp. 361–382, 2022.
https://doi.org/10.1007/978-3-031-17615-9_25

362        Y. Albayram et al.

and many o thers. While monitoring can provide some advantages for employers, it can have numerous disadvantages for employees, such as stress, low employee satisfaction, productivity, lack of trust, and feelings of privacy invasion, and other negative reactions [2,14,25,31,35,39,48,53]. With the increasing prevalence of monitoring use in the workplace, it is important to gain insights into employees' views, perceptions, and concerns about monitoring in order to create more effective monitoring systems and policies, and to ensure that their rights, psychological well-being, and security and privacy are not adversely affected. To investigate the perceptions and opinions of remote workers with respect to some of the monitoring methods that are being implemented to track their productivity, their thoughts on their right to privacy, and the potential effects of these monitoring methods on the workplace, we conducted a survey on Prolific by recruiting remote employees and asked them about their knowledge concerning the methods used by their employers to monitor their work, as well as which methods are currently implemented and which they consider acceptable methods of management.

We found that participants deemed the use of camera, microphone and screen recording as the most concerning monitoring methods that would cause them to refuse a job offer, promotion and even quit their job. Through qualitative analysis, we identified that "Invasion of privacy/concerns about safety" was the most prominent reason as to why participants selected these monitoring methods. While the majority of the participants reported similar perspectives on monitoring their work activities while working remotely and at their employer's office/location, the others participants were more opposed to remote monitoring than monitoring at office/location. Moreover, intention to disclose and trust in employers are found to be strong predictor of employee satisfaction and loyalty. While intention to disclose was not a predictor of right to monitor, trust in employers was a predictor of intention to disclose and right to monitor.

## 2   Related Work

Electronic monitoring systems used by organizations have seen a rise over the past decade [25]. This trend has accelerated recently as more people work remotely due to the COVID-19 pandemic [45]. For example, a 2018 Gartner survey with 239 large companies showed that nearly half of large companies use some type of monitoring techniques (e.g., analyzing texts of emails) [28]. Furthermore, a 2020 Gartner survey revealed that 74% plan to keep some proportion of their workforce in a permanent remote status post-COVID-19 [17,30], while at the same time, another study found that global demand for employee monitoring software increased by 87% in April 2020 [37].

While electronic monitoring is designed to improve performance, reduce liability risks and loss of company assets [16,18,29,46,47], monitoring employees' activities can also have deleterious effects on them. For instance, prior research identified that monitoring can affect employees' self-esteem and cause stress, anxiety, depression, paranoia, carpal tunnel syndrome, as well as nerve disorders [3]. In a study of 1500 service workers, 75% believed that their quality of work suffered from the monitoring practices of their employers [46].

Prior studies found that monitoring can also have a negative impact on employee trust [9,19,25]. The use of monitoring by the employer can signal to employees that they are not trustworthy, which can cause employees to lose trust in their employers [45]. Many articles stressed the importance of explicitly detailing the methods of employers' monitoring systems and discerning what information is needed, relevant and truly required, rather than being overly comprehensive [29,46,52].

As we have just entered a new landscape of "work from home"/"work remotely" due to the pandemic, more research is needed to better understand the impact of remote monitoring in this new digital workspace. Among a limited number of recent studies, Kalischko and Riedl [25] reviewed the literature in the electronic performance monitoring following the COVID-19 induced lock downs and presented a framework for future studies. The framework accounts for the level and the type of monitoring, which can affect job satisfaction, motivation, commitment, performance, and employee trust stress level. Similarly, Galanxhi and Nah [13] presented a research framework that shows the effects of different technological affordances on users' digital well-being and potential areas for understanding digital well-being in the context of remote work. Jandl et al. [23] underlined that the use of tracking and tracing systems (TATS) in working environments creates a dilemma for organizations. As such, organizations need to adopt new technologies to increase their competitiveness and improve employee safety, while ensuring that existing laws on data protection are complied with so that employees are not adversely affected. Thus, the costs and benefits of TATS should be carefully weighed, while considering other important factors (e.g., transparency) for the adoption of monitoring software and tools [23,24].

Towards understanding the privacy and security aspects of working remotely, Nurse et al. [41] analyzed cybersecurity and privacy issues that can arise due to working remotely during the pandemic, such as a lack of security training for remote workers being available due to the sudden shift to work from home, exposing home space and personal information with the use of online communication tools (e.g., Zoom, Webex). The authors also argued that the use of additional monitoring can increase the perception that employees are not trusted, and evidence from prior efforts indicates that employees can be even more productive when they work from home [40,41].

Emami-Naeini et al. [11] investigated users' privacy attitudes and concerns towards communication tools such as Zoom and WebEx during the events of the pandemic in the context of working, socializing and learning from home. In the same vein, Obada-Obieh et al. [42] pointed out how telecommuting can impact employees' security and privacy (e.g., an always-on video camera request during work meetings can be an invasion of employee privacy).

While these papers contributed to the literature, little is known about the opinions and perceptions of remote workers on different monitoring methods as well as what factors influence employees' perceptions of monitoring in the workplace. Building upon prior work, our study makes an important contribution to the body of literature by providing both a qualitative analysis of remote workers' perceptions regarding monitoring and their attitudes towards different monitoring methods commonly used by employers, and quantitative analysis identifying factors influencing trust, employee satisfaction, loyalty, and openness to employee monitoring.

## 3    Methodology

The goal of this study was to gain a better understanding of remote workers' perceptions, concerns, and attitudes about employee monitoring. Towards that, we seek to answer the following research questions through both quantitative and qualitative analysis.

- **RQ-1:** How do employees view remote monitoring compared to monitoring at office/location?
- **RQ-2:** How do employees approve/disapprove of different monitoring methods commonly used by employers, and would these methods have any impact on quitting, and refusal of a promotion/job offer?
- **RQ-3:** What factors influence employees' decisions towards remote monitoring?
- **RQ-4:** What are the relationships among trust in employer, intention to disclose, and participants' opinions on "employers' right to monitor", as well as employee satisfaction, loyalty, and faith in intentions of management?

To answer these research questions, we conducted an online survey by recruiting participants who were currently working remotely for an employer either full-time or part-time, and working in profit, non-profit, local government, state government or federal government. These criteria allowed us to recruit participants who were not self-employed workers (monitoring would not apply for these individuals as they are technically employers) so that we can explore their perceptions of remote working and monitoring.

### 3.1   Survey Measures and Recruitment

The survey started with demographic questions asking about their gender, age, level of education, marital status, race, computers knowledge in general. Participants were then asked about their work details such as employment status, where/how they work (e.g., office or remotely), their role (e.g., employee, middle management), their remote work details such as equipment used, and whether they had proprietary software on their personal equipment or not.

To measure level of satisfaction and loyalty each participant has with their employer as well as faith in intentions management of their employer, we adapted three scales: 1) six-item employee satisfaction scale from [21], 2) five-item employee loyalty scale from [34], and 3) three-item faith in intentions of management scale from [10]. Participants rated their agreement with each statement using a 5-point Likert scale.

Next, participants rated "Intention to disclose information scale", which was adapted from [26]. This scale included 11 types of different information such as chronic conditions, religious and political beliefs (excluding age, employment status, income and number of sexual partners) and measured the extent which participants would be willing to disclose this information. We calculated a total score for each participant by giving 1 point to the participants who selected "I would disclose" and 0 points who selected "I would prefer not to say" [26].

To measure the level of trust participants have in their employer, we used a trust beliefs scale, which was adopted from [32]. This five-item trusting belief scale was originally used to assess the degree to which people believe a firm is trustworthy in protecting consumers' personal information. In our case, the scale aimed to measure workers' level of trust they have in their employer when monitoring their remote work activity. Participants rated these items on a 7-point Likert scale where higher scores indicate a higher level of trust.

Next, participants were asked if they knew whether they were being monitored. If so, participants were asked if their employers use commonly used monitoring methods and their privacy concerns associated with these methods. Moreover, we asked participants for their opinions about whether their employers had the right to monitor them remotely or in the office. As some of the monitoring methods used by employers may be deemed as an invasion of privacy and their usage can potentially negatively influence employee-employer relationships, these monitoring methods may affect the stability of staff for employers, weaken recruitment of potential staff and even stifle the career growth of employees. Towards that, participants were asked whether monitoring would have a potential impact on situations such as quitting a job, refusal of a promotion/job offer, and which monitoring method would have an impact on them. These were followed by open-ended questions to further understand underlying reasons for disapproving these monitoring methods in each scenario. An attention check question was also included in the survey to filter out inattentive participants.

To recruit participants for this study, we used Prolific Platform. We restricted participants to those aged 18 years or older, living in the US or UK, and having at least 95% approval rate. Participants were compensated with $3.50 for completing the survey. The study was approved by our university's IRB.

### 3.2  Survey Data Analysis

**Qualitative Analysis:** We used a bottom-up inductive coding approach [38] to analyze participants' open-ended responses elaborating the reasons behind their ratings on the several survey questions, and to identify different themes and possible relationships between them.

Three researchers were involved in the coding process. Initially, two researchers individually went through all the comments of participants to compose themes and codes. All researchers then met online to create the final codebook. The codebook was finalized through several meetings in which the third researcher who was not involved in the initial coding acted as moderator to help reach agreement. Subsequently, the two researchers updated their codebooks to match with the finalized codebook. Finally, one of the researchers consolidated the codes and calculated inter-rater reliability (i.e., Krippendorff's alpha) between the two coders using the ReCal OIR software package [12] for each open-ended response.

Krippendorff's alpha values were 0.80 (employer right to monitor), 0.83 (refuse job offer), 0.78 (refuse a promotion), and 0.79 (quit a job), which are within reasonable bounds for agreement [27].

**Statistical Analysis:** We performed linear regressions to identify the factors associated with 1) employee satisfaction, 2) employee loyalty, 3) faith in intentions of management, and 4) employees' openness to employer monitoring. We also performed a path analysis to determine the relationship among the important factors identified in the regression analysis.

**Reliability of Scales:** Before running the regression analysis, we verified the reliability of our scales using Cronbach's $\alpha$. The 6-item employee satisfaction scale ($\alpha = 0.89$), the 5-item employee loyalty scale ($\alpha = 0.88$), and the 3-item faith in intentions of management scale ($\alpha = 0.87$) had good reliability [15]. Moreover, as participants' opinions about whether their employers have the right to monitor them remotely or in the office were significantly correlated (see Sect. 4.3), responses to these two statements ($\alpha = 0.90$) were combined into a single dependent variable, which we refer as "Employers right to monitor".

## 4    Evaluation

### 4.1    Sample Statistics

**Demographics:** A total of 209 participants completed the study. We removed data of 12 participants who were self-employed or did not correctly answer the attention check question, resulting in 197 participants in total. Of the 197 participants, 53.3% (105) were female, 45.7% (90) were male, and 1% (2) were non-binary. Our participants were remote workers either from the UK (70%) or the US (30%). The mean age of the participants was 37.64 (median = 36, SD = 9.77). 47.7% reported having a 4-year/3-year college degree, 15.7% Master's degree, 11.7% some level of college education, 8.6% high school/GED/high school equivalency level of education, 6.1% trade/technical/vocational training/certification, 4.6% had a Doctorate degree, 4.6% 2-year college degree, and 1% Professional/Medical degree.

The vast majority of our participants (92%; 180) reported their ethnicity as white or Caucasian. The next highest ethnicity was Asian with 8 responses (4%), followed by African American (2%; 4), Hispanic and Mixed (each with 2 responses), and 1 participant selecting "prefer not to say." In terms of marital status, 52.3% of the participants were single, 41.6% married, 5.1% divorce, and 1% widowed.

51.7% of the participants indicated their level of knowledge about computers in general as proficient, 30.9% as competent, 14.7% as expert, 2% as beginner, and 0.5% as novice.

**Work Details:** In terms of employment status, 176 participants reported working full-time (89.3%), 19 part-time (9.6%), and 2 students (1%). 67.5% of the participants reported that they work in the role of employee, 31% in the role of middle manager, 1% in the role of executive manager, and 0.5% in the role of independent researcher. The participants were also asked how many hours per week they work. 72.1% participants reported working 35–40 h a week, 10.7% between 1 and 34 h, and 17.3% more than 40 h.

In terms of work status, 93.9% of the participants reported working remotely for an employer, 5.1% working a combination of working remotely and at their employers location, and 1.0% working at their employers' location/office. In response to "Do you prefer working remotely or at your employer's location/office?", 84.3% participants answered that they prefer to work remotely, 4.6% prefer to work in the office, 6.1% have no preference, and 2.5% prefer a mixture of office and remote working. Additionally, 2.5% of participants reported that they always worked remotely. The participants were also asked whether they worked remotely before the COVID-19 pandemic. While 56.3% participants had not worked remotely prior to the pandemic, 43.7% participants had.

### 4.2   Monitoring Methods Used by Employers

Participants were asked if their employer uses any monitoring method to track their activities while working remotely. The majority of participants (66.5%) reported that their employers do not monitor their remote activities, and 14 participants (7%) reported that they are unsure whether they were being monitored or were not aware of any monitoring methods in use. This result is inline with a recent survey conducted by EDUCAUSE [6] where 55% of remote workers reported that they were not monitored during their work. One possible reason for this high response rate could be a lack of awareness of existing monitoring systems, as some organizations may not be fully transparent to their employees. The increase in the number of remote workers caused by the COVID-19 pandemic may also mean that organizations will begin implementing monitoring methods at a higher rate as they now rely on remote working more than ever.

Among the monitoring methods used by employers, "monitoring emails" was the most common (17%), followed by keyboard recorder (4.1%), screen recorder (4.1%), microphone (2.5%), and camera (1.5%). Additionally, 7% of the reported method were other methods, including methods such as third-party monitoring software or task monitoring programs. The participants were also asked if they had any of their employer's proprietary software on their personal equipment or computer. 63.5% responded "No", 33.5% "Yes", 2.5% did not know, and 1 participant (0.5%) chose to not respond.

## 4.3   Employees' Views on Remote Vs. Monitoring at Office

To understand how open/tolerable participants were to monitoring and if there was any difference between the participants' views on remote monitoring vs. monitoring at the employer's office/location (RQ-1), we asked participants to rate their agreement with the following two statements on a 5-point Likert scale with an option to choose not to respond. This was followed by an open-ended question asking them to explain the reasoning behind their answers.

- I believe my employer has the right to monitor my work activities while I work for them at their office/location
- I believe my employer has the right to monitor my work activities while I work remotely

For the quantitative part, using Spearman's coefficient, we found that participants have very similar perspectives on monitoring their work activities while working remotely and at their employer's office/location ($\rho = 0.823$, $p < 0.001$). The first statement had a mean value of 3.13 (Median = 4, SD = 1.23), while the second statement had a mean value of 2.89 (Median = 3, SD = 1.28).

We also computed the direction and extent of the shift in participants' answer between the two statements. For this variable, the range goes from $-4$ to $+4$, and it is positive for participants who are more tolerant with monitoring at office compared to remote monitoring and negative suggests the opposite (e.g., if a participant rated remote monitoring 1 (strongly disagree) and office monitoring 5 (strongly agree), the difference would be $-4$). The majority of the participants (80%) have a similar view for monitoring remotely and at their employer's office/location. However, more participants obtained positive score (34 vs. 5), suggesting that participants were less opposed to employer monitoring them in office/location than remote monitoring. One possible explanation for participants being less tolerant of remote work monitoring may be their expectations of having greater freedom to work remotely/work from home, or perhaps their concerns about privacy (e.g., with the prevalence of video monitoring, various aspects of employees' private lives can be captured on screen [24,41,42].)

For the qualitative part, we received 197 comments and organized these comments into 7 codes based on the reasons the participants gave for their ratings (i.e., employers right to monitor). The most common theme was "Employers have expectations for their paid work" with 99 comments (50.25%). The second most mentioned theme was "Work output should take precedence" with 66 comments (33.5%), followed by "Employers should trust their employees" with 63 comments (31.98%). "Employees have a right to privacy at home" had 38 comments (19.29%) and "Invasion of privacy" had 29 comments (14.72%). We also had 8 responses that we coded as "Unsure/prefer not to say/none" (4.06%) and 4 comments that were coded as "Other" (2.03%).

Comments such as *"I feel like I ought to have a right to privacy, but it is their machine that I am working on"* and *"They are paying me to work so I feel that it is within their own interest to monitor this is some way should they choose to do so. I do appreciate that currently they do not do this."* show some of the sentiments of the remote workers regarding employers' reasonable expectations for their paid work. These participants felt that it would be reasonable for their employers to monitor their work activities, as their employers own the equipment and are paying them their salaries.

Some participants felt that the results of their work should matter more to their employers than their specific actions. For example, they expressed things like *"I think that as long as I am producing results and meeting targets, monitoring my day to day activity is just a way to get more power and control.",* *"Outputs rather than work activities/time/intensity should be measured regardless of location.".*

Many participants also stressed the importance of trust within the workplace through comments such as *"It feels too invasion and unnecessary, like they don't trust their own employees"* and *"I believe if I sign a contract agreeing, they can do it. However, I dislike it and feel it indicates distrust. It would be easier to be disproportionate in monitoring if someone is working remotely - e.g. listening to their home life.".*

Additionally, since many participants were working from home, we identified many employees who felt they had the right to privacy when at home or when they used their personal devices. This sentiment was found in comments like *"They do not have the right to monitor me while I work from home because it would be an intrusion on my household's privacy."* and *"I use a personal desktop computer for the majority of my work activities while I work remotely, so I don't believe that entitles my employer to monitor my work. I would be concerned about the potential security implications of their monitoring of my work activities."*

Overall, these comments suggest that many of our participants understand their employers' reasoning behind monitoring their remote work, as their employers provide salaries and should act in the best interests of their businesses. However, while they understood the utility, the extent to which they would permit this monitoring had its limitations. We found many instances where monitoring would not be acceptable to these employees, as some believed this action showed a lack of trust in the workplace or constituted an invasion of their right to privacy. The process of remote working also leads to complications in the relationship between the supervisors and the supervised, with many believing that it would be unjust to be monitored within personal spaces on the same level they would be monitored in the office.

### 4.4   The Impact of Monitoring

To better understand which monitoring methods employees approve/disapprove and their potential impact on quitting, and refusal of a promotion/job offer (RQ-2), participants were presented with a list of monitoring methods commonly used by employers and asked to select those methods (multiple selections were permitted) in different situations such as refusing a job offer, promotion or quitting a job. In particular, the participants were asked the following questions with options 1) Keyboard Recorder, 2) Screen Recorder, 3) Listening and/or recording via a microphone, 4) Watching and/or recording via a camera, 5) Monitor and/or record emails and 6) No/None for each question.

1. Would you refuse a job offer if the potential employer used any of the following monitoring methods?
2. Would you refuse a promotion if the new position at your employer used any of the following monitoring methods?
3. Would you quit your job if you found out that your employer used any of the following monitoring methods?

Each of these questions were followed with an open-ended question that asked them to explain their reasons for choosing those monitoring methods, if any.

For the quantitative part, as shown in Fig. 1, we found that camera, microphone, and screen recorder were the the three most selected monitoring methods that would cause participants to refuse a job offer, refuse a promotion, or quit a job. Specifically, as a reason for refusing a job offer, 84% of participants selected being watched via a camera, 80% being recorded with a microphone, 58% a screen recorder being used, 56% a keyboard recorder being used, and 28% emails being monitored. Similarly, as a reason for refusing a promotion, 80% of participants selected being watched via a camera, 75% being recorded with a microphone, 54% a screen recorder being used, 51% a keyboard recorder being used, and 28% emails being monitored. The percentages are slightly lower when it comes to quitting a job. As a reason for quitting a job, 60% of participants selected being watched via a camera, 56% being recorded with a microphone, 40% a screen recorder being used, 37% a keyboard recorder being used, and 22% emails being monitored. On the other hand, 13% of participants selected that they would not refuse a job offer, 16% would not refuse a promotion, and 32% would not quit their job if any of the above monitoring methods were used by their employers.

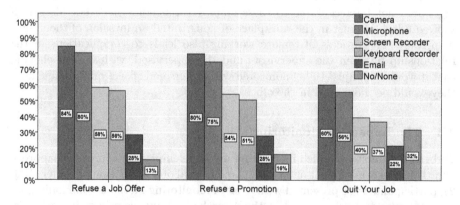

**Fig. 1.** Frequencies of participants' responses to whether they would refuse a job offer, a promotion or quit the job if the potential employer used 5 different monitoring methods. Note that percentages do not add up to 100% as a participant was allowed to select more than one options or none if that apply.

For the qualitative part, we received 197 comments for each open-ended question. Based on the reasons the participants gave for their ratings, we organized the comments into 6 codes for refusing a job offer and refusing a promotion, and 8 codes for quitting a job. The full list of codes with respect to each open-ended question can be found in the Table 1.

**Table 1.** Codes' frequency of occurrence in participants' reasoning behind their decision to approve or disapprove of a variety of monitoring methods in 3 different situations: 1) Refuse a Job Offer, 2) Refuse a Promotion, and 3) Quit a Job.

| | Count | | |
|---|---|---|---|
| | Refuse a Job Offer | Refuse a Promotion | Quit a Job |
| Invasion of privacy/concerns about security | 94 | 75 | 56 |
| Trust in the workplace | 49 | 46 | 44 |
| Monitoring methods are excessive/unnecessary | 45 | 53 | 24 |
| Monitoring is acceptable | 42 | 35 | 58 |
| Stressful | 29 | 17 | 23 |
| Transparency is crucial | N/A | N/A | 26 |
| Yes I would quit/start looking for a new job | N/A | N/A | 37 |
| Other/prefer not to say/none | 7 | 18 | 18 |

The most common theme we found was "Invasion of privacy/Concerns about security", with 48% of participants stated as a reason for refusing a job offer, 35% for refusing a promotion, and 28% for quitting their job. "Monitoring methods are excessive/unnecessary/invasive" and "Trust in the workplace" were also commonly mentioned by participants as a reason for refusing a job offer, promotion and quitting job.

Comments such as *"I would not like to be monitored while I work from home because it would be a violation of my right to privacy in my own home."*, and *"I work remote, a microphone or camera would capture things outside of my work device. They do not need to see my spouse, pets, kids (if I had any), etc. or hear anything said in my home."* reflect the participants' view on how some of the monitoring methods could compromise/jeopardize employee privacy.

Some of the participants also pointed out that monitoring would be unnecessary and intrusive, and also indicative of a low level of trust, which can endanger employee-employer relationship, job satisfaction and increase staff turnover as employees are more likely to search for more trusted employers [5]. For example, participants wrote the following: *"This [monitoring] is unnecessary and intrusive. On a deep evolutionary psychological level feeling that you are being watched all of the time could be damaging."* , *"These [monitoring methods] seem like ways to babysit employees and create a hostile environment for workers. You feel like they don't trust you."*, and *"I would not want to work for a company with such little trust in me. I feel that the above methods are a breach of privacy and should not be allowed in any company."*

The importance of transparency when it comes to monitoring was also echoed in some participants' comments such as: *"If I found out that my employer uses monitoring without me knowing about it, I would feel betrayed and I would not be able to trust my employer again.",* and *"I would quit if I found out that they were using those methods because that is a complete violation of privacy. I work from home, so I feel like my employer should be up front if they are going to record me in my home. I think that is going too far, and I don't feel like my employer needs access to see inside of or hear me inside my home."*

While some participants who were not against employer monitoring left comments such as: *"I feel that this [monitoring] is fair to ensure that all employees are doing the work they are paid to do",* others emphasized the important role of being in control of the monitoring method used. For instance, a participant indicated that *"... I might be willing to use a screen recorder and keyboard recorder, but only if I knew that I could turn off the software at any time without repercussion, as long as I am not specifically working at that time."*

## 4.5   Regression Analysis

**Identifying Factors Influencing Employee Satisfaction, Loyalty and Faith in Intentions Management:** To explore the extent to which different factors affect employee satisfaction, employee loyalty, and faith in intentions management (RQ-3), we performed a linear regression analysis for each of these dependent variables by including several independent variable covering employers' individual differences (e.g., age, gender, education level, annual income, marital status, level of computer proficiency, country they work in (US vs. UK)), trust in employer, and intention to disclose information to employer and ratings of openness for remote monitoring.

The results can be seen in Table 2, where each model's coefficients are presented with the significance level to indicate whether the independent variables are strong predictors of the corresponding dependent variable. The coefficient for each variable represents the outcome (e.g., higher or lower average ratings for employee satisfaction) when the coefficient is increased by one-unit while controlling all other numerical variables at their mean values and categorical variables at their baseline.

Regarding employee satisfaction and loyalty, trust in employer was found to be one of the strongest predictors of employee satisfaction and loyalty with a positive coefficient indicating participants who trust their employer were more likely to report higher employee satisfaction ($b = 0.40$, $p < 0.001$) and loyalty ($b = 0.41$, $p < 0.001$). Participants with a higher intention to disclose information ratings (i.e., more open to disclose information to their employers) were more likely to report higher employee satisfaction ($b = 0.04$, $p = 0.036$) and loyalty ($b = 0.04$, $p = 0.035$). There was also some evidence that participants' gender being female was associated with higher employee satisfaction ($b = 0.20$, $p = 0.090$) and loyalty ($b = 0.19$, $p = 0.091$). Also, participants with higher computer proficiency were marginally more likely to report higher employee satisfaction ($b = 0.14$, $p = 0.079$), while divorced participants were marginally more likely to report higher employee loyalty ($b = 0.44$, $p = 0.078$).

Regarding faith in intentions management, we found that participants who trust their employer were more likely to report higher faith in intentions management ($b = 0.57$, $p < 0.001$). Interestingly, participants who agreed more with "their employers have a right to monitor" were more likely to report lower faith in intentions management ($b = -0.14$, $p = 0.007$) (see the next section for further explanation). Participants currently working in the US were more likely to report higher faith in intentions management compared to participants currently working in the UK ($b = 0.27$, $p = 0.049$).

**Identifying Factors Influencing Employees' Openness to Employer Monitoring:** We also performed another linear regression analysis to better understand what factors influence employees' openness to employer monitoring. Similar to previous analysis, we included a similar set of individual differences as independent variables. Additionally, we included employee satisfaction, employee loyalty, and faith in intentions management as an exploratory variable to evaluate the relationships with employees' openness to employer monitoring (RQ-4). The results can be seen in Table 2.

The results indicate that participants with lower education level were more likely to give higher ratings for the openness to employer monitoring ($b = -0.11$, $p = 0.024$). Participants currently working in the US were more likely to agree that their employers have the right to monitor their work activities compared to participants currently working in the UK ($b = 0.37$, $p = 0.047$). Additionally, trust in employer was once again the strongest predictor of employers' openness to employer monitoring with a positive coefficient indicating that participants who trust their employer were more likely to agree that their employers have the right to monitor their work activities ($b = 0.49$, $p < 0.001$). Interestingly, participants who gave higher ratings for faith in intentions management were less likely to agree that their employers have the right to monitor their work activities ($b = -0.26$, $p = 0.024$). This result may seem counter-intuitive. However, as can be seen from the comments of some participants, although some participants have faith in intentions management, they may be against monitoring because they think that monitoring could potentially violate their privacy. For example, the following comment shed light on this aspect: *"I don't believe that my employer should be monitoring my activity as long as my work is being completed on time and to a sufficient standard. It feels like an infringement on my privacy and personal space, particularly while working remotely.",*

**Table 2.** Coefficients for the four different linear regressions predicting users' agreement with Employee Satisfaction, Employee Loyalty, Faith in Intentions Management, and Right to Monitor (i.e., Openness to Employer Monitoring). $R^2$ value corresponding to each regression is presented in the last line. "—" indicates that the variable was not included in the analysis, but independent variables are shown this way for the sake of brevity.

| | Employee Satisfaction | | Employee Loyalty | | Faith in Intentions | | Right to Monitor | |
|---|---|---|---|---|---|---|---|---|
| | Coeff. | Std. Error | Coeff. | Std. Error | Coeff. | Std. Error | Coeff. | Std. Error |
| **Gender (Baseline: Male** Gender: Female | 0.201 | 0.118 | 0.197 | 0.116 | −0.0096 | 0.127 | 0.0168 | 0.174 |
| Gender: Non-binary | 0.401 | 0.538 | 0.595 | 0.53 | 0.173 | 0.579 | 0.413 | 0.787 |
| Age | 0.004 | 0.006 | 0.004 | 0.006 | −0.002 | 0.006 | 0.011 | 0.009 |
| Education Level | −0.0003 | 0.033 | 0.019 | 0.033 | −0.020 | 0.036 | −0.111* | 0.048 |
| **Country Work In (Baseline: US** Country: UK | −0.135 | 0.129 | −0.164 | 0.127 | −0.276* | 0.139 | −0.377* | 0.188 |
| **Marital Status (Baseline: Single/Cohabiting** Marital Status: Married | 0.161 | 0.122 | 0.185 | 0.120 | 0.048 | 0.131 | −0.018 | 0.179 |
| Marital Status: Divorce | 0.383 | 0.256 | 0.447 | 0.252 | 0.200 | 0.276 | 0.042 | 0.376 |
| Marital Status: Widowed | −0.312 | 0.766 | 0.152 | 0.754 | 0.128 | 0.825 | −0.472 | 1.119 |
| **Employment Status (Baseline: Full-time** Employment Status: Part-time | 0.052 | 0.197 | 0.025 | 0.194 | −0.013 | 0.212 | 0.209 | 0.287 |
| Employment Status: Student | 0.707 | 0.761 | 0.835 | 0.748 | 0.956 | 0.819 | 0.653 | 1.113 |
| **Role (Baseline: Employee)** Role: Executive Management | −0.215 | 0.541 | −0.440 | 0.532 | −0.671 | 0.582 | −1.276 | 0.786 |
| Role: Middle Management | 0.248 | 1.088 | −0.920 | 1.070 | 0.466 | 1.171 | 0.680 | 1.603 |
| Role: Independent Researcher | 0.109 | 0.120 | 0.125 | 0.118 | −0.058 | 0.129 | 0.005 | 0.175 |
| Computer Proficiency | 0.142 | 0.804 | 0.026 | 0.079 | −0.096 | 0.086 | −0.115 | 0.120 |
| Intention to Close | 0.047* | 0.022 | 0.046* | 0.022 | 0.020 | 0.024 | 0.045 | 0.032 |
| Trust in Employer | 0.405** | 0.052 | 0.410** | 0.051 | 0.573** | 0.056 | 0.493** | 0.090 |
| Right to Monitor | −0.079 | 0.051 | −0.064 | 0.050 | −0.149** | 0.054 | — | — |
| Employee Satisfaction | — | — | — | — | — | — | −0.112 | 0.199 |
| Employee Loyalty | — | — | — | — | — | — | 0.094 | 0.206 |
| Faith in Intentions | — | — | — | — | — | — | −0.263* | 0.116 |
| Intercept | 0.476 | 0.541 | 0.945 | 0.532 | 1.708** | 0.58 | 2.016* | 0.787 |
| $R^2$ | 0.37 | | 0.38 | | 0.26 | | 0.27 | |

$** \ p < 0.01, * \ p < 0.05.$

## 4.6   Path Analysis

We performed a path analysis to further explore the relationship among the important factors identified in the regression analysis (see previous section). Figure 2 presents path model's coefficients for all direct effects and relationships among trust, "intention to disclose" and participants' opinions on "employers' right to monitor" as well as employee satisfaction, faith in intentions management and employee loyalty (Table 3 shows the direct, indirect and total effects for each path). The results indicate that trust in employer was a significant positive predictor of "intention to disclose" ($b = .83$, $SE = .15$, $p < 0.001$; $\beta = .36$)

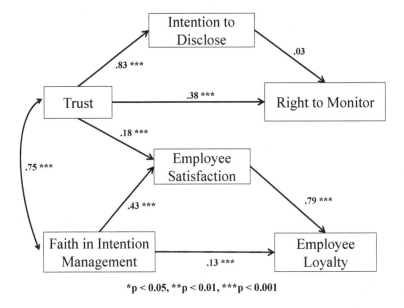

$$*p < 0.05, **p < 0.01, ***p < 0.001$$

**Fig. 2.** Path diagram of the relationships among trust, "intention to disclose" and participants opinions on "employers' right to monitor" as well as employee satisfaction, faith in intentions management and employee loyalty ($n = 194$). The chi-square goodness of fit test was not significant ($\chi^2(7) = 9.78$, $p = 0.20$), suggesting a good fit of the model to the data. The RMSEA (Root mean squared error of approximation) value was .045 and the pclose test was not significant (p = .48), values < .05 are considered indicative of close fit [51]. The CFI (Comparative fit index) and TLI (Tucker-Lewis index) were both > .95, while the SRMR (Standardized root mean squared residual) was .03. All of these metrics suggest a good fitting model.

and "employers' right to monitor" ($b = .38$, $SE = .07$, $p < 0.001$; $\beta = .38$). However, the path coefficient from "intention to disclose" to "employers' right to monitor" was not significant ($b = .03$, $SE = .03$, $p = .28$; $\beta = .07$), thus 'intention to disclose" was not found to be as the mediator of the association between trust in employer and "employers' right to monitor".

We also found that trust in employer was a significant predictor of employee satisfaction ($b = .18$, $SE = .05$, $p < 0.001$; $\beta = .24$). The indirect effect of trust on employee loyalty was also significant ($b = .14$, $SE = .04$, $p < 0.001$). The path coefficients from faith in intentions management to employee satisfaction ($b = .43$, $SE = .04$, $p < 0.001$; $\beta = .48$) and from employee satisfaction to employee loyalty were significant ($b = .79$, $SE = .05$, $p < 0.001$; $\beta = .78$). There was a significant effect of faith in intentions management predicting employee loyalty, mediated by employee satisfaction (total effect $b = .47$, $SE = .05$, $p < 0.001$, $95\%CI = [.36, .58]$).

**Table 3.** Path model's coefficients along with standard errors (in parentheses), significance level and 95% confidence intervals. (Paths are shown in Fig. 2.)

| Effect | Coef. (Std. Err) | p | 95% CI |
|---|---|---|---|
| Trust->Intention to disclose (direct effect) | .83 (.15) | <0.001 | [.53, 1.12] |
| Intention to disclose->Right to monitor (direct effect) | .03 (.03) | 0.289 | [−.02, .09] |
| Trust->Right to monitor (direct effect) | .38 (.07) | <0.001 | [.24, .51] |
| Trust->Employee satisfaction (direct effect) | .18 (.05) | <0.001 | [.08, .28] |
| Faith in intentions management->Employee satisfaction (direct effect) | .43 (.05) | <0.001 | [.30, .54] |
| Employee satisfaction->Employee loyalty (direct effect) | .79 (.04) | <0.001 | [.70, .86] |
| Faith in intentions management->Employee loyalty (direct effect) | .13 (.03) | <0.001 | [.06, .20] |
| Faith in intentions management->Employee loyalty (indirect effect) | .34 (.05) | <0.001 | [.23, .43] |
| Faith in intentions of management->Employee loyalty (total effect) | .46 (.05) | <0.001 | [.36, .57] |
| Trust->Employee loyalty (total effect) | .14 (.04) | <0.001 | [.06, .22] |

Additionally, the correlation between trust and faith in intentions management was significant (covariance coeff = .75, correlation = .62, $p < 0.001$).

## 5    Discussion

Because of the sudden adoption of "work from home" trend due to the COVID-19 pandemic, practices related to monitoring have become an even more important topic in society today [25]. Towards that, this study makes an important contribution to the literature about remote workers' perceptions on employee monitoring by providing both quantitative and qualitative analysis. Our findings can have important implications not only for employers to develop or design better policies, but also for them to learn how employees perceive monitoring. We present implications of our findings and limitation of our study below.

### 5.1    Findings and Implications

We observed that while the majority of participants ( 80%) had similar views about being monitored in their home office versus being monitored at their employer's office/location, those with differing views were more opposed to being monitored in their home than being monitoring at office/location. Participants justified this by saying they do not want their home's privacy to be invaded by the work/employer. Moreover, participants' disapproval for several monitoring methods in various contexts were observed. In particular, the majority of our participants deemed the use of camera, microphone and screen recorder as the most concerning monitoring methods that would cause them to refuse a job offer, promotion and even quit their job (RQ-2). We have found that even email monitoring, which was indicated by the participants as the least intrusive monitoring method, had a significant negative impact on employee perceptions. 28% of our participants would refuse a job offer or a promotion, and 22% would quit their current jobs. Less acceptable monitoring methods than email monitoring, such as camera, microphone and screen recording, can have even more detrimental effects on employees. Thus, organizations planning to implement these monitoring methods should consider the potential impact on the productivity and stability of their workforce before they are used.

Our results also indicate that employees who trust their employers are more likely to have higher employee satisfaction, employee loyalty, and faith in intentions management. Additionally, we observed that although participants with high trust in their employers are more likely to be open/tolerable for employer monitoring and to disclose more information to their employer, higher intention to disclose ratings does not necessarily mean they are more comfortable with being monitored. This suggests that intention to disclose has little bearing on employers' right to monitor. As noted in previous research [1, 26], we surmise that controllability can affect the value people place on personal information, and impact information disclosure. When individuals choose to disclose private information about themselves to their employer, it is in their control. However, some forms of monitoring methods can relinquish control to employers. For instance, if a camera and/or microphone is used to monitor, it is much more difficult for an employer to control what information is captured in the monitoring process. In this case, since controllability is limited, information such as activity of their family in the background may be disclosed regardless of whether the employee is comfortable with it or not. This can be especially concerning with the growing use of always-on webcam policies employed in organizations to encourage spontaneous chats among employees and even being photographed without employees' knowledge using tools like Sneek [20], since refusing this type of surveillance can potentially increase the risk of unemployment during the pandemic [8, 11, 22]. Thus, designing monitoring methods that allow employees to have a higher level of usable control can make employees tolerable for employer monitoring.

Previous studies [2, 14, 25] have shown that employees typically perceive monitoring negatively and monitoring can have negative effects on them (e.g., increased stress and a reduction in job satisfaction). To increase job satisfaction and a stable and productive workforce, employers should carefully determine what monitoring methods are needed and justified before implementing them [50, 53]. These decisions should also take into account the industry in which they operate, including their regulations, the job roles being affected, and the sensitivity of the information being monitored. In line with previous work [49, 53], we found that trust in employer was a significant predictor of employee satisfaction and loyalty. Participants' comments highlighted that the transparency of monitoring, and clearly communicating the rationale for the monitoring method used can have significant impacts on how employees react and accept monitoring methods. This finding, once again, reinforces that trust is the most important pillar of a healthy employee-employer relationship, which can improve performance and productivity in workplace [36, 44].

## 5.2 Limitations and Future Work

While this study shed light on the perceptions of remote workers with respect to various monitoring methods and the potential effects of these monitoring methods on the workplace, our study had several limitations that could be addressed in future work.

First, as this study focused on the employee perspective, employers' perspectives on various monitoring methods were not observed. Future studies considering both employee and employer perspectives can provide a full view of the effects of remote work monitoring on the workplace. This can also help to obtain more accurate results regarding the types of monitoring methods that are actually used. Our current results may also have been influenced by employee self-report biases as some participants may be unaware of certain monitoring methods implemented by their employers.

Second, our study focused on a limited number of monitoring methods to keep the study tractable. Although the monitoring methods chosen in this study are commonly used by employers [6], there are additional monitoring methods such as monitoring the use of employer-provided mobile device, monitoring phone calls with clients or customers, tracking location using GPS devices to in employer-owned vehicles, and opening of mails addressed to the workplace [7], which can be investigated in future studies.

Third, while Prolific users are known to be demographically diverse subjects [43], participants from Prolific might be more tech savvy and more competent regarding monitoring technologies than the general population. Moreover, our study included remote workers employed in the US or UK. The working conditions, privacy concerns and attitudes in these areas may differ significantly from the rest of the world. Both of these factors can limit the generalizability of our findings. A larger sample size along with a wider range of participants can be beneficial towards providing a broader view of the perception of monitoring methods on remote workers.

Finally, opinions on monitoring remote work may also be influenced by the industry in which it takes place. For example, a governmental employee may have a different point of view than an employee in a private company regarding the need for monitoring to check productivity. To account for these potential differences, future studies may be conducted on remote employees in specific fields. To capture more interesting insights concerning this topic, there may also be a benefit from conducting an interview study where employees can elaborate on their ideas in-person.

# 6   Conclusion

We conducted an online survey with 197 remote workers to better understand their perceptions, concerns and attitudes regarding employee monitoring. We found that the most disapproved monitoring methods by the participants were the use of cameras, microphones and screen recorders that would cause them to refuse a job offer or a promotion or to quit their current job. Our qualitative findings indicated that concerns about invasion of privacy and safety were the main reasons behind their disapproval decisions. While the majority of participants (80%) had a similar view about being monitored in their home office and being monitored at their employer's office/location, those with different views thought that their employers have less right to monitor them at their home. Trust in employers was found to be the most important factor behind employee satisfaction, employee loyalty, and faith in intentions management. Also, our findings suggest that while high trust in employers was a predictor of both openness for employer monitoring and the amount of information to disclose, higher ratings for intention to disclose was not a predictor of being comfortable with employee monitoring. We discussed the implications of our findings in the context of new landscape of remote working and provided insight into how remote workers view or approve/disapprove of different monitoring methods. Our findings could be beneficial for employers considering implementing monitoring methods for their remote workers, researchers/practitioners studying in the field of security and privacy technologies, and monitoring software developers to design monitoring systems and policies with usable control and transparency of monitoring in mind.

**Acknowledgments.** This work was supported by the Central Connecticut State University Faculty & Student Research Grant (No. AFALZP).

# References

1. Acquisti, A., et al.: Nudges for privacy and security: Understanding and assisting users' choices online. ACM Comput. Surv. **50**(3), 1–41 (2017)
2. Aiello, J.R., Svec, C.M.: Computer monitoring of work performance: extending the social facilitation framework to electronic presence 1. J. Appl. Soc. Psychol. **23**(7), 537–548 (1993)
3. Alder, G.S.: Employee reactions to electronic performance monitoring: a consequence of organizational culture. J. High Technol. Manag. Res. **12**(2), 323–342 (2001)
4. Barbuto, A., Gilliland, A., Peebles, R., Rossi, N., Shrout, T.: Telecommuting: Smarter Workplaces (2020)
5. Brett, A.: The effects of low trust in the workplace (2015). https://cutt.ly/RHLM2SJ
6. Brooks, D.C.: EDUCAUSE QuickPoll Results: Privacy and the Remote Workforce (2021). https://er.educause.edu/blogs/2021/2/educause-quickpoll-results-privacy-and-the-remote-workforce
7. Clearinghouse, P.R.: Workplace Privacy and Employee Monitoring (2019). https://cutt.ly/4HL1JGu

8. Cohen, P., Hsu, T.: Rolling Shock' as Job Losses Mount Even With Reopenings (2020). https://www.nytimes.com/2020/05/14/business/economy/coronavirus-unemployment-claims.html
9. Cole-Laramore, A., et al.: Trust and technology in the virtual organization. In: SAM, vol. 67, pp. 22–25 (2002)
10. Cook, J., Wall, T.: New work attitude measures of trust, organizational commitment and personal need non-fulfilment. J. Occupat. Psychol. 53(1), 39–52 (1980)
11. Emami-Naeini, P., Francisco, T., Kohno, T., Roesner, F.: Understanding privacy attitudes and concerns towards remote communications during the covid-19 pandemic. In: Seventeenth Symposium on Usable Privacy and Security (SOUPS 2021), pp. 695–714. USENIX Association (2021)
12. Freelon, D.: Recal oir: ordinal, interval, and ratio intercoder reliability as a web service. Int. J. Internet Sci. 8(1) (2013)
13. Galanxhi, H., Nah, F.F.-H.: Addressing the "Unseens": digital wellbeing in the remote workplace. In: Nah, F.F.-H., Siau, K. (eds.) HCII 2021. LNCS, vol. 12783, pp. 347–364. Springer, Cham (2021). https://doi.org/10.1007/978-3-030-77750-0_22
14. George, J.F.: Computer-based monitoring: common perceptions and empirical results. MIS Quart. 459–480 (1996)
15. Gliem, J.A., Gliem, R.R.: Calculating, interpreting, and reporting Cronbach's alpha reliability coefficient for likert-type scales. In: Midwest Research-to-Practice Conference in Adult, Continuing, and Community Eduction. Midwest Research-to-Practice Conference in Adult, Continuing, and Community Eduction (2003)
16. Haag, C.D.: Instructor's manual to accompany: management information systems for the information age (1998)
17. Hill, S.: Employers are spying on remote workers in their homes (2020). https://cutt.ly/BHLN5op
18. Hodson, T.J., Englander, F., Englander, V.: Ethical, legal and economic aspects of employer monitoring of employee electronic mail. J. Bus. Ethics 19(1), 99–108 (1999)
19. Holland, P.J., Cooper, B., Hecker, R.: Electronic monitoring and surveillance in the workplace: the effects on trust in management, and the moderating role of occupational type. Person. Rev. (2015)
20. Holmes, A.: Employees at home are being photographed every 5 minutes by an always-on video service to ensure they're actually working (2020). https://cutt.ly/IHLMo84
21. Homburg, C., Stock, R.M.: Exploring the conditions under which salesperson work satisfaction can lead to customer satisfaction. Psychol. Market. 22(5), 393–420 (2005)
22. Jagannathan, M.: Like "punching a time clock through your webcam": how employers are keeping tabs on remote workers during the pandemic (2020). https://cutt.ly/EHLMQFi
23. Jandl, C., Taurer, F., Hartner-Tiefenthaler, M., Wagner, M., Moser, T., Schlund, S.: Perceptions of using tracking and tracing systems in work environments. In: Nah, F.F.-H., Siau, K. (eds.) HCII 2021. LNCS, vol. 12783, pp. 384–398. Springer, Cham (2021). https://doi.org/10.1007/978-3-030-77750-0_24
24. Jeske, D.: Monitoring remote employees: implications for hr. Strategic HR Review (2021)
25. Kalischko, T., Riedl, R.: Electronic performance monitoring in the digital workplace: conceptualization, review of effects and moderators, and future research opportunities. Front. Psychol. 12 (2021)

26. Kitkowska, A., Warner, M., Shulman, Y., Wästlund, E., Martucci, L.A.: Enhancing privacy through the visual design of privacy notices: exploring the interplay of curiosity, control and affect. In: Sixteenth Symposium on Usable Privacy and Security (SOUPS 2020), pp. 437–456. USENIX Association (2020)
27. Krippendorff, K.: Testing the reliability of content analysis data. The Content Analysis Reader, pp. 350–357 (2009)
28. Kropp, B.: The Future of Employee Monitoring (2019). https://cutt.ly/yHLNBLx
29. Latto, A.: Managing risk from within: monitoring employees the right way. Risk Manag. **54**(4), 30 (2007)
30. Lavelle, J.: Gartner CFO Survey Reveals 74% Intend to Shift Some Employees to Remote Work Permanently (2020). https://cutt.ly/hHLNKfj
31. Lee, S., Kleiner, B.H.: Electronic surveillance in the workplace. Manag. Res. News (2003)
32. Malhotra, N.K., Kim, S.S., Agarwal, J.: Internet users' information privacy concerns (IUIPC): the construct, the scale, and a causal model. Inf. Syst. Res. **15**(4), 336–355 (2004)
33. Marinova, I.: 28 Need-To-Know Remote Work Statistics of 2021 (2021). https://review42.com/resources/remote-work-statistics/
34. Matzler, K., Renzl, B.: The relationship between interpersonal trust, employee satisfaction, and employee loyalty. Total Quality Manag. Bus. Excellence **17**(10), 1261–1271 (2006)
35. McNall, L.A., Roch, S.G.: Effects of electronic monitoring types on perceptions of procedural justice, interpersonal justice, and privacy 1. J. Appl. Soc. Psychol. **37**(3), 658–682 (2007)
36. McNall, L.A., Roch, S.G.: A social exchange model of employee reactions to electronic performance monitoring. Human Perform. **22**(3), 204–224 (2009)
37. Migliano, S.: Employee Surveillance Software Demand up 58% Since Pandemic Started (2020). https://cutt.ly/xHLmaok
38. Miles, M.B., Huberman, A.M.: Qualitative Data Analysis: An Expanded Sourcebook. SAGE (1994)
39. Moorman, R.H., Wells, D.L.: Can electronic performance monitoring be fair? Exploring relationships among monitoring characteristics, perceived fairness, and job performance. J. Leadership Organ. Stud. **10**(2), 2–16 (2003)
40. Nagy, A.: Business Wire: Productivity Has Increased, Led By Remote Workers (2020). https://www.businesswire.com/news/home/20200519005295/en/
41. Nurse, J.R. C., Williams, N., Collins, E., Panteli, N., Blythe, J., Koppelman, B.: Remote working pre- and post-COVID-19: an analysis of new threats and risks to security and privacy. In: Stephanidis, C., Antona, M., Ntoa, S. (eds.) HCII 2021. CCIS, vol. 1421, pp. 583–590. Springer, Cham (2021). https://doi.org/10.1007/978-3-030-78645-8_74
42. Obada-Obieh, B., Huang, Y., Beznosov, K.: Challenges and threats of mass telecommuting: a qualitative study of workers. In: Seventeenth Symposium on Usable Privacy and Security (SOUPS 2021), pp. 675–694. USENIX Association (2021)
43. Palan, S., Schitter, C.: Prolific. ac-a subject pool for online experiments. J. Behav. Exp. Financ. **17**, 22–27 (2018)
44. Ravid, D.M., Tomczak, D.L., White, J.C., Behrend, T.S.: EPM 20/20: a review, framework, and research agenda for electronic performance monitoring. J. Manag. **46**(1), 100–126 (2020)
45. Schawbel, D.: How Covid-19 has Accelerated the Use of Employee Monitoring (2020). https://cutt.ly/9HLNIsa

46. Schumacher, S.: What employees should know about electronic performance monitoring. ESSAI **8**(1), 38 (2011)
47. Smith, T.: Monitoring employee e-mails: is there any room for privacy? Acad. Manag. Perspect. **23**, 33–48 (2009)
48. Stanton, J.M.: Reactions to employee performance monitoring: framework, review, and research directions. Human Perform. **13**(1), 85–113 (2000)
49. Stanton, J.M., Barnes-Farrell, J.L.: Effects of electronic performance monitoring on personal control, task satisfaction, and task performance. J. Appl. Psychol. **81**(6), 738 (1996)
50. Stanton, J.M., Sarkar-Barney, S.T.: A detailed analysis of task performance with and without computer monitoring. Int. J. Human Comput. Interact. **16**(2), 345–366 (2003)
51. Stevens, J.P.: Applied multivariate statistics for the social sciences. Routledge (2012)
52. Tabak, F., Smith, W.P.: Privacy and electronic monitoring in the workplace: a model of managerial cognition and relational trust development. Employee Respons. Rights J. **17**(3), 173–189 (2005)
53. Wells, D.L., Moorman, R.H., Werner, J.M.: The impact of the perceived purpose of electronic performance monitoring on an array of attitudinal variables. Human Resour. Develop. Quart. **18**(1), 121–138 (2007)

# Usability Evaluation Towards a Cultural Perspective: Design Guidelines for Peruvian Government Websites

Yoluana Gamboa[(✉)], Juan Jesús Arenas, and Freddy Paz

Pontificia Universidad Católica del Perú, San Miguel, Lima 32, Peru
{a20140058,fpaz}@pucp.pe, jjarenas@pucp.edu.pe

**Abstract.** Usability currently plays an essential role in the software development process. Companies are increasingly concerned with offering understandable, attractive, and easy-to-use websites to ensure their success in the market. However, based on usability studies, cultural factors can affect how people interact with the systems. Although multiple investigations have been conducted to determine the best design settings for each cultural context, there is no evidence of research that analyses the perspective of Latin American countries. In this study, we have analyzed the Cultural Models to establish guidelines that can guide the design of web usable user interfaces oriented to Peruvian citizens. Including cultural factors with which Peruvians are familiar could increase satisfaction with the website. The proposed guidelines were established and validated through a systematic methodology that involved several structured and well-defined steps. In this process, and using the proper cultural model, prominent design elements were identified as those that must represent the cultural identity and, therefore, must guide the design process of a Peruvian website. The selection of featured design elements was based on analyzing cultural factors and design elements presented on Peruvian websites and from countries with similar cultural characteristics. This work intends to serve as a reference to increase the quality of the software systems offered to citizens in Latin America.

**Keywords:** Human-computer interaction · Usability heuristics · Case study · Cultural-oriented heuristics · Web interfaces

## 1 Introduction

Currently, software products are essential in people's daily lives and are topics of interest for various companies in multiple sectors [23]. Because of this, specialists in the field of Human-Computer Interaction have developed several guidelines and methods that allow development teams to determine if a website reaches an adequate level of usability [13]. The purpose of developers and designers is to achieve a set of interfaces that are understandable, easy to use, and attractive to end-users. Likewise, providing interfaces aimed at achieving the user's objectives has a significant impact on the software product's success in the market.

© The Author(s), under exclusive license to Springer Nature Switzerland AG 2022
M. Kurosu et al. (Eds.): HCII 2022, LNCS 13516, pp. 383–395, 2022.
https://doi.org/10.1007/978-3-031-17615-9_26

To increase the degree of usability of websites, the specialists are incorporating cultural characteristics of societies in the design of the interfaces. In addition, considering cultural aspects allows a better understanding of users' needs and goals and, at the same time, a better analysis of the context of use [4]. In this sense, multiple studies have been carried out in various countries to obtain outstanding social characteristics. Likewise, different cultural models have been formulated and are currently the theoretical basis to address the issue of design and user experience in software interfaces in a more appropriate way [15].

Some proposals of design guidelines that address cultural aspects have been applied and validated on websites of Electronic Commerce, Electronic Government, Academics, and others [27]. The usage of these guidelines with a cultural approach is being increasingly recognized as a value proposition for the design and evaluation of websites aimed at improving the level of usability [24]. Websites that should reflect cultural load are those belonging to government entities. Their target audience is mainly delimited by people who live in the same country and share heritage characteristics. However, usability studies oriented to the cultural field have not been applied to evaluate the design of these websites based on the cultural characteristics of the Peruvian society [15]. There are no studies on the suggested guidelines for designing Peruvian government websites that involve local social aspects. Including these characteristics in the design and evaluation of the different sites belonging to government entities in Peru will allow a broader analysis of the differences in user satisfaction compared to the strategy without considering the cultural issue.

This research intends to provide a design or evaluation tool that can be used both in academia and the industrial field to obtain high-quality software products. The premise that we are corroborating with this study is that considering cultural aspects in the design of interfaces generates a feeling of familiarity in users that produces satisfaction and, at the same time, allows the achievement of their objectives with efficiency and efficacy.

## 2   Theoretical Background

### 2.1   Cultural Models

In a previous work [15], a systematic review was carried out with the aim of identifying cultural models that have been used for the design of graphical interfaces of software products. This literature review was performed applying the methodology proposed by B. Kitchenham [22]. Several cultural models were found, which are described as follows:

- **Cultural dimensions** (Hofstede, Geert) [19]: Hofstede's study focuses on analyzing the culture, mainly in the work environment. It presents a comparative classification between countries.
- **Cultural factors** (Hall, Edward) [18]: Hall's approach focuses on non-verbal communication, specifically about context, time and space.

- **Cultural factors** (Trompenaars, Fons and Hampden-Turner, Charles) [29]: Trompenaars and Hampden-Turner's study focuses on aspects of the individual, communication styles, temporal orientation, and environment control. It presents percentages by country according to respondents for situations related to the components of the cultural model.
- **LESCANT model** (Victor, David) [30]: Victor's work presents seven areas to which reference is made when addressing business communication on an international scale.
- **Cognitive model** (Nisbett, Richard) [25]: Nisbett's research focuses on the relationship between people, the context, and the preferences to explain and predict events. Predictions can be explained by analyzing the relationships or through rules.

These findings have made it possible to identify an overview of the various approaches that could guide the graphical user interface design process. Based on these models, the next step was to identify the most appropriate cultural model to build a set of design guidelines specific to the Peruvian context. The models were subsequently compared and thoroughly analyzed based on explicit criteria to determine the most suitable.

## 3   Cultural Models in Usability Studies

In usability studies, it is established that specialists employ cultural models to incorporate cultural concepts into design elements of a graphical user interface. The frequency of cultural model usage depends on several factors, such as the country under study, the technology to be designed, the cultural aspect to be addressed, and the specialists' experience regarding the model. In this section, an analysis of each identified cultural model will be detailed, as well as the result of the selection process that was carried out to select the most appropriate proposal to establish design guidelines for the Peruvian cultural context.

### 3.1   Analysis of Cultural Models

The studies on usability with a cultural approach were obtained through a systematic literature review (SLR) conducted in the Scopus, IEEExplore, and Web of Science search engines in which scientific articles published since 2000 were considered [15]. The search retrieved 109 documents, and by using previously established inclusion and exclusion criteria, 14 relevant and primary studies were selected, which are presented in Table 1. Usability studies commonly reference one or more cultural models in order to use them as a guide to incorporate cultural aspects into web design. As shown in Table 1, even though few authors have addressed the issue of the cultural aspect in the interfaces design, there are studies regarding this topic. In these studies, the specialists propose design guidelines based on cultural models. References of each cultural model in usability studies found are presented in Table 2.

Table 1. Complete list of primary studies that were selected

| Study ID | Author(s) | Year |
|---|---|---|
| A01 [20] | Hu, J., Shima, K., Oehlmann, R., Zhao, J. et al. | 2004 |
| A02 [14] | Fraternali, P., Tisi, M | 2008 |
| A03 [31] | Wan Mohd Isa, W.A.R., Md Noor, N.L., Mehad, S | 2010 |
| A04 [21] | Jano, Z., Noor, S.M., Ahmad, R., Md Saad, M.S., et al. | 2015 |
| A05 [5] | Alostath, J.M., Almoumen, S., Alostath, A.B | 2009 |
| A06 [2] | Alexander, R., Murray, D., Thompson, N | 2017 |
| A07 [3] | Alexander, R., Murray, D., Thompson, N | 2017 |
| A08 [26] | Park, J.Y | 2015 |
| A09 [9] | Cyr, D., Head, M., Larios, H | 2010 |
| A10 [1] | Aladwani, A.M | 2013 |
| A11 [6] | Burgmann, I., Kitchen, P.J., Williams, R | 2006 |
| A12 [11] | Díaz, J., Rusu, C., Pow-Sang, J.A., Roncagliolo, S | 2013 |
| A13 [17] | Gould, E., Zalcaria, N., Yusof, S.A.M | 2000 |
| A14 [28] | Snelders, D., Morel, K.P., Havermans, P | 2011 |
| A15 [7] | Chu, J., Zhu, X | 2010 |

According to the results shown in Table 2, it is possible to establish that the most recognized cultural model by the scientific community is the Geert Hofstede proposal [19]. This fact could be because Hofstede, unlike the other authors, has established numerical values for each country, including Latin America, in each of the cultural components that define his model. In this way, it is easy for specialists to make comparisons and identify, according to the defined components, the cultural peculiarities of the citizens of a given country. For example, Fig. 1 shows the values of each cultural component for Peru. Based on these findings, which are the result of applying a large set of surveys, Peruvians respect hierarchies of power, are collectivist, have gender equality, and have a medium rejection of uncertainty, which means that people not necessarily avoid taking risks. Identifying the characteristics of people helps to make better design decisions as it allows the creation of interfaces with which users feel identified, especially in government websites that should be necessarily citizen-oriented. Likewise, it is necessary to consider that many companies are already taking these characteristics of the culture and country to place images that represent correctly to citizens [8]. Similarly, they distribute the graphic elements in the interfaces depending on whether the population is high or low context and requires a lot of text or explanation for products or preference for animations and interactions [10].

It is essential to mention that although article A01 is not listed in Table 2, it is because it did not state the usage of a specific cultural model for the study of usability. However, within the systematic review process that was carried out, this paper allowed to answer other formulated research questions [15]. The remaining research questions in the systematic review process were oriented to identify usability evaluation proposals related to cultural aspects reported in the literature and design guidelines that address cultural elements. From these results obtained, we can affirm that there are very few studies in which cross-cultural design has been addressed, focusing on Latin America and non-existent evidence, specifically in Peru.

**Table 2.** Cultural models in usability studies

| Cultural model | References | Total |
|---|---|---|
| Cultural dimensions (Hofstede, Geert) | A02, A03, A04, A05, A06, A07, A08, A09, A10, A11, A12, A13, A14, A15 | 14 |
| Cultural factors (Hall, Edward) | A04, A05, A06, A07, A08 | 5 |
| Cultural factors (Trompenaars, Fons and Hampden-Turner, Charles) | A05, A08, A13 | 3 |
| LESCANT model (Victor, David) | A05, A08 | 2 |
| Cognitive model (Nisbett, Richard) | A08 | 1 |

### 3.2  Selection of Cultural Model

Once the cultural models were identified through the literature review, the most appropriate model was selected as the basis to elaborate the design guidelines proposal. In this sense, a set of criteria was established to determine the model that provides the most significant characteristics of the cultural aspects of the Peruvian population. The criteria for the selection of a cultural model was the following:

- **Scope of the study:** Both Hofstede [19] and Trompenaars [29] conducted and compared cross-country studies among more than 40 countries. However, Hall [18] includes countries such as the US, Germany, France and Japan, and mentions some characteristics of Latin America, but does not include specific information about Peru. In the case of Victor's approach [30], not enough information was found about the countries and cultures involved. Conversely, Nisbett studies the difference in the cognitive processes for Asians and Westerns [25].
- **Constitution of the cultural model:** Hofstede presented five dimensions for the classification of countries, which are used in studies on web design guidelines. For Hall's model, the studies found mainly take into account two

of its factors: Context (High Context vs Low Context) and Perception of time (Monochronic/Polychronic) [17]. For Nisbett's model, holistic and analytic perspectives of cognitive processes are taken into account in studies on web usability [12].

- **Presence of the Model in the elaboration of design guidelines:** Cultural models by Hofstede, Hall and Trompenaars has been referenced by studies about design guidelines. Hofstede's cultural model is the mostly used by studies on design guidelines with a cultural approach.
- **Inclusion of Peru in the studies:** Hofstede has carried out an extensive comparative study between countries, among which is Peru [16]. Hall [18] mentions cultural characteristics of Latin America, but does not specify anything regarding the Peruvian cultural context. In the case of the other cultural models, not enough information was found on the inclusion of Peruvian culture in their comparative studies.

Hofestede's Cultural dimensions are the most widely used in studies on usability with a cultural approach and in studies on proposed design guidelines. Likewise, it is the cultural model that includes the Peruvian culture within the scope of its study, which is required due to the nature of research. Based on the previous analysis, the cultural model proposed by Hofstede [19] is the approach that was used for the development of the design guidelines.

### 3.3   Peru According Hofstede's Cultural Dimentions

Hofstede studies gives a score for each of the dimensions of the cultural model [16]. These values have been obtained based on a set of multiple surveys carried out in these countries that aimed to determine their cultural aspects.

Due to this, Peruvian culture can be considered to reflect high Distance to Power, Collectivism, Femininity, high Evasion of uncertainty and low Long-term Orientation. These data are helpful to establish the relationship with the elements of web design according to the procedure used in the studies on the elaboration of web design guidelines with a cultural approach [2]. Likewise, Fig. 1 shows the differences between a Latin American cultures such as Peru, and United States. According to these values, it can be seen that in the North American culture, less importance is given to hierarchies, and horizontal organizational structures are used instead. Similarly, there is a significant difference in the way people are. While in Latin American culture, collectivism and teamwork prevail in achieving goals, in North America, personal purposes and objectives are fundamental. In addition, in the United States, there is a higher rate of masculinity, which means that there is a strongly differentiated gap between men and women, which is evidenced to a lesser degree in Peru. The Latin American culture has a greater predisposition to take and face risks. On the contrary, in North America, there is a preference for controlling situational scenarios, establishing rules, and respecting the tradition. As a final aspect, it can be seen that there are no differences in the dimension of long-term orientation, which means constancy that past traditional ceremonies and procedures are valued equally in both cultures.

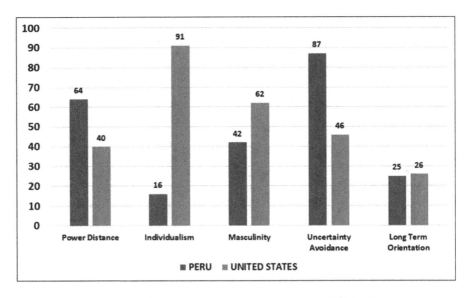

**Fig. 1.** Estimated values for Peru and United States for each of the dimensions established in Hofstede's cultural model. [16]

## 4   Proposal of Design Guidelines

### 4.1   Web Page Elements, Culture, and a Comparative Analysis

Based on the studies obtained in the systematic literature review [1,3,21,31] and through a comprehensive analysis of reported studies, we conclude that there is an existing correlation between Hofstede's cultural dimensions and web design guidelines. Given the previous relation, to obtain web design guidelines applicable to Peru, we performed a country comparison among Peru and other countries included in the previous cited studies.

For each country under analysis, we used Hofstede's estimated cultural dimension values to identify the ones which are more similar to Peru. Thus, Power Distance related guidelines applicable to China and Saudi Arabia are also applicable to Peru due to the similarity in their associated values. The same analysis is used to determine which guidelines are applicable to Peru according to Hofstede's values for Individualism, Masculinity, Uncertainty Avoidance, and Long Term Orientation.

Based on the comparative analysis established in Fig. 2, Peruvian culture is similar to Saudi Arabia in terms of Power Distance. Likewise, Peruvians have a similar perception as the Chinese culture regarding individualism. Also, there are similarities with Saudi Arabia concerning masculinity rates and uncertainty avoidance. As a final result, there are coincidences with the United States, Australia, and Saudi Arabia regarding the long-term orientation dimension. In accordance with these values, the purpose of this study was to consolidate the findings of the various studies identified in the review to propose a set of guidelines that consider good practices found and reported in the literature. The result is the new design guidelines proposal for Peruvian Government Websites.

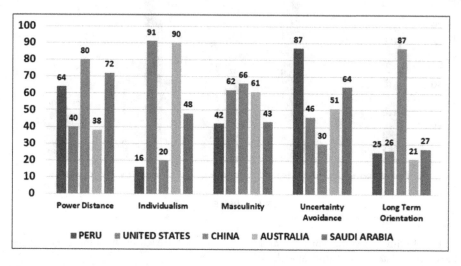

**Fig. 2.** Estimated values for Peru, United States, China, Australia and Saudi Arabia for each of the dimensions established in Hofstede's cultural model. [16]

## 4.2   Design Guidelines Applicable to Peru Web Pages

After a comprehensive analysis, web design guidelines that are currently being applied in other countries with similar cultural backgrounds were selected to be applied when designing Peruvian web pages. Selected guidelines are listed as follows:

### Design Guidelines Associated to Power Distance (PD).

- **PD01.** The interface includes images of leaders or authorities.
- **PD02.** The interface constantly uses images, which can include multiple people.
- **PD03.** The interface presents external information and interaction to emphasize social and organizational relationships.
- **PD04.** The interface presents a structured and hierarchical access to information.

### Design Guidelines Associated to Individualism (IDV).

- **IDV01.** The interface uses images referring to large groups, political and religious images and group achievements.

- **IDV02.** The interface features references to traditions.
- **IDV03.** The interface emphasizes social and organizational achievements.
- **IDV04.** The interface uses links to other institutions in order to demonstrate the strength of the institution.

### Design Guidelines Associated to Uncertainty Avoidance (UAI).

- **UAI01.** The interface features structured navigation with greater control to avoid getting lost on the website.
- **UAI02.** The interface makes use of footers to provide information redundancy and avoid the loss of it.
- **UAI03.** The interface shows only headers on the first level, while sub headers are only visible when selected.
- **UAI04.** The interface separates the information by modules according to topic.
- **UAI05.** The interface maintains a low frequency of information and external interaction.
- **UAI06.** The interface makes use of site maps.
- **UAI07.** The interface makes less use of external links to avoid confusion.
- **UAI08.** The interface uses hints of links.
- **UAI09.** The interface makes use of links that open in a new window infrequently, to avoid loss of information.
- **UAI10.** The interface makes less use of bold text.
- **UAI11.** The interface makes moderate use of bright colors, preference for soft colors.

### Design Guidelines Associated to Long-term Orientation (LTO).

- **LTO01.** The interface shows less complexity of the information with a hierarchical navigation structure for the fulfillment of tasks.
- **LTO02.** The interface shows little amount of initial information.
- **LTO03.** The interface maintains a low frequency of information and external interaction.
- **LTO04.** The interface shows few links in the main menu.

## 5   Conclusions and Future Works

Usability is currently considered a highly relevant aspect for the success of software products in the market. For this reason, development teams nowadays look to offer usable and understandable interfaces to allow end-users to achieve their goals with efficiency and efficacy. Given the importance of usability, some methods and guidelines have been established to design easy-to-use graphical interfaces. However, according to several studies, considering cultural aspects in interface design allows for more positive results since it allows the development of proposals with which people feel more identified.

Through a systematic review of the literature, it has been possible to identify a set of proposals for design guidelines that cover cultural aspects for various countries. However, no evidence has been found on any approach oriented to the Peruvian or Latin American culture. In this sense, the purpose of this work was to analyze the various usability studies with a cultural approach to develop a new proposal oriented to Peru, that can be used with confidence for the design and evaluation of government websites. Considering that government applications are highly relevant because they offer information and services of public interest to Peruvian citizens, this study becomes equally important.

The design guidelines proposal was developed through a methodological process that involved a set of phases. First, the cultural models usually employed to carry out usability studies were identified. From these models, Hofstede's model was selected, which describes a country's culture through dimensions. This selection was made by establishing several criteria that allowed to determine the best proposal. In this comparative analysis, it was concluded that although all models provide relevant perspectives to catalog cultures, Hofstede's model was the only one that had a better description of the cultural characteristics of Peru.

Once the cultural model was identified, the proposal of design guidelines for Peruvian government websites was developed. The guidelines were developed from proposals and best practices established for countries with cultural similarities with Peru. For this reason, an exhaustive analysis of all the studies identified in the systematic literature review was carried out to establish a set of guidelines appropriate to Peru. This work intends to provide a proposal that can be used both by the academy and the industry to design high-quality websites.

As future work, it is proposed to use this instrument to redesign a government website in Peru. Likewise, verifying if this proposal can be used for other similar cultural contexts in Latin America would be relevant. Finally, given the current variety of categories and types of software products, it is possible to adopt this proposal to other domains and carry out experimental case studies to verify if it is viable to generalize the results obtained in this work.

**Acknowledgement.** This study is highly supported by the *Section of Informatics Engineering* of the *Pontifical Catholic University of Peru* (PUCP) - Peru, and the "HCI, Design, User Experience, Accessibility & Innovation Technologies" Research Group (HCI-DUXAIT). HCI-DUXAIT is a research group of PUCP.

# References

1. Aladwani, A.M.: A cross-cultural comparison of Kuwaiti and British citizens' views of e-government interface quality. Gov. Inf. Q. **30**(1), 74–86 (2013). https://doi.org/10.1016/j.giq.2012.08.003
2. Alexander, R., Murray, D., Thompson, N.: Cross-cultural web design guidelines. In: Proceedings of the 14th International Web for All Conference. W4A 2017, Association for Computing Machinery, New York, NY, USA (2017). https://doi.org/10.1145/3058555.3058574
3. Alexander, R., Murray, D., Thompson, N.: Cross-cultural web usability model. In: Bouguettaya, A. (ed.) WISE 2017. LNCS, vol. 10570, pp. 75–89. Springer, Cham (2017). https://doi.org/10.1007/978-3-319-68786-5_6
4. Alexander, R., Thompson, N., McGill, T., Murray, D.: The influence of user culture on website usability. Int. J. Hum Comput. Stud. **154**, 102688 (2021). https://doi.org/10.1016/j.ijhcs.2021.102688
5. Alostath, J.M., Almoumen, S., Alostath, A.B.: Identifying and measuring cultural differences in cross-cultural user-interface design. In: Aykin, N. (ed.) IDGD 2009. LNCS, vol. 5623, pp. 3–12. Springer, Heidelberg (2009). https://doi.org/10.1007/978-3-642-02767-3_1
6. Burgmann, I., Kitchen, P.J., Williams, R.: Does culture matter on the web? Market. Intell. Plan. **24**(1), 62–76 (2006). https://doi.org/10.1108/02634500610641561
7. Chu, J., Zhu, X.: Culture-oriented evaluation method for interaction: applied in Chinese e-commerce website design. In: 2010 3rd International Conference on Computer Science and Information Technology, vol. 2, pp. 331–335 (2010). https://doi.org/10.1109/ICCSIT.2010.5564590
8. Collazos, C.A., Gil, R.: Using cross-cultural features in web design patterns. In: 2011 Eighth International Conference on Information Technology: New Generations, pp. 514–519 (2011). https://doi.org/10.1109/ITNG.2011.95
9. Cyr, D., Head, M., Larios, H.: Colour appeal in website design within and across cultures: a multi-method evaluation. Int. J. Hum Comput. Stud. **68**(1), 1–21 (2010). https://doi.org/10.1016/j.ijhcs.2009.08.005
10. Díaz, J., et al.: Website transformation of a Latin American airline: effects of cultural aspects and user experience on business performance. IEEE Lat. Am. Trans. **17**(05), 766–774 (2019). https://doi.org/10.1109/TLA.2019.8891945
11. Díaz, J., Rusu, C., Pow-Sang, J.A., Roncagliolo, S.: A cultural-oriented usability heuristics proposal. In: Proceedings of the 2013 Chilean Conference on Human - Computer Interaction, pp. 82–87. ChileCHI 2013, Association for Computing Machinery, New York, NY, USA (2013). https://doi.org/10.1145/2535597.2535615
12. Dong, Y., Lee, K.P.: A cross-cultural comparative study of users' perceptions of a webpage: With a focus on the cognitive styles of Chinese, Koreans and Americans. Int. J. Des. **2**(2), 19–30 (2008)
13. Fernandez, A., Insfran, E., Abrahão, S.: Usability evaluation methods for the web: a systematic mapping study. Inf. Softw. Technol. **53**(8), 789–817 (2011). https://doi.org/10.1016/j.infsof.2011.02.007
14. Fraternali, P., Tisi, M.: Identifying cultural markers for web application design targeted to a multi-cultural audience. In: 2008 Eighth International Conference on Web Engineering, pp. 231–239 (2008). https://doi.org/10.1109/ICWE.2008.34
15. Gamboa, Y., Arenas, J.J., Paz, F.: Usability evaluation towards a cultural perspective: a systematic literature review. In: Marcus, A., Rosenzweig, E. (eds.) HCII 2020. LNCS, vol. 12202, pp. 608–617. Springer, Cham (2020). https://doi.org/10.1007/978-3-030-49757-6_44

16. Geert Hofstede: Hofstede Insights. https://www.hofstede-insights.com/ (2022). Accessed 20 May 2022
17. Gould, E.W., Zalcaria, N., Yusof, S.A.M.: Applying culture to web site design: a comparison of Malaysian and us web sites. In: 18th Annual Conference on Computer Documentation. IPCC SIGDOC 2000. In: Proceedings of IEEE Professional Communication Society International Professional Communication Conference on Technology and Teamwork, pp. 161–171, September 2000. https://doi.org/10.1109/IPCC.2000.887273
18. Hall, E.T.: The Dance of Life: The Other Dimension of Time. Anchor Books, United States of America (1984)
19. Hofstede, G., Hofstede, G.J., Minkov, M.: Cultures and Organizations: Software of the Mind - Intercultural Cooperation and Its Importance for Survival. McGraw Hill, United States of America (2010)
20. Hu, J., Shima, K., Oehlmann, R., Zhao, J., Takemura, Y., ichi Matsumoto, K.: An empirical study of audience impressions of B2C web pages in Japan, China and the UK. Electron. Commer. Res. App. 3(2), 176–189 (2004). https://doi.org/10.1016/j.elerap.2003.09.004
21. Jano, Z.: Website usability and cultural dimensions in Malaysian and Australian universities. Asian Soc. Sci. 11(9), 176–189 (2015). https://doi.org/10.5539/ass.v11n9p1
22. Kitchenham, B., Charters, S.: Guidelines for performing systematic literature reviews in software engineering. Technical report. EBSE 2007–001, Keele University and Durham University (2007)
23. Kumar, B., Roy, S.: An empirical study on usability and security of e-commerce websites. In: Kumar, R., Quang, N.H., Kumar Solanki, V., Cardona, M., Pattnaik, P.K. (eds.) Research in Intelligent and Computing in Engineering. AISC, vol. 1254, pp. 735–746. Springer, Singapore (2021). https://doi.org/10.1007/978-981-15-7527-3_69
24. Li, H., Sun, X., Zhang, K.: Culture-centered design: cultural factors in interface usability and usability tests. In: Eighth ACIS International Conference on Software Engineering, Artificial Intelligence, Networking, and Parallel/Distributed Computing (SNPD 2007), vol. 3, pp. 1084–1088 (2007). https://doi.org/10.1109/SNPD.2007.489
25. Nisbett, R.E., Peng, K., Choi, I., Norenzayan, A.: Culture and systems of thought: holistic versus analytic cognition. Psychol. Rev. 108(2), 291–310 (2001). https://doi.org/10.1037/0033-295X.108.2.291
26. Park, J.Y.: Cross-cultural language learning and web design complexity. Interact. Learn. Environ. 23(1), 19–36 (2015). https://doi.org/10.1080/10494820.2012.745427
27. Plocher, T., Rau, P.L.P., Choong, Y.Y., Guo, Z.: Cross-Cultural Design, pp. 252–279. John Wiley & Sons, Ltd., Hoboken (2021). https://doi.org/10.1002/9781119636113.ch10
28. Snelders, D., Morel, K.P., Havermans, P.: The cultural adaptation of web design to local industry styles: a comparative study. Des. Stud. 32(5), 457–481 (2011). https://doi.org/10.1016/j.destud.2011.03.001
29. Trompenaars, F., Hampden-Turner, C.: Riding the Waves of Culture: Understanding Diversity in Global Business. McGraw Hill, United States of America (2012)

30. Victor, D.A.: International Business Communication. HarperCollins, United States of America (1992)
31. Wan Mohd, W.A.R., Md Noor, N.L., Mehad, S.: The Information Architecture of E-Commerce: An Experimental Study on User Performance and Preference, pp. 723–731. Springer, Boston (2010). https://doi.org/10.1007/b137171_75

# Identifying Requirements and Quality Attributes from the Point of View of Users of Mobile Digital Libraries

José Meireles[1], Kennedy Nunes[2], Arthur Passos[2], João Santos[2],
Yandson Costa[2,3], José Durand[2], Rayanne Silveira[1,2],
Alana Oliveira[1,2,4], Davi Viana[1,2,3,4],
Ana Emilia Figueiredo de Oliveira[2], Mario Teixeira[2,3,4],
and Luis Rivero[2,3,4(✉)]

[1] Computer Engineering Department - ECP, Federal University
of Maranhão (UFMA), Sao Luis, Brazil
`jose.victor@discente.ufma.br`,
`{rayanne.silveira,alana.oliveira,davi.viana}@ufma.br`
[2] Directorate of Technologies in Education - DTED/UNA-SUS,
Federal University of Maranhão (UFMA), Sao Luis, Brazil
`{kennedy.anderson,arthur.passos,joao.davi,yandson.jesus,`
`durand.jose}@discente.ufma.br`,
`{ana.figueiredo,mario.meireles,luis.rivero}@ufma.br`
[3] MSc Program in Computer Science - PPGCC, Federal University
of Maranhão (UFMA), Sao Luis, Brazil
[4] PhD Program in Computer Science - DCCMAPI, Federal University
of Maranhão (UFMA), Sao Luis, Brazil

**Abstract.** Due to the COVID-19 pandemic there has been a significant
growth in the adoption of online educational resources, including mobile
digital libraries. Thus, several quality attributes have been indicated
by both industry and academy for designing useful and usable digital
libraries. Nonetheless, we are not aware of a complete list of requirements that could be met to develop high quality digital libraries in the
mobile context. In this paper, we try to meet this gap by identifying
features that digital libraries should provide. To do so, we carried out an
analysis of 20 Brazilian mobile digital libraries in the market, identifying requirements that provide functionalities for users. Also, we analyzed
app comments from the top rated and least rated mobile digital libraries
apps, to extract quality attributes. In all, we identified 14 requirements
through the analysis of the applications and 49 quality attributes considering the opinions on users' comments. The list of requirements and
quality attributes is useful to understand the users' expectations and
understand what to maintain or remove when designing and developing
a mobile digital library.

**Keywords:** Mobile digital libraries · Feature analysis · App comments
analysis · Software requirements · Quality attributes

© The Author(s), under exclusive license to Springer Nature Switzerland AG 2022
M. Kurosu et al. (Eds.): HCII 2022, LNCS 13516, pp. 396–408, 2022.
https://doi.org/10.1007/978-3-031-17615-9_27

# 1    Introduction

Mobile digital libraries belong to a category of mobile applications that has great potential to improve student and researcher access to academic resources [9]. The number of interventions from the use of digital libraries to stimulate learning has increased, as their use can improve the students' and researchers' image by providing a better match with the technologies that younger people are naturally adopting [1]. However, despite the increase interest in this type of applications, users still have difficulty using them [11].

In the past few years, there has been a significant growth in the adoption of online educational resources, including mobile digital libraries [4]. As a result, the interest on the definition of requirements necessary for digital libraries from the point of view of users has increased [16, 17]. Nonetheless, we are not aware of a complete list of requirements that could be met to develop high quality digital libraries in the mobile context. Consequently, there is a need to support software development teams in the definition of requirements that they will include during the design of a mobile digital library or during their validation. It is important to define requirements properly, as poorly performed requirements engineering can lead to the development of low quality software and not meeting the users' expectations [5].

In this paper, we try to meet this gap by identifying features that digital libraries should provide to be complete and deliver functionality, while also analyzing the main complains users have when using these features. To do so, first, we carried out an analysis of 20 Brazilian mobile digital libraries available in the Google Play store. Then, considering a subset of these apps that had the highest and lowest ratings, we analyzed app comments to identify both negative and positive aspects that users complain about or want to maintain in the apps. As a result, we obtained a set of 14 requirements and 49 quality attributes that could be useful to understand the users' expectations and what to maintain or remove to meet their needs.

The remainder of this paper is organized as follows. In Sect. 2, we present a background on mobile digital libraries, while discussing work related with this research. In Sect. 3, we present our research methodology. Section 4 presents our results with a list of requirements and quality attributes for mobile digital libraries. Finally, our conclusions and future work are described in Sect. 5.

# 2    Background

## 2.1    Quality in Mobile Digital Libraries

Mobile applications are getting a great deal of interest among researchers due to their proliferation and pervasiveness, especially in the context of digital libraries of educational institutes [14]. Hence, the use of mobile devices in providing library services is an alternative for satisfying the needs of the users regarding access to educational contents. Mobile digital libraries can support user by [13]: (a) bringing the library closer to the users making it easier to use and increasing its usage; (b) using computing power to find information; (c) making it available to access digital information on a network at lower costs; and (d) updating important information continually.

Due to the COVID-19 pandemic there has been a significant growth in the adoption of mobile digital libraries [4]. As public libraries were affected, mobile digital libraries remained active and available to users so that they could access to their digital content [4]. Thus, several quality attributes have been indicated by both industry and academy for designing useful and usable digital libraries [2].

According to Cane [3], there are several features that impact the satisfaction of users with digital libraries:

**Information Quality** data reliability is a key component in the analysis of an effective computer- based data system. Attributes are usually associated with consistency, design, timeliness, currency, reliability, completeness, accuracy, and significance.

**System Quality** System quality affects the perception of users of the performance of a digital library in knowledge assortment and delivery. In the development of information systems, the quality cycle of the systems is a strong determinant for user satisfaction in various contexts. In this aspect, Accessibility, accuracy, reliability, and quality are the key attributes of performance measurement.

**Service Quality** User perception of the performance of a digital library in the processing and distribution of information is characterized by service quality. One of the prominent qualities of digital service performance is accession, reliability, accessibility, and responsiveness.

**Perceived Ease of Use** The perceived ease of use is defined as the degree to which an individual believes that it would be effortless to use a particular system. In this context, userfriendliness indicates a belief that using DL would require minimal effort. Also, accessibility is sometimes related to ease of use.

Considering the impact of Mobile Digital Libraries in the context of online education, several studies have been conducted regarding the identification and proposal of requirements to meet quality standards so that software development teams have indicators on what users' require [16,17]. Below, we present some researches in which these requirements and/or quality attributes have been presented and/or applied.

## 2.2   Requirements in Digital Libraries

According to Dubbels [6], requirements play a central role in educational platforms since even though having evidence-supported requirements is not possible, there are techniques that can help generate and test insights as part of an iterative process, culminating incremental improvement of requirements, models, and testing. Furthermore, having a list of requirements can be useful for the development team, as it can be used as an early artifact in the software development process which is further mapped into the software requirements specification [15].

In the context of Mobile Digital Libraries, there has been an increased interest in understanding what are the features and attributes that this type of application should provide [7]. For instance, Xie et al. (2020) identified features to enhance the usability of digital libraries for blind and visually impaired users. According to the authors, multiple data collection methods were applied to obtain data on usability problems in digital libraries, including pre-questionnaires, think-aloud protocols, transaction logs, and pre and post search interviews. Among some of the features the authors list for improving usability for visually impaired, we can list: (a) Provide added description or clear labels; (b) Provide instruction and context-sensitive help for features and web pages; (c) Improve ease of navigation and increase access points; (d) Modify text or spacing elements to eliminate confusion of screen reader interpretation; (e) Enhance search functions or add new search features; and (f) Modify multimedia items (e.g., change start time of video to eliminate delay). Although the attributes are applicable to most digital libraries, the improvements can mostly me useful for the visually impaired, and few examples of requirements and attributes for broader users are presented.

In another work, Wei et al. (2015) shows quality attributes that impacted the usability and user experience of a mobile digital library app. The authors applied a usability testing, using pre-test questionnaires, accomplishing tasks, and post-test surveys. The authors make some recommendations, such as: (a) Adjustment of the location and identification label of the functional module; (b) Optimization of search functions and promotion of searching efficiency; and (c) Offer human-oriented and user-friendly operations based on smartphone characteristics. Nevertheless, these features are specific for the application that they evaluated and there are few examples of requirements that could be implemented to provide a positive user experience and/or improve the ease of use of the mobile digital library.

Finally, other researchers have applied traditional usability evaluations to determine whether a digital library met users' expectations [8]. The authors employed traditional usability evaluation heuristics [12] to assess the quality of the app. Although the heuristics are generic and can be applied in mobile digital libraries, they do not allow evaluating the specifics of this type of software. Thus, making it difficult to identify aspects that users of digital libraries could require to improve their experience and achieve their goals.

After considering several research papers on quality attributes of mobile digital libraries, we did not find a complete list of requirements that could be met to develop high quality digital libraries in the mobile context. Also, although there are suggestions of attributes that could improve the usability of mobile digital libraries, these attributes are not specific for this type of software or are not complete, as they are based on the evaluation and analysis of a single application. Consequently, there is a need to support software development teams in the definition of requirements that they will include during the design of a mobile digital library or during their validation.

There are several approaches to evaluate the quality of VLEs and their contents. Mastan et al. (2022) carried out a systematic literature review and identified 38 publications describing approaches evaluating a range of quality criteria in VLEs, such as: usability, quality of service, learning performance, user satisfaction, technology adoption, and others. Within the context of usability and user experience evaluation, several approaches have been developed. To meet this gap, in the following section we describe how we carried out a feature analysis of existing mobile digital libraries in Brazil and the evaluation comments of their users.

## 3   Research Methodology

We carried out an analysis of Brazilian mobile digital libraries available in the Google Play app store. The goal was to read the documentation provided by the developers on the features presented in these applications and explore the applications to experience their features.

In all, we selected 20 mobile digital libraries (due to convenience), prioritizing those with more than 50,000 downloads and a rating 4 or above, to guarantee that these mobile applications where in use and provided useful resources to users to incite download. To reach at least 20 applications with mixed reviews, we also considered those with less downloads or scores, but had at least 100 reviews, indicating improvement opportunities.

Table 1 shows the requirements we identified based and the set of mobile digital libraries that have these features. We highlight that the data for this analysis was obtained in Brazilian app stores in February 2022 and updated in May 2022. The applications that we considered are listed bellow.

- APP01 - Kindle[1]
  APP02 - Árvore Livros[2]
- APP03 - PocketBook reader[3]
- APP04 - Deseret Bookshelf[4]
- APP05 - Let's Read - Digital Library[5]
- APP06 - Skeelo: livros digitais[6]
- APP07 - Biblioteca Virtual by Pearson[7]

---

[1] https://play.google.com/store/apps/details?id=com.amazon.kindle  Accessed  on: May 23rd, 2022.

[2] https://play.google.com/store/apps/details?id=arvoredelivros.com.br.arvore Accessed on: May 23rd, 2022.

[3] https://play.google.com/store/apps/details?id=com.obreey.reader  Accessed  on: May 23rd, 2022.

[4] https://play.google.com/store/apps/details?id=com.deseretdigital.bookshelf Accessed on: May 23rd, 2022.

[5] https://play.google.com/store/apps/details?id=org.asiafoundation.letsread Accessed on: May 23rd, 2022.

[6] https://play.google.com/store/apps/details?id=br.com.gold360.skeelo Accessed on: May 23rd, 2022.

[7] https://play.google.com/store/apps/details?id=com.minha.biblioteca Accessed on: May 23rd, 2022.

- APP08 - Ebook Reader[8]
- APP09 - Biblion: é gratuita, é de SP[9]
- APP10 - Google Play Livros[10]
- APP11 - FBReader[11]
- APP12 - Ler livros digitais - Kobo Books[12]
- APP13 - Aldiko Next[13]
- APP14 - Glose[14]
- APP15 - 50000 eBooks & AudioBooks (Oodles)[15]
- APP16 - Bookplay[16]
- APP17 - Biblioteca Digital Senac[17]
- APP18 - Biblioteca Pública Digital[18]
- APP19 - BDEscolar[19]
- APP20 - Minha Biblioteca[20]

Considering that users' opinions about a mobile application also contain information about its positive or negative aspects [10], we decided to analyze app comments from the top rated and least rated mobile digital libraries apps, to guarantee both positive and negative aspects. Due to a large number of comments from the applications, samples were defined to facilitate collection and analysis. For this, we selected 100 comments for each selected app. In all, we selected 12 apps from the original list of mobile digital libraries in Table 1 (see

---

[8] https://play.google.com/store/apps/details?id=com.ebooks.ebookreader  Accessed on: May 23rd, 2022.

[9] https://play.google.com/store/apps/details?id=es.odilo.saopaulopl  Accessed on: May 23rd, 2022.

[10] https://play.google.com/store/apps/details?id=com.google.android.apps.books  Accessed on: May 23rd, 2022.

[11] https://play.google.com/store/apps/details?id=org.geometerplus.zlibrary.ui. android Accessed on: May 23rd, 2022.

[12] https://play.google.com/store/apps/details?id=com.kobobooks.android  Accessed on: May 23rd, 2022.

[13] https://play.google.com/store/apps/details?id=com.aldiko.android  Accessed on: May 23rd, 2022.

[14] https://play.google.com/store/apps/details?id=com.glose.android  Accessed on: May 23rd, 2022.

[15] https://play.google.com/store/apps/details?id=com.oodles.download.free.ebooks. reader Accessed on: May 23rd, 2022.

[16] https://play.google.com/store/apps/details?id=air.com.mundialeditora.bookplay  Accessed on: May 23rd, 2022.

[17] https://play.google.com/store/apps/details?id=br.com.senac.editoradigital  Accessed on: May 23rd, 2022.

[18] https://play.google.com/store/apps/details?id=es.odilo.dibam Accessed on: May 23rd, 2022.

[19] https://play.google.com/store/apps/details?id=es.odilo.cra Accessed on: May 23rd, 2022.

[20] https://play.google.com/store/apps/details?id=com.minha.biblioteca Accessed on: May 23rd, 2022.

(continued)

**Table 1.** Feature analysis of the 20 selected Brazilian mobile digital libraries

| Score | Code | |
|---|---|---|
| 4,9 | **APP01** | **Kindle** |
| 4,7 | **APP02** | **Árvore Livros** |
| 4,6 | **APP03** | **PocketBook reader** |
| 4,6 | APP04 | Deseret Bookshelf |
| 4,6 | APP05 | Let's Read - Digital Library |
| 4,5 | **APP06** | **Skeelo livros digitais** |
| 4,4 | **APP07** | **Biblioteca Virtual by Pearson** |
| 4,3 | **APP08** | **Ebook Reader** |
| 4,3 | APP09 | Biblion |
| 4,1 | APP10 | Google Play Livros |
| 4,1 | APP11 | FBReader |
| 4 | APP12 | Ler livros digitais Kobo Books |
| 4 | APP13 | Aldiko Next |
| 3,7 | APP14 | Glose |
| 3,3 | **APP15** | **50000 eBooks & AudioBooks (Oodles)** |
| 3,2 | **APP16** | **Bookplay** |
| 3 | **APP17** | **Biblioteca Digital Senac** |
| 2,8 | **APP18** | **Biblioteca Pública Digital** |
| 2,3 | **APP19** | **Biblioteca Digital Escolar CRA** |
| 2,2 | **APP20** | **Minha Biblioteca** |

Table 1. (continued)

| Evaluations | 291 | 1 610 | 8 990 | 119 | 4230 | 58 800 | 2090 | 215000 | 275749 | 222000 | 1910000 | 359 | 92112 | 2 180 | 30600 | 2040 | 2340 | 81300 | 13 700 | 2 440 000 |
|---|---|---|---|---|---|---|---|---|---|---|---|---|---|---|---|---|---|---|---|---|
| RF01 | × | × | × | × | × | × | × | × | × | × | × | × |   | × | × | × | × | × | × | × |
| RF02 | × | × | × | × | × | × | × | × | × | × | × | × | × | × | × | × | × | × | × | × |
| RF03 | × | × | × | × | × | × | × | × | × | × | × | × | × | × | × | × | × | × | × | × |
| RF04 | × | × | × | × | × | × | × | × |   |   | × | × |   | × | × | × | × | × | × | × |
| RF05 | × | × | × |   |   | × | × | × | × |   | × |   |   |   | × |   |   |   |   | × |
| RF06 | × | × | × |   |   | × | × | × | × | × | × |   | × | × | × |   | × | × | × | × |
| RF07 | × | × | × | × | × |   | × |   | × | × | × | × |   | × |   | × | × |   | × | × |
| RF08 | × | × | × | × |   | × | × | × | × | × | × | × | × | × | × | × | × | × | × | × |
| RF09 | × | × | × | × | × |   |   | × | × |   | × | × |   | × |   | × | × | × | × | × |
| RF10 | × | × | × | × |   | × | × | × |   |   | × | × | × | × | × | × | × | × | × | × |
| RF11 |   | × | × |   |   |   | × |   | × |   |   |   |   |   |   | × |   |   |   | × |
| RF12 |   |   |   |   |   |   | × |   |   |   |   |   |   |   |   |   |   |   |   |   |
| RF13 | × | × | × | × | × | × | × | × | × | × | × | × | × |   | × | × | × | × | × | × |
| RF14 | × | × | × |   |   |   | × |   |   |   | × |   |   |   |   |   |   |   |   | × |
| Percentage | 85% | 92% | 92% | 64% | 50% | 64% | 92% | 71% | 71% | 50% | 85% | 64% | 42% | 64% | 64% | 71% | 71% | 64% | 71% | 92% |
| Total | 12 | 13 | 13 | 9 | 7 | 9 | 13 | 10 | 10 | 7 | 12 | 9 | 6 | 9 | 9 | 10 | 10 | 9 | 10 | 13 |

highlighted apps). The apps were selected based on the scores of the apps, guaranteeing having apps with both low and high scores. Also, when scores wee the same and there was the possibility of having another app with a different average score, with more comments, we tried to include it in order to diversify our sample of comments.

Once the apps were selected, their comments were extracted according to the order of appearance. The collection was done manually by two software engineering researchers and the comments were stored in a database. With the set of comments, we applied the following classification process. The texts of the comments were read and labeled in quality attributes considering positive and negative points that can affect the quality of a mobile digital library. The list of quality attributes was initialized empty, and as the sorting process took place, new items were added. If a comment had an association with more than one attribute in the list, it was categorized with all attributes with which it had an association. In addition, the classification was revised by two other researchers to reduce the number of inconsistencies or wrong classifications. Table 2 shows the list of selected mobile digital libraries from which we selected the evaluation comments of the users.

**Table 2.** List of selected apps for extracting users' evaluation comments

|        | Code  | Name                                  | Score | Evaluation |
|--------|-------|---------------------------------------|-------|------------|
| ≥ 3,5  | APP01 | Kindle                                | 4,9   | 2440000    |
|        | APP02 | Árvore Livros                         | 4,7   | 13700      |
|        | APP03 | PocketBook reader                     | 4,6   | 81300      |
|        | APP06 | Skeelo: livros digitais               | 4,5   | 30600      |
|        | APP07 | Biblioteca Virtual by Pearson         | 4,4   | 2180       |
|        | APP08 | Ebook Reader                          | 4,3   | 92112      |
| ≤ 3,5  | APP15 | 50000 eBooks & AudioBooks (Oodles)    | 3,3   | 58800      |
|        | APP16 | Bookplay                              | 3,2   | 4230       |
|        | APP17 | Biblioteca Digital Senac              | 3     | 119        |
|        | APP18 | Biblioteca Pública Digital            | 2,8   | 8990       |
|        | APP19 | BDEscolar                             | 2,3   | 1610       |
|        | APP20 | Minha Biblioteca                      | 2,2   | 291        |

## 4   Results

Table 3 shows the list of 14 requirements we identified through the feature analysis of the mobile digital libraries. For each considered application in the feature analysis, we extracted which functionalities it provided and related them to the app in Table 1. The code of the Requirement/Functionality (RF) is now next to its description in Table 3.

**Table 3.** Identified requirements based on the feature analysis of the considered Brazilian mobile digital libraries

| Code | Requirement description |
|------|-------------------------|
| RF01 | The system must provide general information for each resource (Title, Abstract, Authors, Rating, Image) |
| RF02 | The system must provide a resource catalog |
| RF03 | The system should allow searching for a resource in the catalog |
| RF04 | The system must present information about the Terms and Conditions of Use |
| RF05 | The system must provide a dictionary function |
| RF06 | The system should allow creating, editing, highlighting of notes/comments |
| RF07 | The system must have a shelf with favorite features |
| RF08 | The system must have a shelf with a history of consumption to facilitate access to resources consumed and with consumption in progress |
| RF09 | The system should provide a list of news |
| RF10 | The system should provide a list of recommendations |
| RF11 | The system should present information on resource consumption statistics |
| RF12 | The system must have features to engage the student, such as competition and gamification |
| RF13 | The system should allow using the resources offline |
| RF14 | The system should allow the user to evaluate a resource |

Note that even though some applications provide the same number of functionalities (e.g. APP01, APP14, APP18 and APP19) in Table 1, their scores are not the same. Therefore, analyzing the users' evaluations comments could be useful for identifying further quality attributes. Hence, Table 4 shows the 49 Quality Attributes (QA) we identified. Each of the quality attributes was categorized in either Functionality or Quality of Use. In terms of functionality, we considered attributes that denoted new functionalities that the application should provide, such as: providing notifications (QA01), providing further information on the consumption process of a resource within the library (QA03), generating reports (QA09), and others. Also, in terms of quality in use, we considered aspects that made it easier to use the application and/or (could) improved the user experience, such as: visual support in terms of colors (QA19), customization of page size (QA29), or provide shortcuts for experienced users (QA42), and others.

**Table 4.** Identified quality attributes based on the analysis of comments made during evaluations of mobile digital libraries

| Code | Category | Quality attribute |
|------|----------|-------------------|
| QA01 | Functionality | The system must send notifications when receiving files |
| QA02 | Functionality | The system must support different file formats |
| QA03 | Functionality | The system must show reading progress such as pages read and total pages |
| QA04 | Functionality | The system must allow searching for terms within a resource |
| QA05 | Functionality | The system must allow importing resources |
| QA06 | Functionality | The system must allow to create handwritten notes |
| QA07 | Functionality | The system must allow to create notes apart from resources |
| QA08 | Functionality | The system must provide automatic translations for resources that do not have official translations |
| QA09 | Functionality | The system must present statistics on resource consumption such as daily/monthly/annual reading time, total reading time of a book |
| QA10 | Functionality | The system must provide an achievement system (gamification) |
| QA11 | Functionality | The system must present to the user new resources available on the platform |
| QA12 | Functionality | The system must provide a bookshelf, arranging the books in: already read, desired and in progress |
| QA13 | Functionality | The system must provide a quick access tab to the chapters and pages of a resource |
| QA14 | Functionality | The system must allow choosing which pdf reading engine to use |
| QA15 | Functionality | The system must allow factory reset the settings |
| QA16 | Functionality | The system must allow auto-scrolling |
| QA17 | Functionality | The system must allow navigating the resource using the cell phone's volume buttons |
| QA18 | Functionality | The system must sync with cloud services and third-party apps and be able to connect to other devices and external web/mobile platforms |
| QA19 | Quality of Use | The system must provide a dark mode to assist the visually impaired |
| QA20 | Quality of Use | The system should allow changing of the marking color a resource's section |
| QA21 | Quality of Use | The system must provide a widget with a shortcut to the feature in use on the home page |
| QA22 | Quality of Use | The system must offer a free demo of the resource within the library so that the reader can decide whether or not to consume the resource |
| QA23 | Quality of Use | The system must allow to adjust the luminosity (brightness scale) |
| QA24 | Quality of Use | The system must allow to highlight the text |
| QA25 | Quality of Use | The system must provide a page with all the bookmarks of the book |
| QA26 | Quality of Use | The system must provide a voice over of the resource |
| QA27 | Quality of Use | The system must allow bookmarks |
| QA28 | Quality of Use | The system must allow to create notes about a section from the book |
| QA29 | Quality of Use | The system must allow to adjust the page size through zoom |
| QA30 | Quality of Use | The system must allow to customize the font, such as format, size and color |

(*continued*)

**Table 4.** (*continued*)

| Code | Category | Quality attribute |
|------|----------|-------------------|
| QA31 | Quality of Use | The system must allow horizontal reading |
| QA32 | Quality of Use | The system must provide the search by author, title or keyword |
| QA33 | Quality of Use | The system must provide the creation of lists, categories or sections for organizing resources |
| QA34 | Quality of Use | The system must allow to download of books for offline access |
| QA35 | Quality of Use | The system must provide an integrated dictionary for searching the meaning of a word |
| QA36 | Quality of Use | The system must provide a wish list in the app |
| QA37 | Quality of Use | The system must allow sharing a link to a title |
| QA38 | Quality of Use | The system must provide the name of the translator who did the localization |
| QA39 | Quality of Use | The system must allow to create folders or categories to classify the notes |
| QA40 | Quality of Use | The system must provide recommendations based on previously consumed resources |
| QA41 | Quality of Use | The system must prevent the screen from turning off while the user is consuming a resource |
| QA42 | Quality of Use | The system must automatically save the position the user was within the resource |
| QA43 | Quality of Use | The system must allow the user to select which languages to find the resources |
| QA44 | Quality of Use | The system must allow the user to find the actual page number for reference purposes |
| QA45 | Quality of Use | The system must present an estimate of time to finish a resource and part of the resource |
| QA46 | Quality of Use | The system must keep the books in its catalog and notify users in advance of the withdrawal of a book |
| QA47 | Quality of Use | The system must smooth the screen transitions and keep them at an acceptable speed |
| QA48 | Quality of Use | The system must resize the text according to the screen size |
| QA49 | Quality of Use | The system must be available in the local language |

# 5   Conclusions and Future Work

To support the design of high quality mobile digital libraries, we carried out an analysis of real applications in the market, identifying requirements that provide functionalities for users. Also, the list of quality attributes from the point of view of users is relevant to understand the users' expectations and understand what to maintain or remove when designing and developing a mobile digital library.

We are currently employing the proposed requirements list for the development of a new mobile digital library. As the next steps of this work, we intend to carry out empirical studies to analyze if by meeting the identified requirements and including the quality attributes, we can improve the effectiveness, efficiency, and the overall acceptance of the new proposed mobile digital library from the point of view of users in real usage scenarios. In addition, we intend to refine this list of requirements and quality attributes to propose a set of heuristics and guidelines for the development of usable and useful mobile digital libraries considering the users expectations. Through this research, we intend to provide a more reliable and robust requirements and quality attributes list suitable for use by the software industry, as well as software engineers in the development of mobile digital libraries.

# References

1. Alfaresi, S.H., Hone, K.: The intention to use mobile digital library technology: a focus group study in the United Arab Emirates. Int. J. Mob. Hum. Comput. Interact. (IJMHCI) **7**(2), 23–42 (2015)
2. Blandford, A., Buchanan, G., Jones, M.: Usability of digital libraries. Int. J. Digit. Libr. **4**(2), 69–70 (2004)
3. Cane, F.K.: Service quality of digital libraries and users satisfaction. Adv. Educ. Manag. Sci. Technol. **4**(3) (2012)
4. Ćirić, J., Ćirić, A.: The impact of the COVID-19 pandemic on digital library usage: a public library case study. J. Web Librariansh. **15**(2), 53–68 (2021)
5. Curcio, K., Navarro, T., Malucelli, A., Reinehr, S.: Requirements engineering: a systematic mapping study in agile software development. J. Syst. Softw. **139**, 32–50 (2018)
6. Dubbels, B.R.: Requirements-based design of serious games and learning software: an introduction to the vegas effect. In: Exploring the Cognitive, Social, Cultural, and Psychological Aspects of Gaming and Simulations, pp. 1–34. IGI Global (2019)
7. Franzini, G., Terras, M., Mahony, S.: Digital editions of text: surveying user requirements in the digital humanities. J. Comput. Cult. Herit. (JOCCH) **12**(1), 1–23 (2019)
8. Fung, R.H.Y., Chiu, D.K., Ko, E.H., Ho, K.K., Lo, P.: Heuristic usability evaluation of university of Hong Kong libraries' mobile website. J. Acad. Librariansh. **42**(5), 581–594 (2016)
9. Høivik, J.: Mobile digital library in the national library of norway. Library Hi Tech News (2011)
10. Khalid, H., Shihab, E., Nagappan, M., Hassan, A.E.: What do mobile app users complain about? IEEE Softw. **32**(3), 70–77 (2014)
11. Li, H., Cai, Z.Q.: Design and implementation of the mobile library app based on smart phone. In: 2016 International Conference on Machine Learning and Cybernetics (ICMLC), vol. 1, pp. 318–322. IEEE (2016)
12. Nielsen, J.: Usability inspection methods. In: Conference Companion on Human Factors in Computing Systems, pp. 413–414 (1994)
13. Oinam, A.C., Thoidingjam, P.: Impact of digital libraries on information dissemination. Int. Res. J. Libr. Inf. Sc. **9**(1) (2019)
14. Rafique, H., Almagrabi, A.O., Shamim, A., Anwar, F., Bashir, A.K.: Investigating the acceptance of mobile library applications with an extended technology acceptance model (TAM). Comput. Educ. **145**, 103732 (2020)
15. Ramdhani, M.A., Maylawati, D.S., Amin, A.S., Aulawi, H.: Requirements elicitation in software engineering. Int. J. Eng. Technol. (UEA) **7**(2.19), 772–775 (2018)
16. Wei, Q., Chang, Z., Cheng, Q.: Usability study of the mobile library app: an example from Chongqing University. Library Hi Tech (2015)
17. Xie, I., Babu, R., Lee, T.H., Castillo, M.D., You, S., Hanlon, A.M.: Enhancing usability of digital libraries: designing help features to support blind and visually impaired users. Inf. Process. Manag. **57**(3), 102110 (2020)

# A Survey on the Usability and User Experience of the Open Community Web Portals

Shabnam Kazemi, Gernot Liebchen, and Deniz Cetinkaya<sup>(✉)</sup>

Department of Computing and Informatics, Faculty of Science and Technology,
Bournemouth University, Poole BH12 5BB, UK
{skazemi,gliebchen,dcetinkaya}@bournemouth.ac.uk

**Abstract.** Web-based portals enable a new communication paradigm that could provide variety of benefits and support to both the customers and companies. Customers can have continuous access to the services, information, support, and payments on the portal with the possibility of personalisation. This paper presents a survey on the usability and user experience studies relevant to open community web portals and information sharing platforms. The objective of the work presented in this paper was to produce an overview of how literature reported on usability in relation to information sharing web portals. A systematic mapping method has been applied to identify and quantify primary studies focusing on the usability and user experience of the open community web portals.

**Keywords:** Usability · User experience · Open community web portal · Usability of web systems · Human computer interaction

## 1 Introduction

Web-based portals enable a new communication paradigm that could provide variety of benefits and support to both the customers and companies. Customers could have 24/7 access to the services, information, support, and payments on the portal with the possibility of personalisation. Thus, portals have gained a considerable attention in businesses and governments due to widespread functionality [12,19]. In the recent years, due to the development of network infrastructures and sources, the expansion and evolution of web portals have been also influenced [17,20]. On the other hand, usability and user experience aspects are still challenging as satisfying the needs of different users is an open problem for such systems.

This paper presents a survey on the usability and user experience studies relevant to open community web portals and information sharing platforms. The objective of the work presented in this paper was to produce an overview how literature reported on usability in relation to information sharing web portals.

M. Kurosu et al. (Eds.): HCII 2022, LNCS 13516, pp. 409–423, 2022.
https://doi.org/10.1007/978-3-031-17615-9_28

The usability considerations for these information sharing portals were considered to be a non-trivial undertaking since multiple user groups with varying backgrounds are interacting with the system simultaneously. That means that creators of information sharing portals will need to apply usability techniques. Which ones have been used and reported on, and how much impact these techniques had, and ultimately reported on, was one of the key questions this work aimed to answer. Additionally, we focused on finding out the trends in user experience of information portals and open community websites during this study.

The work presented in this paper provides an overview of how usability is dealt with in relation to information sharing portals. Considering these portals require user interaction through sharing of user created content, and the user participation, this study provides information of how usability has been discussed in recent publications.

The remaining of the paper is structured as follows: Next section presents the literature review and related work. Research methodology is explained in Sect. 3. Results and findings are presented in Sect. 4. Conclusions and potential future work are presented in Sect. 5.

## 2   Related Work

Usability evaluation is an important topic in user interface design practice and research. Many different methods have been specifically developed for web sites while the most prominent example is still user testing [14]. However, it is very time consuming and heavily constrained by available time, money and human resources so various tools have been proposed for automated usability testing over the years [13, 15].

We have recently presented a case study evaluating the usability and user experience of the SPEED (Smart Ports Entrepreneurial Ecosystem Development) open community web portal [8]. The SPEED portal is an open community information portal, and its main purpose has been the promotion of innovation and efficiency in the smart port domain by building an ecosystem for smart port application development. This open community platform provides services to port stakeholders (such as port authorities, customs and excises), logistic companies (including ships, road, train), technology entrepreneurs, start-ups, students and members of the public.

Throughout the literature we found many examples for research on the usability of web applications [2, 3, 5, 10]. User-experience (UX) has become a major area in open community portals which can be characterized as "users' judgment of product quality arising from their experience of interaction, and the product qualities which engender effective use and pleasure" [21]. Good usability and better user experience are essential as the use of the system should enhance the workflow and encourage active engagement [4]. An engaging user experience design can increase the likelihood of users' motivation to disclose thoughts and views [22]. From the user's point of view, there are various dimensions related to a web portal including quality, design and community support. For example, regarding the quality, content's creditability and usefulness are essential aspects, i.e. user's reliability to the portal's content and services in terms of usefulness, trustworthiness and accuracy. Content organization and clarity are also very important in terms of an efficient and effective journey for the visitors. Community support has also gained interest lately facilitating the required tools and services for communication, interaction and collaboration within the network between the portal's users.

To better understand the various aspects of the usability and user experience of the open community web portals and information sharing platforms, we present a systematic mapping study in this paper. Critical to this effort is to determine the focus of the work, so this study focuses on open community web portals and online web platforms for information sharing and building knowledge collaboratively. Although review studies about usability and user experience evaluation are presented in the literature [6,11], they are not specifically focused on open community information sharing portals or platforms. Sharing information is important for the scientific community. Over the years the internet became the main information source due to its actuality, interactivity and flexibility [7]. User-centered design significantly impacts the knowledge-sharing processes [18].

## 3   Methodology

### 3.1   Process

A systematic mapping method has been applied to identify and quantify primary studies focusing on the usability and user experience of the open community portals [16]. The results were gained from the four repositories, assessed, and then aggregated to provide an objective overview of the relevant evidence. The method applied for the presented review study consisted of four steps, namely setup, search, screening, and classification. Each step resulted in a list of identified publications, and the final step resulted in the outcome of the systematic mapping exercise as shown in Fig. 1.

To provide an effective overview of the primary studies and research areas, the coverage and the presence of a thesaurus for choosing databases are crucial [1,9]. Figure 1 shows that four bibliographic databases/repositories (ACM Di-gital Library, IEEE Xplore, Science Direct, and Scopus) were chosen to conduct the search for publications. They were selected primarily based on data accessibility, resource stability, and full functionality of application of the chosen search string. Additionally, these resources are considered the main bibliographic databases/repositories for the subject of computer science.

### 3.2   Keywords

The authors aimed to keep the search as inclusive as possible, but ultimately decided to focus on "web" rather than "online" to allow for web portals/sites.

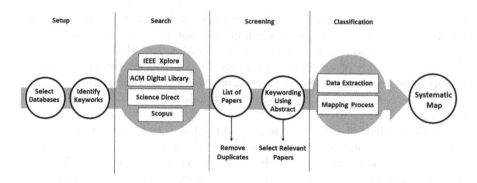

**Fig. 1.** Mapping process.

The keyword "online" was considered to be too open, and it would have resulted in too many non - computer science related publications. In the screening step of the overall process the focus was on "web" in relation to the terms "site", "page", "system", "portal", and "platform". Figure 2 shows the search strings from three different point of views, namely user, system and functionality. The keywords were searched in the title and keywords of the papers as well as within the abstract and metadata if available.

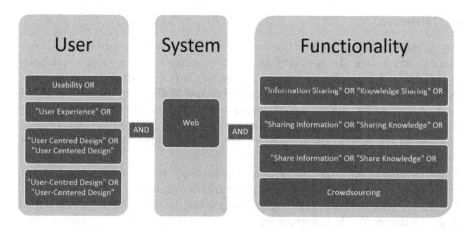

**Fig. 2.** Keyword selection.

For example, following query was used on the IEEE database: ("All Metadata": Usability OR "User Experience" OR "User Centred Design" OR "User Centered Design" OR "User-Centred Design" OR "User-Centered Design") AND ("All Metadata": Web) AND ("All Metadata": "Information Sharing" OR "Know-ledge Sharing" OR "Sharing Information" OR "Sharing Knowledge" OR "Share Information" OR "Share Knowledge" OR Crowdsourcing).

### 3.3    Paper Selection

398 papers were initially identified after applying the search strings in the selected databases. Table 1 indicates the initial paper count from each repository. We included research articles published as a journal paper, conference paper or book chapter between January 2010 and December 2021 in this mapping study. So, full proceedings, newsletters, etc. were excluded.

**Table 1.** Initial paper count from each repository.

| Database | Initial results |
|---|---|
| IEEE Xplore | 67 |
| ACM Digital Library | 42 |
| Science Direct | 9 |
| Scopus | 280 |
| Total | 398 |

After the initial screening step, 234 papers were selected in the first round according to the following exclusion criteria:

- repeated studies in different repositories (same results in different search results),
- not accessible papers (if we cannot access the full paper after searching online or contacting the authors),
- multiple publications (only the latest or most complete one such as journal paper was selected),
- identified as completely out of context by title or abstract.

In the second round, we excluded irrelevant papers per contribution as they should be related to user experience or usability aspects for web portals. As a result, 98 papers were used for classification and mapping study after applying the established protocol used to search, select, and evaluate the primary studies.

At the last round of selection, after the data extraction, papers presenting studies in the context of generic web development or using crowdsourcing as a means to assess websites were excluded because those were not focus of this review study. After the last round of screening, 42 publications were considered to be relevant per context and functionality, i.e. related to information or knowledge sharing systems and focusing on usability in some way. Figure 3 shows the number of papers in each round. Selected papers are briefly listed in the Bibliography with paper title and year. The mapping file is available upon request from the authors.

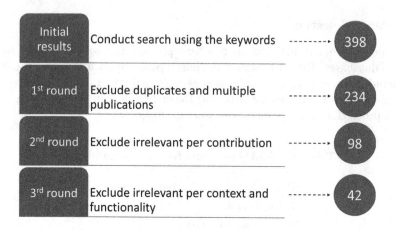

**Fig. 3.** Number of selected papers in each round.

## 3.4 Questions

Our main research question in this research was "What are the methods and important aspects on the usability and user experience of the open community web information portals?". After a planning stage, we conducted the search and completed the mapping study by analysing the findings and reporting the results.

During the mapping study all authors were involved in the analysis of the papers and checked for validity. Following questions were investigated for each paper:

- Contribution Type: What is the type of the contribution in the paper? e.g. new method, case study, software implementation, etc.
- Application Domain: What is the application domain? e.g. health, transportation, education, etc.
- Research Method: Which research methods have been used?
- Usability Methods/Frameworks/Standards: Have any specific usability related methods, frameworks or standards been used in the study? e.g. Nielsen's, System Usability Scale, user testing, etc.
- Usability-UX Features/Best Practices: Which specific usability/user experience aspects, features or best practices are considered in the paper?
- Usability-UX Issues/Challenges: Which specific usability/user experience related issues or challenges are considered in the paper?
- Developers/Admin Experience: Does the paper discuss any aspects related to developers or admin experience?
- Portal's Features: Have any specific features of the portal been mentioned?

The results show that different assessment strategies and development techniques were used. They also indicate that there is no unified approach available to deal with usability for information web portals. Detailed analysis of the results and findings are presented in the next section.

## 4   Results

This section will present the results of the mapping study and our findings for the questions listed in the previous section. Figure 4 shows the distribution of publications over the years. It is noticeable that 2015 produced most of the publications. That may be explained through a relative maturity of web development, and that web portals are not considered separately from general web sites in academic literature. However, for the purpose of this mapping study, the decision was taken to consider web portals as special due to their crowdsourcing and knowledge sharing capabilities.

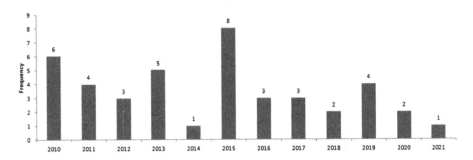

**Fig. 4.** Number of papers identified per year.

Contribution types of the papers were different in the papers but most of them presented system design and development studies including software implementation. Figure 5 shows the various contribution types of the selected studies and the count of how many papers are categorised into those types.

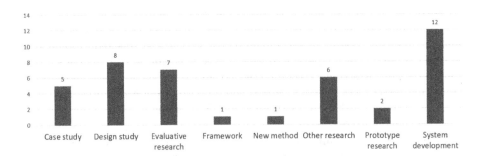

**Fig. 5.** Contribution types of the papers.

Most publications about web-based portals and knowledge sharing sites considered and discussed in the literature were focusing on Education (11 explicit mentioning). Knowledge Sharing had the second strongest representation (8). In fact, knowledge sharing was the purpose for most portals even if other domains had the main focus. Two of the publications focusing on Knowledge Sharing portals mentioned Wikis specifically. The other two domains worth mentioning are Health (7) and Government (4). Further domains did feature, but were limited to one or two instances. Table 2 lists the number of papers per domain.

**Table 2.** Number of papers identified per domain/theme.

| Domain/Theme | Count |
| --- | --- |
| Architecture | 1 |
| Content management system | 1 |
| Commerce | 2 |
| Defence | 1 |
| Education | 11 |
| Environment | 1 |
| Geographic information/mapping | 1 |
| Government | 4 |
| Health | 7 |
| Knowledge sharing | 8 |
| News | 1 |
| Non specific | 1 |
| Social networking | 1 |
| Software engineering | 1 |
| Tourism | 1 |

27 out of 42 publications selected employed some form of usability method or assessment of web portals. This may appear as a relatively low number, but in the remaining publications usability may not have been the main focus of the research. Figure 6 shows the various methods used in the selected studies and the count of how many papers used each method. It can be seen that a variety of methods and assessments were employed and some papers used more than one method. The most utilised method was the use of questionnaires, and user testing was the second most used approach. This seems logical as usability is dependent on the users of a system.

Table 3 lists the usability or quality aspects influencing if users are engaging with a web portal so judged to be important for user experience. It can be seen that some aspects are incorporate others. Specifically, *functionality* is actually also encompassing *interactivity, searchability, crowdsourcing, sharing information, feedback mechanism, help functionality, communication facilities, recommendation mechanism, collaborative,* and *competition/reward,* and it appears logical that a functionality would impact users' desire to interact with a web portal.

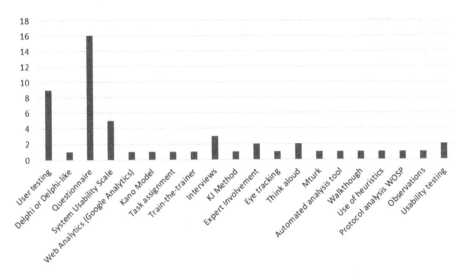

**Fig. 6.** Usability method or assessment technique used.

*Aesthetics* also encompasses *use of colour, symmetry, layout arrangement (balance and grouping), consistency* and *data hierarchy. Portability/compatibility* also incorporates *adaptability*. That is the reason *functionality, aesthetic,* and *portability/compatibility* have higher counts. Other aspects could have been grouped too, but these are somewhat judgement calls of the researchers. Apart from the groupings *accessibility* and *ease of use* were the most mentioned aspects to be important for usability of a web portal.

The challenges to usability and user involvement identified by literature in Table 4 mirror the aspects in Table 3. For instance *functionality* is seen as important for users to engage with a web portal. It may be counter intuitive to suggest a connection between *usability* and *functionality* and *lack or quality of functionality*, which also featured relatively strongly in Table 4, but without a perceived use or purpose a system may not be used, and as such *usable*. It could be argued that *quality of content* could be related to the *usability* since the quality of any information can frustrate users.

*Security*, although not directly related to *usability*, could be considered similarly related to *functionality* since perceived *security* will affect if users engage with a system. *Uncertainty and trust* are also related to *security. Performance* and *latency*, which impact waiting time are clearly impacting perceived *usability*.

For designers of web portals catering for *different types of users*, it would be interesting that there is *no central metric of usability*, and that there are different national usability indexes. These challenges could clearly also be seen as issues for developers and administrators of web portals, and they could have been featuring in Table 5 which shows challenges for web portal developers and administrators. *Maintainability* and *security* were the most prominent challenges for developers and administrators. *Ease of administration* could be considered

**Table 3.** Portal usability and quality aspects judged to be important.

| Usability/Quality aspect | Count | Paper identifier |
|---|---|---|
| Ease of use | 8 | 2, 15, 17, 23, 24, 27, 40, 42 |
| Accessibility | 9 | 4, 8, 9, 12, 31, 34, 37, 38, 42 |
| Understandability | 2 | 6, 13 |
| User satisfaction | 1 | 6 |
| Usefulness | 7 | 6, 7, 12, 13, 16, 27, 40 |
| Simplicity | 6 | 7, 12, 16, 31, 34, 42 |
| Usability | 7 | 6, 9, 10, 19, 25, 27, 38 |
| Easy navigation | 6 | 15, 25, 30, 31, 34, 37 |
| Responsiveness | 2 | 16, 31 |
| Performance | 2 | 16, 31 |
| Content | 2 | 27, 34 |
| Learnability | 3 | 30, 34, 40 |
| Task efficiency | 2 | 30, 39 |
| Satisfaction | 3 | 31, 33, 35 |
| System efficiency | 4 | 31, 33, 35, 40 |
| Effectiveness | 2 | 33, 35 |
| Reliability | 3 | 13, 23, 42 |
| Legitimacy | 1 | 37 |
| SEO friendly | 1 | 38 |
| Functionality | 9 | 13, 14, 19, 21, 23, 27, 34, 37, 41 |
| - Interactivity | 1 | 27 |
| - Searchability | 1 | 23 |
| - Crowdsourcing | 1 | 21 |
| Sharing information | 1 | 10 |
| - Feedback mechanism | 2 | 34, 37 |
| - Help | 1 | 37 |
| - Communication facilities | 1 | 41 |
| - Recommendation mechanism | 1 | 41 |
| - Collaborative | 2 | 14, 19 |
| - Competition/Rewards | 1 | 17 |
| Portability/Compatibility | 5 | 14, 16, 25, 41, 42 |
| - Adaptability | 2 | 25, 41 |
| Aesthetic | 6 | 18, 22, 30, 31, 34, 37 |
| - Use of colour | 1 | 22 |
| - Symmetry | 1 | 22 |
| - Layout | 1 | 22 |
| - Consistency | 1 | 31 |
| - Data hierarchy | 2 | 22, 37 |
| Social Factor/Good story | 1 | 17 |
| Community focused | 1 | 9 |

**Table 4.** Identified challenges.

| Usability challenges | Count |
| --- | --- |
| Latency | 2 |
| Different types of users | 2 |
| Age disparity | 1 |
| Attitude of users | 1 |
| Quality of content | 3 |
| Quality of user interface | 1 |
| Authorship and copyright | 1 |
| Privilege customisability | 1 |
| Uncertainty and trust | 3 |
| Performance | 4 |
| Reliability | 1 |
| Network availability | 1 |
| Complexity | 1 |
| Security | 4 |
| Security transparency | 1 |
| Developer limitations | 1 |
| Users' interpretations | 1 |
| Users' calculations of the utility of a resource | 1 |
| Information overload | 1 |
| Fragmentation of data | 1 |
| Personalisation of data | 1 |
| Clarity of usage | 1 |
| Lack of learnability | 1 |
| Functionality/usefulness | 5 |
| Lack or quality of functionality | 3 |
| Lack of portability | 1 |
| Lack of flexibility/customisability | 1 |
| Insufficient accessibility | 1 |
| Information not up-to-date | 1 |
| Poor feedback mechanism | 1 |
| Integration with other systems | 1 |
| No central metric of usability | 2 |

as related to *maintainability*, and in fact *maintainability* could be described as the *usability* of a system from the perspective of developers and administrators.

**Table 5.** Challenges for developers and administrators.

| Dev./Admin. challenges | Count |
|---|---|
| Ease of administration | 1 |
| Extensibility | 1 |
| Deployment | 1 |
| Information representation | 1 |
| Maintainability | 4 |
| Requirement elicitation | 1 |
| Security | 3 |

Table 6 shows features and qualities of the web portals discussed. One of the key features is *content sharing*, which seems to be the main purpose of web portals. This combined with the importance of *ease of use* as indicated in Table 3 highlights that the tasks a user can carry out need to be easily achievable. The second most noted quality in Table 6 is *engaging* which is difficult to achieve as this may change depending on user groups and possibly even changing attitudes to what is considered to be engaging.

**Table 6.** Noted portal features and characteristics.

| Feature/Characteristics | Count |
|---|---|
| Content sharing | 6 |
| Focus on social nature of portal | 3 |
| Consensus support system | 1 |
| Communication facilities | 3 |
| Recommendation mechanism | 1 |
| Engaging | 5 |
| Visually appealing | 1 |
| Searchable | 1 |
| Reliable | 1 |
| Flexible | 3 |
| Privacy | 1 |
| Accessibility features | 4 |
| Assistive services | 1 |
| Collaboration tools | 1 |

### 4.1 Limitations

As with any systematic literature review the work presented in this paper has some threats to validity. The main issue could be linked to the selection of keywords. There may be synonyms that were not included in the search due to non-standardised terminology. However, in this study the search terms were purposely left open to include as many relevant publications as possible.

We would like to also note that ACM search feature and user interface have changed while we were working on this study. Search results were different with the new version and included more irrelevant papers based on keywords search, but we included those new results and repeated the study for the ACM repository. In addition, ScienceDirect search feature did not allow more than eight operators, so search is repeated to include all keywords and results were merged.

Another possible thread to validity could be the interpretation of the categories presented in Sect. 4. Classifying is a non-trivial process, and categories may not be universally agreed on. However, the results presented in Sect. 4 still indicate aspects that may impact user engagement which is the core purpose of web portals.

## 5 Conclusion

Understanding how users interact with the knowledge sharing platforms is very important to realise the issues that users may encounter when visiting a portal. The ultimate experience of a portal can only be judged by the portal's users themselves, and not by the developers only even if they are experienced usability experts. In this paper, we presented a systematic mapping study with the objective of identifying the trends in usability and user experience of information portals and open community websites.

Our findings have been utilised in the SPEED (Smart Ports Entrepreneurial Ecosystem Development) project. The project's main purpose was toward efficiency and innovation. If the ports' needs coordinates with the advanced data science, it could be an important step in expediting the developments. Therefore, SPEED portal was developed to build a network community connecting high-tech start-ups with ports and ports stockholders.

Future work would be related to what attracts users to web portals, and what engages their participation. Usability is clearly an important part to maintain users' participation, but it is not entirely clear yet how successful web portals encourage users to interact with the web portal.

**Acknowledgments.** SPEED (Smart Ports Entrepreneurial Ecosystem Development) Project is funded by EU Interreg 2 Seas Mers Zeeën programme. The authors would like to thank Aikaterini Kakaounaki and Prof Reza Sahandi for their help and support.

# References

1. Bramer, W.M., de Jonge, G.B., Rethlefsen, M., Mast, F., Kleijnen, J.: A systematic approach to searching: an efficient and complete method to develop literature searches. J. Med. Libr. Assoc. JMLA **106**(4), 531–541 (2018). https://doi.org/10.5195/jmla.2018.283
2. Dingli, A., Cassar, S.: An intelligent framework for website usability. Adva. Hum.-Comput. Interact. **2014**, 1–13 (2014). https://doi.org/10.1155/2014/479286
3. Distante, D., Risi, M., Scanniello, G.: Enhancing navigability in websites built using web content management systems. Int. J. Softw. Eng. Knowl. Eng. **24**, 493–515 (2014). https://doi.org/10.1142/S0218194014500193
4. Estuar, M.R.J., De Leon, M., Santos, M.D., Ilagan, J.O., May, B.A.: Validating UI through UX in the context of a mobile - web crowdsourcing disaster management application. In: 2014 International Conference on IT Convergence and Security (ICITCS) (2014). https://doi.org/10.1109/ICITCS.2014.7021823
5. Fernandez, A., Insfran, E., Abrahão, S.: Usability evaluation methods for the web: a systematic mapping study. Inf. Softw. Technol. **53**(8), 789–817 (2011). https://doi.org/10.1016/j.infsof.2011.02.007
6. Følstad, A.: Users' design feedback in usability evaluation: a literature review. HCIS **7**(1), 1–19 (2017). https://doi.org/10.1186/s13673-017-0100-y
7. Hellmers, J., Thomaschewski, J., Schön, E.M., Wriedt, T.: Usability evaluation methods for a scientific internet information portal. J. Univ. Comput. Sci. **18**, 1308–1322 (2012)
8. Kazemi, S., Cetinkaya, D., Liebchen, G., Sahandi, R.: Usability and user experience in open community web portals: a case study in smart ports domain. In: Proceedings of the 20th International Conference in E-Society (2022)
9. Lefoe, G., O'Reilly, M., Parrish, D., Bennett, S., Keppell, M., Gunn, C.: The carrick exchange: not just another repository. In: Montgomerie, C., Seale, J. (eds.) Proceedings of the World Conference on Educational Multimedia, Hypermedia and Telecommunications EdMedia + Innovate Learning 2007, pp. 108–113. Association for the Advancement of Computing in Education (AACE), June 2007. https://www.learntechlib.org/p/25365
10. Lew, P., Olsina, L., Zhang, L.: Quality, quality in use, actual usability and user experience as key drivers for web application evaluation. In: Benatallah, B., Casati, F., Kappel, G., Rossi, G. (eds.) ICWE 2010. LNCS, vol. 6189, pp. 218–232. Springer, Heidelberg (2010). https://doi.org/10.1007/978-3-642-13911-6_15
11. Maia, C.L.B., Furtado, E.S.: A systematic review about user experience evaluation. In: Marcus, A. (ed.) DUXU 2016. LNCS, vol. 9746, pp. 445–455. Springer, Cham (2016). https://doi.org/10.1007/978-3-319-40409-7_42
12. Maligat, D.E., Torio, J.O., Bigueras, R.T., Arispe, M.C., Palaoag, T.D.: Web-based knowledge management system for camarines norte state college. In: IOP Conference Series: Materials Science and Engineering - International Conference on Information Technology and Digital Applications (ICITDA 2019), vol. 803 (2019)
13. Meier, F., Bazo, A., Burghardt, M., Wolff, C.: Evaluating a web-based tool for crowdsourced navigation stress tests. In: Marcus, A. (ed.) DUXU 2013. LNCS, vol. 8015, pp. 248–256. Springer, Heidelberg (2013). https://doi.org/10.1007/978-3-642-39253-5_27
14. Nebeling, M., Speicher, M., Grossniklaus, M., Norrie, M.C.: Crowdsourced web site evaluation with CrowdStudy. In: Brambilla, M., Tokuda, T., Tolksdorf, R. (eds.) ICWE 2012. LNCS, vol. 7387, pp. 494–497. Springer, Heidelberg (2012). https://doi.org/10.1007/978-3-642-31753-8_52

15. Nebeling, M., Speicher, M., Norrie, M.C.: Crowdstudy: general toolkit for crowd-sourced evaluation of web interfaces. In: Proceedings of the 5th ACM SIGCHI Symposium on Engineering Interactive Computing Systems, EICS 2013, pp. 255–264. Association for Computing Machinery, New York (2013)
16. Petersen, K., Vakkalanka, S., Kuzniarz, L.: Guidelines for conducting systematic mapping studies in software engineering. Inf. Softw. Technol. **64**(C), 1–18 (2015). https://doi.org/10.1016/j.infsof.2015.03.007
17. Pinho, C., Franco, M., Mendes, L.: Web portals as tools to support information management in higher education institutions: a systematic literature review. Int. J. Inf. Manag. **41**, 80–92 (2018). https://doi.org/10.1016/j.ijinfomgt.2018.04.002
18. Reychav, I., Wu, D.: The role of user-centered design and usability on knowledge sharing: a school website field study. Int. J. Knowl. Learn. **10**(1), 16–28 (2015). https://doi.org/10.1504/IJKL.2015.071051
19. Shekh.Khalil, N., Dogruer, E., Elosta, A.K.O., Eraslan, S., Yesilada, Y., Harper, S.: Eyecrowdata: towards a web-based crowdsourcing platform for web-related eye-tracking data. In: ACM Symposium on Eye Tracking Research and Applications (ETRA 2020). Association for Computing Machinery, New York (2020)
20. Subramanian, D.V., Geetha, A., Shankar, P.: An effective assessment of knowledge sharing and e-learning portals. Int. J. Web-Based Learn. Teach. Technol. **10**(2), 1–12 (2015). https://doi.org/10.4018/IJWLTT.2015040101
21. Sutcliffe, A.: Designing for User Engagement: Aesthetic and Attractive User Interfaces, vol. 2. Morgan & Claypool, San Rafael (2009)
22. Walser, K.: Engaging citizens with UX design. In: Marcus, A. (ed.) DUXU 2013. LNCS, vol. 8012, pp. 427–436. Springer, Heidelberg (2013). https://doi.org/10.1007/978-3-642-39229-0_46

# Anchoring Effect Mitigation for Complex Recommender System Design

Dionisis Margaris[1] , Dimitris Spiliotopoulos[2]([⊠]) , and Costas Vassilakis[3]

[1] Department of Digital Systems, University of the Peloponnese, Sparta, Greece
margaris@uop.gr

[2] Department of Management Science and Technology, University of the Peloponnese, Tripoli, Greece
dspiliot@uop.gr

[3] Department of Informatics and Telecommunications, University of the Peloponnese, Tripoli, Greece
costas@uop.gr

**Abstract.** The adoption of a recommender system depends mostly on the accuracy of the computation of the rating predictions from the users. The user rating prediction accuracy has been a main topic in recent research. Collaborative filtering is one of the most prevalent algorithms for rating prediction, where ratings from close users, Near Neighbours, are used for the prediction of item ratings. For the collaborating filtering algorithm implementation, researchers utilise a large set of parameters, such as the number of close users and user proximity calculation metrics, to automatically determine these users, resulting in time-consuming decision conflicts over the most appropriate selections. This paper explores an approach that enables scientists to make informed selections for the metrics, parameters, and setups, using a prototype user interface with preloaded tools for the scientist to explore close users and attributes. The end users may create simulations to gain insight into the rating prediction process. The user study verifies that the designer anchoring effect of conflict of decision may be mitigated using the proposed approach, enabling transparency for the recommendations and informed decisions from the simulations.

**Keywords:** User interface · Recommender systems · Collaborative filtering · Rating prediction · Conflict of decision · Anchoring effects in designing complexity · User evaluation · Usability evaluation

## 1 Introduction

The persistent growth of the content available in web applications, nowadays, has created an abundant amount of information for the users to consume. Recommender systems (RSs) can be used to overcome this issue, by limiting and/or prioritising the information displayed to the users, based on their perceived value [1–3]. One of the most widely used RS techniques is Collaborative Filtering (CF), whose overall goal is to produce accurate rating predictions for items unrated by the users [4–6]. Then, the items scoring

© The Author(s), under exclusive license to Springer Nature Switzerland AG 2022
M. Kurosu et al. (Eds.): HCII 2022, LNCS 13516, pp. 424–436, 2022.
https://doi.org/10.1007/978-3-031-17615-9_29

the higher rating prediction values, and hence the highest probability that those items will be desirable, are typically recommended to the users [7–9]. As expected, the closer these rating predictions are to the real rating values, the more accurate the RS is.

CF RS designers use existing datasets to simulate output using RS models and algorithms. This allows them to select the most appropriate approach and finetune it, using low and high cut-off parameters [10–12]. In the absence of appropriate user interfaces (UIs) and visual feedback, this work would traditionally be done programmatically using custom code. With the increase of the available datasets, research approaches and fine-tuning methods, in the recent years, the task of manual parameterisation for multiple datasets and subsets has been shown to yield suboptimal results in several situations [13–15]. The designer is required to try out approaches and multitudes of parameters per dataset to determine the optimal setup for the recommendation engine [16–18].

Apart from the fatigue and the human errors, it is hypothesised that anchoring effect manifests itself on the designer decision process. Based on the above, the first research hypothesis (RH1) is that designers experience conflict of decision between possibly optimal setups more often than expected. A second hypothesis (RH2) is that conflict resolution (due to task complexity) may be mitigated through visual decluttering of the model/parameter settings and no-code comparative overview.

This paper reports on the user study of 30 participants on the design and evaluation of the model/parameter decision making process for item rating prediction, using (implementing) CF, which is one of the most prevalent algorithm categories for rating prediction in RSs.

The rest of this paper is structured as follows: Sect. 2 summarizes related work, while Sect. 3 overviews the necessary foundations from the CF research area. Section 4 introduces the user interface (UI) and analyses the design and functionalities, while Sect. 5 presents the user evaluation results. Finally, Sect. 6 concludes the paper and outlines the future work.

## 2   Related Work

Over the recent years RSs has been of major interest by many research works [19–22]. Luo et al. [23] perform unconstrained non-negative latent factor analysis on high-dimensional and sparse matrices by transferring the non-negativity constraints from the decision parameters to the output latent factors and connect them using a dependent mapping function. Afterwards, they theoretically prove that the resulting model precisely represents the original one, by making a mapping function fulfil specific conditions. Lastly, they design efficient unconstrained non-negative latent factor analysis RSs algorithms. Qin et al. [24] generalise the classic position bias model to an attribute-based propensity framework. Their methods allow propensity estimation across a wide range of implicit feedback scenarios and estimate propensity scores based on offline data. These are demonstrated by applying their framework to a Google Drive RS with millions of users. Shin [25] examines how users perceive news recommendations issues and the way they engage and interact with algorithm-recommended news. Furthermore, he introduces an underlying algorithm experience model of news recommendation, integrating the heuristic process of affective, behavioural, and cognitive factors. The proposed algorithm affects the user's perception and system trust, in different ways. The heuristic aspects transpire when the users' subjective beliefs about accuracy and transparency act as a mental shortcut. The mediating role of trust is an indication that the algorithmic performance could be enhanced by establishing algorithmic trust between news recommendation systems and users. The model illustrates the motivation behind user behaviours, as well as the users' cognitive processes of perceptual judgment. Shambour [26] introduces a deep learning-based algorithm for multi-criteria RS that exploits the nonlinear, non-trivial and hidden relations between users, regarding multi-criteria preferences, by the employment of deep auto-encoders, which generates more accurate recommendations. The algorithm produces accurate rating predictions, when compared with state-of-the-art rating prediction algorithms, based on experiments on the TripAdvisor and Yahoo! Movies multi-criteria datasets. Tian et al. [27] introduce a RS that automatically selects a best-suited metaheuristic method without trial and error on a given problem. This algorithm explores the intricacies of optimisation problems, by developing a generic tree-like data structure. It trains a deep recurrent neural network which makes automated algorithm recommendation, by learning to choose the best metaheuristic algorithm. This algorithm makes metaheuristic optimisation techniques accessible to policy makers, industrial practitioners, as well as other stakeholders having no prior knowledge of metaheuristic algorithms. Alhijawi and Kilani [28] introduce a novel genetic-based RS, that operates using historical rating data and semantic information. This genetic algorithm finds the best list of items to the active user, by hierarchically evaluating the individuals using three fitness functions. The first one estimates the strength of the semantic similarity between items, utilising the semantic information on items. The second one estimates the satisfaction level similarity between users, while the last one selects the best recommendation list, based on the predicted ratings.

Accuracy is an important aspect of CF RSs [10, 29, 30]. Singh et al. [31] seek to overcome the issue of CF recommendation inaccuracy, due to the fact that the predicted rating may tend towards the average rating value of the user. This is achieved by mitigating the issues of (i) the consideration of different value of k nearest neighbour per user and (ii) dataset sparsity. To predict the target item, for each item, they select the nearest neighbour, due to the high computational cost of finding k for each/different item. Yan and Tang [32] present a model that uses Gaussian mixture to cluster items and users. Furthermore, their model builds a new interaction matrix, by extracting new features, which solves the rating data sparsity impact on CF algorithms. Lastly, they present a new similarity calculation method that combines the Jaccard and the triangle similarities. Jain et al. [33] present an Enhanced Multistage User-based CF algorithm that predicts the unknown user ratings in two stages, using the active learning concept. This algorithm predicts the anonymous ratings for each stage using the traditional User_CF algorithm. However, it uses the Bhattacharyya Coefficient based nonlinear similarity model for the similarity computations among users. The presented algorithm uses an extension of the simple Enhanced multistage user-based CF algorithm, which achieves to increase the prediction accuracy, by progressively increasing the density of the original rating matrix. Margaris et al. [34] introduce the Experiencing Period Criterion rating prediction algorithm which enhances the prediction accuracy of CF RSs, based on the combination of the time period the rating to be predicted belongs to, in a certain product category, and the users' experiencing wait period in the same product category. The rationale behind this algorithm is that a user may apply different experience practices on different product categories, that is, being reluctant to experience new products in certain categories, while being keen to experience new products in others. Chae et al. [35] present a Rating Augmentation framework with GAN, targeting at alleviating the data sparsity problem in CF, which achieves to improve recommendation accuracy. Also, they identified that the naive Rating Augmentation GAN tends to generate values biased towards high ratings when applying GAN to CF for rating improvement. This issue is addressed by introducing a refined version of RAGAN.

HCI and RS research has started to grow over the last years [36–38]. Braham et al. [39] present a RS for selecting the most relevant design patterns in the HCI domain, by combining ontology-based and text-based techniques and by using ontology models and semantic similarity to retrieve appropriate HCI design patterns. They also validate the presented RS regarding its acceptance, by evaluating the perceived accuracy and perceived experience by users. Dominguez et al. [40] provide a perspective of the many variables involved in the user perception of several aspects of a RS, such as relevance, explainability, domain knowledge and trust. They study several aspects of the user experience with a RS of artistic images, from both HCI and algorithmic perspectives, and then they conduct user studies to evaluate the levels of explainability. Margaris et al. [41] introduce a UI for WS-BPEL designers that supports personalised recommendation and selection of business process functionalities, based on user generated criteria. More specifically, the UI gives the WS-BPEL designers the opportunity, based on either particular or total scores, to ask for web service recommendations and select specific web services out of ordered lists. This allows the users to have the final selection choice, thus overcome the automatic system selection issue that leads to adaptation failure. Locatelli Cezar et al. [42] introduce a RS for the HCI community, recommending papers from the Brazilian Symposium on Human Factors in Computing Systems. This RS applies a post-processing strategy, focused on fairness to balance the users' interests, in order to recommend papers related to each user's profile. Margaris et al. [43] present a specialised UI for WS-BPEL designers, which allows personalised recommendation and business process functionalities selection based on user generated criteria. The UI supports user-specified restrictions, based on non-qualitative criteria, WS preselection, as well as tuning of the number of retrieved candidate web services presented to the WS-BPEL designer.

However, none of the above-mentioned works explores how RS scientists can be enabled to make informed selections for the metrics, parameters, and setups of a CF RS, for example, the number of Near Neighbours (NNs) to consider and user similarity calculation metrics. This work introduces a UI with preloaded tools that enables the users to create simulations, to gain insight into the rating prediction process and, ultimately, increase the rating prediction accuracy, to essentially lead to higher recommendation accuracy.

## 3  Prerequisites

The major concepts from the areas of CF RSs, which are used in our work, are summarized in the following paragraphs.

First and foremost, the ultimate goal of a CF RS is to produce accurate predictions for the products that users have not yet evaluated [6]. Then, the RS typically recommends the products achieving the higher prediction values, to each user, assuming that higher prediction values usually drive to higher probability that the user will actually be interested in these products [44, 45]. Obviously, the more accurate these rating predictions are, the more reliable the recommendations will be, and hence the more successful the RS will be.

The first step of a typical CF RS is to find users y, who share similar tastes with the active user x (that is, the user for whom the rating prediction is being formulated), by comparing the real ratings that both x and y have already entered to common products p. In order to quantify the closeness of similar tastes between users, a user similarity function must be used, such as the Pearson Correlation Coefficient and the Cosine Similarity, the selection of which is made by the RS scientist [46, 47].

Afterwards, all users y, who are found to have (to a large extent) similar ratings with active user x, are considered x's candidate NNs. At this moment, the RS scientist must again select the exact number of NNs that each user x will use for prediction formulation [18, 48].

Lastly, in order to formulate the rating prediction of user x to product p, the existed ratings of x's NNs to the same product are used. This happens under the rationale that, in the real world, humans trust people close to them (close friends, family, etc.) when suggestions for a new experience/commodity are demanded (Fig. 1).

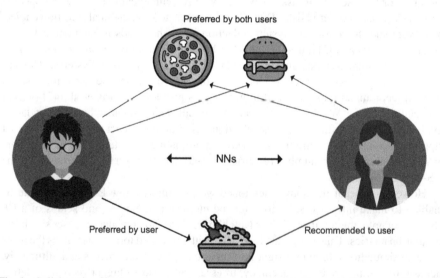

**Fig. 1.** Collaborative filtering recommender systems use near neighbours to recommend items to users.

Based on the aforementioned steps, both the user similarity function and the exact number of NNs directly affect the rating prediction value and, hence, accuracy, which ultimately affects the recommendation success. As a result, the selections that the RS scientist must take are of critical importance. Scientists spend time researching the optimal setups and are asked to make decisions between multiple seemingly adequate options. Decision conflicts are time consuming and hinder productivity. This necessitated the implementation of a UI with preloaded tools for the RS scientist to support these selections and resolve decision conflict.

## 4  User Interface Design and Functionalities

The proposed UI was designed and implemented with the following functionalities:

- Selection of the similarity function between the CF users.
- Selection of the exact number of NNs that each user x will use for prediction formulation.
- Real time simulation for selected setups and metrics and graphical representation of accuracy

In the following subsections the above functionalities will be analysed. The UI is depicted in Fig. 2.

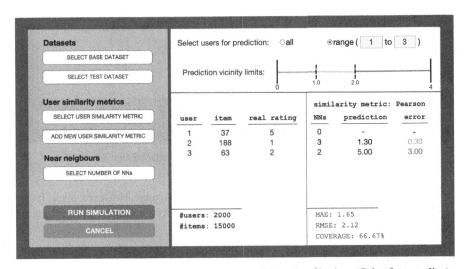

**Fig. 2.** The UI for rating prediction analysis for collaborating filtering. (Color figure online)

On the left-hand-side, the RS scientist selects all the necessary information a CF algorithm needs, that is, the base dataset, the test dataset, the user similarity metrics, and the number of NNs used. On the upper part of the screen, the scientist selects the users (all or a range of users) which the rating prediction procedure will formulate predictions for. The UI allows the RS scientist to select the exact number of NNs that will take part, for each user, to the rating prediction formulation. If a user has less NNs than the selected number, all of his NNs will be used for the rating prediction formulation.

According to the vicinity between the rating prediction and the real user rating, the user can select the limits for which the UI displays the prediction error in colours (the red colour indicates large prediction errors, the yellow colour indicates medium prediction errors, and the green colour indicates small prediction errors) so that the user can easily locate the cases to focus on.

Lastly, after the simulation is run, the rating predictions are displayed on the right-hand side. The predictions also incorporate statistics that may help the user interpret the results of the rating prediction procedure. These include the number of users and items the dataset contains, the Mean Average Error and the Root Mean Square Error, as well as the prediction coverage of the prediction process.

The UI allows the user to select from the preloaded user similarity functions, such as the Pearson Correlation Coefficient and the Cosine Similarity. Apart from the already implemented user similarity metrics, the user may add, edit, or delete custom metrics (Fig. 3). These add to the flexibility of the UI, since many users prefer to utilise their own code implementations.

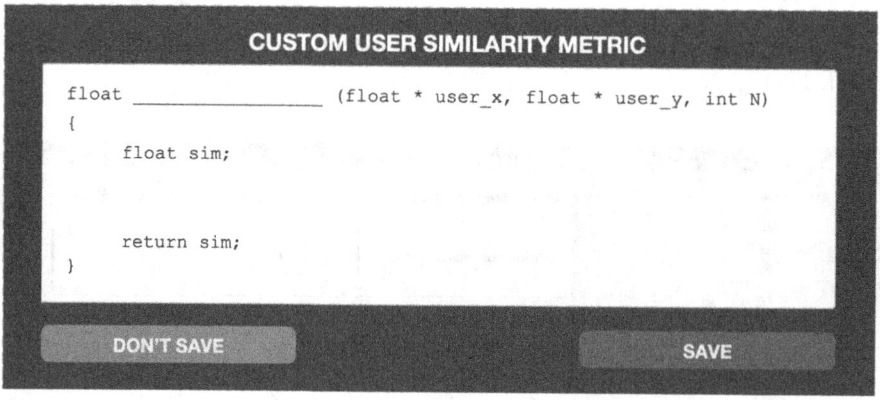

```
CUSTOM USER SIMILARITY METRIC

float _____  (float * user_x, float * user_y, int N)
{
    float sim;


    return sim;
}
```

DON'T SAVE                                          SAVE

**Fig. 3.** User-created custom similarity metrics for recommendation simulations

At the moment, the UI supports the C programming language. However, in our future work we are planning to extend it so that it also supports JAVA and Python programming languages, which many RS scientists use, as well.

## 5 Evaluation

This section reports on the user study of 30 computer science literate participants on the design and evaluation of the model/parameter decision making process for the rating prediction, implementing the CF algorithm. The mean age of users was 20.7 years, 70% male and 30% female.

For RH1, think aloud testing was applied to monitor and register decision conflicts. Time to task completion and number of individual trials per dataset (including backtracking to former datasets and setups when optimal parameters were found) were also logged. This was studied for 5 datasets, randomly selected out of the 10 trial datasets, widely used in CF research, for the study, namely the Amazon datasets [49, 50] and the MovieLens datasets [51].

The RH2 investigation was contacted as follows. For the remaining half of the datasets, the users explored the selection set of model and parameters for the RS and simulated the applied setups using a prototype UI that implemented the following functionalities:

- Selection of input/simulation base and test datasets.
- Selection of user vicinity metric.
- Capacity to add new, custom vicinity metrics by the user.
- Selection of number of NNs for output prediction.
- Selection of range of target users (i.e., from the datasets) which the prediction output is computed for. This allows for insight into the algorithm and better explainability.
- Colour coded vicinity prediction to real values.

All the aforementioned metrics were also applied and actions were recorded. In addition, a usability evaluation was performed on the latter approach using the moderated feedback, namely the think aloud method and user behaviour and perception metrics, as in similar works [43, 52]. The sessions were run for up to 30 m per task for the total of two tasks per user.

RH1 was found true. The users reported between six and twenty conflicts of decision per session (Fig. 4). The main findings were:

- Time consuming actions: the users attempted to run multiple tries on a dataset, make deductions on the optimal setup and proceed to try the setup for the next dataset (termed as "traditional developer" approach). This resulted in several re-tries of similar parameters and lack of insight on the datasets that followed the ones tested, since they would be examined anew.
- Conflict of decision: the users experienced most conflicts when similar positive results were evaluated, since no insight on the performance of the setups for the other datasets (sparse and dense) could be known.

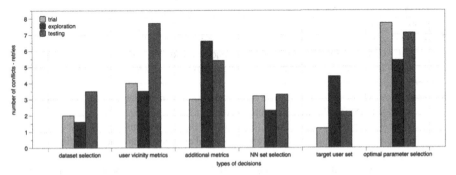

**Fig. 4.** User-reported average decision conflict breakdown. The results clearly depict the activities and types of decisions that trigger conflicts. Those conflicts are mitigated through the proposed approach.

RH2 was also found true. The users reported that the colour-coded vicinity prediction to real values in a comparative manner was helpful for making informed decisions regarding setups that worked well for groups of datasets (two or more). Since dataset performance varies due to dataset content differences, the target user range selection was helpful in grouping setup performance even better for groups of datasets. In addition, the users reported very high acceptance (behaviour metrics: task completions and confidence; perception metrics: task completion and task difficulty).

The approach that utilised the UI prototype reduced the conflicts by 4.71 times on average, while the maximum reduction was over 6 times on average for the five most problematic types of decisions.

## 6    Conclusion

This work presented a UI with preloaded tools for RSs scientists, targeting at mitigating the anchoring effect of conflict of decision that the scientists face. More specifically, the scientists can make informed selections for the metrics, parameters and setups, as well as create simulations to gain insight into the rating prediction process. A user study verified that the RS designers face the anchoring effect of conflict of decision. This may be mitigated using the proposed approach, enabling transparency for the recommendations and informed decisions from the graphical results from the recommendation process simulations.

In our future work, we are planning to extend the set of languages that the UI supports, including JAVA and Python programming languages, which many RS scientists use [53, 54]. Furthermore, we are planning the UI to include graphical representation of the rating prediction results. Last, we are planning to extend the rating prediction error metrics, including the most used ones in RS research [10, 12, 55].

## References

1. Alslaity, A., Tran, T.: Goal modeling-based evaluation for personalized recommendation systems. In: Adjunct Proceedings of the 29th ACM Conference on User Modeling, Adaptation and Personalization, pp. 276–283. ACM, Utrecht Netherlands (2021). https://doi.org/10.1145/3450614.3464619
2. Berkovsky, S., Freyne, J.: Web personalization and recommender systems. In: Proceedings of the 21th ACM SIGKDD International Conference on Knowledge Discovery and Data Mining, pp. 2307–2308. ACM, Sydney, NSW, Australia (2015). https://doi.org/10.1145/2783258.2789995
3. Aivazoglou, M., et al.: A fine-grained social network recommender system. Soc. Netw. Anal. Min. 10(1), 1–18 (2019). https://doi.org/10.1007/s13278-019-0621-7
4. Margaris, D., Spiliotopoulos, D., Vassilakis, C.: Social relations versus near neighbours: reliable recommenders in limited information social network collaborative filtering for online advertising. In: Proceedings of the 2019 IEEE/ACM International Conference on Advances in Social Networks Analysis and Mining, pp. 1160–1167. ACM, Vancouver, British Columbia, Canada (2019). https://doi.org/10.1145/3341161.3345620
5. Veras De Sena Rosa, R.E., Guimaraes, F.A.S., da SilvaMendonca, R., de Lucena, V.F.: Improving prediction accuracy in neighborhood-based collaborative filtering by using local similarity. IEEE Access 8, 142795–142809 (2020). https://doi.org/10.1109/ACCESS.2020.3013733

6. Herlocker, J.L., Konstan, J.A., Terveen, L.G., Riedl, J.T.: Evaluating collaborative filtering recommender systems. ACM Trans. Inf. Syst. **22**, 5–53 (2004). https://doi.org/10.1145/963 770.963772

7. Balabanović, M., Shoham, Y.: Fab: content-based, collaborative recommendation. Commun. ACM. **40**, 66–72 (1997). https://doi.org/10.1145/245108.245124

8. Cechinel, C., Sicilia, M.-Á., Sánchez-Alonso, S., García-Barriocanal, E.: Evaluating collaborative filtering recommendations inside large learning object repositories. Inf. Process. Manage. **49**, 34–50 (2013). https://doi.org/10.1016/j.ipm.2012.07.004

9. Margaris, D., Kobusinska, A., Spiliotopoulos, D., Vassilakis, C.: An adaptive social network-aware collaborative filtering algorithm for improved rating prediction accuracy. IEEE Access **8**, 68301–68310 (2020). https://doi.org/10.1109/ACCESS.2020.2981567

10. Kluver, D., Ekstrand, M.D., Konstan, J.A.: Rating-based collaborative filtering: algorithms and evaluation. In: Brusilovsky, P., He, D. (eds.) Social Information Access. LNCS, vol. 10100, pp. 344–390. Springer, Cham (2018). https://doi.org/10.1007/978-3-319-90092-6_10

11. Cunha, T., Soares, C., de Carvalho, A.C.P.L.F.: Selecting collaborative filtering algorithms using metalearning. In: Frasconi, P., Landwehr, N., Manco, G., Vreeken, J. (eds.) ECML PKDD 2016. LNCS (LNAI), vol. 9852, pp. 393–409. Springer, Cham (2016). https://doi.org/ 10.1007/978-3-319-46227-1_25

12. Jalili, M., Ahmadian, S., Izadi, M., Moradi, P., Salehi, M.: Evaluating collaborative filtering recommender algorithms: a survey. IEEE Access **6**, 74003–74024 (2018). https://doi.org/10. 1109/ACCESS.2018.2883742

13. McNee, S.M., Riedl, J., Konstan, J.A.: Making recommendations better: an analytic model for human-recommender interaction. In: Proceedings of the CHI 2006 Extended Abstracts on Human Factors in Computing Systems, pp. 1103–1108. ACM, Montréal, Québec, Canada (2006). https://doi.org/10.1145/1125451.1125660

14. Miller, B.N., Albert, I., Lam, S.K., Konstan, J.A., Riedl, J.: MovieLens unplugged: experiences with an occasionally connected recommender system. In: Proceedings of the 8th International Conference on Intelligent User Interfaces - IUI 2003, p. 263. ACM Press, Miami, Florida, USA (2003). https://doi.org/10.1145/604045.604094

15. Kunkel, J., Loepp, B., Ziegler, J.: A 3D item space visualization for presenting and manipulating user preferences in collaborative filtering. In: Proceedings of the 22nd International Conference on Intelligent User Interfaces, pp. 3–15. ACM, Limassol, Cyprus (2017). https:// doi.org/10.1145/3025171.3025189

16. Chae, D.-K., Lee, S.-C., Lee, S.-Y., Kim, S.-W.: On identifying k -nearest neighbors in neighborhood models for efficient and effective collaborative filtering. Neurocomputing **278**, 134–143 (2018). https://doi.org/10.1016/j.neucom.2017.06.081

17. Li, S., Karatzoglou, A., Gentile, C.: Collaborative filtering bandits. In: Proceedings of the 39th International ACM SIGIR Conference on Research and Development in Information Retrieval, pp. 539–548. ACM, Pisa, Italy (2016). https://doi.org/10.1145/2911451.2911548

18. Verstrepen, K., Goethals, B.: Unifying nearest neighbors collaborative filtering. In: Proceedings of the 8th ACM Conference on Recommender Systems - RecSys 2014, pp. 177–184. ACM Press, Foster City, Silicon Valley, California, USA (2014). https://doi.org/10.1145/264 5710.2645731

19. Jannach, D., Manzoor, A., Cai, W., Chen, L.: A survey on conversational recommender systems. ACM Comput. Surv. **54**, 1–36 (2022). https://doi.org/10.1145/3453154

20. Nikolakopoulos, A.N., Ning, X., Desrosiers, C., Karypis, G.: Trust your neighbors: a comprehensive survey of neighborhood-based methods for recommender systems. In: Ricci, F., Rokach, L., Shapira, B. (eds.) Recommender Systems Handbook, pp. 39–89. Springer, New York, NY (2022). https://doi.org/10.1007/978-1-0716-2197-4_2

21. Karimi, M., Jannach, D., Jugovac, M.: News recommender systems – survey and roads ahead. Inf. Process. Manage. **54**, 1203–1227 (2018). https://doi.org/10.1016/j.ipm.2018.04.008

22. Deldjoo, Y., Schedl, M., Hidasi, B., Wei, Y., He, X.: Multimedia recommender systems: algorithms and challenges. In: Ricci, F., Rokach, L., Shapira, B. (eds.) Recommender Systems Handbook, pp. 973–1014. Springer US, New York, NY (2022). https://doi.org/10.1007/978-1-0716-2197-4_25

23. Luo, X., Zhou, M., Li, S., Wu, D., Liu, Z., Shang, M.: Algorithms of unconstrained non-negative latent factor analysis for recommender systems. IEEE Trans. Big Data. **7**, 227–240 (2021). https://doi.org/10.1109/TBDATA.2019.2916868

24. Qin, Z., Chen, S.J., Metzler, D., Noh, Y., Qin, J., Wang, X.: Attribute-based propensity for unbiased learning in recommender systems: algorithm and case studies. In: Proceedings of the 26th ACM SIGKDD International Conference on Knowledge Discovery & Data Mining, pp. 2359–2367. ACM, Virtual Event, CA, USA (2020). https://doi.org/10.1145/3394486.340 3285

25. Shin, D.: How do users interact with algorithm recommender systems? The interaction of users, algorithms, and performance. Comput. Hum. Behav. **109**, 106344 (2020). https://doi.org/10.1016/j.chb.2020.106344

26. Shambour, Q.: A deep learning based algorithm for multi-criteria recommender systems. Knowl.-Based Syst. **211**, 106545 (2021). https://doi.org/10.1016/j.knosys.2020.106545

27. Tian, Y., Peng, S., Zhang, X., Rodemann, T., Tan, K.C., Jin, Y.: A recommender system for metaheuristic algorithms for continuous optimization based on deep recurrent neural networks. IEEE Trans. Artif. Intell. **1**, 5–18 (2020). https://doi.org/10.1109/TAI.2020.302 2339

28. Alhijawi, B., Kilani, Y.: A collaborative filtering recommender system using genetic algorithm. Inf. Process. Manage. **57**, 102310 (2020). https://doi.org/10.1016/j.ipm.2020.102310

29. Rendle, S., Krichene, W., Zhang, L., Anderson, J.: Neural collaborative filtering vs. matrix factorization revisited. In: Proceedings of the Fourteenth ACM Conference on Recommender Systems, pp. 240–248. ACM, Virtual Event, Brazil (2020). https://doi.org/10.1145/3383313.3412488

30. Koren, Y., Rendle, S., Bell, R.: Advances in collaborative filtering. In: Ricci, F., Rokach, L., Shapira, B. (eds.) Recommender Systems Handbook, pp. 91–142. Springer, New York, NY (2022). https://doi.org/10.1007/978-1-0716-2197-4_3

31. Singh, P.K., Sinha, M., Das, S., Choudhury, P.: Enhancing recommendation accuracy of item-based collaborative filtering using Bhattacharyya coefficient and most similar item. Appl. Intell. **50**(12), 4708–4731 (2020). https://doi.org/10.1007/s10489-020-01775-4

32. Yan, H., Tang, Y.: Collaborative filtering based on gaussian mixture model and improved jaccard similarity. IEEE Access **7**, 118690–118701 (2019). https://doi.org/10.1109/ACCESS.2019.2936630

33. Jain, A., Nagar, S., Singh, P.K., Dhar, J.: EMUCF: enhanced multistage user-based collaborative filtering through non-linear similarity for recommendation systems. Expert Syst. Appl. **161**, 113724 (2020). https://doi.org/10.1016/j.eswa.2020.113724

34. Margaris, D., Spiliotopoulos, D., Vassilakis, C., Vasilopoulos, D.: Improving collaborative filtering's rating prediction accuracy by introducing the experiencing period criterion. Neural Comput. Appl., 1-18 (2020). https://doi.org/10.1007/s00521-020-05460-y

35. Chae, D.-K., Kang, J.-S., Kim, S.-W., Choi, J.: Rating augmentation with generative adversarial networks towards accurate collaborative filtering. In: Proceedings of The World Wide Web Conference on - WWW 2019, pp. 2616–2622. ACM Press, San Francisco, CA, USA (2019). https://doi.org/10.1145/3308558.3313413

36. Jesse, M., Jannach, D.: Digital nudging with recommender systems: survey and future directions. Comput. Hum. Behav. Rep. **3**, 100052 (2021). https://doi.org/10.1016/j.chbr.2020.100052

37. Jannach, D., Pu, P., Ricci, F., Zanker, M.: Recommender systems: past, present future. AIMag. **42**, 3–6 (2021). https://doi.org/10.1609/aimag.v42i3.18139
38. Vultureanu-Albisi, A., Badica, C.: Recommender systems: an explainable AI perspective. In: Proceedings of the 2021 International Conference on INnovations in Intelligent SysTems and Applications (INISTA), pp. 1–6. IEEE, Kocaeli, Turkey (2021). https://doi.org/10.1109/INI STA52262.2021.9548125
39. Braham, A., Khemaja, M., Buendía, F., Gargouri, F.: A hybrid recommender system for HCI design pattern recommendations. Appl. Sci. **11**, 10776 (2021). https://doi.org/10.3390/app 112210776
40. Dominguez, V., Donoso-Guzmán, I., Messina, P., Parra, D.: Algorithmic and HCI aspects for explaining recommendations of artistic images. ACM Trans. Interact. Intell. Syst. **10**, 1–31 (2020). https://doi.org/10.1145/3369396
41. Margaris, D., Spiliotopoulos, D., Vassilakis, C., Karagiorgos, G.: A user interface for personalized web service selection in business processes. In: Stephanidis, C., et al. (eds.) HCII 2020. LNCS, vol. 12427, pp. 560–573. Springer, Cham (2020). https://doi.org/10.1007/978-3-030-60152-2_41
42. Cezar, N.L., de Borba, C., Gasparini, I., Lichtnow, D.: Applying a post-processing strategy to consider the multiple interests of users of a paper recommender system. In: Proceedings of the XVII Brazilian Symposium on Information Systems, pp. 1–7. ACM, Uberlândia, Brazil (2021). https://doi.org/10.1145/3466933.3466985
43. Margaris, D., Spiliotopoulos, D., Vasilopoulos, D., Vassilakis, C.: A user interface for personalising WS-BPEL scenarios. In: Nah, F.-H., Siau, K. (eds.) HCII 2021. LNCS, vol. 12783, pp. 399–416. Springer, Cham (2021). https://doi.org/10.1007/978-3-030-77750-0_25
44. Sarwar, B., Karypis, G., Konstan, J., Reidl, J.: Item-based collaborative filtering recommendation algorithms. In: Proceedings of the Tenth International Conference on World Wide Web - WWW 2001, pp. 285–295. ACM Press, Hong Kong, Hong Kong (2001). https://doi.org/10.1145/371920.372071
45. Xue, F., He, X., Wang, X., Xu, J., Liu, K., Hong, R.: Deep item-based collaborative filtering for top-N recommendation. ACM Trans. Inf. Syst. **37**, 1–25 (2019). https://doi.org/10.1145/3314578
46. Herlocker, J., Konstan, J.A., Riedl, J.: An empirical analysis of design choices in neighborhood-based collaborative filtering algorithms. Inf. Retrieval **5**, 287–310 (2002). https://doi.org/10.1023/A:1020443909834
47. Elahi, M., Ricci, F., Rubens, N.: A survey of active learning in collaborative filtering recommender systems. Comput. Sci. Rev. **20**, 29–50 (2016). https://doi.org/10.1016/j.cosrev.2016.05.002
48. Margaris, D., Vasilopoulos, D., Vassilakis, C., Spiliotopoulos, D.: Improving collaborative filtering's rating prediction accuracy by introducing the common item rating past criterion. In: Proceedings of the 2019 10th International Conference on Information, Intelligence, Systems and Applications (IISA), pp. 1–8. IEEE, PATRAS, Greece (2019). https://doi.org/10.1109/IISA.2019.8900758
49. He, R., McAuley, J.: Ups and downs: modeling the visual evolution of fashion trends with one-class collaborative filtering. In: Proceedings of the 25th International Conference on World Wide Web, pp. 507–517. International World Wide Web Conferences Steering Committee, Montréal, Québec, Canada (2016). https://doi.org/10.1145/2872427.2883037
50. McAuley, J., Targett, C., Shi, Q., van den Hengel, A.: Image-based recommendations on styles and substitutes. In: Proceedings of the 38th International ACM SIGIR Conference on Research and Development in Information Retrieval., pp. 43–52. ACM, Santiago, Chile (2015). https://doi.org/10.1145/2766462.2767755
51. Harper, F.M., Konstan, J.A.: The movielens datasets: history and context. ACM Trans. Interact. Intell. Syst. **5**, 1–19 (2016). https://doi.org/10.1145/2827872

52. Spiliotopoulos, D., Margaris, D., Vassilakis, C.: Data-assisted persona construction using social media data. BDCC. **4**, 21 (2020). https://doi.org/10.3390/bdcc4030021
53. Ortega, F., Mayor, J., López-Fernández, D., Lara-Cabrera, R.: CF4J 2.0: adapting collaborative filtering for java to new challenges of collaborative filtering based recommender systems. Knowl-Based Syst **215**, 106629 (2021). https://doi.org/10.1016/j.knosys.2020.106629
54. Ekstrand, M.D.: LensKit for python: next-generation software for recommender systems experiments. In: Proceedings of the 29th ACM International Conference on Information & Knowledge Management, pp. 2999–3006. ACM, Virtual Event, Ireland (2020). https://doi.org/10.1145/3340531.3412778
55. McLaughlin, M.R., Herlocker, J.L.: A collaborative filtering algorithm and evaluation metric that accurately model the user experience. In: Proceedings of the 27th annual International Conference on Research and Development in Information Retrieval - SIGIR 2004, p. 329. ACM Press, Sheffield, United Kingdom (2004). https://doi.org/10.1145/1008992.1009050

# Research on the Cognitive Performance of Color Difference in Bank Self-service Terminal Interface Based on Visual Perception

Jiaran Niu and Zehua Li[✉]

Nanjing University of Science and Technology, Nanjing 210094, China
lizehuawy@163.com

**Abstract.** The wide application of self-service mode in banks reduces the conflicts between service supply and service demands. With the continuous development of digitization and informatization, the intelligent service terminal has been popularized in banks, and human-computer interaction interface plays an important part in intelligent terminal system, its scientific and reasonable interface design closely correlated with user experience and efficiency, so it is beneficial to improve the cognitive performance of intelligent terminal interface by studying the design elements. In this paper, the authors attempt to study the visual search behavior of users when browsing terminal interface by an eye movement experiment from the perspective of visual perception. Besides, the relationship between the color difference of intelligent terminal interface and cognitive performance was analyzed based on eye-tracking. Results showed that whether the color of the information module was the same as the main color of the intelligent terminal interface or not would affect performance of users. Specifically, If the two colors kept the same, the search performance was better, and it is helpful to improve the performance when the key module was color-differentiated in the interactive interface.

**Keywords:** Self-service terminal · Interaction design · Cognitive performance · Eye movement research

## 1 Introduction

With the continuous development of digitization and informatization, the application of intelligent service terminal equipment is rapidly popularized in banks, which reduces the conflicts between limited-service supply and huge service demand. However, an intelligent human-computer interaction interface can show massive and complex information in a recognizable, orderly and beautiful form. Reasonable and friendly information interface design can greatly improve the cognitive performance of users and enhance the accuracy and efficiency of information processing [1], and color has a very important impact on visual information acquisition and cognitive performance. Despite the rapid development of public terminals, there are still many people unable to access these services due to the interface design of interactive service terminals[2]. Douglas [3] was the forthgoer to propose the design of the self-service passenger system used by airlines.

© The Author(s), under exclusive license to Springer Nature Switzerland AG 2022
M. Kurosu et al. (Eds.): HCII 2022, LNCS 13516, pp. 437–449, 2022.
https://doi.org/10.1007/978-3-031-17615-9_30

The main functions of the self-service terminal system include handling flight inquiries, checking in and providing passes, etc. In the interface design of terminal system, he proposed to use a VDU screen to establish a user interface and cooperate with computer graphics dialogue display. Robert L [4] put forward that the perception of visual channels is more important from the perspective of cognitive psychology compared with other senses, and they are closely related to the rapid progress of reading. Zhang et al. [5] classified the information stimulus of visual perception in digital interface information into layout, color, text, icon and picture, they also divided the whole process of acquiring information into several stages from the perspective of cognitive psychology. The reasonable use and collocation of colors in the human-computer interaction interface can not only greatly improve cognitive ergonomics, but also enrich the interface [6]. Many scholars have investigated the relationship between color elements of information interface and user cognition from cognitive psychology and design. Some people analyzed the interface design of bank self-service terminal from the perspective of interface color coding and user cognition to improve the rationality and usability of its design. Numerous studies showed that we should not only solve problems from the point of professional design, but also integrate psychology with other comprehensive considerations to make the interface suitable for more users to improve the machine adaptability to humans [7].

Based on theories related to cognitive psychology and design, this paper is designed to study the cognitive performance of users in browsing and searching information in the intelligent interface based on the background color of the interface information module, combined with eye movement and the terminal interface of a bank self-service machine is selected as a case. The paper is organized into the following three parts. The first part is the background introduction and summarization of the current situation of self-service terminal interface; Secondly, the role of color elements in visual perception and the user's visual behavior, cognitive characteristics and behavior pattern is analyzed in detail. Thirdly, a physiological evaluation was carried out on the terminal interface of a bank self-service counter machine with eye-tracking, and suggestions on improving the color design of the information module of the interface are provided, followed by certain implications for the color design of subsequent human-computer interfaces.

## 2    Visual Perception and Color Analysis of Interactive Interfaces

### 2.1    Overview of Visual Perception Theory

The sensory system is composed of receptors and connected neurons of five senses (hearing, vision, touch, taste and smell), among which vision is very important [8]. The beginning of information acquisition and cognition is the contact with external stimuli, then the corresponding eye movements will be produced, which is usually called visual perception. Generally speaking, the visual behavior of users in the information interface mainly includes information searching and browsing [9]. It works by sending stimuli in the form of images to the brain and controlling the movement of the human eye through the brain's visual cortex. This process is composed of searching, exploration, differentiation and recognition [10]. In other words, visual stimuli are returned to the organism after processing by the visual and nervous system, and then muscles and glands make clear reactions [11], as shown in Fig. 1. The physiological reactions and functions of the eyes can reflect the activities of the human brain. For example, staring reflects the thinking process in the cognitive process. The human eye is the main organ for acquiring and capturing information. In the process of acquiring and processing information, light enters the lens and vitreous and is projected to the retina [12]. In the cognitive process, visual gaze is not only an inherent physiological characteristic of the eye, but also closely related to the cognitive activities of the brain. For example, when looking at a screen, human eyes first see the part at the horizontal line of the sight rather than the part below. When human eyes observe the information on the interface, they usually stare at the left and upper parts longer [13]. Due to the objective limitations, human eyes can only receive limited visual information within a limited perceptual span. Therefore, users' browsing pattern is related to cognitive behavior, information type and information display [14]. In terms of sensory perception, in recent years, scholars tend to study the physiological mechanism of human brain's reaction functions affecting behavior, as well as the relationship between implicit memory and explicit sensory perception. In practical applications, most of the researchers focus the correlation on sensory with characteristics of products and sensory stimulation. Li et al. [15] Based on Munsell color space and solid attributes to classify the level of color and the theories related to visual perception and attention, with the premise of a black background, it's concluded that when the brightness and saturation were gradually reduced, the level of the visual perception also decreased and the recognition efficiency was higher with the low brightness color. Guo et al. [16] studied the perceptual quantization of visual interface color coding based on recognition task driving. By analyzing the perception rule of color difference in the visual system, the quantitative study of color-coding perception is realized by using the ladder method and quantitative method to figure out the differentiation.

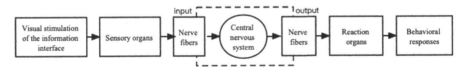

**Fig. 1.** Interface information stimulus elements and user cognitive behavior.

To sum up, most experimental studies on cognitive performance use eye tracking to study human gaze, fixation and other behaviors to judge the ergonomics of human-computer interaction. Furthermore, the appropriate color design of the information module of the interface can correctly and quickly guide users to perceive and operate efficiently. Users should perceive and pay attention to the interface information before cognition. The research on the information elements of the interactive interface has a certain referential role in improving the information acquisition speed, reducing operation reaction time and enhancing cognitive ergonomic efficiency when using the interface.

## 2.2 Interactive Interface Color Element Analysis

In the visual elements of an interactive interface, color is an element that can easily attract people's attention, many relevant types of research in psychology show that when making observations in the original 20 s when stimulated by color, the color perception can account for about 80%. And color can be impressive [17], so it is necessary to study cognitive performance from the perspective of color element stimulus. In the information interface, adopting the same hue with different lightness and purity to distinguish key parts or functional areas by means of strong contrast can better attract attention and help improve performance [18]. The color of information presented and its background color is important elements that affect users' perception and information acquisition, and the different level of color attributes will also affect searching performance. In terms of color design researches of interactive interfaces, relevant scholars started from the perspective of color's impact on visual hierarchy and the impact of color difference on visual saliency through eye movement experiments or other psychological evaluation experiments. Wu [19] found that when the foreground color and background color of the same hue were combined, the reading efficiency was lower when the foreground color had lower brightness and saturation than the background color. When the foreground and background colors of different hues were combined, the reading speed would be affected but the above rule was still followed. Zhang et al. [20] studied the performance of human recognition when different background colors were matched with different targeted colors. The time of eye pause in the process of acquiring information can reflect the performance of cognitive processing. Max [21] proposed a method to quantify the salience of the targets based on color space, and studied the influence of difference between the color of icons and their background colors on user search performance. Peter [22] found that the contrast between colors is an important factor affecting the visual saliency and searching efficiency. Bhattacharyya et al. [23] also demonstrated through eye movement experiments that the larger the color difference between the graphics color and the background color, the shorter the visual search time and the higher the visual salience of the target.

In conclusion, the color of interactive interface has an important influence on the rationality and usability of interface design. In the information interface, we can analyze the hue, saturation, chromatic aberration and lightness of the color, and carry out specific research on the color of the information module or the foreground and background color, aimed to obtain the optimal color element, so that users can notice the most useful information in the shortest time.

## 3 Eye Movement Study of Color Visual Perception in Interactive Interface

After analyzing the main theories of visual perception, as well as the visual physiological behavior of users to the different color elements of the interactive interface, an eye movement experiment is designed to analyze the influence of color elements on users' searching and browsing behavior on the self-service terminal interface in banks. When analyzing the data of this experiment, the cognitive performance of color vision elements in the information interface is utilized. The eye movement experiment paradigm adopted in this study is to analyze the process of information acquisition and cognitive processing under the physiological function and characteristics of human eyes, and to reach the data, such as the Time to First Fixation (TFF), Reaction Time (RT) and gaze plot.

## 3.1  Experimental -Objectives

The self-service terminal interface of a bank is selected as the experimental material of the study, and the color elements of the original interface are extracted. The color of the font of the information module and the background color of the module are seen as a single variable. The main color of the original interface is blue, the color of the information font is black, and the module has no color filled. Two experiments are conducted to explore the influence on the changes of font color and module background color and the cognitive performance of the self-service terminals.

## 3.2  Experimental Design

With the use of eye-tracking, experimental material is 5 pictures provided to per experiment, each image containing nine information modules, the position of each image information module offered randomly. The participants perform the experiment of target by searching task, by collecting data such as time to first fixation, reaction time to analyze the most efficient way to present information. After the experiment, the data of the subjects is processed, and the search physiological behavior of the user behavior is analyzed so as to explore the influence of the information color of the interactive interface of the self-service terminal of the bank on the searching efficiency. This research is in the single-task situation for target identification in order to prevent the influence of other factors. Each image's background and its main color adopt the blue of a certain bank. When the font color of the information module does not change, the background color saturation of the lower information module is set to 5 levels and appears randomly; Each experimental material picture has 9 fixed information modules but are randomly positioned. The color variable of the experiment is based on The HSB Color systems, as shown in Fig. 2. Color visual stimuli in the experiment are presented through saturation changes. In order to increase the randomness, the appearance order of each picture is random, and the location of targeted information is also random. Under each experimental condition, the subjects are required to complete 5 searching tasks. The subjects only obtain the target information through text, and then look for the corresponding module of the information in the interface.

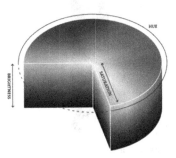

**Fig. 2.** The HSB color systems (also known as HSV).

### 3.3   Participants

There were 10 participants in total, including 5 boys and 5 girls; the average age was between 22 and 25 years old, and they were all postgraduates of the School of Design Art and Media at Nanjing University of Science and Technology. All participants' naked vision or corrected vision were above 1.0, without color blindness or color weakness. Each participant carried out a pre-experiment training before the experiment, and the formal experiment was conducted after completing the exercise test.

### 3.4   Experimental Equipment and Materials

All the experimental materials were presented on a 15.6-in.LCD screen with a resolution of 1280 pixels $\times$ 1024 pixels. The screen brightness is 92 cd/m$^2$. Two groups of experiments were conducted. The first group of material information module was blue background color with five levels of saturation. The second group was a gray background color, also containing 5 saturation levels of experimental materials. All experimental materials were presented randomly, and the positions of the target items were also presented at random positions in the visual field. The experiments were carried out in the laboratory of School of Design Art and Media at Nanjing University of Science and Technology. The experimental materials are taken from a bank self-service terminal interface. The experimental material contained ten pictures, one of which was the original interface without any change, and the other nine were designed for color adjustment and change based on the original interface. The experiment was divided into two parts, each part containing searching tasks for five pictures. The font colors of the five images in the first group were consistent with the blue tone style of the original interface, and the blue had the same color attribute (#5779B8). The experimental materials were shown in Fig. 3. The fill color of the background in the information module in the five images was divided into five grades below the blue saturation value of the main tone, as shown in Table 1.

**Fig. 3.** Sample diagram of experimental materials.

**Table 1.** Experimental group 1 interface information module background color information.

| Color grade | H | S | B |
|---|---|---|---|
| I | None | None | None |
| II | 219 | 15 | 93 |
| III | 219 | 25 | 93 |
| IV | 219 | 35 | 93 |
| V | 219 | 45 | 93 |

### 3.5 Experimental Process

The experiment was carried out in the form of individual tests. Participants sat in front of the test instrument, and Tobbi Studio software was used to ensure that participants' eyes were captured by the eye tracker. The table and chair were not moved during the experiment, but they were permitted to move the head in a small range. Before the experiment, participants would be explained the simulated scene, experimental process, tasks to be completed and other matters needing attention before the experiment started. Practicing experiments were conducted before the formal experiment began. First of all, participants were asked to read the experiment guide. Before the formal experiment began, participants were told that the task in the following interface was to search the targeted information module, and then pressed any key on the keyboard. After ensuring that participants understand the whole procedure, they would conduct a set of practice experiments as required. After the practice experiment was completed, participants would be told to take a break for one minute. The formal experiment was carried out after the break. Participants were required to complete tasks according to pictures of experimental materials, and it took about 10 min for each participant to complete all tasks. The whole experimental process is shown in Fig. 4.

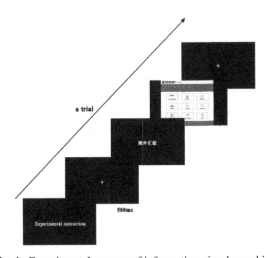

**Fig. 4.** Experimental process of information visual searching.

### 3.6  Data Analysis of Eye Movement Experiment

The First experiment task was to search target information. Based on this task, the target information modules in the pictures were marked and divided, and then added to the analysis list to generate time to first fixation data. The TFF data of the first group are shown in Table 2.

The color of the information module for the first group was consistent with the main color, namely blue, and the variable was the saturation of the background color of the information module, which was divided into five grades. One level has no background color, and the other four modules have four levels of background color saturation based on a saturation lower than the main color blue. Experimental results show that the average time of the first fixation time on the information interface module with background color is generally lower than that of the interface without background color, which indicates that the module color discrimination of key information has an impact on the search performance, and the color distinction with different saturation helps the participants to search and capture information faster. In this experiment, it can be seen from the data that participants used less time to search in material 3 and material 5, and the average value is obtained after removing the two extreme values from the two sets of data. When the color saturation of the information module in material 5 was 45, the target search task took the shortest time and the search performance was higher.

**Table 2.** Time to first fixation data sheet for material Group 1.

|        | Material 1 |      | Material 2 |      | Material 3 |      | Material 4 |      | Material 5 |      |
|--------|------------|------|------------|------|------------|------|------------|------|------------|------|
|        | M          | SD   | M          | SD   | M          | SD   | M          | SD   | M          | SD   |
| TFF(s) | 1.91       | 1.31 | 1.84       | 0.79 | 1.25       | 1.00 | 1.78       | 0.74 | 1.23       | 0.88 |

The color of the information module of the second group was inconsistent with the main color blue. The original interface was adopted and variables were added to the background color of the module. The variables were the hue of the background color of the information module, divided into five grades. One level was no background color, that is, the color of original unchanged interface, and the other four modules were divided into four levels of background color based on a hue higher than black. The experimental results show that in three of the four groups, the mean time of the first fixation time with background color in the information interface module is lower than that of the interface without background color, which again indicates that the color distinction of the key information module has an impact on the search performance, which helps the participants to search and capture information faster.

When the first group ended, a short rest was taken and the second group started to conduct the experiment. Five pictures of the second group were basically the same as those of group 1, with the same experimental process and indicators, but the original unchanged interface was also included, namely the black interface of information module. Secondly, in the other four experimental materials, the information module was also given to fill the background color to distinguish the key information. The background color is filled based on the original interface. The filling color is different levels of black, that is, the hue value is 15,25,35,45 four levels of color. The TFF data in the second group is shown in Table 3.

**Table 3.** Time to first fixation data sheet for lab material group 2.

|        | Material 1 | | Material 2 | | Material 3 | | Material 4 | | Material 5 | |
| --- | --- | --- | --- | --- | --- | --- | --- | --- | --- | --- |
|        | M | SD | M | SD | M | SD | M | SD | M | SD |
| TFF(s) | 2.58 | 0.89 | 3.10 | 2.30 | 1.54 | 1.15 | 1.79 | 0.99 | 1.91 | 0.73 |

A comprehensive comparison of the two groups shows that whether the main color of the information interface is consistent or not, the average time of target searching for experimental materials with background color in the information module is shorter than that without background color, which indicates that color differentiation of key information is conducive to faster target searching, as shown in Fig. 5. Secondly, group 1, that is, experimental material with consistent interface tone, takes less time to search the target than group 2, as shown in Fig. 6. Except for the fourth group, all the other groups have significant differences. The experimental results show that the color of the information module and the interface can achieve the same tone by using the same color system, and the two keeping the same color is conducive to search to the target quickly.

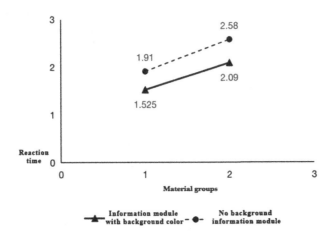

**Fig. 5.** Information module with or without background color response diagram.

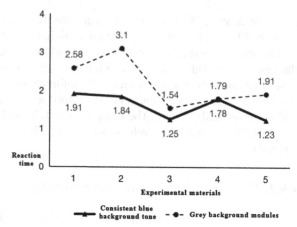

**Fig. 6.** Reaction time data of whether the information module is consistent with the main color of the interface.

After completing the experiment, eye-movement fixation point diagrams of different interfaces were obtained, as shown in Fig. 7. The fixation point plot reflects the path of fixation, duration and number of fixation points, and the larger the fixation point is, the longer the fixation time is. The fixation path can also be used to determine the rate of return of the participants. By comparing the two groups of fixation points, it is found that when the main color of the interface is consistent with the color of the information module, there are few fixation points outside the searching area. It's reflected that when the color of the interface and information module keeps the same, users would pay more attention to searching the information module. When the main color of the interface is inconsistent with that of the information module, the number of fixation points in the information module increases, and there are more fixation paths between the information modules, indicating that the regression rate is higher, and there are more fixation points outside the reading area. It can be considered that the color of the information module has certain visual guidance for users to read and search information, as well as reasonable and appropriate color configuration helps users to find and obtain information quickly.

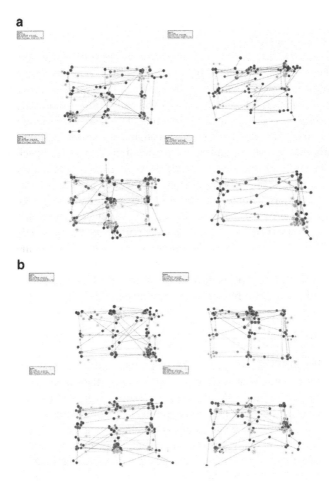

**Fig. 7.** a. Main tone consistent group eye movement fixation diagram. b. Eye movement fixation diagram of the group with inconsistent dominant tone.

## 4    Results and Discussion

The above experiments are analyzed from the perspective of color coding of the interactive interface information module, and the cognitive performance differences of color elements at different levels in the interactive interface information module of intelligent banking terminals are comprehensively investigated through experiments. The experimental results show that different colors of information module can better attract the attention of the participants and search the information faster, and whether the color of the information module is consistent with the main color of the interface will also affect the search performance. The search performance is significantly higher when the color with lower saturation of the same color system is used to distinguish information, and the color differentiation of key information is helpful to improve the search performance.

The same color palette helps users focus on effective information modules and search for information more intently.

In the digital interface design, visual perception and cognition physiological characteristics have been an important topic of cognition studies. With the rapid development of informatization and intellectualization, the information levels and amount of human-computer interaction interface were increased. This article just explores the background color by controlling the variables in the information of the self-service terminal interface. In recent years, many scholars have studied readability, comfort and other perceptual attributes of brightness, contrast and color combination from the perspective of cognitive performance and user experience [24, 25]. Existing researches not only start from the theory of visual perception, but also from the theories of attention mechanism and cognitive workload. For example, Andersen [26] et al. studied the guidance of attention and the prediction of color capture in complex interfaces based on the theory of visual attention. Most existing studies evaluate cognitive ergonomics and performance by studying color coding [27, 28]. In the future, we can not only study the ergonomics level of color elements in-depth, but also improve the design level of cognitive demand, aesthetic demand and other aspects through quantitative calculation and other methods from the perspective of sensibility and user experience.

## 5 Conclusion

In the self-service terminal interface of the bank, there are still many problems to be solved. For example, with the increase in service business, the amount of information in the system increases rapidly, resulting in user operation errors. Unreasonable interface information layout, module and font color Settings do not conform to aesthetics and ergonomics, etc. which are the contents and topics that designers and scholars need to consider and investigate in many aspects. At present, there are still some defects in this study. For example, there is no comprehensive analysis and research on other attributes of the information module color. This paper only studies the background color of the information module, without involving other aspects such as layout and text; the age and educational level of the subjects were not fully covered, which was a limitation of this experimental study. In addition, this study only analyzes the interactive interface of a certain bank terminal as experimental materials, lacking more diversified materials and research samples, which need to be improved and further explored in the later stage.

## References

1. Xue, C.Q., Wang, L.L.: Review of human-computer integration interaction in intelligent human-computer system. Packag. Eng. **42**(20), 112–124 (2021)
2. Shi, W.H., Xin, X.Y.: University J. usability of public terminal interface. Packag. Eng. **37**(6), 62 (2016)
3. Kelley, D.F.: Skylink self-service ticketing terminal: design and ergonomics. Behav. Inf. Technol. **3**(4), 391–397 (1984)
4. Solso, R.L., Maclin, M.K., Maclin, O.H.: Cognitive Phychology (2008)
5. Zhang, W.W., Xiao-Li, W.U., Hua, F.: A survey of visualization of digital interface user information acquisition. Sci. Technol. Vis. (2018)

6.  Tallon-Baudry, C.: Attention and awareness in synchrony. Trends Cogn. Sci. **12**(8), 523–528 (2004)
7.  Kahneman, D.: Attention and Effort. Prentice Hall Inc, New Jersey (1973)
8.  Sully, J.: The question of visual perception in germany. Mind **3**(10), 167–195 (1878)
9.  Solso, R.L.: Cognitive Psychology, 7th ed. Pearson Education, New Zealand (2005)
10. Brookhuis, K., Hedge, A., Hendrick, H., et al.: Handbook of human factors and ergonomics models (2005)
11. Ning, L., Wang, H., Feng, X., Du, J.: The browsing pattern and review model of online consumers based on large data analysis. Chin. J. Electr. **24**(01), 58–64 (2015)
12. Treisman, A., Gelade, G.: A feature integration theory of attention. Cogn. Psychol. **12**(3), 97–136 (1980)
13. Van Orden, K.F., Divita, J., Shim, M.J.: Redundant use of luminance and flashing with shape and color as highlighting codes in symbolic displays. Hum. Factors, **35**(2), 195–204 (1993)
14. Xiao-li, W.U.: Error-Cognition Mechanism of Task Interface Complex Information System—A New Design Method of System Interface by Introducing Error Factors. Science Press, Beijing (2017)
15. Jing, L.I.: Color encoding research of digital display interface based on the visual perceptual layering. J. Mech. Eng. **52**(24), 201 (2016)
16. Guo, Q., Xue, C., Zhou, X., et al.: Experimental study on quantization perception of color coding based on visualization interface recognition task. J. Southeast Univ. (Natl. Sci. Ed.) **49**(6), 1048–1053 (2019)
17. Zhan, Q.C.: Research on colors for logo design and its application. Art Des. (03), 53–55 (2009)
18. Wang, MH.: Study on design of visual information interface based on visual cognition. Packag. Eng. (2011)
19. Wu, J.H., Yuan, Y.: Improving searching and reading performance: the effect of high-lighting and text color coding. Inf. Manag. **40**(7), 617–637 (2003)
20. Zhang, L., Zhuang, D.: Color matching of aircraft interface design. J. Beijing Univ. Aeronaut. Astronaut. **35**(08), 1001–1004 (2009)
21. Friedrich, M., Vollrath, M.: Urgency-Based color coding to support visual search in displays for supervisory control of multiple unmanned aircraft systems. Displays, **74**(102185), 0141–9382 (2022)
22. Peter, B.: Chromaticity contrast in visual search on the multi-color user interface. Displays **24**(1), 39–48 (2003)
23. Bhattacharyyad, C.B., Chatterjee, T., et al.: Selection of character/background color combinations for onscreen searching tasks: an eye movement, subjective and performance approach. Displays **35**(3), 101–109 (2014)
24. Li, Y., Huang, Y., Li, X., Ma, J., Zhang, J., Li, J.: The influence of brightness combinations and background colour on legibility and subjective preference under negative polarity. Ergonomics, 1–11 (2022)
25. Huan, T.: Research on Visual Comfort of Color Design in Digital Interface. Southwest University of Science and Technology (2019)
26. Andersen, E., Goucher-Lambert, K., Cagan, J., Maier, A.: Attention affordances: applying attention theory to the design of complex visual interfaces. J. Exper. Psychol. Appl. **27**(2), 338–351 (2021)
27. Ming, C, Wu, Z, Gu, H, et al.: The effects of luminance contrast and color combination on icon cognitive performance. Color Res. Appl. **47**(2), 498–506 (2021)
28. Wu, X., Xu, P., Jiang, X.: Color level coding on industrial monitoring interface based on attention capture. Indus. Eng. Manag. 1–13 (2022)

# Assessment of Static and Dynamic Image Presentation for User Cognition and Understanding

Pankati Patel[1], Patricia Morreale[1]([✉]) [iD], and George Avirappattu[2] [iD]

[1] School of Computer Science and Technology, Kean University, Union, NJ 07083, USA
{patpanka,pmorreal}@kean.edu
[2] School of Mathematical Sciences, Kean University, Union, NJ 07083, USA
gavirapp@kean.edu

**Abstract.** The internet supports users who want to locate information with minimal search while remaining engaged. Using a graphical approach for data presentation supports both information and engagement, but it is unknown if static or dynamic graphical display improves cognitive function. Both displays provide information to the viewer, but they are different in functionality and implementation. Static images are still images represented as a PNG, JPEG or PDF, without hidden layers and interactivity. In contrast, dynamic or Scalable Vector Graphics (SVG) images have more flexibility, and different approaches can support interaction with the image. Layers can be hidden which can be revealed by the viewer. Dynamic images hold data that tell the same story but from different viewpoints. In this research, pandemic data including case rate, vaccination rate, and mortality rate data for different states is used. The scope of the data remains the same, with the values varying based on the geographic region or state. The research investigates the effectiveness of interactive visuals to improve cognitive function. Two images, one static and one dynamic, were sequentially presented to viewers, followed by a series of questions after each image to test the user's cognition. The analyzed responses to the questions conclude whether the dynamic image improved cognition when compared to the static image. The research showed that users preferred dynamic images by a factor of 2 to 1, with the users preferring the interactivity of the image. Further research will fully determine changes in user cognition and understanding.

**Keywords:** Data visualization · Cognitive function · Usability

## 1 Introduction

Data collection is an important factor to gain insight into a specific subject. Data visualizations turn text and numbers into a graphical format. A graphical approach allows viewers to have a visual representation of the data which, when compared to text and numbers, allow information to be extracted and easily applied. Recently, there has been a need to display massive amounts of data in a way that is easily accessible, and comprehensible. It is even more important that users understand the information presented.

M. Kurosu et al. (Eds.): HCII 2022, LNCS 13516, pp. 450–459, 2022.
https://doi.org/10.1007/978-3-031-17615-9_31

## 1.1 Visualization Approaches

Visualizations allow the viewer to look at data differently. There are two approaches to data visualization: static and dynamic. All data visualizations fall within these two categories. The goal of the research question motivating this study was to determine if the approach used for data visualization affects user cognition and understanding.

**Static Images.** Static images are presented when a static visual focus on a single viewpoint is needed. The static image remains unchanged, and the data is concise [1]. Static images are best when used with small sized data. Since there are no dimensions to web graphics, static images are flat images: pie charts, line graphs, infographic posts are just a few examples. Using a combination of visuals and words allows the user to comprehend the data being presented [2]. While static graphical illustrations remain perfectly adequate in many instances, they become problematic as larger and more complex data sets evolving over time are used.

**Dynamic Images.** A dynamic image, also be referred to an interactive image, has multiple viewpoints but tells the same story. The different layers in a dynamic image allows the viewer to display information they find useful [3]. A reader-driven approach supports the role of the reader to both view the data and to interact with the data as well. Interactive visualizations usually take the form of a Scalable Vector Graphic (SVG) [4]. A SVG image is an XML format for describing two dimensional (2-D) graphical displays that also support interactivity, animation, and filters for special effects on different elements within the display. SVGs are separated by paths. Each path represents a complex shape by combining straight or curved lines, which is then capable of manipulation to give interactivity or animation. There are three methods to give an SVG interactivity, as shown in Fig. 1.

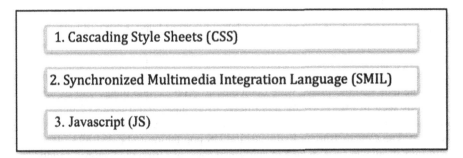

**Fig. 1.** Interactive methods

## 2  Related Work

To test user cognition between static and dynamic images, an earlier research project investigated which approach resulted in better user recall [6]. Participants were instructed to form either static or dynamic images for subsequent free recall of concrete nouns. The study defined static images as a graphic that does not move and a dynamic image as images that involve action and movement. From the study it was concluded that the number of recalled words correlated positively with percentage use of dynamic images.

A second study was conducted which discusses the influence of dynamic and static images on user perception in web interface visualizations [7]. This study experimented with eye movement and the results show that the visual cognitive effect was better for the dynamic image then the static image, and how the efficiency of visual search was improved. The study identifies how dynamic images may involve different cognitive processes and perceptions than viewing static images.

## 3  Methodology

Interactive visuals give the viewer the ability to interact with the data, but it is not clear if interactive visuals improve cognitive function. Using both the static and interactive approaches, we conducted a comparative study with 22 users (n = 22) between the ages of 18–25. Two images were developed and populated with two different COVID-19 data sets. Datasets were kept separate to avoid memorization of the values for the preceding questions asked for both images. Appropriate human subjects and university IRB protocols were followed, with user consent obtained prior to administering surveys. Survey respondents were recruited at a university and participation was voluntary.

### 3.1  Static Image

For the static approach an image of New Jersey was used and presented to the viewer with the most recent COVID-19 data set. The information was extracted from the U.S. Census Bureau data set [8] and include the number of Covid cases, mortality cases, Covid case percentage by gender and demographics. Using the open-source photo editing tool GIMP, the data and the image were combined to produce one image and exported as a JPEG as seen in Fig. 2. Using this image, users answered a series of questions to test their cognitive functions with the data shown. One example of the questions being asked is: "The Census Bureau Estimates the US population to be 331,893,745. Using this information, what percentage of confirmed cases are from the featured county?".

## New Jersey
Union County

**Cases:** 125,393

**Mortality:** 30,253

*Find futher information about NJ Covid 19 rates below*

### Cases by Gender
**Female:** 52.8%

**Male:** 47.2%

### Cases by Race
**Caucasian:** 42.9%

**Hispanic:** 21.4%

**African American:** 13.0%

**Asian:** 5.3%

**Other:** 17.4%

## 30.1%
**The highest confirmed cases was for people between the age 30-49**

**Fig. 2.** Static image of New Jersey

### 3.2  Interactive Image

For the interactive image an SVG of the United States was used. Each of the states are broken into paths to allow each state to stand alone, as shown in Fig. 3. To make the image interactive JavaScript and CSS were used. For the states that have data present they are filled in with a color based on the legend in Fig. 4.

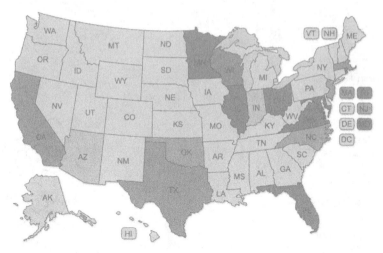

**Fig. 3.** Interactive United States map

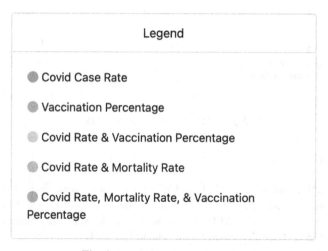

**Fig. 4.** Legend for interactive map

Clicking on the non-gray states reveals an ArcGIS map as seen in Fig. 5. The ArcGIS map can be searched by address, zip code, or county.

**Fig. 5.** ArcGIS map

The users were asked to search for Union County, NJ, USA and view the data for the zip code 07061 displayed in Fig. 6. They are presented with a window with a COVID-19 dataset from 2021. Using this information, the user is asked to answer questions that will test their cognitive function. An example of the question being asked is "Of the total population in Union County what percentage of people are of Asian descent?".

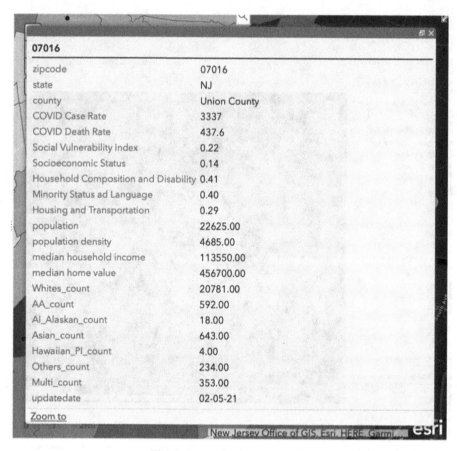

**Fig. 6.** Interactive image data set

## 4 Results

During the survey, the user was presented with the static image first, followed with questions to test their cognition. There was a combination of direct, easier questions, followed by questions that would require use of cognition and understanding in percent conversion. Next, the dynamic, or interactive image was presented, followed by questions. Analysis of the close-ended question survey results showed that 68.2% of the users preferred the interactive image, as shown in Fig. 7.

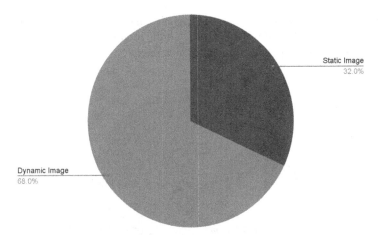

**Fig. 7.** User preferred image

Each question has three options which the user could choose from, as well as another option for a user-provided answer if the users felt the correct answer was not among the three options. The answers received were consistent for the static image and the other option was used once. Responses for a static image are shown in Fig. 8. The question being asked is "What is the percentage of confirmed cases in NJ for people between the ages 50–65?".

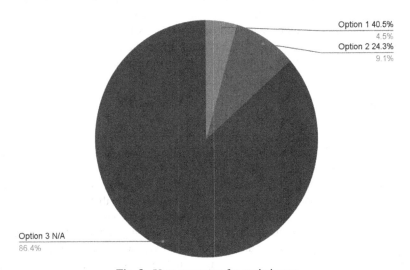

**Fig. 8.** User responses for static image

When the user proceeded to the dynamic image the answers were more varied and the "other" option was selected as the answer for most of the questions. It can be inferred that the user either did not search the image properly, used the internet to answer the questions, or the user did not correctly understand percent conversion. An example of the user responses to the survey for the dynamic image can be seen in Fig. 9. The question that was asked for this dataset was "Of the total population in Union County what percentage of the population are of Asian descent?".

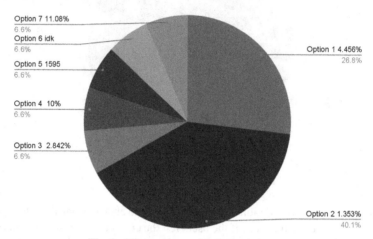

**Fig. 9.** User responses for dynamic image

The user feedback was very informative, with viewers preferring the dynamic map over the static map. Users felt that in the dynamic map they had more control over the information they wanted to view. Unlike the static image, where all the information was provided at one, the dynamic image did not provide all the information at first. The dynamic image had room for using JavaScript event handlers to hide and show objects as there was mouse movement or clicking events on objects revealed hidden layers.

## 5   Conclusion

From the survey responses it can be concluded that the users did not refer to the dynamic images. The users also had trouble calculating percentages. After viewing the results there are some concepts that were left out of the study. The responses for the static image were positive but it is not clear if this is due to the merits of the static image or the fact that the static image was displayed first. It is possible that the user might lose motivation or interest in answering the questions as they proceed to the dynamic image. Future research will use two groups, with one group viewing only the static image then responding to survey questions and the other group viewing only the dynamic image and responding to survey questions. Keeping the user groups surveyed separate will not affect user motivation to answer two sets of questions but will avoid any possible impact of survey fatigue or presentation bias in the responses received. Comparison of both the static and dynamic results received will provide a clearer understanding of which image improves cognitive function.

# References

1. Mahajan, K., Gokhale, L.: Comparative study of static and interactive visualization approaches. Int. J. Comput. Sci. Eng. **10**(3), pp. 85–91 (2018). https://doi.org/10.21817/ijcse/2018/v10i3/181003016
2. Ellis, D., Merdian, H.: Thinking outside the box: developing dynamic data visualizations for psychology with shiny. Front. Psychol. **6**, 1782, (2015). https://doi.org/10.3389/fpsyg.2015.01782
3. Segel, E., Heer, J.: Narrative visualization: telling stories with data. IEEE Trans. Vis. Comput. Graph. **16**(6), 1139–1148 (2010). https://doi.org/10.1109/TVCG.2010.179
4. Nolan, D., Temple Lang, D.: Interactive and animated scalable vector graphics and R data displays. J. Statis. Softw. **46**(1), 1–88 (2012). https://doi.org/10.18637/jss.v046.i01
5. Dougherty, J., Ilyankou, I.: Hands-on Data Visualization: Static Image vs Interactive iframe. https://handsondataviz.org/static.html. Accessed April 28 2022
6. Reed, S., Kazemi, S.: Effect of Static Versus Dynamic Images on Recall (2004). www.academia.edu/7282977/Effect_of_Static_versus_Dynamic_Images_on_Recall. Accessed 27 May 2022
7. Pei, H., Huang, X., Ding, M.: Image visualization: dynamic and static images generate users' visual cognitive experience using eye-tracking technology. Displays, **73**, 102175 (2022). https://doi.org/10.1016/j.displa.2022.102175
8. U.S. Census Bureau, COVID-19 Demographic and Economic Data Resources. https://covid19.census.gov/. Accessed 26 May 2022

# A Framework for Designing Relationship Strengthening Digital Money Gifts in Close Friendships

Freya Probst[1]([✉]), Martin Maguire[1], Cees de Bont[1], and Hyosun Kwon[2]

[1] School of Design and Creative Arts, Loughborough University, Loughborough, UK
{f.x.probst,m.c.maguire,c.j.de-bont}@lboro.ac.uk
[2] Department of Industrial Design, Kookmin University, Seoul, South Korea
hyosun.kwon@kookmin.ac.kr

**Abstract.** Receiving a money gift can be bound to potential awkwardness and money gifts are also often regarded to show little effort and thought or surprise and thus leaves little impression on a relationship. We developed a framework presenting some of the key influential design considerations. This framework was transformed into a brief and design cards that was further applied in co-design workshops. This resulted in three low-fidelity interactive prototypes: Reborn Game, Fictional Wedding, and Guardian Angel. The design factors of the framework are evaluated in their effect to be potentially relationship-strengthening. Based on 20 interviews the perception of money gifts was explored. The application of factors was found to achieve a more effortful, careful gift, and also awkwardness of receiving money could be relieved through the design. The digital gift also showed an ability to convey the giver's thoughts and feelings in an experience, but it also could feel artificial.

**Keywords:** Digital gifts · Digital money · Framework

## 1 Introduction

We define a digital money gift as digitally transmitted money adapted to function as a personal gift in connection with new financial technologies. Current examples are monetary gifts exchanged in PayPal, in form vouchers, subscriptions, or wedding registries. Based on testing two speculative gifting scenarios in focus groups [8] we observed possible limitations of such gifts in supporting personal relationships, a key quality of gifts [9, 11]. To express it with the words of one of our participants: *"I have the concern, that if this becomes very mainstream... that you are just not as personally involved anymore, and that this is also how you distance yourself from each other... I think that also has to do something with how much time people would then invest in something like this."* Further literature [7] indicates the interest of givers in digital gifts that would achieve a relationship reinforcement.

There has been previous work exploring the design of money in closer personal relations [2, 5, 13] they did not explore the application of factors that are particular to gift exchange (i.e., personalization, or a surprise) that might enhance the perception of money in the digital surrounding. Much of the exploration of digital wrapping has taken place in the presentation of digital files in general, but these did not address potential relations of the wrapping with the monetary gift.

To evaluate the framework that aims to achieve a better understanding of the digital monetary gift, we evaluated three prototypes from workshops: *Reborn Game, Virtual Wedding*, and *Guardian Angel*. 'Reborn Game' describes a monetary gift collected and spent through a video chat and shared personalized game. 'Virtual Wedding' plays in a future virtual reality network, where people can prepare fictional places as a gift, where the recipient can travel to. 'Guardian Angel' is a gift embedded into the daily communication platform of the recipient, where the giver can set up a guardian angel mode, filtering and overlaying potential negative messages, and also send monetary gifts. The key aim is to understand the effect of the applied factors from our framework.

## 2 Background

To receive money as a gift can be awkward [1] found money can risk being insulting; it can fail to show much effort or be construed as a lazy way to gift. Also, the giver's or recipient's financial possibilities play a role. It may be awkward to receive money from someone less affluent as a gift. Such kind of problems continue in the digital realm. In non-family relations, literature observed possible discomfort in the receipt of digital monetary or voucher gifts [6, 8] also observed its limits to convey effort and care, due to its convenience and simplicity. However, there are also practices that can affect money and its perception positively [14] observed how physical money was 'earmarked' or wrapped through different currencies, stories, or meaningful amounts, framed to give a personal impression. Due to its limitations, money might not function well as a relationship-supporting gift. Thus, money needs special adaptation and contextual conditions to work and be appropriate also in the digital circumstances.

Recent work in HCI discussed the role and form of digital money and its adaption to function in the exchange also in closer personal relations [2] for instance described how users would sometimes add emojis to lighten up the need of sending money in an online payment service Venmo [13] described incidences where small monetary transactions could take the meaning of symbolic care, support, or apologies and thus have a positive relationship impact [5] analysed existing situations of two Chinese payment applications. They explored how digital monetary services were used in several social frames that led to differentiations. Their key factors were 'Actors', 'Context', 'Representation', 'Quantity', 'Timing', 'Flow' (whether the spending is restricted). These factors depict how money can be designed but leaves room for exploration in which ways money can be wrapped.

There has been work into wrapping digital gifts in HCI, not distinguishing between those of monetary value and those without. This also involved explorations into how digital gifts can be influenced by physical, 'hybrid' forms of wrapping to generate new forms of gifts [4].

Our addition to this body of work is to explore certain important gifting factors applied to the design of money. Aim is a better understanding of the possibilities of a digital wrapping for monetary gifts in close friendships and how it affects the perception of money.

## 3   The Framework

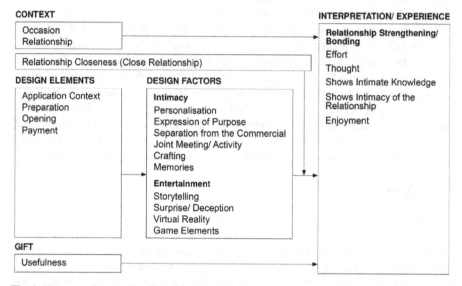

**Fig. 1.** Framework to design digital money gifts (with a focus on close friendship-relationships)

The framework is divided into the contextual influences (occasion, relationship, relationship closeness), the design elements are the experiential phases or points that are to be designed, the gift itself, the design factors that indicate the immediate design aims or user needs based on literature and previous experience [8], and factors that impact the relationship supporting perception such as effort or thoughtfulness. In this paper the main evaluated factors are the design factors in the framework, while the other factors still need more in-depth exploration.

**The Context.** Gifts are exchanged in a specific contextual influence (occasion, relationships) where certain gifts might be more appropriate culturally speaking. For instance, a monetary gift from a child to its mother might be more unusual [12]. Or a money gift might be usual in one culture on New Year in China, while it would be inappropriate in another culture.

**Design Elements.** They describe the phases of the gifting process or experience the designers want to incorporate in the design [see 5, 6] (i.e., the preparation, representation of the money).

**The Gift.** Money has the advantage to never not be a burdensome gift (when not liked by the recipient), as an overabundance of one type of gift can be perceived useless by recipients. Also [6] emphasized the usefulness of the gift as something that differentiated digital files as gifts.

**The Design Factors.** The design factors derived from our previous gifting study [8] and compiles intimate and entertaining factors, to achieve a positive and personal experience for the recipient.

*Intimacy* is Defined as the Conveyance of the Perceived Intimacy of the Relationship, the Personal Affection and Meaning

- Personalization (Adapt the gift to the recipient/giver/shared qualities)
- Expression of Purpose (Show positive intent, convey purpose)
- Separation from the Commercial (Avoid commercial impressions)
- Joint Meeting/Activity (Add a meeting/activity)
- Crafting (Enable the giver's invested time and effort)
- Memories (Create new and use old memories, remind of the giver)

  *Entertainment* intends to make the gift enjoyable, special, and elicit stronger feelings.

- Storytelling (Add/tell a story with the gift)
- Surprise/Deception (Mislead recipient/add something unexpected)
- Virtual Reality (Impossible become possible such as meeting one another)
- Game Elements (Take inspiration from games)

**The Interpretation/Experience.** One of the main outcomes of gifts is a relationship effect and in this way the framework follows [9] and [11].

## 4   Evaluation

To evaluate the framework, it was applied by the author working with other co-designers, who had a professional or educational background, in seven design workshops (with 13 designers). The designers were given a design brief, the framework, and cards and asked to develop innovative designs for digital money gifting the resulting ideas were summarized in three prototypes that would best reflect the variety of ideas generated. Afterwards they were implemented in form of basic interactive prototypes. These were later tested with potential users.

### 4.1   Content Creation Workshops

The ideation was oriented around a brief that would fix the contextual factors of the framework (occasion where a close friend experienced a relationship-break up/divorce, and a gift is sent across distance to cheer them up a while later) and the phases of the gifting experience (application context, preparation, opening, payment phase). Money was also meant to be unbound to any store (such as in vouchers), leaving the recipient the freedom to buy anything they would like to buy. The design factors were then presented form of inspirational cards (see Fig. 2) in addition to the framework (see Fig. 1).

**Fig. 2.** Inspirational cards were designed for the Workshop. The design factors were presented on different color-coded cards, pink (left hand card), green (right hand card). (Color figure online)

The three prototypes created are presented below, each based on the design brief of the workshop.

**Reborn Game – Money Gift exchanged and spent in a Live Video Chat and Game.** The first prototype referred to as *Reborn Game* (Fig. 3) is a money gift that takes place during an online video call between two friends. They play through two game levels previously personalized by the gift giver. GIFT OPENING: In the first level, the recipient goes through a process of rebirth. The level presents previous memories of the recipient from their lifetime before the divorce, which they can then symbolically take forward or leave behind through selecting 'take along' or 'let go' for each memory (see Fig. 3, left picture). Through this process they collect energy points that represent real money. PAYMENT: The credit derived from the first gaming level is now spent in a second level, where the game application is able to generate a matching gift for the recipient based on their input. In this second theme the giver builds a new self (future identity) through the creative personalization of an avatar and its environment. The system automatically determines a gift. At the start of this process, the recipient can limit the product suggestions based on their personal interests and preferences. If the system suggests something the recipient did not like as much, he can go back to try another combination.

**Fictional Wedding – Gift a Better Place in the Virtual Reality.** This second prototype (Fig. 4) embeds money into a fictional, virtual reality story and world. In the future, people will be part of a virtual reality network. They can send one another gifts in form of fictional places to visit. In this scenario the recipient travels to a Martian community in a parallel reality, that traditionally marry, divorce, and switch partners on a yearly basis. GIFT OPENING: The recipient receives an invitation by a secret gift giver and travels to the fictional place. He explores the world step by step to understand the underlying story the gift tells. It consists of interactions with other locals that report of the merits of their

**Fig. 3.** Prototype 1 (Reborn Game): In the first game level during the video call the recipient collects energy points that represent the money (left). In the second level the recipient arranges a future persona or avatar to receive an automatic gift proposition by the system (right).

local coupling traditions, and the recipient also takes part in their tradition on that day by marrying another local Martian. The recipient also meets the masked gift giver who hands over their monetary wedding gift, in form of the local currency. PAYMENT: The Martian money can be spent in local stores the giver personalized with local products to buy. If a fictional product or memory is bought from the fictional world, the real monetary gift value in this real world would automatically be transferred to the recipient's general account or credit. So, he would end up with a fictional gift token and money that can be freely spent. Alternatively, the Martian currency can be spent in any online shop in the virtual reality network.

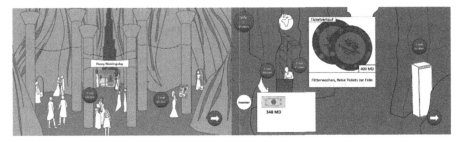

**Fig. 4.** Prototype 2 (virtual wedding): recipient experiences a better parallel reality, the giver designed for them and their situation (left). The recipient can also fictionally buy certain self-designed virtual gifts while the real monetary value ends up in their regular account (right).

**Guardian Angel – Lighten the Recipient Mood with Filtered Messages and a Money Gift over Time.** The last prototype (Fig. 5) consists of a gifting system that is situated in context of the daily messaging and wallet platforms of the gift recipient. The giver can enter the guardian angel mode to protect their friend from any incoming messages relating to the topic of divorce. The friend can set up filter words, personalize an avatar, and write positive messages throughout the time the recipient is shielded for. The positive messages also overlay negative incoming messages. GIFT OPENING: In context of this procedure, the giver also sends a monetary gift brought by the angel figure to the recipient. PAYMENT: When the recipient pays with the money from that guardian angel folder, a message/commentary arrives adapted to the thing that they bought from that money (i.e., 'I will protect you from further bills of this kind in the future').

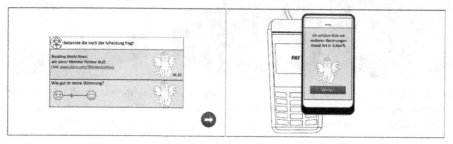

**Fig. 5.** Prototype 3 (guardian angel): The guardian angel can filter out divorce-related messages based on filter words chosen by the giver, and present positive messages and gifts instead (left). During payment with the gift the guardian angel makes a comment on what the recipient bought (right).

## 4.2  Participants

As much literature has focused on monetary gifts as potentially problematic and bound to specific expectations in Western cultural contexts [1, 12] participants were all from a German cultural background (nationality and place of birth). We were also interested in younger participants who are digitally skilled, aged 18–40. All participants had experienced digital gifts or digital monetary exchange i.e., through PayPal before (see Table 1). They were recruited via convenience sampling.

**Table 1.** Participant: Gender, Age, and experience with digital money/gifts

| Participant | Gender | Age | Previous Usage of digital gifts/money |
|---|---|---|---|
| P1 | F | 24 | Digital gift card |
| P2 | F | 26 | Digital greeting cards |
| P3 | F | 22 | Digital gift card from partner |
| P4 | F | 24 | Digital gift card from friend |
| P5 | M | 28 | Used PayPal for transactions |
| P6 | F | 34 | Digital greeting cards, uses PayPal App |
| P7 | F | 23 | Digital gift card |
| P8 | F | 38 | Digital gift card from friend |
| P9 | F | 24 | Digital gift cards from friends, Christmas and Birthday |
| P10 | F | 26 | Digital gift card code via e-mail |

*(continued)*

**Table 1.** (*continued*)

| Participant | Gender | Age | Previous Usage of digital gifts/money |
|---|---|---|---|
| P11 | M | 25 | Monetary birthday gift via E-mail from friend |
| P12 | F | 22 | PayPal birthday gift from friends |
| P13 | F | 25 | Digital gift card from parents |
| P14 | M | 27 | Uses PayPal |
| P15 | F | 30 | Gift card code via email from family member |
| P16 | F | 30 | Gift through code via email |
| P17 | F | 19 | Uses PayPal app |
| P18 | M | 30 | Digital podcasts, e-books as gifts |
| P19 | F | 27 | Digital gift card |
| P20 | F | 33 | Digital voucher from friend, podcast service subscription |

### 4.3  Procedure

Before each interview took place, participants received the information and participant consent form. The interviews took place via video call through Microsoft Teams, while the three prototypes were in form of an online PowerPoint file. The PowerPoint file allowed basic animations and interactivity and could easily be opened by participants online. Participants would share the window with the prototype when clicking through. In-between each prototype the researcher asked questions and also shared Likert-type questions in form of a presentation.

Participants were initially introduced to the fictional scenario in which the gifting prototypes they viewed would take place (occasion: gift from a close friend after a divorce situation, relationship: close friend that lives across distance). Participants were asked to empathize with the recipient role in the prototypes and to imagine a real close friend of theirs as the giver. Each gifting prototype was therefore personalized to the viewer, as if they were the recipient by incorporating their name. The characters were presented in a gender-neutral fashion so all participants could better relate to receiving the prototype. Also, each time, the sequence in which the designed prototypes were shown was alternated (i.e., 123, 312, 231…).

This study is part of a larger study, and the questions presented in the following, were those analysed in this paper. In the beginning of the study and after each shown prototype participants were presented the following Likert-type question (1–7, strongly disagree to strongly agree). They were asked to relate it to the seen scenario while ignoring previous scenarios. Based on their rating, follow-up questions were asked (first open-endedly, then also probingly for potentially relevant design factors):

- Money gifts can be relationship-strengthening in close friendships

For further differentiation they were also asked Likert-type with follow-up questions about their perception of the wrapping and the perception of the money gift in context of the wrapping:

- The way the money was given is relationship-strengthening in close friendships
- The monetary gift is relationship-strengthening in close friendships

At the end of the interview, they were also asked which prototype they would like to best receive.

## 4.4  Analysis

A deductive content analysis [10] was conducted. First, a coding frame was established based on the key design factors from the framework (see Table 2) The interviews were transcribed and then analysed using NVivo. A second coder independently analysed half of the interviews, and the codes were reconciled. The analysis focused on the mentioned design factors that were seen as potentially relationship supporting (or weakening), so there was a differentiation between positive and negative factors. Moreover, there was a differentiation in positive factors between spontaneous and prompted mentioning to weigh their relevance. The importance of a concept was determined by how many different participants they were mentioned rather than their overall frequency.

**Table 2.**  Coding frame with

| Code | Description | Rule | Example |
| --- | --- | --- | --- |
| Personalization | There is an adaptation/relation to the recipient | | |
| Expression of purpose | The gift expresses/ the recipient becomes aware of the purpose/ intention | | |
| Separation from the commercial | The monetary aspect is hidden | | |
| Joint meeting/Activity | A design element that involves a joint meeting or activity, ranging from a live to asynchronous or implied meetings | This does not mean an abstract feeling of togetherness based on non-related design-elements | i.e., "this virtual reality is perhaps also an expression that you experience something together..., my friend may have thought about it and has already run through it mentally before me."(Prototype 2, P20): |

*(continued)*

**Table 2.** (*continued*)

| Code | Description | Rule | Example |
|------|-------------|------|---------|
| Crafting | A notable involvement/preparation by the giver | | |
| Memories | Memories placed in the gift, and what makes the gift memorable | | |
| Game elements | A playful element and quality of the gift | | |
| Surprise/Deception | The gift has design elements that make the gift more surprising | | |
| Virtual reality | Perception of the virtual reality and represented fictional representations | | |
| Storytelling | Involves story elements | | |

## 5 Results

Initially, participants were neutral on the stance that monetary gifts can be relationship strengthening in close friendships (Mean = 4). Their rating was best based on seeing Prototype 1 (see Table 3). This also aligned with their most preferred prototype (10 participants liked to receive the 'Reborn Game' scenario in the final rating question best).

**Table 3.** Participant ratings (Mean) on whether money gifts could be relationship strengthening (prior to and based on seeing the respective prototype)

| | Prior to any prototypes | Reborn game | Virtual wedding | Guardian angel |
|---|---|---|---|---|
| Relationship strengthening | 4 | 6 | 5 | 5 |

**Joint Meeting/Activity:** Nearly all participants spontaneously mentioned a potential relationship-fostering effect of a personal meeting and shared activity as presented in Prototype 1 which included a live video chat. The most common reasons mentioned was the interaction, to share time together, and the communicative exchange.

"it promotes interaction, that's why I find it relationship strengthening, friendship is based on giving and taking, so interaction, communication." (P12)

Seven participants appreciated that the giver organized a personal meeting as part of the gift. It depicted an interest to spend time online together and listening to their personal difficulties. It also showed more care, knowing what happens to the recipient:

> "because then I see the person is present and they are interested in what happens to their gift and not that it is just thrown… 'Do what you want', but rather that they are interested in me." (P4)

The gift bound to be spent together in their meeting. Some participants felt the gift was more connected to the giver in their memory in that way:

> "Because somehow this makes it clear to the recipient in that moment that the other has given you this… When he buys a book or he does something, at that moment he would be more reminiscent of the person than if it is a gift card with 15 € and 'do what you want, and I don't really know which product you got in the end'." (P6)

**Memories:** Half of the participants appreciated the memories as relationship-strengthening. This was because it elicited a reflection about their relationship and its intimacy of their relationship.

> "That you go through these experiences together again and thus earn these points, this friendship is emphasized by the gift of money… Because that's just something between me and the person and not between me and other people… that the person just knows what is going on in my life, what maybe other people do not know… This level of intimacy… And there you just see with whom you just have a stronger bond or friendship and with whom not?" (P9)

Selecting the memories also showed effort, and personalization by the giver.

> "he thought about it, he picked out fragments of memory that fit together with the game and I notice he thought about it" (P12)

**Expression of Purpose:** Nearly half of the participants spontaneously noticed the expressed intention or purpose of the gift as a relationship strengthening factor. For instance, the guardian angel expressed care and thought about what the recipient would need in that moment.

> "because the person then simply supported me in the situation, showed me that I am important to him, showed me that he knows me, that he knows what I need now, what is good for me and what may not do me any good" (P10)

**Personalization:** Most participants had the opinion that personalization expresses effort and thought and the giver's considerations regarding the recipient.

> "The person has thought about it, has taken time to write something personal that applies to my situation, and I also find that very appreciative, also strengthening the relationship." (P16)

**Separation from the Commercial:** The importance of this aspect mainly became apparent in cases where money was not sufficiently hidden and registered by participants. Yet, participants had quite different perceptions how to hide money. This became especially clear in Prototype 3, where a money gift was brought by the guardian angel in connection with filtering their messages. While some understood money positively how it was brought to the recipient in a playful manner:

"Because simply through this guardian angel the money was indirectly mediated... This is not so formal, but in a nice way, a very loving way shown 'here you have a bit of what you can redeem or what you can spend'. It's just not as formal." (P9)

Others did not find the money well enough wrapped:

"money is sent, but there is nothing behind it... so the avatar has nothing to do with the money." (P1)

**Crafting:** Other participants also noticed the involved creations by the giver. The main effect of crafting was for those participants that it showed effort, thoughtfulness, or also something more personalized. In prototype 3, for instance the avatar of the guardian angel could be personalized, and hand drawn.

"The Avatar... he just upgrades everything a bit... Because I just know that the person has created something that really belongs only to me. This was really just made for me and something no one else has in the world... it's just such an expression of affection, of friendship, that I don't just not matter to the person." (P18)

**Game Elements:** Four participants also spontaneously noted the playful game-related elements as somewhat distracting from the monetary gift, but also due to the action that they need to do to collect it in the game level.

"… somehow with this playful surrounding I have the feeling I do not have such a problem to accept the money... I think because I have the feeling that the focus is not on the money, but on the game, because the person has put so much energy and time and resources into it and because I just think I do something for it and don't get the money just like that" (P16)

**Storytelling:** To a few participants the story in prototype 2 indicated the giver's effort in how to present the gift.

"The fact that this money gift is embedded, that shows for me simply that someone has made so much effort not only to transfer money to my account. But to integrate it so creatively into the story... And also, the thoughts, and that it was just not enough for the person to just transfer the money to the account, but to put one on top of it" (P13)

**Virtual Reality:** A few participants described the virtual reality and its potential relationship effect. They perceived fictional interactions and processes in the virtual reality rather diversly. While for some participants noted more positively the thoughtfulness and invested time as well as personal character of the self arranged virtual world. They also expressed how this form of gift would be visually presenting the thought world of the giver:

"in fact, somehow, did I perceive it as even closer than when a person somehow gives a gift to a person directly... I think, because maybe then somehow this personal world was created by the person, and you were let into this world and so you were invited... She shares her own thoughts and allows you to participate in her own thoughts and feelings, That then expresses a kind of trust" (P14)

Others were more deterred by a perceived impersonal character of the virtuality and mentioned the artificiality of the prototype:

"the way is just too artificial for me... Yes, that's just the way that the person is not so close to me in this process." (P9)

**Surprise:** Three participants also felt greater enjoyment and happiness by the way money was hidden as or connected to suspense and surprise. In Prototype 1 for example this participant found it surprising to receive a monetary gift in addition to a non-monetary game activity:

"because it also triggered this surprise effect with me, there I now get 20 € from my friend ... Simply because it just triggers in me this inner joy... Because you just connect this relationship with something good" (P18)

**Specialness:** Another factor noted in the prototypes was also their specialness, which was a sign of effort and particularly appropriate for a close friendship:

"Because I think that's something very special. And that's something you don't get all the time... Because that shows to me that it is a close relationship. If someone thinks of something so special for me, I wouldn't expect that from a normal friendship... I wouldn't expect someone to put so much effort into the money gift" (P13)

## 6  Discussion

In this paper we presented a framework to provide an overview of the most relevant influential factors we see to be considered in the design of digital money gifts. It was applied in the design of three prototypes. Particularly, we applied design factors from the framework (i.e., the personalization, a shared activity). There has been little prior research on the experience of digital money in regard to these gift-related design factors and how it would affect people's opinion of the receipt of pure money as a gift in its wrapping.

Overall, participants had a positive understanding, that monetary gifts could strengthen close friendships after experiencing the prototypes. It indicates that applying the design factors to the money gift may enhance even pure money as a gift (it was not bound to any stores). This aligns with prior literature, describing how people earmarked physical money in different ways [14]. Yet, we also add a differentiation to the influential factors in the wrapping and find new digital forms.

A key insight of this study is the potential of our factors to reframe or enhance money gifts. For instance, the shared meeting/activity and the presence by the giver during the exchange and spending of the money showed more care in the gift and in its effect, compared to leaving the recipient on their own spending the money. The derived interpretation was the interest of the giver in the recipient and the gift. The presence to which the exchange and spending of the money was bound also reframed the money gift as a shared activity. The wrapping could also change the feeling about the money gift when participants were possibly shy to receive money as a gift: for instance, when embedded in a game and having to work for it, by collecting money like points in Prototype 1. This could help address certain limitations observed in previous applications contexts, where feelings of indebtedness could lead to negative experiences [13]. Yet, some ways in which money was connected to the prototypes was perceived differently by participants. For instance, in Prototype 3 participant views were more divided on its effectiveness. This might need more detailed further research.

Other factors showed effort and thought such the act of wrapping the money itself (i.e., through storytelling, through personalization). It is the specialness of the gift, the particular, that participants further noticed as effortful (similar to previous research [3]). This indicates the limits of current gifts which are very similar and there is no difference between a close friend or an employer, except the type of store in the best case, and a personal message.

At the same time, there is still some distancing element in spending time online, especially when being alone, as some participants felt the overwhelming digitality and fictionality of the virtual reality of the second prototype was somehow artificial. We suggest in these cases to better connect the digital with the reality of the recipients, such as real places or people that would be present.

## 7  Conclusion

In this paper we present a framework to support the design of digital money as a gift. We explore the functioning particularly in context of close friendships. This work aims to indicate further options of designing money not bound to certain stores and to enhance its effect in closer personal relations across distance. The finding of this paper is the indication that simple money can be presented and reframed in a manner to be positively accepted and relationship-strengthening as a gift even in intimate friendship relations. Yet, it is important how to apply those factors to the design. The results show that both, the design of the payment phase, how the money is used would also need to be considered when applying these factors. We also found indications for potentially different wrapping needs in participants.

**Acknowledgement.** The research was funded by Loughborough University. We thank all co-designers in our workshops for their interesting contributive discussion. We also gratefully thank the participants for their very thorough responses.

# References

1. Burgoyne, C.B., Routh, D.A.: Constraints on the use of money as a gift at Christmas: the role of status and intimacy*. J. Econ. Psychol. **12**(1), 47–69 (1991). https://doi.org/10.1016/0167-4870(91)90043-S

2. Caraway, M., Epstein, D.A., Munson, S.A.: Friends don't need receipts: the curious case of social awareness streams in the mobile payment app venmo. In: Proceedings of ACM Human-Computer Interaction, vol. 1, CSCW, Article 28, pp. 1-17 (2017). https://doi.org/10.1145/3134663

3. Kelly, R., Gooch, D., Patil, B., Watts, L.: Demanding by design: supporting effortful communication practices in close personal relationships. In: Proceedings of the 2017 ACM Conference on Computer Supported Cooperative Work and Social Computing, pp. 70–83. ACM, New York (2017). https://doi.org/10.1145/2998181.2998184

4. Koleva, B., et al.: Designing hybrid gifts. ACM Trans. Comput.-Hum. Interact. **27**(5), Article 37, 33 (2020). https://doi.org/10.1145/3398193

5. Kow, Y.M., Gui, X., Cheng, W.: Special digital monies: the design of alipay and wechat wallet for mobile payment practices in China. In: Bernhaupt, R., Dalvi, G., Joshi, A., K. Balkrishan, D., O'Neill, J., Winckler, M. (eds.) INTERACT 2017. LNCS, vol. 10516, pp. 136–155. Springer, Cham (2017). https://doi.org/10.1007/978-3-319-68059-0_9

6. Kwon, H., Koleva, B., Schnädelbach, H., Benford, S.: It's not yet a gift: understanding digital gifting. In: Proceedings of the 2017 ACM Conference on Computer Supported Co-operative Work and Social Computing, pp. 2372–2384. ACM, New York (2017). https://doi.org/10.1145/2998181.2998225

7. Mamonov, S, Benbunan-Fich, R.:'Exploring factors affecting social e-commerce service adoption: the case of facebook gifts'. Int. J. Inf. Manag. **37**(6), 590–600 (2017). https://doi.org/10.1016/j.ijinfomgt.2017.05.005

8. Probst, F., Kwon, H., de Bont, C.: Euros from the heart: exploring digital money gifts in intimate relationships. In: Stephanidis, C., et al. (eds.) HCII 2021. LNCS, vol. 13094, pp. 342–356. Springer, Cham (2021). https://doi.org/10.1007/978-3-030-90238-4_24

9. Ruth, J.A., Otnes, C.C., Brunel, F.F.: Gift receipt and the reformulation of interpersonal relationships. J. Consum. Res. **25**(4), 385–402 (1999). https://academic.oup.com/jcr/article-abstract/25/4/385/1785887

10. Schreier, M.: Qualitative Content Analysis in Practice. SAGE Publications (2012)

11. Sherry, J.F.: Gift giving in anthropological perspective. J. Consum. Res. **10**(2), 157–168 (1983). https://www.jstor.org/stable/2488921

12. Webley, P., Lea, S.E.G., Portalska, R.: The unacceptability of money as a gift. J. Econ. Psychol. **4**(3), 223–238 (1983). https://doi.org/10.1016/0167-4870(83)90028-4

13. Wu, Z., Ma, X.: Money as a social currency to manage group dynamics: red packet gifting in Chinese online communities. In: Proceedings of the 2017 CHI Conference Extended Abstracts on Human Factors in Computing Systems, pp. 2240–2247. ACM, New York (2017). https://doi.org/10.1145/3027063.3053153

14. Zelizer, V.A.: The Social Meaning of Money: Pin Money. Poor Relief, and Other Currencies. Princeton University Press, Paychecks (1997)

# Predictions on Usefulness and Popularity of Online Reviews: Evidence from Mobile Phones for Older Adults

Minghuan Shou[✉], Xueqi Bao, and Jie Yu

Business School, University of Nottingham Ningbo China, Ningbo 315100, China
minghuan.shou@nottingham.edu.cn

**Abstract.** This paper aims to propose an effective method to locate valuable reviews of mobile phones for older adults. After collecting the online reviews of mobile phones for older adults from JD mall, we propose a three-step framework. Firstly, Topic Modeling models and linguistic inquiry and word count (LIWC) methods are employed to extract latent topics. Secondly, regression models are used to examine the effect of variables obtained from the first step on the popularity (number of replies) and usefulness (number of helpful counts). Thirdly, seven machine learning models are adopted to predict the popularity and usefulness of online reviews. The results indicate that although older adults are more interested in the exterior, sound, money, and communication functions of mobile phones, they still care about the touch feel, work, and leisure functions. In addition, Random Forest performs the best in predicting the popularity and usefulness of online reviews. The findings can help e-commerce platforms and merchants identify the needs of the targeted consumers, predict which reviews will get more attention, and provide some early responses to some questions.

**Keywords:** Online review · Older adult · Mobile phone

## 1 Introduction

Information and communication technologies (ICT) have shifted the social interactions (Jara et al. 2015) and the fabric of economic life (Song et al. 2020). However, serious inequalities in access to and use of ICT have appeared among the categories of persons in one group (Park et al. 2015). For example, some of the public may have problems making use of the various digital devices. Scholars call this unequal disparity in ICT diffusion a digital divide. Whereas the digital divide occurring in society can create and aggravate economic as well as social inequalities. It has also been regarded as one of the most important barriers to social inclusion and fostering a strong and creative economy (Park et al. 2015). Thus, it is urgent to propose some methods to solve the digital divide. Digital divides are now understood to be complicated with several dimensional situations (Cruz et al. 2017) like accessibility, affordability, reliability, speed, and utilization (Loo 2012). More seriously, digital divides have been proved to exist in many countries (Szeles 2018) and have become a global problem. Current findings of the influential factors mainly

M. Kurosu et al. (Eds.): HCII 2022, LNCS 13516, pp. 475–489, 2022.
https://doi.org/10.1007/978-3-031-17615-9_33

contain gender (Mumporeze and Prieler 2017; Potnis 2016), age (Ball et al. 2019; Hall et al. 2015), economic development (Fuchs 2009), and education (Estacio et al. 2019).

On the other hand, the increasing number of older adults (aged 65+) makes the age-based digital divide more serious. Older adults always discontinue adopting digital communication technologies (Neves et al. 2018). For example, older people in Greece and Bulgaria are more than 11 times less likely to be online than the overall population (Niehaves and Plattfaut 2014). Additionally, a survey exploring computer and internet experience among younger adults (n = 430, aged 18–28 years) and older adults (n = 251, aged 65–90 years) found the difference significant. The percentages of older people showing experience with computers and the internet are 80% and 50%, respectively, compared to 99% and 90% for the younger adults (Olson et al. 2011). Psychological aging theory and processing-speed theory suggest that older adults may have some cognitive limitations on using new technologies, which explains the lower proportion of older adults with computer and internet experience.

Since only very few older adults are using the internet and the number of older adults is rapidly growing, mobile phone designers and merchants can make more profits if the future products can attract older adults. Besides, online reviews are regarded as a source of information for decision-making because of the abundance and ready availability of information. However, the sheer volume of online reviews makes it hard for consumers, especially older adults who perceive more difficulties in reading reviews and obtaining information compared to younger adults, to locate the useful ones. If merchants can locate the online reviews, which will receive more attention from the public in advance, they can increase older adults' satisfaction by placing the useful ones in a prominent place to help the public get better access to information and save time.

Thus, there are two main purposes of this paper. The first aim is to understand what characteristics of the technology are applicable to older adults, and the second one is to predict the popularity (number of replies) and usefulness (number of helpful counts) of online reviews via machine learning models. A three-step research framework is designed. Firstly, we crawl the online reviews of mobile phones from JD Mall (https://www.jd.com/), and then construct the Topic Modeling models and linguistic inquiry and word count (LIWC) to investigate what characteristics older adults prefer. Secondly, regression models are employed to explore what characteristics obtained from the first step can significantly affect the popularity (number of replies) and usefulness (number of helpful counts) of online reviews. Thirdly, machine learning models are adopted to predict the popularity and usefulness of online reviews based on their significantly influential characteristics.

Our study deviates from previous studies in some aspects. The main contributions are as follows.

Firstly, this paper provides a guideline for scholars on how to solve the age-digital divide. By adopting Topic Modelling models and analyzing the data of online reviews, this paper accurately obtains the characteristics of mobile phones older adults prefer. Scholars can take advantage of the preference to continue their studies and avoid some useless experiments. This can effectively save time and resources. Besides, because the age-digital divide has not currently been solved, merchants struggle to explore what product value customers want. What this paper finds can provide evidence for designers by clearly showing the contribution of comment information to the public attention, and merchants can make use of the results to design the products.

Secondly, the findings of this paper argue that the cognitive limitations of older adults on new technologies are decreasing. This provides an oppositive view to the current theories which present that older adults are more likely to refuse to use new technologies. Besides, the findings can also provide support to the work published by Ghasemaghaei et al. (2019) that older adults do not always mean simpler IT products. In some cases, they may perceive IT products with other features.

Thirdly, the results of this paper indicate that it can be possible to locate useful online reviews in advance via machine learning models. For merchants, they can better manage their time and effort in dealing with consumers' responses based on the results of predictive models. In addition, they can be alerted and take precautions measures against negative consumer comments.

The paper is structured as follows: the following section shows the theoretical foundation of this paper and some studies on how to solve the digital divide. Section 3 details the research framework and the data information. A presentation of results follows. The conclusion and some suggestions are drawn in Sect. 5. Finally, this paper summarizes the limitations and the future work.

## 2 Literature Review

This section covers two parts. The first part is a summary of the previous studies on the digital divide. The second part is to present the development of the model we use in this article.

### 2.1 Studies About the Digital Divide

Just as we can see from section one, the digital divide has become a global problem, and its development of it has strongly affected social and economic development. Thus, it is urgent for scholars to think of some methods to change the status. However, by summarizing the previous studies, we are surprised to find that there are only a few studies on how to solve the problem, and the existing papers mainly focus on the following two aspects.

On the one hand, scholars spent much time building models to evaluate the digital divide. Pertrovic et al. (2012) proposed an innovative procedure for benchmarking the digital divide. Classifying countries into hierarchical levels of their performance and selecting the benchmarks for less successful ones are two main innovations. Cruz-Jesus et al. (2012) addressed the European digital disparities by building multivariate statistical models and cluster analysis. Park et al. (2015) and Billon et al. (2010) also dedicated to studying the digital divide between countries. But they took advantage of the similar method used by Pertrovic et al. (2012) as well to categorize the countries into several different groups and explained the specific appearance of the digital divide in each group. Kiss et al. (2020) and Chang et al. (2012) both collected data by questionnaire, but the first one took advantage of the cluster method, and the latter chose to use the analytic hierarchy process (AHP).

On the other hand, exploring the conditions where the digital divide may occur is also one of the focuses. Except for the factors mentioned in section one, there are more others. Reddick et al. (2020) conducted a survey to explore the influence of affordability factors on the broadband digital divide. They found that geographical disparities play an important role. Besides, the digital divide was not exclusively a rural/urban digital divide but also appeared in an intra-city context. Jiang et al. (2019) paid attention to analyzing the appearance of cancer survivors. They found that some patients had problems using online patient-provider communication (OPPC), which meant that there were significant digital divide barriers existing in the adoption and actual usage of OPPC. Duplaga (2017) and Sachdeva et al. (2015) also found evidence of a digital divide among patients.

By reading the papers about the solutions to the digital divide, we find that the existing research mainly focused on providing general suggestions for the governments. Akca et al. (2007) and Huang and Cox (2014) proposed the design of web pages and internet access could be a method. Loo and Ngan (2012) suggested that governments should implement some measures to encourage the use of mobile phones and personal computers. Similarly, Townsend et al. (2013) also mentioned that a growing digital divide would make it more dangerous, and increasing broadband usage would be necessary.

As a basis for summarizing the above papers, it was not difficult to find that there were so many methods to evaluate the digital divide and the digital divide occurred in various conditions. However, only a few scholars focused on providing evidence for governments to make policies to solve the digital divide, but their suggestions were not targeted. Thus, it was urgent to explore some new methods.

## 2.2 Researches on Online Reviews

Online reviews have become indispensable information sources that can provide useful information to customers (Mudambi and Schuff 2010). Customers can obtain information about the products that they want to buy before purchasing from either the review content or the communicative interaction between the product review author and other consumers (Cao 2020; Li and Huang 2020). Due to the sufficient information from the online reviews, scholars have started to build some models to make some analyses on them, aiming at obtaining the preference of customers. Wang et al. (2020) developed a novel approach based on Bayesian statistics to explore the prior belief in online reviews and solved the problem that review-hosting firms could not detect the helpfulness of reviews. Choi et al. (2020) created an aging theory-based EDT algorithm to build the groups of similar reviews and tracked their development. Finally, by using sentiment analysis and evaluating time-evolving events, people could identify time-evolving product opportunities. Linguistic issues, sentiment analysis, and content analysis were also performed by Teso et al. (2018). Besides, they suggested that retailers could adapt the offer to the gender of customers. In summary, online reviews obtained much information, and taking advantage of the information could bring more opportunities.

## 3 Research Framework

This section introduces our research model and methods for data collection, processing, and measurement (Fig. 1). Before making some analyses, we plan to mine the online reviews of mobile phones for older adults from JD mall. LDA and NMF methods can be performed to reveal the latent dimensions that express the customer's priorities. These dimensions present what customers prefer while purchasing the products. Besides, the results of LIWC can help us test the results obtained by the Topic Modelling models. After that, this paper explores whether the characteristics obtained from the Topic Modeling models can significantly affect the popularity and usefulness of online reviews. Eventually, seven machine learning models are employed to predict the popularity and usefulness of online reviews. To display the results, we divide the entire data into two parts based on the median of the output features. For example, the median output (number of replies to online reviews) is 5, so this paper converts the number ($>= 5$) to 1 and the number ($<5$) to 0, representing 43.67% and 56.33%, respectively. The median output (number of helpfulness) is 4, so this paper converts the number ($>= 4$) to 1 and the number ($<4$) to 0, representing 38.19% and 61.81%, respectively.

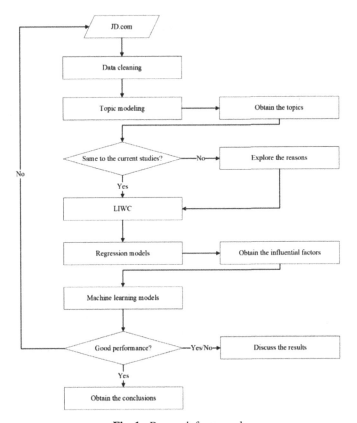

**Fig. 1.** Research framework

A web crawler has been designed to obtain the online reviews of mobile phones for elders from JingDong mall. Some data cleaning methods have been performed. We mainly followed the steps suggested in (Tirunillai and Tellis 2014). In the first step, some irrelevant characters and words, such as HTML, tags, URLs, and punctuation marks are eliminated due to their no information content about the product or the dimensions of quality that we are interested in extracting. After that, the presence of characters (e. g. ".", "!", "?") is used to break the reviews into several sentences. Then we apply the part-of-speech method to retain words that are adjectives, nouns, or adverbs. The above steps are to collect the words with sufficient information about the product and its quality. Finally, stop-words are also deleted, and function words are numbered to support the following analysis. A total of 284527 comments have been collected after data cleaning.

Besides, seven popular machine learning models were chosen to predict the "usefulness" and "popularity" of online reviews, including Random Forest, Logistic Regression, Decision Tree, Naive Bayes, Neural Network, Support Vector Machine (SVM), and K-Nearest Neighbor (KNN). Their performances were mainly measured by accuracy. The confusion matrix is shown in Table 1. Besides, we also calculate AUC and draw ROC curves to compare the results.

**Table 1.** Confusion matrix

|  |  | Prediction value | |
| --- | --- | --- | --- |
|  |  | Positive | Negative |
| Real value | Positive | True positive (TP) | False negative (FN) |
|  | Negative | False positive (FP) | True negative (TN) |

$$Accuracy = \frac{TP + TN}{TP + TN + FP + FN}$$

## 4 Results

### 4.1 Results of Topic Modeling Models

Two different models (LDA & NMF) are employed to obtain what characteristics of mobile phones older adults prefer, which can prove the robustness of the results. To foster our understanding, we also divide the whole data into two groups based on the number of stars. We only show the first nine topics summarized from the detailed information to show the results clearly.

**Table 2.** Results of topic modeling model (LDA & NMF)

|  | Data | | Data (Star > = 3) | | Data (Star < 3) | |
| --- | --- | --- | --- | --- | --- | --- |
| Topic | NMF | LDA | NMF | LDA | NMF | LDA |
| 1 | Function | Battery | Function | Old | Function | Quality |

*(continued)*

**Table 2.** (*continued*)

| Topic | Data | | Data (Star > = 3) | | Data (Star < 3) | |
| | NMF | LDA | NMF | LDA | NMF | LDA |
|---|---|---|---|---|---|---|
| 2 | Exterior | Price | Operation | Battery | Operation | Sound |
| 3 | Feel | Communication | Feel | Communication | Feel | Communication |
| 4 | Money | Old | Battery | Money | Exterior | Operation |
| 5 | Sound | Exterior | Sound | Exterior | Sound | Storage |
| 6 | Delivery | Delivery | Parent | Sound | Delivery | Delivery |
| 7 | Parent | Feel | Delivery | Signal | Parent | Function |
| 8 | Operation | Parent | Exterior | Delivery | Font | Exterior |
| 9 | Quality | Sound | Money | Function | Quality | Price |

Table 2 shows the detailed information obtained from two topic modeling models (LDA & NMF). There is nearly no difference between the results from the two models, which means that it is reasonable to make some analysis on these topics. The results indicate that older adults are still concerned more about the communication function, exterior, touch feel, and sound of mobile phones. Besides, they are still concerned about the work, leisure, and money of the products.

This paper considers using LIWC to get consumers' attention from online reviews. The results of this component can help us verify the conclusions obtained above. The findings are shown in Fig. 2 support the results of Topic modeling. While among these seven features, older adults pay more attention to the money, sound, exterior, and communication function than the rest.

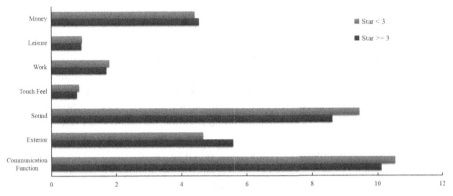

**Fig. 2.** Results of LIWC

## 4.2 Results of Regression Models

Before employing these features obtained from Topic Modeling models to predict the popularity and usefulness of online reviews, regression models are adopted to examine whether these features have a significant effect.

As shown in Table 3, the average word count of the comment is 14.53, and the variables (7–13) refer to consumers' attention towards each aspect. According to the correlation analysis results, there is no strong relationship between the independent variables, which means the regression results are not affected by the multicollinearity when predicting the popularity and usefulness of online reviews.

**Table 3.** Statistical description and correlation analysis of the variables

|    |                        | Mean  | 1     | 2     | 3     | 5     | 6     | 7     | 8     | 9     | 10    | 11   | 12   | 13   |
|----|------------------------|-------|-------|-------|-------|-------|-------|-------|-------|-------|-------|------|------|------|
| 1  | Star                   | 3.52  | 1.00  |       |       |       |       |       |       |       |       |      |      |      |
| 2  | Popularity             | 0.44  | −0.77 | 1.00  |       |       |       |       |       |       |       |      |      |      |
| 3  | Usefulness             | 0.38  | −0.16 | −0.07 | 1.00  |       |       |       |       |       |       |      |      |      |
| 5  | Sentiment              | 0.79  | 0.11  | 0.04  | −0.05 | 1.00  |       |       |       |       |       |      |      |      |
| 6  | Word Count             | 14.53 | 0.00  | −0.10 | −0.06 | 0.10  | 1.00  |       |       |       |       |      |      |      |
| 7  | Communication Function | 10.33 | −0.03 | 0.04  | 0.01  | −0.01 | −0.03 | 1.00  |       |       |       |      |      |      |
| 8  | Exterior               | 5.1   | 0.06  | −0.04 | −0.02 | 0.22  | 0.04  | −0.12 | 1.00  |       |       |      |      |      |
| 9  | Sound                  | 9.04  | −0.03 | 0.05  | 0.00  | −0.01 | −0.01 | 0.46  | 0.04  | 1.00  |       |      |      |      |
| 10 | Touch Feel             | 0.83  | −0.02 | 0.00  | 0.01  | −0.03 | −0.01 | −0.03 | −0.03 | −0.05 | 1.00  |      |      |      |
| 11 | Work                   | 1.74  | −0.01 | 0.01  | −0.01 | 0.01  | 0.03  | 0.01  | −0.07 | −0.05 | −0.01 | 1.00 |      |      |
| 12 | Leisure                | 0.95  | −0.01 | 0.00  | 0.01  | 0.01  | 0.01  | 0.04  | −0.05 | 0.00  | 0.00  | 0.01 | 1.00 |      |
| 13 | Money                  | 4.47  | 0.00  | 0.02  | 0.00  | 0.05  | −0.04 | 0.08  | −0.13 | −0.10 | −0.03 | 0.04 | 0.07 | 1.00 |

In the regression models, three control variables are located, including star, sentiment, and word count. After examining the effect of control variables on the dependent ones (column (1) in Tables 4 and 5), the effect of the seven independent variables is tested (columns (2–8) in Tables 4 and 5). Before examining whether these variables can significantly affect the popularity and usefulness of online reviews, the significance of the models is tested first. In Tables 4 and 5, all the models are statistically significant at a 0.01 level, and all the control variables are significantly related to the dependent ones. When we predict the popularity of online reviews, we do find that only six independent variables show a significant effect, including the exterior, sound, touch feel, leisure, money, and communication functions. When we predict the usefulness of online reviews, only sound, touch feel, work, and leisure show a significant effect. Accordingly, we combine all the control variables and the significant independent variables to construct machine learning models.

**Table 4.** Results of predicting the popularity (number of replies) of online reviews

|  | (1) | (2) | (3) | (4) | (5) | (6) | (7) | (8) |
|---|---|---|---|---|---|---|---|---|
| Exterior |  | −0.0010*** |  |  |  |  |  |  |
|  |  | (0.0001) |  |  |  |  |  |  |
| Sound |  |  | 0.0013*** |  |  |  |  |  |
|  |  |  | (0.0001) |  |  |  |  |  |
| Touch feel |  |  |  | −0.0008*** |  |  |  |  |
|  |  |  |  | (0.0001) |  |  |  |  |
| Work |  |  |  |  | 0.0001 |  |  |  |
|  |  |  |  |  | (0.0001) |  |  |  |
| Leisure |  |  |  |  |  | −0.0010*** |  |  |
|  |  |  |  |  |  | (0.0001) |  |  |
| Money |  |  |  |  |  |  | 0.0005*** |  |
|  |  |  |  |  |  |  | (0.0001) |  |
| Communication function |  |  |  |  |  |  |  | 0.0007*** |
|  |  |  |  |  |  |  |  | (0.0000) |
| Star | −0.2445*** | −0.2442*** | −0.2242*** | −0.2445*** | −0.2445*** | −0.2445*** | −0.2445*** | −0.2243*** |
|  | (0.0004) | (0.0004) | (0.0004) | (0.0004) | (0.0004) | (0.0004) | (0.0004) | (0.0004) |
| Sentiment | 0.2190*** | 0.2253*** | 0.2191*** | 0.2188*** | 0.2190*** | 0.2192*** | 0.2183*** | 0.2190*** |
|  | (0.0018) | (0.0019) | (0.0018) | (0.0018) | (0.0018) | (0.0018) | (0.0018) | (0.0018) |
| Word count | −0.0016*** | −0.0016*** | −0.0016*** | −0.0016*** | −0.0016*** | −0.0016*** | −0.0016*** | −0.0016*** |
|  | (0.0000) | (0.0000) | (0.0000) | (0.0000) | (0.0000) | (0.0000) | (0.0000) | (0.0000) |
| _cons | 1.1475*** | 1.1469*** | 1.1344*** | 1.1485*** | 1.1473*** | 1.1484*** | 1.1455*** | 1.1399*** |
|  | (0.0019) | (0.0019) | (0.0020) | (0.0019) | (0.0019) | (0.0019) | (0.0019) | (0.0020) |
| R-square | 0.6201 | 0.6204 | 0.621 | 0.6201 | 0.6201 | 0.6201 | 0.6202 | 0.6204 |
| Prob > F | 0.0000 | 0.0000 | 0.0000 | 0.0000 | 0.0000 | 0.0000 | 0.0000 | 0.0000 |
| Number of obs | 284527 | 284527 | 284527 | 284527 | 284527 | 284527 | 284527 | 284527 |

Notes: N = 284527. * $p < 0.10$, ** $p < 0.05$, *** $p < 0.01$

### 4.3 Results of Machine Learning Models

Seven machine learning models, namely Random Forest, Logistic Regression, Decision Tree, Naïve Bayes, Neural Network, SVM, and KNN, are employed in this part. Table 6 and Figs. 3 and 4 present that the accuracy values of all models are higher than 0.9, suggesting that machine learning models can be well used to predict the popularity of online reviews based on the number of stars, sentiment, and word counts of online reviews. In addition, after combining the control variables with independent variables, the performance of the majority of the machine learning models becomes better, except for the SVM and KNN when predicting the popularity of online reviews.

**Table 5.** Results of predicting the usefulness (number of helpful counts) of online reviews

|  | (1) | (2) | (3) | (4) | (5) | (6) | (7) | (8) |
|---|---|---|---|---|---|---|---|---|
| Exterior |  | 0.0001 |  |  |  |  |  |  |
|  |  | (0.0001) |  |  |  |  |  |  |
| Sound |  |  | −0.0003*** |  |  |  |  |  |
|  |  |  | (0.0001) |  |  |  |  |  |
| Touch feel |  |  |  | 0.0007*** |  |  |  |  |
|  |  |  |  | (0.0002) |  |  |  |  |
| Work |  |  |  |  | −0.0011*** |  |  |  |
|  |  |  |  |  | (0.0002) |  |  |  |
| Leisure |  |  |  |  |  | 0.0006** |  |  |
|  |  |  |  |  |  | (0.0002) |  |  |
| Money |  |  |  |  |  |  | −0.0000415 |  |
|  |  |  |  |  |  |  | (0.0001) |  |
| Communication function |  |  |  |  |  |  |  | 5.73E-06 |
|  |  |  |  |  |  |  |  | (0.0001) |
| Star | −0.0498*** | '−0.0498*** | − 0.0499 | −0.0498*** | −0.0499*** | −0.0498*** | −0.0498*** | −0.0498*** |
|  | (0.0006) | (0.0006) | (0.0006) | (0.0006) | (0.0006) | (0.0006) | (0.0006) | (0.0006) |
| Sentiment | −0.0400*** | '−0.0406*** | −0.0400*** | −0.0398*** | −0.0398*** | −0.0401*** | −0.0399*** | −0.0400*** |
|  | (0.0029) | (0.0029) | (0.0029) | (0.0029) | (0.0029) | (0.0029) | (0.0029) | (0.0029) |
| Word count | −0.0009*** | −0.0009*** | −0.0009*** | −0.0009*** | −0.0009*** | −0.0009*** | −0.0009*** | −0.0009*** |
|  | (0.0000) | (0.0000) | (0.0000) | (0.0000) | (0.0000) | (0.0000) | (0.0000) | (0.0000) |
| _cons | 0.6010*** | 0.6011*** | 0.6038*** | 0.6002*** | 0.6029*** | 0.6005*** | 0.6011*** | 0.6009*** |
|  | (0.0030) | (0.0030) | (0.0031) | (0.0030) | (0.0030) | (0.0030) | (0.0030) | (0.0031) |
| R-square | 0.0324 | 0.0324 | 0.0324 | 0.0324 | 0.0325 | 0.0324 | 0.0324 | 0.0324 |
| Prob > F | 0.0000 | 0.0000 | 0.0000 | 0.0000 | 0.0000 | 0.0000 | 0.0000 | 0.0000 |
| Number of obs | 284527 | 284527 | 284527 | 284527 | 284527 | 284527 | 284527 | 284527 |

Notes: N = 284527. * $p < 0.10$, ** $p < 0.05$, *** $p < 0.01$

**Table 6.** Results of machine learning models on predicting the popularity of online reviews

|  | Control variables | | Control variables + independent variables | | Difference | |
|---|---|---|---|---|---|---|
|  | Accuracy | AUC | Accuracy | AUC | Accuracy | AUC |
| Random forest | 96.11% | 96.07% | 96.95% | 96.94% | 0.84% | 0.87% |
| Logistic regression | 92.83% | 93.24% | 92.94% | 93.30% | 0.11% | 0.06% |
| Decision tree | 96.06% | 96.00% | 96.39% | 96.33% | 0.33% | 0.33% |
| Naive bayes | 93.43% | 94.03% | 93.43% | 94.03% | 0.00% | 0.00% |
| Neural network | 94.10% | 94.18% | 94.40% | 94.61% | 0.30% | 0.43% |
| SVM | 92.48% | 93.13% | 92.40% | 93.09% | −0.08% | −0.04% |
| KNN | 94.58% | 94.57% | 90.76% | 90.68% | −3.82% | −3.89% |

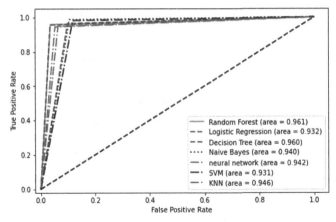

**Fig. 3.** Results of predicting the popularity of online reviews with control variables

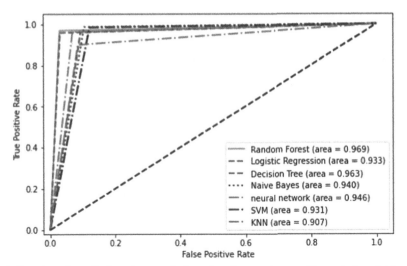

**Fig. 4.** Results of predicting the popularity of online reviews with control variables and independent variables

Table 7 and Figs. 5 and 6 focus on predicting the usefulness of online reviews via seven machine learning models. The results indicate that there is a large difference in the performance of machine learning models, with the Random Forest and Decision Tree performing the best. In addition, after combining the control variables with the independent variables to construct the machine learning models, we do find that for Random Forest, Logistic Regression, Decision Tree, Naïve Bayes, Neural Network, and KNN, the improvement is significant and positive. While for SVM, the effect is diverse.

**Table 7.** Results of machine learning models on predicting the usefulness of online reviews

| | Control variables | | Control variables + independent variables | | Difference | |
|---|---|---|---|---|---|---|
| | Accuracy | AUC | Accuracy | AUC | Accuracy | AUC |
| Random forest | 77.01% | 74.88% | 78.56% | 77.02% | 1.55% | 2.14% |
| Logistic regression | 62.00% | 50.14% | 62.03% | 50.25% | 0.03% | 0.11% |
| Decision tree | 77.09% | 75.09% | 78.36% | 76.91% | 1.27% | 1.82% |
| Naive bayes | 51.20% | 53.93% | 53.37% | 55.29% | 2.17% | 1.36% |
| Neural network | 63.26% | 53.45% | 63.42% | 54.44% | 0.16% | 0.99% |
| SVM | 51.43% | 50.09% | 44.31% | 49.53% | –7.12% | –0.56% |
| KNN | 68.49% | 66.12% | 68.52% | 66.25% | 0.03% | 0.13% |

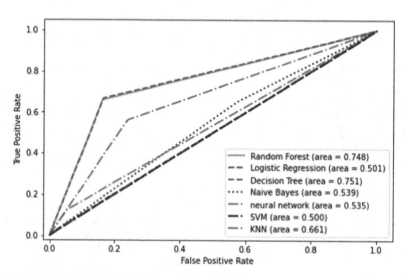

**Fig. 5.** Results of predicting the usefulness of online reviews with control variables

## 5   Discussions and Limitations

After conducting the Topic Modeling models, we obtain that the older adults not only care about the exterior, communication function, touch feel, sound, and money of the mobile phones but also pay attention to the leisure and work. Although the current theories state that older adults have cognitive limitations on using new technologies, what this paper obtains proposes an opposite view. Older adults' requirement for the multi-functions of mobile phones is rising. Traditional mobile phones, which can only be used for phone calls, can no longer meet the requirements of older adults nowadays. The findings also provide support to the work published by Ghasemaghaei et al. (2019). Two possible reasons can be used to explain it. Firstly, economic development provides

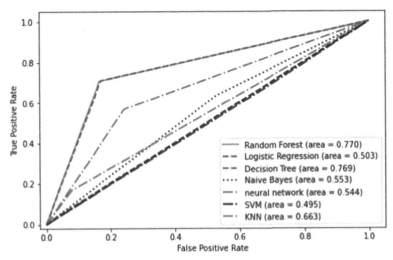

**Fig. 6.** Results of predicting the usefulness of online reviews with control variables and independent variables

older adults more opportunities to access new technologies, which can contribute to the reduction in their cognitive limitations. Secondly, public library constructions can provide rich physical infrastructural resources and free training sessions for the public, which can help reduce the digital divide (Manzuch and Maceviciute 2020). Older adults have more free time to access the resources provided by libraries than younger ones, suggesting that the age-based digital divide can be well reduced.

The main limitation of this paper is that the data collection in this paper is mainly on smart mobile phones. Due to the lack of data about non-smart mobile phones, some comparisons cannot be made. This means that this study cannot investigate whether there is a significant difference in product value between smart mobile phones and non-smart ones. The difference can be meaningful for increasing the sales of smart mobile phones. To solve this problem, collecting more data is necessary. Making some comparisons between phones with different product values can be beneficial for obtaining the effect of the product value. Besides, designing some experiments to explore the influence mechanism of these two variables while people purchase mobile phones can be useful.

## 6 Conclusion and Suggestions

The findings indicate that currently, although older adults pay more attention to mobile phones' exterior, money, sound, and communication function while purchasing mobile phones, they are still concerned about the touch feel, week, and leisure. Besides, we do find that machine learning models can be used to predict the popularity and usefulness of online reviews accurately based on the number of stars, sentiment, and word counts. After combining the independent variables, the performance of the majority of machine learning models improves.

Some suggestions are made in this paper. Firstly, since the growing requirement of older adults for the multi-functions of mobile phones, manufacturers should make some adjustments to their innovation plans and spend some resources on exploring ways to improve the quality of leisure and work functions. Secondly, machine learning models have been successfully adopted to predict the popularity and usefulness of online reviews. Merchants can employ this method to locate useful comments in advance. If there are some problems mentioned in these useful reviews, merchants can respond in a timely manner.

# References

Akca, M. Sayili, K.: Theory and practice: Esengun challenge of rural people to reduce digital divide in the globalized world. Gov. Inf. Q. **24**, 404–413 (2007)

Ball, C., Francis, J., Huang, K.T., Kadylak, T., Cotten, S.R., Rikard, R.V.: The physical-digital divide: exploring the social gap between digital natives and physical natives. J. Appl. Gerontol. **38**(8), 1167–1184 (2019)

Billon, M., Lopez, F.L., Marco, R.: Differences in digitalization levels: a multivariate analysis studying the global digital divide. Rev. World Econ. **146**, 39–73 (2020)

Cao, H.H.: Online review manipulation by asymmetrical firms: is a firm's manipulation of online reviews always detrimental to its competitor? Inf. Manag. **57**(6), 103244 (2020)

Chang, S.I., Yen, D.C., Chang, I.C.: Study of the digital divide evaluation model for government agencies - a Taiwanese local government's perspective. Inf. Syst. Front. **14**, 693–709 (2012)

Choi, J., Oh, S., Yoon, J., Lee, J.M., Coh, B.Y.: Identification of time-evolving product opportunities via social media mining. Technol. Forecast. Soc. Chang. **156**, 120045 (2020)

Cruz-Jesus, F., Oliveira, T., Bacao, F., Irani, Z.: Assessing the pattern between economic and digital development of countries. Inf. Syst. Front. **19**(4), 835–854 (2016). https://doi.org/10.1007/s10796-016-9634-1

Duplaga, M.: Digital divide among people with disabilities: analysis of data from a nationwide study for determinants of internet use and activities performed online. PLoS ONE **12**(6), e0179825–e0179825 (2017)

Estacio, E.V., Whittle, R., Protheroe, J.: The digital divide: examining socio-demographic factors associated with health literacy, access and use of internet to seek health information. J. Health Psychol. **24**(12), 1668–1675 (2019)

Fuchs, C.: The role of income inequality in a multivariate cross-national analysis of the digital divide. Soc. Sci. Comput. Rev. **27**(1), 41–58 (2009)

Ghasemaghaei, M., Hassanein, K., Benbasat, I.: Assessing the design choices for online recommendation agents for older adults: older does not always mean simpler information technology. MIS Q. **43**(1), 329–346 (2019)

Hall, A.K., Bernhardt, J.M., Dodd, V., Vollrath, M.W.: The digital health divide: evaluating online health information access and use among older adults. Health Educ. Behav. **42**(2), 202–209 (2015)

Huang, S.-C., Cox, J.L.: Establishing a social entrepreneurial system to bridge the digital divide for the poor: a case study for Taiwan. Univ. Access Inf. Soc. **15**(2), 219–236 (2014). https://doi.org/10.1007/s10209-014-0379-7

Jara, I., et al.: Understanding factors related to Chilean students' digital skills: a mixed methods analysis. Comput. Educ. **88**, 387–398 (2015)

Jiang, S., Hong, Y.A., Liu, P.L.: Trends of online patient-provider communication among cancer survivors from 2008 to 2017: a digital divide perspective. J. Cancer Surviv. **13**(2), 197–204 (2019). https://doi.org/10.1007/s11764-019-00742-4

Kiss, H., Fitzpatrick, K.M., Piko, B.F.: The digital divide: risk and protective factors and the differences in problematic use of digital devices among Hungarian youth. Child Youth Serv. Rev. **108**, 104612 (2020)

Li, M.X., Huang, P.: Assessing the product review helpfulness: affective-cognitive evaluation and the moderating effect of feedback mechanism. Inf. Manag. **57**, 103359 (2020)

Loo, B.P.Y., Ngan, Y.L.: Developing mobile telecommunications to narrow digital divide in developing countries? Some lessons from China. Telecommun Policy **36**, 888–900 (2012)

Loo, B.P.Y.: The e-society. Nova Science, New York (2012)

Manzuch, Z., Maceviciute, E.: Getting ready to reduce the digital divide: scenarios of Lithuanian public libraries. J. Am. Soc. Inf. Sci. **71**, 1205–1217 (2020)

Mudambi, S.M., Schuff, D.: What makes a helpful online review? a study of customer reviews on Amazon.com. MIS Q. **34**(1), 185 (2010)

Mumporeze, N., Prieler, M.: Gender digital divide in Rwanda: a qualitative analysis of socioeconomic factors. Telematics Inform. **34**, 1285–1293 (2017)

Neves, B.B., Waycott, J., Malta, S.: Old and afraid of new communication technologies? reconceptualising and contesting the 'age-based digital divide.' J. Sociol. **54**(2), 236–248 (2018)

Niehaves, B., Plattfaut, R.: Internet adoption by the elderly: employing IS technology acceptance theories for understanding the age-related digital divide. Euro. J. Inf. Syst. **23**, 708–726 (2014)

Olson, K.E., O'Brien, M.A., Rogers, W.A., Charness, N.: Diffusion of technology: frequency of use for younger and older adults. Ageing Int. **36**, 123–145 (2011)

Park, S.R., Choi, D.Y., Hong, P.: Club convergence and factors of digital divide across countries. Technol. Forecast. Soc. Chang. **96**, 92–100 (2015)

Petrovic, M., Bojkovic, N., Anic, I., Petrovic, D.: Benchmarking the digital divide using a multi-level outranking framework: evidence from EBRD countries of operation. Gov. Inf. Q. **29**, 597–607 (2012)

Potnis, D.: Inequalities creating economic barriers to owning mobile phones in India: Factors responsible for the gender digital divide. Inf. Dev. **32**(5), 1332–1342 (2016)

Reddick, C.G., Enriquez, R., Harris, R.J., Sharma, B.: Determinants of broadband access and affordability: an analysis of a community survey on the digital divide. Cities **106**, 102904 (2020)

Sachdeva, N., Tuikka, A.M., Kimppa, K.K., Suomi, R.: Digital disability divide in information society. J. Inf. Commun. Ethics Soc. **13**(3/4), 283–298 (2015)

Song, Z.Y., Wang, C., Bergmann, L.: China's prefectural digital divide: spatial analysis and multivariate determinants of ICT diffusion. Int. J. Inf. Manage. **52**, 102072 (2020)

Szeles, M.R.: New insights from a multilevel approach to the regional digital divide in the European Union. Telecommun. Policy **42**, 452–463 (2018)

Teso, E., Olmedilla, M., Martinez-Torres, M.R., Toral, S.L.: Application of text mining techniques to the analysis of discourse in eWOM communications from a gender perspective. Technol. Forecast. Soc. Chang. **129**, 131–142 (2018)

Tirunillai, S., Tellis, G.J.: Mining marketing meaning from online chatter: strategic brand analysis of big data using latent dirichlet allocation. J. Mark. Res. **51**(4), 463–479 (2014)

Townsend, L., Sathiaseelan, A., Gorry, F., Wallace, C.: Enhanced broadband access as a solution to the social and economic problems of the rural digital divide. Local Econ. **28**(6), 580–595 (2013)

Wang, J.N., Du, J.Z., Chiu, Y.L.: Can online user reviews be more helpful? evaluating and improving ranking approaches. Inf. Manag. **57**, 103281 (2020)

# AI-Driven User Interface Design for Solving a Rubik's Cube: A Scaffolding Design Perspective

Dezhi Wu[1]([✉])(iD), Hengtao Tang[2], Cassidy Bradley[1], Brittany Capps[1], Prathamjeet Singh[1], Katelyn Wyandt[1], Karen Wong[1], Matthew Irvin[2], Forest Agostinelli[1], and Biplav Srivastava[1]

[1] College of Engineering and Computing, University of South Carolina, Columbia, SC 29208, USA
dezhiwu@cec.sc.edu
[2] College of Education, University of South Carolina, Columbia, SC 29208, USA

**Abstract.** In this paper, we describe an AI-driven platform, ALLURE, with an embodied chatbot that teaches the user how to solve a Rubik's Cube. Our AI algorithm consists of macro-actions, which refer to a set of moves that are not transparent or usable to users as a black box. Through the integration of explainable AI and conversational user interface designs, we created a novel AI-driven visual user interface inspired by scaffolding design paradigms to engage users. We conducted a set of initial usability testing with ten users, and usability findings imply some important AI-driven user interface designs to engage users for problem solving.

**Keywords:** Human-AI interaction · HAI · Chatbot · Conversational user interface · CAI · Multimodal interaction · Explainable artificial intelligence · XAI · Pathfinding · Human-computer interaction · HCI · AI

## 1 Introduction

Recent technological innovation, especially with the advancement in artificial intelligence (AI), has changed how we live, work, and learn. The primary challenge is that AI technology is still mainly a black box that cannot directly engage users, so having explainable and trustworthy AI is critical to making a real impact. Integrating AI into education is a promising way to transform today's education [1] due to its capability to uncover the most efficient ways of problem-solving. Drawing upon a knowledge base grounded in large volumes of data, AI can adapt to its end user, thereby identifying and improving student learning patterns [2]. Although AI-transformed education is promising, we have only scratched the surface of this new phenomenon. There are many unknowns concerning how AI is built into the learning system, and what AI-driven user interface design can effectively engage learners to learn and why. Thus, we are motivated to create a novel design strategy through a scaffolding design paradigm that decodes the

M. Kurosu et al. (Eds.): HCII 2022, LNCS 13516, pp. 490–498, 2022.
https://doi.org/10.1007/978-3-031-17615-9_34

black box of AI through an AI-enabled platform called ALLURE with an embodied chatbot (Fig. 1). Our goals are to not only guide users to use AI, but to also engage users in learning by solving complicated problems, such as solving a Rubik's Cube. Our use case, the Rubik's cube, has $4.3 \times 10^{19}$ possible configurations, and each method for solving has its own high-level step-by-step plan and algorithms for achieving that plan [3]. While AI is often able to solve a Rubik's cube and solve it in the most efficient way [3], the complexity of the solutions often surpasses AI's ability to explain these solutions [4]. This problem-solving is facilitated by a multimodal chatbot design embedded in the ALLURE platform with visualized scaffolds (Fig. 2, Fig. 3, and Fig. 4).

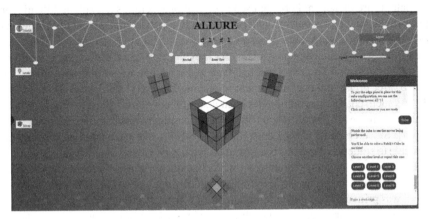

**Fig. 1.** AI-Enabled ALLURE platform snapshot.

In this paper, we will first conduct a brief literature review, and then explain our user interface design. Following our usability study description and the preliminary usability testing results, we will provide AI-driven chatbot design implications and future directions for this research.

## 2  Literature Review

The concept of scaffolding is rooted in works by Vygotsky on social constructivism [5], especially his influential notion about the zone of proximal development [5]. Scaffolding is defined as providing learners with instructional support to obtain knowledge/skills or complete academic tasks that they otherwise cannot accomplish [6, 7]. Research has indicated that scaffolding helps college students understand advanced concepts [8], solve complex problems [9], and develop higher order thinking skills [10]. Specifically, scaffolding supports student learning by providing conceptual, strategic metacognitive, and motivational support [6, 11]. Conceptual scaffolding provides students with guidance on knowledge or concepts relevant to the tasks at hand [9], while strategic scaffolding, usually in the form of questions and prompts, engages students to search for efficient problem-solving strategies for those tasks [11]. Metacognitive scaffolding prompts students to metacognitively monitor and control their problem-solving progress as they complete tasks [6, 12], and motivational scaffolding students' interest and self-efficacy in solving a problem [12]. Various types of scaffolding may tap into different aspects of learning. For example, the meta-analysis on various types of scaffolding by Kim et al. [12] indicates that conceptual scaffolding can improve student cognitive outcomes, but it is inferior to strategic scaffolding and metacognitive scaffolding in this aspect. In addition, Kim et al. [11, 12] found that strategic scaffolding and metacognitive scaffolding develop students' higher order thinking skills. In this study, we focused on four types of scaffolding--conceptual, motivational strategic, and metacognitive scaffolding--and integrated them into our developed system. Namely, we used an embodied chatbot to teach users how to solve a Rubik's Cube on the ALLURE platform.

Chatbots are increasingly being used in educational settings to explain difficult concepts, provide practice problems, and offer tailored feedback to learners [14]. They can also help students monitor their progress and stay on top of their assignments when integrated in learning management systems. As they develop, chatbots are expected to not only adopt colloquial language and language patterns that are similar to humans [15], but also offer praise and encouragement in response to users' successful completion of tasks. As such, chatbot instruction has been just as, if not more, effective than traditional instructor training [16], and students often prefer learning with chatbots over other methods [14]. Since chatbots can be customized in aspects like pace and content, they are accessible to students of various backgrounds, experience levels, and learning styles [14, 15]. Furthermore, students who interact with chatbots are generally more interested and intrinsically motivated than those in traditional learning settings [17]. In this study, our chatbot was primarily designed to provide users with scaffolding that engages users and provide feedback for complicated problem-solving tasks, i.e., solving a Rubik's Cube.

While current literature surveys the affordances of chatbots in academic environments, little research has focused on the use of chatbots for extra-curricular learning that takes place outside of the classroom. To that point, most chatbots are intended to deliver a set type or amount of content, usually through modules or step-by-step instruction. What's more, these chatbots tend to assume all learners are novices with the same level of background knowledge and therefore require them to start at the same place and work through the same content. Finally, existing chatbots combine multimodal elements like text, images, video, and audio [18], but do not incorporate engaging AI that users can interact with in real time. The ALLURE platform fills these gaps in the literature by using a chatbot to help users solve a Rubik's cube. Unlike academic content that is required by teachers for class credit or a grade, the content in the ALLURE platform relates to an activity users choose to pursue in their leisure time. With an optional tutorial and levels that are accessible in any order and at any time, the interface is also designed for learners with varying degrees of background knowledge; Thus, we designed a set of *conceptual scaffoldings* to support users on the ALLURE platform (Fig. 2). Plus, while the chatbot on the ALLURE platform does offer step-by-step instruction with motivational scaffolding, the goal is for users to gain foundational knowledge about the Rubik's cube that they can later apply when engaging with cubes outside of the platform (Fig. 4). Finally, in addition to text and static images, the ALLURE platform implements *metacognitive scaffolding* through highlighting and 3D movements to engage users, as well as arrows that initiate *strategic scaffolding mechanisms* to teach users how to solve problems on a Rubik's cube (Fig. 3 and Fig. 4).

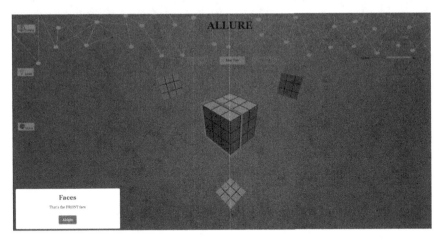

**Fig. 2.** ALLURE platform tutorial design

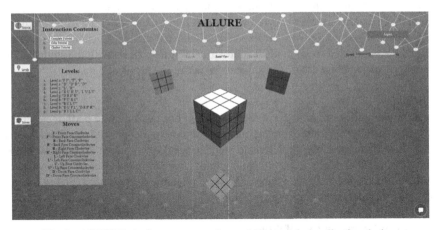

**Fig. 3.** ALLURE platform macro-action and 3D model visualization designs

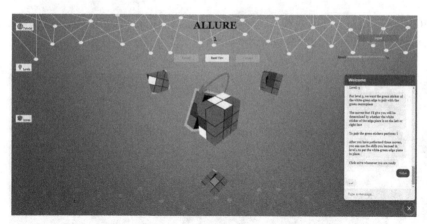

**Fig. 4.** ALLURE platform arrow and highlighting visualization and chatbot design

## 3 Usability Study Design and Preliminary Results

A concurrent mixed-methods study was conducted, with quantitative and qualitative data being collected and analyzed separately to gain an integrated understanding of college students' perception of the effectiveness of the chatbot in our ALLURE system [19]. Quantitative research used a validated chatbot usability scale with a focus on inquiring about students' perception of their experience with the chatbot. Qualitative inquiries included data collected by individual semi-structured interviews with the students, the researchers' observation notes, and students' think-aloud protocol data.

### Participants
A total of ten college students were recruited from our institution to participate in this study. The participants' demographics and their prior experience with the Rubik's cube varied. Five male students, four female students, and one student who chose not to specify their gender, were included. Additionally, five participants rated themselves as intermediate skill-level Rubik's cube users, two rated themselves as skilled users, and three rated themselves as beginners.

### AI Platform Design and Scaffolding
Scaffoldings were provided via the chatbot for the participants to solve problems on a Rubik's cube. The problem in this study was solving a Rubik's Cube white cross. To support the participants, four types of scaffolding were available: conceptual, motivational, metacognitive and strategic [6, 11]. Specifically, conceptual scaffolding was given by providing an explicit tutorial on solving problems via relevant "moves" on the Rubik's cube [12] (Fig. 2). These tutorials presented essential information the participants needed to solve the problem. Using motivational scaffolding techniques, the embodied chatbot would serve as a virtual tutor to motivate and engage users. Strategic scaffolding was also provided via the function of macro actions (see Fig. 3). Macro actions showcased the strategies that can be used to solve the problem, including identifying the problem, representing the problem, and developing the solutions to the problem. Participants were

able to interact with macro actions, which informed the participants of efficient strategies to solve the problem. Metacognitive scaffolding was delivered via arrows that recorded the moves completed by the participants (see Fig. 4). By tracking the moves, the arrows were expected to engage the participants in both metacognitive monitoring and control to identify what they had completed and whether they were on the right track towards solving the problem.

**Data Collection**

The instruments used to collect quantitative and qualitative data in this round of usability testing sought to gauge users' experience with chatbots and seek their perception of the usability of the chatbot. Particularly, the Chatbot Usability Scale [20] was used to collect quantitative data, while researcher observation notes and post-interview protocols were used to collect qualitative data. The chatbot usability scale included five-point Likert-type scale items with a focus on the participants' perceived usefulness, perceived ease of use, perceived ease for learning, satisfaction, effectiveness, and their experience with the chatbot. For qualitative data, each interview was semi-structured with an interview protocol provided and recorded for 45 to 60 min. Each interview was audio- or video-recorded per the consent of the participants. The interview was transcribed using an online transcription service, Otter.ai, and validated by three of the researchers with an acceptable level of mutual agreement. Observation notes were taken by the research team while observing the usability testing experience. Then, the researchers reviewed their notes together to mitigate any disparities.

**Data Analysis**

Quantitative data was assessed using the descriptive statistics to determine the participants' perception of their experience with the chatbot and also the usability of the chatbot. For qualitative data, thematic analysis [19] was conducted to seek the participants' perceptions. In the end, the findings from two sources of data were integrated to evaluate the effectiveness of the chatbot in scaffolding the participants' problem solving on the Rubik's cube.

**Results**

**Table 1.** User survey results

| Constructs | Mean | Standard deviation |
|---|---|---|
| Perceived usefulness | 3.26 | 1.20 |
| Perceived ease of use | 3.7 | 1.19 |
| Perceived ease of learning | 4.27 | 0.91 |
| User satisfaction | 3.31 | 1.22 |
| Chatbot effectiveness | 3.85 | 1.20 |

Overall, the participants reported a moderate-to-positive perception of the usability of the ALLURE platform with an embodied chatbot (Table 1). Specifically, the mean value for each subscale fell in the range between neutral (3) and agree (4). Participants found it easy to use the chatbot for learning (M = 4.27, SD = 0.91), but their perception of the usefulness and the ease of use for the chatbot as well as their satisfaction with the chatbot remained at a moderate level, indicating room for user interface improvement.

## 4 Study Findings and AI-Driven User Interface Design Implications for Problem-Solving Domains

Our preliminary usability study findings for the ALLURE platform and its embodied chatbot design provide important design implications for AI, HCI, and education researchers as well as user interface/user experience design practitioners who are interested in using the problem-solving domain to effectively engage users. Since we implemented scaffolding design strategies for this project, this study contributes to the emerging human-AI interaction field through a novel theoretical lens. We highlight our design implications in multiple ways:

(1) Using different types of *scaffolding mechanisms* for the user interface design, we can holistically engage users in learning hard concepts. Then, through interacting with AI algorithms, we can help users foster their own novel problem-solving solutions at different phases of the learning processes through interacting with the AI algorithms. For example, implementing conceptual scaffolding designs for hints and key notions allows users, especially novice users, to be more engaged and comfortable during the initial learning phase. This is critical for complicated problem-solving, as initial cognitive engagement can be intimidating for those who are not familiar with the problem. Our usability study implies that, through effective conceptual scaffolding designs, users will gradually place trust in the AI system and gain the confidence they need to prepare for the cognitively demanding problem-solving task. When users begin the learning process and require more explicit hints or guidance, metacognitive scaffolding can effectively bridge the gap between the problem and the users. If users need more directional guidance, strategic scaffolding designs can provide additional hints to guide them towards problem-solving without providing direct solutions.

(2) Engaging and retaining users for complicated problem-solving is a challenge, and thus motivational scaffolding strategies are critical. In our study, we implemented a novel AI-driven chatbot that works in synchronization with the AI algorithm to enable useful feedback when users require more information for their problem-solving. Additionally, using more human-like conversations, such as "John, great job!" and "Ah, don't be frustrated, let's try another alternative" further intrigues and encourages users in problem-solving. Users are also more likely to feel less embarrassed or judged with a chatbot than they might be with a human tutor, especially when they are stuck. Therefore, our study established a solid use case that begins to transparentize the black box of AI for complicated problem-solving, while identifying novel scaffolding design strategies to engage users in that learning process.

(3) Explainable AI (XAI) and trustworthy user interfaces are also critical to bridge the gap between AI and humans in educational settings. Our case study offers some insightful XAI design implications for human-AI interactions in problem-solving. First, user interface designs must establish trust in order to engage the user. In our usability testing, users perceived that XAI algorithms efficiently explained the solutions. For example, one user indicated that an algorithm that helped the user solve a Rubik's Cube in a more efficient way would be useful. One user stated, "Yes, I saw one (Rubik's Cube), like five years ago, and I was confused. Well, now that I understand what the commands mean, yeah. I think the ALLURE program gives me a good foundation." Second, the ability of user interface designs to explain the underlying rationale in an explicit and concise way will further in complicated problem solving engage users. As an example, one of users said "[About the moves and explanations] Oh, I liked having both. I like that it explained what was happening and then kind of broke it down to just that. Like the letters because then you got your brain thinking like that. Just the shorthand of it." Third, to make user engagement most effective, user interface designers need to carefully pace each step to account for user processing. In our case, a few users felt the learning process moved too quickly, which prevented them from fully understanding the tasks. A user control design thus needs to be in place, so users can personalize their problem-solving process. Fourth, user feedback design plays a key role in retaining users during the problem-solving process. We observed that users would get frustrated if they could not elicit a human-like answer from our chatbot, since they expected the interface to function similarly to a human tutor. Thus, we need "conversational user interfaces to integrate" more advanced human-AI interaction, natural language processing, machine learning and pedagogical design strategies to satisfy users' needs.

## 5 Future Research

Based on the current usability findings, we plan to conduct a large, controlled user experiment to empirically examine the effectiveness of our AI-driven platform along with its embodied chatbot for optimal user engagement and problem-solving outcomes. Overall, our study laid the foundation for human-AI interaction research on complicated problem-solving. Our Rubik's Cube use case offers inspiring insights to advancing this emerging and exciting field.

**Acknowledgement.** The authors would like to acknowledge the generous funding support from ASPIRE II grant at the University of South Carolina (U of SC), and partial funding support provided by UofSC's Grant No: 80002838.

## References

1. Cheng, X., Sun, J., Zarifis, A.: Artificial intelligence and deep learning in educational technology research and practice. Br. J. Edu. Technol. **51**(5), 1653–1656 (2020). https://doi.org/10.1111/bjet.13018

2. Beardsley, M., Santos, P., Hernández-Leo, D., Michos, K.: Ethics in educational technology research: Informing participants on data sharing risks. Br. J. Edu. Technol. **50**(3), 1019–1034 (2019)

3. Agostinelli, F., et al.: Designing Children's new learning partner: collaborative artificial intelligence for learning to solve the rubik's cube. In: Interaction Design and Children, pp. 610–614. Athens, Greece (2021). https://doi.org/10.1145/3459990.3465175

4. Agostinelli, F., Panta, R., Khandelwal, V., Srivastava, B., Muppasani, B., Wu D.: Explainable Pathfinding for Inscrutable Planners with Inductive Logic Programming (2022)

5. Vygotsky, L.S.: Mind in Society: The Development of Higher Psychological Processes. Harvard University Press (1978)

6. Belland, B.R., Glazewski, K.D., Richardson, J.C.: A scaffolding framework to support the construction of evidence-based arguments among middle school students. Educ. Tech. Res. Dev. **56**(4), 401–422 (2008)

7. Wood, D., Bruner, J.S., Ross, G.: The role of tutoring in problem solving. J. Child Psychol. Psychiatry, **17**(2), 89–100 (1976). https://doi.org/10.1111/j.1469-7610.1976.tb00381.x

8. Lange, C., Gorbunova, A., Shmeleva, E., Costley, J.: The relationship between instructional scaffolding strategies and maintained situational interest. Interactive Learn. Environ. 1–12 (2022)

9. González-Calero, J.A., Arnau, D., Puig, L., Arevalillo-Herráez, M.: Intensive scaffolding in an intelligent tutoring system for the learning of algebraic word problem solving. Br. J. Edu. Technol. **46**(6), 1189–1200 (2015)

10. Hannafin, M., Land, S., Oliver, K.: Open learning environments: foundations, methods, and models. Instruct.-Des. Theor. Mod. New Paradigm Instruct. Theory **2**, 115–140 (1999)

11. Kim, N.J., Vicentini, C.R., Belland, B.R.: Influence of scaffolding on information literacy and argumentation skills in virtual field trips and problem-based learning for scientific problem solving. Int. J. Sci. Math. Educ. **20**(2), 215–236 (2022)

12. Kim, N.J., Belland, B.R., Walker, A.E.: Effectiveness of computer-based scaffolding in the context of problem-based learning for STEMeducation: Bayesian meta-analysis. Educ. Psychol. Rev. **30**(2), 397–429 (2018)

13. Kim, N.J., Belland, B.R., Lefler, M., Andreasen, L., Walker, A., Axelrod, D.: Computer-based scaffolding targeting individual versus groups in problem-centered instruction for STEM education: meta-analysis. Educ. Psychol. Rev. **32**(2), 415–461 (2020)

14. Cai, W., et al.: Bandit algorithms to personalize educational chatbots. Mach. Learn. **110**(9), 2389–2418 (2021). https://doi.org/10.1007/s10994-021-05983-y

15. Gupta, & Chen, Y.: Supporting inclusive learning using chatbots? A chatbot-led interview study. J. Inf. Syst. Educ. **33**(1), 98–108 (2022)

16. Yuan, C.C., Li, C.-H., Peng, C.-C.: (in press). Development of mobile interactive courses based on an artificial intelligence chatbot on the communication software LINE. Interactive Learn. Environ. 1–15 (2021)

17. Yin, J., Goh, T.-T., Yang, B., Xiaobin, Y.: Conversation technology with micro-learning: the impact of chatbot-based learning on students' learning motivation and performance. J. Educ. Comput. Res. **59**(1), 154–177 (2021)

18. Jain, M., et al.: FarmChat: A conversational agent to answer farmer queries. Assoc. Comput. Mach. **2**(4), 1-22 (2019)

19. Borsci, S., et al.: The chatbot usability scale: the design and pilot of a usability scale for interaction with AI-Based conversational agents. Pers. Ubiquit. Comput. **26**(1), 95–119 (2022)

20. Creswell, J.W., Plano Clark, V.L.: Designing and Conducting Mixed Methods Research (3rd ed.). Sage (2018)

# Mobile Applications Usability Evaluation: Systematic Review and Reappraisal

Jiabei Wu and Vincent G. Duffy[(✉)]

Purdue University, West Lafayette, IN 47906, USA
{wu1660,duffy}@purdue.edu

**Abstract.** To be more competitive in the mobile applications market, designing the mobile applications that users tend to use is of great significance. Usability plays an indispensable role in affecting usage intention. Therefore, mobile applications usability evaluation is vital in the designing process. This report is a systematic review of mobile applications usability evaluation by bibliometric analysis. We used Scopus and Web of Science to search documents. Trend analysis, co-occurrence keywords analysis, co-authorship analysis, co-citation analysis, leading table, and word cloud were conducted to do the systematic review. Research related to this topic has become popular in recent years. Mobile applications usability can be influenced by the user, environment, task/activity, and technology, evaluated by different usability attributes from different perspectives, and influence technology acceptance, adoption, retention, etc. [7] Lab experiments and field study were frequently used mobile applications usability evaluation methods [5–7]. The subjective questionnaire, such as SUS (System Usability Scale) [12] and USE (Usefulness, Satisfaction, Ease of use) questionnaire [17], were frequently applied to investigate participants' subjective feelings after using mobile applications. Another subjective method is the heuristic evaluation [15]. Then, objective metrics, such as task completion time, task completion rate, time spent on the first use, and so on, were frequently used in mobile applications usability evaluation [5, 6, 35]. In future work, we can find papers from more databases and include more papers in the literature review. Next, differences in contexts, users, and goals, should be considered in mobile applications usability evaluation. Finally, security is a prominent factor in mobile applications development.

**Keywords:** Mobile applications · Usability · Evaluation · Bibliometric analysis

## 1 Introduction

Mobile devices are widely used in our daily life and lead to the rapid development of mobile applications [1]. The commonly used mobile applications include mobile commerce, mobile social media, mobile health, and so on [2]. From the perspective of mobile application developers, designing the mobile application that people tend to use is of great significance in the highly competitive market. Based on TAM3 (Technology Acceptance Model 3), objective usability is one determinant of the perceived ease of use and then influence the perceived usefulness and usage intention of technology [3].

© The Author(s), under exclusive license to Springer Nature Switzerland AG 2022
M. Kurosu et al. (Eds.): HCII 2022, LNCS 13516, pp. 499–516, 2022.
https://doi.org/10.1007/978-3-031-17615-9_35

Therefore, usability has an indirect influence on the usage intention. To enhance the usage intention, usability improvement is an effective way, and research related to mobile applications usability evaluation has become popular.

Based on the definition by International Organization for Standardization, usability is the ability that the system can enable a specific user to accomplish a specific goal under a specific context [4]. Wei & Dong defined the mobile system usability as the ability that the mobile system helps the user meet the intended goals under a specific context [2]. Compared to the usability evaluation of other systems, the following issues should be considered in the context of mobile applications due to the characteristic of mobile devices [5–7]. The first issue is the small screen size [2, 5–7]. Because of the limited size of the screen, what information should be displayed [2] and how to effectively organize the information are essential in improving mobile applications usability. The second issue is the mobile context [5, 6]. Mobile applications are frequently used in the dynamic environment that contains many interactions between the user and the context [5, 6]. For example, when using the mobile map app while driving, driver should pay attention to both road condition and mobile map app. The third issue is the input method [2, 5–7]. This issue is due to the small screen size [2, 5, 6]. Buttons on mobile devices can't be as large as other devices due to the screen size constraint. However, the small button can increase the operation difficulty and errors, and lower the input speed and efficiency [6]. The remaining issues include connectivity [5, 6], display resolution [5–7], etc.

This report is a systematic review related to mobile applications usability evaluation by bibliometric analysis. Scopus and Web of Science were applied to search literature. Three tools, including VOSviewer, CiteSpace, and MAXQDA, were used in this report to do the bibliometric analysis. This part is the introduction, which comprises the background information and topics were going to analyze. The second part shows the procedure of searching related documents and search results. The third section is the analyses results. The fourth section is the discussion. The fifth section is the conclusion, which presents the main work in this report. The last section is the future work, which points out possible directions for further research.

## 2 Procedure

In this report, documents related to mobile applications usability evaluation were analyzed. Scopus and Web of Science were used for searching papers. The published year is between 2010 to 2021. There are three search terms, including mobile applications, usability, and evaluation. Table 1 is the search results. Based on Table 1, more papers can be found in Scopus.

**Table 1.** Table of databases and search results.

| Topic | Database | Year | Search terms | Number of papers |
|---|---|---|---|---|
| Mobile applications usability evaluation | Scopus | 2010–2021 | Mobile applications, usability, evaluation | 1174 |
| | Web of Science | | | 292 |

After searching papers, trend diagram was generated based on the number of documents per year. Next, co-occurrence keyword analysis, co-authorship analysis, and co-citation analysis were performed in VOSviewer based on the search results. Moreover, CiteSpace is another effective tool for doing the co-citation analysis. Then, leading authors and leading sources related to mobile applications usability evaluation were summarized based on the papers searched by Scopus. Finally, the word cloud was generated by MAXQDA.

## 3   Results

### 3.1   Trend Analysis

Papers searched by two databases were analyzed. Figure 1 shows the number of documents per year. For the papers searched by Scopus, the number of published papers in each year almost keeps increasing from 2010 to 2019, decreases in 2020, and increases again in 2021. For the papers searched by Web of Science, the number of published papers in each year decreases from 2010 to 2012, increases from 2013 to 2017, decreases in 2018 and 2020, and increases in 2019 and 2021. The almost increasing trend represents the popularity of this topic in recent research.

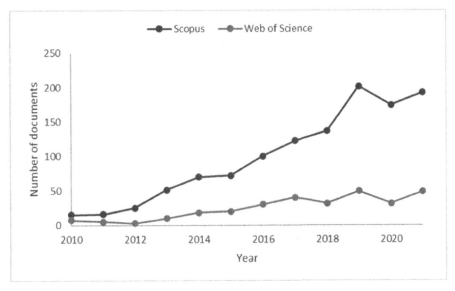

**Fig. 1.**   Trend diagram based on the number of documents per year from 2010 to 2021.

### 3.2   Co-occurrence Keywords Analysis

Papers searched above were used to do the co-occurrence keyword analysis. The minimum occurrence for each term was 20. Next, 342 terms were selected based on the papers searched by Scopus and 64 terms by Web of Science. Then, 205 terms based on Scopus and 38 terms by Web of Science were chosen as the most relevant terms. Figure 2 is the co-occurrence keyword diagram based on Scopus, and Fig. 3 is the co-occurrence keyword diagram based on Web of Science.

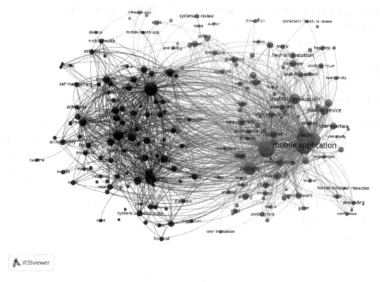

**Fig. 2.** Co-occurrence keyword diagram based on Scopus.

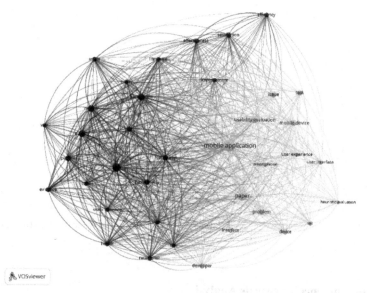

**Fig. 3.** Co-occurrence keyword diagram based on Web of Science.

Figure 2 and Fig. 3 are the co-occurrence keyword diagrams related to mobile applications usability evaluation. In the co-occurrence keyword diagram, the term circle size is related to the occurrence times in these papers' abstracts or titles [8]. The term circle size will be large if this term appear frequently in the title or abstract of papers [8]. "Mobile application" has the most considerable circle size in Fig. 2 and Fig. 3, which indicates this term is most frequently occurred in the abstract or title based on the documents searched by two databases. Next, the distance between two terms would be closer if they frequently co-occurred [8]. For example, the distance between "mobile health" and "diabete" in Fig. 2 and the distance between "effectiveness" and "satisfaction" in Fig. 3 are close, which means they frequently co-occurred in papers. Then, terms with the same color were divided into the same cluster, and the terms in the same cluster had a similar research topic [8]. For instance, Fig. 2 has four clusters and Fig. 3 has three clusters. In Fig. 2, there are many terms related to mobile health in the red cluster, such as "mobile health", "mhealth", "diabete", "patient", "treatment", and so on, which represent the main topic in this cluster. In Fig. 3, three terms are related to usability evaluation attributes in the blue cluster, including "efficiency", "effectiveness", and "satisfaction".

To be more clear about the importance of different terms, terms were ranked by occurrence generated from VOSviewer. Table 2 shows the top terms searched by co-occurrence keyword analysis based on two databases. The top terms based on the documents searched by Scopus are "Mobile application", "Application", "Paper", "App", "System", "Participant", "Usability evaluation", "Patient", "Model", and "Score". The top terms based on the documents searched by Web of Science are "Mobile application", "Paper", "App", "Usability evaluation", "Quality", "Participant", "Review", "Mobile device", "Patient", and "Problem".

**Table 2.** Table of the top terms by co-occurrence keyword analysis in VOSviewer.

| Scopus top occurrence term | Occurrence | WOS top occurrence term | Occurrence |
| --- | --- | --- | --- |
| Mobile application | 703 | Mobile application | 217 |
| Application | 645 | Paper | 115 |
| Paper | 421 | App | 98 |
| App | 421 | Usability evaluation | 71 |
| System | 368 | Quality | 63 |
| Participant | 278 | Participant | 62 |
| Usability evaluation | 254 | Review | 60 |
| Patient | 242 | Mobile device | 58 |
| Model | 190 | Patient | 51 |
| Score | 179 | Problem | 51 |

### 3.3 Co-authorship Analysis

The papers searched above were used for the co-authorship analysis, and the analysis was conducted by VOSviewer. The minimum number of documents was 3. Finally, 122 authors were selected based on Scopus, and 17 authors were selected based on Web of Science. Figure 4 and Fig. 6 are the detail of the co-authorship diagrams, and Fig. 5 and Fig. 7 are the co-authorship diagrams. In the co-authorship diagram, the size of the circle indicates the number of documents the author has [9]. For the papers searched by Scopus, Hussain A has 41 papers with the largest circle in Fig. 5. For the papers searched by Web of Science, Hussain A is also the leading author based on the circle size and the number of documents. Total link strength in this part represents the sum of link strength the author has [10]. Hussain A has the most significant total link strength in both papers searched by Scopus and Web of Science.

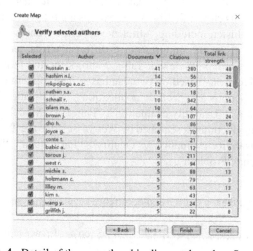

**Fig. 4.** Detail of the co-authorship diagram based on Scopus.

**Fig. 5.** Co-authorship diagram based on Scopus.

| Selected | Author | Documents ⌄ | Citations | Total link strength |
|---|---|---|---|---|
| ☑ | hussain, azham | 11 | 53 | 12 |
| ☑ | cho, hwayoung | 4 | 43 | 4 |
| ☑ | schnall, rebecca | 4 | 43 | 4 |
| ☑ | barker, trevor | 3 | 15 | 9 |
| ☑ | caro-alvaro, sergio | 3 | 6 | 9 |
| ☑ | de-marcos, luis | 3 | 6 | 9 |
| ☑ | garcia-cabot, antonio | 3 | 6 | 9 |
| ☑ | garcia-lopez, eva | 3 | 6 | 9 |
| ☑ | jefferies, amanda | 3 | 15 | 9 |
| ☑ | joyce, ger | 3 | 15 | 9 |
| ☑ | lilley, mariana | 3 | 15 | 9 |
| ☑ | mohd, haslina | 3 | 14 | 6 |
| ☑ | zahra, fatima | 3 | 14 | 6 |
| ☑ | hashim, nor laily | 3 | 18 | 3 |
| ☑ | mkpojiogu, emmanuel o. c. | 3 | 10 | 3 |
| ☑ | idri, ali | 3 | 271 | 0 |
| ☑ | soui, makram | 3 | 13 | 0 |

Create Map ✕

Verify selected authors

< Back    Next >    Finish    Cancel

**Fig. 6.** Detail of the co-authorship diagram based on Web of Science.

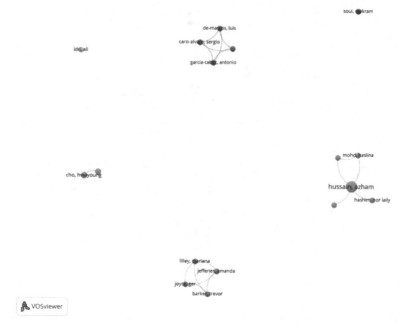

**Fig. 7.** Co-authorship diagram based on Web of Science.

## 3.4   Co-citation Analysis

Papers searched by Scopus were used. The minimum number of citations was 7, and 12 cited references were selected. Figure 8 is the co-citation diagram, and Fig. 9 is the selected references. In Fig. 8, 12 cited references were divided into 7 clusters. From Fig. 9, paper [6] has the enormous citations and total link strength, which indicates the importance of this paper in this area. Since the information of one paper in Fig. 8 is not adequate, we selected 11 papers (6 clusters) in Fig. 9 for further analysis.

The first cluster contains three papers which are related to SUS [11–13]. Brooke developed SUS to conduct the effective usability evaluation in different contexts [12], and conducted a review of SUS in 2013 [13]. There are ten statements in SUS and participants are required to fill in the questionnaire based on their user experience immediately after using a system in the experiment [12]. Bangor et al. investigated the relationship between SUS score and usability by adding one statement in SUS [11]. The second cluster contains three papers which focus on the usability evaluation model [5, 6, 14]. Paper [5] and [6] are reviews of mobile applications usability evaluation model, which have discussed usability evaluation methods, usability evaluation attributes, and so on. Seffah et al. proposed an integrated usability evaluation model by considering the existing usability evaluation models [14]. The third cluster has two papers [7, 15]. Coursaris & Kim conducted a review related to mobile applications usability evaluation based on previous empirical studies [7]. Nielsen & Molich used heuristic evaluation to search for usability problems in different user interfaces [15]. The remaining three clusters contain one paper each [16–18]. Bangor et al. analyzed SUS based on empirical studies and testified the effectiveness of SUS [16]. Lund proposed the USE questionnaire, which is also a subjective usability evaluation questionnaire [17]. Stoyanov et al. designed MARS (Mobile App Rating Scale) to testify the usability of mobile health [18].

**Fig. 8.** Co-citation diagram based on Scopus.

**Fig. 9.** Selected papers in Fig. 8.

Another effective tool is CiteSpace. In this part, papers searched by the second database were used. Figure 10 is the co-citation diagram by CiteSpace. This figure is part of the co-citation diagram. In Fig. 10, some nodes were marked with the author name and year, and some clusters were marked with keywords. In this figure, several keywords, "mobile applications", "usability testing", "digital psychiatry", "health care evaluation mechanisms", "older adults", "technology acceptance", "software", and "information technology" were identified. Moreover, citation burst in CiteSpace is an effective way to search essential papers on the given topic. As shown in Fig. 11, four important papers related to mobile applications usability evaluation were found, and three of them [5, 7, 18] were identified in Fig. 9. The red line in Fig. 11 represents the paper that was frequently cited during these years [19]. For instance, the paper written by Harrison et al. [5] was frequently cited from 2016 to 2018.

**Fig. 10.** Co-citation diagram by Citespace based on Web of Science.

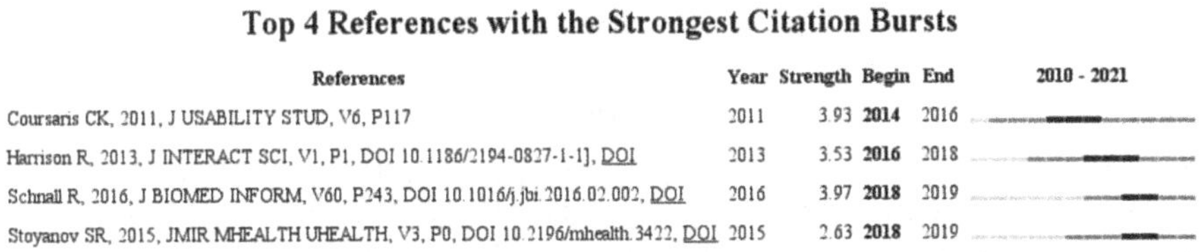

**Top 4 References with the Strongest Citation Bursts**

| References | Year | Strength | Begin | End | 2010 - 2021 |
|---|---|---|---|---|---|
| Coursaris CK, 2011, J USABILITY STUD, V6, P117 | 2011 | 3.93 | **2014** | 2016 | |
| Harrison R, 2013, J INTERACT SCI, V1, P1, DOI 10.1186/2194-0827-1-1], DOI | 2013 | 3.53 | **2016** | 2018 | |
| Schnall R, 2016, J BIOMED INFORM, V60, P243, DOI 10.1016/j.jbi.2016.02.002, DOI | 2016 | 3.97 | **2018** | 2019 | |
| Stoyanov SR, 2015, JMIR MHEALTH UHEALTH, V3, P0, DOI 10.2196/mhealth.3422, DOI | 2015 | 2.63 | **2018** | 2019 | |

**Fig. 11.** Citation bursts based on Web of Science.

## 3.5 Leading Table

The first leading table is the leading author table based on papers searched by Scopus. This table is ranked by the number of papers that the author published between 2010–2021. From Table 3, Hussain A has the most significant number of published papers related to this topic from 2010 to 2021. The second leading table is the leading source table based on papers searched by Scopus. In Table 3 and Table 4, we can get both the leading information and the popular research topics for each leading author and source based on keywords. From Table 4, research related to mobile health was popular.

**Table 3.** Leading author table.

| Author (Scopus) | Keywords | Count |
|---|---|---|
| Hussain, A | Mobile application, Usability, Evaluation, Usability evaluation, Usability testing | 41 |
| Hashim, N.L | Mobile application, Evaluation, Usability, Deaf, Deaf people | 14 |
| Mkpojiogu, E.O.C | Mobile application, Mobile app, Perceived usability | 12 |
| Nathan, S.S | Mobile application, Usability model, Deaf, Deaf people, Usability evaluation model | 11 |
| Islam, M.N | Usability, Mobile applications, Mobile computing, Mobile application, Usability evaluation | 10 |

## 3.6 Word Cloud

Content analysis was conducted by MAXQDA. Four papers from Fig. 9 [5–7, 14] and two chapters related to mobile applications usability evaluation from the book [2, 20] were selected. In MAXQDA, the minimal frequency of words was 50, and the number of words in the image was 50. The word cloud was generated after removing some irrelevant words and repetitions. In the word cloud, the size of the term represents the occurrence of this term in the selected materials. In Fig. 12, the size of "usability" and "mobile" are large, which means these two terms frequently appear in the above documents.

**Table 4.** Leading source table.

| Source | Keywords | Count |
|---|---|---|
| Lecture notes in computer science including subseries lecture notes in artificial intelligence and Lecture notes in bioinformatics | Mobile applications, Human computer interaction, Usability engineering, Mobile computing, Usability evaluation | 87 |
| Jmir Mhealth and Uhealth | Mobile applications, Human, Humans, Mobile application, MHealth | 63 |
| Studies in Health Technology and Informatics | Mobile applications, Mobile application, Human, Humans, MHealth | 61 |
| ACM International Conference Proceeding Series | Mobile applications, Mobile computing, Usability evaluation, Usability engineering, Mobile application | 47 |
| Advance in Intelligent Systems and Computing | Mobile applications, Usability engineering, Mobile computing, Usability, Human engineering | 29 |

**Fig. 12.** Word cloud generated by MAXQDA.

# 4   Discussion

## 4.1   Mobile Applications Usability

Based on the definition by ISO, if one or more than one of these three factors (user, goal, and context) change, the usability of this system may be different [4]. Coursaris & Kim proposed a mobile usability framework [7]. Their mobile usability framework contains three layers. The first layer has four factors (user, environment, task/activity, and technology) that can influence mobile usability, the second layer includes several usability attributes that can represent mobile usability from different perspectives, and the third layer shows the effect of usability [7]. Some keywords identified by co-citation analysis in Fig. 10 is related to the above framework. For example, "older adults" is related to the user in the first layer, and "technology acceptance" is the effect of usability.

In the first layer, usability can be influenced by the above four factors. Users can be divided into different clusters based on their age, gender, culture, etc. [7] When asking different users to use the same system to complete the same task in the same context, system usability might be varied. Therefore, user difference should be considered in mobile applications usability evaluation to meet different groups' requirements. For example, some factors, such as visual acuity, hearing, memory, etc. should be emphasized when designing for the elderly [21]. Next, the usability of a system may not be the same due to the environment. Taking the mobile map app as an example, even though some mobile map apps are easy to use in a static environment, their usability might change when using in a dynamic environment, such as walking, driving, etc. Then, the task or activity has an impact on usability. With the increment of difficulty or number of tasks, the usability of mobile applications may be varied. Harrison et al. pointed out that mobile application developers tend to add additional functions to achieve as many goals as possible [5]. However, some redundant functions may have negative effects on the original and primary goals [5]. Finally, technology is an essential factor that can influence usability. In the framework proposed by Coursaris & Kim, technology contains device type and interface [7]. Mobile devices include mobile phones, tablets, and wearable devices [2, 22]. Kortum & Sorber found that the usability of phone applications is better than tablet applications [23]. The main difference between the phone and the tablet is the screen size. For the same mobile application, the tablet can display more information than the phone on one page. However, the large amount of information will lead to trouble in proper information selection and decreasing the usability. Additionally, mobile application developers consider more in the necessity of functions due to the limited screen size and capacity [23].

The second layer is the usability attributes. Table 5 shows the usability attributes in previous papers. The first and the second row of Table 5 are usability attributes, and the third and the last row of Table 5 are mobile applications usability attributes. Based on Table 5, the frequently used mobile applications usability attributes are effectiveness, efficiency, satisfaction, learnability, memorability, and error [4–6, 24]. Effectiveness evaluates the ability of mobile applications that can enable users to accomplish specified goals with completeness and accuracy [4–6]. Efficiency reflects the resources required to achieve goals with speed and accuracy [4–6, 24]. Satisfaction is the user's subjective feeling after using a specific mobile application [4–6, 24]. Learnability requires the mobile application should be easy to learn, and the user can achieve a specific level in using this mobile application in the short term [5, 6, 24]. Memorability represents the extent the user can use the mobile application after not using it for a given period [5, 6, 24]. Error can be calculated by the number of errors that occur in the usability testing, and well-designed mobile applications should promise the low error while using them [5, 6, 24].

**Table 5.** Usability attributes in previous papers.

| Paper | Usability attributes |
|-------|----------------------|
| [4]   | Effectiveness, Efficiency, Satisfaction |
| [24]  | Learnability, Efficiency, Memorability, Errors, Satisfaction |
| [5]   | Effectiveness, Efficiency, Satisfaction, Learnability, Memorability, Errors, Cognitive load |
| [6]   | Learnability, Efficiency, Memorability, Error, Satisfaction, Effectiveness, Simplicity, Comprehensibility, Learning performance |

The third layer is the effect of usability. Well-designed mobile applications can promise users to accomplish tasks with accuracy, speed, and low effort. Improving mobile applications usability can attract more users since people tend to use the easy operating mobile applications. Based on the model related to technology acceptance, objective usability is one factor that has an impact on perceived ease of use, and perceived ease of use is one attribute that can influence perceived usefulness and usage intention [3, 25]. Therefore, the usability improvement can stimulate and keep customers' usage intention of mobile applications.

### 4.2  Mobile Applications Usability Evaluation Methods

Lab experiment and field study are two frequently used mobile applications usability evaluation methods [5–7]. The difference between these two methods is the lab experiment is conducted in the controlled context while the field study is conducted in a real-world context [5, 6]. Moreover, it is easier to control and record the testing process in the lab experiment than in the field study [6].

After completing the tasks, participants' subjective feelings toward the usability of the mobile application can be collected by questionnaire. SUS is an effective way to do usability evaluation [12, 13] and is frequently used in mobile applications usability evaluation [26–29]. It contains ten statements that participants can assess the system usability from different perspectives and participants are required to grade each statement to show their agreement immediately after completing all tasks [12]. Nevertheless, how to use the final grade to interpret the usability is a question [11, 16]. Bangor et al. added one statement related to the overall feeling of the product in SUS, investigated the relationship between the SUS score and the overall feeling, and found they are highly co-related [11, 16]. USE questionnaire, which can evaluate usability from three perspectives, is another subjective usability evaluation questionnaire proposed by Lund [17]. There are several statements in each perspective and participants are required to grade each statement after using a product [17].

Another subjective method is heuristic evaluation. Heuristic evaluation is an effective and efficient way to do the software usability evaluation [30]. Participants can raise usability problems based on different heuristics and their user experience. Nilsen & Molich pointed out that five evaluators can find most of the usability problems based on nine interface usability heuristics, and more usability problems can be identified as the number of evaluators increases [15]. They also proposed ten interface usability heuristics in 1994, and the latest update was in 2020 [31]. However, usability heuristics proposed by Nilsen focused mainly on desktop interfaces rather than mobile applications, which should take the small screen size, input methods, and some other characteristics of mobile devices into consideration [32]. Therefore, Joyce & Lilley developed usability heuristics for mobile applications based on previous literature and experts' assessments [32]. Joyce et al. have also testified the effectiveness of their usability heuristics in identifying mobile applications usability problems [33]. Inostroza et al. have also contributed to the development of mobile applications usability heuristics [34].

Mobile applications usability can be evaluated by some objective metrics. Different metrics can evaluate mobile applications usability from different perspectives, such as effectiveness, efficiency, learnability, memorability, error, and so on [5, 6, 35]. For example, effectiveness is usually represented by the task completion rate, efficiency is often evaluated by task completion time and task success rate, learnability is frequently assessed by the time spent on achieving a specific level or the time spent on the first trial, memorability can be evaluated by the time spent on the second use, and error can be measured by the error frequency [5, 6, 35].

## 5  Conclusion

To be more competitive in the mobile applications market, research related to mobile applications usability evaluation has become popular. Therefore, this report analyzed this topic based on recent literature. From the trend analysis, the number of papers related to mobile applications usability evaluation searched by Scopus keeps increasing from 2010 to 2021, except for 2020. The increasing number of papers represents the popularity of this topic in recent years, customers' demands for mobile applications with high usability, and developers' awareness of improving the usability of mobile applications. Co-occurrence keyword analysis can indicate both the importance of each term and the relationship between different terms [8]. Based on the co-occurrence keyword analysis, some important terms were identified. What's more, different terms with a close relationship were also identified, such as mobile health and diabete. Co-authorship analysis and co-citation analysis have a similar function as the co-occurrence keyword analysis. In the co-authorship analysis, the importance of the author can be ranked by the number of documents, citations, and total link strength. The relationship between different authors can be assessed based on the distance and link in the co-authorship diagram. In this report, Hussain A has the most significant number of documents and total link strength in papers searched by both databases. Co-citation analysis was performed by VOSviewer and CiteSpace. Both tools can identify the frequently cited references and the relationship between different references. Additionally, citation burst generated by CiteSpace can represent the frequently cited references in different periods. Based on co-citation analysis, papers related to the usability evaluation model, SUS, USE questionnaire, and usability heuristics were identified. Then, two leading tables were constructed based on the number of documents the author had and the number of documents in each source. Finally, word cloud generated by MAXQDA was based on the previously searched materials, which shows the leading terms directly in the selected material.

## 6 Future Work

This report is a literature review on mobile applications usability evaluation based on bibliometric analysis methods. However, the papers analyzed in this report are limited since most are from the co-citation analysis based on two databases. Therefore, more databases can be used to search papers and more papers can be included in the review. Next, the mobile usability evaluation framework, including usability attributes and usability evaluation methods, might be different due to the different users, contexts, and goals. In future work, for mobile applications usability evaluation, the choice of usability attributes, evaluation methods, and evaluation heuristics, should be emphasized based on these differences. Finally, the objective of this topic is to detect and improve the usability problems that will influence technology acceptance during the design process. However, some other factors can influence technology acceptance either. One prominent factor related to mobile applications pointed out by Wei & Dong is security [2]. How to prevent security problems and recover immediately after encountering security problems to avoid loss are of great significance in future work.

## References

1. Hoehle, H., Viswanath, V.: Mobile application usability: conceptualization and instrument development. MIS Q. **39**(2), 435–472 (2015)
2. Wei, J., Dong, S.Y.: Mobile systems design and evaluation. In: Handbook of Human Factors and Ergonomics, 5th edn., pp. 1037–1057. Wiley, Hoboken (2021)
3. Venkatesh, V., Hillol, B.: Technology acceptance model 3 and a research agenda on interventions. Decis. Sci. **39**(2), 273–315 (2008)
4. International Organization for Standardization: Ergonomics of human-system interaction - Part 11: Usability: Definitions and concepts. https://www.iso.org/obp/ui/#iso:std:iso:9241:-11:ed-2:v1:en
5. Harrison, R., Derek, F., David, D.: Usability of mobile applications: literature review and rationale for a new usability model. J. Interact. Sci. **1**(1), 1–16 (2013)
6. Zhang, D.S., Boonlit, A.: Challenges, methodologies, and issues in the usability testing of mobile applications. Int. J. Hum. Comput. Interact. **18**(3), 293–308 (2005)
7. Coursaris, C.K., Kim, D.J.: A meta-analytical review of empirical mobile usability studies. J. Usability Stud. Arch. **6**, 117–171 (2011)
8. Ding, Y., Rousseau, R., Wolfram, D. (eds.): Measuring Scholarly Impact. Springer, Cham (2014). https://doi.org/10.1007/978-3-319-10377-8
9. Kurniawan, J., Duffy, V.G.: Systematic review of the importance of human factors in incorporating healthcare automation. In: Duffy, V.G. (ed.) HCII 2021. LNCS, vol. 12778, pp. 96–110. Springer, Cham (2021). https://doi.org/10.1007/978-3-030-77820-0_8
10. Van, E.N.J., Waltman, L.: VOSviewer Manual, pp. 1–54. Univeristeit Leiden, Leiden (2021)
11. Bangor, A., Kortum, P., Miller, J.: Determining what individual SUS scores mean: adding an adjective rating scale. J. Usability Stud. **4**(3), 114–123 (2009)
12. Brooke, J.: SUS - a quick and dirty usability scale. In: Usability Evaluation in Industry, vol. 189, no. 3 (1996)
13. Brooke, J.: SUS: a retrospective. J. Usability Stud. **8**(2), 29–40 (2013)
14. Seffah, A., Mohammad, D., Rex, B.K., Harkirat, K.P.: Usability measurement and metrics: a consolidated model. Softw. Qual. J. **14**(2), 159–178 (2006)

15. Nielsen, J., Molich, R.: Heuristic evaluation of user interfaces. In: Proceedings of the SIGCHI Conference on Human Factors in Computing Systems, pp. 249–256 (1990)
16. Bangor, A., Kortum, P.T., Miller, J.T.: An empirical evaluation of the system usability scale. Intl. J. Hum. Comput. Interact. **24**(6), 574–594 (2008)
17. Lund, A.M.: Measuring usability with the use questionnaire12. Usability Interface **8**(2), 3–6 (2001)
18. Stoyanov, S.R., Hides, L., Kavanagh, D.J., Zelenko, O., Tjondronegoro, D., Mani, M.: Mobile app rating scale: a new tool for assessing the quality of health mobile apps. JMIR mHealth uHealth **3**(1), e3422 (2015)
19. Chen, C.M.: The citespace manual. College of Computing and Informatics, pp. 1–84 (2014)
20. Lewis, J.R., Sauro, J.: Usability and user experience: design and evaluation. In: Handbook of Human Factors and Ergonomics, 5th edn., pp. 972–1015. Wiley, Hoboken (2021)
21. Holzinger, A., Searle, G., Nischelwitzer, A.: On some aspects of improving mobile applications for the elderly. In: Stephanidis, C. (ed.) UAHCI 2007. LNCS, vol. 4554, pp. 923–932. Springer, Heidelberg (2007). https://doi.org/10.1007/978-3-540-73279-2_103
22. Poynter, R.: The utilization of mobile technology and approaches in commercial market research. In: Mobile Research Methods, pp. 11–20. Ubiquity Press, London (2015)
23. Kortum, P., Sorber, M.: Measuring the usability of mobile applications for phones and tablets. Int. J. Hum. Comput. Interact. **31**(8), 518–529 (2015)
24. Nielsen, J.: Usability Engineering. AP Professional, Boston (1994)
25. Venkatesh, V.: Determinants of perceived ease of use: integrating control, intrinsic motivation, and emotion into the technology acceptance model. Inf. Syst. Res. **11**(4), 342–365 (2000)
26. Beul, L.S., Christian, S., Maximilian, W., Karl, H.K., Eva, M.J., Martina, Z.: Usability evaluation of mobile passenger information systems. In: Marcus, A. (ed.) Design, User Experience, and Usability. Theories, Methods, and Tools for Designing the User Experience, pp. 217–228. Springer, Cham (2014). https://doi.org/10.1007/978-3-319-07668-3_22
27. Arain, A.A., Hussain, Z., Rizvi, W.H., Vighio, M.S.: Evaluating usability of M-learning application in the context of higher education institute. In: International Conference on Learning and Collaboration Technologies, pp. 259–268. Springer, Cham (2016). https://doi.org/10.1007/978-3-319-39483-1_24
28. Islam, M.N., Khan, S.R., Islam, N.N., Rezwan, A.R.M., Zaman, S.R., Zaman, S.R.: A mobile application for mental health care during Covid-19 pandemic: development and usability evaluation with system usability scale. In: Suhaili, W.S.H., Siau, N.Z., Omar, S., Phon-Amuaisuk, S. (eds.) International Conference on Computational Intelligence in Information System, pp. 33–42. Springer, Cham (2021). https://doi.org/10.1007/978-3-030-68133-3_4
29. Islam, M. N., Karim, Md.M., Inan, T.T., Islam, A.K.A.M.: Investigating usability of mobile health applications in Bangladesh. BMC Med. Inf. Decis. Making **20**(1), 19 (2020)
30. Joyce, G., Lilley, M., Barker, T., Jefferies A.: Mobile application usability heuristics: decoupling context-of-use. In: Marcus, A., Wang, W. (eds.) Design, User Experience, and Usability: Theory, Methodology, and Management, pp. 410–423. Springer, Cham (2017). https://doi.org/10.1007/978-3-319-58634-2_30
31. Nielsen Norman Group: 10 Usability Heuristics for User Interface Design. https://www.nngroup.com/articles/ten-usability-heuristics/#poster
32. Joyce, G., Lilley, M.: Towards the development of usability heuristics for native smartphone mobile applications. In: Marcus, A. (ed.) Design, User Experience, and Usability. Theories, Methods, and Tools for Designing the User Experience, pp. 465–474. Springer, Cham (2014). https://doi.org/10.1007/978-3-319-07668-3_45
33. Joyce, G., Lilley, M., Barker, T., Jefferies A.: Mobile application usability: heuristic evaluation and evaluation of heuristics. In: Amaba, B. (ed.) Advances in Human Factors, Software, and Systems Engineering, pp. 77–86. Springer, Cham (2016). https://doi.org/10.1007/978-3-319-41935-0_8

34. Inostroza, R., Rusu, C., Roncagliolo, S., Rusu, V., Collazos, C.A.: Developing SMASH: a set of smartphone's usability heuristics. Comput. Stand. Interfaces **43**, 40–52 (2016)
35. Saleh, A., Ismail, R., Fabil, N.: Evaluating usability for mobile application: a MAUEM approach. In: Proceedings of the 2017 International Conference on Software and e-Business, pp. 71–77. ACM (2017)

# Cognition and Interaction

# Quantifying the Rating Performance of Ambiguous and Unambiguous Facial Expression Perceptions Under Conditions of Stress by Using Wearable Sensors

Jakub Binter[1,2]([✉]) [iD], Silvia Boschetti[1,2] [iD], Tomáš Hladký[1,2] [iD],
Hermann Prossinger[3] [iD], Timothy Jason Wells[1] [iD], Jiřina Jílková[1] [iD],
and Daniel Říha[1,2] [iD]

[1] Faculty of Social and Economic Studies, University of Jan Evangelista Purkyně, Ústí nad Labem, Czech Republic
jakub.binter@ujep.cz
[2] Faculty of Humanities, Charles University, Prague, Czech Republic
[3] Department of Evolutionary Anthropology, University of Vienna, Vienna, Austria

**Abstract.** *Background*: In real-world scenarios humans perceive the world contextually, relying on previous information to modify their responses. During interactions with a machine, missing contexts may decrease the accuracy of judgements. In the realm of human-computer interactions (HCI), relatively easy tasks as controls may not be relevant.

To evaluate the impact of stress we increased the cortisol level by the safe but reliable procedure Cold Pressor Task. We used five stimuli represented by facial expressions: 'neutral', 'laughter', 'fear', 'pain', and 'pleasure'.

*Aim*: We intend to find out how the responses to stimuli are altered by stress and statistically quantify the BVP (Blood Volume Pulse) signals.

*Materials*: 27 raters rated these five stimuli presented by 5 actors and 5 actresses, while BVP was being registered.

*Methods*: Each physiological response was a six-second time series after the rater rated the stimulus. A nontrivial model includes lag dependencies on either previous states or previous noise. The simplest models would be $ARMA(p, q)$ models with to-be-determined parameters $\varphi_1, \ldots \varphi_p$ and $\theta_1, \ldots \theta_q$.

*Inferences*: In this study, we find that the wearables' sampling for six seconds cannot separate signal from noise significantly. Only one response was found to be significantly affected by the condition of stress: the perception of fear.

**Keywords:** ARMA time series · 'Wearables' · BVP · Maximum likelihood distributions · Bayesian likelihood · Emotion perception · Fear · Pain · Pleasure · Stress

## 1 Introduction

In real-world scenarios, humans estimate a large proportion of their perceived world contextually and use previous information to adjust or modify their expectations and

© The Author(s), under exclusive license to Springer Nature Switzerland AG 2022
M. Kurosu et al. (Eds.): HCII 2022, LNCS 13516, pp. 519–529, 2022.
https://doi.org/10.1007/978-3-031-17615-9_36

responses. During interactions with a machine, contexts may be missing and, therefore, it is claimed, the accuracy of judgements decreases [6].

Furthermore, many applications using human-machine-interfaces rely on the premise that ratings and responses are in concordance and, consequently, requesting a response for a rating would not be necessary, since the signal can be directly obtained from the sensors (installed, for example, in wearables) [2, 7].

However, in the realm of human-computer interactions (HCI), using relatively simple tasks as controls may not be relevant; in the real world, ambiguous situations and stress presumably negatively impact the measurable response.

To evaluate the impact of stress we have employed a procedure commonly used in psychological experiments called Cold Pressor Task (see below). It reliably, but safely, increases the cortisol level. The participants were not informed that stress will be induced (so as to eliminate any possible bias) [4].

To evaluate the impact of possible ambiguity we used five stimuli present in human faces: two of which are easily identified by the raters ('neutral' and the basic emotion 'laughter'), one basic emotion that is often misinterpreted ('fear'), as well two affective states ('pain' and 'pleasure').

One of the main reasons for using the sensors for the communication between human and machine is to create a short-cut and allow for multiple channels to detect the state of the human responder or, alternatively, to categorize the response directly without explicitly asking the human via interviews or questionnaires [9].

There are certain tasks that are automatic for humans, many of which are visual-based e.g., the gaze oriented towards moving target. [5] As stimuli, the use of facial expressions is an ideal task since this is a process that is automatic and triggers a response. Indeed, allocation of attention towards face or face-like stimuli is one of the automatic, fast processes that develops from early childhood onwards [9].

In this study we aimed to test whether the condition of increased arousal affects physiological responses, namely Blood Volume Pulse (BVP), to the displayed stimuli.

Previous articles have shown that for similar tasks the stationary measuring devices (sampling rate of 256 Hz) are necessary for at least 5 s of exposition to the stimulus. [5] Usually multiple sensor data are required (BVP, EDA, temperature) but the wearables we used had a presumably insufficient sampling rate other than for BVP.

## 2 Materials and Methods

### 2.1 Data Collection

This sample consists of 27 students ($N_{\male} = 14$ and $N_{\female} = 13$) aged 19–30 years. Some of them ($N_{stress} = 15$) underwent a procedure called Cold Pressor Task which consists of immersing a subject's limb in ice water (2–4 °C) for 90 s. This procedure causes an elevation of the stress hormone cortisol causing an increase of the sympathetic nervous system activation. The sympathetic nervous system is functionally related with the psychological concept of arousal. [4] Consequently, the participant responded under a physiological state of high arousal (stress). The control group underwent the same procedure but the water was of room temperature so there was no effect on physiological arousal.

The participants were wearing E4 Empatica® (MIT) bracelets to collect data about their physiological reaction during the procedure. In this study, we focus on the output from the photoplethysmography (PPG) sensor with a sampling frequency of 64 Hz, namely the Blood Volume Pulse (BVP). BVP is derived from a PPG process, which uses the infrared light reflected by the skin to estimate blood vessel diameter. Diameter changes of the peripheral blood vessels, which are regulated by the sympathetic neural system, affect the amount of light reflected back to the photo-sensor; this changes the amplitude of the signal, corresponding to sympathetic activation. Figure 1 shows ten signals for one stimulus for one individual.

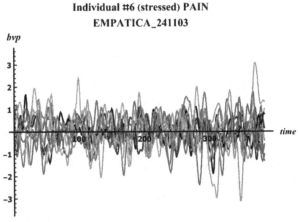

**Fig. 1.** Ten time-series of a stressed rater while assessing the stimulus 'pain' exhibited by five actors and five actresses. Different time series are rendered with a different color. Unit of time is $\frac{1}{64}$ s. The first measurement is 'immediately' (i.e. within 1 ms) after the rater has pressed the enter button that registers his/her rating of the stimulus; the last measurement is 384 pulses later. (Color figure online)

The procedure consisted of presentation of visual stimuli. In total 50 stimuli were displayed: five types of facial expressions representing emotions and affective states (laugh, pain, pleasure, and pain), along with neutral. Each facial expression was displayed by five actors and five actresses and each participant rated them on a scale A–C. For this study, we only analysed the BPV signal, not the ratings.

## 2.2 Statistical Analyses

Some of the time series had extraordinary positive and negative values. These, furthermore, did not meet the criterion of weak stationarity. They were discarded. We also tested whether the (rare) discarded time series were uniformly distributed across all stimuli and whether the raters were control or stressed. We used the Bayesian approach to test for significant differences. If $n_1$ is the number of discarded time series for control raters (for a given stimulus) and $n_2$ the number of discarded time series for the stressed raters, then the Bayesian likelihood of the probability $s$ that the number of discards is greater for the controls is $\Lambda(s) = \frac{\Gamma(n_1+n_2+2)}{\Gamma(n_1+1)\Gamma(n_2+1)} s^{n_1}(1-s)^{n_2}$ where $\Gamma(\cdot)$ is the Gamma function. [1] If the mode is close to $s = \frac{1}{2}$, and the $HDI_{95\%}$ uncertainty interval [3] overlaps the probability $s = \frac{1}{2}$, then there is no significant difference between the discarded time series for control versus stressed.

We use this Bayesian method of computing the likelihood function $\Lambda(s)$ [1] and determining the uncertainty interval $HDI_{95\%}$ [3] for numerous other comparisons below.

Distribution of peaks: we subtracted a Laplacian filter of each time series from the time series to identify the peaks. First, we simply inventoried the number of peaks in each signal for each stress. We estimated the ML distribution for each signal from a suite of three distributions: lognormal, Weibull and Gamma. We then used the log-likelihood of the ML distribution of peaks for control and stressed and Wilks lambda to find the probability that the control and stressed peaks were derived from the same statistical population. Formally: if $\ln\Lambda_C$ is the log-likelihood for the control, and $\ln\Lambda_S$ is the log-likelihood of the stressed, then Wilks lambda $\Lambda_{Wilks} = -2(\ln\Lambda_{CS} - (\ln\Lambda_S + \ln\Lambda_C))$. is $\chi^2$-distributed with $df = df_S + df_C - df_{CS}$ degrees of freedom. (The index CS refers to the data set formed by combining the data set for C with that for S.)

We constructed a matrix: the (ten) rows were the ratings by a participant of a specific stimulus and in each row were the 384 sequential registrations by the wearable. We first tested whether smoothing via Singular Value Decomposition (SVD) could be used to eliminate noise. None of the scree plots of the squares of the singular values showed a knee. In fact, the square of the first singular value never explained more than 20% of the square of the Frobenius norm of the matrix.

We therefore used time series analysis to investigate the signal for each rating by each individual for each stimulus—a total of $27_{raters} \times (5_{stimuli} \times (5_{\male} + 5_{\female})) = 1350$ time series, minus the 32 discarded ones. We used an ARMA $(p,q)$ time series model for each time series. In an ARMA$(p,q)$ model, the signal is modeled as $y_t = c + \varphi_1 y_{t-1} + \varphi_2 y_{t-2} + \cdots + \varphi_p y_{t-p} + \theta_1 w_{t-1} + \theta_2 w_{t-2} + \cdots + \theta_q w_{t-q}$ with both $p > 0$ and $q > 0$. The functions $w_{t-k}$ are Gaussian white noise contributions with finite variance $\sigma_w^2 > 0$. [8] The $p$ coefficients (amplitudes) $\varphi_1 \cdots \varphi_p$ describe the contributions of the $p$ past values of the underlying signal and the $q$ coefficients (amplitudes) $\theta_1 \cdots \theta_q$ describe the previous/lagged white noise contributions to the observed signal; $c$ is a constant. We use a software package (MATHEMATICA v12.4 from WOLFRAM Technology) to find a fit for the maximum $p$ and $q$ (and their numerical estimators) using AICc (Akaike's Information Criterion, corrected for finite sample size) as the optimality criterion. We also tested for weak stationarity.

Since we are interested in whether the time series of the raters depended on whether they were controls or were stressed, we tallied all numbers of amplitudes $p$ for each stimulus, both for the stressed and for control. Because the largest number (by far) was for $p = 3$ (see below), using a $\chi^2$-test for homogeneity is not meaningful, because we will find the probability of homogeneity to be very low. Instead, we use a Bayesian approach by comparing, for each $p = 0 \ldots p = 6$ for each stimulus, the frequencies of the stressed and the controls. We then use the machinery of computing the likelihood function $\Lambda(s)$ [1] and determining the uncertainty interval $HDI_{95\%}$ [3].

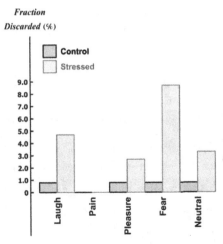

**Fig. 2.** A bar chart of fractions of time series that had to be discarded, prior to statistical analyses, because of extremely large departures from the predominantly occurring amplitudes. We note that these departures occurred more often when the raters were stressed, but the fractions were still small. No time series needed to be discarded for the stimulus 'Pain'. A Bayesian analysis of the fractions 'control' versus those 'stressed' showed a significant difference only for 'Laugh' and 'Fear' (at 5% significance level).

**Table 1.** The results of the Wilks lambda test of whether the peaks for one stimulus versus that of another stimulus is significantly (at 5% significance) different: control (light blue background) versus stressed (light orange background) raters. The percentages are the fractions of the compared stresses that were significantly different.

|          | Laugh | Pain  | Pleasure | Fear  | Neutral |
|----------|-------|-------|----------|-------|---------|
| **Laugh**    |       | 16.7% | 33.3%    | 33.3% | 41.7%   |
| **Pain**     | 33.3% |       | 33.3%    | 16.7% | 25.0%   |
| **Pleasure** | 33.3% | 26.7% |          | 41.7% | 8.3%    |
| **Fear**     | 46.7% | 40.0% | 40.0%    |       | 33.3%   |
| **Neutral**  | 33.3% | 40.0% | 40.0%    | 40.0% |         |

## 3  Results

A bar chart of the 32 discarded time series is shown in Fig. 2. Table 1 shows the fractions of pairwise significant differences in peak distributions of stimuli. A tests for significance (using Wilks lambda) of numbers of peaks control versus stress show that only one pair ('Fear' control versus 'Fear' stress) is significantly different (results not shown). Likewise, a test for a significant difference for intervals/gaps between peaks showed no significant difference (results not shown). Per individual, the ML distributions of numbers of peaks as well as the modes of their distributions are most often Weibull distributed, a few Gamma distributed and only one log-normally distributed (Fig. 3).

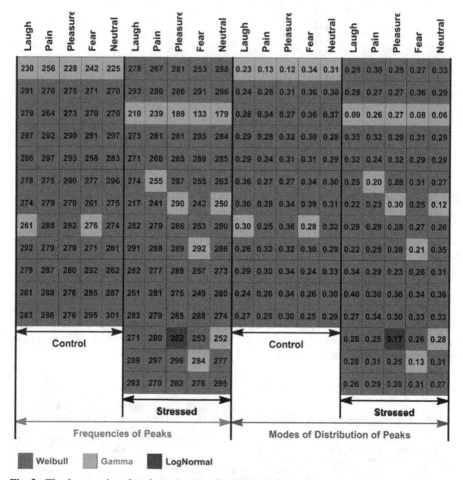

**Fig. 3.** The frequencies of peaks and modes for each individual for each stimulus, along with the ML distributions of these peaks. The largest number of peaks is Weibull distributed, very few are Gamma distributed, and only one is log-normally distributed. Most modes are Weibull distributed, very few are Gamma distributed, and only one is log-normally distributed. No modes are greater than 1.

Very rarely was the observed signal dependent on more than three previous signals (as opposed to the noise component of the signal; Fig. 4). For all stimuli, the amplitudes $\varphi_p$ ($p \leq 3$) are collinear and do not significantly differ between controls and stressed (Fig. 5). For every $p$ (the number of nonzero contributions $\varphi_p$ to the AR part of the ARMA($p,q$) time series), there was no significant difference between control and stressed individuals (Fig. 6).

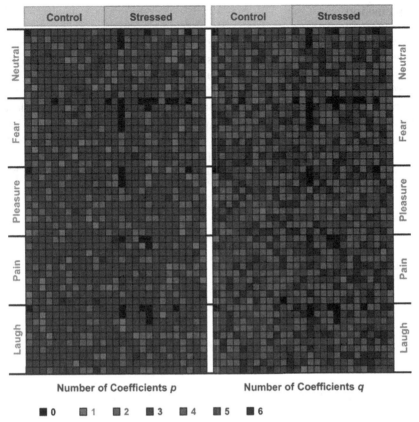

**Fig. 4.** The heat map of the frequencies of the coefficients $\varphi_k \ k = 1 \ldots p$ and $\theta_j \ j = 1 \ldots q$ in the ARMA($p,q$) time series models for the signals supplied by the wearables' data sets. The numbers of coefficients for $\theta$ are randomly distributed, whereas those for $\varphi$ are not. In fact, by far the most $\varphi_k k = 1 \ldots p$ are for $p = 3$. There is no significant statistical difference between the frequency distribution of coefficients for $\theta$ between 'control' and 'stressed'; nor is there any for the coefficients for $\varphi$. In this latter case, very, very many are $p = 3$.

These results show that the BVP signal for each individual provides no evidence that inducing stress altered the distribution of peaks nor the distribution of the amplitudes $\varphi_k$ in the ARMA($p,q$) time series, except for some features of 'Fear'.

## 4  Discussion

The data set we analyze here is large: there are 1350 time series with 384 data points each. The measurement routine can be considered reliable, as only 32 of 1350 (2.4%) time series had to be discarded. It is remarkable that the non-noise amplitudes $\varphi_k$ in the ARMA($p,q$) time series are co-linear (Fig. 5). We cannot explain this and have found no reference to such a relation in the literature. This linearity implies, for example, that the amplitudes $\varphi_1$ and $\varphi_2$ are anti-correlated with each other and anti-correlated with $\varphi_3$. In other words, if a BVP signal (without noise) is strongly dependent on the previous amplitude, then the dependence on the 'pre-previous' amplitude is strongly suppressed, and by almost the same amount. Whether this effect depends on latencies in the blood vessel dilation, we do not know (yet).

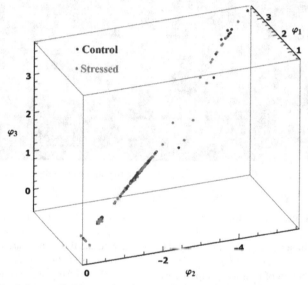

**Fig. 5.** A graph of the amplitudes $\varphi_k$ $k = 1 \ldots 3$ for all ARMA(3,$q$) time-series registered by the wearables as the raters rated the stimuli showing 'Pain'—color-coded according to whether the raters were control or stressed. Not all time-series are rendered in this graph, because some have been discarded, and some have ARMA($p,q$) models with $p > 3$. Displayed are 110 'control' time-series and 146 'stressed' time-series. In this graph, for all $\varphi_k$ $k = 1 \ldots p < 3$ we observe that $\varphi_k = 0 \,\forall\, 2 \leq k < 3$. These (few) $\varphi_k$ can be seen as a short row of dots at $\varphi_3 = 0$. (Color figure online)

The primary goal of the study was to investigate whether the wearables can detect an alteration in the time series, after the cortisol level is raised. We find no significant effect. One possible explanation for this may be that 6.00 s (384 measurements) is too short for the circulatory system to respond. Another possibility is that effects are only detectable in a multivariate setting: we have not investigated a vector time series. In any case, the univariate signal BVP provides no evidence for a significant difference between stimuli for an individual (control versus stressed). Outside a laboratory setting, the decision to decrease the sampling frequency is probably motivated by extending battery life and maintaining state tracking, which lasts longer than stimulus exposure.

The outcome regarding the distribution of the ML distributions is important for the development of algorithms that will be applied in future computations. We expect most ML distributions to be Weibull.

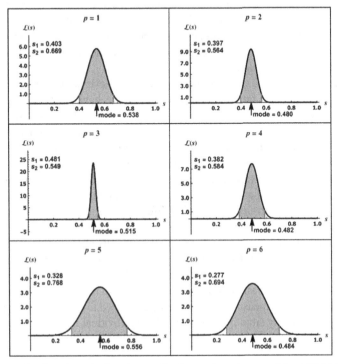

**Fig. 6.** The result of testing whether the amplitudes $\varphi_k$ $k = 1 \ldots p$ of the ARMA($p,q$) are significantly different for the controls versus the stressed. The probability $s$ is the probability that amplitudes for a given $p$ are more probable for the 'controls'. For all six $p$, the HDI$_{95\%}$ uncertainty interval $(s_1, s_2)$ overlaps the probability $s = \frac{1}{2}$, so there is no evidence of a significant difference between the amplitudes $\varphi_k$ $k = 1 \ldots p$ for 'stressed' versus 'controls'. All modes are very close to $s = \frac{1}{2}$. The short, red, vertical lines show the borders of the HDI$_{95\%}$ interval. (Color figure online)

We point out that in one case a significant difference was found, namely in case of 'Fear'. This is an important finding involving several research fields. In the field of psycho-physiological research, there is an ongoing debate about the problem of fear perception regarding categorization (positive vs. negative), and classification (labeling the stimulus with a correct name). It is present in many sensory fields (visual-facial perception, and acoustic-vocalization perception). Our study may resolve this problem by providing support for involvement of an inner state (in our case stress) in ambiguous stimuli perceptions.

## 5  Conclusion

This paper shows that there are shortcomings when using wearables related to monitoring stimuli data. Although their use is on the increase, it should be pointed out that, currently, wearables are not precise laboratory devices; they have limitations due to short battery life, sensitivity to movement artifacts (accelerations), and data gathering frequencies incompatible with several physiological variations (such as blood vessel dilation). In our case, the sampling rate only allowed us to use one sensor output, namely BVP.

It should be pointed out though that the proportion of discarded data is below 3%, which is a very good result, indicating that the wearables could handle almost any challenges posed by the wearer.

Usually, wearables are used in applications that last several minutes or more. While we argue that the six-second period is insufficient, we have no conclusive evidence other than the hint of a very small signal-to-noise ratio (Fig. 4). We point out that this novel approach (using time series analyses) is one rigorous method of quantifying noise. We have not found literature analyzing noise in wearables applications with such short sampling times. The oftentimes used analysis deals with amplitudes of peaks; we point out that perhaps too many (noise-related) artefacts are then included in the analyses. If wearables are to be used as assistance to human-computer-interaction, the sampling rate needs to increase, with sufficient battery-life, the wearables all the while remaining sufficiently unobtrusive for the wearer. It should be further noted that the future use of human-computer-interaction should also include rapidly changing signals, e.g., EEG, combined with several signals from wearables so as to generate a multivariate time series. Thus, high-sampling rate wearables could supply valuable input about the individual´s psychological state, such as stress-level, which will inform researchers about the central-nervous system response measures. There is an urgent need to develop the methods in the near future since in many situations the state of the individual may be a life-threatening one.

**Acknowledgements.** The research and data collection was supported by Czech Science Foundation (Grant No. 19-12885Y "Behavioral and Psycho-Physiological Response on Ambivalent Visual and Auditory Stimuli Presentation"). Part of the research team (JB, SB, TH, JJ) is employed by the Project SMART reg. no. CZ.02.1.01/0.0/0.0/17_048/0007435 Smart City-Smart Region-Smart Community. D.Ř. is funded by the Ministry of Education, Youth and Sports, Czech Republic and the Institutional Support for Long-term Development of Research Organizations, Faculty of Humanities, Charles University, Czech Republic (Grant COOPERATIO "Arts and Culture").

**Conflict of Interest.** The Author(s) Declare no Competing Interests.

**Ethics Statement.** The Project Was Evaluated and Approved by the Ethical Committee of the Faculty of Science, Charles University, as Part of Broader Project (7/2018). GDPR Regulations Were Followed at All Times.

## References

1. Bishop, C.M.: Pattern Recognition and Machine Learning. Springer, New York (2006)

2. Gao, R., Islam, A., Gedeon, T., Hossain, M.: Identifying real and posed smiles from observers' galvanic skin response and blood volume pulse. In: Yang, H., Pasupa, K., Leung, A.C.-S., Kwok, J.T., Chan, J.H., King, I. (eds.) ICONIP 2020. LNCS, vol. 12532, pp. 375–386. Springer, Cham (2020). https://doi.org/10.1007/978-3-030-63830-6_32

3. Kruschke, J.K.: Doing Bayesian Data Analysis. A Tutorial with R, JAGS, and STAN. Elsevier, San Diego (2015)

4. Lamotte, G., Boes, C.J., Low, P.A., Coon, E.A.: The expanding role of the cold pressor test: a brief history. Clin. Auton. Res. **31**(2), 153–155 (2021). https://doi.org/10.1007/s10286-021-00796-4

5. Maaoui, C., Pruski, A.: Emotion recognition through physiological signals for human-machine communication. Cutting Edge Rob. **11**, 317–332 (2010)

6. Santos, L.R., Rosati, A.G.: The evolutionary roots of human decision making. Annu. Rev. Psychol. **66**, 321 (2015)

7. Sindhu, N., Jerritta, S., Anjali, R.: Emotion driven mood enhancing multimedia recommendation system using physiological signal. In: IOP Conference Series: Materials Science and Engineering, vol. 1070, no. 1, p. 012070. IOP Publishing, February 2021

8. Shumway, R.H., Stoffer, D.S.: Time Series Analysis and its Applications. With R Examples. Springer, New York (2006). https://doi.org/10.1007/978-3-319-52452-8

9. Tcherkassof, A., Dupré, D.: The emotion-facial expression link: evidence from human and automatic expression recognition. Psychol. Res. **85**(8), 2954–2969 (2021)

# The Effect of Age on Mental Status of Air Traffic Controllers During Intensive Simulation Training

Zhenling Chen[1], Jianping Zhang[1]($\boxtimes$), Hangshi Shan[2], Yiyou Chen[1], Peng Hu[1], and Xiaoqiang Tian[1]

[1] The Second Research Institute of Civil Aviation Administration of China, Chengdu 610041, China
zhangjp@caacsri.com

[2] Shanghai New Jinshan Century Aviation & Development Co. Ltd., Shanghai 201506, China

**Abstract.** Air traffic controllers (ATCOs) are one kinds of key personnel for aviation safety. They often accept training for learning new knowledge and skills of advanced technologies related on aviation safety. The aim of this study was to learn the age effect on the perception, mood and fatigue of ATCOs for learning. An investigation with 3 × 2 levels of two factors including load of training and age on simulators was carried out at one training center in China. 234 effective questionnaires (78 person times) were collected and analyzed with statistical methods. Results of Pearson correlation test showed that ATCOs' perception had correlativity with their mood and their fatigue. Results of repeated measure variance analysis showed that the accumulation of load of training led to ATCOs perception decreased, mood worse, and fatigue increased very significantly. The results also showed that the age effect was significant to ATCOs' perception, mood and fatigue, and the elder ATCOs were easier to feel perception decreased, mood worse, and fatigue than the younger ones. These results indicated that it was more difficult for elder ATCOs to learn new knowledge and skills. And the results promote to give more help to the elder ATCOs for their training on new knowledge and skills.

**Keywords:** Air traffic controller · Age · Load · Perception · Mood · Fatigue

## 1 Introduction

Air traffic controllers (ATCOs) are key personnel for civil aviation safety. They are responsible for preventing collisions between aircrafts, between aircraft and obstructions in the maneuvering area, as well as expediting and maintaining an orderly flow of air traffic [1]. In order to improve the levels of aviation safety, the technology and instruments related to the safety keep iterating and improving. Therefore, ATCOs often accept trainings of new knowledge and skills related to the advance technology and instruments for their duties. The civil aviation organization also emphasize the importance of ATCOs training. For example, the Federal Aviation Administration of United States

© The Author(s), under exclusive license to Springer Nature Switzerland AG 2022
M. Kurosu et al. (Eds.): HCII 2022, LNCS 13516, pp. 530–538, 2022.
https://doi.org/10.1007/978-3-031-17615-9_37

(FAA) has laid down regulations and professional institutions for ATCOs training, and keeps improving the training instruments and course content [2, 3]. In China, the Civil Aviation Administration has also set up rules and professional institutions for ATCOs training, and keeps developing instruments and courses [4].

In order to enhance training effect, researchers and institutions often review and evaluate the ATCO training. In January 2013, the FAA conducted a review of ATCO training at the FAA Academy and evaluated the curriculum provision and the ability to meet developmental ATC demands [5]. Brudnicki et al. (2006) provided an in-depth overview of the training technologies utilized in the FAA Academy and on-site facility training [6]. Redding and Seamster (1997) analyzed and summarized the application of the cognitive task analysis in aviation settings for air traffic controller curriculum redesign [7]. Bernhardt et al. (2019) tried to apply the electroencephalography to ATC training to monitoring cognitive workload and engagement [3]. However, there are few studies pay attention to natural characteristics of ATCOs, such as age. Many studies on aging effect paid attention to learning and memory field. For example, Chiviacowsky et al. (2008) found that age stereotypes effected motor learning in adults [9, 10]. Muffato et al. (2019) found that the young adults gained better performance than the old adults in spatial learning regardless of the learning methods and conditions [11, 12]. However, studies of aging effect of ATCOs learning are still lacking. The aim of this paper is to learn the aging effect on the perception, mood, and fatigue of ATCOs during training for learning new knowledge and skills with a field investigation.

## 2  Method

### 2.1  Participants

ATCOs who accepted training at a training center in China during November in 2020 were recruited in this study. The training course included a new airspace structure and a new series of control procedures containing new control instructions. The training course were performed during day time from 9 am to 5 pm, and had a rest for lunch for 60 to 90 min. The ATCOs worked at a terminal control units and had rested for 2 days to get enough rest before taking the training course. All the participants had certificates of competency and III A health certificates. The general information of ATCO volunteers was showed in Table 1.

**Table 1.** General information of ATCO volunteers in this study.

| Gender | Age | N |
|--------|-----|---|
| Male | ≤31, mean 28.7 | 43 |
| | >31, mean 33.9 | 35 |

## 2.2  Questionnaires

Stanford Sleepiness Scale (SSS) was used in the present study. The SSS includes 7 items describing the feeling of sleepiness with 7-point liker score. The SSS was widely used for the investigations of ATCOs fatigue with a high reliability and validity [15].

The seven-item FMP scale developed by [13, 14] was used. It has been found to have good reliability and validity with ATCOs in the previous works. The scale has 7 items and the participants were asked to indicate their current feelings on a 10-point scale ranging from 10 to 100. The scale has three subscales, namely, the mood subscale (MS, 3 items, e.g. "irritable"), the perception subscale (PS, 3 items, e.g. "able to concentrate") and the sleepiness subscale (SS, 1 item, e.g. "sleepy"). The Cronbach's coefficients for the two sub-scales were 0.74 and 0.86 for the emotion subscale and the perception subscale, respectively.

## 2.3  Procedure

The ATCO volunteers were asked to fill in the questionnaire just before the training course in the morning, in the middle of the course in the noon, and just after finishing the course in the afternoon. Nighty ATCOs were recruited and eighty-five of them completed the scales all three times as before, in the middle of and after their training.

To investigate the aging effect, we set two levels of age. Participants older than 31 were set as elder level and participants younger than or equals to 31 were set as younger level. The training stage when participants complete questionnaires was also an independent variable in our study, which has three levels: before training, in the middle of training, after training.

The study protocol was approved by the Ethics Committee of the Second Research Institute of Civil Aviation Administration of China. All ATCOs participating in the investigation was provided with and signed an informed consent form. All relevant ethical safeguards have been met with regard to subject protection.

# 3  Results and Discussion

## 3.1  Preliminarily Analysis

The Pearson correlation analysis was applied to the items of the both scales. The results showed that the Pearson correlation of each SSS item and each item of the second scale were very significant (all $p < .001$, 2-tailed), and the absolute value of correlation coefficients were from .18 to .56. These results indicated that the measurement results of two scales were related very significantly.

## 3.2  The Effect of Training Stage

The repeated measure analysis of variance with training stage as an independent variable with 3 levels were employed to the PS of the second scale. The results showed a significant main effect ($p < .001$). The post-hoc analysis of the repeated measure data found that the PS values in the middle of training (mean 70.9) and after training (mean 65.0) were very significant decreased compared with that before training (mean 80.0), respectively ($p < .001$), and the PS values after training decreased significantly compared to that in the middle of training ($p = .011$) (Fig. 1).

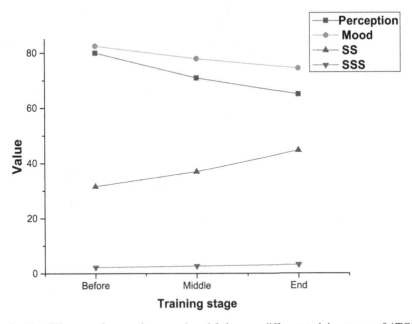

**Fig. 1.** The difference of perception, mood, and fatigue on different training stages of ATCOs.

The influence of the training stage on the mood of ATCOs for learning was also investigated. Similar to the PS, the repeated measure variance analysis was employed to the MS of the second scale. The results showed a significant main effect ($p < .001$). The post-hoc analysis discovered that the MS values in the middle of training (mean 77.9) and after training (74.4) decreased compared with that before training (mean 82.5) significantly ($p = .050$) and very significantly ($p = .001$), respectively. But the changes of the MS values between those in the middle of training and after training were not significant ($p = .141$) (Fig. 1).

Then the influence of the training stage on the fatigue of ATCOs for learning was investigated. The fatigue measurement of the two scales were very similar. The repeated measure variance analysis discovered that the effect of the training loads to the ATCOs fatigue was very significant within-subjects either with the SSS ($p < .001$) or the SS of the second scale ($p < .001$). As for SSS, the multiple comparison analysis found that the fatigue values in the middle of training (mean 2.7) and after training (mean 3.1) increased compared with that before training (2.2) very significantly ($p = .003$, $p < .001$), respectively. The increase of fatigue values was also significant ($p = .043$) from that in the middle of training to that after training. As for the SS of the second scale, the multiple comparison analysis showed that the difference of fatigue values in the middle of training (mean 36.9) and before training (21.5) was not significant ($p =$

.220), and the fatigue values increased very significantly ($p < .001$) after training (mean 44.6) compared with that before training. The change between the values in the middle of training and after training was not significant ($p = .053$).

The above analysis results indicated that perception and mood of the ATCO volunteers decreased, and their fatigue increased significantly as time went by when they accepted the training course for learning. The training course of the ATCOs contained an extensive new airspace structure for control, a series control procedures and corresponding instructions. Obviously, these training loads were heavy enough for the ATCOs to make much effort to study and master the course contents. Therefore, when they completed a day's training, their perception values and mood values decreased, and they also became fatigue.

### 3.3    The Influence of Age

The ATCO volunteers were separated into age groups using age median as the cutoff point. The younger group was below 31 years old and the elder group was over 31).

The repeated measure analysis of variance with age as an independent variable employed to the PS of the second scale (Fig. 2). The results showed that the age effect was significant ($p = .032$).

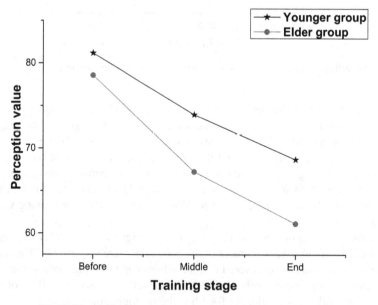

**Fig. 2.** Age influence on the perception of ATCOs for learning.

The age influence on the mood of ATCOs for learning was also investigated. The repeated measure variance analysis also employed to the MS of the second scale (Fig. 3). The results showed that the age effect was significance ($p = .027$).

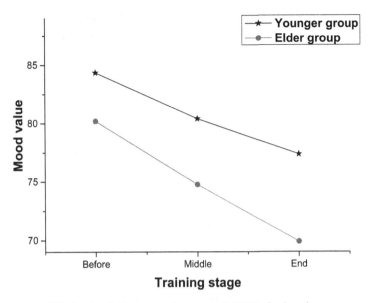

**Fig. 3.** Age influence on the mood of ATCOs for learning.

The repeated measure variance analysis employed to the SSS (Fig. 4) and the SS of the second scale (Fig. 5). The age effect was very significant with the SSS ($p = .007$), and significant with the SS of the second scale ($p = .029$).

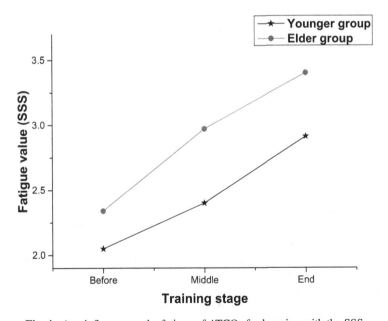

**Fig. 4.** Age influence on the fatigue of ATCOs for learning with the SSS.

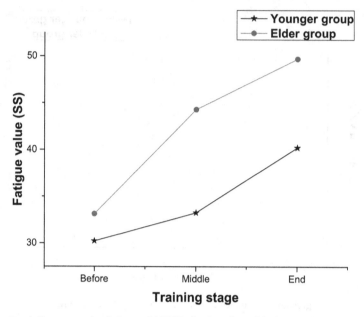

**Fig. 5.** Age influence on the fatigue of ATCOs for learning with the SS of the second scale.

During the learning for new knowledge and skills, the above results indicated that the elder ATCOs had lower values of the perception and mood, and higher values of the fatigue than the younger ones. These results illustrated that the elder ATCOs spent more efforts than the younger ones. Recent studies have demonstrated that aging coincides with a decline in spatial learning, and age stereotypes also impede the learning of performance and motor skills [7–12]. In the training course of this field investigation, the airspace structure renewed which challenged the elder ATCOs declined spatial learning compared with the younger ones. The series of new control procedures and instructions challenged the elder ATCOs age stereotypes including knowledge structure and memory.

## 4  Conclusion

In conclusion, the ATCOs are very important for ensuring aviation safety. In the face of developing flight flow and advancing safety technologies, ATCOs must keep learning new knowledge and skills in the training institutions. The institutions and related investigations paid most attention to the course design and instrument development, seldom cared of the natural characteristics of ATCOs like age. In recent years, researchers discovered that the age influence several aspects of learning for adults [7–12]. Civil aviation air traffic control work requires ATCOs have clear airspace structure in minds and have good memory for control procedures and instructions. In this paper, we primarily demonstrated that the training stage, which is a possible indicator of training load, influenced ATCOs perception, mood, and fatigue during their control training course for learning with a field investigation. What's more, our results, for the first time, provided the evidences with the field investigation that the age influence on ATCOs perception, mood and fatigue for learning. The results of the study were only preliminary. Future studies could use larger samples and more objective measurements.

The results indicate that in addition to training course design and organization of teaching form, the characteristics of ATCOs such as age was an important fact to pay attention to. Further explanations for elder ATCOs will help them integrate the new things into their knowledge structure and decrease the difficult to understand and successfully master new knowledge and skills.

**Acknowledgement.** We would like to thank all air traffic controllers who participated in this study. This study was supported by the National Natural Science Foundation of China (No. 22074157 and No. 52072406), Safety Foundation of Civil Aviation Administration of China (No. [2021]89) and Chengdu Science and Technology Project (2020-XT00-00001-GX).

# References

1. International Civil Aviation Organization: Procedures for Air Navigation Services Air Traffic Management. Doc 4444, 16th edn. (2016)
2. Updegrove, J.A., Jafer, S.: Optimization of air traffic control training at the federal aviation administration academy. Aerospace **4**, 50 (2017). https://doi.org/10.3390/aerospace4040050
3. Bernhardt, K.A., Poltavski, D., Petros, T., et al.: The effects of dynamic workload and experience on commercially available EEG cognitive state metrics in a high-fidelity air traffic control environment. Appl. Ergon. **77**, 83–91 (2019)
4. Lin, Y., Wu, Y.K., Guo, D., et al.: A deep learning framework of autonomous pilot agent for air traffic controller training. IEEE Trans. Hum. Mach. Syst., 442–450. IEEE Press (2021). https://doi.org/10.1109/THMS.2021.3102827
5. Federal Aviation Administration: Review and Evaluation of Air Traffic Controller Training at the FAA Academy. https://www.faa.gov/airports/runway_safety/news/congressional_repo rts/media/Review%20and%20Evaluation%20of%20Air%20Traffic%20Controller%20Trai ning%20at%20the%20FAA%20Academy.pdf
6. Brudnicki, D., Chastain, K., Ethier, B.: Application of advanced technologies for training the next generation of air traffic controllers. MITRE Corporation (2006). https://www.mitre.org/ sites/default/files/pdf/06_0978.pdf
7. Redding, R.E. Seamster, T.L.: Cognitive task analysis in air traffic controller and aviation crew training. In: Aviation Psychology in Practice, p. 33 (1997). Imprint Routledge. eBook ISBN 9781351218825
8. Montero, L., Serrano, R., Llanes, A.: The influence of learning context and age on the use of L2 communication strategies. Lang. Learn. J. **45**, 117–132 (2013). https://doi.org/10.1080/ 09571736.2013.853824
9. Chiviacowsky, S., Cardozo, P.L.: Age stereotypes' effects on motor learning in older adults: the impact may not be immediate, but instead delayed. Psychol. Sport Exerc. **36**, 209–212 (2018). https://doi.org/10.1016/j.psychsport.2018.02.012
10. Lamont, R.A., Swift, H.J., Abrams, D.: A review and meta-analysis of age-based stereotypes, not facts, do the damage. Psychol. Aging. **30**, 180–193 (2015)
11. Muffato, V., Meneghetti, C., De Beni, R.: Spatial mental representations: the influence of age on route learning from maps and navigation. Psychol. Res. **83**(8), 1836–1850 (2018). https:// doi.org/10.1007/s00426-018-1033-4
12. Gazova, I., Laczo, J., Rubinova, E., et al.: Spatial navigation in young versus older adults. Front. Aging Neurosci. **5**, 94 (2013). https://doi.org/10.3389/fnagi.2013.00094

13. Chen, Z., Zhang, J., Ding, P., et al.: A scale to assess fatigue, concomitant mood and perception of air traffic controllers: a field study. In: 2020 IEEE 2nd International Conference on Civil Aviation Safety and Information Technology, pp. 874–877. IEEE Press, Weihai (2020)
14. Chen, Z., Zhang, J., Jing, W., et al.: A preliminary field study of air traffic controllers' fatigue for interface design. In: Harris, D., Li, W.C. (eds.) Engineering Psychology and Cognitive Ergonomics. HCII 202, LNAI 12767, pp. 119–129. Springer, Cham (2021). https://doi.org/10.1007/978-3-030-77932-0_10
15. Nealley, M.A., Gawron, V.J.: The effect of fatigue on air traffic controllers. Inter. J. Aviat. Psychol. 25(1), 14–47 (2105)

# Study of Operational Capability Attributes of Complex Information Systems Based on ANP Sensitivity Theory

Yuhan Jin[1], Hua Liu[3], Ximing Zhu[3], and Wenjun Hou[1,2(✉)]

[1] School of Digital Media and Design Art, Beijing University of Posts and Telecommunications, Beijing 100876, China
3115890439@qq.com
[2] Beijing Key Laboratory of Network System and Network Culture, Beijing University of Posts and Telecommunications, Beijing 100876, China
[3] The Twenty-Seventh Research Institute of China Electronics Technology Group Corporation, Zhengzhou 450052, China

**Abstract.** As modernization accelerates, various new technologies and new ways of operation proliferate, and the complexity of human-computer interaction systems continues to increase. The gradual complication of functions and tasks of complex information systems places special training demands on the operator's operational capabilities. How to develop individualized training programs for different types of operators on the basis of identifying the differences in each ability attribute has become an important issue to improve training efficiency and train specialized and high-fit operator teams.

In this study, firstly, on the basis of analyzing the operational tasks of complex information systems, a model of the competence indicator system for operators of different seats in complex information systems is established. The weights of the indicator system are evaluated by using the ANP model, and the weights of the three operator alternatives are obtained, on the basis of which the characteristics of the relative magnitude of change in the proportion of the three alternative options are identified using the method of sensitivity analysis. The results of the subjective clustering of the various characteristics show that the characteristics of the magnitude of variation of these competencies can be finally classified into four categories, namely, "experienced, knowledgeable, fixed, and cumulative competencies." Finally, the proposed competency training program for operators of different levels and individual characteristics can be used as a reference for efficient training of operating competencies of complex information systems.

**Keywords:** Capability system · ANP · Capability index system · Weight sensitivity analysis

## 1 Introduction

The establishment of the operator capacity indicator system, it is an important tool for the comprehensive evaluation of the performance of the operational process; and the

M. Kurosu et al. (Eds.): HCII 2022, LNCS 13516, pp. 539–551, 2022.
https://doi.org/10.1007/978-3-031-17615-9_38

determination of the weights is the core of the comprehensive evaluation problem. The Analytic Hierarchy Process (AHP) is a widely used method for determining weights. However, The Analytic Hierarchy Process (AHP) method assumes that the evaluated index system is a linear recursive hierarchy and that the various index systems are independent of each other [1]. In some systems with a strong correlation between indicator systems. For example, in the complex information system operator capability indicator system involved in this study, the capability indicators are interwoven into a network. They are both interdependent and constrained by each other. This is not only reflected in the decomposition and convergence between the indicator levels but also in the mutual dependence and support within the indicators of the same level. The Analytic Network Process (ANP) proposed on the basis of AHP can better solve the problem of calculating weights when there is a strong connection between indicators, which is more in line with the characteristics of "non-linear, open and dynamic" of complex information system operator capability index system, and can take into account the dependency and feedback between evaluation indicators, and can better solve the problem of calculating weights when there is a strong connection between indicators.

A commonly used analysis tool is sensitivity analysis based on the weighting analysis of the indicator system. Sensitivity analysis can be used to study the degree of influence of changes in factors on the target and to analyze the magnitude of risk in decision making and can provide modelers and decision-makers with a method to determine the input and output data and relevant parameters of the decision problem. It is more commonly used in areas such as investment project evaluation and business management decisions [2]. For example, Han Yapin [4] used vector entropy cosine, preference structure of weighted sum method, and weight sensitivity analysis to solve the multi-objective decision-making problem of PPP projects. In the study about the weight of the index system, Shi Hongwei [3] conducted a sensitivity analysis on the ecological safety evaluation results of the mining area. The study was able to identify the key factors affecting ecological safety in mining areas, analyze the trend of ecological safety changes and predict ecological risks, and propose scientific theoretical guidance for ecological construction and sustainable development in mining areas. By analyzing the five criterion layers and the associated pairwise comparison matrix, Yun Chen [5] et al. identified the most sensitive elements of the matrix to help relevant decision-makers reduce uncertainty and perform more effective measures in the spatial multicriteria decision-making process.

After analyzing the relevant literature, it is found that most of the studies use the weight sensitivity method to obtain quantitative weight sensitivity coefficient results after modeling the study area and collecting subjective and objective data, and calculating the weights. However, this research method is highly specific to the field under study, and the results are difficult to be generalized to other related fields. In this study, the operational competencies of operators of complex information systems are studied. In order to identify the characteristics of each competency indicator of operators of complex information systems using the theory of sensitivity analysis, a method of differentiating the characteristics of competency attributes in combination with subjective analysis is proposed. Unlike the previous approaches that only focus on the current research field and rely on raw data and expert scoring, the extraction of competency characteristics in this study has certain universal characteristics. It can be used as an idea for the application of related competency index systems and the formulation of operator training programs to help identify the attributes of competency indicators in various related studies and can be used as a reference for the formulation of subsequent competency training programs.

## 2   Research Process

This study is based on the competency index system of complex information systems for electronic reconnaissance. First, the operator capability index system is established by analyzing the operator's operational tasks and mapping them to "task-competency." Using a combination of the subjective and objective scoring process, the weights of the index system are obtained. The sensitivity theory is used to analyze the changing trend of the alternatives after changing the weights of each index. Subjective clustering analysis is conducted to extract the implied attribute characteristics of this capability index.

### 2.1   Operator Competence Index System Establishment

In order to ensure the completeness and relevance of the competency index system at the same time, a large amount of relevant literature was firstly reviewed in the construction process of the index system [6–23]. And through the bottom-up clustering process, 40 initial competency indicators covering the general competency indicators of operators were formed to obtain the operator competency dictionary. The lexicon is a three-tier structure, with the primary competencies being basic competency A1 and professional competency A2. The secondary competencies are basic physiological competency B1, basic cognitive competency B2, theoretical knowledge level B3, information acquisition competency B4, information processing competency B5, task integration competency B6, operational management competency B7, and collaborative competency B8. The secondary competencies are subdivided into detailed competency indicator layers, which constitute a three-tier structure of the competency lexicon. The detailed competency indicator layers are subdivided into a three-layer structured competency dictionary.

Since the above-mentioned capability dictionary is a large and comprehensive capability indicator system, which contains a variety of fields and types of capability indicators, including some capability indicators that do not fit the electronic reconnaissance task process, or the description of certain capability indicators cannot fit the task content of radar electro-reconnaissance, so targeted word adjustment and reorganization are needed. In order to accomplish the above adjustments in a targeted manner, the task logic of the complex information system involved in this study is sorted out, the important task boards are extracted, and the task processes are split up article by article with appropriate granularity. The competency words that can characterize each task process are selected from the above competency dictionary and corresponded to each task content one by one to achieve the purpose of being able to comprehensively describe the competency indicators in the task process. Upon completion of the above task-competency index correspondence, the competency indexes involved in this complex information system are again integrated from the bottom up, clustered according to the categories they belong to, and finally form the respective competency index system for each seat.

The following is an example of a seat in a complex information system for electronic reconnaissance to form a system of indicators. A good operator mainly demonstrates the following capabilities: the amount of information in the situational chart is large and multidimensional. The operator has to monitor the current situation in real-time and give timely attention to any abnormalities that may appear in the situational chart at any time. This requires good attention capabilities, including breadth of attention and sensitivity of attention. As the basis of situational awareness, it is important to perceive situational changes and grasp the overall situational situation in a timely manner. At the same time, the operator needs to have good logical reasoning and evaluation decision-making ability, to efficiently analyze, understand and judge the information obtained from the situational chart and make reasonable decisions based on the judgment of the current situation to ensure the smooth implementation of the task. In addition, the operator needs to have a high level of system familiarity and system parameter control to be able to quickly and accurately complete radar resource management, target-related settings, and other operations in the situational chart system to ensure the efficient completion of the mission. Since the operator needs to collaborate with other seat operators during the mission to synchronize the current situation or collaborate to detect key targets, the operator needs to have good command understanding and language expression ability to ensure the smooth collaboration process and accuracy of message delivery.

The first-level competence indicators of active seat operators are divided into five major categories, namely, theoretical knowledge level, information acquisition ability, information processing ability, system operation and management ability, and collaborative ability. There are 11 secondary competence indicators under them, and the corresponding relationships are shown in Table 1.

**Table 1.** Capability index system

| Tier 1 indicators | Tier 2 indicators |
|---|---|
| Theoretical knowledge level | Basic theoretical knowledge (K1) |
| | Task performance experience (K2) |
| Information Acquisition Capability | Breadth of attention (A1) |
| | Sensitivity of attention (A2) |
| Information Processing Capability | Logical reasoning ability (P1) |
| | Decision-making judgment ability (P2) |
| System operation and management capabilities | System familiarity (O1) |
| | Parameter control level (O2) |
| | Ability to control the timing of operation (O3) |
| Synergy | Clarity of information presentation (S1) |
| | Verbal ability (S2) |

## 2.2 ANP Model Establishment and Weight Determination

The ANP consists of two parts. The first part is called the control factor layer, which includes the problem objective and decision criteria. All decision criteria are determined to be independent of each other and governed only by the objective factors. The second part is the network layer, which consists of all factors governed by the control layer, with interdependence, mutual influence, and feedback among them.

Based on the above process of constructing the active capability indicator system and the ANP hierarchy, the ANP model of the operator's capability indicator system is drawn separately in the yaanp software. The model drawn in the software is shown in Fig. 1.

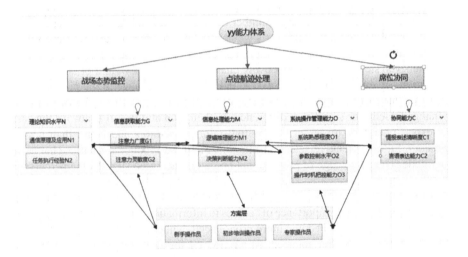

**Fig. 1.** Model built in yaanp software

In the "Solution Layer" of the ANP model, we set up three options: "Novice Operator", "Initial Training Operator" and "Expert Operator". The criteria for differentiating the three types of operators are shown in Table 2, which can be adjusted according to the actual usage scenarios.

**Table 2.** Different level of operator classification basis

| Operator type | Training level | Flight time |
|---|---|---|
| Novice operator | No training in electro-detection | None |
| Initial training operator | Trained in electro-surveillance but with little experience in practical training | Less |
| Expert operator | Trained in electro-detection and experienced in practical training | More |

Next, the two-by-two judgment matrix of the control layer indicator weights and the calculated results are calculated using yaanp software, the two-by-two judgment matrix of the network layer indicator weights, and the resulting final weights of each indicator. Among other things, the theory of sensitivity analysis is used. In the case where the scoring of indicator weights has been obtained, by artificially changing the proportion of weights for each indicator and observing the change in the proportion occupied by the three alternatives, in this case, several attributes of this capacity indicator can be characterized.

## 2.3 Sensitivity Analysis

Using the sensitivity analysis function in the yaanp software, the change in the weights of the three operators' options is examined one by one after changing the weights of each indicator. As there are a large number of competency indicators, this paper takes the example of changing the operator's weight for "information acquisition capability," as shown in Fig. 2. On the basis of the operator's ANP competency system and its competency system weights, subjectively change the indicator weight of "information acquisition capability" from 0% to 100% and observe the change in the proportion of the three alternative options. The ranking of the three categories of operators remains unchanged due to the significant differences in their own abilities. It is always the case that expert operators are larger than initial training operators and larger than novice operators. Still, the relative selection ratios of the three produce a smaller change in magnitude. The percentage of professional operators increased slightly, the percentage of novice operators decreased slightly, and the percentage of initially trained operators remained essentially unchanged. The implication behind the magnitude of the above relative choice is that as the importance of "access to information" increases, the advantages of professional operators become more pronounced, while the disadvantages of novice operators become more pronounced. At a ratio of 1 for all three groups, no particular advantage or disadvantage is revealed for this ability of the initial training operators.

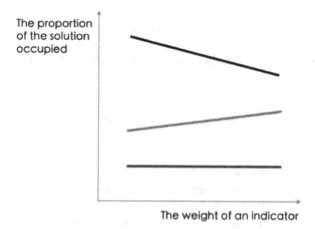

**Fig. 2.** The black lines represent expert operators; The orange line represents an operator who has undergone initial training; The blue lines represent novice operators (Color figure online)

# 3   Results Analysis

## 3.1   Sensitivity Clustering

In accordance with the above analysis process, we selected 9 competency indicators corresponding to each of the three task processes from the total number of competency indicators involved in this study, for a total of 27 indicators. We conducted a sensitivity study on each of these competencies. The results of all sensitivity line graphs are shown in Fig. 3.

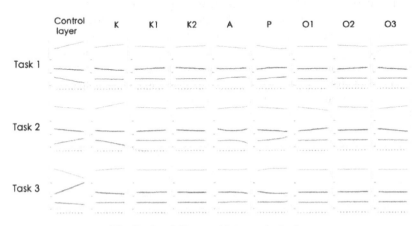

**Fig. 3.** Capability sensitivity analysis chart

It can be found that the magnitudes of change of these line graphs present different performance profiles. After subjective clustering of the different manifestations of the magnitude of change, it is found that their magnitude of change characteristics can be clustered into four types. These four types of competencies are named "Experiential Competencies," "Knowledge Competencies," "Fixation Competencies," and "Accumulative Competencies" based on the difference in the magnitude of change of these competencies and the difference in the meaning behind them "and" cumulative ability. The following is an explanation of each of them.

## 3.2   Interpretation of Clustering Results

**Experience-Based Ability.** For this type of competency, the magnitude of the sensitivity change can be abstracted as the sample shown in Fig. 4. This is shown by the fact that as the weight of a competence indicator is artificially increased, the proportion of choices of novice operators remains essentially constant. At the same time, the proportion of choices of expert operators increases, and the proportion of choices of initially trained operators decreases.

The reason for this change is that this type of competency requires a certain basic knowledge background, which novice operators do not have at all. Therefore, the proportion of novice operators selected remains essentially the same as the indicator weights increase. However, for the initially trained operators with a certain degree of knowledge background and the expert operators with a rich knowledge background, the advantages of the expert operators are magnified and reflected after the corresponding index weights are increased. The gap between them and the remaining two types of operators gradually widens. This indicates that such abilities can be accumulated and improved after initial training, and the effect of improvement becomes more and more obvious after getting professional training.

Competencies that show such trends in the current analysis include operational timing control ability; operational timing control ability; task execution experience; task execution experience; level of theoretical knowledge; information processing ability; and level of theoretical knowledge (each metric also includes differences across task contexts that are not detailed here). An analysis of these capabilities shows that they do require some background knowledge of radar electro-surveillance, and with the gradual improvement of mission experience and the gradual increase of mission operation time, strong professionalism will become the core advantage to be reflected. Therefore, these capabilities are named as "experience-based capabilities."

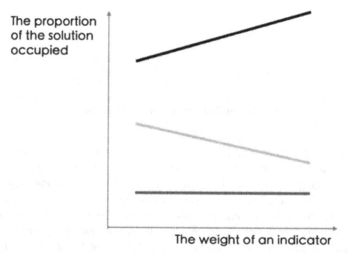

**Fig. 4.** The black lines represent expert operators; The orange line represents an operator who has undergone initial training; The blue lines represent novice operators (Color figure online)

**Knowledge-Based Capabilities.** For this type of competency, the magnitude of the sensitivity change can be abstracted into the sample shown in Fig. 5. This is shown by the fact that as the weight of a competence indicator is artificially increased, the selection percentage of novice operators remains essentially constant, while the selection percentage of expert operators decreases and the selection percentage of initially trained operators increases. The decrease in the selection ratio of expert operators does not mean that the expert operators have become less competent, but rather that the sum of the ratios of competence of expert, novice, and initial training operators in the analysis is 1. Since the increase in such competence after initial training is very significant, the ratio of expert operators decreases slightly in relative terms to maintain the overall sum of the selection ratios of the three options at 1.

The reason for the above change is that this type of competency also requires a certain basic background in electro-sleuthing, which novice operators do not have at all. Therefore the proportion of growth with indicator weights remains largely unchanged. However, unlike the above-mentioned "experience-based competencies," the proportion of initially trained operators increases significantly after the weighting of the corresponding indicators increases, while the advantage of expert operators is not obvious. This means that this ability can be improved significantly after initial training but not significantly after long-term training.

Capabilities in the current analysis that exhibit such trends include the level of parameter control, level of parameter control; system familiarity; application of communication principles; and application of communication principles (individual metrics also include differences with different task contexts that are not detailed here). After analyzing these capabilities, it can be found that they all require some background in radar electro-surveillance. Still, they are all expressed in the proficiency of operating systems and some capabilities involving the basic theoretical knowledge of radar electro-surveillance, which are limited and fixed, and therefore can be mastered by ordinary operators after some training. This type of capability is named "Knowledge-based capabilities."

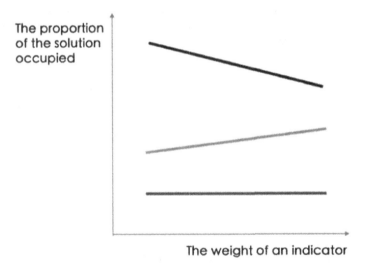

**Fig. 5.** The black lines represent expert operators; the orange line represents an operator who has undergone initial training; the blue lines represent novice operators (Color figure online)

**Curing Type Capability.** For this type of competency, the magnitude of sensitivity change can be abstracted as the sample shown in Fig. 6. This is shown by the fact that as the weight of a competence indicator is artificially increased, the proportion of novice operators' choices increases. At the same time, the difference in competencies between expert operators and initially trained operators gradually decreases, and the gap in competencies between the three decreases. The decrease in the selection ratio of expert operators does not mean that the expert operators become less competent, but rather that the sum of the competence ratios of expert, novice, and initial training operators in the analysis is 1. Since the increase in such competence after initial training is very significant, the ratio of expert operators decreases slightly in order to keep the overall sum of the selection ratios of the three options at 1.

The reason for the above change is that this type of ability is inherent to novice operators and can be performed to some extent without training, which is reflected in the graph by the increase in the percentage of novice operators selected. However, after initial and specialized training, the competencies of initial training operators and expert operators do not increase significantly but remain basically at the same level as before. Thus, the difference in competence between the three gradually decreases as the indicator ratio rises.

Capabilities that exhibit such trends in the current analysis include information processing capability, information processing capability, and information acquisition capability (individual metrics also include differences across task contexts that are not detailed here). An analysis of these capabilities reveals that they do not require a technical background in radar electro-detection and that people with normal vision can complete tasks such as multi-target tracking and specific information search as required. This is related to the individual's breadth of vision, the ability to focus attention, and other basic qualities. The magnitude of improvement after training is not obvious and can only be maintained within the level of ability that one can achieve. Therefore, this type of ability is named "Curing type capability."

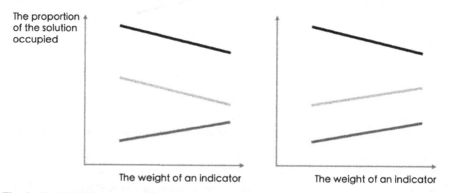

**Fig. 6.** The black lines represent expert operators; The orange line represents an operator who has undergone initial training; The blue lines represent novice operators (Color figure online)

**Cumulative Capabilities.** For this type of competency, the magnitude of its sensitivity change can be abstracted as the sample shown in Fig. 7. This is shown by the fact that as the weight of a competence indicator is artificially increased, the selection ratio of initially trained operators remains basically the same, while the selection ratio of expert operators rises and that of novice operators falls, and the competence gap between the three gradually enlarges.

The reason for the above changes is that the gap between the competencies of all three types of operators gradually widens after initial and specialized training. It indicates that this ability can be sufficient to distinguish the difference in ability between different operators and that the ability can be significantly improved after training as well as professional training.

The competencies that show such trends in the current analysis include the level of theoretical knowledge; and access to information (individual indicators also include differences with different task contexts, which are not detailed here). An analysis of these capabilities reveals that although there is an overlap between the fixed and knowledge-based capabilities, there are differences in task context that lead to such performance. For example, the task process of "point-track trajectory processing" relies heavily on task experience, and the longer the flight time, the more likely it is that one will develop suitable information acquisition habits and a theoretical knowledge base, which becomes an important influencing factor for the difference between new and experienced pilots. Therefore, this type of capability is named "Cumulative capabilities."

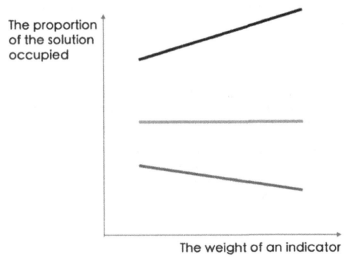

**Fig. 7.** The black lines represent expert operators; The orange line represents an operator who has undergone initial training; The blue lines represent novice operators (Color figure online)

### 3.3  Training Program Determination

After the above analysis, it can be found that different competency indicators will reflect different changes in the process of training. When training, it should be organized rationally, considered, and laid out in advance in order to obtain the highest possible training effect with limited training resources.

Curing type capability is a capability that the operator already has and is related to the operator's personal qualities, which are not obvious after training. Therefore, sufficient attention should be paid to this type of capability during the initial operator selection process, and operators with significant advantages should be focused on it.

Experience-based, knowledge-based, and Cumulative capabilities can be gradually improved through later training. For Knowledge-based capabilities, as the foundation of the other types of capabilities and the type of capabilities with obvious short-term training effects, we should make more efforts at the beginning of the training and follow up the learning situation of the training cases to carry out personalized checking and remediation of certain knowledge points that are not mastered well.

For both experienced and Cumulative capabilities, since both involve the significant advantages of expert personnel, expert opinions should be actively adopted in the initial training process to enhance training efficiency and avoid the training resource consumption caused by a large number of meaningless exploration trials error processes for novice operators. In particular, for Cumulative capabilities, the development of efficient operating habits of individuals with different operators may be involved in the current system capabilities, so attention should be given to such capability characteristics after a certain degree of training to provide suggestions for the development of individualized system design and development adapted to unique operating characteristics that will contribute to the overall task performance.

# References

1. Hongwei, S., Lei, T.: Evaluation of ecological safety in mining areas based on ANP and sensitivity analysis of index weights. J. Hebei Eng. Univ. (Nat. Sci. Ed.) 37(03), 75–81 (2020)
2. Yan, J., Xuejun, X., Ning, L.: Sensitivity analysis of weights in multi-objective decision making. J. Three Gorges Univ. (Nat. Sci. Ed.) 05, 447–449 (2004)
3. Hongwei, S., Lei, T.: Evaluation of ecological safety in mining areas based on ANP and sensitivity analysis of index weights. J. Hebei Eng. Univ. (Nat. Sci. Ed.) 37(03), 75–81 (2020)
4. Yapin, H., Genmou, J.: Application of weight sensitivity analysis in multi-objective decision making of PPP projects. Shanxi Archit. 35(01), 7–8 (2009)
5. Jia, Y., Yun, C., Jingyi, L., et al.: Sensitivity analysis of weights in OAT-based spatial multicriteria decision making. Resour. Sci. 9, 10 (2014)
6. Qian, F., Xuan, S., Hongbin, S., Yuliang, F., Zhencheng, H.: Study on the maturity model and training model of fintech talent capability in the data center. China Financ. Comput. 07, 75–80 (2021)
7. Yina, W.: Analysis, description, and assessment of teachers' educational technology competence. Beijing University (2008)
8. Shuang, L.: Assessment of operators' cognitive abilities based on KLEE and fuzzy integrated evaluation. Hum. Ergon. 16(01), 30–31+73 (2010)
9. Ruishan, S., Ning, Z., Jingqiang, L., Wei, W.: Structural analysis of air traffic controllers' competency quality model. Chin. J. Saf. Sci. 24(10), 8–14 (2014)
10. Yang Fan, Y., Minjian, L.Y., Mingliang, C.: Research on flight controllers' job competency under the reform of tower command model. J. Inf. Eng. Univ. 22(01), 112–118 (2021)
11. Gardner, H.: Multiple Intelligences, p. 5. Xinhua Publishing House, Beijing (2003)
12. Li Xuehua, L., Tianshu, L.J., Rui, G.: Construction of a standardized casualty core competency system in nursing rescue capacity training. Chin. J. Nurs. 51(09), 1101–1104 (2016)
13. Yang, Z., Yin, J., Song, Y.: Accounting talent competence needs and undergraduate accounting education reform: a stakeholder's survey analysis. Acc. Res. (01), 25–35+97 (2012)

14. Xiaorong, H., Wenjie, S., Liping, Z., Wei, L., Chen, L., Yun, L.: Construction of the core competency evaluation index system for hemodialysis specialist nurses in Jiangsu Province. Chin. J. Nurs. **50**(12), 1510–1514 (2015)
15. Ailing, W., Ying, J.: Exploration of teacher competence system in the new century. Educ. Theory Pract. **20**(4), 41–44 (2000)
16. Jing, Q., Jiang, X., Yang, J., Zhou, Y.: Research on the index system of coal mine safety production capacity based on hierarchical analysis (AHP). China J. Saf. Sci. **16**(9), 74–79+145 (2006)
17. Yanfei, W., Keran, Z., Meihua, C., Ji, L.: Research analysis of intelligence perception. Intell. Theor. Pract. **41**(08), 1–4 (2018)
18. Qiaoyu, D., Zhixue, W., Zhongwei, W.: Research on the evaluation model of ZZ organization command and control capability. Command Control Simul. **41**(5), 16–20 (2019)
19. Deng, B., Jiang, X., Tao, Y., Lu, Y.: Modeling and analysis of intelligent security capability requirements for commander's key information needs. China Command and Control Society. In: Proceedings of the Ninth China Command and Control Conference. Chinese Command and Control Society: Chinese Command and Control Society (2021)
20. Hu Jinhui, H., Dabin, X.J.: Research on the comprehensive assessment method of crew members' job operation ability. Comput. Digit. Eng. **45**(7), 1287–1293 (2017)
21. Fei, L., Weibo, C., Kexuan, L., Zhaoning, Z., Bilian, L.: Comprehensive quality evaluation of controllers based on ternary interval number. J. Saf. Environ. **18**(5), 1876–1880 (2018)
22. Yanhong, L., Shuzheng, J.: Construction of competence model for civil aviation flight attendants. J. Civil Aviat. Univ. China **33**(5), 60–64 (2015)
23. Zhao, Y., Xiaofeng, X.: ANP-based joint force ZZ capability assessment. Command Inf. Syst. Technol. **8**(05), 43–48 (2017)

# Effects of Different Instructions on Subjective Flow State and Physiological Responses Induced by the Same Mental Task

Hiroyuki Kuraoka[✉] and Mitsuo Hinoue

University of Occupational and Environmental Health, Japan, Kitakyushu, Japan
h-kuraoka@health.uoeh-u.ac.jp

**Abstract.** This study investigated the effects of different instructions on the subjective flow state and physiological responses induced by a mental arithmetic task. Eighteen male undergraduate students were asked to perform a mental arithmetic (MA) task for 15 min. They were given the following two conditions under which they performed: "self-paced (SELF)" and "Always do more calculations than in the previous line (FLOW)." Electrocardiograms (ECG) were recorded during the resting (REST) and the MA tasks. Low-frequency components (LF), high-frequency components (HF), and the LF/HF ratio of heart rate variability (HRV) were derived from ECGs. Skin gas from the back of the neck and left palm was monitored during the REST and the MA task. A flow-state scale was adopted to evaluate participants' flow state during the task. NASA–Task Load Index (NASA-TLX) was used to assess subjective mental workload. Results indicated that there were no significant differences in flow scores. The Pattern 1 response, in which the heart rate increased during the MA task, was observed under the FLOW condition. The results of HRV indices indicated that the LF and HF decreases were significantly decreased for the MA task during both conditions. There was no significant main interaction with conditions and blocks (resting period, task periods) found in physiological responses except for the LF/HF and skin gas. Therefore, although it was not possible to not induce the flow state by the task instructions, it was suggested that the heart rate responses induced by instructions might be more susceptible than other indices.

**Keywords:** Flow state · Heart rate · Skin gas · Mental arithmetic task

## 1 Introduction

The flow theory, which was proposed by Csikszentmihalyi, has been increasingly employed to improve workplace productivity and motivation [1–3]. Flow is a state of being fully absorbed in a certain activity, so the sense of time and the self-consciousness of the ego are lost. Subjective assessments such as the flow state scale (FSS) [4] have been used frequently to measure the flow state. Although subjective scales such as FSS have been able to evaluate the overall state of flow regardless of task duration, they cannot monitor the flow state continuously and in real time.

M. Kurosu et al. (Eds.): HCII 2022, LNCS 13516, pp. 552–562, 2022.
https://doi.org/10.1007/978-3-031-17615-9_39

Several previous studies have reported that physiological signals in the brain wave activity and cardiac activity are useful in quantitatively evaluating the flow state. Katahira examined experimentally the electrocardiogram (EEG) activities when the flow was evoked, and it was suggested that the theta activity in the frontal area was associated with the flow state [5]. Regarding cardiac activity, de Manzano et al. [6] demonstrated that the R-R interval decreases and the LF/HF increases in the heart rate variability (HRV) might be related to an increased flow in an experiment targeting professional piano players. Previous studies have indicated that there was a significant inverted U-shaped relationship between the LF and the flow state during stress situations [7–9]; thus, these results also suggest that the flow state may be associated with moderate sympathetic activation. However, there are only a few studies examining was little research on the effects of flow state on the ANS activity.

A previous study of ours focused on the effects of task characteristics on HR and HRV by instructing them to perform the sensory intake task "without any hurry" and "as precisely as possible" [10]. The sensory intake/rejection hypothesis suggests that physiological responses such as the heart rate change depends on task characteristics [11]. Therefore, this study investigated the effects of different instructions on the flow state and physiological responses during a mental arithmetic (MA) task as a sensory rejection task.

## 2 Method

### 2.1 Participants

Eighteen healthy undergraduate students (mean age: $21.9 \pm 0.28$ years) participated in the study. Three participants were excluded from the analysis due to failure in Electrocardiogram (ECG) recording and frequent arrhythmia. Therefore, data from 15 participants were analyzed. This study was approved by the Ethics Committee of the University of Occupational and Environmental Health, Japan.

### 2.2 Procedure

Upon the arrival of the participants to the laboratory, after obtaining their informed consent, ECG electrodes and skin-gas sensors were attached. First, during the resting period (REST), participants were asked to watch a video of a forest scene (Fig. 1) on a 49-inch LED display in a sitting position. A previous study suggested that there were no differences between baseline and the VIDEO conditions regarding HR and HRV responses [12, 13]. Therefore, we applied physiological data in REST as a baseline. After resting for 5 min, the participants were asked to perform a mental arithmetic task for 15 min. The subjective flow state and mental workload assessments were conducted after the task.

**Fig. 1.** Forest scene in the video [13]

## 2.3 Task

The Uchida–Kraepelin performance test [14] was used as the mental arithmetic task. The participants were required to perform calculations on the pre-printed paper for 15 min. This paper contains in 15 lines of random, single-digit, and horizontally aligned numbers. In this task, participants were asked to start a new line regardless of their current progress in a certain line. All participants were administered to two conditions in which they performed under the different instructions, that is, "self-paced (SELF)" and "Always do more calculations than that of the previous line (FLOW)." The order of the tasks was counterbalanced.

## 2.4 Physiological Measurement

The ECGs from lead II were recorded during the tasks and the rest period. The HF, LF, LF/HF ratio, coefficient of variation of RR intervals (CV-RR), and HR were obtained.

This study monitored skin gas, which is a remarkable biomarker, for evaluating psychological states such as mental stress [15]. No studies have reported the relationship between the skin gas and the flow state, to the best of our knowledge. An overview of the experimental apparatus is shown in Fig. 2. An odor-measuring monitor (OMX-ADM, Shinyei Technology Co., Ltd) with a good response to ammonia was used for skin gas measurements, which were taken at two sites on the back of the neck and the back of the hand. Before the start of the experiment, the laboratory was ventilated until the acclimatization began. For cleaning and calibration, activated carbon was attached to the air intake of the odor-measuring monitor, which was cleaned and calibrated for several minutes. The collection portion of the experimental apparatus was then attached to the subject's measurement site and the end of the tube was attached to the odor-measuring monitor. After the above preparations were completed, the measurements of the odor monitors were started, measurements were confirmed to be stable, and the experiment was initiated. The odor intensity was monitored using an odor monitor. In this experiment, the odor intensity from the left palm of more than half of the participants exceeded the upper response. Thus, this study used the odor intensity from the back of the neck.

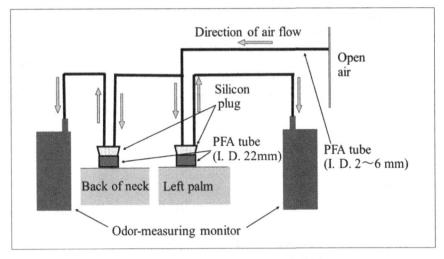

**Fig. 2.** Schematic diagram of the experimental method of skin gas measurement

## 2.5   Subjective Assessment

Subjective mental workload (MWL) scores were obtained using the National Aeronautics and Space Administration Task Load Index (NASA-TLX). This index contains the following six subscales: mental demand, physical demand, temporal demand, performance, effort, and frustration. The weighted mean (Adaptive Weighted Workload: AWWL) of these six subscales was calculated; it is a weighted average score of the six subscales calculated using the weighting coefficients defined by the rank order of the raw scores without the paired comparisons [16].

Flow scores were assessed by the flow state scale (FSS) [4]. It consists of the following nine items as follows: "challenge–skill balance," "action-awareness merging," "clear goals," "unambiguous feedback," "concentration on task," "sense of control," "loss of self-consciousness," "transformation of time," and "autotelic experience." However, we used four items, that is, Clear Goals (CG), Challenge–Skill Balance (CS), Unambiguous Feedback (UF), and Transformation of Time (TT) to verify "entering a flow state." Each item was rated on a 7-point scale ranging from "very strongly disagree" to "very strongly agree." The total scores for the four items were calculated. Participants answered questions on time perception during the task on a visual analog scale ranging from 0 ("feeling very short") to 100 ("felt very long").

## 2.6 Statistical Analysis

Averaged data during resting and the task were used to analyze the effects of instructions on physiological indices. The task periods were divided into three blocks (one block for 5 min) to evaluate the change. All physiological indices were standardized among the four blocks of each condition (REST, TASK-1, TASK-2, and TASK-3) for each participant. Two-way repeated-measures analysis of variance with task conditions (2) × blocks (4) was used to analyze the differences between factors and interactions with task conditions and blocks. Degrees of freedom were applied using the Greenhouse–Geisser correction. *Post-hoc* analysis using the Bonferroni correction was conducted. Paired *t*-tests were applied to test the differences in MWL scores between the SELF and FAST conditions.

# 3   Results

## 3.1   Subjective Scores

In the FSS results FSS, there were no significant differences in any subscale and total score. Furthermore, although the time perception score was <50 in the FAST condition, no significant difference was observed between task conditions.

The NASA-TLX score showed that TD was significantly higher in the FLOW condition than in the SELF condition (Fig. 3). However, there were no significant differences in the average workload scores.

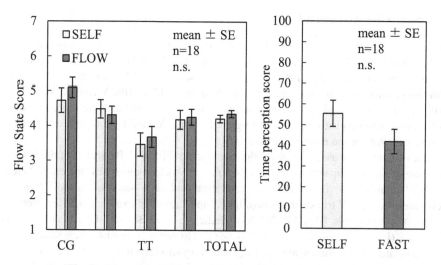

**Fig. 3.** Changes in the flow state score and time perception score

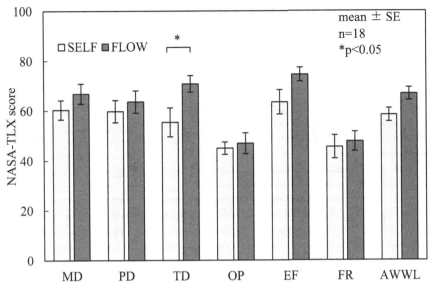

**Fig. 4.** Changes in NASA-TLX scores

## 3.2 Physiological Indices

The changes in the HR and HRV indices are shown in Figs. 4, 5, 6, 7 and 8. The HR in the TASK-3 in the SELF condition was significantly greater than that in the REST condition ($p < 0.05$). Furthermore, in the FLOW condition, the HR in all TASK blocks was significantly greater than that in the REST condition ($p < 0.01$). In the HRV indices, the results of the SELF condition showed that the LF in REST was significantly lower than that in some TASK blocks (TASK-1, $p < 0.05$; TASK-3, $p < 0.05$). The HF in the REST was significantly higher than that in the TASK-3 ($p < 0.05$). In contrast, in the FLOW condition, the LF during REST was significantly smaller in all TASK blocks (TASK-1, $p < 0.01$; TASK-2, $p < 0.01$; TASK-3, $p < 0.05$). The HR in REST was significantly greater than that in some TASK blocks (TASK-1 and TASK-2: $p < 0.05$). No significant main effects were observed for LF/HF ratio. Although no significant interaction between the task condition and block for LF, HF, and HR, a significant interaction was observed for LF/HF ($p < 0.05$). The skin gas results are shown in Fig. 9. Although there were no significant main effects, a significant interaction between the condition and block was observed ($p < 0.05$).

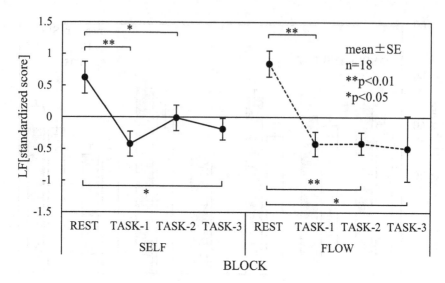

**Fig. 5.** Changes in the standardized score of LF

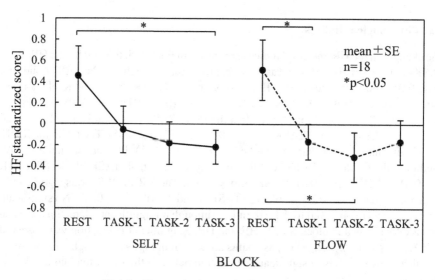

**Fig. 6.** Changes in the standardized score of HF

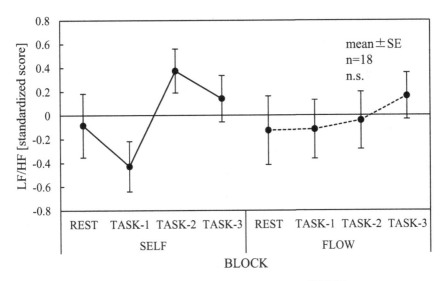

**Fig. 7.** Changes in the standardized score of LF/HF

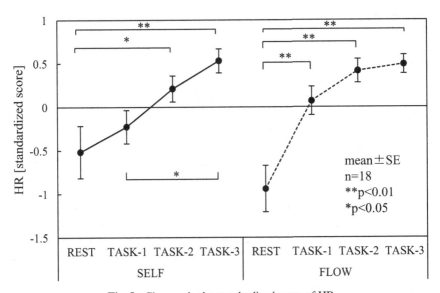

**Fig. 8.** Changes in the standardized score of HR

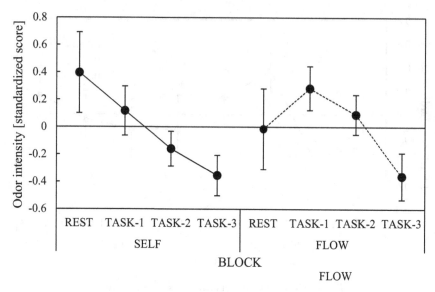

**Fig. 9.** Changes in the standardized score of skin gas

## 4 Discussion

The FSS results in this study suggest that the flow state might not be affected by the instructions. The TD score in the NASA-TLX was significantly higher in the FLOW condition, so the participants might have felt time pressure rather than "entering a flow state." As for the physiological indices, our results showed that the Pattern 1 response [16], including an increased HR during the MA task, was clearly confirmed. The HR in TASK-1 increased significantly only in the FLOW condition compared to the baseline (REST). These results are consistent with those of previous studies [17, 18]. However, an increase in the heart rate during the first 5 min after the starting task (TASK-1) may suggest a relationship between the flow state and enhancement of cardiac sympathetic nervous system activity. Although there was no significant difference between the REST and TASK blocks in both conditions, this result implies that the LF/HF does not reflect an index of the SNS activity but the balance between the SNS and PNS activity [19]. The LF and HF decreased significantly decreased in the MA task under both conditions. These results indicate that the inhibition of the parasympathetic nervous system activity was induced not by the content of the instruction, but by the task. Thus, the HR was affected more by task instructions than HRV parameters. In contrast, compared to the results of HR and HRV, there was no significant difference between the resting and task periods in skin gas. In monotonous tasks, such as the U-K test, a higher mental workload might be required to observe more gas emissions.

# 5   Conclusion

This study confirmed that the flow state during the mental task might not be affected by the content of instructions. However, the Pattern 1 response, where the heart rate increased during the MA task, was observed clearly when instructions to evoke the flow state was given. Further studies are necessary to investigate and clarify these physiological responses by comparing them in an experimental design.

# References

1. Csikszentmihalyi, M.: Beyond Boredom and Anxiety, pp. 38–43. Josey-Bass Publishers, San Francisco (1975)
2. Csikszentmihalyi, M.: Flow: the psychology of optimal experience. J. Leis. Res. **24**(1), 93–94 (1990)
3. Jackson, S.A., Ford, S.K., Kimiecik, J.C., Marsh, H.W.: Psychological correlates of flow in sport. J. Sport Exerc. Psychol. **20**, 358–378 (1998)
4. Jackson, S.A., Marsh, H.W.: Development and validation of a scale to measure optimal experience: the flow state scale. J. Sport Exerc. Psychol. **18**, 17–35 (1996)
5. Katahira, K., Yamazaki, Y., Yamaoka, C., Ozaki, H., Nakagawa, S., Nagata, N.: EEG correlates of the flow state: a combination of increased frontal theta and moderate Frontocentral alpha rhythm in the mental arithmetic task. Front. Psychol. **9**, 1–11 (2018)
6. De Manzano, Ö., Theorell, T., Harmat, L., Ullén, F.: The psychophysiology of flow during piano playing. Emotion **10**(3), 301–311 (2010)
7. Peifer, C., Schulz, A., Schachinger, H., Baumann, N., Antoni, C.H.: The relation of flow-experience and physiological arousal under stress-Can u shape it? J Exp. Soc. Psychol. **53**, 62–69 (2014)
8. Tian, Y., Bian, Y., Han, P., Wang, P., Gao, F., Chen, Y.: Physiological signal analysis for evaluating flow during playing of computer games of varying difficulty. Front. Psychol. **8**, 1–10 (2015)
9. Micheal, S.C., Stefano, N.K.: Is there an optimal autonomic state for enhanced flow and executive task performance? Front. Psychol. **10** (2019)
10. Kuraoka, H., Tsuruhara, K., Wada, C., Miyake, S.: Effects of a sensory intake task on heart rate variability. In: Proceedings 19th Triennial Congress of the IEA (IEA), Paper 2004 (2015)
11. Lacey, J.I.: Psychophysiological approaches to the evaluation of psychotherapeutic process and outcome. In: Rubinstein, E.A., Parloff, M.B. (eds.) Research in Psychotherapy. Washington, DC: American Psychological Association, pp. 160–208 (1959)
12. Brown, D.K., Barton, J.L., Gladwell, V.F.: Viewing nature scenes positively affects recovery of autonomic function following acute-mental stress. Environ. Sci. Technol. **47**, 5562–5569 (2013)
13. Kurosaka, C., Kuraoka, H., Sakamoto, H., Miyake, S.: Physiological responses induced by mental workload simulating daily work. In: Stephanidis, C., Antona, M. (eds.) HCI International 2020, pp. 359–366. Springer, Cham (2020). https://doi.org/10.1007/978-3-030-50726-8_47
14. Tsukuda, M., Nishiyama, Y., Kawai, S., Okumura, Y.: Identifying stress markers in skin gases by analysing gas collected from subjects undergoing the Trier social stress test and performing statistical analysis. J. Breath Res. **13**(3), 036003 (2019)
15. Kashiwagi, S., Yanai, H., Aoki, T., Tamai, H., Tanaka, Y., Hokugoh, K.: A factor analytic study of the items for the personality description based on the principle of the three traits theory for the work curve of addition of the Uchida-Kraepelin psychodiagnostic test. Shinrigaku Kenkyu (Jpn. J. Psychol.). **56**, 179–182 (1985)

16. Miyake, S., Kumashiro, M.: Subjective mental workload assessment technique-an introduction to NASA-TLX and SWAT and a proposal of simple scoring methods. Jpn. J. Ergon. **29**, 399–408 (1993)
17. Kasprowicz, A.L., Manuak, S.B., Malkoff, S.B., Krantz, D.S.: Individual differences in behaviorally evoked cardiovascular response: temporal stability and hemodynamic patterning. Psychophysiology **27**(6), 605–619 (1990)
18. Gendolla, G.H.E., Richter, M.: Ego Involvement and effort: cardiovascular, electrodermal, and performance effects. Psychophysiology **42**, 595–603 (2005)
19. Reyes del Paso, G.A., Langewitz, W., Mulder, L.J.M., Roon, A.V., Duschek, S.: The utility of low frequency heart rate variability as an index of sympathetic cardiac tone: a review with emphasis on a reanalysis of previous studies. Psychophysiology **50**, 477–487 (2013)

# Extravehicular Intelligence Solution for Lunar Exploration and Research: ARSIS 5.0

Megan Laing, Caleb Cram, Marc Frances, Akiah Tullis, Digno JR Teogalbo, and Karen Doty[✉]

Boise State University, 1910 W University Dr, Boise, ID 83725, USA
karendoty@boisestate.edu

**Abstract.** Augmented Reality Space Informatics System (ARSIS) 5.0 is a prototypal system designed to help astronauts on Extravehicular Activity (EVA), per the 2022 NASA SUITS (National Aeronautics and Space Administration) (Spacesuit User Interface Technologies for Students) Challenge. ARSIS employs a Ground Station and a HoloLens 2 application that cohesively collaborate to improve autonomy, efficiency, and efficacy of communication between Mission Control and an astronaut on the moon.

The core of the ARSIS system is in its interactive menu navigation. These menus are implementations of the mixed reality toolkit that have redundant interaction control methods employing hand tracking, eye tracking, and voice commands. A few examples of the interactive menus within the ARSIS system include procedures, biometrics, a geology sampling tool and field notes.

The Mini Map is a persistent dismissible panel that displays real-time environmental information, as well as waypoints and beacons set by mission control. This overlay can be expanded into an interactive panel (Mega Map) allowing the user to resize, zoom, set waypoints, and ultimately guide an RC assistant all utilizing hand tracking control methods. Utilizing the Mega Map, the HoloLens 2 user will be able to select destinations in the environment for an RC car, which utilizes self-driving to reach the selected destination. The user receives visual feedback in the HMD via static images and video feed.

Information overload is avoided by utilizing Arm-Retained Menus which are virtual informational overlays rendered over the user's forearms for easy visibility and access. ARMs provide additional access to commonly used features and functions such as Navigation, Emergency, Tools, and System Access. The Navigation ARM is located on the back of the left hand and provides quick access to the Mega Map as well as functionalities related to the Map Navigation Beacons. The Emergency ARM is located on the back of the user's right hand and provides quick access to Biometrics and LunaSAR system functionalities. The Tools ARM is located on the left palm and provides access to various tools. Included is the Record Path tool which allows the user to record their physical path of movement through an environment visualized as an AR annotation as well as the measurement tool which allows the user to place points to

M. Kurosu et al. (Eds.): HCII 2022, LNCS 13516, pp. 563–580, 2022.
https://doi.org/10.1007/978-3-031-17615-9_40

measure distance.

Mission Control is equipped with the Ground Station which includes virtual reality (VR) and desktop software portals affording Mission Control three major functionalities. The HoloLens 2 HMD records topological data about the user's surroundings and transmits that data to the Ground Station. Utilizing point cloud matching, a low-resolution version of the environment is rendered. This function provides the Ground Station users the ability to better understand the immediate environment. Future plans include implementing cloud anchors to increase the accuracy of this simulated environment to combat the problem of drift over time. This function supports the primary purpose of the Ground Station to provide Telestration to the HoloLens 2 user. The Ground Station user has the ability to create icons or paths, which are placed in the HoloLens 2 field of view via augmented reality (AR) annotation. Annotations are placed in accordance with the topology received by the Ground Station ensuring they are properly rendered in the HoloLens 2 user's real-world environment. The Ground Station is also capable of adding or removing Navigational Beacons as well as procedures at run time to allow for flexible problem solving and communication. Topology reconstruction, Telestration, and Mission Updates can all be performed in real-time with minimal latency affording improved effectiveness and efficiency between Mission Control and an Astronaut on EVA.

**Keywords:** Augmented reality · Extended reality · Virtual reality · Telestration · Bio-metrics

## Terms

| | |
|---|---|
| AR: | Augmented Reality |
| ARMs: | Arm Retained Menus |
| ARSIS: | Augmented Reality Space Informatics System |
| CRUD: | Create, Read, Update, Delete |
| EVA: | Extravehicular Activity |
| HITL: | Human In The Loop |
| HMD: | Head Mounted Display |
| HUD: | Heads-up Display |
| MRTK: | Mixed Reality Toolkit |
| NASA: | National Aeronautics and Space Administration |
| LunarSAR: | Lunar Search and Rescue |
| RC: | Remote Controlled |
| SLAP: | Situational and Locational Awareness Package |
| SUITS: | Spacesuit User Interface Technologies for Students |
| UI: | User Interface |
| VR: | Virtual Reality |
| XR: | Extended Reality |

# 1   Introduction and Background

We are a team of students and faculty at Boise State University that engage in the annual NASA SUITS challenge from the NASA Microgravity University challenges. The challenge focuses on XR technologies for use on Extravehicular Activities (EVAs).Recently, the focus of the challenge shifted to lunar excursions and research efforts.

Our project, ARSIS, is a prototypal system to answer this challenge. ARSIS uses an Augmented Reality HMD, a VR HMD, and a desktop computer. It was built primarily in the Unity Game Engine with the MRTK2 and Photon plugins. ARSIS is on its fifth iteration, or ARSIS 5.0.

The XR HMD is the primary device. We are currently developing on a Microsoft Hololens 2. This device is worn by the astronaut, and is the main window into the functionality of ARSIS. The XR HMD is used to display contextual information to the astronaut, to interact with the system, and to send information back to Mission Control.

The VR HMD and the desktop environment are the portals for Mission Control. We are currently developing with an Oculus Quest 2. Mission control uses the portals to see a VR mesh representing the astronaut's environment, gain current information about the astronaut and mission, and to send mission-relevant visual data to the astronaut via their AR HMD.

## 1.1   Design Requirements (based on NASA's 2021-2022 Challenge Description)

Accepting the challenge NASA gives us comes with an outline of things they expect to see each year. This includes 2 sections; primary and secondary. Primary objectives is the area they expect all groups to develop UI towards, while secondary objectives is for returning teams, like us, to have an opportunity to do extra work that NASA is hoping to see, however is not required.

**Primary Objectives.** Per participation requirements, all teams are expected to develop UI encompassing, Navigation, Terrain Sensing, EVA System State, and User Interface and Controls. For navigation the requirements specifically outline a resource that will safely direct the AR device through planned and unplanned terrain, including long range and short range distances. The UI must also include a way to familiarize itself with its surroundings in order to chart data correctly and keep the user safe through Terrain Sensing. Teams must introduce new ways of collaboration between the system and the suit's telemetry stream. And finally NASA asks the teams to display a User Interface and Controls that the astronaut can navigate with functions that will be useful to the user for their EVA missions.

**Secondary Objectives.** A heavy emphasis is placed on tele-robotics, and inclusion of a robotic assistant aid, for returning teams this year. NASA challenges returning teams to implement the use of an auxiliary device. In addition, peripheral devices are recommended to provide functions in data collection and device functionality. Lastly, NASA recommended implementation of geology research through data recognition or sampling in order to assist in the large scope of lunar research.

## 2  UI Navigation

The ARSIS 5.0 UI takes advantage of Microsoft's Mixed Reality Tool Kit. MRTK is a Unity-based tool that provides the developer with an impressive range of features and components that allow the developer to rapidly prototype cross-platform mixed reality content for any headset capable of it. MRTK recognizes a multitude of inputs. These include eye tracking, voice commands, and hand tracking. This will provide the user with multiple redundant input methods to navigate our UI.

### 2.1  Voice Commands

Voice commands are one of the main inputs we use for ARSIS 5.0. Each of our UI menus and included buttons can be called to just by using your voice. Each UI element is designed to display the command intended to trigger that element. For example, if the user see's the close button, it will say "close".

### 2.2  Gaze and Voice

As mentioned above, each UI element is designed with the trigger word displayed. ARSIS 5.0 uses gaze tracking as a form of confirmation to the user when using voice input. When a user wants to close a menu with their voice, they need to look at the close button before they it can be executed.

### 2.3  Hand Gestures

Hand gestures are an essential input method to ARSIS 5.0. MRTK has multiple recognized gestures to help the user navigate. This includes pinch and hold, double pinch and hold, flat palm, tap, and tap and hold. MRTK also uses physics based interactions with UI elements such as buttons, scroll menus, and models.

### 2.4  Eye-Tracking

Eye tracking is intended to allow users to select UI elements with just their eyes. We experimented with this functionality in previous iterations of ARSIS, however eye tracking was found to be tedious which increased the difficulty of navigating the UI drastically.

# 3   Informational Displays

The interfaces in ARSIS 5.0 leverage the HoloLens' ability to display and represent data and information through a tactile and visual appearance ability to implement user interfaces which are used in redundancy, promote efficiency, and allow ease of use. These interfaces appear virtually and can be anchored to locations in real space to provide useful contexts for the AR participant.

## 3.1   Arm Retained Menus (ARMS)

We are developing ARMs as a user interface that leverage the unique ability of the HoloLens to track hand and wrist locations to anchor user interfaces in an accessible and easily identifiable location. ARMs aid the user in avoiding information overload and clutter by storing information into distinguishable areas. The Navigation ARM will contain access points to our Mini-Map and Mega-Map interfaces and navigation beacon controls. The Emergency ARM will contain quick access to Biometrics and LunarSAR (Lunar Search and Rescue) system functionalities. The Tools ARM will provide access to the record path tool, built-in measurement tools, and field notes access (Fig. 1).

## 3.2   Mini-Map

The MiniMap is a widget anchored on the user's screen space that changes and updates in real-time with environmental information, and includes information about waypoints and beacons set by mission control. This provides a visual indicator of the user in physical space and enables ease of use when navigating by providing visual cues to movement.

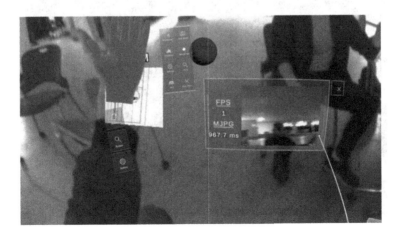

**Fig. 1.** Information display

### 3.3   Mega-Map

The MegaMap is a manipulatable interface that occupies virtual space for use in navigation and communication. This interface provides a tactile interface for resizing, zooming, setting waypoints, and guiding an RC assistant with hand tracking control methods. When accompanied with annotations provided by telestration, the MegaMap improves collaboration between users.

### 3.4   Lunar Search and Rescue (LunarSAR)

LunarSAR is a module that enables users to register and record their location so that the AR participant can calculate the proper heading and bearing to the downed crew member(s).

## 4   Lighting in Harsh Enviroments

We have tested ARSIS in a wide range of harsh environments from desert sand dunes to frozen lakes in both high and low lighting scenarios. While the HoloLens 2 is a surprisingly robust piece of hardware that handles various environments with relative ease, it struggles to the point of non-functionality in low light conditions due to the depth sensor's inability to function adequately in darkness. In low light situations, the Windows 10 Holographic operating system overrides the ARSIS software to display a warning regarding being unable to spatially map out your surroundings (Fig. 2).

**Fig. 2.** Windows 10 holographic operating system

## 4.1  Low Light

In testing, we found that environments with low light conditions are not ideal for the HoloLens 2. Its ability to receive meshes from the depth sensor are faltered due to the inadequate lighting. Without proper illumination, the HoloLens 2 will just refuse to work along with all of its core functionalities such as articulated hand tracking and mesh gathering.

**Rover Equipped with Floodlights.** As a returning team of the SUITS challenge, we were given an a secondary goal of implementing an RC robotic assistant that can be controlled via the HoloLens 2. We plan to mount diffused lighting on the assistant too aid the user in providing adequate illumination. This heavy lighting should allow the user to see any obstacles that may be in the users way.

**HMD Mounted Lights.** The solution we came up with involved zip tying five LED pen lights to the HoloLens 2. In testing, we found that the HMD mounted lights work very well. It allowed us to see our hands and effectively capture meshes. In some instances, the intense light reflecting off surfaces can mess with your meshes and tracking if situated in a small space or corner. The solution we plan to implement in the near future would be diffusing the HMD lights to cover an area rather than using a direct beam.

## 4.2  High Light

Low light however is not the only environmental concern for the HoloLens 2. In testing, our team has found that intense lighting situations can prove to be just as disastrous in the HoloLens 2 as low light scenarios if not worse due to the fact that Windows 10 Holographic operating system has no form of warning for when the lighting is too intense as it does for low light. A consistent issue that we faced in our tests at Bruneau Sand Dunes and the frozen Cascade lake is that the intense sunlight coupled with the relatively reflective ice and sand surfaces led to the waveguide holograms in the HoloLens 2 viewport being completely washed out. Many virtual objects simply aren't bright enough to be overlayed on top of the bright sunlight.

**Photochromic Tint/film from Holotint to Block Light.** Our solution to this issue is relatively simple, however has proven to be quite effective in our early testing. We have chosen to apply a photochromic film to the HoloLens 2 which acts as sunglasses for the device by blocking out the harshest sun rays allowing the user to clearly see the virtual objects being displayed in their viewport. This tint can be added or removed from the display of the HoloLens 2 for usage in both high and low light environments allowing us to employ ARSIS in more diverse conditions.

# 5   Features

## 5.1   Interactive Menus

The core of ARSIS 5.0 is its interactive menus. The interactive menus are persistent augmented reality windows that display text, images, and interactive buttons. The menus are accessed through voice commands or via a persistent hand menu. There are four primary menus in ARSIS: procedures, biometrics, and field notes.

## 5.2   Procedures

The procedures menu displays a list of recorded procedures using CRUD (create, read, update, delete) guidelines. The astronaut can select any of these procedures to display. Once selected, the astronaut can see images and text describing each step of the procedure. The user can navigate hands-free via voice commands. Additionally the user can navigate via touch controls if desired.

## 5.3   Biometrics

ARSIS is a prototypal tool for spacewalks, thus it contains a spacesuit integrity menu. The biometrics menu displays all metrics of interest concerning a spacesuit. It additionally provides information over whether their measurements are currently in the acceptable and safe range. Biometrics out of the acceptable range (or close to it) will display in red. Otherwise they will display in green. ARSIS's menu currently uses simulated data from a telemetry stream, rather than a functioning suit.

## 5.4   Field Notes

The field notes menu presents a series of prompts concerning a geology sample. The astronaut can click through these prompts to record notes of the sample's structure, color, and other characteristics. At the end of the questionnaire, the astronaut can record a voice recording and take a picture. All of this data is saved to the device and is accessible to view at a later time.

## 5.5   Spacial Awareness

One of the primary goals of ARSIS is to aid astronauts in navigation. A priority of this objective is to allow the astronaut to see their location in relation to the mission at all times. To this end, a Situational and Locational Awareness Package (SLAP) was created. SLAP has several tools for helping the astronaut traverse terrain, navigate to locations, and send locational information to mission control. The parts of SLAP are: map, minimap, beacons, telestration, notifications, breadcrumb trail.

**Map.** This is a map of the mission location. It includes as much detailed information as can be provided in an image file. The astronaut's current position is recorded on the map, as well as the position of all current beacons.

**Mini-Map.** A smaller, more contextual map sits persistently in the astronaut's field of view. This map shows the astronauts current position, facing, and relative distance to all active beacons. The minimap can be disabled and re-enabled via voice command.

**Beacons.** Beacons represent a location relevant to the current mission. They are displayed as colored orbs that float in augmented reality. On the minimap, they are represented via a direction arrow and a distance.

**Telestration.** A spatial mesh of the environmental topography is gathered from the Augmented Reality (AR) Head Mounted Display (HMD) and transferred to mission control over a wifi network. A map is then built from this data, and displayed in 3D for mission control in a desktop or Virtual Reality environment. Mission Control can see the environmental topography as well as the AR HMD user's location. In either one of these portals, Mission Control can create text, icons, and lines to transmit to the astronaut. This essentially allows mission control to 'draw' on the astronaut's environment.

**Notifications.** If an event occurs that could cause later issues if not immediately resolved, a notification appears in the astronaut's field of view. This notification can be accompanied by a sound effect or a visual effect, depending on its urgency.

**Breadcrumb Trail.** This is a tool that allows the HMD user to record their location as they travel, allowing efficient backtracking.

## 5.6    Misc

Camera Streaming for Remote Controlled Vehicles One of the considerations of this challenge is implementing RC vehicles. We have figured out how to stream webcam data over a network and display it in ARSIS, proving that we can provide this data wherever we have a wifi connection.

# 6    Testing Results (Human in the Loop Testing in Variable Environments)

## 6.1    High Light Test of ARSIS and VR Ground Station in a Sandy Environment

After the enlightening lessons learned from testing our software at the Bruneau Sand Dune, we sought out other extreme scenarios to test the limitations of our solution and found the perfect challenge in snowmobiling across the frozen lake Cascade. We attempted a few methods to try shielding the Quest 2 from the sun enough to allow for positional controller tracking with some moderate success ultimately deciding that we need to run the VR Ground Station from indoors moving forward until we can implement effective hand tracking controls which should work effectively in high light environments. We knew that highlight washing out the HoloLens 2 viewport was a definitive issue based on our testing at Bruneau sand dunes, however this was our first opportunity to attempt utilizing the HoloLens at a relatively high speed. For this test the VR Ground Station mapped out a rough path to follow and the ARSIS user attempted to follow that path while driving a snowmobile. While the HoloLens 2 performed relatively well at low speeds, as soon as we began to encroach 10 - 15 mi per hour on the snowmobile the HoloLens began to lose positional tracking. Additionally it appeared to begin mixing up the spatial mesh understanding placing parts of the virtual scene far beneath the surface of the snow and ice. While rebooting ARSIS fixed this issue, it does not provide an effective solution at high rates of movement and fast acceleration which is something we will need to keep in mind moving forward with this project (Fig. 3).

## 6.2    High Speed and Reflectively Test of ARSIS and Ground Station on Snow.

Throughout the course of developing ARSIS, we had heavily tested our system throughout a variety of indoor spaces and even some outdoor locations such as backyards, however we needed to find a place to test the absolute limitations of our solution. This entailed performing a test of our VR Ground Station running on the Quest 2 and ARSIS running on the HoloLens 2 at Bruneau Sand Dunes which provided the perfect opportunity to test the lighting limitations. Prior to testing we were unaware of any potential issues, however we rapidly encountered some important limitations. The VR Ground Station proved to be nearly infunctional due to an inability to track the controllers. Oculus uses IR lights in their Oculus Touch controllers to track their respective positions from the HMD. Unfortunately the sun was so bright that the light reflecting off the surface of the sand dune was enough to completely wash out those IR lights leading to no positional tracking in the Quest 2. From a software standpoint, the VR ground station worked flawlessly, however without being able to track controller positions, our telestration tools proved to be incredibly difficult to effectively utilize. ARSIS also operated flawlessly from a software standpoint, but we

**Fig. 3.** Sand dune test 2

quickly encountered some serious limitations to the hardware itself. Specifically, the sunlight beaming down and reflecting off the sand completely washed out the waveguide display making it incredibly difficult to see any of the virtual objects being placed in the environment by the VR Ground Station (Fig. 4).

### 6.3 Testing ARSIS on the Quest 2 with Ground Station on Quest 2 to Test the Limitation of Oculus Passthrough and Various Hardware Options

Since Oculus released their passthrough API for the Quest in late July of 2021, our development team has been heavily experimenting with its obvious limitations as well as its surprising use cases. One such demonstration we've assembled is a version of ARSIS, originally built for the HoloLens 2, running in the Quest 2 using passthrough as well as a version of our VR Ground Station that has Oculus passthrough enabled instead of a virtual skybox. This proved to work surprisingly well with absolutely all of the functionality we'd built for the HoloLens 2 working flawlessly in the Quest 2 with the exception of mesh gathering from the real world environment due to the lack of a depth sensor on the Quest 2 and some materials needing to be modified to accurately display over the Oculus passthrough layer. The VR Ground Station worked so well in passthrough on

**Fig. 4.** Snowmobile test

the Quest 2 that we are now making that a core feature in our primary VR Ground Station project. The ability to visually bring the ARSIS user's environment into your real world space is incredibly useful for giving informed guidance to the ARSIS user (Fig. 5).

**Fig. 5.** Hardware options

## 7 Testing Results (Human in the Loop Testing in Controlled Environments)

Prior to testing ARSIS 5.0, the principal investigator provided guidance on how to wear the HoloLens 2. The principal investigator demonstrated the proper way of viewing the interface in the HoloLens 2 HUD. In order to gain accurate data during testing it was important to ensure all participants wore the HoloLens

2 correctly and could view the user interface in the correct manner. Using the Hololens Device Portal, the principal investigator has the ability to view what the participant sees while experiencing ARSIS 5.0. The HoloLens Device Portal is described in the next section (Figs. 6 and 7).

**Fig. 6.** UI test transfer

**Fig. 7.** UI field note

## 7.1 HoloLens Device Portal

Using the HoloLens Device Portal, the principal investigator has the ability to see how participants view the interface. If participants were unable to view the ARSIS 5.0 interface accurately, the Hololens 2 was adjusted accordingly to fit the participant correctly. The Mixed Reality Portal allowed the principal investigator to view the experience through the eyes of the participant. Additionally, the HoloLens Device Portal provided a way to record the experience thus providing information for quantitative analysis. In order to gain accurate data on the usability and function of the ARSIS 5.0 user interface, participants experienced the application in a controlled environment. The environment used for testing was an open room with limited furniture. Lighting in the environment was limited to low light therefore testing the effectiveness of the interface in a low light environment. The testing environment has limited distractions thus providing an ample space to test the application without interruptions.

## 7.2   Participants

For testing purposes, participants with moderate experience in extended reality or virtual environments were recruited for testing. All participants were accustomed to wearable HUDs and had experienced immersive environments prior to testing the ARSIS 5.0 application on the Hololens 2. All participants tested are adults and were over the age of 18 at the moment of testing. Gender data and accessibility data was not gathered for this test. However, in future testing, additional information may provide insight on demographic characteristics and user testing correlation to the ARSIS 5.0 interface. In total, seven participants were tested for this part of the study (Fig. 8).

## 7.3   User Testing Procedures

Participants were provided a series of directions to follow while experiencing the application.

## 7.4   Controlled Environment Test Results

All participants successfully followed the tasks asked of them. Additionally, all participants were able to operate the user interface as predicted. When testing the voice commands, all participants successfully operated the voice interface. Finally, all participants were able to locate and document the field object and provide a summary in the field notes. Gathered qualitative data is listed below in Fig. 12 (Fig. 9).

## 8   Limitations

It is important to note the limitations of the HITL tests that may have impacted the user testing results. The limitations for variable environment tests include For the controlled testing procedures, additional information over participant characteristics may provide insight on data patterns in response to the ARSIS 5.0 interface. Since data was not gathered on certain participant characteristics such as accessibility needs or gender, it is possible that future tests may benefit from

**Testing Environment Preparation**
- Clean the HoloLens 2 & Oculus Quest 2
- Place X or arrow on the floor for orientation
- Place furniture in different locations to provide obstacles in test environment
- Open Windows Mixed Reality Portal and prepare it to record the test from the HoloLens 2 point of view
- Place field note sample in the space. It is recommended to use the mascot.

**UI Navigation**
The UI Navigation portion of the test requests participants experience the user interface by testing both the interactive touch and voice commands

**User Interface Testing Type**
- Voice: ARSIS 5.0 includes voice commands as an additional interactive element used in the interface. Voice commands provide a redundant form of interaction in addition to providing a way to interact with multiple interfaces simultaneously. While there are many voice commands to test. The voice command "follow me" was chosen as a consistent voice interface test for the controlled environment testing. Participants are asked to focus on a menu UI vocally say the "follow me" command.

- Hand Tracking: ARSIS 5.0 uses hand tracking as a way for participants to interact with the user interface of the application. It is suggested that all participants wear gloves if possible in order to emulate a more accurate example of the user interface use scenario

- Touch: During testing, participants are asked to use hand tracking and touch commands to interact with multiple UIs. Below lists the UIs tested in the controlled environment testing.

**MiniMap User Interface**
- Participants are asked to locate the minimap UI
- Participants are asked to toggle the map on and off

**Telestration**
- Participants are asked to toggle telestration on and off
- Participants are requested to follow the path previously created by the ground station user. The path will lead the participant to the field note location.
- Participants are requested to test the path interface by asking them to both enable and disable path recording as well via voice command

**Field Notes**
- Prior to testing, the principal investigator chooses an object to use for field note sampling. The principal investigator places that object in a location in the testing environment. For adequate testing of the user interface, the object should be placed out of sight in order to test the telestration and navigation user interfaces.
- Participants are requested to locate and navigate toward the field sample
- Participants are requested to inspect the field sample and respond to Mission Control with a voice recording summary of the sample in the field notes

**Fig. 8.** ARSIS 5.0 test scenario

more detailed participant demographic information. Additionally, due to current time constraints, seven participants was the maximum number of participants tested for the first controlled testing experience on the ARSIS 5.0 interface. It would be beneficial to test a larger number of participants in the future in order to gain more detailed data. Finally, the controlled environment testing focused solely on testing the interface from the HoloLens 2 point of view. Thus, participants tested in the position of astronauts in the field. However, ARSIS 5.0

- Over half of the participants commented that they were able to navigate accurately with the minimap and made a point to mention that the behavior of the interface responded intuitively to their movements.
- Multiple participants noted the voice commands were easy to understand and utilize
- One participant suggested that the menu UI distracted them during testing
- One participant commented that the minimap obscured their vision during part of the test
- All participants enjoyed the navigation process of the application and were successful in navigating to the planned location.
- Multiple participants commented that the design of the 3D UIs were easy to understand
- Multiple participants commented that hand tracking worked well and was intuitive to use
- Two participants said they had difficulty in reading the maps at times. They both suggested this may be due to a needed adjustment when wearing the device.

**Fig. 9.** Controlled results

additionally functions as an application usable from the Ground Station point of view. Participants in the controlled environment test were not granted the ability to experience the application from the Ground Station interface. Future tests may benefit by testing both collaborative interfaces in the ARSIS 5.0 interface.

## 9   Future Plans

One massive update to our system we are currently working on is building an ERA (Extravehicular Robotic Assistant) to assist the ARSIS user on EVA's. Commands will be delivered to the assistant from the VR Ground Station or ARSIS allowing both mission control and an astronaut on EVA to pilot the ERA. The robotic assistant will be equipped with a suite of lighting, cameras and sensors to illuminate and capture the environment for transcription to the VR Ground Station and the ARSIS system. Currently this takes the form of a simple webcam feeding data back to our software portals, however we plan to experiment with 360 footage, automated hazard detection, point clouds and mesh generation all of which will be used to more effectively inform the VR Ground Station as well as the ARSIS user.

Currently, in ARSIS, we are using MRTK V2 to handle our input methods such as hand and eye tracking. Microsoft has announced plans to release MRTK V3 to the community in the near future at which point we will begin upgrading our systems to fully leverage the new toolkits as it's released.

Hand tracking has proven to be an absolutely incredible input method for the Quest 2 in our initial experimentation, and we're elated to implement it at a deeper level throughout our project. However, hand tracking on the Quest 2 does have its limitations and our team recently learned about UltraLeap's Gemini hand tracking system which can be implemented into the Quest 2 via the Ultraleap Stereo IR 170 depth sensor. This could allow for significantly increased accuracy and refresh rate of hand tracking allowing us to move away from the need for controllers entirely.

### 9.1 Additional Testing

Additional testing is planned to test a larger control group on the interface functionality and response. Three added testing dates are planned over the next three months in order to gain data on the interface and provide time to improve the experience. Final testing for the ARSIS 5.0 iteration will commence at the Johnson Space Center in Houston, Texas.

In addition to testing more participants, other areas of functionality are planned as an included portion in future tests. Testing the ground station interface is planned as a future user experience test. Incorporating the robotic assistant to the ARSIS 5.0 interface additionally provides new testing opportunities for future user experience testing.

## 10 Conclusion

This year has allowed for many new developments to our XR solution as we strive to achieve NASA's requests and beyond. The capabilities provided by ARSIS improves situational awareness and more effectively equips astronauts for the unpredictable environments they will face while helping mission control maintain a clear understanding of what is transpiring during a mission via telepresence so that they can more effectively guide and communicate with the astronaut. ARSIS has been a working project for our team for the last 5 years and as we grow more in our prototype we look forward to seeing it's implementation in real lunar research.

**Acknowledgements.** The achievements our team have and will continue to make are in large part due to our advisors Dr. Steve Swanson and Dr. Karen Doty. We appreciate all their contributions and thank you, the reader, as well for supporting our efforts and to HCI for inviting our team to participate in HCI International 2022.

## References

1. Arora, R., Kazi, R. H., Anderson, F., Grossman, T., Singh, K., Fitzmaurice, G. W.: Experimental evaluation of sketching on surfaces in VR. In: CHI, vol. 17, pp. 5643–5654 (2017)
2. Barnes, R., Press, R.: Self-driving RC car using tensorflow and opencv. The MagPi magazine. Accessed 22 Oct 2021. https://magpi.raspberrypi.com/articles/self-driving-rc-car
3. Bowman, D., Kruijff, E., La Viola, J., Poupyrev, I.: 3D user interfaces theory and practice. Boston, MA: Addison-Wesley. Kindle Edition (2004)

4. Hsieh, C.-Y., Chiang, Y.-S., Chiu, H.-Y., Chang, Y.-J.: Bridging the virtual and real worlds: a preliminary study of messaging notifications in virtual reality. In: Proceedings of the 2020 CHI Conference on Human Factors in Computing Systems (CHI 2020). Association for Computing Machinery, New York, NY, USA, 1–14 (2020). https://doi.org/10.1145/3313831.3376228

5. Mahalil, I., Yusof, A.M., Ibrahim, N., Mahidin, E.M.M., Rusli, M.E.: Virtual reality mini map presentation techniques: lessons and experience learned. In: 2019 IEEE Conference on Graphics and Media (GAME), pp. 26–31, Polar-kev et al., July 1, 2021. What is the Mixed Reality Toolkit, Microsoft (2019). https://docs.microsoft.com/en-us/windows/mixed-reality/mrtk-unity/. https://doi.org/10.1109/GAME47560.2019.8980759

6. Pell, M.: Envisioning holograms: design breakthrough experiences for mixed reality. New York, Apress (2017). https://doi.org/10.1007/978-1-4842-2749-7

7. Yoshinaga, T.: HoloLens2 Point Cloud App. Github Repository. https://github.com/TakashiYoshinaga/HoloLens2-Point-Cloud-App (2021)

# A Study of Driver Fatigue States in Multiple Scenarios Based on the Fatigue and Sleepiness Indicator

Minxia Liu[1] ⓘ, Xintai Song[1](✉) ⓘ, and Mohammad Shidujaman[2] ⓘ

[1] School of Mechanics and Vehicles, Beijing Institute of Technology, Beijing 100081, China
1433626140@qq.com
[2] American International University- Bangladesh, Dhaka 1229, Bangladesh

**Abstract.** In order to solve the problem that the fatigue indicators of both EEG and ECG are not in the same evaluation dimension in the study of driver fatigue state under different emotions, this paper introduces the conceptual formula of the Fatigue and Sleepiness Indicator for conducting the processing of fatigue indicators in the late data, and normalizes the data of several types of different evaluation dimensions to get the data in the same evaluation dimension, which facilitates the integration of EEG and ECG data. In this paper, $(\alpha + \theta)/\beta$ was used as the EEG fatigue index, and LF/HF was used as the ECG fatigue index; the EEG fatigue index and ECG fatigue index were processed using the conceptual formula of the Fatigue and Sleepiness Indicator to obtain the EEG and ECG exertional fatigue values. Finally, the data were fused using principal component analysis to obtain the integrated fatigue index, i.e., the Fatigue and Sleepiness Indicator. The comparison of the values of the degree of fatigue showed that in the two kinds of brain load driving tasks, the emergence of emotions that distinguish the envisaged will increase the driver's brain load, thus increasing the degree of fatigue of the driver, the performance of the degree of fatigue of the driver in the usual scenario without emotional fluctuation state is between the pleasant emotion and sad emotion, the fatigue of the driver in the pleasant emotion is the lowest, and the effect of the happy group on the degree of fatigue in the fatigue driving stage is significantly higher than the effect of the sad group on the degree of fatigue. By this study, differences in driver fatigue performance under different emotions were obtained, and the applicability of the conceptual formula of fatigue degree in the fusion of EEG and ECG data was tested.

**Keywords:** Fatigue and Sleepiness Indicator · EEG · ECG · Fatigued driving · Mood

## 1 Introduction

As the most common problem in human-computer interaction, fatigue has the most extensive impact on production life, and devices such as EEG and ECG can monitor human fatigue, brain load and other states, and then decode human state information to achieve dynamic work task allocation, adjustment or provide fatigue and overload

M. Kurosu et al. (Eds.): HCII 2022, LNCS 13516, pp. 581–596, 2022.
https://doi.org/10.1007/978-3-031-17615-9_41

warning, effectively improving the friendliness, safety and work efficiency of human-computer interaction. For example, Ker-Jiun Wang et al. used a BCI biosensing algorithm to translate the "feeling of missing someone" into perceptible images and tactile sensations that were communicated remotely to a friend, providing immediate telepathy and a sense of calmness, and improving the friendliness of human-computer interaction [1].

Based on this, this paper used EEG and ECG to monitor the fatigue state of drivers in different emotional states in two brain load scenarios, recorded the EEG and ECG changes data of several drivers in the whole process of simulated driving, and extracted from them the EEG fatigue index - the power spectral density ratio of $\alpha$, $\theta$ and $\beta$ waves $(\alpha + \theta)/\beta$, the ECG fatigue index - the ratio of low frequency variation to high frequency variation in the N-N interval LF/HF. Then the data in different evaluation dimensions were sorted and fused using the concept formula of the Fatigue and Sleepiness Indicator to obtain the comprehensive fatigue indicator – the Fatigue and Sleepiness Indicator (FSI), and the fatigue state laws of drivers in different emotional states were found through the comparison of driver fatigue degree, and some practical suggestions were given according to these laws.

## 2  Background of the Study

### 2.1  Bioelectrical Signal Generation Mechanisms

Electrical signals such as EEG and ECG are essentially bioelectrical signals, which are changes in potential activity and polarity that occur in organs, tissues and cells. When the cell membrane of the tissue cell in question is subjected to a specific stimulus, its permeability to tiny ions such as $Na^{+1}$, $Cl^{-1}$, $Ca^{+2}$, $K^{+1}$, etc. changes, and special channels on it open, causing ions on both sides of the membrane to flow in a certain direction, and the resting potential is periodically disrupted and reestablished, during which the cell membrane with the changed potential produces a periodic local potential difference with the neighboring cell membrane that is still in the resting state. It is transmitted along the axon to the axon terminal, where the synaptic vesicles in the axon terminal are released into the synaptic gap and then captured by the postsynaptic membrane, thus altering the excitability of the next neuron. A detectable bioelectric signal is formed when the firing activity of some neuronal cells is synchronized and the electric field activity they form is consistent and the amount of energy accumulated in the signal exceeds a certain domain value [2].

### 2.2  EEG Signal Analysis

EEG signal analysis methods can be broadly classified into five categories, namely, time domain analysis, frequency domain analysis, time/frequency domain analysis, artificial neural network (ANN) analysis and nonlinear dynamics analysis [3].

Among them, the frequency domain analysis methods include power spectrum estimation, coherence analysis, bispectrum analysis, etc. The commonly used one is power spectrum analysis, which can be divided into two major categories: the first category is the classical power spectrum calculation methods, including the direct method and the indirect method, the direct method is to calculate the power spectrum of the signal directly by using the square of the magnitude of the transform coefficient of the Fourier transform of the EEG signal, and the indirect method is to first estimate the self-intercorrelation function of the EEG signal, and then find the power spectrum of the signal; the second category is modern power spectrum calculation methods, including power spectrum calculation based on AR model, ARMA model, MA model, MUSIC algorithm and eigenvectors [4].

Since EEG signals are more concise and intuitive in the frequency domain, many scholars use frequency domain analysis for signal processing. For example, Yabing Zhu et al. extracted the rhythm signals in the EEG signal, selected the energy values of $\delta$, $\theta$, $\alpha$ and $\beta$ waves as the characteristic values of fatigue driving, and used the ratio of the sum of the energy values of $\delta$ and $\theta$ waves to the energy value of $\beta$ waves as the fatigue index, and found that the fatigue index increased gradually as the subject's fatigue increased. The fatigue index was found to increase gradually with the increase of the fatigue level of the subject [5]; Tianjiao Liu et al. extracted the three frequency bands of $\alpha$, $\beta$ and $\theta$ waves in the EEG signal, and fitted the EEG signal fitting index $(\theta + \alpha)/\beta$ with the subjective fatigue level of the subject, and the two were positively correlated, thus verifying that the brain electrical activity signal fitting index $(\theta + \alpha)/\beta$ can make real-time estimation of the fatigue state of the driver [6]; Aftanas L I et al. used Fourier transform to map the raw EEG signal to theta, alpha and beta bands and derived the power spectral density of each electrode as EEG features on the basis of power spectrum [7]; Nie D et al. used video stimulation in the delta band (1–4 Hz), theta band (4–8 Hz), the alpha frequency band (8–13 Hz), beta frequency band (13–30 Hz) and gamma frequency band (36–44 Hz) using fast Fourier transform and combined with linear dynamics and other methods to identify emotions and fit emotion curves using stream learning [8]; Reza Khosrowabadi et al. filtered the raw EEG signal to 4 Hz –13 Hz and then extracted the EEG features of the corresponding brain regions using kernel density estimation and Gaussian mixture model, respectively [9].

### 2.3   ECG Signal Analysis

Typical ECG indicators include heart rate and heart rate variability. Unlike heart rate analysis, which studies the number of heart beats, heart rate variability analysis analyzes the differences and patterns of consecutive cycles of heart beats to find out the differences in heart beat cycles and thus discover some physiological or psychological changes in the human body, so heart rate variability analysis is more valuable for research [10].

The main methods of heart rate variability (HRV) analysis include time domain analysis, frequency domain analysis and nonlinear (chaotic) kinetic analysis [11].

Among them, the frequency domain analysis method can extract and analyze the R-R interval as components of different frequency bands with accurate data, high sensitivity, and quantitative decomposition analysis, which can accurately evaluate the estimated sympathetic and vagal nerve activity levels [12]. For example, Yushu Yang et al. found that four ECG indicators have a certain correlation with fatigue level by conducting virtual driving experiments, which can be used to quantify the fatigue level [13]; PIOTROWSKI et al. used heart rate variability analysis for drowsiness state classification and drowsiness check state detection, the most important parameter from the point of view of drowsiness classification came from the different frequency bands that would be extracted from the R-R interval [14]; Muhammad et al. achieved fatigue state classification by extracting HRV features from ECG signals of subjects and using radial basis function neural network for fatigue detection based on microcontroller unit [15]; Khalil et al. proposed a fast ECG classification method based on extreme learning machine (ELM) algorithm to classify frequency rhythms in heartbeat with 97.55% classification accuracy [16]; Murugan et al. filtered ECG data and extracted 13 statistically significant features, after which they used three classifiers (SVM, KNN and Ensemble) were trained, SVM and KNN achieved high classification accuracy, Ensemble performed poorly and needs further optimization and improvement [17].

### 2.4  Emotion Elicitation

Since there are different explanatory theories for the mechanism of emotion generation, there are various criteria for classifying emotions. In daily life, we are accustomed to the simplest method of classifying emotions, which divides emotions into three categories: positive emotions, neutral emotions and negative emotions. What is widely adopted now is the two-dimensional emotion model proposed by Lange, which maps different emotions into a two-dimensional space, in which the horizontal axis represents the degree of pleasure of emotion and the vertical axis represents the degree of excitement of emotion, and emotions are no longer presented in discrete states such as happy and calm, but become a continuous state [18].

Emotion elicitation is the achievement of a specific emotional state by a subject through a specific external environmental stimulus or an internal response of the body, and the commonly used materials for emotion elicitation are text, pictures, videos, etc. Among them, when using text and pictures for emotion elicitation, the experimental conditions are simple and easy to achieve but the elicitation intensity is limited and the elicitation time is longer. The use of video can stimulate the subject to enter a specific emotional state quickly, which is easy to implement and has a shorter elicitation time [19]. In addition, there is another type of emotion elicitation called the self-evoked approach, which measures subjects' spontaneous emotions, however, it is difficult to determine the timing and content of emotions at this time, and therefore, this approach is not common in emotion elicitation.

At the same time, researchers have encountered some problems in studying emotions based on different emotion-evoking experiments because the evaluation criteria are not uniform. For this reason, Soleymani M built a multimodal database for emotion recognition using emotion video clips as well as label-consistent experiments [20]; Koelstra S constructed a database for emotion recognition (DEAP) using music clips as stimuli and processed it for statistical analysis and other purposes to ensure the validity of emotion elicitation in this dataset [21].

### 2.5  Fatigue Driving Detection

Fatigue driving detection methods can be roughly divided into four categories, which are based on subjective assessment, physiological parameters, driving behavior characteristics and information fusion detection technology, of which, the common one is fatigue detection technology based on physiological parameters, which can be further divided into detection based on EEG signal, EMG signal, ECG signal, pulse beat, etc. Because it is directly connected to the human body through the instrument and collects human bio-signals in real time, it can more accurately reflect the fatigue state of the human body [22]. For example, Artanto D et al. invented a device to detect early drowsiness in drivers, which can attach a myoelectric signal acquisition device to the skin around the eyelids, which can detect the closing of the eyes and face without hurting the eyes, and designed the ESP8266 system based on this method, which was finally used for the purpose of detecting fatigue [23]; Brandt T et al. fused information from the monotonicity judgment of the road with the detection of the driver's face and eye state to discern whether the driver was fatigued, achieving a better detection of the driver's fatigue level [24].

## 2.6 Fatigue and Sleepiness Indicator (FSI)

The fatigue indicators obtained from the analysis of many different signals in the detection of driving fatigue based on physiological parameters are different, and although some indicators are formally ratios without units, the meanings they represent are still not in the same evaluation dimension, such as EEG $(\theta + \alpha)/\beta$ and ECG LF/HF, for which the concept of FSI is proposed in this paper to incorporate these different signals reflecting fatigue status into the same fatigue state evaluation dimension.

$$FSI = \left| \frac{Driving\ status\ indicator - Awake\ indicator}{Awake\ indicator - Fatigue\ state\ indicator} \right| \tag{1}$$

Taking the EEG fatigue index as an example, the specific establishment process is: firstly, to make multiple measurements of EEG features on subjects in the awake or fatigue state; secondly, to perform signal processing on a fatigue-related index (e.g., power spectral density ratio $(\alpha + \theta)/\beta$) of these features and find the mean value of the largest (smallest) few values; this mean value is used as its standard value of fatigue (wakefulness), and the data of this indicator during normal driving are subjected to the operation of the conceptual formula of the FSI to obtain data that are between 0 and 1. The closer the fatigue is to 0, the more sober it is, and the closer the fatigue is to 1, the more fatigued it is, and the closer it is to the standard value of its own fatigue.

The introduction of the concept of the FSI in this study has three benefits.

1. Since there are small differences in the values of EEG, ECG and other characteristics of each individual, the FSI can provide a uniform standard for different drivers to compare based on their own fatigue level, which somewhat counteracts the drawbacks of experimental studies with differences in the absolute values of physiological signals in different populations.
2. The FSI can normalize multiple physiological signal data, transforming several data in different evaluation dimensions into data in the same evaluation dimension, simplifying the fusion processing of experimental data.
3. The concept of the FSI allows scholars in different fields to have a simple, intuitive and quick understanding of fatigue levels.

# 3  Experiments on Typical Driving Tasks

## 3.1  Purpose of the Experiment

During the execution of the driving tasks under different emotions, the EEG and ECG devices were used to track and record the driver's EEG and ECG signals, and then to investigate the difference in the change of fatigue state during the driver's driving task under different emotions.

## 3.2  Experimental Equipment

BD-C-1 wireless EEG acquisition and analysis system, BD-C-2 wireless ECG acquisition and analysis system, driving simulator, timer, medical alcohol, alcohol cotton balls, wet wipes, audio playback equipment, emotion evoking video, light source with infinitely dimmable light, illuminance meter, marker (to record the position of the light source), tape (to prevent electrodes from falling off), etc.

## 3.3  Experimental Subjects

Eighteen BIT students aged 20–24 years (16 males, 2 females).

- No sleep problems such as poor sleep, insomnia, etc.
- Absence of heart diseases such as arrhythmia and heart attacks.
- Emotional richness.
- Honesty, integrity and responsibility.
- Understanding of traffic signs and driving rules and driving experience.
- No events that caused dramatic mood swings in the month prior to the experiment.
- No other psycho-stimulating beverages such as coffee within twenty-four hours prior to the experiment.
- Seven to eight hours of sleep were ensured prior to the experiment.
- No food or strenuous activity within one hour prior to the experiment.

Subjects were asked preliminarily about what trigger conditions would elicit happy and sad emotions, and the selection of emotion-evoking audio and video was based on the relevant situations obtained from the questioning, and they were trained to use the driving equipment.

## 3.4  Construction of a Typical Driving Task Scenario

This experiment was completed using UC win Road 8.1 to build two virtual scenarios of typical driving tasks, a low-load high-speed scenario and a high-load town scenario. In this paper, the experimental task was adjusted in order to shorten the length of the experiment, so that the subjects showed a high level of fatigue within 90 min, which is somewhat different from the actual driving process in the same time driver fatigue performance.

**Fig. 1.** High-speed road scene

High-speed road scenario (shown in Fig. 1): the scene is sparse, the road scene is single and spacious, the whole process is two-way three lanes and the road is closed, the driver's operational task is small, the brain load is also small, the overall driving task is one and a half hours.

Town road scenario (shown in Fig. 2): the scenario has dense traffic flow, multiple road scenes, including sidewalks, jaywalking pedestrians, haphazardly parked trucks, etc., two lanes in both directions, the road is not closed, the driver has a large operational task and a large brain load, and the overall driving task is one and a half hours.

**Fig. 2.** Town road scene

In addition to the above virtual scene construction, the entire experimental cycle of the laboratory temperature and humidity to maintain consistent, do not produce significant fluctuations, indoor curtains are all drawn, try to avoid the interference of external environmental light, relying on fluorescent lamps (to provide the basic needs of indoor brightness) and stepless dimming of the light source (to adjust the light at the driver) to control the indoor brightness, so that there is no significant difference in light intensity and irradiation direction at the driver for each experiment conducted.

## 3.5   Experimental Procedure

Before the start of the formal experiment, the experimental subjects were explained the specific experimental procedure and the precautions to be taken, and they were allowed to enter the simulated driving equipment and adjust the seat position angle, etc. [25].

**Emotion Elicitation.** Three representative emotions were selected for this experiment, namely pleasure, usual (calm) and sadness. After a preliminary survey of the subjects, we found that the subjects were all emotionally rich and easy to perform emotional elicitation, so we played the corresponding videos for about fifteen to thirty minutes, depending on the changes in the subjects' emotional states.

**Completion of the Fatigue Subjective Rating Scale.** There was a waiting period of three to five minutes after the end of the emotional elicitation, which was used mainly for the relative calming of emotions and the completion of the subjective fatigue rating scale. This subjective assessment scale of fatigue is derived from the Stanford Drowsiness Scale, which is a subjective fatigue assessment tool commonly used in fatigue driving studies (Table 1).

**Table 1.**  Fatigue subjective rating scale

| Level of fatigue | Fatigue level (score) |
|---|---|
| Very refreshed and physically energetic | 1 |
| Mental levels are high but not at their peak, allowing for concentration | 2 |
| Clear thinking, mentally relaxed, able to respond in a more timely but less responsive manner | 3 |
| A little weary and a little relaxed | 4 |
| Full of tiredness, no longer mentally awake, especially lax | 5 |
| Begin to feel drowsy, dizzy, and just want to end the current state or lie down to rest | 6 |
| Entering a light sleep | 7 |

**Conducting Driving Simulations.** Timing was started and the subject was made to perform a simulated driving for one and a half hours, during which the subject was not allowed to make significant body part movements, such as swinging, twisting, etc., and the subject was given a reminder that the experiment was nearing completion with fifteen minutes remaining until the experiment was completed.

**Completion of the Fatigue Subjective Rating Scale Again.** The timing was stopped, the subjective evaluation of fatigue was performed again, and the collection device was turned off and the data collection device was removed.

**Data Collection.** Collecting and backing up the collected EEG and ECG data, the experiment was completed.

The above process need to be carried out three times in six scenarios: happy low load, happy high load, normal high load, normal low load, sad low load, sad high load, and each subject also had to be collected the most values of EEG and ECG indexes for their waking state and fatigue state several times, the waking state measurement time was usually one hour just after waking up in the morning, the fatigue state measurement time was usually the time when you were extremely fatigued after a day of work or when you felt very fatigued by yourself, and the data was saved after collection to prepare for later data processing.

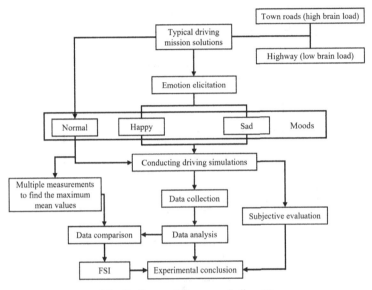

**Fig. 3.** Research framework diagram

The research framework for the entire experimental cycle is shown in Fig. 3.

## 4 Data Analysis

### 4.1 EEG and ECG Data Processing

The EEG data collected by the EEG device would get the data series of theta wave, low alpha wave, high alpha wave, low beta wave and high beta wave after the pre-processing of the TGAM module, and since the TGAM module can filter the interference such as the Electrooculographic signals, noise and 50/60 Hz AC during the experiment, the anti-interference ability was strong, so these data series obtained could be directly analyzed by power spectrum to find the power spectrum density [26].

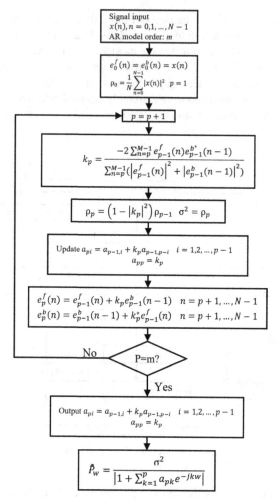

**Fig. 4.** Flow chart for solving power spectral density using AR model estimation method

In this paper, the power spectral density of EEG signals was calculated using the Burg method based on the AR model estimation method, and the calculation flow is shown in Fig. 4.

The power spectral density of θ wave, low α wave, high αwave, low β wave, and high β wave could be obtained by the above calculation process, and let α = (low α + high α)/2 and β = (low β + high β)/2 [27]. The power spectral density ratio (α + θ)/β, which was commonly used in domestic research, was chosen as the index of EEG equipment to evaluate driver fatigue, and an average value was taken for every five minutes to represent its integrated level in five minutes.

The ECG data collected by the ECG device could directly output the LF, HF, LF/HF and other indicators commonly used in domestic driving fatigue research through the BD-C-2 wireless ECG acquisition and analysis system, and LF/HF was selected as the indicator for evaluating driver fatigue by the ECG device, and an average value was taken for every five minutes to represent its integrated level in five minutes.

## 4.2 Data Fusion

The above two types of data were processed using the concept formula of FSI to obtain EEG FSI and ECG FSI, respectively, and the new data obtained were subjected to Pearson correlation tests with the subjective fatigue evaluation scores, which resulted in the data tables shown in Table 2 and Table 3.

From the table, it can be seen that EEG FSI and ECG FSI have significant correlation with subjective fatigue evaluation scores, and both can be used as indicators to evaluate driver fatigue degree. However, the two indicators have their own emphasis, and due to the subject's own differences and many other external environmental factors, the ECG and EEG data measured during the experiment may have different fluctuations, therefore, establishing a comprehensive fatigue evaluation index - the Fatigue and Sleepiness Indicator (FSI) based on EEG FSI and ECG FSI can eliminate some interfering factors and reflect the fatigue degree of the subjects more accurately, and also facilitate the comparison of the data.

**Table 2.** Table of EEG correlation data

|  |  | Subjective evaluation score | EEG FSI |
|---|---|---|---|
| Subjective evaluation score | Pearson correlation | 1 | $0.990^{**}$ |
|  | Sig. (two-tailed) |  | 0.000 |
|  | Number of cases | 36 | 36 |
| EEG FSI | Pearson Correlation | $0.990^{**}$ | 1 |
|  | Sig. (two-tailed) | 0.000 |  |
|  | Number of cases | 36 | 36 |

$^{**}$ At the 0.01 level (two-tailed), the correlation was significant.

**Table 3.** Table of ECG correlation data

|  |  | Subjective evaluation score | ECG FSI |
|---|---|---|---|
| Subjective evaluation score | Pearson Correlation | 1 | $0.985^{**}$ |
|  | Sig. (two-tailed) |  | 0.000 |
|  | Number of cases | 36 | 36 |
| ECG FSI | Pearson Correlation | $0.985^{**}$ | 1 |
|  | Sig. (two-tailed) | 0.000 |  |
|  | Number of cases | 36 | 36 |

$^{**}$ At the 0.01 level (two-tailed), the correlation was significant.

In this paper, Pearson correlation coefficient was used to calculate the correlation coefficient between EEG FSI and ECG FSI, and the correlation degree of the two was very significant and the change trend was the same, so the principal component analysis could be used to select the comprehensive fatigue index. Through the results of total variance decomposition of principal components, as shown in Table 4, it can be concluded that the cumulative contribution rate of principal elements has reached more than 90%, which can meet the requirements of principal element feature extraction.

**Table 4.** Total variance explained

| Ingredients | Initial eigenvalue | | | Extraction of the sum of squares of loads | | |
|---|---|---|---|---|---|---|
| | Aggregate | Percentage variance | Cumulative % | Aggregate | Percentage variance | Cumulative % |
| 1 | 1.997 | 99.850 | 99.850 | 1.997 | 99.850 | 99.850 |
| 2 | 0.003 | 0.150 | 100.00 | | | |

In turn, its component matrix can be found, and the eigenvector values of the principal elements are obtained as $u_{EEG} = 1.413$ and $u_{ECG} = 0.002$, and then *the composite index* $= 1.413 \times EEG\ FSI + 0.002 \times ECG\ FSI$ ($1.415 \geq$ the composite index $\geq 0$), considering the practical meaning of strain, here let $FSI =$ *the composite index*$/1.415$ ($1 \geq FSI \geq 0$), we can get the subject's FSIs, as shown in Fig. 5 and Fig. 6.

## 5  Discussion

Under the condition of uniform brain load variables, it can be seen from Fig. 5 and Fig. 6 that the fatigue state pattern of drivers in different emotional states in the early stage is

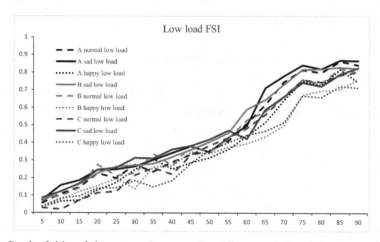

**Fig. 5.** Graph of driver fatigue state changes under different typical emotional scenarios (low load)

not obvious, but the later it is, the fatigue state of drivers under pleasant emotional scenes are lower than that of normal and sad emotional load scenes, and the time of substantial change of exertion is also delayed to some extent, and the fatigue state of drivers under normal emotional scenes is between the pleasant and sad emotional load scenes, which is different from the emergence of emotions envisaged before the experiment that will increase the brain load of drivers.

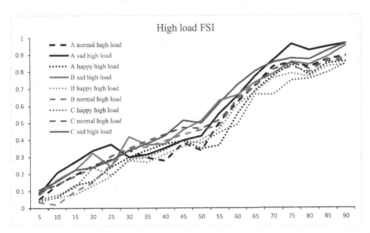

**Fig. 6.** Graph of driver fatigue state changes under different typical emotional scenarios (high load)

First of all, the sharp changes of fatigue in the low load scenario were concentrated between 60–65 min, i.e., in this time period, the fatigue level of the subjects had a greater change, while the sharp changes of fatigue in the high load scenario were concentrated between 50–55 min, and the comparison of the time periods of concentrated changes of fatigue showed that different brain load scenarios had a greater effect on the changes of fatigue level of the subjects. This indicates that the experiment is very reasonable in dividing the different brain load scenarios. In the two different brain load scenarios, the change pattern of driver fatigue under different typical emotions showed the same change pattern, which also increased the credibility of the experimental conclusion to a certain extent.

Secondly, before the sharp change of exertional fatigue, the exertional fatigue of the sad group in the low load scenario was 2%–4% higher than the normal group as a whole, the exertional fatigue of the sad group in the high load scenario was 3%–5% higher than the normal group as a whole, while the exertional fatigue of the normal group in the low load scenario was 2%–5% higher than the happy group as a whole, and the exertional fatigue of the normal group in the high load scenario was 1%–5% higher than the happy group as a whole, that is, the difference between different emotional groups in the high load scenario The gap between different emotional groups of high load scenes is roughly comparable to the gap between different emotional groups of load scenes, and the gap between different emotional groups of the same scenes is between 2%–5%, which indicates that at the early stage of driving tasks, the influence of emotions on the degree of driver fatigue is limited, and there is only a small fine-tuning of normal performance; after a sharp change in the degree of exertional fatigue, the degree of exertional fatigue of the low load scenes sad group is 1%–4% higher than the normal group as a whole, and the high load scenes sad group The fatigue level was 2%–5% higher than that of the normal group, while the fatigue level of the normal group was 5%–9% higher than that of the happy group, and the fatigue level of the normal group was 3%–7% higher than that of the happy group, i.e., the difference between different emotional groups in the same scene was larger, and the effect of the happy group on fatigue level was significantly higher than that of the sad group on fatigue level.

Finally, in the time period of 75–80 min, the fatigue level tended to decrease more or less, and the decrease was concentrated in the range of 2%–4%, which may be related to the fact that we gave the subjects a voice reminder that the experiment was about to end at 75 min, but the change in fatigue level in this 75–80 min was relatively small, and after 80 min, the fatigue level of more than 90% of the subjects This suggests that the effect of the voice reminder was limited. We speculate that the voice reminders may have made the subjects aware that the experimental task was coming to an end and their brains were slightly awake, but the subsequent 15 min of driving time was still relatively long and the subjects returned to the fatigue driving stage again.

Based on the above experiments, this paper gives the following recommendations.

1. According to the performance of driver fatigue in different brain-load scenarios, it is recommended that drivers should try to stagger their trips when performing driving tasks, avoid moments of heavy traffic flow, and if they need to drive vehicles at times of heavy traffic flow, they should minimize the time spent driving and take timely rest.
2. Based on the manifestation of the driver's fatigue state in different emotional scenarios, the driver is advised to reduce driving behaviour during adverse emotions or to take a longer period of time after the onset of adverse emotions before engaging in driving activities.
3. The superimposition of high-load scenarios and sadness can make drivers in the midst of driving activities more likely to approach a state of exhaustion after a day's work, so try to avoid high brain-load driving activities while in a sad mood.
4. The experiment in this paper made a time of voice reminder to the driver in the last fifteen minutes towards the end of the experiment, and the driver's fatigue was somewhat relieved after the voice reminder, but the relief was still limited. Therefore, for drivers, appropriate voice stimulation (e.g., a full task end countdown in navigation) can be helpful for drivers in a fatigued state, but it is still important to schedule time for rest.

# 6 Conclusion

In this paper, the fatigue states of drivers under different typical emotions were collected and analyzed using EEG and ECG equipment, and the power spectral density ratios ($\alpha + \theta$)/$\beta$ and LF/HF were processed separately using the conceptual formula of the Fatigue and Sleepiness Indicator (FSI), and the data of two different evaluation dimensions were processed into the data of the same evaluation dimension, which simplified the subsequent data fusion process and provided a new idea for the fusion of multiple different criteria data in fatigue research, and finally we got the conclusion that drivers in pleasant emotions performed better than usual emotions and sad emotions in both brain-load driving tasks in terms of fatigue, and the effect of pleasant emotions on driver fatigue was significantly higher than that of sad emotions.

Due to the conditions, there are certain limitations in this paper, such as the research content of this paper is based on young school students aged 20–24 with insufficient driving experience, so truck drivers, taxi drivers and other long-term driving activities are not very applicable to this study; there are certain gaps between the constructed virtual scene and the real scene, such as the noise outside the window, the angle change of outdoor light, the task volume setting, etc., which cannot be fully restored, and because the time of fatigue change is generally long, this paper adjusted the experimental task in order to shorten the length of the experiment, so that the subjects showed a high degree of fatigue within 90 min, which is somewhat different from the fatigue performance of the same time in the actual driving process.

# References

1. Wang, K.-J., Zheng, C.Y., Shidujaman, M., et al.: Jean Joseph v2.0 (REmotion): make remote emotion touchable, seeable and thinkable by direct brain-to-brain telepathy neurohaptic interface empowered by generative adversarial network. In: 2020 IEEE International Conference on Systems, Man, and Cybernetics (SMC), pp. 3488–3493 (2020)
2. Xu, X., Wang, P., Fu, D.: Brief analysis of bio-signal and its application in ergonomics. Indu. Des. **09**, 28–29 (2021)
3. Yao, J., Wu, C.: Review of brain-computer interface technology research. Mod. Comput. **27**, 80–84 (2017)
4. Feng, T.: Principles of EEG time-frequency analysis and Matlab operation. Think Tank Era (04), 230–231 (2020)
5. Zhu, Y., Zeng, Y., Feng, Z., et al.: The detection method for driving fatigue based on EEG signals. J. Changchun Univ. Sci. Technol. (Nat. Sci. Ed.) **39**(05), 119–122 (2016)
6. Liu, T., Jinfei, M.A.: Analysis of EEG detection of driver active fatigue on expressway. China Saf. Sci. J. **28**(10), 13–18 (2018)
7. Aftanas, L.I., Golocheikine, S.A.: Non-linear dynamic complexity of the human EEG during meditation. Neuroence Lett. **330**(2), 143–146 (2002)
8. Nie, D., Wang, X.W., Shi, L.C., et al.: EEG-based emotion recognition during watching movies. In: 2011 5th International IEEE/EMBS Conference on Neural Engineering, pp. 667–670 (2011)
9. Khosrowabadi, R., Wahab, A., Ang, K.K., et al.: Affective computation on EEG correlates of emotion from musical and vocal stimuli. In: 2009 International Joint Conference on Neural Networks, vol. 2, pp. 573–1172 (2009)
10. Li, J., Zhang, F., Liu, X., et al.: Mechanism of heart rate variability and research advance in its relevance to cardiovascular diseases. J. Pract. Electrocardiol. **30**(04), 293–296 (2021)
11. Wang, F.: Analysis of driving b ehavior based on physiological and psychological factors. Chinese Master's Theses Full-text Database, pp. 10–14 (2020)
12. Li, Y.: Analysis of heart rate variability of plateau highway drivers. China Transp. Rev. **41**(08), 78–82 (2019)

13. Yang, Y., Yao, Z., Li, Z., et al.: Investigation on correlation between ECG indexes and driving fatigue. Mach. Des. Manuf. **05**, 94–95 (2002)
14. Piotrowski, Z., Szypulska, M.: Classification of falling asleep states using HRV analysis. Biocybernetics Biomed. Eng. **37**(2), 290–301 (2017)
15. Hendra, M., Kurniawan, D., Chrismiantari, R.V., et al.: Drowsiness detection using heart rate variability analysis based on microcontroller unit. J. Phys. Conf. Ser. **1153**, 012047 (2019)
16. Khalil, K., Asgher, U., Ayaz, Y., et al.: Efficient extreme learning machine (ELM) based algorithm for electrocardiogram (ECG) heartbeat classification. In: Ayaz, H., Asgher, U. (eds.) International Conference on Applied Human Factors and Ergonomics, pp. 312–318. Springer, Cham (2020). https://doi.org/10.1007/978-3-030-51041-1_41
17. Murugan, S., Selvaraj, J., Sahayadhas, A.: Detection and analysis: driver state with electrocardiogram (ECG). Phys. Eng. Sci. Med. **43**(2), 525–537 (2020). https://doi.org/10.1007/s13246-020-00853-8
18. Russell, J.A.: A circumplex model of affect. J. Pers. Soc. Psychol. **39**(6), 1161–1178 (1980)
19. Yi, H., Chen, R., Deng, G., et al.: Research on emotion recognition based on heart rate variability. J. Biomed. Eng. Res. **39**(02), 128–132 (2020)
20. Soleymani, M.: A multimodal database for affect recognition and implicit tagging. IEEE Trans. Affect. Comput. **3**(1), 42–55 (2012)
21. Koelstra, S.: DEAP: a database for emotion analysis; using physiological signals. IEEE Trans. Affect. Comput. **3**(1), 18–31 (2012)
22. Xiao, S., Lei, Y.: Research on the causes for driver fatigue and the monitoring technology progress. Technol. Econ. Areas Commun. **19**(04), 14–19+63 (2017)
23. Artanto, D., Sulistyanto, M.P., Pranowo, I.D., et al.: Drowsiness detection system based on eye-closure using a low-cost EMG and ESP8266. In: 2017 2nd International Conferences on Information Technology, Information Systems and Electrical Engineering (ICITISEE), pp. 235–238. IEEE (2017)
24. Brandt, T., Stemmer, R., Rakotonirainy, A.: Affordable visual driver monitoring system for fatigue and monotony. In: 2004 IEEE International Conference on Systems, Man and Cybernetics, vol. 7, pp. 6451–6456. IEEE (2004)
25. Li, J., Pan, X.-D.: High-risk period of fatigue in long-time driving based on EEG. J. Transp. Sci. Eng. **28**(04), 72–79 (2012)
26. Pei, Y., Jin, Y., Chen, H.: Fatigue characteristics in drivers of different ages based on analysis of EEG. China J. Highw. Transp. **31**(04), 59–65+77 (2018)
27. Zhao, X., Fang, R., Rong, J., et al.: Experiment study on comprehensive evaluation method of driving fatigue based on physiological signals. J. Beijing Univ. Technol. **37**(10), 1511–1516+1523 (2011)

# Research on the Relationship Between the Aesthetics of Interface Elements Layout and Visual Working Memory

Changyun Ma, Haiyan Wang[✉], and Chengqi Xue

School of Mechanical Engineering, Southeast University, Nanjing 211189, China
whaiyan@seu.edu.cn

**Abstract.** The aesthetics of the element layout in the human-computer interface (HCI) play a positive role in the understandability, learnability, and operation efficiency. However, whether and in what aspects the aesthetics of interface layouts could promote visual working memory (VWM) has not been explored clearly. An interface with an easy-to-remember layout can provide a better user experience with a reduction in cognitive load, especially serving the increasing aging users. It was found that the website interfaces with higher subjective aesthetic rating scores are easier to be remembered. In addition to the subjective scoring, which the evaluator group greatly influences, plenty of studies have proposed mathematical calculation models to calculate the aesthetics of the interface layout by proposing multiple factors that affect the visual perception and their calculation formulas. This paper aims to investigate whether the memorability of interface element layout is affected by its aesthetics through objective evaluation. The influence of various visual features in the objective evaluation system is explored which can be used as an indicator to reduce the memory cost and improve user experiments when designers make layout arrangements.

**Keywords:** Visual working memory · Human-Computer Interface (HCI) · Aesthetics evaluation · Interface layout design

## 1 Introduction

The human-computer interface (HCI) is the medium that enables the transfer of information between man and machine. The interface layout refers to the arrangement of elements in an interface following functional and aesthetic requirements and constraints for the enhanced efficiency and experience of human-machine interaction [1].

Visual aesthetics of interface had been shown to critically affect a variety of constructs such as perceived acceptability, learnability, and productivity [2–4]. Tullis [2] proved that the worst layout arrangement required 128 percent that much time to retrieve features than the best. Aspillage [3] applied visual aesthetics to schooling, showing that a more visually appealing interface design leads to improved concentration and comprehension of course content. Grabinger [4] discovered that the organization of visual interest

M. Kurosu et al. (Eds.): HCII 2022, LNCS 13516, pp. 597–607, 2022.
https://doi.org/10.1007/978-3-031-17615-9_42

which is related to the aesthetic affected reading fluency and learning expenses, suggesting monotony, unbalanced, and bareness are unfavorable. However, these studies have focused on the final outcome of the interaction and less on the cognitive processes that underpin the interaction process. Contrasting perceived aesthetics without usage, Tuch et al. [5] indicated that post-use perceived aesthetics has a stronger impact on usability which indicates that aesthetics continue to influence usability during the using process. Using an interface is dependent on a diverse range of cognitive processes, including attention, memory, and logic. This paper speculates that interface aesthetics are beneficial for the cognitive processes leading to a reduction in cognitive load, which may contribute to the ease of use improved in the aforementioned findings.

A lot of investigations on the effect of visual aesthetics on cognitive activity have focused on the. Working memory. Numerous research that has focused on images have examined the parameters that influence the memorability of images and demonstrated its neural correlates to the population response magnitude variation that emerges in the high-level visual cortex [6]. In the case of interface, recent research has shown that web interfaces with better subjective beauty scores are more likely to be remembered [7]. However, this finding relied heavily on the interface's content, which is not the domain of the design for some interfaces. In terms of interface elements layout without semantic information, it can be postulated that aesthetics have an influence on its memorability, analogous to images as visual stimuli. Miura [8] proposed a gamified application to measure interface layouts' memory difficulty for a wide range of ages clarifying the relations between age and the volume of visuospatial memory and suggesting that minimizing its memory difficulty could lessen the cognitive strain on users, especially the older and juvenile populations. Based on previous studies, this article investigates whether aesthetics influence the working memory of interface elements' layout.

With the growth of Kansei engineering, there has been an emergence of research on the aesthetics of interfaces, which can be classified as subjective and objective. Although subjective evaluations can reflect a person's perception of beauty, they are highly dependent on the group of evaluators which has low stability of results [9]. In contrast, objective evaluation has received increasing attention from interface design researchers due to its quantifiability and stability. These studies extract multiple factors that affect visual aesthetic perception and quantification methods. Ngo et al. [1] proposed 14 layout features and their calculation formulas quantified each of the components and the overall aesthetic degree, which are the measure of balance (BM), the measure of equilibrium (EM), the measure of symmetry (SYM), the measure of sequence (SQM), the measure of cohesion(CM), the measure of unity(UM), the measure of proportion (PM), measure of simplicity (SMM), the measure of density (DM), the measure of regularity (RM), the measure of economy (ECM), the measure of homogeneity (HM), the measure of rhythm (RHM) and the measure of order and complexity (OM). Zhou et al. [10] explored the superiority of each aesthetic variable using a grey correlation method in an effort to determine the interface's overall aesthetic degree. There is no uniform position now on the calculation of the overall beauty value, as there is no reference value against which to compare the advantages of each aesthetic factor, which has not produced a broadly approved approach in current studies.

Instead of one specific overall aesthetics value, the indicators in these assessment models which cover diverse aspects of visual aesthetics are in line with the purpose of this research to reveal how aesthetics influences working memory in cognitive processes by examining the various parts of visual aesthetics perception. Therefore, for the aesthetics scores of interface layout, this study employs the methodology from objective aesthetics evaluation research which is achieved in two main steps: extraction of the layout information and calculation of aesthetic values. The approach for extracting layout data is depicted in Fig. 1. We abstract the functional partition as the smallest rectangle that can contain its internal elements in black (R:0, G:0, B:0) and the background is shown in gray (R:128, G:128, B:128). The top left corner of the interface's general framework is designated as the starting point. From the starting point, the positive X-axis extends to the right and the positive Y-axis extends downward. Each rectangle is positioned according to the interface's overall frame by four parameters: the X-coordinate, Y-coordinate, height H, and width W of the starting point.

**Fig. 1.** Original Interface(www.lib.seu.edu.cn)

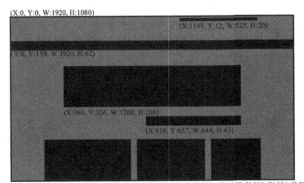

**Fig. 2.** Simplified Interface

For the calculation step, we choose 13 aesthetic indicators with OM excluded from the 14 aesthetic indicators proposed by Ngo to conduct a thorough evaluation. The OM referring to the overall aesthetic value was removed because its calculation is unclear as the contribution of each aesthetic indicator to it was ambiguous.

Working memory is a form of information storage in the cognitive system and refers to the temporary storage of information for current information processing, lasting between 5 and 60 s [11]. In contrast to the storage of information for later information processing, also known as long-term memory, working memory occurs more frequently for the usage of the interface, particularly for the initial use of the interface. Lindgaard et al. [12] demonstrated that aesthetic judgments are formed steadily within a relatively brief period of time following the appearance of the object, usually 50 ms–500 ms, which precedes the end of working memory. Therefore, the aesthetics of the interface layout as perceived by the observer may have an impact on the memory effect in the time dimension. For the measurement of the visual working memory, we applied the widely-used change detection task named change-detection paradigm, in which participants have to identify whether the stimulus has changed in the second presentation compared to the first presentation.

All in all, the aim of this research was to ascertain whether the aesthetics of interface layout has an influence on its visual working memory. Specifically, 13 aesthetics indicators from the objective evaluation model are selected to measure the various parts of the layout aesthetics and the memorability of interface layout is measured through the memory test. The relationship between aesthetics and working memory is examined, which could be used to offer a reduction in memory difficulty while relieving the cognitive load of the interface and may explain the impact of aesthetics on usability stated in earlier work.

## 2   Pilot Experiment

As the most salient feature of working memory, limited capacity has a substantial influence on the difficulty of memory. The amount of information in memory, however, was not the focus of this investigation. Therefore, we kept the number of elements in all stimuli identical to avoid overriding the effect of aesthetic factors. To avoid ceiling and floor effects, the optimum number of elements was chosen from 5 to 9 which is the consensus VWM capacity agreed upon by the majority of studies [13].

### 2.1   Methods

**Stimulus.** 35 web interfaces with 7 interfaces for each quantity type were collected and kept at a consistent size of $1920 \times 1080$ pixels. The interfaces were simplified in Photoshop 2021 (Adobe Photoshop, 22.5.6, Adobe, US.) until only layout information remained.

**Participants.** Twenty participants were enrolled to take part in the pilot experiment, with 10 male and 10 female students at Southeast University whose ages range from 19 to 26 years old(M=23.352, SD=1.02). All the participants were right-handed and had normal and correct-to-normal visual acuity, and were volunteered to participate in the experiment with signed consent forms.

**Procedure.** The pilot experiment is carried out in the form of the change detection paradigm same as the formal experiment. Participants were asked to memorize the lay-out of the interface (memory array) and make judgments about whether the layout changed when it reappeared (test array) again. Fifty percent of the interface remained the same when presented again, while others showed a clearly recognizable change of one element's position with consistent movement distance.

Trials began with the presentation of a black fixation cross ($0.4° \times 0.4°$, 1,000 ms), followed by the presentation of a memory array ($7° \times 11°$) for 3000 ms. After a delay period (1,000 ms), the test display appeared. The test display remained on the screen until the participants made a keypress. The participants were asked to press the left control key with their left index finger if they detected a change and to press the right control key on the number keypad with their right index finger if they did not detect any change. The two keys were labeled with the words "Different" and "Same", respectively. The order in which all stimuli were presented was randomized. Prior to the experiment, there will be exercises that provide correct and incorrect feedback, which does not appear in the formal experiment. Participants were encouraged to respond accurately and immediately and the memory performance measures included accuracy and reaction time.

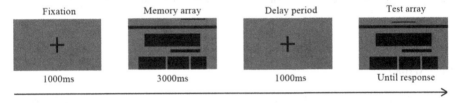

| Fixation | Memory array | Delay period | Test array |
| 1000ms | 3000ms | 1000ms | Until response |

**Fig. 3.** Experiment stimuli and task sequence.

**Apparatus.** The experiment was programmed using E-prime3.0(Psychology Soft-ware Tools, Pittsburgh, PA)and displayed on a 24-in widescreen monitor with a re-fresh rate of 100 Hz. The viewing distance was 58 cm from the monitor. In order to control for the effect of different levels of arousal on the memory effect, all subjects were subjected to the experiment in the same time period and in the same laboratory environment.

**Table 1.** Average and standard deviation of the accuracy of each category

| Number of elements | 5 | 6 | 7 | 8 | 9 |
| --- | --- | --- | --- | --- | --- |
| Average (s) | 0.828 | 0.724 | 0.714 | 0.513 | 0.463 |
| SD | 0.062 | 0.112 | 0.231 | 0.083 | 0.048 |

## 2.2 Result

The memory scores of each category of interfaces including the accuracy and reaction time were collected, excluding extreme data (M-3SD < Xi < M + 3SD). The mean and standard deviation of the accuracy are shown in Table 1. It can be seen that the standard deviation of the memorability of the two types of interfaces with 5 and 9 elements is significantly smaller than that of the other three types of images.

## 2.3 Conclusion

From the mean values, it can be seen that the amount of information memorized could strongly influence the difficulty of remembering it, with more information making it more difficult. It can be surmised from the standard deviation that when there are too much or too few elements, there may be a ceiling or floor effect that the effect of other factors on memory especially aesthetics in this research may be overrode and difficult to be detected. Therefore, in the formal experiment, the interfaces with the number of elements of 7 were chosen for the formal experiment with the largest standard deviation of memorability. At this point, the quantity component does not fully dictate the ease of memorization, and there is scope for it to be influenced by other factors.

# 3 Experiment

## 3.1 Method

**Stimulus.** 16 simplified interfaces that all have a number elements of 7 were prepared. These stimuli were not present in the previous pilot experiment.

**Participants.** Twenty participants were enrolled to take part in the formal experiment, with 10 male and 10 female students at Southeast University whose ages range from 21 to 29 years old(M = 24.21, SD = 1.45). All the participants were right-handed and had normal and correct-to-normal visual acuity, and were volunteered to participate in the experiment with signed consent forms. Subjects who participated in the formal experiment had not taken part in the pilot experiment.

**Procedure & Apparatus.** The procedure and apparatus keep consistent with the pilot experiment.

## 3.2 Result

**Aesthetics degree.** The 13 aesthetic degrees of the layout of the interface is objectively evaluated based on the most widely used objective evaluation model proposed by Ngo, which includes balance (BM), equilibrium (EM), symmetry (SYM), sequence (SQM), cohesion(CM), unity(UM), proportion (PM), simplicity (SMM), density (DM), regularity (RM), economy (ECM), homogeneity (HM) and rhythm (RHM), are calculated by MATLAB (Mathwork, Natick, MA).

**Table 2.** The aesthetic scores of 16 stimulus

|    | BM | EM | SYM | SQM | CM | UM | PM | SMM | DM | RM | ECM | HM | RHM |
|----|------|------|------|-------|------|------|------|------|------|------|------|------|------|
| 1  | 0.793 | 0.972 | 0.446 | 0.750 | 0.721 | 0.224 | 0.224 | 0.728 | 0.728 | 0.265 | 0.143 | 0.073 | 0.375 |
| 2  | 0.944 | 0.973 | 0.481 | 1.000 | 0.744 | 0.214 | 0.214 | 0.750 | 0.750 | 0.308 | 0.143 | 0.261 | 0.388 |
| 3  | 0.938 | 0.996 | 0.281 | 0.500 | 0.585 | 0.249 | 0.249 | 0.579 | 0.579 | 0.089 | 0.143 | 0.069 | 0.367 |
| 4  | 0.468 | 0.949 | 0.369 | 0.750 | 0.578 | 0.525 | 0.525 | 0.693 | 0.693 | 0.191 | 0.143 | 0.078 | 0.436 |
| 5  | 0.749 | 0.981 | 0.427 | 0.750 | 0.680 | 0.214 | 0.214 | 0.678 | 0.678 | 0.245 | 0.167 | 0.059 | 0.494 |
| 6  | 0.593 | 0.997 | 0.354 | 0.500 | 0.591 | 0.352 | 0.352 | 0.695 | 0.695 | 0.145 | 0.143 | 0.069 | 0.349 |
| 7  | 0.709 | 0.993 | 0.418 | 0.750 | 0.665 | 0.214 | 0.214 | 0.760 | 0.760 | 0.223 | 0.143 | 0.042 | 0.427 |
| 8  | 0.814 | 0.992 | 0.472 | 1.000 | 0.727 | 0.214 | 0.214 | 0.730 | 0.730 | 0.271 | 0.143 | 0.147 | 0.450 |
| 9  | 0.835 | 0.977 | 0.328 | 0.500 | 0.523 | 0.525 | 0.525 | 0.683 | 0.683 | 0.113 | 0.143 | 0.146 | 0.479 |
| 10 | 0.738 | 0.956 | 0.583 | 1.000 | 0.718 | 0.405 | 0.405 | 0.833 | 0.833 | 0.345 | 0.143 | 0.261 | 0.210 |
| 11 | 0.749 | 0.976 | 0.472 | 1.000 | 0.692 | 0.461 | 0.461 | 0.762 | 0.762 | 0.311 | 0.200 | 0.156 | 0.460 |
| 12 | 0.408 | 0.951 | 0.490 | 1.000 | 0.564 | 0.545 | 0.545 | 0.687 | 0.687 | 0.279 | 0.143 | 0.047 | 0.346 |
| 13 | 0.740 | 0.979 | 0.368 | 0.500 | 0.647 | 0.214 | 0.214 | 0.674 | 0.674 | 0.154 | 0.167 | 0.052 | 0.408 |
| 14 | 0.709 | 0.993 | 0.418 | 0.750 | 0.665 | 0.214 | 0.214 | 0.760 | 0.760 | 0.223 | 0.143 | 0.042 | 0.427 |
| 15 | 0.810 | 0.994 | 0.389 | 0.750 | 0.538 | 0.618 | 0.618 | 0.665 | 0.665 | 0.217 | 0.200 | 0.015 | 0.410 |
| 16 | 0.791 | 0.974 | 0.373 | 0.500 | 0.724 | 0.214 | 0.214 | 0.750 | 0.750 | 0.172 | 0.143 | 0.063 | 0.535 |

**Table 3.** The memory performance of 16 stimuli

| Stimuli number | 1 | 2 | 3 | 4 | 5 | 6 | 7 | 8 | 9 | 10 | 11 | 12 | 13 | 14 | 15 | 16 |
|---|---|---|---|---|---|---|---|---|---|---|---|---|---|---|---|---|
| Accuracy (Proportion Correct) | 0.722 | 0.792 | 0.421 | 0.634 | 0.702 | 0.518 | 0.691 | 0.752 | 0.487 | 0.910 | 0.838 | 0.766 | 0.538 | 0.691 | 0.689 | 0.591 |
| Reaction Time (s) | 2.435 | 2.411 | 3.184 | 2.846 | 2.481 | 3.173 | 2.485 | 2.549 | 3.056 | 2.346 | 2.572 | 2.461 | 2.759 | 2.485 | 2.541 | 2.956 |

**Memory score.** Table 3 shows the memory performance including accuracy and reaction time with the extreme data ($m-3sd < Xi < m + 3SD$) is removed and the average is calculated.

**Correlation analysis.** It can be seen from Table 2 that all of the 12 aesthetic factors are continuous values, with the exception of the SQM factor, which is a discontinuous number. To examine the correlation between aesthetics and memory, a one-way ANOVA was used to compare SQM and memory correctness, while the other components were each analyzed to a unary linear regression analysis with memory accuracy.

The one-way ANOVA on the 3 different levels of SQM showed a significant effect on memory accuracy [$F(3, 12) = 27.967$, $p < 0.05$]. The result of the unary linear regression is shown in Table 4. It finds out that the *p-value* of SYM, SMM, CM, and RM are lower than 0.05, indicating that these three indicators have a significant effect on memory. In contrast, the other 8 measures' p-values are higher than 0.05.

The unary linear regression equation for these four indicators with the accuracy score are: $y = -0.036x + 1.702$ (SYM); $y = 0.089x + 0.89$ (CM); $y = -0.789x + 9.003$ (SMM); $y = 0.276x + 1.779$ (RM). Figure 4 depicts the residual plots. As can be seen, the regression equations' predictive quality is dependable.

Excluding the seven factors that did not have a strong effect, a multiple linear regression of SYM, CM, SMM, and RM on memory accuracy was conducted to investigate the extent to which these three metric factors had an effect on memory. However, the

**Table 4.** $R^2$ and $p$-Value of unary linear regression for the aesthetics indicators and memory score

|  | BM | EM | SYM | CM | UM | PM | SMM | DM | RM | ECM | HM | RHM |
|---|---|---|---|---|---|---|---|---|---|---|---|---|
| $R^2$ | 0.015 | 0.187 | 0.911 | 0.267 | 0.011 | 0.477 | 0.938 | 0.050 | 0.982 | 0.1146 | 0.021 | 0.088 |
| $p$-Value | 0.650 | 0.095* | 0.001** | 0.040** | 0.702 | 0.060* | 0.006** | 0.403 | 0.010** | 0.1997 | 0.059* | 0.264 |

*$p < 0.1$

**$p < 0.05$

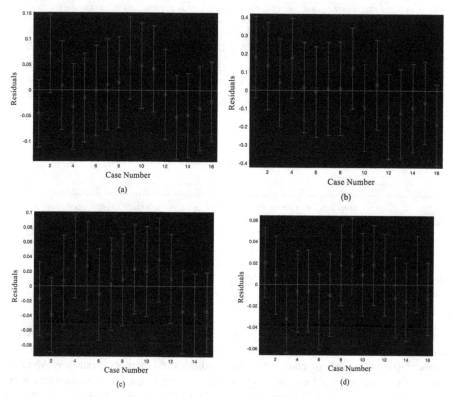

**Fig. 4.** Plots of Residuals. (a) refers to SYM; (b) refers to CM; (c) refers to SMM; (d) refers to RM

results showed that there was multicollinearity between SYM, CM, SMM, and RM (VIF > 10), suggesting a correlation between the four aesthetic factors.

### 3.3 Conclusion

Based on the results of the above analysis, it can be concluded that SYM, SQM, CM, SMM, and RM have a strong correlation with memory; EM, PM, and HM have a generally not strong enough correlation with memory; while BM, UM, DM, ECM, and RHM show no correlation with memory in this study. Accordingly, symmetry, sequence, simplicity, and regularity that constitute the aesthetics of an interface are likely to influence the difficulty of remembering the interface layout. In interface layout design, these aspects can be used to enhance aesthetics while achieving a reduction in memory difficulty and hence a reduction in cognitive load and better service to users. When developing the interface layout, make the elements more symmetrical, organize them in size order from left to right and top to bottom, and align the edges of the elements, especially the start points, as much as possible to make them easier to be remembered and reduce cognitive workload.

## 4  Discussion

This paper explores whether the aesthetics of the human-machine interface layout has an influential effect on its memory. Based on the objective evaluation model of aesthetics, the correlation between 13 aspects of aesthetics and working memory was explored, revealing a significant effect of symmetry, sequence, cohesion, simplicity, and regularity on memory among them, while balance, equilibrium, unity, proportion, density, economy, homogeneity, and rhythm were not tested for its effect on memory in this study.

Based on the aesthetic factors which showed a significant effect on memory in this finding, and the fact that the main factors influencing working memory include the memorizer's level of arousal, the difficulty of the blocks of memorized content, and the depth of cognitive processing [13], this paper makes the following three hypotheses about why aesthetics has a facilitating effect on memory. First of all, it is probable that the generation of aesthetics influences the individuals' state of arousal and motivates them to perform the memory task. Subjects preferred interfaces with a higher score of proportion, simplicity, and homogeneity because they were more visually pleasant. This is consistent with prior research showing that more visually appealing interfaces might boost students' enthusiasm for learning. Albeit less important to balance, equilibrium, proportion, and homogeneity factors showed influence on working memory in this research, this could be due to the fact that the effect of these factors on the degree of arousal is rather weak, but this does not mean that there is no influence. Secondly, some of the aesthetic factors had a significant effect on blocking, to the extent that they facilitated memory. Symmetry, cohesion, simplicity, and regularity which showed a significant effect on memory in the results, and the economy, which did not show a significant correlation, are all consistent with the principle of similarity in the Gestalt block principles [13]. The unity, density, homogeneity, and rhythm principle, on the other hand, did not show an effect in this study but is consistent with the proximity principle of the remaining Gestalt principles. The construction of chunks enables the combination of multiple pieces of information into a single memory unit, considerably reducing the difficulty of remembering while also enhancing memory capacity. Finally, this article speculates that another aspect of the aesthetic component has a major effect on cognitive processing. The sequence factor, for example, which corresponds to the order of human visual processing, can be positioned in such a way that helps individuals to acquire information more quickly and easily.

These findings can be used to improve the VWM of HCI through a practical layout design from the five layout aspects, which are proven to have a significant effect on memory performance, thereby reducing the cognitive load. It is known that the shorter the time required to memorize the interface layout, the lower the user's learning cost, the shorter the time for searching for targets and operations, and the improved efficiency and experience. Studying the influencing factors of the memorability of interface layout is of great help in reducing the interface's memory cost and optimizing the user's experience.

This paper examines the role of aesthetics in facilitating the memory component of the cognitive process. It can be hypothesized that the enhancement of usability by aesthetics may stem from its contribution to cognitive processes. The pursuit of aesthetics, the reduction of memory difficulty, and the enhancement of usability are consistent. Form and function can remain united without contradiction [14]. The ultimate objective of aesthetics and functions remains the same to offer a better user experience.

A limitation of this study is the small sample size, which may have led to the lack of independence between some of the beauty factors in the analysis. At the same time, due to the indeterminacy of the independence and relevance between the aesthetic indicators, it is hard to analyze the interaction effect of multiple indicators on memory effect, which needs further research. Future research could invest in larger samples and participants and the relationship may be analyzed using multivariate statistical approaches.

# References

1. Ngo, D., Byrne, J.G.: Application of an aesthetic evaluation model to data entry screens. Comput. Hum. Behav. **17**(2), 149–185 (2001)
2. Tullis, T.S.: An evaluation of alphanumeric, graphic, and colour information displays. Hum. Factors **23**, 541–550 (1981)
3. Aspillaga, M.: Screen design: location of information and its effects on learning. J. Comput. Based Instruction (1991)
4. Grabinger, R.S.: Computer screen designs: viewer judgements. Educ. Tech. Res. Dev. **41**(2), 35–73 (1991)
5. Tuch, A.N., Roth, S.P., Hornbæk, K., Opwis, K., Bargas-Avila, J.A.: Is beautiful really usable? toward understanding the relation between usability, aesthetics, and affect in HCI. Comput. Hum. Behav. **28**(5), 1596–1607 (2012)
6. Rust, N.C., Mehrpour, V.: Understanding image memorability. Trends Cogn. Sci. **24**(7), 557–568 (2020)
7. Douneva, M., Jaron, R., Thielsch, M.T.: Effects of different website designs on first impressions, aesthetic judgements and memory performance after short presentation. Interacting with Computers, iwv033 (2016)
8. Miura, T., Yabu, K.I., Tanaka, K., Ueda, K., Ifukube, T.: Visuospatial working memory game and measured memory performances at various ages. In: 2016 IEEE International Conference on Systems, Man, and Cybernetics (SMC). IEEE (2016)
9. Altaboli, A., Lin, Y.: Objective and subjective measures of visual aesthetics of website interface design: the two sides of the coin. In: International Conference on Human-Computer Interaction, pp. 35–44. Springer, Berlin, Heidelberg, July 2011
10. Zhou, L., Xue, C., Tang, W., Li, J., Niu, Y.: Aesthetic evaluation method of interface elements layout design. J. Comput.-Aided Des. Comput. Graph. **25**, 758–766 (2013)
11. Peterson, D.J., Berryhill, M.E.: The Gestalt principle of similarity benefits visual working memory. Psychon. Bull. Rev. **20**(6), 1282–1289 (2013). https://doi.org/10.3758/s13423-013-0460-x

12. Lindgaard, G.: Aesthetics, visual appeal, usability and user satisfaction: what do the user's eyes tell the user's brain? Australian J. Emerg. Technol. Soc. **5**(1) (2007)
13. Woodman, G.F., Vecera, S.P., Luck, S.J.: Perceptual organization influences visual working memory. Psychon. Bull. Rev. **10**(1), 80–87 (2003)
14. Kurosu, M., Kashimura, K.: Apparent usability vs. inherent usability. Human Factors in Computing Systems. In: CHI 1995 Conference Companion: Mosaic of Creativity, Denver, Colorado, USA, May 7–11, DBLP (1995)

# The Simon Effect in Driving

Alexander Boudreau[1] and Thomas Z. Strybel[2](✉)

[1] California State University, Long Beach, USA
[2] Department of Psychology, 1250 Bellflower Blvd, Long Beach, CA 90840, USA
thomas.strybel@csulb.edu

**Abstract.** It is anticipated that automobiles will become fully autonomous at some time in the future. To achieve this outcome, designers and manufacturers are introducing new automated driving aids incrementally which should improve the safety and efficiency of surface transportation, but could potentially increase the complexity of driving. As more automation is added, both for driving (i.e., adaptive cruise control) and non-driving (i.e. entertainment console) purposes, the location of displays and controls will become increasingly important to ensure rapid and accurate responses to time-critical events. One factor that has been shown to affect response latency and accuracy in many task settings is stimulus-response (S-R) compatibility: when stimulus and response locations are spatially congruent, response times are lower that when the spatial locations are incongruent. This S-R compatibility effect has been demonstrated even when stimulus location is not relevant to the task, known as the Simon Effect. In the present experiment, we investigated the Simon Effect using a dynamic driving task known as the Lane Change Test (LCT). We found partial support for a Simon effect that was modified by the position of the vehicle on the road.

**Keywords:** Simon Effect · S-R compatibility · Driving

## 1 Introduction

Norman (1988) observed that the introduction of early automation in automobiles resulted in the standardization of several aspects of car design, for example, the left-right position of the driver in the vehicle, the left-right position of the vehicle on the road, and driving controls such as steering wheel, clutch, brake and accelerator. The benefits of standardization to driving, according to Norman, was that "… Once you have learned to drive one car, you feel justifiably confident that you can drive any car, any place in the world… (p202) [1]." Today's automobiles are being equipped with more advanced automation systems for driving (e.g. adaptive cruise control) and non-driving (e.g. entertainment systems) purposes. Currently, the locations of displays and controls for these systems are determined by the manufacturer and it is possible that one's confidence in the ability to drive any car any place in the world may be diminishing.

Early design decisions evolved over time, and explanations for these decision rely mostly on folklore [2, 3]. For example, early automobile manufacturers such as the Ford Motor Company in the U.S. placed the driver on the left side of the vehicle closest to the

M. Kurosu et al. (Eds.): HCII 2022, LNCS 13516, pp. 608–616, 2022.
https://doi.org/10.1007/978-3-031-17615-9_43

center of the road so that drivers could determine the amount of space between oncoming vehicles and passengers could enter/exit the vehicle on the curb side of the road. Modern vehicle technologies are aimed at automating the driving task itself, with the ultimate goal creating fully autonomous vehicles. Until that goal is achieved, however, automation is being implemented incrementally, meaning that until fully autonomous vehicles are achieved, the driver is faced with additional information displays and controls regarding these automated subsystems.

Driving is essentially a spatial perceptual-motor task, in which the driver controls the direction and speed of the vehicle as it moves through space. With increased autonomy, however, the driver is burdened with detecting, understanding and remembering the current state of the vehicle, and its automation. In effect, the driver's task is becoming more like that of an airline pilot, who inputs information regarding the direction, speed and altitude of their aircraft, supervises the automated systems and ensures that they are performing as the pilot intended.

For driving, the semi-autonomous systems require additional controls for setting the states of these systems, and responding to system failures. One design solution currently used in most automobiles is to place controls directly on the steering wheel, although the exact location for each function varies somewhat by manufacturer. There are some reports in the human factors literature on driver preference for steering-wheel-mounted controls. Mossey (2013), for example, reported that drivers from several user groups preferred non-essential radio-related controls on the left side of the steering wheel, and driving–related cruise controls on the right side [4]. The rationale behind the drivers' preferences were not determined. This arrangement is consistent with some current automotive designs (e.g., Honda) although other manufactures (e.g., Buick) use an opposite arrangement.

## 1.1 Simon Effect and S-R Compatibility

Control-display location has been shown to affect human performance in other task domains. One principle related to button placement, that should affect driving performance is stimulus-response (S-R) compatibility, in which response times to stimuli that vary in location are faster when the location of the response corresponds to the location of the stimulus. That is, response times to stimuli located on the right are faster when the response button is also located on the right, compared with response times to right-side stimuli that are made with a response button on the left side. This effect also occurs when the stimulus location is irrelevant to the task. Even if location of the stimulus is unrelated to the task, known as the Simon effect [5]. For example, responses to the color of a stimulus is faster when the response location corresponds to the location of the stimulus. In general compatibility effects are determined by a spatial referent, often this is relative to the individual respondent, but also other referents may interact with the human spatial referent.

A common explanation for S-R compatibility and Simon effect is Kornblum et al.'s dual process model that emphasizes dimensional overlap between the stimulus and response locations, regardless of whether the overlap is task relevant [6]. Essentially, a stimulus produces automatic activation of a spatially corresponding response. If this response is identical to the correct response, activation occurs, but when they are different, response conflict can delay the response. Correspondence is related to a spatial frame of reference. In the simplest case, the observer serves as their own spatial referent and correspondence can mean whether the stimulus and response locations are to the left or right of the participant. It has been shown repeatedly that multiple frames of reference can determine the amount of facilitation or interference.

Because S-R compatibility and Simon effects are determined by spatial referents, identifying these referents and designing for them becomes important. Reference points and their salience can be external objects, location codes, or combinations of them [7]. For example, when wrists were crossed in a standard S-R compatibility task by placing the participant's left hand on the right button and the right hand on the left button there was little difference in the compatibility effect compared to when wrists were uncrossed [8]. Additionally, Nicoletti et al., (1982) found the same pattern of compatibility effects when both the stimuli and response options were placed to the left or right side of the body midline. It was more important that the stimuli and response options were spatially located relative to the task than when they were physically located with regard to the person [9].

## 1.2 Simon Effect in Driving

Multiple frames of reference and S-R compatibility have been studied in the context of driving. Bayliss (2007) measured response times to images of automobile turn signals, when the location of the turn indicator light was either more lateral than the headlight, indicating compatibility with the location of the observer and the approaching automobile, or closer to the center of the car relative to the approaching automobile [10]. In the latter case, the signal was compatible with respect to the observer, but incompatible with respect to the approaching vehicle. In two experiments, Bayliss showed that participants responded more slowly and less accurately to turn indicators located to the inside of headlights than when the turn indicators were on the outside of the headlights. This was explained by conflicting location codes. For a left response on an inside turn indicator, the code is left with respect to the car but has a right code with respect to the headlight. For a turn indicator on the outside of the headlight the code is left with respect to the car and the headlight. The inside placed turn indicator creates a conflict between the left and right codes and it takes longer for the brain to sort out which is the correct response for the task.

Xiong and Proctor (2015) investigated the effects of multiple frames of reference on the compatibility effect for response buttons positioned on the steering wheel using a Simon task. These authors hypothesized that left and right buttons on the steering wheel could be compatible or incompatible depending on the frame of reference. The buttons would be spatially compatible with the steering wheel and driver, but in some cases incompatible relative to the location of an infotainment display located in the center of the vehicle but to the right/left of the steering wheel based on whether the driver was positioned on the left (as in the U.S.) or right side (as in many European countries) of the vehicle. In the initial experiment, the infotainment center was not present and participants responded to the pitch of a tone that could be presented to the left or right side of the steering wheel. The left-right button attached to the steering wheel could be therefore congruent with the tone (e.g., tone presented from the left speaker responded with the left button) or incongruent with the tone (e.g., tone presented from left speaker is responded with the right button). A compatibility effect was obtained, in that congruent responses were on the average 10–13 ms faster than incongruent responses. In subsequent experiments, the location of an infotainment display located in the center of the vehicle, modified the size of the compatibility effect based on the position of the steering wheel and participant.

### 1.3  Purpose

Xiong and Proctor therefore showed S-R compatibility effects in that when the location of the response was incongruent with the stimulus location, reaction times were elevated, suggesting that designers should consider spatial compatibility relative to these frames of reference when laying out displays and controls. Note, however, that in both Bayliss and Xiong and Proctor, performance was measured in stationary vehicles, meaning the outside environment was unchanging and the participant was not actually engaged in driving. Therefore, the salience of these inside frames of reference may have been elevated compared to when the driver is allocating most of their attentional resources to controlling the vehicle as it moves through space. Moreover, with a dynamic driving task, position of buttons on wheel will change slightly based on current rotation of the steering wheel. That is, right/left turns will add a vertical dimension to the relative location of the steering wheel buttons (e.g., turning to the left places the left button lower vertically and right button higher vertically). Therefore, in the present experiment, we measured response times in a Simon task to high and low pitch tones with compatible and incompatible response buttons located on the drivers steering wheel, while the participant was driving, using a simple driving simulation known as the Lane Change Test (LCT) [12].

## 2  Method

### 2.1  Participants

Fourteen undergraduate students participated, 11 males and 3 females, all but one being right handed. Participants were licensed drivers in the State of California between the ages of 20 and 33 years (M = 26.6, SD = 3.5). All participants had normal or corrected-to- normal vision and reported no known hearing deficits. Participants received payment for two hours of participation in the form of a $20 electronic gift cards.

### 2.2  Apparatus and Stimuli

The experiment was run in a sound attenuated room having a large screen on which the driving simulation was projected. Participants sat at a small desk placed in front of the projector 1.4 m from the screen. On the desk was a G27 Logitech Force-Feedback Racing Wheel and pedal system; only the steering wheel was used in the experiment, however. Two response buttons were mounted on the steering wheel at roughly the 10-o'clock and 2-o'clock positions, thus enabling the participant to rest their left and right thumbs on the buttons while gripping and turning the steering wheel. The auditory stimuli were 200-Hz and 500-Hz sine waves at 60 dB A-weighted and 200 ms in duration. The tones were presented through loudspeakers located behind the projector screen, on the left and right edges of the projected LCT image (approximately ± 30° from the center of the screen).

The Lane Change Test (LCT) was projected on the screen from an adjacent control room. The LCT is an otherwise empty, 3-lane highway 18 km long (see Fig. 1). Participants drive the highway at 60 km/hr with speed controlled by the software, thus requiring 3 min to complete a track. Road signs were located on each side of the highway roughly every 150 km; these instructed the participants to change lanes. Participants were instructed to respond to lane change instructions as quickly and efficiently as possible. Each track of the LCT contains 18 lane change signs with 6 instructing a change to each of the 3 lanes, meaning that the vehicle occupied each lane the same amount of time on each track. Performance on the LCT is measured by the mean lane deviation (MDev) the average distance between the vehicle's path and a normative optimal path. MDev has been shown to measure capture aspects of driving performance including detection, maneuver quality, and lane keeping ability [12].

**Fig. 1.** Screen shot of the Lane Change Test (LCT) with road sign instructing move to left lane

### 2.3  Experimental Design

The experimental design was a 2 (Button Location: left vs. right) X 2 (Congruency: congruent vs. incongruent response) within-subjects design, with the dependent variables MDev and response time to the tone stimulus. In addition, baseline conditions of the LCT with no tone task, and the tone discrimination task without driving were also run.

## 2.4  Procedure

Each participant completed two one-hour sessions over two days. On the first day, participants completed 3 practice trials of the LCT. This was followed by the baseline LCT with no responses to the tones required, and then practice driving the LCT and responding to the target tone stimulus. Five experimental trials were then run in which the LCT was driven while simultaneously responding to tones that were played through one of the loudspeakers. The researcher designated one of the tones (200 Hz or 500 Hz) as the target tone for each participant and the participant was instructed to respond to the target tone using one of the two buttons on the steering wheel. On the first day of testing, the participant was assigned either the left or right button as the required response, and on the second day, the opposite button was assigned. On both days, the participant's target tone frequency did not change. Participants were instructed not to respond to the non-target tones, a go-no-go task. Participants completed 5 tracks for each button condition. Within a track, 54 tones were presented, 27 target tones, with half of the target tones spatially congruent (emitting from the same side as the response button) and half spatially incongruent (emitting from the opposite side). Auditory tones were presented at random intervals with the restriction that they did not occur while the driver was changing lanes. Participants were instructed to give equal weight to both the driving and tone response tasks.

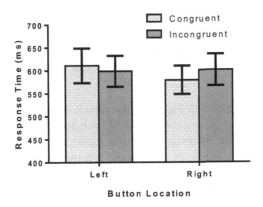

**Fig. 2.** Mean response times as a function of Button Location and Congruency.

One the second day of testing, participants also completed a brief tone response baseline task, consisting of 20 target tones (10 congruent) and 20 non-target tones that were presented when the participant was not driving. This was followed by practice with the LCT while using the opposite response button, and then 5 experimental trials.

## 3  Results

The mean reaction time for each participant was computed and a two way repeated measures analysis of variance was performed with the factors Button Location (left vs.

right) and Congruency (congruent vs. incongruent). For response times, the main effects of Button Location and Congruency were non-significant (ps > .28), but the two-way interaction was significant (F(1,13) = 6.97; p = .02). As shown in Fig. 2, a significant Simon Effect of 22 ms was found for right button presses (t(14) = 2.64; p = .02). For the left button condition, incongruent responses were on average 15 ms faster than congruent responses although this difference was non-significant (p = .20) Of course, for this analysis, congruency was based on the relative positions of the steering wheel button and tones. As previously discussed, however, it is possible that congruency for driving could be influenced by spatial referents external to the vehicle. For the simple LCT, one possible referent is the highway itself, as other vehicles, road signs other than lane change instructions or road intersections were not present. Therefore, we ran separate two-way ANOVAs for response times when the vehicle was in the left, center and right lanes to determine the influence of lane positions.

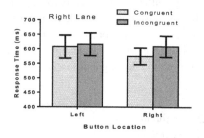

**Fig. 3.** Mean response times as a function of Button Location and Congruency when the Vehicle was in the right lane. Image on right shows driver's view from right lane.

Response times are shown in Fig. 3 for the vehicle in the right lane. A significant main effect of Congruency was obtained (F(1,13) = 6.54; p = .02) but the main effect of Button Location and the interaction was non-significant (ps > .29). For right lane driving, incongruent response times were on the average 21 ms higher than congruent responses. As shown in Fig. 3, differences in response times between congruent and incongruent conditions are slightly larger for right buttons.

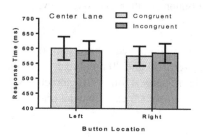

**Fig. 4.** Mean response times as a function of Button Location and Congruency when the vehicle was in the center lane. Image on right shows the driver's view from the center lane.

Figure 4 shows response times when the vehicle was in the center lane. Here, all effects were non-significant (ps > .27). As shown in the Fig. 4, response times were roughly equivalent for both congruency conditions and button locations. Figure 5 shows response times when the vehicle was in the left lane. Here, the interaction between Button Location and Congruency was significant (F(1,13) = 11.53; p = .005) but all main effects were non-significant (ps > .35) As shown in Fig. 5, response times increased 24ms on the average for incongruent right button conditions, which was marginally significant (t(13) = 1.99; p = .07). However for left buttons, response times for incongruent conditions significantly decreased 35 ms on the average (t(13) = 3.51; p = .002).

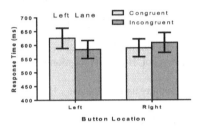 

**Fig. 5.** Mean response times as a function of Button Location and Congruency when the vehicle was in the left lane. Image on the right shows driver's view from the left lane.

## 4  Discussion

Caution should be taken regarding the findings here because the small sample size and number of trials was much lower compared with those typically used in S-R- compatibility and Simon-effect experiments [11]. Nevertheless, it appears that response times in a dynamic driving task can by influenced by spatial referents outside the vehicle, although the magnitude and direction of the effect is unclear. For the right lane, the suggestion of a greater Simon effect for right buttons is consistent with Xiang and Proctor, as the left button would be incompatible with the road referent. On the other hand, when the left button is used while driving in the left lane should produce the greatest Simon Effect, yet incongruent responses were in fact faster than congruent responses.

In this experiment, the external driving view was quite sparse, consisting only of the 3-lane highway and road signs. Moreover, the internal referents were limited to that of the steering wheel, as the driving platform consisted of a steering wheel on a small table. Therefore, internal spatial referents were limited to the steering wheel and driver, and external spatial referents were limited to the highway itself. At best, these findings suggest that S_R compatibility and Simon effects should be investigated further in a dynamic driving environment and with both internal and external spatial referents.

## References

1. Norman, D.A.: The Psychology of Everyday Things. Basic Books Inc, New York (1988)

2. Lucas, B.: Which side of the road do they drive on?, August 2018. http://brianlucas.ca/roadside/

3. Norman, D.: Which side is the steering wheel?, November 2008. https://jnd.org/which_side_is_the_steering_wheel/

4. Mossey, M.: Designing a novel steering wheel for Generation-Y, Baby Boomers, and engineers (Doctoral Dissertation) (2013)

5. Retrieved from https://tigerprints.clemson.edu/all_theses

6. Lu, C.H., Proctor, R.W.: The influence of irrelevant location information on performance: a review of the Simon and spatial Stroop effects. Psychon. Bull. Rev. **2**, 174–207 (1995)

7. Kornblum, S., Hasbroucq, T., Osman, A.: Dimensional overlap: cognitive basis for stimulus-response compatibility – a model and taxonomy. Psychol. Rev. **97**, 253–270 (1990)

8. Hommel, B.: The Simon effect as a tool and heuristic. Acta Physiol. (Oxf) **36**, 139–202 (2011)

9. Brebner, J., Shephard, M., Cairney, P.: Spatial relationships and S-R compatibility. Acta Physiol. (Oxf) **36**, 1–15 (1972)

10. Nicoletti, R., Anzola, G.P., Luppino, G., Rizzolatti, G., Umilta, C.: Spatial compatibility effects on the same side of the body midline. J. Exp. Psychol. Human Perception Perf. **8**(5), 664–673 (1982)

11. Bayliss, A.P.: Mixed signals; stimulus-response compatibility and car indicator light configuration. Appl. Cogn. Psychol. **21**, 669–676 (2007)

12. Xiong, A., Proctor, R.W.: Referential coding of steering-wheel button presses in a simulated driving cockpit. J. Exp. Psychol. Appl. **21**, 418–428 (2015)

13. Mattes, S., Hallen, A.: Surrogate distraction measurement techniques: the lane change test. In: Regan, M.A., Lee, J.D., Young, K.L. (Eds.) Driver Distraction: Theory, Effects and Mitigation. CRC Press, Boca Raton ( 2009)

# Vector-Based Data Improves Left-Right Eye-Tracking Classifier Performance After a Covariate Distributional Shift

Brian Xiang[(✉)] and Abdelrahman Abdelmonsef

Swarthmore College, Swarthmore, PA 19081, USA
{bxiang1,ayahia1}@swarthmore.edu

**Abstract.** The main challenges of using electroencephalogram (EEG) signals to make eye-tracking (ET) predictions are the differences in distributional patterns between benchmark data and real-world data and the noise resulting from the unintended interference of brain signals from multiple sources. Increasing the robustness of machine learning models in predicting eye-tracking position from EEG data is therefore integral for both research and consumer use. In medical research, the usage of more complicated data collection methods to test for simpler tasks has been explored to address this very issue. In this study, we propose a fine-grain data approach for EEG-ET data collection in order to create more robust benchmarking. We train machine learning models utilizing both coarse-grain and fine-grain data and compare their accuracies when tested on data of similar/different distributional patterns in order to determine how susceptible EEG-ET benchmarks are to differences in distributional data. We apply a covariate distributional shift to test for this susceptibility. Results showed that models trained on fine-grain, vector-based data were less susceptible to distributional shifts than models trained on coarse-grain, binary-classified data.

**Keywords:** HCI Theories and Methods · Machine learning · Covariate distributional shift · RBF SVC · Linear SVC · Random forest · XGBoost · Gradient boost · Ada boost · Decision tree · Gaussian NB

## 1 Introduction

### 1.1 Problem Statement

Eye-tracking (ET) is the process of predicting a subject's point of gaze or robustly detecting the relative motion of the eye to the head [28]. Electroencephalography (EEG) signals are brain signals that correspond to various states from the scalp surface area, encoding neurophysiological markers, and are characterized by their high temporal resolution and minimal restrictions [27].

Recently, predicting eye-tracking data using EEG has received increasing interest because of the recent hardware and software technological advancements

M. Kurosu et al. (Eds.): HCII 2022, LNCS 13516, pp. 617–632, 2022.
https://doi.org/10.1007/978-3-031-17615-9_44

and its versatile applications in different fields [10,37,38]. For instance, EEG-ET data can be used to identify shopping motives relatively early in the search process [11], to detect workload strain in truck drivers [36], and to assess the diagnosis of many neurological diseases such as Autism Spectrum Disorder and Alzheimer's [12–14].

With the broad array of EEG-ET data applications, accuracy and efficiency are of utmost importance. The collection of both EEG and ET data, however, involves challenges such as finding invariant representation of inter-and intra-subject differences as well as noise resulting from the unintended interference of brain signals from multiple sources [16]. Increasing the robustness of machine learning models in making accurate eye-tracking predictions from EEG data is therefore integral for both research and consumer use.

## 1.2   Literature Review

EEG is a type of highly individualized time-series data [17,23,29,47]. Machine Learning approaches perform adequately on computer vision, bioinfomatics, medical image analysis and usually have potential in EEG analysis as well [15,22,31,34]. Machine Learning and Deep Learning methods have been implemented in EEG classification research with promising results [44–46,48]. Recent works in this area have focused on determining what machine learning models are more capable of predicting eye position from EEG signals. In that pursuit, [44] has shown that Riemannian geometry and tensor-based classification methods have reached state-of-the-art performances in multiple EEG-based machine learning applications. Previous work has also been done in collecting large datasets that combine EEG and ET data. A good example is the multimodal neurophysiological dataset collected by [43] and EEGEyeNet [10]. Finally, other work has been done to eliminate the noise associated with EEG data collection automatically, such as [39,40]. Also, [41] showed the potential of using machine learning for noise elimination. Soon after, Zhang et al. collected EEGde-noiseNet, a dataset suitable to train machine learning models in noise elimination [42]. These benchmarks include ocular artifacts; thus, they apply to EEG data collected simultaneously with eye-tracking data.

While much work has been done to improve the accuracy of ET-based EEG applications, there is a lack of previous work that focuses on examining the effects of data collection methods on eye position prediction accuracies. In particular, we are interested in comparing coarse-grain and fine-grain data collection techniques for simultaneously collecting EEG and eye-tracking data. In other fields of medical research, fine-grain data collection methods have been explored with great success [7,30]. That is using more complicated data collection methods to test for less complicated tasks. Often, systems developed in "lab conditions" only work in controlled environments, causing difficulties when utilized in uncontrolled conditions [8,9]. With consumer EEG-ET applications becoming increasingly prevalent, the importance of assessing whether finer-grain data collection methods improve upon the accuracy and robustness of EEG-ET machine learning classifiers is magnified. To narrow down this assessment, this study focuses on the effects of training machine learning models on fine- versus coarse-grain EEG data in predicting the binary direction (left or right) of eye-tracking position.

### 1.3  Purpose of Study

Previously, benchmarks for left-right eye-tracking predictions were established utilizing data from binary-classified data collection methods [10]. In this study, we train machine learning models for left-right eye-tracking classification using data from a vector-based collection framework. We then compare the results to the models trained by Kastrati et al. and determine whether finer-grain data is beneficial to the robustness of EEG-ET machine learning models. Robustness is determined by the accuracy after a covariate distributional shift. This attempts to mimic realistic data with varying distributional patterns. The purpose of this study is to verify whether machine learning models trained using vector-based, fine-grain eye-tracking data obtain higher accuracies in left-right gaze classification than models trained using binary-based, coarse-grain eye-tracking data after a covariate shift is applied.

## 2  Data

In our experiments, we used the EEGEyeNet dataset [10]. The EEGEyeNet dataset gathers EEG and eye-tracking data from 356 (190 female and 166 male) healthy subjects of varying ages (18–80). Data were collected for 3 different experimental tasks according to the Declaration of Helsinki Principles. The tasks are Pro- and Antisaccade, Large Grid, and Visual Symbol Search. The recording setup was similar across all experimental tasks. EEG data were recorded using a 128-channel EEG Geodesic Hydrocel system at a sampling rate 500 Hz. Eye position was simultaneously recorded using an infrared video-based ET EyeLink 1000 Plus also at a sampling rate 500 Hz. Between trials, the eye-tracking device would be reset with a 9-point grid. Subjects were situated 68 cm away from a 24-inch monitor with a resolution of $800 \times 600$ pixels. In this study, we directly use data from the pro-antisaccade paradigm and manipulate data from the large grid paradigm to use for the analysis.

### 2.1  Pro-Antisaccade Task

In this task, each trial starts with a central square on which the participants were asked to focus for a randomized period that doesn't exceed 3.5 s. Then, a dot appears horizontally to the left or the right of this central square, as shown in Fig. 1. Subjects were asked to perform a saccade towards the opposite side of the cue and then look back to the center of the screen after 1 s. Thus, gaze positions in pro-antisaccade were restricted to the horizontal axis and were binary-classified either left or right (relative to the dot at the screen's center).

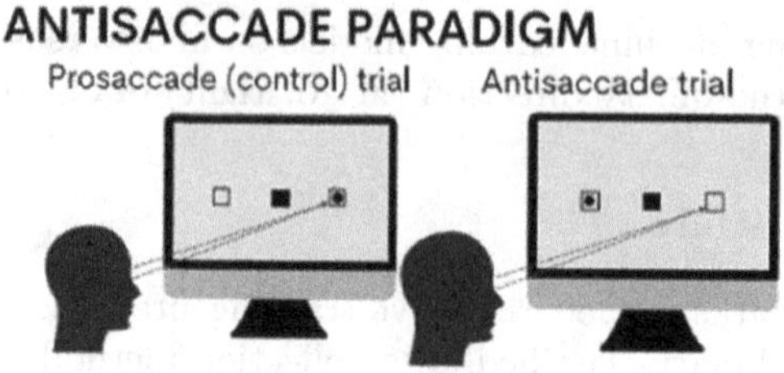

**ANTISACCADE PARADIGM**

Prosaccade (control) trial       Antisaccade trial

**Fig. 1.** Schematic for the location of the cues on the screen in the pro-antisaccade paradigm [10]

## 2.2 Large Grid Task

For this task, subjects were asked to stare at a blank screen and focus on the appearing dots. A set of well-distributed dots in 25 positions would then appear one at a time for 1.5 to 1.8 s, as shown in Fig. 2. The center dot would appear three times for a total of 27 trials per block. Subjects perform 5 blocks and repeat the procedure 6 times for a total of 810 trials per subject. Thus, large grid's framework enabled fine-grain EEG-ET data collection as gaze positions were encoded using both angle and amplitude.

## 3    Experiment Design

The learning objective of the machine learning models trained in our experiment was to use EEG brain signals to predict the direction of a subject's gaze along the horizontal axis (whether they are looking to the left or the right). Although predictions for this task using the same dataset were made by [10], they were performed exclusively using data from the prosaccade trials of the pro-antisaccade task for both training and testing.

In this paper, we train 8 machine learning models on both the pro-antisaccade and large grid data and perform a covariate distributional shift by comparing their performance based on the accuracy when tested on data from a different experimental task. As per the author's recommendation, we used the minimally

**LARGE GRID PARADIGM**

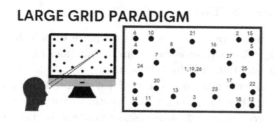

**Fig. 2.** Schematic for the location of the dots on the screen in the large grid paradigm [10]

preprocessed EEG data. To split the data, data from 70% of the participants were assigned to the training set, data from 15% of the participants was assigned to the cross-validation set, and 15% for the testing. No single participant's data was shared among different sets; each participant's data is entirely assigned to one set.

## 3.1  Data Processing

Given the classification nature of our learning problem, data from the large grid paradigm, encoded as Angle and Amplitude, should be translated and labeled into the expected format for training left-right classification models. The expected format for our labels, or data in the algorithm we used, was a lookup table with the subject ID to identify unique participants and 1 or 0 to encode left or right.

**Angle to Direction:** The angle value for each training set will be used as an indication of the gaze direction. Given that the angle values in the dataset range from $-\pi$ to $\pi$, the translation logic is only concerned about the values in this range; angles with absolute values larger than $\pi$ are ignored because they are not represented in the dataset. To perform the transformation from angle to left and right, the adopted convention for conversion is that for angle $\alpha$, $|\alpha| \leq \pi/2$ will be assigned the right direction; $|\alpha| > \pi/2$ will be assigned the left direction. As shown in Appendix A, the logic for this transformation has been confirmed by the dataset authors and is shown in Fig. 3.

**Amplitude and ID:** Given the role of ID in properly splitting the data, the subject ID will be kept and used the same as in the original format. We plan on adding amplitude later to the translated left-right values to determine if weighting data points increases or decreases accuracy.

The processing code implementing the logic above can be found here.

## 3.2  Models Training

Experiments were conducted for 4 different combinations of training and testing datasets: models trained on pro-antisaccade data and tested on pro-antisaccade data, models trained on pro-antisaccade data and tested on large grid data, models trained on large grid data and tested on large grid data, and models trained on large grid data and tested on pro-antisaccade data. The EEGEyeNet code was used as an interface for feature extraction and running the machine learning models on the extracted features. Since our task is a classification problem, regression machine learning models were excluded from running this task. The included models are the Decision Tree, Random Forest, XGBoost, Radial Basis Function kernel SVC, Gradient Boost, Gaussian Naive Bayes, AdaBoost, and Linear Support Vector Classification (SVC). Data processing was done using the NumPy library and the model implementations were installed from the SKlearn

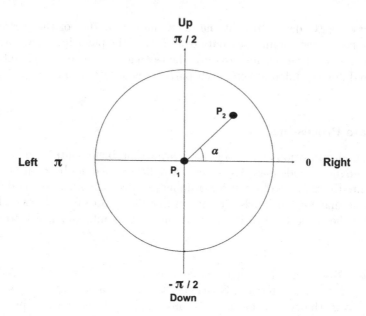

**Fig. 3.** Illustration of angle $\alpha$. $P_1$ represents the initial gazing position of the eye and $P_2$ represents the end gazing position of the eye. The line between them represents the movement of the eye.

library [4]. Specifications regarding the test environment, actual runtime of the models, and total space occupied by the dataset are provided in Appendix B.

## 4   Models

### 4.1   Machine Learning Models

In this study, machine learning models operate on features extracted from the data rather than the data itself. Feature extraction has been applied in two steps. First, [10] applied a band-pass filter in frequencies in the range [8–13 HZ] on the acquired signals through all trials. This choice of frequencies is based on [3] suggestions. Following the filtering step, the Hilbert transform was applied, resulting in a complex time series from which targeted features were extracted for learning models. Since we are considering a classification problem, we experimented with classification-only models (Linear SVC) and models that can be applied to both classification and regression problems, such as ensemble classifiers.

**SVCs:** SVC isan abbreviation for Support Vector Classifier. These are machine learning algorithms that are commonly used for supervised classification problems and sometimes regression problems, which are called Support Vector Regression. The classification decision relies on finding the best hyperplanes in the feature space. These planes are, then, used to differentiate the predictions' classes based on their orientation to the planes. A simple example in a 2d feature space might be a line that distinguishes two groups and classifies predictions based on whether the point in the 2d feature space lies to the left or the right of the plane. In our paper, we will be using Linear SVC and RBF. These algorithms still perform well after several decades since they were first implemented in this field [1, 2]

**Ensemble Classifiers:** Ensemble (or voting) classifier is a machine learning classification algorithm that trains with different classification models and makes predictions through ensembling their predictions to make a stronger classification. These algorithms have been the gold standard for several EEG-based classification experiments [45]. In our study, we used Random Forest, XGBoost, GradientBoost, and AdaBoost.

**Naive Bayes and Decision Tree Classifier:** Naive Bayes (NB) Classifier is the statistical Bayesian classifier [6]. It assumes that all variables are mutually correlated and contribute to some decree towards classification. It is based on the Bayesian theorem and is commonly used with high dimensional inputs. On the other hand, a decision tree is not a statistically based one; rather, it is a data mining induction technique that recursively partitions the dataset using a depth-first greedy algorithm till all the data gets classified to a particular class. Both NB and the decision tree are relatively fast and well suited to large data. Furthermore, they can deal with noisy data, which makes them well suited for EEG classification applications [5].

### 4.2 Deep Learning Models

Deep learning is a subfield of machine learning algorithms in which computational models learn features from hierarchical representations of input data through successive non-linear transformations [47]. Deep learning methods, especially Convolutional Neural Network (CNN), performed well in several previous EEG band power (feature) based research [45]. Still, these methods have not demonstrated convincing and consistent improvements [44]. Given so and their high run time, they are excluded from analysis in this paper.

## 5 Results

We trained the machine learning models using the two datasets (pro-antisaccade and "translated" large grid), tested each of them on data from the two datasets, and compared the results. Thus, we had 4 combinations of training and testing datasets: pro-antisaccade - pro-antisaccade (PA-PA), large grid - large grid (LG-LG), pro-antisaccade - large grid (PA-LG), and large grid - pro-antisaccade (LG-PA). PA-PA is essentially a recreation of the work of [10] and LG-LG compares whether training and testing on large grid will obtain higher accuracies than that of PA-PA.

**Table 1.** Left-right task trained and tested on the pro-antisaccade data

| Model | Accuracy (%) | Standard deviation | Mean Run time (s) |
|---|---|---|---|
| XGBoost [25] | 97.9 | 1.11E−16 | 0.062 |
| GradientBoost [18] | 97.4 | 3.8E−4 | 0.016 |
| RandomForest [24] | 96.5 | 5.15E−4 | 0.121 |
| AdaBoost [18] | 96.3 | 1.11E−16 | 0.142 |
| DecisionTree [21] | 96.2 | 1.11E−16 | 0.012 |
| LinearSVC [19] | 92.0 | 1.55E−4 | 0.007 |
| RBF SVC [26] | 89.4 | N/A | 1.864 |
| GaussianNB [20] | 87.7 | 1.11E−16 | 0.012 |

Comparing PA-LG and LG-PA is the main objective of the paper since it will give insight into whether models trained on fine-grain data (the vector-based eye tracking large grid data) will be more accurate when tested against unfamiliar data from the pro-antisaccade experiment, or vice versa.

Results regarding accuracies, standard deviation for accuracies, and mean run time for each algorithm in all combinations are provided in Tables 1, 2, 3, and 4. Some of the standard deviations could not be calculated because some of the models did not converge. A summary table of the results is presented in Table 5.

### 5.1   Comparison of PA-PA, LG-LG, PA-LG and LG-PA

**PA-PA vs LG-LG.** Looking at Tables 1 and 2, we can see that in all 8 models, the prediction accuracies for models trained and tested on pro-antisaccade data were greater than those trained and tested on large grid data. The average difference in accuracy, as shown in Table 5, was around 1.8%. Despite this difference, the accuracies of models trained and tested on large grid remained relatively high; all the tested models except GaussianNB and RBG SVC, have accuracies that are higher than or equal to 92%. On another note, data in Table 1 resembles results found by [10], proving the reproducibility of their work.

**Table 2.** Left-right task trained and tested on the large grid data

| Model | Accuracy (%) | Standard deviation | Mean Run time (s) |
|---|---|---|---|
| GradientBoost | 95.6 | 3.6E−4 | 0.013 |
| XGBoost | 95.5 | 1.11E−16 | 0.082 |
| RandomForest | 94.6 | 1.55E−3 | 0.081 |
| AdaBoost | 93.5 | N/A | 0.086 |
| DecisionTree | 92.0 | N/A | 0.009 |
| LinearSVC | 92.0 | 2.94E−4 | 0.006 |
| RBF SVC | 88.9 | N/A | 1.071 |
| GaussianNB | 87.2 | N/A | 0.013 |

**Table 3.** Left-right task trained on pro-antisaccade and tested on large grid

| Model | Accuracy (%) | Standard deviation | Mean Run time (s) |
|---|---|---|---|
| XGBoost | 93.4 | 1.11E−16 | 0.054 |
| GradientBoost | 92.1 | 3.8E−4 | 0.019 |
| LinearSVC | 91.4 | 1.55E−4 | 0.005 |
| RandomForest | 91.2 | 5.15E−4 | 0.071 |
| AdaBoost | 91 | 1.11E−16 | 0.080 |
| RBF SVC | 87.2 | N/A | 1.043 |
| GaussianNB | 85.4 | 1.11E−16 | 0.009 |
| DecisionTree | 88.4 | 1.11E−16 | 0.007 |

**PA-LG Vs LG-PA.** Comparing Tables 3 and 4, we see that except for RBF SVC and GaussianNB, models trained on large grid data have higher accuracies when tested on pro-antisaccade data compared to the reverse. As shown in Table 5, the average improvement in accuracy is around 1.9%. This result aligns with the hypothesis that in general, models trained on finer-grain data will perform better when covariate shifts are applied, specifically in terms of varying data complexity. It also aligns with previous work regarding the influence of higher complexity EEG data on machine learning [33].

**Implications of LG-PA > PA-LG in General.** Although previous eye-tracking classifiers report higher accuracies (95.5% ± 4.6%), their models assume distributionally similar data [35]. The models trained on large grid in this study, on the other hand, retain accuracy even after a distributional shift. This means that regardless of distributional patterns, large grid trained models are able to identify similarity traits in eye-tracking data. Therefore, in general, models trained on vector-based data, rather than binary-classified data, are more adaptable to day-to-day EEG-ET data collection.

**Table 4.** Left-right task trained on large grid and tested on pro-antisaccade

| Model | Accuracy (%) | Standard deviation | Mean Run time (s) |
|---|---|---|---|
| XGBoost | 96.5 | 1.11E−16 | 0.050 |
| GradientBoost | 96.0 | 6.07E−4 | 0.0123 |
| AdaBoost | 95.0 | N/A | 0.138 |
| RandomForest | 95.0 | 3.57E−4 | 0.085 |
| DecisionTree | 91.9 | N/A | 0.006 |
| LinearSVC | 90.8 | 1.66E−4 | 0.006 |
| RBF SVC | 86.3 | 1.11E−16 | 1.892 |
| GaussianNB | 83.7 | N/A | 0.013 |

# 6  Discussion

This paper utilizes the benchmark data from the EEGEyeNet dataset and 8 machine learning models to create left-right classifiers trained on both coarse-grain and fine-grain data. The accuracies of the models are then tested and compared using two different testing sets of different distributional complexity. In this way, the effects of a covariate distributional shift on the performance of the machine learning models are observed. This provides useful insights into the experimental models and the nature of the data.

## 6.1  Models Trained on Pro-Antisaccade

As expected from the results of [10], making left-right predictions using data from the pro-antisaccade paradigm is highly accurate. This is shown by Table 5 as the average accuracy of the models trained using pro-antisaccade data are 94.2% and 90%. Although these models are accurate, there is a lack of consistency because the average dropped 4.2% after covariate shifting. This means that models trained on pro-antisaccade data are susceptible to distributional shifts. All of the classifiers dropped in accuracy. DecisionTree, RandomForest, XGBoost GradientBoost, and AdaBoost were the most susceptible, dropping in accuracy by 7.8%, 5.3%, 4.5% 5.3%, and 5.3% respectively. RBF SVC, GuassianNB, and LinearSVC were the least susceptible, dropping in accuracy by 2.2%, 2.3%, and 0.6% respectively.

## 6.2  Models Trained on Large Grid

As shown in the results, making left-right classification predictions using data from the large grid paradigm has similarly high accuracies as the predictions

**Table 5.** Accuracy of machine learning models on left-right classification. PA-PA indicates trained on pro-antisaccade and tested on pro-antisaccade, LG-LG indicates trained on large grid, tested on large grid, PA-LG indicates trained on pro-antisaccade, tested on large grid, LG-PA indicates trained on large grid, tested on pro-antisaccade.

| Models | PA-PA (%) | LG-LG (%) | PA-LG (%) | LG-PA (%) |
|---|---|---|---|---|
| **XGBoost** | 97.9 | 95.5 | 93.4 | 96.5 |
| **GradientBoost** | 97.4 | 95.6 | 92.1 | 96.0 |
| RandomForest | 96.5 | 94.6 | 91.2 | 95.0 |
| AdaBoost | 96.3 | 93.5 | 91.0 | 95.0 |
| DecisionTree | 96.2 | 92.0 | 88.4 | 91.9 |
| **LinearSVC** | 92.0 | 92.0 | 91.4 | 90.8 |
| RBF SVC | 89.4 | 88.9 | 87.2 | 86.3 |
| GaussianNB | 87.7 | 87.2 | 85.4 | 83.7 |
| Average | 94.2 | 92.4 | 90.0 | 91.9 |

made by models trained on pro-antisaccade data. The performance of these machine learning models is, however, more consistent as shown by comparatively minimal decrease in accuracy after covariate shifting. While the acccuracy of models trained on pro-antisaccade data dropped by 4.2% on average after covariate shifting, classifiers trained using large grid data dropped in accuracy only by 0.5%. In fact, some of the classifiers increased in accuracy when tested on data from a different, simpler distributional pattern. DecisionTree, RBF SVC, GaussianNB, and LinearSVC decreased in accuracy by 0.1%, 2.6%, 3.5%, and 1.2% respectively. RandomForest, XGBoost, GradientBoost, and AdaBoost increased in accuracy by 0.4%, 1%, 0.4%, and 1.5% respectively.

### 6.3 Comparison of the Models and the Best Model for EEG-ET Classification

DecisionTree was the most susceptible classifier when trained on coarse-grain data and did not really change in accuracy when trained on fine-grain data. RandomForest, XGBoost, GradientBoost, and AdaBoost were all high susceptible machine learning models when trained on course-grain data. They were all, however, the best performing when trained on fine-grain data. This suggests that data distribution and representation is most important for DecisionTree, RandomForest, XGBoost, GradientBoost, and AdaBoost. Out of these 5 classifiers XGBoost and GradientBoost performed the best, having high accuracies as well as performing the best after covariate shifting.

As shown in Table 5, RBF SVC, GaussianNB, and LinearSVC dropped in accuracy a somewhat consistent amount between PA-LG and LG-PA. This shows that regardless of coarse-grain and fine-grain data, these classifiers will drop in accuracy after a covariate shift is applied. Out of these classifiers, LinearSVC was the least susceptible to distributional shifts.

To summarize the results, the most consistent classifier, regardless of coarse-grain and fine-grain data, is LinearSVC whereas the best performing classifiers, after covariate distributional shifting, are XGBoost and GradientBoost, but specifically when trained on fine-grain data. Since the benchmark results of this classification task were already relatively accurate, the variation in performance was not very large. For a benchmark with less accurate results, the variation can only increase, magnifying the results found in this study. These results portray the importance of fine- versus coarse-grain data as well as the types of machine learning models that should be used for EEG-ET classification given a dataset of some consistent/random distributional complexity. We encourage future EEG and eye-tracking research to keep fine- versus coarse-grain data in mind as well as in general, be conducted utilizing fine-grain data collection methods to more accurately emulate real-world stimuli.

### 6.4 Future Recommendations and Improvements

To further advance the work provided in this study, three steps are highlighted for future exploration.

Although deep learning models were excluded due to inconsistent results [44], the main reason was due to restraints in time and resources. As deep learning models, especially CNN, have shown promising results in regards to EEG-ET classification, it is important to thoroughly explore the effects of fine- versus coarse-grain data on the robustness of such models.

Additionally, the angle value is currently the only indicator used to determine whether the saccade is towards the left or the right. The amplitude was completely ignored in data processing. The amplitude could be incorporated by using it as a weighting/scaling factor to indicate the left-right extension and solve this as a regression problem. Based on the predictions made by the regression value, we can then classify it as either left or right utilizing finer-grain data.

Furthermore, a testing set was not properly compiled as a dataset made up of both fine-grain and coarse-grain data, in other words a dataset of purely unfamiliar data, was not used. An idea to make this paper more comprehensive would be to pool both complex and simple data into one dataset and then train/test the machine learning models on that. This would confirm whether it is better to train a machine learning model using coarse-grain, binary-classified data or fine-grain, vector-based data to classify EEG-ET data after a covariate distributional shift is applied.

It is also worth mentioning that our results are derived from training only 8 machine learning models for the specific application of EEG-ET gaze classification; thus, further investigation may be needed to confirm whether the trend will persist for other applications of machine and deep learning models.

## 7   Conclusion

The motivation behind this work was to check whether training machine learning models on finer-grain data leads to more robust models. Our results indicated that when tested on data of similar data-collection complexity, prediction accuracy does not increase. On the other hand, models trained on the fine-grain, vector-based eye-tracking data performed better in general than those trained on the coarse-grain, binary-classified data after a covariate shift is applied. This suggests that training models on vector-based, fine-grain data is more reliable for building practical, day-to-day Human-Computer Interfaces as opposed to binary-classified, coarse-grain data.

**Author contributions.** Brian Xiang and Abdelrahman Abdelmonsef–The two authors contributed equally to the paper

## 8   Appendix

### 8.1   Appendix A

After emailing Ard Kastrati, Ard verified that for angle $\alpha$ in radians:

$\alpha = 0$ is right

$\alpha = \frac{\pi}{2}$ is down

$\alpha = \pi$ is left

$\alpha = -\frac{\pi}{2}$ is up

## 8.2    Appendix B

The models were trained and tested on this environment settings:

OS: Mac 12.2.1
Cuda: 9.0, Cudnn: v7.03
Python: 3.9.0
cleverhans: 2.1.0
Keras: 2.2.4
tensorflow-gpu: 1.9.0
numpy: 1.22.1
keras: 2.2.4
scikit-learn 1.0.2
scipy 1.8.0

The total space occupied by the dataset on the device is 69.0574 GB, and the total time for training and testing was 3 min on average.

# References

1. Bashivan, P., Rish, I., Heisig, S.: Mental state recognition via wearable EEG. arXiv preprint arXiv:1602.00985 (2016)
2. Lotte, F.: Signal processing approaches to minimize or suppress calibration time in oscillatory activity-based brain-computer interfaces. Proc. IEEE **103**(6), 871–890 (2015)
3. Foster, J.J., Sutterer, D.W., Serences, J.T., Vogel, E.K., Awh, E.: Alpha-band oscillations enable spatially and temporally resolved tracking of covert spatial attention. Psychol. Sci. **28**(7), 929–941 (2017)
4. Pedregosa, F., et al.: Scikit-learn: machine learning in Python. J. Mach. Learn. Res. **12**, 2825–2830 (2011)
5. Jadhav, S.D., Channe, H.P.: Comparative study of K-NN, naive Bayes and decision tree classification techniques. Int. J. Sci. Res. (IJSR) **5**(1), 1842–1845 (2016)
6. Duda, R.O., Hart, P.E.: Pattern classification and scene analysis, vol. 3, pp. 731–739. Wiley, New York (1973)
7. Higginson, C.I., Arnett, P.A., Voss, W.D.: The ecological validity of clinical tests of memory and attention in multiple sclerosis. Arch. Clin. Neuropsychol. **15**(3), 185–204 (2000)
8. Marcotte, T. D., Scott, J. C., Kamat, R., Heaton, R.K.. Neuropsychology and the prediction of everyday functioning. The Guilford Press (2010)
9. Wilson, B.A.: Ecological validity of neuropsychological assessment: do neuropsychological indexes predict performance in everyday activities? Appl. Prevent. Psychol. **2**(4), 209–215 (1993)
10. Kastrati, A., et al.: EEGEyeNet: a Simultaneous Electroencephalography and Eye-tracking Dataset and Benchmark for Eye Movement Prediction. arXiv preprint arXiv:2111.05100 (2021)
11. Pfeiffer, J., Pfeiffer, T., Meißner, M., Weiß, E.: Eye-tracking-based classification of information search behavior using machine learning: evidence from experiments in physical shops and virtual reality shopping environments. Inf. Syst. Res. **31**(3), 675–691 (2020)

12. Thapaliya, S., Jayarathna, S., Jaime, M.: Evaluating the EEG and eye movements for autism spectrum disorder. In: 2018 IEEE international conference on big data (Big Data), pp. 2328–2336. IEEE, December 2018
13. Sotoodeh, M.S., Taheri-Torbati, H., Hadjikhani, N., Lassalle, A.: Preserved action recognition in children with autism spectrum disorders: Evidence from an EEG and eye-tracking study. Psychophysiol. **58**(3), e13740 (2021)
14. Kang, J., Han, X., Song, J., Niu, Z., Li, X.: The identification of children with autism spectrum disorder by SVM approach on EEG and eye-tracking data. Comput. Biol. Med. **120**, 103722 (2020)
15. Qian, P., Zhao, Z., Chen, C., Zeng, Z., Li, X.: Two eyes are better than one: exploiting binocular correlation for diabetic retinopathy severity grading. In: 2021 43rd Annual International Conference of the IEEE Engineering in Medicine and Biology Society (EMBC), pp. 2115–2118. IEEE, November 2021
16. Wu, F., Mai, W., Tang, Y., Liu, Q., Chen, J., Guo, Z.: Learning spatial-spectral-temporal EEG representations with deep attentive-recurrent-convolutional neural networks for pain intensity assessment. Neuroscience **481**, 144–155 (2022)
17. Qu, X., Hall, M., Sun, Y., Sekuler, R., Hickey, T. J. (2018). A Personalized Reading Coach using Wearable EEG Sensors-A Pilot Study of Brainwave Learning Analytics. In CSEDU (2), pp. 501–507
18. Freund, Y., Schapire, R.E.: A decision-theoretic generalization of on-line learning and an application to boosting. J. Comput. Syst. Sci. **55**(1), 119–139 (1997)
19. Bhuvaneswari, P., Kumar, J.S.: Support vector machine technique for EEG signals. Int. J. Comput. Appl. **63**(13), 1–5 (2013)
20. Carrión-Ojeda, D., Fonseca-Delgado, R., Pineda, I.: Analysis of factors that influence the performance of biometric systems based on EEG signals. Expert Syst. Appl. **165**, 113967 (2021)
21. Aydemir, O., Kayikcioglu, T.: Decision tree structure based classification of EEG signals recorded during two dimensional cursor movement imagery. J. Neurosci. Methods **229**, 68–75 (2014)
22. Qian, P., et al.: Multi-target deep learning for algal detection and classification. In: 2020 42nd Annual International Conference of the IEEE Engineering in Medicine and Biology Society (EMBC), pp. 1954–1957. IEEE, July 2020
23. Qu, X., Sun, Y., Sekuler, R., Hickey, T.:. EEG markers of STEM learning. In: 2018 IEEE Frontiers in Education Conference (FIE), pp. 1–9. IEEE, October 2018
24. Edla, D.R., Mangalorekar, K., Dhavalikar, G., Dodia, S.: Classification of EEG data for human mental state analysis using Random Forest Classifier. Procedia Comput. Sci. **132**, 1523–1532 (2018)
25. Tiwari, A., Chaturvedi, A.: A multiclass EEG signal classification model using spatial feature extraction and XGBoost algorithm. In: 2019 IEEE/RSJ International Conference on Intelligent Robots and Systems (IROS), pp. 4169–4175. IEEE, November 2019
26. Satapathy, S.K., Dehuri, S., Jagadev, A.K.: EEG signal classification using PSO trained RBF neural network for epilepsy identification. Inform. Med. Unlocked **6**, 1–11 (2017)
27. Kumar, J.S., Bhuvaneswari, P.: Analysis of Electroencephalography (EEG) signals and its categorization-a study. Procedia Eng. **38**, 2525–2536 (2012)
28. Klaib, A.F., Alsrehin, N.O., Melhem, W.Y., Bashtawi, H.O., Magableh, A.A.: Eye tracking algorithms, techniques, tools, and applications with an emphasis on machine learning and Internet of Things technologies. Expert Syst. Appl. **166**, 114037 (2021)

29. Qu, X., Liukasemsarn, S., Tu, J., Higgins, A., Hickey, T.J., Hall, M.H.: Identifying clinically and functionally distinct groups among healthy controls and first episode psychosis patients by clustering on EEG patterns. Frontiers in psychiatry, 938 (2020)

30. Plancher, G., Tirard, A., Gyselinck, V., Nicolas, S., Piolino, P.: Using virtual reality to characterize episodic memory profiles in amnestic mild cognitive impairment and Alzheimer's disease: influence of active and passive encoding. Neuropsychologia 50(5), 592–602 (2012)

31. Gu, J., et al.: Multi-phase cross-modal learning for noninvasive gene mutation prediction in hepatocellular carcinoma. In 2020 42nd Annual International Conference of the IEEE Engineering in Medicine Biology Society (EMBC), pp. 5814–5817. IEEE, July 2020

32. Li, L., Abu-Mostafa, Y.S.: Data complexity in machine learning (2006)

33. Burns, T., Rajan, R.: Combining complexity measures of EEG data: multiplying measures reveal previously hidden information. F1000Research, 4 (2015)

34. Xu, K., et al.: Multi-instance multi-label learning for gene mutation prediction in hepatocellular carcinoma. In: 2020 42nd Annual International Conference of the IEEE Engineering in Medicine and Biology Society (EMBC), pp. 6095–6098. IEEE, July 2020

35. Nilsson Benfatto, M., Öqvist Seimyr, G., Ygge, J., Pansell, T., Rydberg, A., Jacobson, C.: Screening for dyslexia using eye tracking during reading. PLoS ONE 11(12), e0165508 (2016)

36. Lobo, J.L., Ser, J.D., De Simone, F., Presta, R., Collina, S., Moravek, Z.: Cognitive workload classification using eye-tracking and EEG data. In: Proceedings of the International Conference on Human-Computer Interaction in Aerospace, pp. 1–8, September 2016

37. Sabancı, K., Köklü, M.: The classification of eye state by using kNN and MLP classification models according to the EEG signals (2015)

38. Hollenstein, N., Rotsztejn, J., Troendle, M., Pedroni, A., Zhang, C., Langer, N.: ZuCo, a simultaneous EEG and eye-tracking resource for natural sentence reading. Scientific data 5(1), 1–13 (2018)

39. Plöchl, M., Ossandón, J.P., König, P.: Combining EEG and eye tracking: identification, characterization, and correction of eye movement artifacts in electroencephalographic data. Front. Hum. Neurosci. 6, 278 (2012)

40. Oikonomou, V.P., Nikolopoulos, S., Kompatsiaris, I.: Machine-learning techniques for EEG data. Signal Processing to Drive Human-Computer Interaction: EEG and eye-controlled interfaces, p. 145(2020)

41. Roy, S. (2019). Machine Learning for removing EEG artifacts: setting the benchmark. arXiv preprint arXiv:1903.07825

42. Zhang, H., Zhao, M., Wei, C., Mantini, D., Li, Z., Liu, Q.: Eegdenoisenet: a benchmark dataset for deep learning solutions of EEG denoising. J. Neural Eng. 18(5), 056057 (2021)

43. Langer, N., et al.: A resource for assessing information processing in the developing brain using EEG and eye tracking. Sci. Data 4(1), 1–20 (2017)

44. Lotte, F., et al.: A review of classification algorithms for EEG-based brain-computer interfaces: a 10 year update. J. Neural Eng. 15(3), 031005 (2018)

45. Qu, X., Liu, P., Li, Z., Hickey, T.: Multi-class time continuity voting for EEG classification. In: Frasson, C., Bamidis, P., Vlamos, P. (eds.) BFAL 2020. LNCS (LNAI), vol. 12462, pp. 24–33. Springer, Cham (2020). https://doi.org/10.1007/978-3-030-60735-7_3

46. Qu, X., Mei, Q., Liu, P., Hickey, T.: Using EEG to distinguish between writing and typing for the same cognitive task. In: Frasson, C., Bamidis, P., Vlamos, P. (eds.) BFAL 2020. LNCS (LNAI), vol. 12462, pp. 66–74. Springer, Cham (2020). https://doi.org/10.1007/978-3-030-60735-7_7

47. Roy, Y., Banville, H., Albuquerque, I., Gramfort, A., Falk, T.H., Faubert, J.: Deep learning-based electroencephalography analysis: a systematic review. J. Neural Eng. **16**(5), 051001 (2019)

48. Craik, A., He, Y., Contreras-Vidal, J.L.: Deep learning for electroencephalogram (EEG) classification tasks: a review. J. Neural Eng. **16**(3), 031001 (2019)

# Workload Evaluation Model of Nuclear Power Plant Operator in Integrated System Validation

Xuegang Zhang[1], Yu Gan[2], Ming Jia[1], and Yijing Zhang[1,2,3]($\boxtimes$)

[1] State Key Laboratory of Nuclear Power Safety Monitoring Technology and Equipment, China Nuclear Power Engineering Co., Ltd (CNPEC), Shenzhen 518172, Guangdong, China
[2] Department of Industrial Engineering, Tsinghua University, Beijing 100084, China
[3] Department of Industrial Engineering, Beijing University of Civil Engineering and Architecture, Beijing 100044, China

**Abstract.** Integrated system validation (ISV) is an important part of Human Factors Engineering Review of a nuclear power plant (NPP) employed to evaluate whether the design of function systems of NPPs support safe operations of operators. Workload evaluation of NPPs operators for ISV remains a problem due to a lack of objective indices and low creditability of subjective ratings. This study aims to establish one workload evaluation model based on physiological and activity indices. An ISV experiment of digitalized main control room was conducted on Yangjiang NPP Full-Scope Simulator. A task scenario of Diverse Human Interface Panel (DHP) and Severe Accident Panel (SAP) was selected from real NPPs task scenarios. Four operators participated in this experiment and finished the task scenario. Physiological and activity data were collected during the experiment and 14 indices were calculated. Task complexity were analyzed using VACP (Visual, Auditory, Cognitive and Psychomotor) theory. The result correlation analysis between task complexity and physiological & activity indices showed a significant positive relation with all p-value $< 0.05$. Finally, a workload evaluation model is constructed. This model can be used in ISV to evaluate the task complexity and workload during human reliability analysis based on the physiological response of NPPs operators.

**Keywords:** Workload evaluation · Nuclear power plant · Physiological indices · Integrated System Validation (ISV) · Task complexity (TC)

## 1 Introduction

Nuclear power plants (NPPs) are safety critical systems. To ensure system safety and human health, human factors engineering review (HFER) is needed in the design, construction and operation of NPPs. Integrated system validation (ISV) is the key step of HFER before NPPs put into practice. ISV is employed to evaluate whether the design of the integrated system can satisfy performance requirements or support safe operations of NPPs. ISV is based on the operator performance under high simulation operation conditions to verify whether the system is safe and reliable. Workload was recommended by some standards like NUREG-0711 [1] as one of important indices in ISV. However,

© The Author(s), under exclusive license to Springer Nature Switzerland AG 2022
M. Kurosu et al. (Eds.): HCII 2022, LNCS 13516, pp. 633–648, 2022.
https://doi.org/10.1007/978-3-031-17615-9_45

researches and surveys on the ISV in-operation NPPs in China found that workload evaluation of operators in NPPs were conducted using subjective ratings, and little physiological data or other objective indices were collected or used, resulting in a lack of objectivity in the evaluation results.

High workload is one of the main causes of human error. Researches showed that workload can be used to judge whether the system is safe, the operator perform at a high level of performance, and whether it is necessary to improve and optimize the function and design of the system [2]. Regulations and standards in the nuclear industry have specific requirements on the evaluation of workload, both during the analysis stage and validation stage [3–6]. Usually, workload is classified as mental workload and physical workload. Mental load is understood as a kind of mental stress and burden [7], while physical load is understood as physiological stress. According to this definition, task scenarios of ISV experiments consist mainly of mental activities, such as observation, analysis, judgment, and decision-making. Therefore, no detailed distinction is made between mental workload and physical workload in this study, and they are all collectively referred to workload.

Methods of workload evaluation are mainly classified into three categories: subjective ratings, performance measures, and physiological measures [8]. Among subjective ratings, NASA-TLX (NASA Task Load Index) is most widely used [9–11]. Its scales can well reflect workload changes, and they are positively related to task complexity and task difficulty [12, 13]. However, in practical applications of ISV, the reliability and validity of NASA-TLX can be impaired by the arbitrariness of the raters. Performance measures mainly evaluate personnel performance during task execution. Some indices have certain universality, such as operating time, accuracy, and operating frequency. Some are closely related to tasks, such as completion status of NPPs operating procedures. The performance data collected in ISV experiments are generally rough indicators, such as task completion status, and cannot be analyzed in detail. As numerous physiological indicators such as eye movement, heart rate, and EEG can reflect changes in workload and were commonly used in NPPs, shipping, aerospace and other fields [13–15], this study will collect multiple physiological indices for analysis in the experiment.

With the development of measurement techniques, more continuous and objective measurements were used to evaluate mental workload [16]. Among those measurements, neurological and physiological indices were shown to have a great potential for assessing workload in complex tasks [17]. Moreover, comprehensive evaluation models were established to predict workload based on multiple indicators. A mental workload model was established using three kinds of indicators: physiological indexes (heart rate and heart rate variability), subjective indicators (NASA-TLX) and performance indexes (response time and accuracy rate) [18]. Cluster data processing (GMDH) integrates multiple physiological indicators into an arithmetic model to obtain a total mental workload [8, 14, 19]. Walter et al. [20] and Borghetti, giametta & rusnock [21] established a mathematical model using machine learning based on EEG data to evaluate the changes of mental workload.

This study conducted an ISV on Yangjiang NPP Full-Scope Simulator. A task scenario of Diversity HSI Panel (DHP) and Severe Accident Panel (SAP) was selected from real NPPs task scenarios. Four operators of different positions participated in this experiment and finished the task scenario. Physiological and activity data were collected during the experiment and 14 physiological & activity indices were calculated. Finally, a workload evaluation model was established to objectively and comprehensively reflect the workload of NPP operators in ISV. Factor analysis method was used to integrate all physiological indices into a synthesized index. The physiological indices include the eye activities (pupil dilation, blink rate, blink duration, fixation duration) and cardiac activities (heart rate, heart rate variability). The task complexity of task units was calculated as the benchmark for evaluating the model.

## 2 Experimental Design of Integrated System Validation

This section clarifies all aspects of the ISV experiment, including purposes, participants, procedure, apparatus and task scenarios. During the experiment, physiological data including cardiorespiratory indices and activity indices were collected. Moreover, there were audio/video recordings for behavior analysis, which are not included in this paper.

### 2.1 Purposes

This ISV experiment was conducted on digitalized main control room (MCR) DHP and SAP in accident condition scenarios. The main purpose was to collect physiological data and explore correlation between physiological response and deduced workload (illustrated in Sect. 2), and develop a workload evaluation model based on physiological indices.

### 2.2 Participants and Procedure

Participants with relevant qualifications were recruited, such as licensed operators, supervisors and safety engineers. Specifically, they were required to a) understand information on MCR human-system interfaces, controllers and instruments; b) be familiar with the interfaces and able to operate all the systems and equipment correctly; c) be able to smoothly follow the operation procedures; and d) can react to alarms correctly and timely.

The recruited participants were operators of Yangjiang NPP and they satisfied all the requirements listed above. There were 4 of them, insisting of one operator for primary loop systems, one operator for secondary loop systems, one unit supervisor and one safety engineer. Their personal information was collected before experiments. Their conversations and behaviors were recorded throughout the experiment. And after the experiment, they were interviewed. This paper only describes and analyzes data that are relevant to the research topic.

### 2.3 Apparatus

The ISV experiment took place in Yangjiang NPP and NPP Full-Scope Simulator was used as the experiment platform, which captures the dynamic and integrated features of real MCR systems under accident conditions, thus satisfying the need to evaluate and validate system functions of DHP and SAP panels of MCR. Figure 1 shows the experiment site.

**Fig. 1.** Experiment site

BioHarness telemetry & logging system (Fig. 2) of BIOPAC Systems Inc. were used to collect physiological data. BioHarness combines chest belt with sensors so that it can monitor, record and analyze a variety of physiological parameters including ECG (electrocardiogram), breathing, acceleration and inclination. Data of all the participants were collected simultaneously during the experiment.

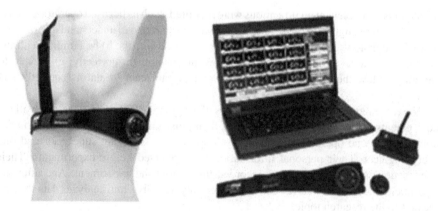

**Fig. 2.** Bioharness telemetry & logging system (from Bioharness manual book)

## 2.4  Task Scenarios

The task scenario was a Small-Break LOCA (Loss of Coolant Accident) combined with a failure in the Reactor Protection Monitoring System (RPMS) which was selected from the real task scenarios of NPPs to cover operations of DHP and SAP panels of MCR. The task scenario comprised two stages: a) initial condition, when the power plant ran normally in full power, and b) accident condition, when there Small-Break LOCA (break flow at 80t/h) in the primary loop systems. Both the conditions have corresponding operation procedures, which the participants were required to follow.

Performance of the participants included important personnel operations, manually trigger protection actions, system monitoring, and reactions according to operation procedures. Important personnel actions included five specific operations: a) AD-SG, which means that operator successfully adjusted SG; b) SD-VLOCA, which means that operator discovered leak; c) SM-30, which means that operator promptly shut down the main pump within 30 min; d) MSS, which means that operator successfully adjusted CHARGE FLOW CONTROL VALVE; and e) RRA-MS, which means operator connect Residual Heat Removal system.

For the task scenario in this experiment, participants on different positions performed different tasks. Task in this paper is defined as all the operations required by one operation procedure. Each task is composed of several task units, which are defined as modules divided from a task according to its operation procedure in order to complete subgoals. A task unit consists of many steps, and each step consists of meta-operations. Meta-operations are defined as measurable minimum operations whose start and end are clearly known. Through the task decomposition, theoretical workload evaluations of higher-order task components such as task units can be synthesized with those of meta-operations, which can be deduced from VACP scales easily.

## 2.5  Data Collection

Physiological data collected in the experiment mainly include:

(1) Heart rate difference (HRD), Heart rate was got from ECG data with sampling rate of 250 Hz, and heart rate difference was the difference of heart rates between task performing and resting;

(2) Heart rate variability (HRV), which measures ECG dynamic complexity and in BioHarness's case, standard deviation of R-R intervals (SDNN);

(3) Breathing rate (BR), detected by pressure sensors on the chest belt. The stabilization of the initial breathing rate requires a breathing cycle of 15–45 s;

(4) Breathing wave amplitude (BWA) measured with the same sensors as BR. Outlier processing should be performed when analyzing data because outliers may appear due to posture changing, speaking or coughing during data collection;

(5) Walk step count (WSC), which is the cumulative number of steps the operator walked during the task;

(6) Peak acceleration (PA), which is the maximum absolute value of three-axis acceleration magnitude achieved during previous one-second period. Three-axis acceleration consists of vertical, lateral and sagittal accelerations;

(7) Activity level (AL), unit of velocity magnitude units (VMU). During walking or running, AL is larger than 0.2 VMU or 0.8 VMU. AL can be calculated with the Formula 1

$$AL = \sqrt{x^2 + y^2 + z^2} \tag{1}$$

where x, y and z are mean acceleration of the three axes with sampling frequency of 100 Hz;

(8) Inclination, which measures the degree of forward or backward tilt degree of the operator, ranging from −180° to 180°, where 0° means the operator is standing or sitting upright, and ±180° is when the operator is upside down. The absolute value of the slope is used during data analysis;

(9) Physiological intensity (PI), which is the intensity value obtained according to the grade score corresponding to HR. When HR is less than 50% of the maximum HR, PI value is 0. When HR is greater than 50% of the maximum HR, PI increases by 1 for each 5% increase of HR over 50% of maximum HR. PI values are numeric and have no units;

(10) Physiological load (PL), which is defined as the cumulative index of cardiac output based on PI, which can better reflect the overall effort level of the operator in a specific training phase;

(11) Mechanical intensity (MI), which is a graded intensity value corresponding to acceleration peak value (APV). When APV is less than 0.5g, MI is 0. And when APV is greater than 0.5g, MI increases by 1 for every 0.05g increase of APV over 0.5g;

(12) Mechanical load (ML), which is defined as the cumulative index of kinetic output based on MI. ML is a measure of the overall amount of exercise;

(13) Training intensity (TI), which is defined as the average of PI and MI;

(14) Training load (TL), which is defined as the average of PL and ML.

## 3   Task Complexity

### 3.1   TC Method

In terms of workload analysis, many researchers have proposed analytical methods for task complexity or workload based on VACP (Visual, Auditory, Cognitive and Psychomotor) [22] theory. VACP method originated from the U.S. air force combat mission and was widely studied and applied at the end of the 20th century [23, 24]. Some researchers believe that task complexity is a task attribute that increases information diversity, changes rate and load [25]. Therefore, task complexity (TC) was defined as the sum of VACP's four resources required to complete a task in nuclear power plants [26, 27]. In this study, TC method (showed as formula 2) was adopted to calculate the complexity of each task unit of the task scenario. It is assumed that the physiological and activity measurements recorded during task performance would be correlated with task complexity.

$$\text{TC} = \sum_{ns=1}^{NS} \sum_{no=1}^{NO} \sum_{nr=1}^{NR} C_{ns,no,nr} \tag{2}$$

In the formula, NR represents the number of resource types for the meta-operation, NO represents the number of meta-operations in the step, and NS represents the number of steps required for the task unit that requires the most resources. $C_{ns,no,nr}$ represents the required level of resource(nr) in the meta-operation(no) of the step(ns).

### 3.2  Meta-operations

Meta-operations and their scores were modified from the work of Wang [28] and evaluated by experts. The results were used in [29] and were shown in Table 1.

### 3.3  Analysis Procedure

TC analysis is divided into the following five steps:

(1) Decompose the tasks of each operator into task units according to the procedures and videos. Based on the analysis of the procedures for the initial and accident conditions, and the videos recorded on-site, this study identified task units for each task through sub-goal recognition. For each task unit, its content, start time and end time were recorded;

**Table 1.** VACP scores for meta-operations (from [29])

| ID | Meta-operations | Resources | V | A | C | P | Sum |
|----|-----------------|-----------|---|---|---|---|-----|
| A | Interpreting procedures | V&C | 5.9 | – | 5.3 | – | 11.2 |
| B | Locating indicators | V | 5 | – | – | – | 5 |
| C | Checking conditions/status | V | 4 | – | – | – | 4 |
| D | Reading parameters/status | V | 5.9 | – | – | – | 5.9 |
| E | Decision making and diagnosing (single decision) | C | – | – | 4.6 | | 4.6 |
| F | Decision making and diagnosing (multiple decisions) | C | – | – | .8 | | 6.8 |
| G | Calculating | C | – | – | 7 | | 7 |
| H | Pressing a button | C&P | – | – | 1 | 2.2 | 3.2 |
| I | Turning a knob | C&P | – | – | 1 | 5.8 | 6.8 |
| J | Selecting a procedure branch | C&P | – | – | 1.2 | 2.2 | 3.4 |
| K | Listening to verbal directions | A | – | 4.9 | – | – | 4.9 |
| L | Transmitting verbal messages | A&P | – | 1 | – | 1 | 2 |
| M | Locating/identifying alarms by sound | A&C | – | 4.2 | 3.7 | – | 7.9 |

(2) Decompose the task units according to the procedures. Each task unit of the operator within a certain period of time is decomposed specifically to steps;

(3) Decompose the steps into meta-operations according to the video. Meta-operations have clear start and end times, as video was employed for their identification. Also, meta-operations cannot be further decomposed, therefore each meta-operation was checked for this feature. Meta-operations list summarized in the Table 1 served as reference for the decomposition;

(4) Score the meta-operations concerning VACP resources. All the meta-operations identified were included in the list summarized in Table 1, so the scores in the table were straightly followed;

(5) Synthesize scores of meta-operations to get scores for steps, task units and the whole task.

**Calculation of an Example.** In order to explain the calculation steps more clearly, the "accident diagnosis" task of the primary loop systems operator is used as an example of calculation. The accident diagnosis procedure guide is shown in Fig. 3. The "accident diagnosis" was the 10th task of the primary loop systems operator. According to the procedures and video analysis, the task was decomposed into 8 specific steps, which were broken down into specific meta-operations. Then score of the whole task was obtained by summing all the meta-operations scores (according to scores of meta-operations in Table 1). Table 2 illustrates the 8 steps of 10th task and their meta-operations, and the scores for the meta-operations.

**Table 2.** Accident diagnosis scores

| Step No | Step Contents | Meta-operation | V | A | C | P | Sum | Total score |
|---------|---------------|----------------|---|---|---|---|-----|-------------|
| 1 | At least one of the three radioactivity alarms rings | A | 5.9 | 0 | 5.3 | 0 | 11.2 | 109.2 |
| | | F | 0 | 0 | 6.8 | 0 | 6.8 | |
| 2 | PRCP > 138bar.g | B | 5 | 0 | 0 | 0 | 5 | |
| | | D | 5.9 | 0 | 0 | 0 | 5.9 | |
| | | E | 0 | 0 | 4.6 | 0 | 4.6 | |
| 3 | The pressure of one SG is lower than the other two | B | 5 | 0 | 0 | 0 | 5 | |
| | | D | 5.9 | 0 | 0 | 0 | 5.9 | |
| | | F | 0 | 0 | 6.8 | 0 | 6.8 | |
| 4 | The pressure of SG is at least higher than the pressure of NI | B | 5 | 0 | 0 | 0 | 5 | |
| | | D | 5.9 | 0 | 0 | 0 | 5.9 | |
| | | E | 0 | 0 | 4.6 | 0 | 4.6 | |
| 5 | At least one SG pressure < = 40bar.g | C | 4 | 0 | 0 | 0 | 4 | |

*(continued)*

**Table 2.** (*continued*)

| Step No | Step Contents | Meta-operation | V | A | C | P | Sum | Total score |
|---------|---------------|----------------|---|---|---|---|-----|-------------|
| | | F | 0 | 0 | 6.8 | 0 | 6.8 | |
| 6 | Three Pressurizers' Depressurization, Pipelines are closed | C | 4 | 0 | 0 | 0 | 4 | |
| | | F | 0 | 0 | 6.8 | 0 | 6.8 | |
| 7 | Containment pressure > 1.2bar.g | B | 5 | 0 | 0 | 0 | 5 | |
| | | D | 5.9 | 0 | 0 | 0 | 5.9 | |
| | | E | 0 | 0 | 4.6 | 0 | 4.6 | |
| 8 | SBLOCA occurs, unit supervisor approves K4 | J | 0 | 0 | 1.2 | 2.2 | 3.4 | |
| | | L | 0 | 1 | 0 | 1 | 2 | |

Following this example showed in Table 2, all tasks were analyzed for their workload scores. There are total 120 task units (3.82 ± 3.64) decomposed from the task scenario. As for the number of task units for four operators, NI has 33 (6.29 ± 4.70) units, CI get 30 (4.33 ± 3.18) units while unit supervisor and safety engineer have to manipulate 31 (2.39 ± 2.22) and 26 (1.81 ± 1.50) task units respectively.

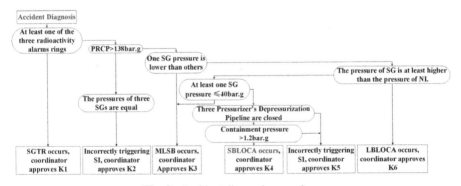

**Fig. 3.** Accident diagnosis procedure.

# 4   Workload Evaluation Model

## 4.1   Factor Analysis Method

Factor analysis (FA) method was used to establish the workload evaluation model. Firstly, correlation analysis between average task complexity and physiological data was conducted to get the suitable indices for building the model. Then, principal components analysis was used to classify closely related variables into one factor. Factors were selected based on the cumulative variance contribution rate. Furthermore, factor weights of the model were based on variance contribution rate. Lastly, SPSS was used for all data analysis.

## 4.2  Correlation Analysis

The correlation between physiological response and task complexity was analyzed in order to screen significantly related variables. The physiological data collected in this study were processed according to the start and end time of each task unit. Task complexity is represented by the average task complexity of one task unit. The results showed that Activity Level, Heart Rate Change, Training Intensity, Training Load, Physiological Load, Physiological Intensity, Breathing Rate, Walk Step Count, Mechanical Intensity and Mechanical Load had significant positive correlations with the average task complexity; breathing wave amplitude (BWA), HRV, and Inclination had significant negative correlations with the average task complexity. Table 3 shows the Spearman coefficients and p values for all the significant correlations.

## 4.3  Principal Component Analysis

Thirteen physiological indices in Table 3 were used for principal component analysis. Firstly, the 13 physiological indices were standardized, then KMO test and Bartlett test were performed. MSA statistic of KMO was 0.758, which was greater than 0.6; and

**Table 3.** Variables related with average workload

| Physiological factors | Spearman $\rho$ | p-value |
| --- | --- | --- |
| Activity Level | 0.483 | <0.001* |
| Heart Rate Change | 0.398 | <0.001* |
| Training Intensity | 0.341 | <0.001* |
| Training Load | 0.332 | <0.001* |
| Physiological Load | 0.327 | <0.001* |
| Physiological Intensity | 0.314 | <0.001* |
| Breathing Rate | 0.256 | 0.005 |
| Walk step Count | 0.242 | 0.008 |
| Mechanical Intensity | 0.182 | 0.047 |
| Mechanical Load | 0.179 | 0.050 |
| Breathing Wave Amplitude | −0.463 | <0.001* |
| Heart RATE VARIABILITY | −0.417 | <0.001* |
| Inclination | -0.243 | 0.007 |

* Significant at the level of 0.05

Bartlett correlation test produced a significant result with $\chi^2 = 1773.268$ and $p < 0.001$. The results showed that the data were suitable for factor analysis.

The eigenvalues of the factors extracted by the principal component method and the corresponding variance contribution rate and cumulative variance contribution rate were calculated. The eigenvalue of factor 1 is 6.069 and the variance contribution rate is 46.687%; while for factor 2 the eigenvalue is 1.977 and the variance contribution rate is 15.210%; for factor 3 and factor 4, the eigenvalue and the variance contribution is 1.245, 9.580% (factor 3) and 1.209, 9.301% (factor 4) respectively. The cumulative variance contribution rate of these four factors reaches 80.777%, which indicates that these four factors can explain the variance of the original indices above 80%.

Table 4 shows the component matrix after rotation with an absolute value of the hidden value less than 0.6. As can be seen from the table, factor 1 mainly relates to "physiological intensity", "training load", "physiological load", "heart rate change", and "heart rate variability". From the aspect of practical meanings, training load is the average of physiological load and mechanical load, physiological load is the accumulation of physiological intensity, and physiological intensity is the intensity value obtained according to the grade score corresponding to heart rate. Heart rate changes and heart rate variability are evaluation indices of cardiac activity. In conclusion, factor 1 mainly reflects the state of heart activity. Factor 2 is associated with "training intensity", "mechanical load", "mechanical intensity", "walking steps" and "activity level". In detail, training intensity is the average of mechanical intensity and physiological intensity. Mechanical load is the accumulative of mechanical intensity, and mechanical intensity is a graded intensity value corresponding to acceleration peak value. Walking steps and activity level are indicators of physical activity. Consequently, factor 2 mainly reflects

**Table 4.** Rotated Component Matrix (Hide the Absolute Value $< 0.6$)

| Variables | Factor 1 | Factor 2 | Factor 3 | Factor 4 |
|---|---|---|---|---|
| Physiological Intensity | 0.901 | – | – | – |
| Training Load | 0.890 | – | – | – |
| Physiological Load | 0.870 | – | – | – |
| Heart Rate Change | 0.861 | – | – | – |
| Heart Rate Variability | –0.686 | – | – | – |
| Mechanical Intensity | – | 0.931 | – | – |
| Mechanical Load | – | 0.929 | – | – |
| Training Intensity | – | 0.859 | – | – |
| Walk Step Count | – | 0.707 | – | – |
| Activity Level | – | 0.630 | – | – |
| Breathing Wave Amplitude | – | – | – 0.823 | – |
| Breathing Rate | – | – | 0.719 | – |
| Inclination | – | – | – | 0.899 |

the state of physical activity. As for factor 3, it mainly involves "breathing wave amplitude" and "breathing rate", which are indicators of respiratory activity. Therefore, factor
3 represents the state of respiratory activity. Lastly, factor 4 interrelates with "slope",
which is an assessment index of Inclination in physical activity.

## 5  Workload Evaluation Model

The corresponding scoring coefficients of the four factors on each index variable were
calculated as the weights of the four factors in bellowing formulas. In the Formula 3,
$X_1, X_2, ..., X_{12}, X_{13}$ represent the 13 standardized indices, and $F_1, F_2, F_3, F_4$ represent
the four factors.

$$F_1 = 0.271X_1 - 0.258X_2 + \cdots - 0.086X_{12} + 0.233X_{13}$$

$$F_2 = -0.027X_1 + 0.118X_2 + \cdots + 0.303X_{12} - 0.046X_{13}$$

$$F_3 = -0.159X_1 + 0.134X_2 + \cdots - 0.079X_{12} + 0.052X_{13} \tag{3}$$

$$F_4 = -0.142X_1 + 0.014X_2 + \cdots 0.094X_{12} + 0.020X_{13}$$

Taking the variance contribution rate of each factor as the weight, the evaluation model
was obtained from the linear combination of four factors.

$$F = 0.3801F_1 + 0.3582F_2 + 0.1428F_3 + 0.1189F_4 \tag{4}$$

Finally, the evaluation model was verified by the correlation analysis of the model
value and average TC. First, normality test (Ryan-Joiner) was performed on the model
value and average TC, and the two data failed the normality test ($p < 0.010$). Therefore,
Spearman correlation analysis was employed and the results showed that Spearman $\rho =
0.376$ and $p < 0.001$, indicating that the model value had a significant positive correlation
with the average TC. The validity of the workload evaluation model was proved.

## 6  Discussion

In the proposed model, four factors contribute to 80.777% cumulative variance and these
factors represent the state of cardiac activity, physical activity, respiratory activity and
physical posture.

The first factor contains physiological intensity, training load, physiological load,
heart rate change, and heart rate variability. Cardiac activities were the most commonly
used physiological measure of mental workload [30] and it was proved that heart activities are significantly correlated to workload. For instance, Jorna [31] reviewed heart rate
as an index for workload and De Waard [32] showed that these differential measures are
indicative of workload. In this study, the heart rate variability decreased as the workload
increased, and the other five metrics showed a negative correlation. These findings were
consistent with previous studies [7, 32].

Factor 2 is associated with training intensity, mechanical load, mechanical intensity, walking steps and activity level. As training intensity, mechanical intensity and mechanical load is indicative of acceleration peak value, and walking steps and activity level corresponds to the physical activity, factor 2 mainly reflects the state of physical workload. The correlation analysis showed a positive correlation between these factors and workload. When the task complexity increases, the operators need to monitor, assess and response more information and instructions, and they have more physical workload to finish the task.

Breathing wave amplitude and breathing rate form the factor 3. It is studied that respiratory rate is the most useful of the respiratory measures for the measurement of mental workload [33]. In this study, breathing wave amplitude decreased as the workload increased and breathing rate increased when the workload raised. The increase in respiration rate may have been a direct result of the increased metabolic demands required to perform the task [30]. The positive correlation between breathing rate and workload is consistent with previous studies [34, 35].

Inclination represents the tilt degree of the operators during the simulation process. In the correlation analysis, Spearman's $\rho$ for inclination is $-0.243$ and p-value is 0.007 (see Table 3), which indicates that although p-value reveals a significant correlation, the Spearman coefficient value indicate that inclination cannot strongly explain workload.

For further application, considering the simplicity of construction and the practical significance of the indices, physiological intensity and mechanical intensity may be enough for operator workload evaluation in practice.

## 7   Conclusion

Workload evaluation of NPPs operators for ISV is essential to assess operators' working situation, however, it remains a problem due to a lack of objective indices and low creditability of subjective ratings. This study summarized the workload evaluation issues in ISV of NPPs, conducted a field experiment for task scenarios under normal and accident conditions, and collected a variety of physiological data based on field investigations, relevant guidelines and standards, and literature research. The task scenarios in ISV were decomposed into tasks, task units, steps and meta-operations, and the TC were calculated based on VACP theory. The correlations between physiological responses and TC were studied: there were significant positive correlation between average workload and physiological indices including heart rate change, respiration rate, walking steps, activity level, physiological intensity, physiological load, mechanical intensity, mechanical load, training intensity, and training load. In addition, there were significant negative correlations between average workload and indices including heart rate variability, breathing wave amplitude, and slope. A workload evaluation model was established based on physiological indices, which provided a quantitative and objective basis for human factors engineers to evaluate operator workload in NPPs.

A major limitation of the study lies in the limited size of the collected data set as conduction of ISV experiments requires the coordination of time, site, equipment, operators and instructors. This research result still needs more task scenarios and more operator experiments for subsequent verification. Moreover, though the correlations between physiological indices and workload are significant, the Spearman coefficient values don't show strong correlation among them. Despite these limitations, we believe that by means of the proposed model we can calculate the workload of NPP operators for given input values of physiological intensity and mechanical intensity. This function enables us to:

(1) Predict performance of nuclear power plant operators: The proposed model can predict the workload of operators, and workload can reflect the future performance of the operators based on their limitations and capabilities. The quantitative results can provide criteria to project overall performance of operators.

(2) Judge whether the system is safe: Based on TC theory and experimental results, operators workload can be obtained based on TC theory and physiological indices. If operators always get high scores based on the proposed model, then the system is unsafe because higher workload causes more human errors. Therefore, the model enables to support identification of a safe or unsafe system.

(3) Improve and optimize better function and design of the system: As the proposed model is composed of four factors, stakeholders can tell which factors contribute the most to the whole workload according to the values, and hence improve and optimize the system's characteristics that is correlated with that factor.

The proposed model provides quantitative results of workload, and we expect that this model can be used in the evaluation and design of nuclear power plants and give other researchers more inspiration.

**Acknowledgments.** This study was supported by China Nuclear Power Engineering Co., Ltd (CNPEC) Science and Technology Innovation Project (Project No. K-A2017.409) and the National Natural Science Foundation of China (No. 71671167), and we would like to thank the important contribution of Professor Zhizhong Li in data analysis and modeling, the contribution of Liang Wang and Shuyu Xie in English translation and proofreading.

# References

1. O'Hara, J., Higgins, J., Fleger, S.: Human Factors Engineering Program Review Model (NUREG-0711) Revision 3: Update Methodology and Key Revisions. Office of Entific & Technical Information Technical Reports (2012)
2. Cain, B.: A review of the mental workload measurement literature. NATO RTO Reprot (RTO-TR-HFM-121-Part-II), NATO OTAN, 4–1~4–34 (2007)
3. IEC-: Nuclear power plants - Main control-room - Verification and validation of design. International Electrotechnical Commission. IEC. 61771 (1995)
4. IEC-: Nuclear Power Plants-Design of Control Rooms-Functional Analysis and Assignment. BS IEC. 61839 (2000)
5. IEC-: Nuclear power plants - Control-rooms - Design. International Electrotechnical Commission. IEC. 60964 (2018)
6. O'hara, J., Higgins, J., Persensky, J., Lewis, P., Bongarra, J.: Human factors engineering program review model. Brookhaven National Lab Upton NY (2004)

7. Young, M.S., Brookhuis, K.A., Wickens, C.D., Hancock, P.A.: State of science: mental workload in ergonomics. Ergonomics **58**(1), 1–17 (2015)
8. Gao, Q., Wang, Y., Song, F., Li, Z., Dong, X.: Mental workload measurement for emergency operating procedures in digital nuclear power plants. Ergonomics **56**(7), 1070–1085 (2013)
9. Hart, S., Staveland, L.: Development of NASA-TLX (Task Load Index): results of empirical and theoretical research. In: Hancock, A., Meshkati, N. (eds.) Human Mental Workload, vol. 52, pp. 139–183. Elsevier Science Publishers B.V., North- Holland (1988). https://doi.org/10.1016/s0166-4115(08)62386-9
10. Colle, H.A., Reid, G.B.: Estimating a mental workload redline in a simulated air-to-ground combat mission. Int. J. Aviation Psychol. **15**(4), 303–319 (2005)
11. Gawron, V.J.: Human Performance, Workload, and Situational Awareness Measures Handbook, 2nd edn. CRC Press, Boca Raton (2008)
12. Gould, K.S., Røed, B.K., Saus, E.R., Koefoed, V.F., Bridger, R.S., Moen, B.E.: Effects of navigation method on workload and performance in simulated high-speed ship navigation. Appl. Ergon. **40**(1), 103–114 (2009)
13. Durantin, G., Gagnon, J.F., Tremblay, S., Dehais, F.: Using near infrared spectroscopy and heart rate variability to detect mental overload. Behav. Brain Res. **259**, 16–23 (2014)
14. Hwang, S.L., et al.: Predicting work performance in nuclear power plants. Saf. Sci. **46**(7), 1115–1124 (2008)
15. Murai, K., Hayashi, Y., Wakabayashi, N.: A basic study on navigator's mental workload by wavelet transform. In: 2003 IEEE Pacific Rim Conference on Communications Computers and Signal Processing (PACRIM 2003) (Cat. No. 03CH37490), vol. 2, pp. 1016–1019. IEEE (2013). https://doi.org/10.1109/PACRIM.2003.1235957
16. Rusnock, C.F., Borghetti, B.J.: Workload profiles: a continuous measure of mental workload. Int. J. Ind. Ergon. **63**, 49–64 (2018)
17. Parasuraman, R., Wilson, G.F.: Putting the brain to work: neuroergonomics past, present, and future. Hum. Factors **50**(3), 468–474 (2008)
18. Wei, Z., Zhuang, D., Wanyan, X., Zhang, H., Liu, C.: A theoretical model of mental workload in pilots based on multiple experimental measurements. In: Harris, D. (ed.) EPCE 2014. LNCS (LNAI), vol. 8532, pp. 104–113. Springer, Cham (2014). https://doi.org/10.1007/978-3-319-07515-0_11
19. Yan, S., Tran, C.C., Wei, Y., Habiyaremye, J.L.: Driver's mental workload prediction model based on physiological indices. Int. J. Occupational Saf. Ergon. (2017)
20. Walter, C., Rosenstiel, W., Bogdan, M., Gerjets, P., Spüler, M.: Online EEG-based workload adaptation of an arithmetic learning environment. Front. Hum. Neurosci. **11**, 286 (2017)
21. Borghetti, B.J., Giametta, J.J., Rusnock, C.F.: Rusnock, assessing continuous operator workload with a hybrid scaffolded neuroergonomic modeling approach. Hum. Factors **59**(1), 134–146 (2017)
22. Wickens, C.D.: Processing Resources in Attention, 1st edn. Academic Press, New York (1991)
23. Little, R., et al.: Crew Reduction in Armored Vehicles Ergonomic Study (CRAVES) Final Report. Alliant Techsystems, Inc., Hopkins, MN, Tech. Rep. ARL-CR-80 (1993)
24. Archer, R.D., Lewis, G.W., Lockett, J.: Human performance modeling of reduced manning concepts for Navy ships. HFES **40**, 987–991 (1996)
25. Campbell, D.J.: Task complexity: a review and analysis. Acad. Manag. Rev. **13**, 40–52 (1988)
26. Liu, P., Li, Z.: Task complexity: a review and conceptualization framework. Int. J. Ind. Ergon. **42**(6), 553–568 (2012)
27. Liu, P., Li, Z., Wang, Z.: Task complexity measure for emergency operating procedures based on resource requirements in human information processing. In: Proceedings of the 11th International Probabilistic Safety Assessment and Management Conference (PSAM11) and the Annual European Safety and Reliability Conference (ESREL 2012), Helsinki, Finland (2012)

28. Chen, T.B., Campbell, D., Gonzalez, F., Coppin, G.: The effect of autonomy transparency in human-robot interactions: a preliminary study on operator cognitive workload and situation awareness in multiple heterogeneous UAV management. In: Chen, C. (ed.) Proceedings of the 16th Australasian Conference on Robotics and Automation 2014. LNCS, pp. 1–10. Australian Robotics and Automation Association (ARAA), Australia (2014). https://doi.org/10.1016/S1525-1578(10)60548-X

29. Gan, Y., et al.: Workload measurement using physiological and activity measures for validation test: a case study for the main control room of a nuclear power plant. Int. J. Ind. Ergon. **78**, 102974 (2020)

30. Charles, R.L., Nixon, J.: Measuring mental workload using physiological measures: a systematic review. Appl. Ergon. **74**, 221–232 (2019)

31. Jorna, P.: Spectral analysis of heart rate and psychological state: a review of its validity as a workload index. Biol. Psychol. **34**(2–3), 237–257 (1992)

32. De Waard, D., Brookhuis, K.A.: The measurement of drivers' mental workload. [Doctor dissertation]. Rijksuniversiteit Groningen (1996)

33. Roscoe, A.H.: Assessing pilot workload. Why measure heart rate, HRV and respiration?. Biol. Psychol. **34**(2–3), 259–287 (1992)

34. Wu, B., Hou, F., Yao, Z., Niu, J., Huang, W.: Using physiological parameters to evaluate operator's workload in manual controlled rendezvous and docking (RVD). In: Duffy, V.G. (ed.) ICDHM 2011. LNCS, vol. 6777, pp. 426–435. Springer, Heidelberg (2011). https://doi.org/10.1007/978-3-642-21799-9_48

35. Zhang, J., Yu, X., Xie, D.: Effects of mental tasks on the cardiorespiratory synchronization. Respir. Physiol. Neurobiol. **170**(1), 91–95 (2010)

# Author Index

Printed in the United States
by Baker & Taylor Publisher Services